T0329614

Magazines and the
Making of America

PRINCETON STUDIES IN
CULTURAL SOCIOLOGY
Paul J. DiMaggio, Michèle Lamont,
Robert J. Wuthnow, and Viviana A. Zelizer,
Series Editors

A list of titles in this series appears at the back of the book.

Magazines and the Making of America

MODERNIZATION, COMMUNITY, AND PRINT CULTURE, 1741–1860

Heather A. Haveman

PRINCETON UNIVERSITY PRESS
Princeton and Oxford

press.princeton.edu
Jacket art from *Parley's Magazine*, June 1836, photographed by Pat Pflieger.

Library of Congress Cataloging-in-Publication Data

Haveman, Heather A.
Magazines and the making of America : modernization, community, and print culture,
1741–1860 / Heather A. Haveman.
     pages cm. — (Princeton studies in cultural sociology)
Includes bibliographical references and index.
ISBN 978-0-691-16440-3 (hardcover : alk. paper)   1. American periodicals—History—
18th century.   2. American periodicals—History—19th century.   3. American
periodicals—Political aspects—United States—History—18th century.   4. American
periodicals—Political aspects—United States—History—19th century.   5. Publishers
and publishing—Social aspects—United States—History.   I. Title.
PN4877.H37 2015
051—dc23
              2014044327

British Library Cataloging-in-Publication Data is available

This book has been composed in Adobe Caslon Pro and Sabon Pro

Printed on acid-free paper. ∞

Printed in the United States of America

10 9 8 7 6 5 4 3 2 1

To Neil

Contents

viii | Contents

Figures and Tables

FIGURES

TABLES

Acknowledgments

N o one who writes a scholarly book (or even a scholarly article) does it alone. All research is collaborative: we are inspired or exasperated by the work we've read, we try to build on or tear down received wisdom, and we depend on or contest concepts and arguments developed by earlier scholars as well as facts uncovered by them. We also benefit from feedback from our peers through presentations, reviews, and comments. I certainly have profited from such feedback over the many years I have been studying the American magazine industry and want to thank all those who helped me.

Librarians at several institutions—Cornell University, Columbia University, the New York Public Library, the Library of Congress, the University of California–Santa Barbara, and UC–Berkeley—helped me track down much of the archival material I used to build the data sets analyzed here. Jane Faulkner of UC–Santa Barbara deserves special kudos for her help in securing reserve library materials when I visited that campus.

Bits and pieces of research that has been incorporated into or influenced the development of this book were presented at annual meetings of the Academy of Management, the American Sociological Association, the Nagymoros Group, and the Social Science History Association. Comments at all of those conferences helped improve this work. I also benefited greatly from comments on presentations at UC–Berkeley (the Center for Culture, Organizations, and Politics; the Center for the Study of Law and Society; the Institute for Research on Labor and Employment; the Institute for the Study of Societal Issues; and the Department of Sociology) and at Boston University, Columbia University, the Copenhagen Business School, Duke University, Emory University, the ESADE Business School, Harvard University, Lugano University, the Massachusetts Institute of Technology, Oxford University, Princeton University, the Stockholm School of Economics, Tilburg University, UC–Irvine, the University of Chicago, the University of Maryland, the University of North Carolina–Chapel Hill, and the University of Southern California.

Some of the material incorporated into this book was shaped by anonymous reviews from the journals to which it was originally submitted: the *Administrative Science Quarterly*, the *American Journal of Sociology*, the *American Sociological Review*, *Organization Science*, *Poetics*, and *Sociological Science*. Alas, those papers didn't always end up in the pages of those journals, but the review process almost always improved them. Two reviewers for Princeton University Press provided incredibly helpful but challenging comments on the entire manuscript; reviewer #2 was particularly assiduous in probing my assumptions and pushing me to up my game while simultaneously supporting my efforts vigorously.

Over the years, many colleagues and several brave students have commented on the papers I was writing on magazines and the grant proposals I wrote to support this work. All of those comments shaped this book, more or less indirectly, by pushing me in new directions and suggesting how to incorporate new perspectives. Thanks to Peter Bearman, Glenn Carroll, John Freeman, Joe Galaskiewicz, William Gallagher, Casey Homan, Mike Hout, Neil Fligstein, Adam Goldstein, Victoria Johnson, Caneel Joyce, David Kirsch, Daniel Kluttz, Jennifer Kurkoski, Chris Marquis, Nydia Macgregor, Debra Minkoff, Phyllis Moen, Giacomo Negro, Chick Perrow, Gabriel Rossman, Chris Ryder, Chuck Tilly, Marc Schneiberg, Jen Schradie, Sarah Soule, Simon Stern, Toby Stuart, and Steve Vaisey.

Chick Perrow read an early version of chapter 1 and urged me to pay more attention to magazine founders' and editors' motives—sometimes crazy, sometimes rational, sometimes self-interested—and, of course, to power. Claude Fischer helped me come up with a title that captures the essence of the book; his insight and wordsmithing also shaped chapter 8 and inspired me to revise several other chapters. Like Claude, Neil Fligstein pushed me to rework both chapters 1 and 8, to highlight key contributions, and to engage readers more deeply in a project he encouraged for years. Chris Bail encouraged me to probe more deeply the connections between my work and those of earlier scholars, especially Gabriel Tarde, and to further develop connections to recent sociological research on the media. Dan Wadhwani offered helpful comments on chapter 1 from the perspective of a business historian. John Meyer read the entire manuscript and provided detailed and highly constructive criticism; John, I'm not sure I followed your advice to be less mundanely realist and "write a bit more like a Canadian explaining to the world why the US is crazy," but I did try to inject a little surprise about how surreal many of the ideals and visions supported by magazines were. Elisabeth Clemens did not read the manuscript, but she did inspire me as I was writing the conclusion and rewriting the introduction; Lis, your talk at the ASA session "The Future of Organizational Sociology" reminded me of things I should have remembered and revealed to me things I didn't know from the work of early historical sociologists. I appreciate you helping me overcome writer's (actually, thinker's) block.

I also want to thank several funding sources. I received financial support for this project from Cornell University's Johnson Graduate School of Management, the Columbia Business School, the University of California–Berkeley, the National Science Foundation (Grant SES-0727502, Magazines and Community in America, 1741–1860; Grant SES-0096016, The Co-evolution of Organizations and Careers) and the William Marion Ewing Kauffman Foundation (Foundings of American Magazines, 1741 to 1860). The funds these institutions provided helped me travel to gather data and present my work; they also helped me purchase computer equipment and books, photocopy old records and book chapters, turn photocopies into electronic files, and pay graduate students to work as research assistants.

Last but certainly not least, I want to thank my graduate students. I have been lucky to work with several brilliant, hardworking, and creative students on this project. Geri Cruz and Robert David at Cornell helped me start gathering data on magazines. Marissa King at Columbia worked with me to gather data on religious denominations, the organized antislavery movement, and the US Post Office. Micki Eisenman and Mukti Khaire at Columbia helped me gather data on printing technology and the economy. Adam Goldstein and Jacob Habinek at UC–Berkeley helped me gather data on educational organizations; Jacob also helped find data on urban areas and magazine founders' backgrounds. Also at UC–Berkeley, Daniel Kluttz helped me plumb the history of copyright law and cultural conceptions of authorship, and Chris Rider helped me gather data on the US Post Office. Five of these students have been coauthors on papers whose findings are incorporated into this book: Marissa King, Adam Goldstein, Jacob Habinek, Daniel Kluttz, and Christopher Rider; without their energy and keen intelligence, this book would have been poorer, if indeed written at all.

Magazines and the Making of America

CHAPTER 1

Introduction

*M*edia have tremendous impacts on society. Most basically, books, newspapers, magazines, radio, television, and the Internet provide us with facts about our world that shape our understanding and our actions: details of political races and sports contests; prices for goods and services; statistics and forecasts about weather and the economy; news of advances in science and medicine; and stories about notable accomplishments, happy occasions, and shameful events. In addition to "just the facts," the media offer us opinions that subtly influence what we know and how we behave: commentaries on politics and the economy; reviews of the arts and literature, entertainment, fashion, and gadgets; praise and criticism of prominent individuals and groups; and advice about health, finances, work, hobbies, romance, and family. Last but not least, the media entertain us with a mix of fact and fiction, both tragedy and comedy. By transmitting facts, opinions, and entertainment, media literally mediate between people, weaving "invisible threads of connection" (Starr 2004: 24) that connect geographically dispersed individuals into cohesive communities whose members share knowledge, goals, values, and principles (Park 1940; Anderson [1983] 1991).

My focus on media leads me away from the view that communities are collections of people with common interests and identities in *particular localities* (towns, cities, or neighborhoods), which is how urban sociologists tend to define community (e.g., Duncan et al. 1960; Warner 1972; Fischer 1982). I am instead interested in how media like magazines make it possible to build *translocal* communities—collections of people with common interests, beliefs, identities, and activities who recognize what they have in common but who are geographically dispersed and cannot easily meet face-to-face. Their interactions are literally mediated by media (Tarde 1969; Thompson 1995).

Media support a realm of social life that lies in between the state and the individual, variously labeled "civil society" (Ferguson 1767) or "the public sphere" (Habermas [1962] 1991). This realm of social life is constituted by openly accessible information and communication about matters of general concern; it springs from conversation, connection, and common action. In this realm, people assemble to discuss and engage with politics and public policy, an exercise that is essential for the functioning of democracy. Starting with Alexis de Tocqueville ([1848] 2000), many scholars have argued that the higher the quality of discourse and the larger the quantity of participation in this realm, the stronger the bonds between citizens and the better democracy is served.[1]

But media are involved in many more realms of social life than formal politics. They also deliver educational content in the arts and humanities, the social and natural sciences, medicine and health, business, and engineering and technology; information for people with many different occupations and in many industries; and material designed to appeal to members of particular ethnic groups, religions, and social reform movements, as well as to sports enthusiasts, lovers of literature and the arts, and hobbyists. In all these realms, which lie outside formal politics and which are the focus of this book, media collectively create and sustain diverse communities of discourse, many of which transcend locality and knit together large numbers of people across vast distances. Thus, the development of media helps propel the transition from a traditional society composed primarily of small, local communities to a modern one composed of intersecting local and translocal communities (Higham 1974; Bender 1978; Eisenstein 1979; Thompson 1995; Starr 2004).

I study America because, by the early nineteenth century, the United States was the leader in mass media even though it was sparsely populated and possessed a small, relatively primitive economy (Starr 2004). Moreover, the United States was always an uncertain union. In 1776 it was just barely possible to imagine a federation of thirteen disparate colonies—if not a fully imagined community, then a community of partial inclusion, centered on white male property owners—only because the colonies were strung along the Eastern Seaboard, connected by rivers and the Atlantic, and migration between the colonies had, by the mid-eighteenth century, engendered an intercolonial creole elite whose members shared an "American" mind-set. But even then, the United States was a daring project: an uneasy amalgam of thirteen societies that varied greatly in terms of religion, ethnicity, politics, and economic organization and that were only loosely bound into a federation with a central government whose powers were quite limited. The new nation covered far more territory than any earlier republic and, compounding the difficulties created by distance, it was fringed by a vast wilderness that had not yet been wrested from the grasp of natives or European powers. Political elites fretted that this republic might dissolve (Nagle 1964; Wood 1969; Wiebe 1984). As one founding father neatly summarized the situation, "The colonies had grown up under constitutions of government so different, there was so great a variety of religions, they were composed of so many different nations, their customs, manners, and habits had so little resemblance, and their intercourse had been so rare, and their knowledge of each other so imperfect, that to unite them the same principles in theory and the same system of action was certainly a very difficult enterprise" (John Adams to Hezekiah Niles, 13 February 1818, quoted in Koch 1965: 228–29).

---

[1] In contrast, see Riley (2010) for a more skeptical view of how and under what circumstances civil society contributes to democracy rather than authoritarianism.

Elites' concern about the fragility of the new nation was well founded. Just three years after the US Constitution was ratified, the Whiskey Rebellion broke out to contest federal excise taxes on distilled spirits. More generally, state legislators quickly began to formulate mercantilist policies to support their own local economies by blocking the inflow of goods and money from other states, based on the assumption that different states in the American "common market" were competing over capital, labor, and entrepreneurial ingenuity (Scheiber 1972). This concern persisted until after the War of 1812. As Henry Adams remarked in his *History of the United States*, "Until 1815, nothing in the future of the American Union was regarded as settled. As late as January, 1815, division into several nationalities was thought to be possible" (1921: 219).

If the original thirteen colonies could be conceivably, if optimistically, unified into a single society, by the middle of the nineteenth century the task of maintaining national unity was far more difficult. The nation had expanded tremendously: the Southwestern Territory (comprising first Tennessee, then Alabama and Mississippi) was created in 1790, Louisiana was purchased in 1803 and Florida in 1821, Texas was annexed in 1845 and Oregon partitioned in 1846, and the territory comprising Arizona, California, western Colorado, New Mexico, Nevada, Utah, and part of Wyoming was acquired between 1849 and 1854. As a result, the landmass of the United States almost quadrupled, from 823,000 square miles in 1790 to 1.72 million square miles in 1803, 2.5 million in 1846, and 3.0 million in 1860. Forging a single community from citizens of thirty-three states and several territories spread over such a vast and varied terrain was almost too much to expect, especially given the lack of east–west waterways, the presence of several mountain ranges, and this era's primitive communication and transportation technologies. It is not surprising then that regional differences in culture and community emerged, separating the North from the South, the East from the Midwest and West, and urban from rural. These cultural schisms were fed not only by immense territorial expansion but also by sparse patterns of settlement along the frontier, which made possible the development of novel community structures, including experimental communal groups such as Zoar in Ohio, Nashoba in Tennessee, and St. Nazianz in Wisconsin, many of which were launched as antimodernist responses to industrialization (Kanter 1972; Hindle and Lubar 1986). Industrialization in the Northeast, which contrasted sharply with the largely agricultural and extractive economy that prevailed elsewhere, also contributed to cultural heterogeneity.

This grand experiment in nation building merits our attention now, as social scientists ponder the future of heterogeneous nation-states (e.g., Paul, Ikenberry, and Hall 2003) and pan-national systems like the European Union (e.g., Fligstein 2008). The last century has seen many nations cleaved by civil war, scores of smaller states emerging, recurrent rumblings of discontent among sectarians in a dozen hot spots, the dismantling of the Soviet Union and the breakup of Yugoslavia, steps toward the unification of Europe into a

transnational community, the possibility of that community being disman-
tled and, most recently, unrest in the Middle East and eastern Europe that may
redraw many national boundaries. These events, and the surprise with which
both their inhabitants and external observers often respond to them, demonstrate a clear need to understand how diverse societies can grow and thrive,
and what role media play in maintaining or undermining comity among subgroups within such societies.

WHY FOCUS ON MAGAZINES?

Scholars have until recently paid far less attention to magazines, especially in
the early years of their history, than to newspapers and books.[2] This neglect
may be due to the contemporary consensus on early magazines, which was
neatly summed by one scholar as: "a kind of literary hinterland or vast record
of not-so-exciting attempts to institutionalize literacy in the colonies and the
early republic vis-à-vis correspondence and news from Europe; amateurish,
heavily didactic essays and poems; reprinted speeches and dry historical biographies; and numerous extracts and miscellaneous trifles concerning a range
of topics as diverse or leaden as 'sleep,' German etiquette, congressional proceedings, or the condition of the Flamborough Man of War and its 20 swivel
guns in 1789. In short ... inaccessible, boring, or simply irrelevant" (Kamrath
2002: 498–99). But magazines—even the earliest ones—are worthy of greater
attention, for five reasons. First, compared to newspapers, magazines' contents
are quite varied, so they forge social ties in realms that extend far beyond politics and public policy. Such variety in contents is fitting, as the word *magazine*
is derived from the Arabic word for storehouse, *makazin*. Thus, studying magazines makes it possible to analyze a wide array of communities—not just in
formal politics but also in religion, literature and the arts, informal politics,
the professions, and among ethnic groups. Second, because their contents are
likely to be of more lasting interest than that of newspapers, magazines are
not discarded as quickly and so have a more enduring impact. That is why
they have long shelf lives, as a visit to any library will attest. Even in the earliest
years of the magazine industry, publishers anticipated that their products
would be bound and kept for future reference; to that end they used better
paper stock than was used for newspapers and offered subscribers indexes,
published at the end of each volume, for inclusion when subscribers bound
each volume for their personal libraries. Some publishers even offered late-
arriving subscribers a full complement of past issues so they would not miss
any part of a volume.

Third, because magazines circulate beyond a single town or city, they reach
geographically wider audiences than do most newspapers. Fourth, because

---

[2] Most recent studies of magazines in this time period, including McGill (2003), Okker (2003),
Nord (2004), and Gardner (2012), focus exclusively on literary life.

helping readers interpret facts rather than merely presenting them is a core function of magazines, they are excellent platforms for oppositional stances on many issues. Finally, magazines are serial publications, which allows them to develop rich reciprocal interactions with their readers, something that newspapers can do but books cannot (Okker 2003; Gardner 2012). Their serial nature not only allows magazine publishers to respond to opponents' salvos and adjust their messages to accommodate feedback from readers but also allows them to manage impressions, modify their images to match shifts in readers' tastes and concerns, and forge strong ties to readers through repetition. Moreover, it allows readers to be active participants in magazines by contributing letters and other content. Thus, through cycles of publishing, magazines and readers mutually construct communal identities.

In sum, magazines' varied contents, relative permanence, broad geographic reach, interpretive mission, and serial nature endow them with the power to influence many aspects of social life: formal politics, commerce, religion, reform, science, work, industry, and education. In short, magazines are a key medium through which people pay attention to and understand the things that affect their everyday lives. It is not surprising that early magazine editors recognized these advantages of magazines over other print media. For instance, in his inaugural address, Thomas Condie, publisher-editor of the *Philadelphia Monthly Magazine*, proclaimed magazines "the literature of the people" (1798: 5.). More grandiosely, Hugh Henry Brackenridge, editor of the *United States Magazine* (founded 1779) declared that his publication would "in itself contain a library, and be the literary coffee-house of public conversation" (Brackenridge 1779b, 9).

MAGAZINES, MODERNIZATION, AND COMMUNITY IN AMERICA

The story of magazines, modernization, and community requires us to understand both society and culture—both the social relations surrounding goods and services and the patterned meanings people attribute to those goods, services, and social relations. As political scientist Karl Deutsch observed, "Societies produce, select, and channel goods and services. Cultures produce, select, and channel information. . . . There is no community nor culture without society. And there can be no society, no division of labor, without a minimum of transfer of information, without communication" (1953: 92, 95). Magazines are central to modernization and community. They are the social glue that brings together people who would otherwise never meet face-to-face, allowing readers to receive and react to the same cultural messages at the same time and, in many cases, encouraging readers to contribute to shared cultural projects.

Magazines can be both instruments of social change and tools of social control that reinforce the status quo. Whenever and wherever the press is free, as it has been in America since the Revolution, magazines are relatively easy to establish. As long as printers have unused capacity, any individual or group with information to disseminate, a point of view to promulgate, a community to build, or a cause to promote can arrange to publish a magazine. Thus magazines, like other communications media, can either reinforce or revolutionize social and cultural patterns (Schudson 1978; Meyrowitz 1985; Fischer 1992; Nord 2004). To the extent that start-up costs are low, magazines are accessible to people in many strata of society, not just socioeconomic elites, as tools of communication and community building.

The story told here begins with the publication of the first magazines in America in 1741 and continues to 1860, the eve of the Civil War, that great cleaving of community, that terrible conflict between a modernizing impulse and a stubborn traditionalism. This temporal scope allows me to trace the institutionalization of this new cultural good to see how magazines evolved from their first appearance, when they were doubtful ventures beset by seemingly intractable problems of supply and demand, into a major communications industry with its own material practices and social conventions. By 1860 magazines had assumed approximately their contemporary print form as bound booklets with covers, issued at regular intervals, and containing a wide variety of reading matter, both verbal and pictorial, that are of more than passing interest and that can be variously narrative, descriptive, explanatory, critical, or exhortative (Wood 1949; Tebbel and Zuckerman 1991). Like their twenty-first-century counterparts, magazine editors in this period identified and wooed authors and illustrators and worked to improve authors' contributions. Starting in 1819 writers were increasingly likely to be remunerated. Publishers throughout this era financed production, sold advertising, managed subscriptions and newsstand sales, and oversaw distribution, while printers created the physical products. Readers paid in advance for subscriptions carried in the mail or purchased magazines when they appeared in local stores, and advertisers paid publishers handsomely to promote their goods and services to readers.

The emergence of the American magazine industry was part of the "rage for reading" (Cavallo and Chartier 1999: 26) that had begun in Europe and the British colonies in North America by the eighteenth century.[3] The proliferation of books, newspapers, and magazines engendered a modern style of reading: extensive rather than intensive, secular rather than religious, and seeking useful knowledge or entertainment rather than moral uplift (Cavallo and Chartier 1999; Griswold 2008).

Magazines in this era constituted an increasingly extensive network for transmitting a wide array of information and opinions; they were passed from reader to reader, and their contents were discussed in private homes and at

[3] The timing of this transition is debated. Some scholars date the transition to Europe in the late Middle Ages, with the rise of scholasticism (Cavallo and Chartier 1999), others to the fifteenth century following the development of the printing press (Eisenstein 1979). More fundamentally, whether this transition constituted an abrupt revolution or merely a gradual evolution in reading style and substance is also debated (Koek 1999).

social gatherings (Mott 1930).[4] Magazines were an especially important source of social cohesion in this era, as the scarcity of long distance transportation systems and the primitive state of other telecommunications media made building community over any distance an arduous task. Thus studying magazines in this era allows us to observe the modernization of America—in particular, the development of translocal communities. Indeed, as one historian noted, magazines fostered a nationwide community of magazine publishers who served as each other's agents, traded copies, and exchanged personal favors:

> It was their shared status as publishers of magazines that bound these printers together . . . and allowed them to create a network of exchange and value around the peculiar currency of their periodicals. They bound each other's magazines, promoted them along with their own, and used them as currency to secure both credit and access to markets far beyond the reach of their local agents. They magazine allowed them to image a *national* literary culture for the first time, and if the realities on the ground lagged behind the vision, it did not prevent them from inhabiting this brave new world together. (Gardner 2012: 100; emphasis in the original)

Studying magazines in this era allows us to observe the shift toward a "society of organizations" (Perrow 1991), an "organizing society" (Meyer and Bromley 2013). The growth of magazines necessitated the development of formal organizations to manage publication and distribution. Putting out a magazine requires sustained, coordinated effort on the part of writers, illustrators, editors, printers, and publishers, which in turn requires formal organizations to manage ongoing, interdependent tasks. Moreover, magazines both benefited from and provided benefits to affiliated organizations: churches, colleges, agricultural and educational societies, literary groups, professional bodies, and reform associations. These organizations provided readers, contributors, and financial support; in turn, magazines provided platforms for broadcasting news and opinions, thereby solidifying bonds among organizational members. Therefore, focusing on the magazine industry in this era offers great insight into the creation and entrenchment of formal organizations in American society as it moved from a traditional social order to a more modern one.

In terms of temporal scale, this study is located between *l'histoire de la longue durée* and *l'histoire événementielle* (Braudel 1980); accordingly, it can shed light on the critical conditions that gave rise to the mosaic nature of American society as well as its melting-pot qualities. Because the starting point is 1741, thirty-five years before the Revolution, the study will provide insights into the origins of contemporary translocal social groups in education, religion, social reform,

---

[4] Notwithstanding their impact on many Americans in this era, it is important to remember that magazines supported only communities of *partial* inclusion—those that always excluded slaves and often excluded free blacks, women, children, Catholics, and Jews.

various occupations, and literature and the arts. Because the ending point is 120 years later, in 1860, the study will demonstrate that this structuring of society into many distinct groups is a slow process and that, as Fernand Braudel noted, social structures "get in the way of history, hinder its flow, and in hindering it shape it" (1980: 31). This study's concern for historical context also fills a gap in sociological research on organizations, where history usually plays only a shady role (Zald 1990, 1996), even though most recent organizational research is oriented toward questions of time and change—grounded in longitudinal data and focused on how organizations are founded, persist, and change.

To explain the simultaneous development of a distinctive, pluralistically integrated American society containing different communities, I craft an institutional demography of eighteenth- and nineteenth-century American magazines. My first concern—demographic—is to describe magazines' vital rates and the distribution of magazines along important dimensions of difference. Rates and distributions are the natural focus of demography; although most demographic work centers on individuals and families, sociologists have adopted its tools to study the evolving number and nature of organizations and their products (for a review, see Carroll and Hannan 2000). My second concern—institutional—is to describe the evolution of social, cultural, and legal institutions in this era and to explain the mutual influences of magazines and these institutions. Sensitivity to institutions is required because history—time and place—is of fundamental importance to the related processes of magazine industry development and social modernization. This approach allows me to move beyond the rich but necessarily limited conclusions drawn from magazine histories covering short time periods or particular industry sectors (e.g., Stearns 1932; Demaree 1941) and from criticism of particular literary movements or authorial communities (e.g., Simpson 1954; Gardner 2012). It also transcends standard histories of the magazine industry (Mott 1930, 1938a, 1938b; Tebbel and Zuckerman 1991) by conducting quantitative analysis of a virtually complete list of magazines, supplemented by quantitative and qualitative analysis of magazines chosen randomly from that list. The conclusions drawn from this kind of analysis are more truly representative of the industry than are conclusions drawn from analysis of nonrandom samples such as the most prominent magazines. Studies that focus on elite-supported or large-circulation magazines provide only a limited, and often biased, picture. For example, if we focus solely on religious magazines affiliated with elite mainline Protestant denominations, we would fail to engage with the dramatic upheaval in American religion that was reflected in and supported by magazines affiliated with upstart religious groups such as the Baptists and Disciples of Christ (Hatch 1989).

Magazines, like all media, and indeed all technologies, both shape their surroundings and are shaped by them (Bijker, Hughes, and Pinch 1987; Boczkowski 2004; Starr 2004). Therefore, my treatment of magazines probes reciprocal causal processes: I examine how developments in American society supported and constrained magazines, how the growing number and variety of magazines promoted and directed modern community building in America, and antimodern reactions to that process. Because this analysis is concerned with the *reciprocal* influence of organizations and society, it answers calls for a return to studying how organizations shape society (Stern and Barley 1996; Perrow 2002). In modern societies, where organizations wield tremendous power and distribute innumerable benefits, all interests—economic, political, and cultural—are pursued through formal organizations (Coser 1974). It is only through such organizations as magazine publishing concerns, churches, and social reform associations that large-scale coordination—for modern states, capitalist economies, and civil societies—become possible. To understand the development and structuring of modern societies, then, we must understand organizations. But we generally study how organizations themselves are shaped by their environments rather than the reverse. Those who have studied the impact of organizations on society have tended to focus on large organizations (e.g., Coleman 1974; Bagdikian [1983] 2004; Perrow 2002; McChesney 2004) and to ignore the impact of small organizations (for a notable exception, see Starr 2004).

The analysis reported here is based on original data collection on 5,362 magazines published between 1741 and 1860. The data were gathered from nine primary and over ninety secondary sources, which are described in appendix 1. These data include virtually all magazines published during this era, according to estimates made by Frank Luther Mott (1930, 1938a, 1938b), whose three-volume history of the industry is still a standard reference work. Data on magazines are complemented by data on key features of American society that affected and were affected by magazines: rapid population growth and urbanization; breakthroughs in printing and papermaking technologies; the development of magazines' principle distribution infrastructure, the postal network; the burgeoning number of religious communities and social reform movements; the evolution of the legal, ministerial, and medical professions; and the growth of educational institutions, the increase in commercial exchange, and the rise of scientific agriculture. Appendix 1 describes how I gathered and prepared these data, while appendix 2 explains how I conducted quantitative data analyses.

Before outlining the book I want to make sure we are (literally) on the same page. To that end I review scholarship on modernization and community and explain how these concepts apply to America in this era.

THE MODERNIZATION OF AMERICA

"Modernization" and "modernity" are complex and often ambiguous phenomena. Historian Richard D. Brown summarized the process of becoming modern neatly as "the movement away from small, localistic communities where family ties and face-to-face relationships provide structure and cohesion, toward the development of a large-scale uniform society bound together by belief in a common ideology, by a bureaucratic system, and by the operation of a large-scale, developed economy" (Brown 1976: 6–7). As this definition indicates, modernity is an omnibus concept that is associated with many related phenomena: rationality, individualism, secularism, mechanized power, large-scale manufacturing, the exchange of goods and services in markets for money, an extensive division of labor, and a highly differentiated array of social statuses and large, bureaucratic organizations.[5] Modernity is often contrasted with tradition. In traditional societies, which were largely hunter-gatherer or agrarian in nature, people were members—by right or custom—of three communal institutions: the family (both kin and kith), the monopolistic religion, and the feudal or monarchical state (MacIver 1917; Weber [1968] 1978). In modern societies, which are to varying extents manufacturing- or service-based, people are members of associative institutions that bring together individuals who may have no connection by birth or custom but who seek to achieve common goals. Because formal, bureaucratic organizations are the most common and most important kind of associative institution, they are the fundamental building blocks of modern societies (Weber [1968] 1978; Galambos 1970; Coleman 1974, 1981; Perrow 1991; Meyer and Bromley 2013).

The modernization of America, which began before the mid-eighteenth century and continued long after the outbreak of the Civil War, proceeded along five related axes. The first was economic: the economy shifted away from family-owned farms where people produced much of what they needed, consumed much of what they produced, bartered some, and sold the remainder for cash and shifted toward a capitalist system of industrial production—a private, profit-seeking system where both ownership and capital investment were formally organized and where markets dictated prices (North 1961; Larson 2010). Observing western Europe, Karl Marx characterized this transformation as one in which "natural relationships" dissolved "into money relationships" ([1846] 1947: 57). The monetary system adopted by the United States after the Revolution itself reflected a modernizing temperament: the decimal currency adopted through the Coinage Act (US Congress 1792b) was highly modern and rational, especially in comparison to the ancient and arcane British system of pounds, shillings, and pence (Linklater 2002).

The second axis of modernization was demographic and geographic: the shift away from living on farms and in small towns toward living in larger urban areas. In many rural areas, vast sections of the nation's growing landmass were organized in an essentially modern geographic pattern. The US Congress's land ordinances of 1785 and 1787 directed that in the new

---

[5] *Modernization* is a contested term; some scholars object to it on the grounds that it is invoked in teleological theories of social change, which have an often unsubtle normative tone. I do not hold such a simplistic and prescriptive view; instead I conceive of modernization as a complex process, one that proceeded haltingly and was not by any means ineluctable or uniformly beneficial to cultural, economic, or political relations, and that may not be complete even today.

states in the West, land was to be divided into sections precisely one mile square, with thirty-six sections forming a township (Treat 1910; Commager 1973; Linklater 2002). This land was sold at public auctions—modern market exchanges.

The third axis of modernization, which is closely related to the second, was social (Tönnies [1887] 1957; Durkheim [1893] 1984; Cooley [1909] 1923; MacIver 1917; Weber [1968] 1978; Tarde 1969). Social relations moved away from undifferentiated, holistic, and personal connections rooted in common values, sentiments, and norms between people who were in similar social positions in small local settlements; they shifted instead toward differentiated, impersonal connections between people who were in different interdependent positions in large, often translocal, communities. Just as work was increasingly divided among distinct but interdependent occupations and productive effort was increasingly divided among chains of specialized enterprises, thought and action were increasingly differentiated: home was increasingly separated from work, production from consumption, the sacred from the secular, art from utility, and private life from public life. But differentiation in social relations was countered by the concentration of people, capital, and trade in a small number of large urban areas, a process that Charles Tilly described as "the implosion of production into a few intensely industrial regions" (1984: 49).

The fourth axis of modernization was technological, which was essential for both the emergence of modern social relations and the development of the modern market-based economy. Technology and the modern capitalist economic system are an ensemble—although technology and economy are analytically distinct concepts, they cannot be fully disentangled empirically because technological change drives economic change and economic change drives technological change (Braudel 1984: 543). Key technological changes implicated in the modernization of American society are the development of communication systems (such as the magazine industry) and transportation systems (such as the post office) as well as the rise of bureaucratic organizations such as schools, religious organizations, reform associations, and business concerns.

The fifth axis of modernization was cultural. At the core of this cultural change was Americans' understanding of time, which shifted away from conceiving the past, present, and future as simultaneous along time (omnitemporal) toward conceiving of these temporal states as links in an endless chain of cause and effect (in which the past was radically separated from the present; Inkeles and Smith 1974; Brown 1976; Anderson [1983] 1991: 22–26). Moreover, impelled by advances in transportation and communication technologies—canals, steamships, railroads, the postal network and, of course, magazines—the place of time in society evolved away from local and shared by community members toward translocal and standardized by outside authorities (Giddens 1990; Zboray 1993). For example, paying people to work at interdependent tasks in artisanal shops and industrial factories focused owners' and workers' attention on time, resulting in novel and highly explicit temporal constraints on everyday life—what E. P. Thompson (1967) termed "time discipline." Outside the economic sphere, educational institutions inculcated in their pupils the virtues of punctuality and regularity—another form of time discipline.

A broader shift in mentality attended this shift in temporal understanding as people moved away from fearing change toward accepting, even welcoming, it (Bellah 1968; Inkeles and Smith 1974). "Modern" people believe they can improve their circumstances, they are open to new experiences; they are ambitious for themselves and their children, so they plan and conserve time; and they are less dependent on traditional authority figures (Inkeles and Smith 1974). Thus "modern" people are calculatingly, instrumentally rational—they work toward long-term goals that are chosen in relation to larger systems of meaning, calculating both the means to their desired ends and the ends themselves (Tönnies [1887] 1957; Weber [1968] 1978; Swidler 1973). "Modern" people are also fundamentally individualistic (Tönnies [1887] 1957; Cooley [1909] 1923): in modern societies, "the social unit . . . is not the group, the guild, the tribe, or the city, but the person" (Bell 1976: 16).

In sum, the modernization of America involved five related transitions: economic, technological, demographic and geographic, social, and cultural. But, as my repeated use of the words "shift away from" and "toward" indicate, these transitions began in some parts of the British colonies before 1740 and ended in most parts of the United States long after 1860—indeed, some parts of the country may be said, even today, to follow highly traditional ways of life. Given the great cross-sectional heterogeneity in the American experience of modernization and the lack of a smooth modernizing trajectory over time, I strive to confine my analysis to carefully delineated time periods, spheres of social life, and geographic regions and make only the most tentative generalizations about America as a whole.

MODERNIZATION AND COMMUNITY IN AMERICA

I am specifically interested in how the media create community—in particular, how they create the kinds of geographically dispersed *translocal* groups that characterize modern societies. The idea of community is particularly important to sociologists because it is "the most fundamental and far-reaching of all sociology's unit-ideas" (Nisbet 1966: 47). Early sociologists, from Ferdinand Tönnies ([1887] 1957) to Émile Durkheim ([1893] 1984), Charles Horton Cooley ([1909] 1923), Robert Morrison MacIver (1917), Max Weber ([1968] 1978) and Gabriel Tarde (1969), were concerned about the nature of community even though they differed greatly in their assessment of the causes and nature of the social bonds holding community members together.[6] They

---

[6] Early sociologists gave the two types of what I am calling community different, sometimes

generally agreed that in modern societies social connections were affiliative, differentiated, and often impersonal and linked people who were in dissimilar but interdependent positions in social structure, and often in very different geographic regions. They contrasted this to community in traditional societies, where connections were communal, undifferentiated, holistic, and personal and where common values, sentiments, and norms linked people who were in similar social positions in the same small local settlement.

Overall, history generally supports these pioneering scholars' predictions. In the wake of the five modernizing transitions described above, the nature and meaning of community was altered in America between 1740 and 1860. In 1740, 95 percent of Americans lived on farmsteads or in small villages and towns; in these small, geographically localized communities, members were bound together by familial relations and face-to-face interactions. By 1860, not only did 20 percent of Americans live in large urban areas but most Americans, including many inhabitants of rural areas, were members of large (sometimes national) translocal communities connected by shared goals, knowledge, values, and principles. These communities were active in many different arenas of social life: specialized occupations, education, religion, social reform, commerce, and literature and the arts. Moreover, by 1860, Americans' interactions in these translocal communities were increasingly mediated by formal organizations—and by magazines. Yet my analysis will reveal that the evolution of community in America from the mid-eighteenth century to the mid-nineteenth was more complex and contingent than these early scholars predicted. Most early sociologists said nothing about how media bind these communities together. Only Cooley ([1909] 1923) and Tarde (1969) made communication media an explicit focus, arguing that mass communication was critical to this transition.

Building on the work of early sociological theorists, many later scholars who studied this time period in America assumed that a largely localized, personal, and communally affiliated society (Tönnies's *Gemeinschaft*) began to be transformed into a translocal, market-oriented society connected through diverse, cross-cutting impersonal affiliations (Tönnies's *Gesellschaft*; see, e.g., Handlin 1959; Wood 1969; Rothman 1971). But, as both historians and I show, this assumption of a highly teleological sequence does not accurately reflect the complex dynamics of American society. The reality is that at every point in this time period, both forms of social interaction, *Gemeinschaft* and

confusingly oppositional, labels. In the following list, the traditional category is given first and the (more) modern one second: community (*Gemeinschaft*) versus society (*Gesellschaft*), held together by organic versus mechanical solidarity (Tönnies); traditional society held together by mechanical solidarity versus modern society held together by organic solidarity (Durkheim); primary versus unlabeled (but presumably secondary) groups (Cooley); community (integral, locational) versus association (partial, intentional; MacIver); communal institution (*Vergemeinschaftung*) versus associative institution (*Vergesellschaftung*) (Weber); and primary versus secondary groups (Tarde). Throughout this book the term *community* can mean a traditional or modern one, something in between, or a complex combination of the two. I will strive to be clear about the characteristics of the specific communities I discuss.

Gesellschaft, were present—albeit in different degrees and affecting different aspects of social life for people in different geographic locations and social positions (Brown 1976; Bender 1978; Rutman 1980; Tilly 1984; Prude [1983] 1999). Localized and highly personal communal relations were not at all times, in all locations, or in all arenas of social life replaced with translocal and impersonal associative relations; instead, the development of *Gemeinschaft* at some times, in some locations, and in some arenas of social life actually reinforced *Gesellschaft*. For example, Frederick Law Olmsted, who is now best known as the codesigner of new York City's Central Park but was also an insightful social critic, observed in his tour of the South between 1853 and 1861 that most whites in Mississippi still wore homespun clothes and most whites in Tennessee went barefoot in winter (Olmsted [1862] 1953). Change coexisted with the absence of change: as Braudel argued, there is a "layer of stagnant history" (1981: 28) that persists in all modernizing societies and resists the penetration of *Gesellschaft* (see also Braudel 1982: 229). Or, as historian Rolla M. Tryon put it, the transition from traditional to modern "was always taking place but never quite completed when the country as a whole is considered" (1917: 243).

In the decades before the Revolution, as the colonies became more settled and "civilized," traditionalism began to reemerge (Brown 1976). On the frontier, the earliest settlers quickly reverted to traditional forms of activity: hunting and subsistence farming, making virtually all of what they needed at home rather than purchasing it from merchants, buying and selling little, if anything, in purely local markets. In political life, the Sabbatarian movement became "America's first great antimodern crusade" (John 1990: 564) in the early nineteenth century. In the rapidly industrializing towns of New England, old and new ways of living and working coexisted in an uneasy tension (Prude [1983] 1999).

A shift away from modernity and toward tradition was especially noticeable in the South (Genovese [1961] 1989; Fox-Genovese and Genovese 1983). As cotton supplanted tobacco on southern plantations, the old quasi-aristocratic system was reinforced and revived (Chaplin 1993). The southern plantation elite came to view agriculture and rural life as ideal and commerce, industry, and urban life as vulgar (Coulter 1930), a decidedly antimodernist sentiment that they shared with the European nobility, who a century earlier had rejected bourgeois claims that economic success should count as much as birth, honor, and tradition (Berger 1986). The growing population of slaves was excluded from modernization: almost all were agricultural laborers or household servants who rarely left the confines of their masters' plantations and thus had highly localized webs of social relations; the few slaves who worked outside agriculture were confined to traditional labor-intensive crafts like carpentry and masonry. Some have argued that the Civil War was, fundamentally, a crisis caused by incompatible social trajectories, with the rapidly modernizing, urbanizing, and industrializing North pitted against the stubbornly traditional, rural, and agrarian South (Luraghi 1962; Foner 1980).

THE PATH FORWARD: THE OUTLINE OF THIS BOOK

I tell the story of magazines, modernization, and community in America in two parts. The first, which is laid out in chapters 2 to 4, examines the history and operations of American magazines—their nature and the determinants of their successes and failures.

Chapter 2: The History of American Magazines, 1741–1860. The earliest American magazines were both few in number and highly precarious ventures. Not until after peace was restored did the industry gain a firm foothold on America. By the 1820s, the industry was flourishing (Tebbel and Zuckerman 1991), growing explosively and becoming popular as tools for social organizing. By 1860, over a thousand magazines were in print; many had long lives and some attracted large nationwide followings.

From their original base in three eastern cities, Boston, New York, and Philadelphia, magazines expanded across the continent. The industry became geographically dispersed in part because dramatic advances in printing technology and the spread of printing presses across the continent lowered barriers to entry and made it possible to publish magazines almost anywhere. But at the same time, magazine publishing became concentrated in New York City due to the metropolis's deep pools of cultural and financial resources: by the 1850s it was home to 25 percent of the magazines then in print.

American magazines in this era were highly eclectic in two regards: the contents of the typical magazine were varied, and many different genres of magazines were published. Moreover, the composition of the magazine industry changed greatly over time. In the eighteenth century, most magazines were general-interest periodicals that published short articles and longer essays on politics, religion, manners and society, literature and art, science and education, and history and geography, as well as poetry and sketches. By the 1820s, religious magazines had come to outnumber general-interest magazines, and the number of literary magazines and specialty medical journals had increased dramatically. At midcentury, religious magazines continued to dominate, followed by general-interest magazines, and agricultural magazines had outgrown literary magazines and medical journals; they were augmented by sizable numbers of magazines devoted to social reform, business, natural science, music, law, and humor.

Chapter 3: The Material and Cultural Foundations of American Magazines. Perhaps the most fundamental fact standing in the way of an American magazine industry in the eighteenth century was that the potential audience was tiny. The colonies were sparsely settled and only a few inhabitants lived in urban areas near the printers who produced magazines and the merchants who sold them. Moreover, the potential reading public had little spare cash or leisure time for such ephemera as magazines. Over the next 120 years, the population exploded, from less than one million in 1740 to over thirty million in 1860, while the number of urban areas (places with over 2,500 inhabitants) rose from 36 in 1760 (the first year reliable data are available on urbanization) to 422 in 1860. This phenomenal increase in the potential reader base made it possible for a wide variety of magazines to thrive.

The evolution of basic production and distribution technologies—specifically, printing technology and the postal system—also facilitated the magazine industry's expansion. In the earliest years, the scarcity of printing presses greatly hampered publishing efforts. The situation was exacerbated by the fact that mid-eighteenth-century printing presses were slow, cumbersome, manually powered mechanisms. By the 1830s smoothly operating, high-volume steam-powered presses had spread to every state and several territories. The earliest magazines' circulations were highly local because they were distributed primarily through nearby merchants. But after passage of the Postal Act of 1794, magazines were increasingly carried through the mails. Wide distribution was facilitated by the exponential growth of the postal network, from 31 offices and fewer than 1,500 miles in 1740 to over 28,000 offices and 240,000 miles in 1860 (Kielbowicz 1989; John 1995). Improvements in the speed and reliability of mail transport kept pace with growth of the postal system, as transportation shifted from horseback over unpaved pathways to horse-drawn carriages over better-maintained roads and as the postal system came to rely more and more on steamboats, canals, and railroads.

The development of copyright law and cultural and economic responses to those changes also affected the magazine industry. Copyright law was nonexistent before 1790 (Bugbee 1967; Patterson 1968; Everton 2005) and almost never applied to magazines until long after the Civil War (Charvat 1968; Haveman and Kluttz 2014). This presented early magazines with both an opportunity and a problem: although they benefited from the freedom to "extract" much of their contents from other publications and so gain access to a wide variety of free material, they had no legal protection for any original material developed by their contributors, and so could not easily differentiate themselves from rival periodicals. This situation was exacerbated by the fact that in the eighteenth century, the few Americans who were authors were conceived of as gentlemen-scholars, not paid professionals. But following cultural shifts in Britain that were promoted by the development of copyright law there, American writers grew in numbers and began to conceive of themselves as professionals who deserved both respect for their skill and remuneration for their output. This cultural shift led magazines to pay authors for their contributions, starting in 1819. In turn, this economic innovation provided magazines with a wealth of original material and made them important outlets for aspiring professional authors.

Chapter 4: Launching Magazines. The men (there were no women) who launched magazines in the eighteenth century were a select few, part of the socioeconomic elite—men like printers Benjamin Franklin and Isaiah Thomas, and Methodist bishop Francis Asbury.[7] But by the time magazines had become

---

[7] Printers had high social status during the eighteenth and early nineteenth centuries: they

a well-established part of American life, their founders had become much more like "everyman"—not only members of the socioeconomic elite, but also many people of middling social stature like novelist Timothy Shay Arthur and spiritualist Uriah Clark, who used magazines to make their reputations and (for a lucky few) their fortunes. Moreover, magazine entrepreneurship became an increasingly organizationally sponsored activity, a fact that reflected the rise of formal organizations created by people banding together in religious, reform, educational, literary, and professional communities.

Magazine founders' espoused goals for their new ventures evolved over time. These goals were expressed in prospectuses and editorial statements that were aimed at convincing both the reading public and potential contributors of magazines' value and thus revealed the cultural schemas underpinning magazines. The vast majority of magazine founders asserted that they sought to benefit society at large or support a particular community. Only a tiny fraction admitted that they sought to earn a profit or otherwise benefit themselves; so strong was the distaste for self-benefit that some sought to demonstrate selflessness by promising that any profits their magazines earned would go to a good cause. While early magazine founders sought to benefit society at large, later ones promoted the interests of particular communities—usually defined in terms of geography or religion, more rarely in terms of demography, occupation, or politics. Thus, although magazines started out as forces for the unification of the colonies into a single society, they soon reflected divisions in this society along geographic, religious, demographic, occupational, and political lines.

Magazine founders used a variety of tactics to legitimate their new ventures. Most basically, they provided detailed explanations of what their publications would contain and why these contents would be valuable to potential subscribers. Such explanations often focused on the enduring value of the contents. Some magazines were legitimated by explicating ties to prominent others—politicians, learned clergy, and college professors—which made observable the "invisible communities" (Park 1940) of subscribers, thereby solidifying the bonds between them and enticing outsiders to join them. Others published encomiums from prominent people; such endorsements allowed founders to "borrow" status from the prominent people who vouched for them and their publications.

The second part of the story of magazines, modernization, and community focuses on the push and pull reflected in and sustained by magazines—the centripetal movement toward a common center and the centrifugal movement toward many distinct, often intersecting, sometimes opposing commu-

---

were highly skilled craftspeople who published official documents for state authorities and often served as postmasters, and were well remunerated, with earnings similar to merchants and others in nonmanual occupations (Wroth 1931; Bailyn 1960; Botein 1981).

nities. This analysis highlights the role that magazines played in promoting discourses replete with principles, symbols, and ideas that community members used to "solve" problems of identity and meaning (Swidler 1986). To elucidate this process, chapters 5 through 7 examine three of the most important areas of social life influenced by magazines—religion, social reform, and the economy—and reveal magazines' role in fostering the pluralistic integration that characterized American society in this era: the awareness and acceptance (sometimes grudging) of others who are different from you in one dimension of social life because they are similar to you in another (Higham 1974; see also Blau and Schwartz 1984). Magazines supported a society that was, paradoxically, unified in a basic way by its distinctiveness from European societies; in doing so, this part of the book will answer long-standing calls to analyze the making of public culture, which stands at the center of the American historical narrative (Bender 1986: 122).

Chapter 5: Religion. Religious heterogeneity has long been the hallmark of America. Before the Revolution, America was home to a wide array of faiths. Although nine of the thirteen British colonies had established (state-sanctioned and state-supported) churches in 1776, a large minority of inhabitants were members of over a dozen "dissenting" denominations. Religious diversity in America became even greater after the Revolution when state churches were disestablished, making it easier for other faiths to gain adherents. Waves of immigration brought more Catholics, Anabaptists, and Lutherans into the mix. Finally, three series of religious revivals further increased the number of distinct faiths, as the leaders of revivalistic religious movements clashed with established religious authorities and seceded from their communities to found dozens of new sects. Religious participation increased as new upstart churches and countermovements within existing churches aggressively courted adherents.

Because of the wide variety of denominations in America, religion in this era was replete with disputes about the nature of faith, which took the form of struggles over meaning, authority, and boundaries. The high level of religious rancor prompted Timothy Flint, prominent western minister and author, to charge in 1830, "Nine pulpits in ten in our country are occupied chiefly in the denunciation of other sects" (quoted in Mott 1930: 369). Religious magazines proved to be powerful platforms for religious partisans. Vicious battles were fought in an ever-increasing number of scholarly theological reviews and newsy magazines for the laity. These debates produced a torrent of talk about faith: news, loud praise and even louder denunciations, emotional exhortations, and eloquent arguments that generated much material for the religious press. Revivalists were particularly likely to use magazines to reinforce their messages, as these leaders of new religious movements sought to reinforce their charismatic authority over recent converts. Indeed, over half of the religious magazines in this era that had an explicit denominational connection were affiliated with revivalist faiths like the Methodists, Baptists, and Disciples of Christ. By 1830, religious periodicals had become "the grand engine of a burgeoning religious culture, the primary means of promotion for, and bond of union within, competing religious groups" (Hatch 1989: 125–26).

Religion was a modernizing force in this era (Bellah 1968): the Protestant denominations that dominated the field of religion in nineteenth-century America pioneered the development of nationwide communities in two ways (Goldstein and Haveman 2013). First, they built modern bureaucracies with nested national, regional, and local structures to manage clergy, recruit and retain members, and preach to the "unchurched" in what became a nationally organized field of religion. Second, they created large and well-funded formal organizations to produce and distribute magazines, tracts, and Bibles across the nation; these were the second example of bureaucracy in America, after the founding of the US Post Office but before the creation of the railroads, and they pioneered the modern nonprofit corporation (Hall 1998; Nord 2004).

By publishing magazines religious communities competed both locally and nationally to recruit and retain adherents. Moreover, competitive mobilization through magazines depended on the extent to which rivalries among faiths played out simultaneously in multiple markets. The analysis presented in chapter 4 shows that three related trends—the development of a pluralistic nationwide field of religion, the competition engendered by pluralism, and the rise of internal competition from schismatic groups—had independent effects on the growth of denominational magazine publishing. But this analysis also shows that magazine publishing efforts grew faster when and where both competition and resources were high: the impetus to mobilize in the face of competition drove religious groups to act only when and where they had the capacity to mobilize substantial resources.

Chapter 6: Social Reform. Between 1740 and 1860, America witnessed a proliferation of associations that advocated a wide array of social reforms: abolition of slavery; temperance in the consumption of alcohol; reform of prostitutes and seamen; strict observance of the Sabbath; protection for widows and orphans; support for Indians and free blacks; relief for debtors and paupers; care of the insane, blind, and deaf and dumb; political and economic rights for women and workers; nonviolence and an end to war; reform of the penal system and elimination of capital punishment; and vegetarianism. Struck by this, Tocqueville famously stated that "Americans of all ages, all conditions, and all minds constantly unite ... if it is a question of bringing to light a truth or developing a sentiment with the support of a great example, they associate" ([1848] 2000: 489).

The supporters of virtually all social reform causes followed the example set by religious groups by seizing on magazines as tools to mobilize the populace in support of their causes. Specialized social reform journals, religious magazines, and general-interest magazines all conveyed information about meetings and public events; confessions of former slave owners, meat eaters, and drunkards; articles bemoaning the plight of slaves, widows, orphans, the poor, the blind, the deaf, and the families of drunkards; fiery essays demanding that those who were wronged be righted; inspirational poetry, moving short stories, and serialized novels; and updates on legal initiatives.

Social reform movements supported the magazine industry in three ways. First and most directly, social reform associations launched magazines. Second, social movements built large bases of interested readers who by virtue of their membership in such associations were subscribers to their publications. Third, reform-association magazines published poetry, fiction, and nonfiction that vividly captured the plight of the unfortunate, which stimulated demand for magazines. Perhaps the most famous example is Harriet Beecher Stowe's novel *Uncle Tom's Cabin*, which was serialized in the antislavery weekly *The National Era* before it was issued in book form.

For their part, the magazines affiliated with social movements in this era helped modernize them. Magazines helped frame and thus theorize movements; they helped observers make sense of the principles on which such movements were built, and so made movement goals appear both appropriate and acceptable (Strang and Meyer 1993). In doing so, magazines reflected as well as created cultural frames around social structures and the ways they might be reformed (Gamson et al. 1992; Gamson and Wolfsfeld 1993). In addition, magazines bound together far-flung communities of activists, making possible modern social movements—those that transcend neighborhoods and are sustained, formally organized, and aimed at distant targets such as the state (Tilly 1986, 1995; Tarrow 1998).

A quantitative analysis focused on the antislavery movement, one of the most important in this era, shows the independent effects of religion and magazines on social movement organizing and reveals that magazines had substantial effects on such organizing, even after taking into consideration their support from reform associations. Thus, the development of magazines was a cause, not merely a consequence or companion, of the growth of antislavery organizations. Second, this analysis extends our thinking about the relationship between religion and reform from a narrow focus on the *strength* of religious belief to include their *content*. Specifically, churches with different theological orientations had different relationships to antislavery societies: this-worldly churches supported them, while otherworldly churches undermined them.

Chapter 7: The Economy. Between 1740 and 1860 the American economy expanded greatly, propelled by the shift from a mostly traditional agricultural and trading economy toward a modern mixture of commerce, manufacturing, and agriculture (North 1961; McCusker and Menard 1991). The path forward was highly turbulent, punctuated by numerous panics, recessions, and embargoes. Although agriculture was during this period always the largest sector of the economy, it became less dominant by 1860 in terms of both the value of production and the number of Americans involved. Agriculture also became increasingly intertwined with commercial markets in urban areas and with industrial manufacturing—not just for farm implements but also for household goods. For its part, industrialization proceeded unevenly—first and fastest in the Northeast, later in the West, and very haltingly in the South. On the eve of the Civil War the manufacturing concerns that had sprung up had changed Americans' personal trajectories, as farmers' daughters flocked to factories in New England and farmers' sons and immigrants to iron works in the mid-Atlantic states and meatpacking plants in the West. The development of a national market for agricultural products and the rise of artisanal and industrial manufacturing to produce goods for personal and farm use was accompanied by a rise in long-distance commercial exchange.

Both business and agricultural magazines played roles in American economic development during this period. But business magazines were few in number and of limited importance until the 1850s; the only exception was bank note reporters and counterfeit detectors, which had mixed effects. On the one hand, this subgenre facilitated commerce and helped bankers, merchants, farmers, artisans, manufacturers, tradespeople, and consumers assess the quality of the bewildering array of bank notes they were offered—most of which were issued by the hundreds of state-chartered banks and could easily be counterfeited (Dillistin 1949; Mihm 2007). Thus, this subgenre wove webs of social relations between many different types of economic actors that often covered large territories. On the other hand, these periodicals undermined economic actors' trust in a basic medium of exchange, and in doing so created barriers to modern commerce.

Agricultural magazines had considerable impact on the economy, in part because agriculture was throughout this time period the largest sector of the economy but also because, starting in the 1820s, agricultural magazines were numerous, broadly distributed, and widely read. The rise of an almost-modern "scientific" agriculture to boost production and keep previously cleared farmland in use—which involved rotating and fertilizing crops, tilling to reduce the erosion of precious topsoil, using new mechanical equipment like rakes and reapers to speed up work, and careful breeding of plants and animals—was supported by almost four hundred magazines, some with large nationwide circulations.[8] For instance, the *American Agriculturist* (1842–1931) had eighty thousand subscribers in 1860, while *Country Gentleman* (1852–1955) had over twenty thousand. In addition to practical advice and information, many agricultural magazines offered farmers and their families an eclectic array of entertainment. Dozens of magazines were launched to meet the needs of the increasing number of farmers who specialized in particular crops and livestock, like silk growers, cotton planters, and fruit orchardists.

---

[8] Circulation figures were generally reported by publishers and editors, and so are likely to be biased upward. But they are all that are available, since the Audit Bureau of Circulations (now the Alliance for Audited Media) did not start work until 1914.

CONCLUSION

Magazines both reflected and effected slow and gradual changes to American society rather than abrupt and radical ones. The emergence and expansion of the magazine industry between 1740 and 1860 was made possible by a series of related contextual shifts that together entrenched magazines in American print culture: population growth (especially the concentration of people in urban areas, increasing numbers of whom participated in market-based monetary exchanges and worked in specialized occupations), advances in printing technologies and the postal system, the gradual development of copyright law, the emergence of the cultural conception of the author as professional, and the practice of paying authors for their contributions. Several other trends both fostered magazines' growth and legitimization and were fostered by them: the disestablishment of state religions, waves of immigration, and outbreaks of religious revivalism that together created a pluralistic but highly competitive national religious field; the efflorescence of a wide array of voluntary social reform societies and the modernization of social reform movements, many of which were supported by religious institutions and theologies; the growth of commerce; and the rise of protoscientific agriculture.

Magazines changed three key areas of American social life: religion, reform, and the economy. These changes came slowly as the costs of manufacturing and distributing magazines dropped and the postal distribution network expanded and became cheaper, as elites figured out what to do with magazines (use them to argue about politics and culture), and as nonelites figured out how magazines could be used to promote their own activities and interests (religion, social reform, agriculture, commerce, specialized manufacturing occupations, cohesion among non-English-speaking immigrants, and new developments in science and industry). It was nonelites who pushed the magazine industry away from politics and serious literature toward entertainment, religion, social reform, agriculture, ethnic cohesion, and occupational and scientific development. But elites did not abandon magazines; instead they continued to promote their own agendas through them.

The complex and highly contingent nature of modernization in America over the 120 years surveyed here has implications for our understanding of community. Social solidarity did not disappear as modernization proceeded but was instead transformed: individuals joined groups that were often parochial in their interests (communities of faith or practice), sometimes local in geographic scope (communities of place), and other times universal or cosmopolitan in their interests and scope (nationwide communities of faith and purpose). Most important, membership in these groups was often literally mediated by magazines: magazines were the social glue keeping many different communities together, especially when their members could not meet face-to-face because they were so numerous and so geographically dispersed.

CHAPTER 2

The History of American Magazines, 1741–1860

I begin this chapter by briefly discussing the origins of magazines in Europe before describing the growth of magazines in America from 1741 to 1860. After that, I detail the evolving distribution of magazines in terms of location, contents, audience, and format.

MAGAZINE ORIGINS

The publication of magazines began in Europe in the late seventeenth century as printing presses became widespread (Eisenstein 1979). The earliest magazines were written for scholars and bibliophiles (Bolton 1897; Ornstein [1938] 1963; Kronick 1962). Although it is difficult to identify the very first magazine, the most likely candidate is *Erbauliche Monaths-Unterredungen* (Edifying Monthly Conversations), a scholarly journal that was published in Germany from 1663 to 1667 by theologian Johann Rist. Two years later, a literary review, the *Journal des Sçavans* (Journal of Learned Men), was launched in Paris by counselor and scholar to Parlement Dennis de Sallo; it continued, with several interruptions due to censoring, until 1792. This weekly published reviews of scholarly books; announcements of scientific inventions and experiments; essays on chemistry, astronomy, anatomy, religion, history, and the arts; obituaries of famous men of letters and science; and news about the Sorbonne. These early periodicals, which targeted very narrow readerships, were followed by magazines that found broader audiences by seeking to entertain rather than edify. *Le Mercure Galant* (Gallant Mercury, a reference to the messenger of the gods) was the first such general-interest magazine; it was founded in Paris in 1672 by the royal historian Jean Donneau de Visé and continued until just before the French Revolution. This monthly was highly successful, not in the least because it was sanctioned by the French court, and it reviewed fine art and literature as well as music and dance, published poetry and anecdotes, critiqued fashion, and dissected manners and society. Notable contributors included the playwrights Pierre Corneille and Pierre Carlet de Chamblain de Marivaux.

The first English-language magazine was the *Philosophical Transactions*. This scholarly journal, which was modeled after the *Journal des Sçavans*, began in 1665 to record investigations into the natural sciences and report news about the activities of English scientists; it later became an organ of the Royal Society of London. The first English review, *A Review of the Affairs of France and of all Europe*, was founded by Daniel Defoe in 1704; this four-page political weekly, which ran until 1713, contained commentary on social issues and acerbic essays about domestic and foreign politics, all written by Defoe himself, and included paid advertising. The most famous of the early English reviews, the *Tatler* (1709–11, founded by Richard Steele) and the *Spectator* (1711–14, founded by Steele and Joseph Addison) were more narrowly focused than Defoe's magazine, eschewing politics and covering only literature; both publications contained essays that sought "to make the polite religious and the religious polite" (Watt [1957] 2001: 51) and were read by a small circle of gentlemen-scholars.

The word *magazine* was first used to describe a periodical in the title of the *Gentleman's Magazine*, founded by London journalist and bookseller Edward Cave in 1731 as "a Monthly Collection, to treasure up, as in a Magazine, the most remarkable Pieces on the Subjects above-mentioned, or at least impartial Abridgements thereof" (Cave 1731). The "subjects above-mentioned" included foreign and domestic affairs; births, deaths, and marriages of prominent persons; civic and ecclesiastical preferments; prices of goods, grain, and livestock; business bankruptcies; newly published books; humor and poetry; and remarkable achievements and occurrences. Like the *Mercure Galant*, the *Gentleman's Magazine* was designed for a wide audience, so it contained not just essays and short pieces on current events but also recipes, advice on housekeeping, and riddles. This venture was amazingly successful, as evidenced by its large circulation, estimated at ten thousand by Samuel Johnson, who wrote for the magazine for three decades (Watt [1957] 2001: 51–52), and by the fact that it survived until 1914, closing only after the outbreak of World War I. Not surprisingly, given its great success, the *Gentleman's Magazine* spawned many imitators in Britain and the colonies.

In America, two pioneering magazines appeared within three days of each other in February 1741, produced by rival printers: Andrew Bradford's *American Magazine, or a Monthly View of the Political State of the British Colonies* and Benjamin Franklin's *General Magazine and Historical Chronicle, for All the British Plantations in America*).[1] Figure 2.1 shows the front page of their first issues.

---

[1] One magazine may have been founded twenty years earlier (Edgar 1975: 55n1). *Telltale* was purportedly issued in 1721 by Ebenezer Turell, a Harvard University student, as a weekly or semi-weekly manuscript magazine (that is, handwritten rather than printed; Edgar cited an article in the *Harvard Graduate Magazine* as his source). Since there is no physical trace of this magazine and no other scholar noted its existence, I omitted *Telltale* from this analysis. Some scholars (e.g., Gardner 2012) have argued that the *New-England Courant*, founded 1721 in Boston by James Franklin, Benjamin Franklin's older brother, and modeled after Addison's *Spectator*, was the first

Figure 2.1. Front pages of the first issues of the first two American magazines: Andrew Bradford's *American Magazine* (source: This image originally appeared as part of ProQuest's American Periodicals product. Reprinted with permission from digital images produced by ProQuest LLC, http://www.proquest.com.) and Benjamin Franklin's *General Magazine* (source: Firestone Memorial Library, Princeton Unversity).

(Although both claimed to have been launched in January, they were delayed by one month.) These pioneering publications, which were modeled on their English predecessors, were quite similar. They were published monthly and their contents included proceedings of government assemblies, speeches in Parliament, and reports from state officials; reprinted essays from British and colonial newspapers on politics, history, religion, paper money, and manners and society; a large selection of poetry; reports of scientific experiments, mathematical puzzles, price lists, commercial articles, and the weather; and long letters to the editor. Their founders expected these fledgling publications to live long lives; indeed, in his first issue, Franklin announced that the twelfth issue of the *General Magazine* would include an index for the year so that subscribers could have easy access to all material published in the first volume. Alas, both periodicals were short-lived: Bradford's *American Magazine* lasted only three issues, while Franklin's *General Magazine* managed to survive for six.

US magazine. Because most historians (e.g., Mott 1941) have classified it as a newspaper, I have omitted the *Courant* from this analysis.

MAGAZINE EVOLUTION

Industry Growth

In the wake of Bradford's and Franklin's pioneering publications, the magazine industry in America grew very slowly. Figure 2.2 charts the number of magazines founded (solid line), failed (dashed line), and published (gray area) each year between 1741 and 1860.[2] Only twenty-three magazines were founded before the end of the Revolutionary War in 1783. Not until peace was restored did magazines gain a firm footing in American society: in the following decade, thirty-six were founded, and the average annual rate of magazine founding increased sevenfold, from one every two years between 1741 and 1783 to 3.6 per year between 1784 and 1793.

After that a steadily increasing number of magazines were launched: 847 between 1794 and 1825, an average of 26.5 per year. The founding rate for magazines began to outstrip the failure rate, and the number of magazines in print rose substantially, from 16 in 1793 to 82 in 1810 and 212 in 1825. The quarter century after 1825—labeled the first golden age of magazines by both contemporary industry participants (*Illinois Monthly Magazine* 1831) and later observers (Mott 1930; Tebbel and Zuckerman 1991)—saw 2,871 magazine foundings (115 per year, on average) and 776 magazines in print by 1850. This golden age was sustained by two trends that will be described in chapters 3 and 4: a general literary boom and the rapid diffusion of the new practice of paying authors for original contributions (Charvat 1968). Magazine foundings continued to accelerate through the last decade before the Civil War, during which 1,585 magazines were launched. By 1860, 1,059 magazines were in print.

This growth trajectory resembles that of many other industries: newspapers, labor unions, telephone companies, restaurants, financial services firms, breweries and wineries, automobile companies, and high-tech manufacturers (for a review, see Carroll and Hannan 2000). This pattern of unfettered growth in the number of magazines in print indicates that the magazine industry became increasingly legitimate—meaning increasingly accepted as reasonable or "normal" cultural goods, taken for granted, or supported by force of law (Meyer and Rowan 1977; Hannan and Freeman 1989). Here I discuss the first two aspects of legitimacy; chapter 3 discusses the third aspect, specifically the increasing acceptance of magazines by US Post Office authorities.

Those who were involved in launching and running magazines were aware of their increasing legitimacy. For instance, just two years after starting *Hopkinsian Magazine* (1824–32), its editor noted, "The peculiar difficulties attend-

---

[2] This figure charts the number of magazines appearing during a calendar year, not the number alive at year's end. Many magazines survived less than six months; indeed, 185 (3.4 percent of the total) published only a single issue. Given their often ephemeral nature, this measure is more appropriate than a "snapshot" taken at year's end.

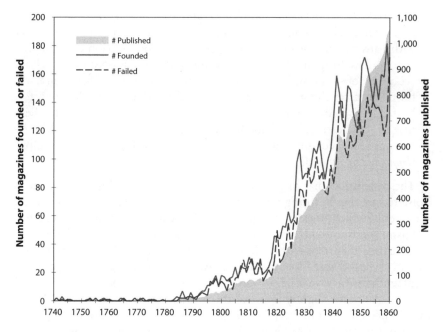

Figure 2.2. Magazines in America, 1741–1860: number founded, failed, and published.

ing the commencement of such a work, if not entirely removed, are greatly diminished. The importance of a cheap, periodical publication ... is more and more felt" (Brown 1826, iii). Another editor commented that magazines were indispensable tools for many groups:

> Nothing can be done without them. Sects and parties, benevolent societies, and ingenious individuals, all have their periodicals. Science and literature, religion and law, agriculture and the arts, resort alike to this mode of enlightening the public mind. Every man, and every party, that seeks to establish a new theory, or to break down an old one, commences operations, like a board of war, by founding a *magazine*. We have annuals, monthlys, and weeklys—reviews, orthodox and heterodox—journals of education and humanity, of law, divinity and physic—magazines for ladies and for gentlemen—publications commercial, mechanical, metaphysical, sentimental, musical, anti-dogmatical, and nonsensical.... They pervade the atmosphere of the country like an epidemic. (*Illinois Monthly Magazine* 1831: 302–3; emphasis in the original)

Still another defended magazines against criticism from an old-fashioned minister and argued that magazines were often more effective teachers of Christian ethics than ministers' sermons:

> Some of the best lessons taught in the great charter of Christian belief are here, in these magazines [the author singles out *Southern Lady's Book*,

Graham's Magazine, Godey's Lady's Book, and *Arthur's Magazine*—all general-interest magazines] contain some of the best reading any where to be met with—instructing the understanding, purifying the affections, refining the taste, and exalting the imagination. Some of the best lessons of household economy; of sweet, and gentle, and unobtrusive charity: of firm and faithful reliance on the goodness and justice of Providence, of Christian forbearance and resignation under insult and wrong... are here, in these magazines, illustrated, explained, made attractive, and enforced, with an efficiency and success not always attained by the teachings form the pulpit. (*Home Magazine* 1853: 236)

The conclusion that magazines were becoming increasingly legitimate is bolstered by the declining reliance on magazine prospectuses and editorial statements, which magazine founders used to explain and justify their new publishing ventures—that is, provide accounts of these ventures that would demonstrate their value to readers and contributors (Mills 1940; Scott and Lyman 1968). These documents are available in the archives for most eighteenth-century magazines (almost 60 percent of magazines founded 1741 to 1800), for slightly fewer of those founded from 1801 to 1825 (just over 50 percent), but for very few magazines founded after about 1825, when the first golden age of magazines began (only 12 percent of those founded from 1826 to 1840 and 2.1 percent of those founded from 1841 to 1860). The decline in the number of these documents available in archives suggests (although certainly does not prove) that early on most magazine founders felt the need to justify their new ventures, but later on such justification seemed less important. In other words, this decline indicates that magazines were increasingly taken for granted—their existence was viewed as routine and commonsensical.

The growing number of magazines also indicates that by 1860 the supply of magazines had not yet outstripped demand for them. I do not mean to suggest that magazines in this era did not compete—they clearly did. Schools of medicine used them to promote their own practices and beliefs, as is mentioned in chapter 3; religious denominations used magazines to vie for adherents' souls, as is described in chapter 5; and, as chapter 6 notes, proponents of abolition used them to fight with proponents of African colonization and defenders of slavery. But this competition seemed to have been mutually beneficial, as it provided exciting material for the pages of magazines and so drew an ever-growing pool of readers. Industry participants perceived that competition had few deleterious effects. For example, the editors of a Boston-based Congregational monthly explained that the launch of a similar periodical in the same city would not harm their own, writing, "It has been supposed ... that the circulation of the Recorder would injure that of the Panoplist. We have never believed that this will be the case ... there is still room for a vast increase of subscribers to each; and, unless we are greatly mistaken, the number of religious publications to be printed and read in this country, is yet to be prodigiously augmented. (*Panoplist, and Missionary Magazine* 1816: 48) A reader of the *Ohio Cultivator* (1845–62) made a similar point in writing to the founders of a new agricultural magazine nearby: "Your valuable periodical has been popular amongst the Hoosiers out in these parts; and although it has a competitor here, (the Indiana Farmer,) I believe it will at least fully maintain its present circulation" (Wesler 1852: 43).

From Precarious Undertaking to Thriving Industry

Along with increases in numbers, the vitality of American magazines improved, as evidenced by their life spans. Over the first 120 years of American magazine history, the median life span increased fivefold, from 0.4 years for magazines founded in the 1740s to 1.9 years for those founded in the 1840s and '50s.[3] Another good indicator of vitality is the percentage of magazines that stayed in print for a long time. In the eighteenth century, 3.4 percent of magazines founded (5 of 148) survived twenty-five years or more, compared with 4.3 percent (21 of 491) founded in the years 1801–20, 8.2 percent (143 of 1,738) in the years 1821–40, and 10.5 percent (314 of 2,985) in the years 1841–60.

Three other indicators of magazine health (or, conversely, frailty)—the number of magazines that ever suspended operations, the number that were published erratically rather than at regular intervals, and the number that put out only a single issue before folding—also improved dramatically. First, consider suspensions: none of the twelve magazines published in the 1740s and '50s ever suspended operations, perhaps because most expired quickly. One magazine suspended operations in the 1760s and none in the 1770s—out of the ten founded in those two decades. After the Revolution ended and magazine publishing picked up, suspensions rose; they peaked in the first decade of the nineteenth century, to include 9.6 percent of magazines published (22 of 229) and then fell gradually to 1.4 percent of magazines published in the 1850s (32 of 2,245). Like suspensions, irregular publication schedules followed a downward trend, dropping from 14 percent of magazines published in the 1750s (1 of 7) to 7.8 percent in the 1800s (18 of 209), and then to 1.3 percent in the 1850s (30 of 2,245). Finally, the fraction of magazines that managed to publish only one issue before folding decreased dramatically after the turn of the nineteenth century: 8.1 percent (12 of 148) published in the eighteenth century put out only a single issue, while only 4.8 percent (25 of 514) of those published between 1801 and 1820 did so. This indicator of magazine frailty continued to decline as the nineteenth century wore on, reaching 3.6 percent (66 of 1,831) of those published between 1821 and 1840 and 2.4 percent (82 of 3,422) of those published between 1841 and 1860.

A final indicator of the increasing vitality of magazines is the fact that by the middle of the nineteenth century many magazines reached large audi-

---

[3] Thirty-six magazines analyzed here were still being published in 2012; for those magazines I calculated life spans using 2012 as the end date. For more information on this calculation, see appendix 2, which describes the methods used in this and all other quantitative data analyses.

ences. Religious magazines, in particular, often had nationwide circulation (Kielbowicz 1989: 123). Data on magazine circulation are available for only a few magazines at scattered moments in time are often of questionable quality, as some editors and publishers offered optimistic, if not downright boastful, numbers. Notwithstanding these limitations, it would seem that between 1841 and 1860, one-third of the magazines for which data are available (101 of 301) had circulations over 10,000, and 4.7 percent (14 of 301) had circulations over 100,000, including *Godey's Lady's Book* (100,000 in 1860), *Ballou's Pictorial Drawing-Room* (103,000 in 1856), *Harper's Monthly Magazine* (130,000 in 1853), the *Temperance Recorder* (200,000 in 1832–43), the *American Messenger* (200,000 in 1852), and *Ballou's Child's Paper* (310,000 in 1857). To put this in perspective, consider that by far the best-selling book in this era, *Uncle Tom's Cabin*, sold 310,000 copies; the next-best-selling novel of the 1850s, Maria Susannah Cummings's *The Lamplighter*, sold fewer than 80,000 copies (Zboray 1993: 122; Winship 2001: 3).

Taken together these statistics suggest that magazines were initially fragile undertakings but they became increasingly robust. This, in turn, indicates that by the middle of the nineteenth century magazines had become a valued means of communication and community building, and thus legitimate cultural and economic products. It also indicates that barriers to entry and continued operation had largely been eroded by the middle of the nineteenth century.

Geographic Expansion

Magazines became not only legitimate cultural and economic products by the middle of the nineteenth century but also quite widespread in circulation. Figure 2.3 charts the spread of magazine publishing across the growing nation, indicating when the first magazine appeared in each state and showing the forty-eight contiguous states.[4] States shaded black first saw magazines published before the Post Office Act of 1794 admitted magazines to the mail; states shaded dark gray first saw magazines published after this act was passed and before the golden age of magazines started in 1825; states with diagonal lines first saw magazines published during the golden age; states shaded light gray first saw magazines published in the decade before the Civil War; and states in white saw no magazines published before the Civil War.

Between 1741, when the first magazines were founded, and 1794, when the US Post Office became a permanent arm of the federal government, most magazines were published in states along the Eastern Seaboard, from New

---

[4] After 1790, new states were carved out of existing ones, created from territories, or established on land purchased from or ceded by colonial powers. To permit longitudinal comparisons, I have imposed modern state boundaries. This means that, for example, magazines founded in Maine before it was carved out of Massachusetts in 1820 were recorded as being in Maine, not Massachusetts. For a more detailed explanation of why I use fixed, contemporary state boundaries in this and other analyses, see appendix 2.

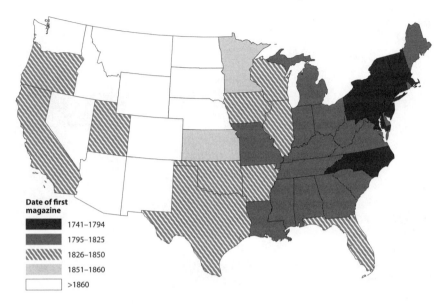

Figure 2.3. The geographic spread of magazines across America, 1741–1860.

Hampshire down to North Carolina. Indeed, the vast majority of magazines published during this period were in the largest American cities (Boston, New York, and Philadelphia), which were also centers of the nascent printing industry (Thomas [1874] 1970) and by far the largest cities. In this time period, these three cities accounted for almost two-thirds (106 of 169) of the annual observations on magazines for which I have data on place of publication. During the next three decades the frontiers of magazine publishing expanded north, south, and west to encompass Alabama, the District of Columbia, Georgia, Indiana, Kentucky, Louisiana, Maine, Michigan, Mississippi, Missouri, Ohio, South Carolina, Tennessee, and Virginia. During the first golden age of magazines, 1826–50, the industry expanded farther west to Arkansas, California, Illinois, Iowa, Oregon, Texas, and Wisconsin as well as the Kansas, Oklahoma, and Utah territories.

As magazines spread across the continent, the industry experienced two opposing pressures: a tendency toward geographic dispersion was countered by a tendency toward geographic concentration. Figures 2.4a–d illustrate how these two pressures played out. In each map, each state shaded dark gray accounted for 20 percent or more of annual observations on magazines during the time period; each state shaded medium gray, 10 percent to less than 20 percent; each state with diagonal stripes, 5 percent to less than 10 percent; each state shaded light gray, 1.5 percent to less than 5 percent; each state with dotted diagonal lines, less than 1.5 percent; and each state in white saw no magazines published before the Civil War. Between 1741 and 1794, over four-fifths of annual observations on magazines were in four states: 26 percent in

(a)

(b)

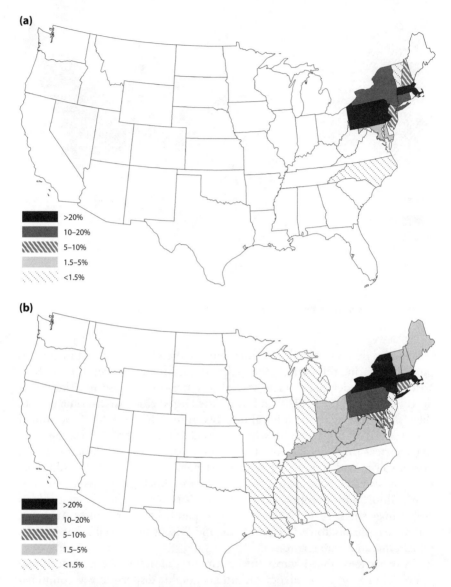

Figure 2.4. (a) The geographic concentration of magazine publishing, 1741–94; (b) the geographic concentration of magazine publishing, 1795–1825; (c) the geographic concentration of

Massachusetts, 25 percent in Pennsylvania, 18 percent in Connecticut, and 15 percent in New York.[5] New York's share of magazine publishing began to rise

[5] Throughout the book I analyze annual observations on magazines rather than one observation per magazine, for two reasons: because some magazines moved, annual observations provide the most reasonable basis for summarizing magazines' locations, and because some magazines

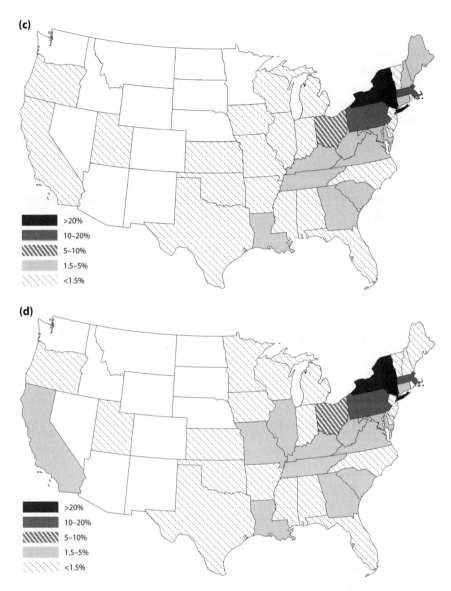

magazine publishing, 1826–50; (d) the geographic concentration of magazine publishing, 1851–60.

after the passage of the Post Office Act of 1794. During the next three decades New York accounted for almost one-fourth of annual observations on magazines, while Massachusetts and Pennsylvania each accounted for about one-

lived a very long time, using annual observations weights long-lived magazines more than ephemeral ones and so provides a more accurate view of the industry at any point in time.

fifth, and Connecticut for less than one-tenth. Around 1800 Ohio began to emerge as the western center of magazine publishing. During the first golden age of magazines, 1826–50, the center of production continued to shift away from Massachusetts and Pennsylvania and toward New York and Ohio. By the 1850s, the battle for dominance was won by New York: the state was home to 28 percent of annual observations on magazines, while Massachusetts and Pennsylvania had 13 percent each and Ohio had 9 percent.

A more nuanced measure of geographic dispersion (or conversely, concentration) is the index of qualitative variation (Mueller and Schuessler 1961: 177–79; Lieberson 1969), which takes into consideration how unevenly (or evenly) magazines were spread over states at various points in time.[6] This index equals 0 for the times when all magazines were published in a single state or colony; it increases for the time period when magazines became more evenly distributed across locations; and its maximum is 1, which would only occur if magazines were spread evenly across all locations (which never happened). This index is not really meaningful until it can chart the more than a handful of magazines that were published in more than a handful of locations—which did not happen until almost a decade after the Revolutionary War ended. In 1790, by which time twelve magazines were published in five states, the index of qualitative variation was 0.97, as the solid line in figure 2.5 shows. After that date, it hovered between 0.88 and 0.99. This pattern indicates that the industry very quickly established a broad geographic presence across states, and this dispersion persisted through the mid-nineteenth century.

As much as we learn about this geographic push and pull by analyzing location at the state level, it actually overstates the extent of geographic dispersion and understates the extent of geographic concentration because magazine publishing activity was not spread evenly within each state. Analyzing location at the municipal level within each state reveals considerably more geographic concentration. To track this, figure 2.5 also plots the index of qualitative variation based on municipality (town or city), averaged across states within each year (the dotted line).[7] In 1790, when ten magazines were published in six locations (including three each in Boston, New York, and Philadelphia), the index was 0.125. It rose slowly but unsteadily over time, first reaching over 0.40 in 1828 and peaking at 0.54 in 1860. Calculating this index of geographic dispersion using towns and cities yields a much lower number than calculating it using states because ten cities accounted for a whopping 59

[6] I calculated this index in steps. I first squared the percentage of magazines published in each state, summed across all states; I then took the square root of this sum and subtracted the result from one. To standardize this index over time and force the maximum to be one, regardless of the number of locations where magazines were published, I then scaled it by $(1—1/n)$, where n is the number of states where magazines were published. For more details on this calculation, and comparisons between this index and other well-known indexes of dispersion and concentration, see appendix 2.

[7] For each state, I squared the percentage of magazines published in each town or city, summed across all towns and cities, took the square root of this sum, and subtracted the result from one. I then took the mean across all states and scaled it by $(1 - 1/n)$, where n is the number of states where magazines were published, to standardize it over time and force the maximum to be one.

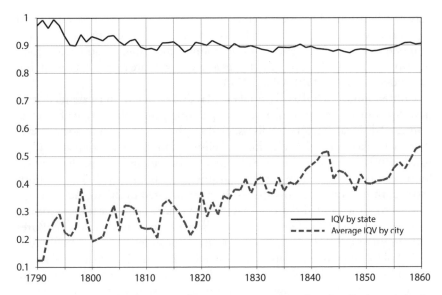

Figure 2.5. The geographic dispersion of magazines, 1790–1860: Index of qualitative variation by state and city.

percent of annual observations on magazines between 1741 and 1860; in descending order, these were New York City, Boston, Philadelphia, Cincinnati, Baltimore, Richmond, Washington, Charleston, Hartford, and New Orleans. Although the share of magazines published in these ten cities declined from 83 percent in 1790 to 51 percent in 1860, indicating that magazines were increasingly published in smaller municipalities as printing presses became cheaper and more widely available, New York City increasingly dominated the industry: the fraction of magazines (based on magazine-year observations) published there rose from 15 percent for the years 1741–94, to 19 percent for 1826–50, and then to 22 percent for 1851–60.

The persistent concentration of magazine publishing in a few cities cannot be explained by mere population trends: the level of concentration among magazines was far greater than that among people. In 1790, New York City accounted for only 0.8 percent of the young republic's population, while the other nine cities combined accounted for another 5.7 percent. In 1820, these percentages were 1.3 percent and 6.2 percent, and in 1860, they were 2.6 percent and 17.4 percent, respectively. Instead, it seems that magazines reflected the rise of centrally important cities (Pred 1973, 1980), regional commercial and manufacturing centers (Warner 1972; Larson 2010) that had deep pools of financial and cultural resources.

Social scientists have long been intrigued by this kind of geographic push and pull. Karl Marx ([1857–61] 2002) has argued that in the modern era, time annihilated space: in the face of technological advances in communication and transportation systems, which are driven by capitalists' continual need for increasing efficiency, geography (both place or location and space or distance between locations) becomes irrelevant. (For a discussion of geography and capitalism, see Harvey [1975] 2001: 237–66.) In this process, magazines serve as modernizing forces: people can be bound into a single nationwide community by reading the same magazines and being aware that others are doing so (Anderson [1983] 1991; Okker 2013).

Contemporary scholars have taken Marx's argument and extended it in new directions. They propose that an expanding geographic scope of interaction can "dislocate" actors by disassociating physical *space* from social *place*, thereby weakening social cohesion and eliminating the "sense of place" (Meyrowitz 1985). As a result, these developments can actually increase demand for local connections (Giddens 1990; Marquis and Lounsbury 2007). In short, easier communication across space—here manifested in the spread of magazines across the United States—may render place (i.e., a local community) even *more* salient by sharpening contrasts between local and nonlocal cultures and amplifying peoples' attachments to their localities (Giddens 1990). Amplified place attachment would feed demand for products such as local magazines that have deep local connections. To the extent that new localisms are produced by the flows of modern communication systems, magazines, which are often characterized as solely modernizing cultural products, can instead serve as bulwarks against the geographic homogeneity of modern society by making place meaningful—that is, by reproducing place-specific cultures (Griswold and Wright 2004; Griswold 2008).

In sum, the analysis of location shows that magazines were subject to opposing forces of geographic dispersion and concentration: although they spread quickly to every corner of America, New York City dominated magazine publishing by the 1830s, as it did book publishing and most forms of commerce. The main forces driving geographic dispersion were the spread of the population across the continent, the increased number of urban areas (settlements with populations over 2,500), and technological advances in printing technology that caused printing presses to spread across the continent—all of which are documented in chapter 3. In combination, these factors made it possible to launch magazines anywhere. The fact that the industry remained concentrated in a few large cities (principally Boston, New York, and Philadelphia, with a much smaller cluster in Cincinnati starting in the early nineteenth century) indicates that at all times during this period people in these cities had access to deep pools of human and financial resources as well as access to superior information about the magazine industry—far deeper than people located elsewhere. But the very success of magazines published in these northeastern cities—in particular, their widespread distribution—pushed many people in smaller communities to publish magazines targeting readers in their particular localities. Chapter 3 details these trends in greater detail.

Geographic Reach

From the issue of how far the magazine industry spread, let us now consider how far individual magazines spread—how far-flung their readers were. Even in the eighteenth century, a few American magazines sought readers over a wide swath of territory. For instance, in the prospectus of his *American Magazine*, Andrew Bradford declared that it was "designed for the equal Use of every Colony, and not for the Service of one in Particular preferable to another" (1740: 3). The subtitle of Franklin's *General Magazine* carried a similar message; it was "for all the British Plantations in America." And the preface to the *American Magazine* (1757–58) declared it would "do equal justice to the affairs of every colony," and stated that it sought readers in all the colonies and in Britain. Some pioneering periodicals were successful in their quest for widespread influence. For instance, the title page of the first issue of the *American Magazine and Monthly Chronicle* (1757–58) noted that it was sold in Boston, New Haven, Newport, New York, and Philadelphia. In the editorial preface published in its inaugural issue, the *United States Magazine* (founded 1794) boasted that subscriptions were handled "by all the Printers and Booksellers in the United States." More convincingly, the *Ladies' Magazine* (1792–93) had subscribers in Albany, New York; Baltimore; Charleston, South Carolina; Boston; New York City; Philadelphia; Richmond, Virginia; and Savannah, Georgia, while the *Medical Repository of Original Essays and Intelligence* (1797–1824) printed a list of subscribers in its first issue; they resided in the mid-Atlantic states, New England, New York, and down the Atlantic coast to Georgia as well as on the island of Martinique in the Caribbean and in London and Nova Scotia.

Notwithstanding these examples, the vast majority of magazines published in the eighteenth century had purely local circulation. I pored over the first year's issues of all magazines in the American Periodical Series (APS) Online for information about where they were sold, where they had agents, or where their subscribers lived, as well as issues of other magazines not available in APS Online that I found in libraries or other Internet archives. Of the fifty eighteenth-century magazines whose pages gave any indication of their geographic reach, two-thirds were sold in a single city or town.

As transportation technologies improved and the US postal network grew, magazines evolved from serving mostly local audiences in a handful of eastern cities to reaching national audiences. Among the 117 magazines founded from 1801 to 1820 whose pages indicated their geographic reach, over half (64) were sold in multiple states, one-sixth (19) were sold throughout the region surrounding their place of publication, and fewer than one-third (34) were distributed only in one city or town. For instance, the *Christian Observer* (1802–66), published simultaneously in Boston and New York, listed in its first issue agents throughout New England and the mid-Atlantic states, as well as the District of Columbia and Virginia, while the *General Repository and Review* (1812–13) was sold in twenty cities from Maine to South Carolina.

Many magazines expanded their geographic reach over time. The *American Journal of Science and Arts* (1818–1938), for instance, was published in New York and was at its inception distributed from Boston south to Georgia and west to Ohio. In November 1820, at the close of its second volume, the editor patted himself on the back and boasted that his was "not a *local* but a *national* undertaking" that was "sustained by *original* communications ... from the East and the West, the North and the South, and even occasionally from other countries" (Silliman 1820, 176). This was no idle boast, as by the mid-1840s this magazine had subscribers as far away as Hamburg, London, and Paris as well as in a host of towns and cities across America. Similarly, the *Journal of Health* (1829–33) was published in Philadelphia and was in its first year of operation sold in Baltimore, Boston, New York, and Philadelphia. Three years later it was sold as far north as Portland, Maine; Middlebury, Vermont; and two towns in upper Canada. It was sold as far south as Mobile, Alabama, and New Orleans, and as far west as Columbus, Cincinnati, and Nashville. The Hartford, Connecticut, *Episcopal Watchman* expanded during its years of publication (1827–33) from serving five cities in Connecticut and New York to serving fifty-four cities on the East Coast, from Maine to Virginia.

After 1825 some noteworthy eastern (mostly New York—based) magazines, including *Harper's New Monthly Magazine, Godey's Lady's Book*, the *Merchant's Ledger*, and *Frank Leslie's Illustrated Magazine*, gained national followings. Even as periodicals from the Northeast circulated widely in the West and South, periodicals from those regions proliferated, but few of them penetrated eastern markets in large numbers. Both western and southern magazines were more likely to have regional circulations than were northeastern ones.

Analysis of magazines' claims about their geographic reach, as signaled by their titles, reinforces this conclusion. Many magazines (36 percent of annual observations) made explicit claims about their geographic reach in their titles or subtitles. These claims can be divided into four nested categories: pancolonial or national (denoted by such terms as *American, national, federal*, and *North American*); multicolony or multistate regional (for instance, denoted by such terms as *Mississippi Valley, New England, Northwestern*, and *Southern*); colonial, state, or large substate regional (for instance, Pennsylvania, Virginia, and western New York); and local (denoted by the name of a county, town, or city).[8] As table 2.1 shows, some 27 percent of southern magazines signaled by their titles that they served their region or state, as did 36 percent of western magazines, compared to 12 percent of magazines published in New England and 4.7 percent of those published in the mid-Atlantic states. The use of the words *southern* and *western* to signal geographic focus in large part reflected regional politics and the existence of distinctive local identities, as chapter 4 will explain in more detail. Magazines published in the Northeast were far

[8] Using titles may understate magazines' geographic reach because many magazines based in large cities reached readers outside their place of publication. For instance, the *New Yorker* (different from the present-day magazine with the same name, this one was published 1836–41) had subscribers all over New York State; from Bangor, Maine, to Savannah, Georgia; from New Orleans to Saint Louis; and from Cincinnati to Toronto. Similarly, the *Boston Quarterly Review* (1838–42) had agents all over New England and in the District of Columbia, New York, Ohio, and Pennsylvania, while the *Baltimore Phenix* [sic] *and Budget* (1841–42) had agents in Alabama, Connecticut, Massachusetts, Ohio, Pennsylvania, and Virginia as well as throughout Maryland.

TABLE 2.1.
Geographic Reach Signaled by Magazine Titles, Overall and by Region

Region	Geographic claims				Total geographic claims	Magazine totals
	National	Regional	State	Local		
New England	651 (10.3%)	294 (4.7%)	451 (7.1%)	605 (9.6%)	2,001 (31.7%)	6,322
Mid-Atlantic states	1,474 (13.9%)	123 (1.2%)	378 (3.6%)	1,298 (12.2%)	3,273 (30.8%)	10,621
South	303 (8.9%)	635 (18.6%)	294 (8.6%)	336 (9.9%)	1,568 (46.0%)	3,410
West	112 (2.5%)	1,025 (23.3%)	568 (12.9%)	301 (6.8%)	2,006 (45.5%)	4,404
United States	2,540 (10.3%)	2,077 (8.4%)	1,691 (6.8%)	2,540 (10.3%)	8,848 (35.7%)	24,757

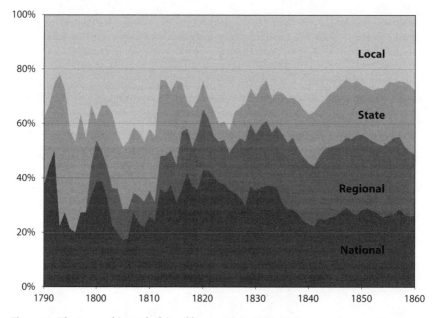

Figure 2.6. The geographic reach claimed by magazines, 1790–1860
Note: This figure shows the percentage of magazines that made explicit claims about geographic reach in their titles.

more likely to signal national geographic reach; 13 percent of them did so, compared to just 5.3 percent of magazines published in the South and the West.

The types of geographic claims magazines made varied greatly over time. Figure 2.6 plots the percentage of magazines making each level of claim over time. The darkest gray area at the bottom is pancolonial and national, the medium gray area is multistate regional, the light gray is colonial or state, and the lightest gray area is local.

In the eighteenth century 40 percent of magazines making an explicit geographic claim styled themselves as pancolonial or national journals, while 25 percent claimed to cover a single colony or state, 32 percent to focus on a local community, and just 3 percent to represent a multistate region. After the turn of the century the share of national magazines fell sharply, bottoming out at 17 percent in 1804, then rising to over 40 percent after the close of the War of 1812. After that it fell slowly, reaching about 25 percent in the late 1850s. In contrast, the share of regional magazines grew after 1800, peaking at 29 percent in 1849, then falling slightly to 22 percent in 1860. The share of state magazines also fell in the first years of the nineteenth century, reaching a low of 7 percent in 1823–24, then rising slowly to 24 percent by 1860. Finally, the share of local magazines rose to 46 percent in 1806 and then fluctuated widely until 1840. After that, it fell slowly from 37 percent in 1840 to 28 percent in 1860. This figure again reveals two opposing forces impinging on the magazine industry in particular and American society in general. On the one hand there was centripetal movement toward a common national center, which was facilitated by the rise of the large cities in the Northeast that were hubs in the fast-developing trade networks (Pred 1973, 1980), the expansion of the postal network, the increasingly reasonable postage rates for magazines, and improvements in printing, all of which are detailed in chapter 3. On the other hand there was a centrifugal push toward many distinct communities, which was impelled by the sheer vastness of the growing nation, the growing number of inland urban areas, and the increasing differentiation (and often contestation) in religion, politics and society, and the economy; these trends are analyzed in chapter 3 and in chapters 5 through 7. And, as chapter 3 shows, the geographic spread of individual magazines was causally connected to the geographic spread of the magazine industry as a whole: the distribution of northeastern magazines through the growing postal network pushed magazines in the hinterlands to focus on serving narrower geographic regions.

VARIETY WITHIN AND AMONG MAGAZINES

American magazines in this era were highly eclectic in two ways: (1) each magazine published highly varied material, and (2) there were many different kinds of magazines catering to different groups of readers and using different publication formats. The remarkable variety of magazines in this era should be of interest to both media scholars and organizational sociologists. Media scholars have long touted the benefits of highly varied media outlets and have debated the impact of concentrated media ownership on media variety. Some have contended that high levels of concentration dampen competition, thereby narrowing the spectrum of political, economic, and social views presented in the media (e.g., Bagdikian [1983] 2004; McChesney 2001; Baker 2006). Others have countered that the uncertainty inherent in media industries, coupled with long-standing antimonopoly regulation and technological change, drives participants to differentiate their products and audiences to seek alternative sources of information (e.g., Elstein 2001; Hale 2003; Hamilton 2003; for a more sociological argument, see also Carroll 1985). Perhaps the most comprehensive analysis of media concentration and variety in the United States is by Paul Starr (2004), who argued that there have always been low levels of concentration among media companies in the United States when compared to Europe, and thus little convergence on a limited range of topics or a narrow set of political perspectives. My analysis of magazines is a complement to Starr's, which focused much more on newspapers.

For organizational sociologists this analysis speaks to the issue of whether the organizations in any industry become more or less varied as that industry evolves. Institutionalists and organizational ecologists have made different claims about organizational variety. Michael T. Hannan and John Freeman (1977: 936) wondered why there are so many kinds of organizations and, following much work in economics, argued that competition drives organizations to differentiate themselves. In contrast, institutionalists Paul DiMaggio and Walter Powell (1983) wondered why organizations resembled each other so closely; they proposed that institutional forces—specifically, interorganizational power structures, socially constructed roles, the state, and the professions—all promote institutional isomorphism (see also White 1981). Not surprisingly, organizational ecologists and institutionalists made starkly different predictions about how the variety of organizations would change over time as a particular industry, its suppliers, and its customers' preferences developed. Building on the work of Amos H. Hawley (1968), Hannan and Freeman proposed that "organizational diversity in a social system depends on the diversity of the agents that control the flow of key resources into the system" (1989: 93) and that as industries develop, deep pools of industry-specific resources build up that make it easier to start and maintain organizations; the upshot is that organizational diversity should increase over time. As DiMaggio and Powell stated, "In the initial stages of their life cycle, organizational fields display considerable diversity in approach and form. Once a field becomes well established, however, there is an inexorable push towards homogenization" (1983: 148). In sum, then, we have divergent predictions. Diversity among industry members should vary over time: it will either increase, according to the ecological argument, or decrease, according to the institutionalist logic.

Institutionalist studies of organizational variety (or isomorphism) have focused on the diffusion of codified organizational structures and practices and the consequent reduction in the variety of organizations in a field. Only a few institutionalists have investigated organizational variety per se (Lehrman 1994; Schneiberg 2002; Berk and Schneiberg 2005; Sine, Haveman, and Tolbert 2005; Haveman, Rao, and Paruchuri 2007); this work has shown that many environmental changes—the rise of social movements, new regulation, demographic trends, and shifts in cultural mores—can alter the array of organizations present. For their part, organizational ecologists have focused primarily on explaining the selection and retention of organizational forms and have largely taken variation as given, thus glossing over the causes of organizational variation (Carroll and Hannan 2000: xxii). My analysis of the variety within and among American magazines will help fill holes in this literature. And in chapters 3 and 5 through 7, I will explain how this variety developed.

Variety within Magazines: Contents

The literary forms published by magazines in this era encompassed long, ponderous essays; short informative or entertaining articles; brief items on the weather, current events, and amusements; many kinds of poetry; anecdotes, tales, short stories, and serialized novels; reviews of books, plays, and music; musical scores; and pictures of fine artworks, plants, animals, landscapes, buildings, machines, and fashion. In addition to publishing many different forms of writing, many magazines covered a wide array of subjects: politics and war, law and crime, philosophy, religion, social reform, manners and society, news and current events, fiction and poetry, music and the performing arts, fine art, education, medicine, agriculture, science and engineering, history and biography, geography and travel, humor and satire, commerce and the economy, sports and other leisure activities, and fashion. Such eclecticism should not be surprising since the term *magazine* originally designated a storehouse that could hold a variety of items.

Some 330 magazines (6.2 percent) signaled their diversity by using in their titles the terms *miscellany, miscellaneous, cabinet, casket, eclectic, sundry, variety, various, compendium, omnibus, olio,* or *(port)folio.*[9] Many others used detailed subtitles. Consider these examples of titles (in italics) and subtitles (in roman script), each taken from a different decade (with founding and failure dates in parentheses):

American Museum or, Universal Magazine (1787–92): Containing Essays on Agriculture—Commerce—Manufactures—Politics—Morals—and Manners. Sketches of National Characters—Natural and Civil History—and Biographical Law Information—Public Papers—Proceedings of Congress—Intelligence. Moral Tales—Ancient and Modern Poetry, &c., &c.

Philadelphia Repository and Weekly Register (1800–1806): Containing Original Essays, Tales and Novels, Interesting Extracts from New Publications and Works of Merit, Amusing Miscellanies, Remarkable Occurrences, Anecdotes, Bon Mots, Jeux d'esprit, Marriages and Deaths, Poetical Essays, Odes, Sonnets, Songs and Generally Whatever is Calculated to Diffuse Interesting and Useful Information, Divert the Fancy, Enlighten the Understanding, Form the Mind, and Mend the Heart

National Register, a Weekly Paper (1816–20): Containing a Series of the Important Public Documents, and the Proceedings of Congress; Statistical Tables, Reports and Essays, Original and Selected, upon Agriculture, Manufactures, Commerce, and Finance; Science, Literature and the Arts; and Biographical Sketches; with Summary Statements of the Current News and Political Events

Cabinet of Literature, Instruction, and Amusement (1828–31): Containing Original Essays, Extracts from New Works, Historical Narratives, Biographical Memoirs, Sketches of Society, Topographical Descriptions, Novels and Tales, Anecdotes, Poetry Original and Selected, the Spirit of Public Journals, Discoveries in the Arts and Sciences, Useful Domestic Hints, etc., etc.

New Mirror of Literature, Amusement and Instruction (1843–44): Containing Original Papers, Tales of Romance, Sketches of Society, Manners, and Every-day Life, Domestic and Foreign Correspondence, Wit and Humour, Fashion and Gossip, the Fine Arts, and Literary, Musical and Dra-

[9] This count does not include "eclectic" medical journals, which promoted botanic-based remedies.

matic Criticism, Extracts from New Works, Poetry Original and Selected, the Spirit of the Public Journals, etc. etc. etc.

Wellman's Literary Emporium (1856–59): Devoted to a Sound, High-Toned
and Healthy Literature, Religion, Freedom, Temperance, Education, and
All Topics Calculated to Expand and Elevate the Mind

Sometimes even extensive subtitles were unable to cover the full range of
magazines' contents; as in three of the six examples above, 111 magazines
ended their lists with the all-purpose promise of *etc.* or with an ellipsis. The
tendency of magazines to use markers of eclecticism in their titles declined
over time, from 19 percent of magazine-year observations in the eighteenth
century to 15 percent between 1801 and 1820, 9.3 percent between 1821 and
1840, and 4.3 percent between 1841 and 1860. This was due in part to the decline in the fraction of general-interest magazines and the increase in the fraction of magazines targeting the those with specialized occupations (doctors,
lawyers, ministers, farmers, workers, engineers, businesspeople, and scientists),
adherents of different faiths, proponents of various social reforms, and lovers
of the fine arts—trends that I describe below.

A prominent example of eclecticism in American magazines is *Port-Folio: A
Monthly Magazine, Devoted to Useful Science, the Liberal Arts, Legitimate Criticism, and Polite Literature* (1801–27), founded by lawyer Joseph Dennie and
bookseller Asbury Dickens and published in Philadelphia. *Port-Folio* covered
politics and government, current events, manners and society, literary criticism, the theater, science and engineering, education, and travel; its contents
included short articles, weighty essays, poetry, fiction (in various forms: brief
sketches, longer tales, and serialized novels), and biography. As a second example, consider the *Literary Magazine and American Register* (1803–7), which
was founded by lawyer and novelist Charles Brockden Brown and published
in Philadelphia. Despite its title's seeming emphasis on literary criticism, this
general-interest periodical also covered politics, law, social reform, fiction, poetry, medicine, agriculture, science and engineering, and travel.

As the industry matured the contents of the typical American magazine
shifted from covering a combination of current events, poetry, religion, politics, and miscellany in the earliest years to having a greater emphasis on religion, fiction, poetry, and literary criticism in the mid-nineteenth century. This
is perhaps best seen by tracing how the contents of individual magazines
evolved. Consider *Port-Folio* again; the first issue contained a travelogue and a
translation of Juvenal by John Quincy Adams, letters from the estate of noted
English author Tobias Smollett, and articles about new publications and discourses on literature by Joseph Dennie. The second issue added a political
department that aired virulent federalist political diatribes written by Dennie
and fellow members of the Tuesday Club, a group of Philadelphia conserva-
tives. After Dennie's ill health forced him to relinquish the editorship of *Port-
Folio* in 1811, the magazine began to focus less on politics and more on fine
art and literature; accordingly, it began to print fine engravings plus travel-

ogues, poetry, and literary criticism. A second example of how magazines' contents evolved is provided by the *Methodist Magazine* (1818–1931). In its first decade it published theological essays, biographies of ministers, expositions of scripture, religious and missionary news, obituaries, and poetry. In the 1830s its contents moved away from a single-minded focus on religion and it came to resemble a general-interest magazine. In the 1840s it regained its focus on religion, viewing literature, politics, history, social reform, education, and science through a theological lens; it maintained this focus throughout the next two decades.

Variety among Magazines: Genre, Audience, Language, and Format

Genre. In addition to variation *within* the pages of individual magazines, there was increasing variation *among* magazines due to the appearance of specialized magazines for those with particular occupations; adherents to various faiths; advocates of over two dozen social and educational reform movements; and lovers of poetry, music, theater, and fine art. Table 2.2 lists magazine genres, provides a brief description of each, and shows the number of annual observations on magazines for each. The most prevalent genres were (in descending order) religious, general interest, literary miscellany, medical, agricultural, and social reform. Together these six genres constituted 82 percent of annual observations on those magazines for which enough data were available to determine genre (20,061 of 24,518).

As with the analysis of geographic dispersion, I calculated an index of heterogeneity (more precisely, an index of qualitative variation) for magazine genre from 1793, when there were enough magazines for this index to be meaningful, to 1860. In 1793 the index equaled 0.60; it rose slowly up to 1812, peaking at 0.80, and then declined to the mid-1820s, when it bottomed out at 0.64. This decline was due in large part to the rapid rise of religious magazines in the early nineteenth century, which increased from one-fifth of magazines published in 1801 (9 of 42) to almost one-half in 1825 (102 of 212). After 1825 the index of qualitative variation slowly rose again; it hovered between 0.77 and 0.80 from 1840 to 1860, which reflects the rise of specialist genres. Overall, this pattern indicates that the magazine industry very quickly became highly varied in terms of genre, which fits with the ecological prediction of increasing heterogeneity as industries develop (Hannan and Freeman 1977) and counters the institutionalist prediction of increasing isomorphism (decreasing variety) as the fields in which industries are embedded becomes increasingly structured (DiMaggio and Powell 1983). For magazine genres the modernization of America—which dramatically increased the array of social statuses (religious, political, and economic), and thus the resources (readers and contributors) available to magazines—seems to have been more important than the growing understanding and increasing legitimacy of magazines as cultural and economic goods and the concomitant institutionalization of magazines.

TABLE 2.2.
Magazine Genres

Magazine type	Description	Year first published	Number of annual observations
1. General interest	A mixture of general news and literature; often touched on politics; occasionally included music and art criticism; often covered science and/or medicine and/or history, biography, geography, and travel.	1741	4,281
2. Literary miscellany	Focused on literature and literary criticism; also included some combination of news, politics, science, drama, music, and the fine arts.	1779	1,904
3. Literary newspaper	Focused on current events, often with a political slant; also included other items, especially literary and scientific.	1793	135
4. Literature and the arts	Almost exclusively fiction, poetry, music, plays and theatre reviews, discussions on art, or some combination.	1786	479
5. Literary review	Focused on literature and criticism, with some philosophy mixed in; occasionally included science.	1792	216
6. Politics	Focused exclusively on politics, especially war and the activities of the government.	1752	317
7. Political miscellany	Focused primarily on politics; also touched frequently on literature and/or science.	1741	156
8. Law/crime	Focused exclusively on law and/or crime.	1808	222
9. Social reform	Advocated a social reform; most common were (in descending order) antislavery reform, women's rights, temperance, pacifism, socialism/worker's rights; less frequent were language reform, African colonization, dress reform, free love, anti-tobacco reform, prison reform, moral reform/antivice reform.	1809	1,494
10. Religion	Written either for lay members of one religious denomination or scholars and clergy; a few almost pure philosophy.	1743	8,803

TABLE 2.2. (*Continued*)

Magazine type	Description	Year first published	Number of annual observations
11. News	General news—not just current events, as in newspapers, but also events with lasting impact.	1764	154
12. Social commentary	Covered society, morality, behavior, gossip.	1831	30
13. Education	Targeted teachers; more rarely, targeted parents and/or students.	1810	548
14. Medicine	Usually targeted physicians or veterinarians; sometimes provided medical information to the general public.	1790	1,855
15. Agriculture	Mostly targeted farmers; sometimes home gardeners; sometimes included farm management and science/engineering.	1801	1,724
16. Science and engineering	Targeted members of particular scientific disciplines (e.g., geographers, biologists, chemists) or engineers (especially canal and railroad engineers); occasionally written to educate a general audience.	1804	620
17. History	Included historical facts, historical essays, memoirs, and/or biographies.	1791	156
18. Geography and travel	Described physical geography and wonders of the natural world; sometimes included travel sketches.	1824	30
19. Humor	Satire, irony; often political, often concerned about local society.	1765	355
20. Business	Focused on commerce, trade, economics, finance, and enterprise management; often targeted people in particular trades (e.g., wine importers, tobacconists, cotton millers).	1794	935
21. Sports and leisure	Focused on gambling, horse racing, fashion, and/or other pastimes.	1829	104

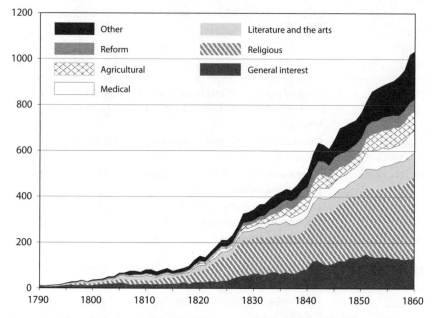

Figure 2.7. The number of magazines in the top six genres by year, 1790–1860.

The distribution of genres changed greatly over time. Figure 2.7, which charts this evolution, shows how many of the six most common genres were published each year from 1790 to 1860.[10] Between 1741 and 1794, when the second Post Office Act was passed, the most common genres were general interest, politics (including political miscellanies, whose contents were broader than pure political journals), and religion. In the early years of the nineteenth century the situation shifted dramatically. Although general-interest magazines continued to grow in numbers throughout the nineteenth century, their share of the industry declined from 35 percent in 1800 to 19 percent in 1830 and 13 percent in 1860. During these six decades, religious magazines began to predominate and political magazines shrank in number. Indeed, by 1813 there were more religious than general-interest magazines—twenty-five versus twenty, respectively—and only five political magazines in print. Religious magazines continued to grow in numbers throughout this era; they constituted over one-third of annual observations on magazines from 1800 onward. Because they constituted such a large share of the US market, chapter 5 is devoted to exploring how religious magazines shaped and were shaped by major developments in American society. The nineteenth century also saw a dramatic rise in magazines devoted to social reform and agricultural magazines (these genres accounted for 6.2 percent and 7.1 percent, respectively, of annual

---

[10] So few magazines were published before 1790 that it is impossible to distinguish genres in any chart for the first five decades.

observations on magazines in the nineteenth century); these trends are detailed in chapters 6 and 7.

After 1800, several small genres grew substantially, becoming a more important part of the industry, even though each individual genre remained small. On the eve of the Civil War, 87 literary periodicals of various types (some quite broad in scope, others narrowly devoted to either fiction, poetry, or literary criticism) were in print, along with 68 business magazines, 36 science and engineering periodicals, 37 education journals, and 16 humor magazines.

The differentiation of magazines into an ever-larger list of specialized genres was part and parcel of the modernization of American society. But not everyone appreciated that trend, as one article reveals: "Formerly when there were fewer periodicals, each one comprised a greater variety of topics, and employed a larger amount of talent; while now, while every department has its separate periodical, the most of them are frittered away into mere trifles.... The poets, philosophers, critics, novelists, wits, and so forth, who are now parcelled out into separate coteries, must call a convention; they must ... combine all their talents and exertion for the amusement and edification of the country" (*Illinois Monthly Magazine* 1831: 304). Similar criticism of the modern trend toward many distinct communities of discourse appeared in other magazines—ironically, sometimes in specialized magazines, such as those that focused on religion, literature, or medicine.

Audiences. In addition to varying by subject matter, magazines in this era varied in terms of their target audiences. The first magazines to target specialized audiences were those for women and children, which began to appear in the late eighteenth century. The monthly *Ein Geistliches Magazien* was the first magazine written for women and children rather than gentlemen, and was also the first German-language magazine in America; it was published sporadically between 1764 and 1772. The first magazine to focus on female readers specifically was *Gentleman and Lady's Town and Country Magazine*, which was published for eight months in 1784. The first for children was *Children's Magazine*, which appeared for three months in 1789. The number of women's and children's magazine grew slowly until 1825, when their number exploded. Women's magazines rose from a total of 22 annual observations on magazines between 1741 and 1794 (0.4 per year, on average) to 559 in the 1850s (56 per year), while children's magazines rose from 10 to 748 annual observations (0.2 to 75 per year). Most women's and children's magazines were general-interest periodicals, but some had a literary, religious, or educational slant.

Other magazines targeted particular racial or ethnic groups. The first magazine for Native Americans, *Muzzinyegun or Literary Voyager*, first appeared in 1826. It was a manuscript magazine (handwritten rather than printed) published in Sault Ste. Marie, Michigan, by Henry Rowe Schoolcraft, who later became famous for his anthropological writings. This literary weekly was written mostly in Ojibwa; its contents ranged over history and biographies of famous Ojibwa leaders, legends, and superstitions; news; essays on the customs and manners of other tribes; the fur trade; travelogues; temperance; poetry; and art. In 1838 the first magazines published by and for African Americans—the *National Reformer* and the *Colored American*—appeared in New York and Philadelphia, respectively. In total, eleven magazines were launched for African Americans; five of these focused on the abolition of slavery, four were primarily religious in nature, one was a literary miscellany, and one was a general-interest magazine.

Many magazines were published by and for members of other ethnic groups, most in languages other than English. Figure 2.8 presents a timeline showing when the first magazine in each language appeared. Magazines published in European languages were launched not long after speakers of those languages immigrated to America. Most numerous were German-language magazines: 307 were published before the Civil War, plus fifteen bilingual German-English magazines and one trilingual German-English-French magazine. Not surprisingly given the geographic distribution of German immigration to America, most German-language magazines were published in Pennsylvania, but they also appeared in Illinois, Indiana, Iowa, Maryland, Missouri, New Jersey, New York, Ohio, Texas, Virginia, and Wisconsin. There were 71 French-language magazines, most published in and around New Orleans, plus 18 French-bilingual magazines (16 French-English, 1 French-Spanish, and 1 French-Italian) and 1 French-German-English magazine. Magazines were also published in Spanish (12, and 2 bilingual Spanish-English), Welsh (12), Czech (2), Danish (2), Norwegian (2), Swedish (2), Hebrew (1, bilingual Hebrew-English), Ojibwa (1, *Muzzinyegan*, described above), Senecan (1, bilingual Senecan-English), Shawnee (1), Santee (1, bilingual Santee-English), and Cherokee (3). These magazines strengthened linguistic communities, reducing their natural tendency to dissolve into the American melting pot. As one scholar commented about the *Philadelphisches Magazin* (1798), the first German-American literary periodical, it "aimed to create a literary community—a space for *writers* (as well as readers) of German-American literature" (Starnes 2009: 87; emphasis in the original).

Finally, specialized magazines for affinity groups—notably, fraternal associations such as the Freemasons and Odd Fellows, also flourished. The first such, *Freemasons Magazine*, was published in Philadelphia in 1811; It was followed by forty-nine other magazines for Masons and thirteen for Odd Fellows.

As with the increasing variety of magazines across genres, the increasing number of magazines targeting specialized audiences—women, children and youth, racial groups, linguistic groups, and affinity groups—fits with the ecological prediction of increasing heterogeneity as the industry developed (Hannan and Freeman 1977) and counters the institutionalist prediction of increasing isomorphism (i.e., decreasing variety; see DiMaggio and Powell 1983). As chapter 3 will explain, magazines' increasing variety was in part a consequence of the nation's economic modernization, as specialized magazines appeared to

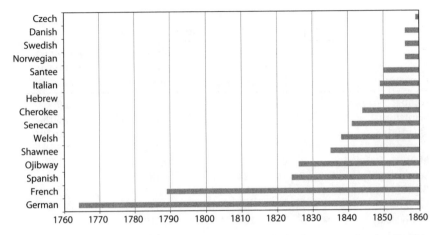

Figure 2.8. Timeline for first appearance of magazines published in languages other than English.

support the increasing array of specialized subcommunities. And as chapter 5 will explain, a second cause of this growing variety of magazines was the increasingly intense competition among the growing number of religious communities, some of which catered to immigrant communities.

Format. Magazines also varied greatly in terms of format, specifically as regards publication frequency. Table 2.3 lists all observed publication formats and, to disambiguate unfamiliar terms, translates them into the number of issues per year. It also shows the number of annual observations on magazines (for magazines not missing data on publication frequency) within each format. Before the Civil War, American magazines used three main formats: weekly (the dominant format), monthly, and quarterly. Together these constituted 82 percent of all annual observations on magazines. A few magazines had unusual formats: semiannual, three or five per year, triweekly, biweekly, bimonthly, quarterly, or semiweekly. Publication formats became standardized by the 1850s, when the three main formats constituted 86 percent of annual observations on magazines. In addition, the number of magazines published irregularly became steadily rarer as time passed: 11 percent for the years 1741–94, 7.3 percent for 1795–1825, 1.8 percent for 1826–50, and 1.5 percent 1851–60.

It is not surprising that magazines settled quickly on three standard publication cycles: weekly, monthly, and quarterly. Most modern Western endeavors are ruled by the inescapable rhythms of the calendar; activities that do not match these socially constructed temporal categories are extremely difficult to maintain (Zerubavel 1981). Even the French Revolution, which sought to overturn all social relations, was unable to destroy the seven-day week and the irregular month. The revolutionary calendar, which divided the year into thirty-six ten-day cycles called *décades*, did not last long (Zerubavel 1985: 28–

TABLE 2.3.
Magazine Formats (Publication Frequency)

Frequency	Number of issues/year	Number of annual observations	Percentage of annual observations
Annual	1	703	2.97%
Semiannual	2	143	0.60%
Quarterly	4	1,669	7.05%
Bimonthly	6	368	1.55%
Monthly	12	9,296	39.3%
Semimonthly	24	1,185	5.00%
Biweekly (fortnightly)	26	657	2.77%
Weekly	52	8,340	35.2%
Semiweekly	104	219	0.92%
Other*		186	0.78%
Irregular		560	2.36%

Note: The category "Other" includes 77 magazines that published only a single issue before folding, and whose intended publication frequency was unknown. Calculations of percentages do not include 1,102 annual observations on magazines for which publication frequency was unknown.

35). Given the resilience of socially constructed temporal categories like weeks and months, it is only to be expected that magazines quickly came to adhere to them. The upshot is that, with respect to format, the history of magazines supports the institutionalist prediction of increasing homogeneity (isomorphism) as the industry developed rather than the ecological prediction of increasing variety.

CONCLUSION

This survey has revealed many important developments between the appearance of the first American magazines in 1741 and the situation prevailing 120 years later. There is a sharp contrast between the short-lived, small-circulation magazines of the mid-eighteenth century and the often long-lived, mass-circulation periodicals of the mid-nineteenth century. In the 1740s and '50s, most magazines were short (four-page) general-interest magazines or political miscellanies read by socioeconomic elites within a single state, and most were exceedingly frail: two-thirds failed within a half year, three-fourths within a year. By 1860, the magazine industry had become both robust and quite similar to its contemporary descendant. Over a thousand magazines were published that year, and while some had narrow circulations within the confines of a single city or county, most had far-flung audiences who eagerly awaited delivery of new issues in the mail. The founders of mid-nineteenth-century magazines could expect their ventures to live for several years: the median life span for magazines founded in the 1850s was 2.0 years. In addition to general-interest magazines, a vast array of specialized journals had appeared to serve particular audiences: women and children, members of different racial and ethnic groups, cultivators of a wide array of crops and livestock, participants in various social and educational reform movements, adherents to a wide array of faiths, members of various occupations, and those who were brought together by their love of literature, art, sports, or fashion. By the mid-nineteenth century magazines had taken on approximately their current form as regards size, shape, layout, and balance between written and pictorial material. Observing the magazine industry up to the Civil War, therefore, allows us to analyze the industry's evolution from its origins to approximately its current state.

By the 1820s American magazines had become highly legitimate: an increasing number were published across the growing nation, and these both lived longer than their eighteenth-century predecessors and had larger circulations. Moreover, as noted in this chapter, the great and sustained variety of magazines in the first 120 years of the industry's history—both the variety of contents within individual magazines and the variety of magazines in terms of genre and audience—is consistent with the ecological prediction of great heterogeneity (Hannan and Freeman 1977) but inconsistent with the institutionalist prediction of increasing isomorphism (decreasing variety) as the industry developed (DiMaggio and Powell 1983). In contrast, the increasing concentration of magazine publication into the weekly, monthly, and quarterly formats is consistent with the institutionalist prediction but inconsistent with the ecological prediction. This difference may be due to the fact that these two aspects of magazine variety evolved in response to very different external forces. With regard to genre and specialized audience groups, American society modernized and Americans became increasingly differentiated in terms of their social positions and interests, which supported magazine variety (Hannan and Freeman 1977). With regard to format, magazines were subject to extremely powerful norms about temporal rhythms—norms that even the architects of the French Revolution were powerless to resist (Zerubavel 1985). The contrasting results for magazine production cycles and magazine genres and audiences indicates that theories of organizational form must become more concrete and more precisely specific regarding which aspects of organization they pertain to: formal structure and forms of authority, management policies and practices, production and distribution technologies, goals, resource bases, or audiences.

Alternatively, we might conclude from the analysis of magazine variety that institutionalist predictions pertain more to internal organizational structure and process whereas ecological predictions pertain more to the attributes of the goods and services produced by those structures and processes and therefore to the array of customers that organizations their products will appeal to.

Scholars of cultural industries—especially the media—are likely wondering, how did magazines become such a common and robust part of American letters and life? This question is answered in chapter 3, which explains how the material and cultural resources needed to support magazines evolved, and chapter 4, which describes how the internal operation of magazines evolved. And scholars of organizations are likely wondering what accounts for the evolving variety of magazines. That question is answered in chapter 3, which shows how magazines' identities and locations were shaped by postal service expansion, and in chapters 5 to 7, which detail the coevolution of magazines and three arenas of American society: religion, social reform, and economic modernization.

CHAPTER 3

The Material and Cultural Foundations of American Magazines

*H*ow did American magazines become so numerous and robust? All productive organizations, including magazine publishing concerns, require raw materials, technologies and skilled employees to transform raw materials into finished products and distribute them, money to pay suppliers and employees, customers to buy them, and acceptance by formal authorities like the state. In the early days of the magazine industry in America, all of these were scarce. Paper was expensive and difficult to make; printing presses were few in number, slow, and difficult to use; there was no ready pool of authorial talent; there was no fast, reliable, or inexpensive way to distribute goods, including magazines, beyond the boundaries of a few towns and cities; there was little free cash available to finance nonessential undertakings like periodical publishing; few people in the sparse population had the time or leisure to read magazines, and even fewer had any interest in literature—and no interesting literature to read—apart from the Bible, Shakespeare, and Milton; and colonial rulers were suspicious of all publishing ventures. For these many reasons, when the American magazine industry was born in Philadelphia in 1741 it was a doubtful venture beset by seemingly intractable problems of supply and demand.

Here I explain how several fundamental changes in American society supported the explosive growth and increasing variety of magazines by providing both the resources necessary to publish magazines and the demand necessary to sustain a wide array of them in locations across the nation. I begin by considering basic material supports: advances in printing and papermaking technologies and the development of the US postal distribution system. I then move on to the more complex demographic, economic, and cultural supports for magazines: the growth of an increasingly urban, better-educated, more prosperous population; the development of a wide array of differentiated religious, political, and economic communities of readers; and the development of copyright law and a culture of the professional author.

While better production and distribution systems were necessary for magazines to thrive in this era, they were not sufficient. New technologies make possible "constitutive moments" in which cultural forces—models from other fields, norms, values, power-dependence relations, and preexisting institutions—can come into play, and it is those cultural forces rather than the intrinsic material features of technologies themselves that determine the form technologies take and the ways they are used (Bijker, Hughes, and Pinch 1987). In particular for the time period under discussion, new communication technologies like the printing press and postal service made it possible for different groups in society to renegotiate power and authority relations, usually in ways that were built on the vestiges of old technologies and relations (Marvin 1987: 4–5; for evidence among a wide array of communication technologies, see Fischer 1992; Kline 2000; Starr 2004). Given the interplay between technical and cultural factors, we must understand how cultural factors—notably, the growth of an increasingly diverse reading public and the parallel developments of copyright law and cultural conceptions of authorship—shaped how magazines in the eighteenth and nineteenth centuries made use of the production and distribution systems and in so doing created the magazine industry we know today.

It is important to recognize also that the causal arrow runs both ways: it was not only that changes in material and cultural conditions supported the development of the magazine industry; the industry itself promoted changes in some material and cultural conditions, in line with what prior research has shown for the newspaper industry (Schudson 1978; Boczkowski 2004).[1] First, just like newspapers, magazines in this era stimulated the development of improved printing and papermaking technologies: the growing number of newspaper and magazine publishing concerns were eager consumers of innovations in printing and papermaking. Second, as magazines began to publish more engaging material, they helped make manifest latent demand for reading as a leisure activity and so created a nation of avid readers. Third, the reading public showed greater interest in becoming literate when there was more to read (Watt [1975] 2001), and magazines helped spread literacy by conveying innovative educational techniques to teachers and offering a platform for edifying and entertaining material that aimed to engage young minds.

[1] I am not arguing that all social changes analyzed in this chapter were promoted by the growth of the magazine industry. The expansion of the postal system was clearly exogenous to the magazine industry. Congress authorized post roads and offices, and within the executive branch the postmaster general authorized funding for them. Although establishing post roads and offices was a form of congressional "pork" (see Rich 1924: 91–126), pressure on Congress came primarily from constituents who sought improved delivery of goods and letters, not magazines (Rich 1924; Larson 1987; Kielbowicz 1989; John 1995). Magazine publishers' influence on Congress was virtually nil because magazines constituted only a tiny portion of the mails (Rich 1924; Kielbowicz 1989; John 1995). Not until the 1850s was the magazine industry able to influence postal officials to secure significant rate reductions (Kielbowicz 1989: 121–39). Therefore, we can be confident that the growth of the magazine industry did not drive postal expansion; instead, postal development supported the magazine industry.

PUBLISHING TECHNOLOGIES

Although we might consider it prosaic today as we rely ever more on electronic communications media, mechanical printing using movable type has
had enormous social impact and has therefore been heralded as one of the
greatest inventions of the modern era, in large part because it brought knowledge and opinions within the reach of a rapidly increasing fraction of the
Western world (Cooley [1909] 1923; Eisenstein 1979). As no less an authority
than Sir Francis Bacon observed, "We should note the force, effect, and consequences of inventions which are nowhere more conspicuous than in those
three which were unknown to the ancients . . . , namely, printing, gunpowder,
and the compass. For these three have changed the appearance and state of the
whole world" (*Novum Organum*, 1620, aphorism 129).

Notwithstanding its already substantial impact on European society, printing technology in mid-eighteenth-century America was in the same stage of
development as the Internet was before the release of the first commercial
web browser, Mosaic, in 1994: available to only a small number of people in a
few places, difficult to use, expensive to access, and of limited and often uncertain utility. The inadequacies of this basic technology made all publishing efforts, including magazines, dubious ventures.

In the century after 1740, many of these inadequacies were rectified. First
and most basic was the fact that printing presses became widely available.
Figure 3.1 charts the diffusion of printing presses across America, showing the
continental United States with modern state boundaries. States where there
were printing presses by 1700 are shaded dark gray. States where there were
printing presses after that date have lighter markings: medium gray shading
for 1701–50, diagonal stripes for 1751–1800, crosshatches for 1801–50, and
white for 1851 onward. By the time the first American magazines were
launched in 1741, only eight of the thirteen colonies had printing presses
(Wroth and Silver 1951: 69–70). At the outbreak of the Revolutionary War all
British colonies had printing presses. By 1800 there were printing presses in
all states of the Union plus the District of Columbia; the Ohio, Michigan, and
Mississippi Territories; French Louisiana; and Spanish Florida. By 1850, printing presses had appeared as far west as California, Idaho, New Mexico, Oregon, and Utah.

Eighteenth-century printing presses were slow and cumbersome; no fundamental improvements had been made in printing technology since the
late fifteenth century (Wroth and Silver 1951: 71). Printing presses in this era
were powered by wooden screws driven by hand that brought inked forms
(platens), filled with wooden or metal type, into contact with damp paper
held in flat beds. Such presses required a great deal of highly skilled physical
labor to produce at most 200 to 250 impressions per hour on one side of a
sheet, which translated to between 100 and 125 double-sided sheets per hour
(Moran 1973).

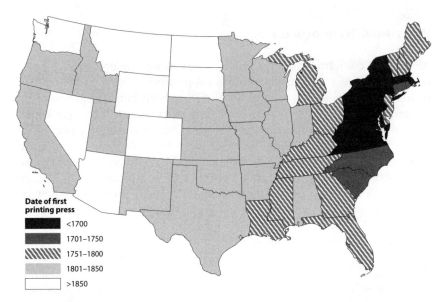

Date of first printing press

- <1700
- 1701–1750
- 1751–1800
- 1801–1850
- >1850

Figure 3.1. The spread of printing presses across America. Source: Lehmann-Haupt (1951: 69–70).

In the first half of the nineteenth century a series of technological advances greatly improved the speed and quality of printing and dramatically reduced printing costs (Berry and Poole 1966; Moran 1973). In 1800 the Earl of Stanhope introduced his eponymous press, which was the first to be made entirely of steel; steel presses could handle higher pressures than wooden ones and so could print faster, producing up to 250 sheets per hour. In 1813 the Columbian press was invented by George Clymer of Philadelphia; Extending the innovations of the Stanhope press, Clymer's machine used a system of levers and fulcrums to provide strong pressure without requiring great physical effort on the part of the printer. The following year the first double-cylinder press was built in Germany; this type of machine first appeared in the United States in the 1820s, and used rotating cylinders rather than flat beds to hold paper, which made it possible to increase printing speeds to 1,100 sheets per hour. In 1829 the Napier press, a greatly improved double-cylinder design, was able to print 3,000 sheets per hour; it was brought to America in 1832. Finally, in 1847 the Hoe rotary press—an American invention—was introduced. It used rolls of paper rather than stacks of sheets, which allowed for faster throughput: 12,000 sheets per hour for the first model, almost double that for later models.

From the 1830s onward, widespread use of steam-powered presses greatly reduced the human effort required to print magazines. In the first decade of the nineteenth century, three men had to work for one full day to print 4,000 sheets; forty years later, three men working with steam-powered machines could produce 56,000 sheets each day—fourteen times as much (Charvat 1968: 46). Technological advances also reduced the weight of printing presses, making them more easily transported, which led to the geographic diffusion of printing presses shown in figure 3.1. As Nathan O. Hatch has noted, "the first half of the nineteenth century was indeed the golden age of regional printing. Almost anyone could set up a printing shop, and publishing was ephemeral, genuinely popular, and virtually uncontrolled" (1989: 144). Advances in printing technology lowered barriers to entry for all kinds of magazines; this had an especially strong impact on the viability of magazines that targeted specialized audience segments, such as children, German-speaking Lutherans, or Freemasons, and those that focused on subjects of interest to a particular group of readers, such as horticulture, horse racing, or history.

Access to printing presses was a basic requirement for the magazine industry to spread to any particular location, and this access varied greatly over time.[2] To take into account this spatial and temporal variation, I calculated the ratio of the number of states or colonies where magazines were published to the number of states or colonies with printing presses. This ratio was 0.125 in 1741, when eight colonies had printing presses but magazines were published in only one of them. It fluctuated between 0.06 and 0.14 during the colonial and Revolutionary War eras, then rose to 0.19 in 1784, the year after the Treaty of Paris ended hostilities between Great Britain and the new republic, when magazines were published in three of the sixteen states and territories that had printing presses. It rose steadily after that, peaking at 0.83 in the mid-1850s, when magazines were published in thirty-five of the forty-two states and territories that had printing presses, before dropping slightly to 0.74. This decline occurred because the spread of printing presses across the continent and into newly settled territories (they were in all thirty-three states plus nine territories) outpaced the spread of the magazine industry (published in all thirty-three states and the Kansas Territory).

Technological innovations transformed printing from a craft to an industry (Lehmann-Haupt 1951), but at the same time they transformed the nature of the work done by print shops—indeed, the nature of print shops themselves. Large, complex steam-powered presses cost far more than simple manual presses. As a result, the printing industry became stratified, with large, highly capitalized print shops in the publishing industry centers (Boston, New York, and Philadelphia) churning out mass market magazines while smaller print shops everywhere produced small-circulation magazines (Stott 1990). For example, the New York–based Harper and Brothers, which published one religious and two literary magazines and was the largest publishing concern in the world (Schlesinger 2000), had a capital base in 1860 of $1.5

[2] There were in existence twenty-one manuscript magazines, which were handwritten rather than printed using movable type. Because these constituted such a tiny fraction of magazines, the existence of printing presses is essentially a limiting technological condition for publishing magazines in any particular location.

million (about $40 million in 2014 dollars) and was housed in its own seven-story building (Stott 1990). Most printers were transformed from highly skilled proprietors of small businesses to less-skilled employees of large firms (Lehmann-Haupt 1951; Blumin 1989; Stott 1990). By the mid-nineteenth century magazine publishers could easily and cheaply hire printers; they did not have to be printers themselves.

Like printing technology, papermaking technology did not change appreciably between the fifteenth and eighteenth centuries: cotton or linen rags were soaked in water and macerated to reduce them to pulp; mesh screens were dipped into the wet mixture, pressed, and set to dry; dried sheets of paper were pulled off the screens, pressed again, and trimmed to size (Weeks 1916; Berry and Poole 1966; Smith 1970). This cumbersome process required highly skilled labor, and the basic ingredients—linen and cotton rags—were costly; therefore paper was very expensive. But like printing technology, papermaking technology improved dramatically in the early years of the nineteenth century, resulting in substantial decreases in paper prices (Moran 1973; Smith 1970). In 1803, the Foudrinier brothers in France developed a machine that replaced hand-held forms for individual sheets of paper with a continuous belt that produced long rolls of paper, increasing production speeds and dramatically reducing production costs. The first papermaking machines appeared in the United States in 1817 (Weeks 1916). In the 1830s, the introduction of a bleaching process made it possible to use colored rags, greatly increasing the supply of raw material used to make paper. A final cost-reducing innovation occurred in the 1850s: straw and soda-wood pulp replaced rags, further increasing the supply of paper. As a result of these technological improvements the price of paper fell dramatically: over 85 percent (in constant dollars) between 1810 and 1865 (Hunter 1952; Starr 2004).

As printing and papermaking technologies improved so did ancillary techniques such as engraving. From the mid-eighteenth to the mid-nineteenth centuries, the materials used in engraving evolved from crude, fragile wooden plates to finer, more durable ones made first of copper and then of steel (Berry and Poole 1966). In the 1790s white-line wood engraving was perfected, which involved using metal engraving tools on the end-grain surface of very hard wood to produce pictures of great clarity. This new technology was complemented by the development of the mezzotint technique, copper-plate engraving that could reproduce subtle gradations of light and shadow, and the aquatint, which simulated watercolor painting. Engraving techniques made a big leap forward in 1810 when steel was first used to make the plates; because steel is harder than copper it was possible to make more impressions from each plate, which reduced costs and made it possible for a wider variety of publications to include illustrations. Lithography, in which prints are made with a plate on which only the image to be printed takes up ink while the nonprinting area is treated to repel ink, was invented in 1789 in Munich and became widespread in the 1820s. This technique provided artists with greater fluidity and scope in the types of illustrations they could create. By 1850 the widespread use of increasingly cheap color lithography further improved the quality of illustrations. Finally, between 1826 and 1839, Frenchmen Joseph Niécephore Niépce and Louis-Jacques Mandé Daguerre invented a way to engrave pictures on metal plates using photography. Their inventions were the basis for all later photoengraving techniques (Greenhood and Gentry 1936).

As was noted in the introduction, it is important to realize that these great technological improvements in printing, papermaking, and engraving were driven in part by the expansion of periodical publishing, including newspapers as well as magazines (Schudson 1978). The rapid increase in the numbers of periodicals and the rise of mass-market periodicals created demand for faster, lighter, easier-to-use printing presses, cheaper paper, and better illustrations. This is just one example of how, as any industry grows, deep pools of industry-specific resources develop (Hannan and Freeman 1989).

DISTRIBUTION INFRASTRUCTURE: THE POST OFFICE

Although reliable, inexpensive, and widely available printing presses, paper, and engraving techniques are necessary to produce print media, they are not enough to guarantee that any print media, including magazines, will thrive. Printed matter must also be transmitted widely, cheaply, reliably, and quickly. Throughout most of the first 120 years of the magazine industry's history, the US Post Office was the key distribution channel for magazines. But at its start in the mid-eighteenth century, the postal system, another technology that today is being supplanted by electronic communications, was quite primitive. There were only a few miles of postal routes connecting a handful of towns along the Northeastern Seaboard, carrying capacity was extremely limited, and the speed of transit was frustratingly slow. Several related developments over the next century transformed the postal system into a rapid and ubiquitous distribution channel that could handle large volumes of magazines and other print media.

The Development of the Postal System

In the colonial era, a slow but reliable postal network extended from Portsmouth, New Hampshire, to Philadelphia, but postal service farther south was irregular (Rich 1924). When Benjamin Franklin became colonial postmaster general in 1753, he established new post roads to the interior and sped up travel on existing roads. Subsequent colonial postmasters general continued in Franklin's footsteps. Between 1740 and 1776, the number of post offices rose from thirty-one to sixty-one, and the network of post roads expanded 20 percent, from 1,462 to 1,778 miles (Rich 1924; Kielbowicz 1989; John 1995). Still, given the inadequacies of the colonial postal network, it is not surprising that many of the earliest magazines were distributed through local merchant establishments—primarily print shops, bookstores, tobacco shops, and general stores.

After the Revolution, political elites were worried that the young republic might dissolve (Nagle 1964; Wood 1969; Brown 1976; Wiebe 1984); they argued that a nationwide plan of internal improvements—a strong postal system and an extensive network of roads and waterways—was necessary to overcome the republic's disintegrative tendencies (Rich 1924; Larson 1987). They viewed the postal system in particular as critical for creating a national community that would transcend state boundaries (Rich 1924; Kielbowicz 1989; John 1995; Starr 2004). Accordingly, the 1794 Postal Act established the Post Office as a permanent arm of the government; after that date magazines gained slow acceptance from postal officials (Kielbowicz 1989; John 1995). The US Congress mandated the postal system's expansion and it grew rapidly, from 75 offices and 1,875 miles of post roads in 1790 to 4,500 offices and 73,492 miles of roads in 1820 (Rich 1924; Kielbowicz 1989; John 1995). This expansion made it easy for magazines to extend their circulation far beyond their points of publication. For instance, the *Military Monitor* (founded 1812) reached subscribers from Maine south to Mississippi and west to Ohio and Kentucky, while the *Columbian Star* (founded 1822) had subscribers in twenty-six states and Washington, DC—in New England, the mid-Atlantic states, all along the western frontier, and as far south as Alabama and Louisiana. Among the magazines founded between 1790 and 1820 for which there are data on the geographic scope of circulation, over half were sold in multiple states, one-seventh were sold throughout their state, and just one-third were sold only in one city or town.

Although the postal system was virtually complete by the late 1820s (John 1995), the federal government continued to invest heavily in expansion to cover the nation's growing landmass. By 1860 there were 28,498 offices and 240,594 miles of post roads (Rich 1924; Kielbowicz 1989; John 1995). The benefit of postal system development for magazines was obvious: by the 1830s several dozen magazines boasted national circulations.

The speed and reliability of mail transport advanced in pace with the expansion of the postal system. In the eighteenth and early nineteenth centuries, the poor state of the roads made travel time from one town to another so long that prompt delivery of magazines was impossible. Before 1825, a stagecoach might average only two miles per hour. This meant that, around 1800, it took four days for mail to travel from Boston to New York and nineteen days (up to a month in bad weather) for mail to be delivered from Philadelphia to Lexington, Kentucky (Mott 1930; Edgar 1975: 14). Even in the late 1830s, six horses pulling a two-wheeled postal cart had trouble traveling on the muddy roads of Ohio at a rate of fifteen miles in three days (Mott 1930).

The first notable improvement was in the roads over which post riders traveled. Dirt roads turned to mud in the winter and spring, slowing the mails to a crawl. Starting in the 1820s, federally funded road projects made use of a new construction technology developed by Scottish engineer John Loudon

MacAdam (Ringwalt 1888; Taylor 1951), who built road surfaces from stones crushed together to form a tough surface that was set above the surrounding ground and graded down the sides so water would run off it. Such "macadamized" roads were far superior to the early mud or "corduroy" (sawed-log) roads. Starting in the 1830s, the addition of tar and pitch as a sealant to create what later became known as tarmac made roads smoother and far less prone to developing potholes or turning into mud.

Improvements in roads were complemented by improvements in modes of transportation. In the 1780s carriage of mail by horseback over rough, unpaved pathways gave way to carriage in horse-drawn sulkies over smoother and better-maintained roads. Then, between 1790 and 1830, stagecoaches eclipsed sulkies. Large-scale transportation of the mails on riverways began on steamboats in 1813, which made upstream travel increasingly fast, cheap, and reliable. For example, in 1815 steamboats on the Mississippi, Missouri, and Ohio Rivers and their tributaries traveled an average of sixty-eight miles per day upstream and 135 miles per day downstream; by 1855 steamboat speeds had more than doubled, to an average of 205 miles per day upstream and 260 miles per day downstream (Haites and Mak 1978: table C-3). As a result, travel time was dramatically reduced. For instance, before the introduction of steamboats, the round-trip between New Orleans and Louisville, by foot and keelboat, took over 150 days; using steamboats, the length of the round trip fell to 39 days by 1815, and then to 11 days by 1860 (Haites, Mak, and Walton 1975: table 16). Transportation costs also dropped precipitously: in 1815, shipping freight on the main western rivers cost 8.05 cents per ton-mile upstream and 1.61 cents downstream; by 1855, freight rates were 0.40 cents per ton-mile upstream and 0.52 cents downstream (Haites and Mak 1978: table 12). Recognizing the enormous benefits created by steamboats, Congress declared all steamboat routes to be post roads.

Canals were constructed as complements to steamboats starting in 1815. They had the great advantage of cutting through large swaths of territory in the western frontier, which had been accessible only overland, and so greatly improved the speed and reliability of transportation across the expanding nation. Canals were built in two spurts, in 1815–34 and in 1836–54. By 1860, over $180 million (in constant 1860 dollars) had been invested in over four thousand miles of canals connecting Atlantic port cities with each other and with inland communities (Cranmer 1960). The investment in canals paid handsome dividends, increasing speed and reducing costs. For instance, the cost per ton of goods shipped up the Erie Canal from Albany to Buffalo dropped over 80 percent, from $18.65 in 1830 to $2.45 in 1860 (Ringwalt 1888).

Railroad construction started in 1826 with three miles of track laid down in Quincy, Massachusetts. Steam engines began to be used in 1830, which greatly enhanced the utility of this new mode of transportation. Until the mid-1840s, railroads were concentrated in New England and along the Northeastern Seaboard. After 1848 railroad construction took off, and by 1860 a

TABLE 3.1.
Travel Times from New York to Selected Cities, 1800–1857

Year	Boston	Charleston	New Orleans	Chicago	San Francisco
1800	4	10	27	42	—
1830	1.5	6	14	19	—
1857	0.5	2	5	2	28

Note: Travel times are given in days.
Source: Carter and Sutch 2006.

network of over thirty thousand miles of track had been woven across the growing nation. By 1860, the railroad was the preeminent mode of mail transport; indeed, as early as 1838, Congress recognized their value and declared railroads to be post roads.

Table 3.1 reveals the overall consequences of these many improvements in transportation infrastructure and technologies, comparing the time required to travel from New York City to cities in different parts of the growing nation in 1800, 1830, and 1857 (Carter and Sutch 2006). Between 1800 and 1857, travel times were reduced by 88 percent for trips to Boston; 80 percent to Charleston, South Carolina; 95 percent to Chicago; and 81 percent to New Orleans.

Acceptance of Magazines by Postal Authorities

Although improved transportation systems promised ever easier and more widespread distribution throughout the expanding postal system, postal officials were not initially sympathetic to carrying magazines in the mails. During the colonial era and in the first decades after the Revolution, local postmasters had discretion about whether to include magazines in the mails. The earliest national postal acts in 1792 and 1794 were ambiguous about whether magazines could be carried in the mails. The Postal Act of 1792, which was intended as an interim measure with only a two-year life span, did not mention magazines at all. After its passage, some magazines (specifically, the *Columbian Magazine* and *American Museum*) were prevented by local postmasters from being mailed to out-of-town subscribers and thus folded, while others (*Massachusetts Magazine* and *New-York Magazine*) were allowed in the mails and thus thrived (Wood 1949: 24). Its replacement, the Postal Act of 1794, which made the post office a permanent arm of the federal government, stated that magazines could be transported "where the mode of conveyance and the size of the mails will admit of it" (US Congress 1794, § 22)—that is, when postmasters perceived that there was enough room. As late as 1804, postmaster general Gideon Granger advised local postmasters that they need not allow magazines in the mails if doing so was inconvenient (Rich 1924: 145).

In 1815, postmaster general Return Jonathan Meigs Jr. declared that all magazines except religious ones were not allowed in the mails unless they

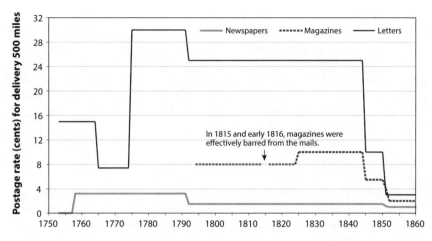

Figure 3.2. Comparing postage rates: newspapers, magazines, and letters, 1750–1860.

paid the letter rate. For a typical sixty-four-page magazine delivered to a sub-scriber five hundred miles from the city of publication, this would amount to a ruinously expensive $1.50. To put this in perspective, the cost to mail one issue of the typical magazine would add more than 60 percent to the average annual subscription rate for magazines published in 1815: the average sub-scription rate in 1815 was $2.56, based on the forty-two magazines (out of seventy-seven published that year) whose subscription rates are known. This virtual ban on carrying magazines was lifted in April 1816, but carriage of magazines in the mails remained at local postmasters' discretion and was not fully regularized until 1845 (Chu 1932: 32).

Distribution of magazines in the mail was also hampered for many years by high postage rates. The 1794 Postal Act set far higher postage rates for magazines than for newspapers: the typical sixty-four-page magazine could be carried less than fifty miles for 4 cents, between fifty and 100 miles for 6 cents, and more than 100 miles for 8 cents; in contrast, newspapers cost 1.5 cents for carriage less than five hundred miles (Kielbowicz 1989: 122). Figure 3.2 charts postage rates for magazines, newspapers, and letters over time in nominal dol-lars. Postage rates for magazines remained fairly constant until 1845; after that point they declined steadily. Before 1845, magazines were subject to consider-ably higher postage rates than newspapers but much lower rates than letters. After 1845, magazine and newspaper postage rates converged.

Although postage rates for magazines before 1845 were high, they were not an insurmountable barrier to the widespread distribution of magazines be-cause much postage due was not paid. Before 1855, magazine publishers did not have to prepay postage and postal officials often did not collect from re-cipients—that is, subscribers. Indeed, correspondence among postmasters in-dicates that many post offices collected less than half of the postage that was owed on periodicals (Kielbowicz 1989: 39, 68). To avoid paying higher magazine postage rates some periodicals, like *Brother Jonathan* (1839–45) and the *Southern Planter* (1841–69), adopted newspaper layouts and called themselves newspapers. For example, *Brother Jonathan* claimed to be "[t]he largest newspaper in the world!!" Such disguises did not always work; for example, Charles Botts, publisher of the *Southern Planter* complained, "On the cover of our paper we have declared that the *Planter* was a newspaper, and subject to postage only as such. We have been directed by the Post Office Department ... to erase this announcement" (1846: 142).

The Impact of the Postal System on Magazines

Postal system development had strong effects on the nature of magazines.[3] Most notably, it spurred competitive differentiation between magazines published in the industry's geographic core (Massachusetts, New York, and Pennsylvania) and those published within the industry periphery (all other states). Two trends are evident. First and most basically, the founding of new magazines became more strongly affected by magazines published farther away and less strongly by those published nearby. Second, magazines founded within the industry core became more likely to adopt universalistic identities, as evidenced by their use of titles signaling national geographic scope (e.g., *American*), while magazines founded within its periphery became more likely to adopt localistic identities, as evidenced by their use of titles signaling local geographic scope (e.g., *Lexington* or *Vermont*). These two trends are related. The increasing scope of interaction among magazines, promoted by the development of the postal system, increased the competition experienced by magazines within the industry periphery and pushed them to emphasize their local roots. At the same time, magazines published within the core differentiated their products from local magazines and expanded their audiences by claiming universalistic identities. Here I detail these intertwined impacts of postal system development on both magazine founding rates and the identities magazines adopted at their founding.

Magazine Founding Rates

Two divergent forces affected the number of magazines founded in the eighteenth and nineteenth centuries. On the one hand, those who founded magazines tended to launch their publishing ventures where they resided for both personal and pragmatic reasons: they preferred not to uproot their families and leave friends, and many of the resources they needed to start and sustain publishing ventures were rooted in place. Much research on the twentieth century has shown that people do not readily relocate for jobs and that infor-

---

[3] The analysis in this section is based on two coauthored papers, "The Spatial Scope of Competition and the Geographic Distribution of Entrepreneurship" (Haveman and Rider 2014a) and "Place *and* Space: The Development of Communication Systems and Competitive Differentiation among Startups" (Haveman and Rider 2014b).

mation networks tend to be highly localized in space (Katan and Morgan 1952; Mueller and Morgan 1962; Sorenson and Audia 2000); in this regard, the situation facing magazine founders in the eighteenth and early nineteenth centuries was similar to that facing many later entrepreneurs. Moreover, research on the late nineteenth and twentieth centuries has shown that the legitimacy of any industry depends on the number of firms operating (Hannan and Freeman 1989). Applying this logic to the eighteenth and early nineteenth centuries suggests that locations where magazines clustered thickly together, like Massachusetts, New York, and Pennsylvania, provided would-be magazine entrepreneurs with greater legitimacy and therefore better access to the resources they needed to start new periodicals. This dynamic meant that the more magazines there were in any location, the higher the founding rates would be.

On the other hand, magazine foundings in any location were also sensitive to the number of magazines in other, nearby locations. Entrepreneurs, including those who published magazines in the eighteenth and early nineteenth centuries, may have moved to locations with many organizations in their industry because those locations signaled good founding conditions; this was especially likely if those locations were not far away from potential entrepreneurs' current ones (Appold 2005; Suire and Vincente 2009). Therefore, dense clusters of organizations located near a particular location would draw entrepreneurs away from that location, attenuating founding rates there (Lomi and Larson 1996). For the magazine industry in the eighteenth and early nineteenth centuries, the upshot is that the more magazines there were outside but nearby any location, the lower the founding rate there. Basically this dynamic would lead locations near dense clusters of magazines (e.g., New Jersey, which was near both New York and Pennsylvania) to have lower founding rates than locations farther away from such clusters (e.g., Kentucky).

The development of the post office reduced spatial barriers to interaction between magazines and their readers and contributors, and so altered the balance between these two dynamics. Like advances in other communication systems (McLuhan 1962; Janelle 1968, 1969; Pred 1973, 1980; Kern 1983; Giddens 1990; Friedland and Boden 1994), postal system development made space "shrink": the distance between newly founded magazines, on the one hand, and resources, customers, and competitors, on the other, mattered less. This happened because postal system development made it easier for magazine entrepreneurs in any location to acquire resources from ever more distant locations—for example, to acquire articles, poems, and illustrations from contributors located far away who could more easily send their contributions through the mail. Postal system development also made it easier for people to receive magazines produced farther away from their local communities. But at the same time, postal development made it easier for magazines in more distant locations to reach readers and acquire resources in any location. The upshot is that magazines published outside any particular location would become increasingly competitive with magazines published in that location.

Advances in communication systems, like those of the postal network, not only heighten competition between local and nonlocal organizations but also make entrepreneurs less dependent on their local communities for customers and inputs because entrepreneurs can more easily reach customers in and acquire inputs from more distant locations. Accordingly, the benefits to entrepreneurs of locating their ventures in places with dense clusters of organizations diminish. For magazines, this meant that as the postal system expanded, the impact of magazines in any location on foundings in that location would diminish.

In work done jointly with Chris Rider, I tested these predictions by analyzing the number of magazines founded in each state each year from 1790 to 1860. (Appendix 2 describes the statistical methods used, while appendix 1 describes variable measures.) Following much previous research (Hannan and Freeman 1989), we measured the influence of magazines within a focal state with the number of magazines published in each state for each year. To account for the influences of nearby magazines in other states, we constructed a distance-scaled count of magazines outside the focal state each year (Sorenson and Audia 2000). We measured postal development through the number of post offices in the United States. We also controlled statistically for other factors that might affect magazine foundings: state population, infrastructure development (roads), literacy, fixed effects for states to capture the effects of otherwise unmeasured state-specific factors, and fixed effects for decades to capture the effects of otherwise unmeasured time-varying factors.

Figures 3.3a–b plot the results of this analysis, showing the effect of the number of magazines published on the subsequent founding rate, net of statistical controls. Figure 3.3a shows the effect for in-state magazines, and figure 3.3b for out-of-state magazines. As expected, magazine foundings increased with the number of magazines published in the focal state and decreased with the number published in other, nearby states. These results reveal the benefits of dense clusters of magazines within the focal location (the focal state) and competitive pressures from dense clusters of nearby magazines outside the focal location (outside of but close to the focal state).[4]

This figure also reveals how the effects of existing magazines on subsequent foundings changed as the postal system expanded by plotting those effects (specifically, multipliers of the founding rate) at three levels of postal development: the mean number of post offices (10,200, a level that was reached around 1833), the mean plus one standard deviation (18,310, reached around 1850), and the mean minus one standard deviation (2,090, reached around 1809). Figure 3.3a shows that the positive effect of in-state magazines on the

---

[4] In results not shown here, we used year dummies in place of decade dummies to more cleanly disentangle the effect of postal system expansion from other historical developments. This required replacing the number of post offices in the United States with the number in the focal state (for analysis of effects of in-state magazines) or the number outside the focal state (for analysis of the effects of out-of-state magazines). Those results, which are shown and discussed in appendix 2, were very similar to those discussed here.

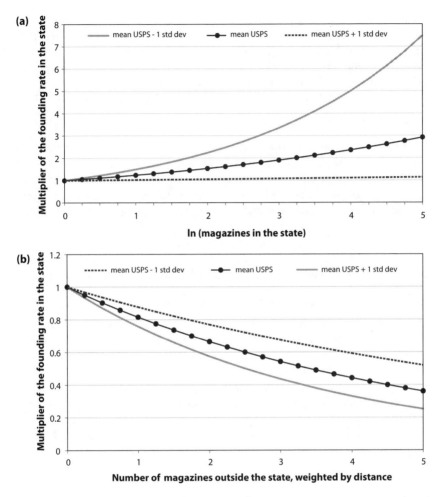

Figure 3.3. (a) The effect of in-state magazines on the magazine founding rate; (b) the effect of out-of-state magazines on the magazine founding rate.

magazine founding rate *decreased* as the postal system expanded. Specifically, as the number of post offices increased between 1809 and 1833, the effect fell from 2.02 to 1.46—a drop of almost 30 percent. Then, as the number of post offices increased further between 1833 and 1850, the effect fell to 1.05—again a drop of almost 30 percent. Figure 3.3b shows that the negative effect of magazines in nearby states on founding rates *increased* as the postal system expanded. Specifically, as the number of post offices increased between 1809 and 1833, the effect rose from 0.65 to 0.72—just over 10 percent. Then, as the number of post offices increased further between 1833 and 1850, the effect rose from 0.72 to 0.81—again, just over 10 percent. Thus, while the expansion of the post office substantially *attenuated* the beneficial effect of the number local magazines on subsequent foundings, it only slightly *accentuated* the competitive effect of the number of nonlocal magazines. This suggests that magazines in any location gained far more from being able to reach readers in other, ever more distant locations than they lost from magazines published in other locations reaching readers in their own locations.

Magazine Identities

Although magazine founding rates increasingly reflected external conditions—specifically, the number of magazines published in nearby states—that does not mean that location ceased to matter. Much research shows that localities can retain distinctive identities even in the face of advances in communication systems like the postal network because social interactions are affected by the local (natural and built) environment, local politicoeconomic factors, and by the demography of local organizations, all of which change very slowly (Molotch, Freudenberg, and Paulsen 2000). Distinctive interaction patterns are channeled through the resulting local culture and shaped by local legal codes and localized information flows and social networks (Saxenian 1994; Marquis 2003; Freeman and Audia 2006; Marquis and Battilana 2009). Localized cultures do respond to human migration and the entry of new organizations, which create new interaction patterns and alter politico-economic systems; however, such changes unfold slowly (Saxenian 1994; Kaufman and Kaliner 2011).

Easy movement across space, made possible by advances in communication systems like the postal network, may actually make location even *more* important by heightening contrasts between local (particularistic) and nonlocal (foreign or universalistic) cultures, thus amplifying local attachments (Giddens 1990). If so, then demand for products with local connections and identities—products that are anchored in particular geographically bounded communities—would increase (Giddens 1990; Marquis and Lounsbury 2007; Barnett, Feng, and Luo 2013), such as magazines produced locally that target local readers with locally focused content. In turn, these developments bind organizations, including magazine publishers, more closely to the particular resources and cultural identities of their sites of production. As the analysis of magazine locations in chapter 2 has shown, this dynamic was reflected in the spread of magazine publishing activity across the country: using states as the geographic unit of analysis, the index of qualitative variation hovered between 0.88 and 0.99 after 1790. But this analysis did not assess the degree to which magazines highlighted their connection to place, which is of central concern here.

All organizations, including magazine publishing ventures, are connected to their sites of production to the extent that their members and activities are embedded in local interactions (Saxenian 1994; Storper 1995). Such embeddedness enables organizations to credibly claim local identities and mobilize resources to support their operations. Owners and managers of local organizations are more dependent on—and therefore more attuned to—the peculiarities of local culture, including local customer preferences, than are owners and managers of nonlocal organizations (Friedland and Palmer 1984; Wheeler 1988). In turn, local organizations' greater dependence on and attention to their community make them more likely than nonlocal organizations to interact with local economic and political elites and more likely to contribute to their community (Molotch 1976; Romo and Schwartz 1995). Therefore, local organizations can more credibly claim local identities and more easily obtain resources from local actors.

In the eighteenth- and nineteenth-century magazine industry, as in many other later industries, not all locations were alike. Instead, a few core locations (Massachusetts, New York, and Pennsylvania) were home to large numbers of magazines, while many more peripheral locations (other states) were home to smaller numbers. Much research on the nineteenth and twentieth century has shown that organizations in their industries' core benefit from agglomeration economies (Marshall 1920; Krugman 1991): deep pools of human and financial resources and superior industry information (Friedland and Palmer 1984; Kono et al. 1998). Industry analysts, media, customers, and suppliers pay more attention to organizations within the industry core than to those within the periphery because it is easier to acquire industry-specific information within the core. But organizations within the core also experience stronger local competition than those within the periphery (Hannan and Freeman 1989; Sorenson and Audia 2000). Therefore, organizations within the industry core have strong incentives to appeal to customers in many locations; they also have the resources necessary to broaden their products' geographic appeal. By marketing products to spatially dispersed customers, organizations within the industry core can reduce their sensitivity to local competition. Relative to organizations within the core, organizations within the periphery face weaker local competition and thus weaker incentives to expand their geographic reach; the resources needed to do so are also in shorter supply. Consequently, organizations within the periphery are likely to target a geographically narrower set of customers than organizations within the core.

Within the core, organizations can best appeal to customers in many places by projecting identities that transcend their place of production—that is, by emphasizing their products' broad, universalistic (national or global) appeal. The emphasis on universalistic appeal should strengthen as communication systems develop because such developments make it easier to reach customers farther away from the site of production. For magazines in the eighteenth and nineteenth centuries, this meant that as the postal system developed those within the core would increasingly emphasize universalistic identities. In contrast, within the periphery the penetration of nonlocal magazines—especially powerful and highly visible ones from the core—might spur a backlash in the form of heightened localism, which would generate demand for local products.

Organizations within the periphery can take advantage of this localistic backlash by signaling their local place attachments—that is, by adopting localistic identities. Such actions are credible because local organizations are embedded in their communities; signaling their localistic roots effectively differentiates local organizations from nonlocal intruders, especially those from the core that adopt universalistic identities. For magazines in the eighteenth and nineteenth centuries, this meant that as the postal system developed, magazines within the periphery would increasingly emphasize localistic identities.

To test these predictions, Chris Rider and I focused on magazine titles, because magazines, like many other organizations and products, signal their connection to place through their names (Fombrun 1996). This is true for print media today; for example, *USA Today* signals its nationwide delivery and readership, while the *San Francisco Chronicle* indicates its focus on that city. It was also true for magazines in the eighteenth and nineteenth centuries; for example, the title *American Journal of Education* signaled that magazine's goal of covering the entire nation, while the title *Schuylkill County School Journal* indicated a focus on that particular county in Pennsylvania. These toponyms anchor people's feelings and thoughts on particular geographic locations while they support communities of place whose boundaries can range from the continent down to a single town. The more magazines identified themselves with local toponyms, the more they signaled connection to their particular location and they more they could appeal to audiences drawn by local place attachments. Conversely, the more magazines identified themselves with nonlocal toponyms, the more they signaled their disconnection from any single location and the more easily they could make universal appeals to audiences in many different locations.

We coded magazines that included the name or nickname of a municipality, county, substate region (e.g., western New York), state, or multistate region (e.g., southern) in their title as adopting a *localistic identity*. We coded magazines whose titles included a nation- or continent-wide term (e.g., American or National) as adopting a *universalistic identity*.[5] Finally, we coded magazines whose titles did not include any geographic identifiers (e.g., *Lady's Magazine*, *Free-Will Baptist Magazine*) as having nongeographic identities. (Appendix 1 provides more details on measurement, and appendix 2 explains how we analyzed the data.)

Figures 3.4a–b show that foundings of magazines with both localistic and universalistic identities increased over time, both within the core (figure 3.4a) and within the periphery (figure 3.4b). But as time passed, localistic magazines became more likely to be founded within the periphery than the core, while universalistic magazines became more likely to be founded within the core than the periphery.

---

[5] We also tried a more restrictive definition of localistic identity (municipality, county, substate region, or state) and a more inclusive definition of universalistic identity (nation, continent, or multistate region). Using these alternative definitions did not change the results.

(a)

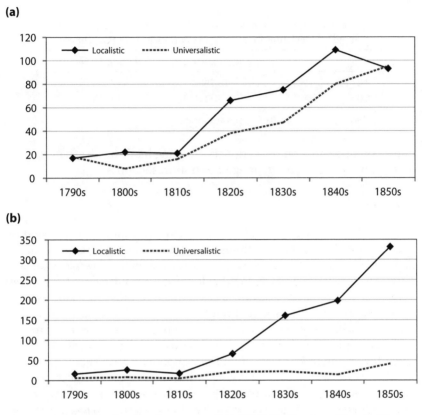

(b)

Figure 3.4. (a) Magazine foundings in core states (MA, NY, PA) by identity and decade; (b) magazine foundings in peripheral states by identity and decade.

Statistical analyses reveal that these temporal trends were due, at least in part, to postal system development. As the postal system developed, magazines in peripheral states became more likely to adopt localistic identities than other (nongeographic) identities, while magazines at the core became more likely to adopt universalistic identities. Table 3.2 shows the magnitude of the effects of postal development on the likelihood of a newly founded magazine adopting a localistic or universalistic identity—specifically, the predicted effect of an increase in the number of post offices of one standard deviation from the mean, such as occurred between 1809 and 1833 or between 1833 and 1850. Such an expansion of the postal system made newly founded magazines on the periphery 22 percent more likely to be founded with localistic identities and newly founded magazines at the core 20 percent more likely to be founded with universalistic identities. These calculations reveal the essentially symmetric nature of this competitive differentiation process: any expansion of the postal system had approximately the same magnitude of

TABLE 3.2.
Increases in Identity Choice Probabilities Associated with a One-
Standard-Deviation Increase in the Number of US Post Offices

	Localistic identity	Universalistic identity
Periphery	16.7%**	−17.9%[n.s.]
Core	−6.7%[n.s.]	14.1%*

Note: ** $p < 0.01$; * $p < 0.05$; [n.s.] not significant.

impact on magazines on the periphery adopting localistic identities as it did on magazines at the core adopting universalistic identities.

Summary

Analysis of the impact of postal system development on magazine founding rates and identities reveals two things: first, reduced spatial barriers to interaction made magazines less influenced by magazines in their own location and more influenced by magazines in other locations; second, reduced spatial barriers to interaction made attachments to place more salient bases for differentiating magazines. This pattern of results accords with analysis by historians and media scholars who view magazines as modernizing forces that propel a shift from particularistic local communities to universalistic national and international communities (McLuhan 1962; Eisenstein 1979; Thompson 1995). In other words, as the US postal system developed, space (distance between locations) mattered less and place (the nature of locations) mattered more. The development of the postal system *did* allow magazines to reach ever more distant readers, but expanding influence *itself* made location more salient to magazine publishers and their readers. Thus we are left with a paradoxical development. Although the earliest magazines sought to be relevant to all of the colonies or states (hence, many called themselves American), the consequence of their legacy was entirely unanticipated: the rise of localistic magazines rooted in and serving specific geographically bounded communities. In this regard, magazines were both modernizing forces (sustaining translocal communities) and bulwarks against modernization (fostering distinctive local communities).

The Reading Public

In the first 120 years of the US magazine industry's history, audiences for magazines changed greatly: they grew in numbers and became more urban and more likely to earn wages (rather than subsist on forestry, fishing, and agriculture); they also became divided among many distinct interest groups. All of these trends made it increasingly easy for magazines to thrive.

Population Growth and Urbanization

Like all enterprises, magazine publishing houses need customers (readers) to buy their products. But the British colonies in North America were quite sparsely populated, which inhibited the earliest American magazines. In 1740 the population of the thirteen colonies was just over 900,000 (US Census Bureau 1975). Sixty years later the new republic still had fewer than four million inhabitants. In addition, only a tiny fraction of eighteenth-century Americans lived in urban areas near the printers, booksellers, and other merchants who sold magazines. In 1760, the first year for which we have reasonable data on urban areas, the urban population constituted only 6.6 percent of the total and there were only seventeen urban areas (defined as settlements with populations above 2,500); all but one (Charleston, South Carolina) were located in coastal New England and the Middle Colonies. (Data sources for the analysis of urbanization are described in appendix 1.) These scattered towns (only Boston, New York, and Philadelphia, which had populations over 15,000, were large enough to be called cities) were administrative centers for the colonies. The number of urban areas grew very slowly over the next six decades, reaching twenty-eight in 1800 and forty-nine in 1820, and urban dwellers grew to 7.4 percent of the American population.

Between 1820 and 1860 urbanization proceeded more rapidly than in any earlier or subsequent time period (Warner 1972; Callow 1982): while the total population increased by 226 percent, the urban population increased by 667 percent; thus urban dwellers as a fraction of the total population increased from 8.5 percent to 20 percent (US Census Bureau 1975). The number of urban areas doubled from eighty-nine in 1820 to 175 in 1840, and then more than doubled again, reaching 422 in 1860. Figure 3.5 charts these trends; the solid line shows the population of the three largest cities, Boston, New York, and Philadelphia; the dashed line shows the population of all other urban areas; and the solid line with dots shows the number of urban areas.

Urban areas not only became more numerous but also became larger. Figure 3.6 plots the number of urban areas within selected size ranges from 1760 to 1860: 15,000–25,000 inhabitants; 25,000–50,000; 50,000–100,000; and over 100,000.[6] Philadelphia grew to over 25,000 inhabitants by 1770, New York by 1790, and Boston around 1800. Philadelphia was also the first city to have over 50,000 inhabitants, a threshold it passed shortly after 1790. Despite Philadelphia's head start, New York outgrew it by 1805, while Boston lagged far behind. Indeed, shortly before 1800 Baltimore displaced Boston as the third largest city. On the eve of the War of 1812, New York had over

---

[6] The bottom range was chosen because in 1760, only Philadelphia (population 18,756), Boston (15,631), and New York (15,393) had more than 15,000 inhabitants. The top range was chosen because in 1860, only nine cities had crossed the 100,000-inhabitant threshold.

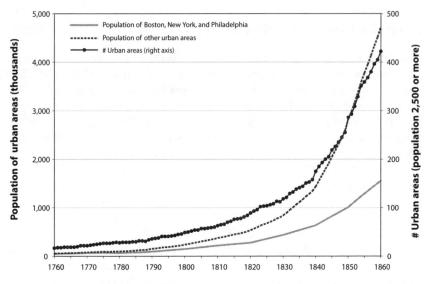

Figure 3.5. Urbanization, 1760–1860.

100,000 inhabitants; Philadelphia 95,000; Baltimore 50,000; Boston 36,000; and Charleston 25,000.

After 1820, urban areas grew even larger. In 1820, only 6 cities (the 5 mentioned above, plus New Orleans) had populations over 15,000, and the median size of all 89 urban areas that year was 4,300 inhabitants. By 1840, the number of cities with populations over 15,000 had swollen to 22, and the median size of all 135 urban areas had risen 20 percent, to 5,200 inhabitants. In 1860, there were 60 cities with populations over 15,000, while the median size of all 422 urban areas was 5,000 inhabitants. In that year, 9 cities boasted populations over 100,000: New York had over 800,000 inhabitants; Philadelphia about 550,000; Brooklyn (a separate city until 1890) 270,000; Baltimore 210,000; Boston 180,000; New Orleans 170,000; Cincinnati and St. Louis 160,000 each; and Chicago 110,000. As these statistics indicate, the cities that became the largest before the Civil War grew rapidly: between 1790 and 1860, population growth for Brooklyn averaged 7.3 percent per year, Baltimore 4.5 percent, New Orleans 4.4 percent, New York City 3.7 percent, Philadelphia 3.2 percent, and Boston 2.0 percent; Chicago grew by 16.3 percent (for 1830–60 only), St. Louis 10.0 percent (for 1810–60 only), and Cincinnati 8.8 percent (for 1800–1860 only). It is notable that the oldest cities on the Eastern Seaboard grew much more slowly than the newer ones to the west.

Urbanization occurred first and most extensively in the Northeast. In 1760 there were thirteen urban areas (areas with populations over 2,500) in the six New England colonies (Connecticut, Maine, Massachusetts, New Hampshire, Rhode Island, and Vermont) and three in the four Middle Colonies (Delaware, New Jersey, New York, and Pennsylvania), compared to just one (Charles-

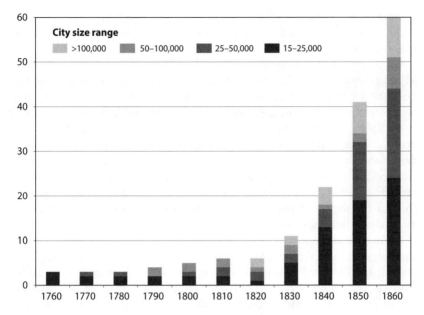

Figure 3.6. The size distribution of urban areas, 1760–1860 (number of communities in each size range). Sources: Moffatt (1992, 1996), Purvis (1995), US Census Bureau (1998).

ton) in the South. By 1820 there were thirty-eight urban areas in New England and twenty-two in the mid-Atlantic states, compared to twenty-one in the South (Alabama, Georgia, Louisiana, Maryland, Mississippi, North Carolina, South Carolina, and Virginia). (This list does not include the District of Columbia and Georgetown, the latter at that time a separate city.) In that year urban dwellers constituted 16 percent of people in New England, 13 percent in the mid-Atlantic states, and only 5 percent in the South. Even the West urbanized at a faster pace than the South: by 1843 there were more settlements with populations over 2,500 in the West (Arkansas, Illinois, Indiana, Iowa, Kentucky, Missouri, Ohio, and Tennessee) than in the South.

From 1820 to 1860 a national system of cities developed (Pred 1973, 1980) as what had been scattered villages and farms were folded into a network of regional commercial and manufacturing centers (Warner 1972). The largest cities—not just Boston, New York, and Philadelphia, but also smaller regional hubs such as Baltimore, Chicago, Cincinnati, New Orleans, and St. Louis—came to dominate the economy. These metropolises produced goods, including magazines, that were distributed widely to smaller settlements; in exchange they absorbed an increasing fraction of agricultural production, as will be described in chapter 7. In their banks, insurance companies, and merchant houses, these cities also accumulated the capital that fueled the growing industrial concerns; these cities were also home to most of the joint stock companies that pooled individuals' savings to launch large, capital-intensive

manufacturing concerns such as textile mills and machine shops and transportation facilities such as turnpikes, bridges, canals, and railroads (Cochran
1981; Seavoy 1982).

Urbanization fundamentally altered the nature of social life in America.
Although much research has documented the consequences of urbanization
from the 1870s onward, its roots date back to the first decades of the nineteenth century (Rothman 1971; Mohl 1972; Warner 1972; Brown 1974; Boyer
1978). In the colonial era, rural and urban areas alike were quite homoge-
neous, with residents belonging to two communal associations, the extended
family and the church. In the nineteenth century the rapidly growing urban
areas began to experience housing shortages as newcomers, mostly farmers
and artisans emigrating from Europe and young people migrating from rural
parts of the nation, crowded into existing structures and enterprising landlords hastily built new ones.

Immigration fragmented urban areas along three axes: ethnicity, religion,
and language. Social fragmentation in urban areas was also increased by industrialization, which transformed many who would have been (or who formerly were) self-employed artisans and merchants into mere employees of
manufacturing and retailing concerns (Blumin 1989; Stott 1990). As a result,
class distinctions became increasingly pronounced. Social fragmentation was
further increased by the generally high rates of geographic mobility into and
out of urban areas (Thernstrom and Knights 1970; Blumin 1973), which
eroded the traditional bases of social relations (Brown 1974; Zucker 1986). In
their place formally organized civic associations, including the many social
reform societies that will be analyzed in chapter 6, became the basis of urban
dwellers' social relations (Brown 1974; Mazzone 2004). Because many of these
civic associations were organized into federated structures, with nested national, regional, and local units (Skocpol 1997; Skocpol, Ganz, and Munson
2000), these associations forged large, translocal communities whose leadership was concentrated in the largest cities, accentuating these cities' dominance of the national system of cities.

Literacy

Audiences for magazines not only grew in numbers and become more urban
but also became more literate. In the colonial era literacy rates among the
free population were quite high, especially in New England (Kaestle 1991a).
After the Revolution the westward push spawned frontier communities and
homesteads whose inhabitants were less literate than those in the more settled seaboard areas. Rates of literacy rose again starting around 1800. Reliable data are hard to find prior to 1840, but in 1800 the average literacy rate
of the free population was estimated to be 75 percent in the North and
50–60 percent in the South (Soltow and Stevens 1981: 189). By 1840 literacy
rates had risen to over 90 percent in the North and to over 80 percent in the

South. From 1840 onward literacy rates for the United States as a whole hovered around 95 percent.

Data on educational institutions offer another perspective on the increased attention to education and the concomitant rise in literacy (Kaestle 1991a, 1991b)—in particular, the shift from mothers educating their children at home to teachers instructing local students in schools (Douglas 1977). In the late eighteenth and early nineteenth centuries, privately and publicly funded primary and secondary schools spread across the land, prompting a substantial rise in enrollments by 1830 (Kaestle 1983). Conditions varied by state, but in the rural areas of the Northeast and Midwest, where the majority of Americans lived, most elementary schools were organized into local districts and funded by a combination of property taxes, tuition, and state aid; in contrast, in the mostly rural South, schools were more heavily dependent on tuition and consequently enrolled a smaller fraction of children (Kaestle 1983: 13–29). In growing urban areas there was a mix of elementary pay schools, "dame schools" (for small children, operated in ladies' homes), and free (often church-sponsored) charity schools (Kaestle 1983: 30–61).

There were two big pushes to build schools, from the Sunday school and common school movements. The Sunday school movement initially sought not only to save the unconverted but also to teach basic literacy so that students could read the Bible themselves and become good Christians—and therefore good citizens of the republic (Soltow and Stevens 1981; Kaestle 1983; Boylan 1988). This movement began in 1791 in Philadelphia under the auspices of the First Day Society but did not spread far until after 1800 (Boylan 1988). The First Day schools grew out of a somewhat secular concern for poor children who received no education during the week, when they were hard at work, and whose disruptive behavior on Sundays constituted both a public nuisance and moral affront to pious Christians (Boyer 1978). Taking them off the streets and putting them in school on Sundays solved both problems. By the first decade of the nineteenth century these First Day schools faced direct competition from a new breed of more evangelical Sunday schools sponsored by competing denominations whose mission was more overtly religious; reading and writing were conceived of as means to a religious end rather than inherently virtuous and republican goals (Boylan 1988). Over time, Sunday schools became complements to common schools; they came to focus exclusively on religious education, while common schools took responsibility for basic literacy and numeracy. In 1824, Sunday schools were organized into an interdenominational association, the American Sunday School Union (ASSU), which included the vast majority of such schools.

The number of Sunday schools rose exponentially, from 43 in 1818 to 8,237 in 1832 and to over 68,000 in 1875 (Boylan 1988), and there was great regional variation in their development. Massachusetts and Pennsylvania share the honor of having the first Sunday schools, founded in 1791; the movement then spread across New England, to New York in 1803 and New

Jersey in 1805, down the Atlantic coast between 1810 and 1815, and westward from 1810 onward. By 1832 (the last year for which good state-level data are available), there were 1,983 Sunday schools in New England, 3,149 in New York and New Jersey, 960 in the other mid-Atlantic states, 336 along the southern coast from Virginia to Georgia, and 1,799 along the Gulf of Mexico and across the West.

The common school movement sought to build institutions that would teach all children; it began in the 1830s and culminated in state legislation establishing funding (a central state fund or, more commonly, local taxes) for free schools in all existing states plus federal funding, via land grants, for free schools in new states (Cremin 1970; Soltow and Stevens 1981; Kaestle 1983; Tyack, James, and Benavot 1987). This movement greatly increased the number of schools, the percentage of children enrolled, and the average number of days students attended school; it also imposed consistent—generally higher— standards on teachers and curricula (Kaestle 1983: 104–35).

Figures 3.7a–b chart census data to show the uneven distribution of common school enrollments across the nation (Haines 2008). Figure 3.7a maps data for 1840, and figure 3.7b for 1860. The states shaded dark gray enrolled less than 12 percent of whites ages five to nineteen; the states shaded medium gray, 12 percent to 30 percent; the states with diagonal stripes, 30 percent to 50 percent; the states shaded light gray, 50 percent and over; and the states shaded white had not yet entered the Union. In 1840 there were over 47,000 common schools with a total enrollment of 1.85 million pupils—35 percent of whites ages five to nineteen.[7]

As figure 3.7a shows, enrollment rates were highest in New England (88 percent in Maine and 86 percent in New Hampshire) and lowest in the South (7 percent in Louisiana, and 8 percent in the District of Columbia and North Carolina). In 1850, 81,000 public schools enrolled 3.35 million pupils—46 percent of all whites ages five to nineteen. By 1860 the number of common schools had risen to over 107,000 and the number of pupils to 4.96 million—52 percent of all whites ages five to nineteen.[8] As figure 3.7b shows, some southern states saw substantial gains in the number of schools and students. In contrast to the extremely low levels reported for 1840, enrollments in 1860 included 44 percent of whites ages five to nineteen in North Carolina, 25 percent in Louisiana, and 12 percent in the District of Columbia. By 1860 the Midwest states had slightly higher enrollments than the states of the Northeast: on average, 68 percent of whites ages five to nineteen were enrolled

---

[7] This is the most reasonable age range for common-school pupils, but using this age range likely understates enrollment rates because many people fifteen years and older did not attend school (Kaestle 1983: 106). Moreover, a small fraction of students in that age range were enrolled in academies, private schools that generally offered elementary and secondary level curricula (Burke 1982: 36). If we include private academies, the fraction of whites ages five to nineteen enrolled in 1840 was 38 percent.

[8] If we include private academies, 57 percent of whites ages five to nineteen were enrolled in 1860.

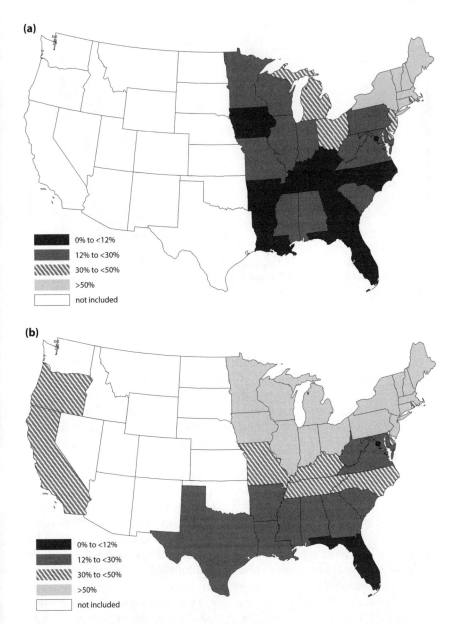

Figure 3.7. (a) The percentage of whites ages five to nineteen enrolled in common schools in 1840, by state; (b) the percentage of whites ages five to nineteen enrolled in common schools in 1860, by state. Source: Haines (2008).

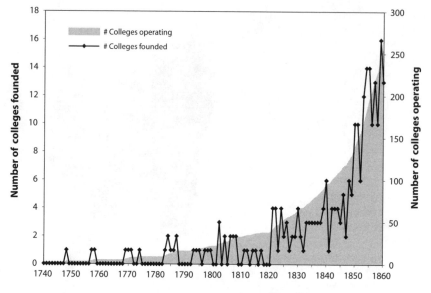

Figure 3.8. The growth of colleges, 1740–1860. Source: Marshall (1995).

in public schools in the Midwest, while 66 percent were enrolled in the Northeast. This difference is due in part to the fact that there were more children working in factories, and thus not attending school, in the Northeast than in the Midwest. Enrollment in the Midwest outpaced that in the Northeast even after taking into consideration private academies, pay schools, dame schools, and charity schools, which were more common in more heavily settled regions like the Northeast.

The establishment of colleges followed a pattern similar to that of the Sunday schools and common schools. In 1741, the year the first magazines were published, there were only three colleges: Harvard College (founded in 1636), the College of William and Mary (1693), and Yale College (1701). The number of colleges grew very slowly until after the Revolutionary War, as figure 3.8 shows: the line plots the number of four-year colleges founded each year, while the solid gray area plots the number of four-year colleges in operation. As peace was restored in 1783, there were ten colleges in the new republic. The number of colleges doubled by the year 1800 and then redoubled every twenty years thereafter, reaching 258 in 1860—a twentyfold increase. The expansion of college enrollment kept pace with the increase in the number of institutions; between 1800 and 1859, college enrollment rose more than twentyfold, from 1,421 to 31,917 (Burke 1973: 22, table 2.3). Because college enrollment grew faster than the overall population, college students constituted an increasing, albeit still tiny, fraction of the American populace: by 1859 there were 10.4 college students per 10,000 Americans, compared to 2.7 in 1800.

Basic Economics: Magazine Prices Relative to Wages

When the first magazines were founded the American population was tiny, and even those few Americans who had cash to spare were hard-pressed to afford magazines. I analyzed all magazines published in the eighteenth century whose subscription prices I could determine (94 of 148). Subscription prices were given in several different currencies: the systems of pounds, shillings, and pence issued by different colonies and states; the system of pounds, shillings, and pence sterling issued by the British government; the Spanish dollar; and the system of dollars, dismes (dimes), and cents issued by the US government. Using a method developed by John J. McCusker (2001), I translated all these currencies into the Spanish dollar (the *peso de ocho reales*, or "pieces of eight").[9] The average annual subscription price for eighteenth-century magazines was $2.21. To take inflation into account, I converted contemporary (nominal) prices to modern price equivalents (constant dollars as of 31 March 2014). Adjusted for inflation, these magazines cost, on average, the equivalent of just over $45 in 2014 dollars. Even those few founders who were so well off that they did not depend on their publications for income, such as William Livingston of the *Independent Reflector* (1752–53), had to charge high rates just to cover printing and distribution costs. Livingston's magazine cost 10 shillings per year Pennsylvania currency, equal to $1.33 in nominal dollars, or just over $40 in 2014 dollars.

To grasp the meaning of these subscription prices for eighteenth-century Americans, it is helpful to compare them to incomes. Andrew Bradford's and Benjamin Franklin's pioneering magazines cost 8 pence and 6 pence per issue, respectively. The average, 7 pence per monthly issue, translates to an annual subscription price of 7 shillings, at 12 pence to the shilling. This equaled about 1 percent of the annual wages of free journeymen in Philadelphia in the middle of the eighteenth century, who earned on average 35 pounds, or 700 shillings (Moss 1972: 144). By 1800 magazines cost subscribers $1.77 per year on average, an amount that skilled artisans like carpenters, masons, painters, bricklayers, and blacksmiths could earn in a little less than one day and common laborers could earn in less than two days (Adams 1968: 406). Thus, although between 1741 and 1800 average annual subscription prices for magazines had dropped from about 1 percent to 0.3 percent of skilled workers' annual wages (assuming five and a half days worked per week for fifty weeks), they were still quite expensive. For a skilled worker of today who earns $40,000 per year, 0.3 percent of his or her annual wages would equal $120—many

<hr />

[9] Largely because of the long-term stability of its value, the Spanish dollar was both the de facto and the de jure world currency standard from the sixteenth century to the nineteenth (McCusker 1992). For American shopkeepers, "their [colonial or state] pounds were money of account. Dollars were their real money" McCusker (2001: 62). Indeed, when the national currency of the fledgling republic, the Continental dollar, was first issued, it was set equal to the Spanish dollar.

times the typical annual subscription rate for a contemporary magazine. Yet because there were far fewer entertainment options in the eighteenth century than there are today, and because magazines were passed around and read by several people (Mott 1930; Albaugh 1994), magazine subscription prices may not have been insurmountable costs.

Over the next six decades wages rose steadily and magazine prices fell. By the early 1850s the daily wages of skilled workers ranged from $1.45 in the Northeast to $1.71 in the South Atlantic states, in nominal dollars (Margo and Villaflor 1987: 893), while annual subscription rates for those magazines founded in this time period for which price data were available averaged $1.87 in nominal dollars.[10] In other words, magazines founded during this time period cost about what a skilled worker earned in little more than an hour. Dorothy S. Brady (1964: 169) estimated that overall, magazine prices dropped 41 percent between 1809 and 1834 and another 32 percent between 1834 and 1860.[11] Moreover, as the number of households that were economically self-sufficient fell, and as the basis of economic transactions shifted from barter to cash (North 1961), the number of people earning cash wages increased dramatically. Thus, by the middle of the nineteenth century the combination of higher wage levels, a transition toward a money economy, and lower magazine prices made it possible for an increasing number of Americans to subscribe to magazines. One contributor to an agricultural magazine made clear how low the price of a magazine had fallen relative to wages by the 1840s, declaring that "a day's labor—a thing so often *thrown* away—will pay for it for a *year*, and thus bring it easily within the reach of the poorest farmer" (Randall 1844: 3; emphasis in the original).

Specialized Audiences

Demand for magazines also increased because new audiences developed—first among the members of the many different religious communities that flourished in this era. America's great religious diversity created opportunities for magazine entrepreneurs, who created specialized periodicals for different faiths. Virtually all faiths embraced magazines—not just large ones like the Baptist, Congregationalist, and Presbyterian churches but also tiny ones like

[10] I could find data on subscription prices for only 31 percent of annual observations on magazines published in this five-year period (1,363 of 4,399) because many magazines published then are not available in the archives. This statistic should therefore be viewed with some caution.

[11] I have limited data on magazine subscription prices in later years. I could determine subscription prices for 65 percent of magazines founded in the eighteenth century, as well as for magazines founded 1801–20, but only for 49 percent of magazines founded 1821–40, and for 32 percent of magazines founded 1841–60. In all years these data are likely to be biased toward higher-priced, more prominent, more "serious" magazines, which were better covered in archives and more likely to be discussed by contemporaries and historians alike; they are thus likely to be overrepresented. Brady's (1964) estimates are likely superior to any I could produce using these data, as they are based on local and national survey data.

the Adventist, Christadelphian, Moravian, Mormon, Plymouth Brethren, and Swedenborgian faiths. By the middle of the nineteenth century religious magazines dominated the industry: they rose from 15 percent of magazines published in the eighteenth century to 35 percent of those published in the 1840s and '50s. In these two decades, religious magazines outnumbered general-interest periodicals in magazine-year observations, 5,543 to 2,510; some, like the *American Messenger* (1843–1923), gained nationwide audiences. Chapter 5 documents these trends in more detail.

Religious fervor also spawned almost two hundred magazines in the 1840s and '50s that were devoted to social reform efforts, including the abolition of slavery, temperance, protection for widows and orphans, and strict observance of the Sabbath (King and Haveman 2008). Most prominent were the *Anti-Slavery Record*, the flagship journal of the American Anti-Slavery Society, and the *Journal of Humanity*, published by the American Temperance Society. Chapter 6 documents the rise of social reform movements and their affiliated magazines.

As education became more formalized and scientific, shifting from home to school and involving developing elaborate pedagogical systems, specialized education magazines appeared, starting in 1810, to broadcast the new pedagogical theories and practices involved with the many different formal systems that competed for the attention of the new education profession (Kaestle 1983). Up to 1840, forty-two education periodicals were published; in the 1840s and 1850s, the genre expanded greatly and 123 more were founded. The most famous educational periodicals of this era were Henry Barnard's *Connecticut Common School Journal* (1838–66) and Horace Mann's Boston-based *Common School Journal* (1838–52; see Mott 1930: 490–92).

Magazines helped the members of emerging and specialized occupations develop common standards of practice and distinct identities. Where most colonial homesteaders played a variety of roles—farmer and forester; spinner, weaver, and seamstress; butcher, cook, and canner; teacher and nurse; carpenter, engineer, and mechanic—nineteenth-century Americans were increasingly likely to work in narrowly defined occupations. In the eighteenth century only two magazines were published for specialized occupations; both were medical magazines. In contrast, in the 1840s and '50s, 475 occupation-specific magazines were launched, not just for physicians but also for lawyers, merchants, manufacturers, and journeymen. As with religious communities, occupational communities were often cleaved by debates, and many of these debates were carried in the pages of their magazines. For example, among members of the evolving medical profession, homeopaths, Thomsonians, eclectics, mesmerists, magnetists, hydropaths, Grahamites, phrenologists, and osteopaths vied for legitimacy with allopaths (Starr 1982). All of these camps launched magazines to promote their view of medical practice.

The growing concern for "scientific" solutions to social problems led to and was reinforced by the publication of sixty-four scientific and engineering magazines in the 1840s and '50s (compared to none in the eighteenth century). Magazines in this genre were very heterogeneous; some, like *Scientific American* (founded 1845) and the *Proceedings of the American Academy of Arts and Sciences* (founded 1846, now titled *Daedalus*), were produced for gentlemen-scholars and academics, while others, like *Eureka: The Journal of the National Association of Inventors* (1846–48), were aimed at more down-to-earth engineers and tinkerers. The increasing valorization of science also promoted the founding of specialty agricultural magazines. Agriculture was the largest sector of the economy from the colonial era to the Civil War, but it changed tremendously over that time period. The rise of scientific agriculture, which involved rotating crops, tilling to reduce the erosion of precious topsoil, speeding up work with new mechanical equipment like rakes and reapers, and the careful cultivation of plants and breeding of animals, boosted production and kept previously cleared farmland in use (McClelland 1997). This agricultural revolution was supported by the publication of over four hundred agricultural magazines, starting in 1801. Some thirty agricultural magazines were founded between 1801 and 1830; after that, the genre grew rapidly, and another 381 magazines were launched. Several of these saw nationwide circulation; for instance, *Country Gentleman* (1852–1955) had over 25,000 subscribers between 1852 and 1860, while *American Agriculturist* (1842–1931) had 50,000 in 1860. Others, like the *American Silk Grower's Magazine* (1844) and the *Pomologist Magazine* (1842–43), targeted narrow audiences. Chapter 7 documents the rise of specialized magazines for farmers.

As was explained in the introduction, the development of the magazine industry affected the reading public. By publishing engaging essays, short articles, fiction, poetry, and illustrations, magazines created a nation of avid readers. In doing so, magazines supported many communities—of faith, purpose, and practice.

PROFESSIONAL AUTHORS AND COPYRIGHT LAW

Although the growth of a literate population with cash to spend on such non-necessities as magazines solved the problems of limited demand for magazines, the earliest magazines were also beset by problems of supply: in the mid-eighteenth century, few people were willing to contribute engaging original material.[12] Between 1741 and 1860 three institutional changes occurred that together created a ready supply of original material for magazines: the emergence of the cultural conception of the author as professional, the development of literary property rights, and the spread of the practice of paying authors for their contributions. In the next section I describe each change; I

---

[12] This section is based in part on two papers: "Antebellum Literary Culture and the Evolution of American Magazines" (Haveman 2004) and "Property in Print: Copyright Law and the American Magazine Industry" (Haveman and Kluttz 2014).

also discuss Britain because cultural conceptions of authorship and developments in copyright law in America echoed the British experience.

Cultural Conceptions of Authorship in Britain

To be an author today means to write and own what you write, but that meaning developed very slowly. As early as the fourteenth century, some English writers claimed a special status for themselves, using the term *auctor* to signify their right to the title of *laureate*, or literary master (Helgerson 1983). This status did not, however, confer ownership of texts because until the eighteenth century people generally thought of texts as actions rather than things and valued them for their ability to move people to think or act (Rose 1993). As actions, rather than objects, texts could not be "owned."[13]

In the mid-seventeenth century Thomas Hobbes, building on the early modern notion of authorial honor and reputation and combining it with the medieval notion of author as actor, argued for authorial ownership of literary work:

> A person, is he, *whose words or actions are considered, either as his own, or as representing the words or actions of another man, or any other thing, to whom they are attributed, whether truly or by fiction.* When they are considered as his own, then he is called a *natural person*: and when they are considered as representing the words and actions of another, then he is a *feigned* or *artificial person* .... Of persons artificial, some have their words and actions *owned* by those whom they represent. And then the person is the *actor*; and he that owneth his words and actions is the AUTHOR: in which case the actor acteth by authority. For that which in speaking of goods and possessions, is called an *owner*, ... is called the author. And as the right of possession, is called dominion; so the right of doing any action, is called AUTHOR-ITY. (Hobbes [1651] 1962: 125; emphasis in the original)

Hobbes's argument, which linked authorship (the act of creating a text) with authority (power over that text), meshed with John Locke's justification of ownership of property through labor in which "every man has a property in his own person: this no body has any right to but himself. The labour of his body, and the work of his hands, we may say, are properly his. Whatsoever then he removes out of the state that nature hath provided, and left it in, he hath mixed his labour with, and joined to it something that is his own, and thereby makes it his property" (Locke 1690a, chapter 5, section 27). Hobbes's argument was also compatible with Locke's conception of the mind as a blank page—a *tabula rasa* (1690b, 87)—on which experience writes a self.

---

[13] It is true that during the sixteenth century the spread of printing presses prompted the development of a norm whereby printers obtained writers' permission to publish. This norm, however, was intended to safeguard authors' honor and reputation from "the stigma of print" (Saunders 1951), not to secure any economic interest they might have had in printed texts (Rose 1993).

Further development of the notion of the author as owner was, however, hindered by the economics of publishing. Until the mid-eighteenth century most British writers depended for their livelihood on patrons, either wealthy aristocrats or powerful printers, who claimed ownership of the texts produced by their writer-clients. Aristocrat-patrons received honor and status through their writer-clients' service, while printer-patrons received from their writer-clients goods they could sell profitably in the developing marketplace; in return, both kinds of patrons offered their clients cultural and material rewards (Febvre and Martin [1976] 1990; Lucas 1982; Rose 1993). The notion that writers "owned" what they wrote was simply not congruent with this economic and social system (Rose 1993).

Early in the eighteenth century Daniel Defoe (1704) and Joseph Addison (1709, 1711) invoked a new metaphor: literary property as landed estate and author as gentleman-farmer. This metaphor required that authors be accepted as possessive individuals (Macpherson 1962) and recognized as creators of objects, rather than actions (Patterson 1968; Woodmansee 1984; Rose 1993). Four decades later William Warburton (1747) took the first steps toward conceiving of a professional writer as an exalted figure whose ownership of his work merited protection in the law. He held that literary works were property because they were "useful to mankind," which obligated society to give authors the right to protect them. Indeed, he viewed literary works as a special kind of property—the production of the mind.

This nascent conception of author as owner was fostered by the late eighteenth-century Romantic movement. The Romantics began to incorporate the notion that individuals could be the authors of their lives, and thus of all the artistic works they produced (Abrams 1953; Woodmansee 1984; Jaszi 1991; Saunders 1992; Rose 1993). To assert one's ownership of original creations was to assert one's *self*, one's unique personality. Yet achieving this understanding of author as creator was by no means inevitable; instead, it required a series of conceptual inventions; as David Saunders notes, "An emerging group of 'literary' writers had to *acquire* an expressible interiority, such that a certain mode of printed work could be recognised and experienced as both 'mine' and 'me'. . . . [A]n emerging category of 'literary' writing in print . . . had to *become* a specialised ethical and aesthetic activity using print. A new manner of relating to one's self had itself to *establish* a manner of relating to print replication and dissemination. . . . [This] required nothing less than a new form of ethical-literate persona" (Saunders 1992: 73; emphasis in the original). Writing that was new to the world came to be seen as the product and property of the writer—a very Lockean conception. And, as in Hobbes's analysis, authorship became linked to authority.

This conceptual shift was enabled by the development of a market-oriented society in the late seventeenth and early eighteenth centuries that directed authors' economic and social relations away from patronage ties to wealthy elites and toward market ties to booksellers and, through them, to an expanding reading public (Febvre and Martin [1976] 1990; Feather 1988).[14] Perhaps the most famous example is Samuel Johnson's 1754 letter rejecting Lord Chesterfield's patronage for his *Dictionary*, which has been called "the *Magna Carta* of the modern author" (Kernan 1987: 105). The letter signaled that professional authorship as we understand it today was becoming both economically feasible and culturally acceptable. Johnson could reject Chesterfield's patronage because the development of a market for books made it possible for him to earn a profit from his dictionary. His widely publicized claim of sole authorship helped spread acceptance of authorial ownership.

Cultural Conceptions of Authorship in America

When the first magazines were launched, most of the few Americans who produced literature were gentlemen-scholars whose output was an avocation, a natural by-product of their learning. For example, *Longworth's American Almanack, New-York Register, and City Directory* (1799) does not list anyone who was employed as an author or any other occupation related to literature except a few bookbinders, booksellers, and printers. Eighteenth-century patricians like lawyer-polemicist William Livingston and minister-essayist Aaron Burr Sr. wrote to further their own political, artistic, religious, or scientific objectives, not to make money (Charvat 1968; Dauber 1990), so they were generally unconcerned with claiming property rights over their writing. Indeed, they generally shunned publicity: their writings, including those in the pages of magazines, were usually published anonymously or pseudonymously to avoid any taint of "vulgar" public or mercenary ambition and thus preserve their reputations as gentlemen (Charvat 1968; Davidson 1986; Bender 1987). Perhaps most notable is the case of Thomas Jefferson, who publicly disavowed and threatened to burn the entire first edition of his only book, *Notes on the State of Virginia*, when it was published in 1781: "Do not view me as an author, and attached to what he has written," he cautioned James Madison (quoted in Ferguson 1984: 34).

The twin conceptions of author as gentleman and author as amateur (someone who wrote for the love of it, not someone who was unskilled) were reinforced by the economics of authorship in the eighteenth century, when there were few wealthy aristocrats to flatter with prose and poetry or powerful printers who could turn profits by selling books. Even in the nineteenth century, only a tiny fraction of American authors found wealthy patrons to underwrite their literary aspirations. Most notably, several transcendentalist writers, including Margaret Fuller and Henry David Thoreau, were sponsored by Ralph Waldo Emerson (Dowling 2011), while Herman Melville's father-in-

---

[14] This cultural-cognitive shift was analogous to the changing conception of painters in late nineteenth-century France, from learned men under the academy system to middle-class professionals under the dealer-critic system (White and White 1965).

law supported him so he could write full-time (Charvat 1943). A few more, including essayist Robert Walsh and novelist Nathaniel Hawthorne, received remunerative political appointments that freed them to write—a distinctly American form of political and literary patronage that persisted from the Revolution through the nineteenth century (Charvat 1968; Brubaker 1975).

As America became a more market-oriented society and literature evolved to connote commodities created by professionals and traded for profit, American understandings of what it meant to be an author changed. A letter written in 1795 by magazine founder Joseph Dennie (*Tablet*, founded 1795) revealed a nascent conception of authorship as a potentially lucrative profession: "My grand object ... was money. The ways & means were Authorship" (quoted in Pedder 1936: 145). Charles Brockden Brown (founder of the *Monthly Review*, 1799–1800; the *American Review and Literary Journal*, 1801–2; and the *Literary Magazine and American Register*, 1803–7) stated that "pecuniary profit is acceptable ... this is the best proof which [the editor] can receive that his endeavours to amuse and instruct have not been unsuccessful" (Brown 1803: 5). And in a letter to the publisher of the *Southern Literary Messenger*, editor Edgar Allan Poe declared that "to be appreciated you must be *read*" and argued that a tale he had submitted should be judged on economic, not aesthetic, grounds and claimed that the quality of tales like these "will be estimated better by the circulation of the Magazine than by any comments upon its contents" (Poe 1835; emphasis in the original).

Although the conception of author as professional emerged in the late eighteenth century, professional writers were not then held in high esteem. One essay denigrated those who wrote for pay as possessing a "degenerate ambition" that "would work no good" (*Museum of Foreign Literature, Science, and Art* 1828: 92). Another ranked four motives for becoming an author in descending order of value. The top rank was the gentleman-amateur, who was lauded as a "public benefactor" who spreads his "knowledge and attainments" that "may be beneficial to the rest of mankind." The second rank, the professional, included "many praiseworthy, estimable individuals, and persons possessing talents of even high rank" but "the writings of this second class are worth 'as much as they will bring.'" (Herbert and Patterson 1833: 3).

The social rankings of amateur and professional writer were reversed by the 1840s, as this example attests:

> Few can do well "for love" which can be better done for money.... If it be true in the common concerns of life, that the laborer is worthy of his hire, it is much more to be so considered when we ascend in the scale of labor, and come finally to that which most tasks the intellect and requires the greatest number of choice thoughts.... An amateur in almost every walk is regarded as much inferior to a working member of the craft. A man rarely puts his heart or invests the whole stock of his faculties in a pursuit which he takes up casually to while away an hour or two of an idle day. (Mimin 1845: 62–63)

This reveals a conception of professional authors as people who possess specialized expertise and confers upon them exclusive authority over literature (Larson 1977). It also reveals a change in the definition of amateur authors— no longer people who wrote purely for the love of it but now those who produced "faulty and deficient" literary work (Bledstein 1976: 31).

There were, of course, reactions against acceptance of the idea of author as professional. In the 1830s and '40s, the transcendentalists maintained a stalwartly anticommercial stance (Dowling 2011: 91–96). Their leader, Ralph Waldo Emerson, characterized the task of serious scholars as "the slow, unhonored, and *unpaid* task of observation" and asserted that they "must relinquish display and immediate fame" (Emerson 1837; emphasis added). (Of course, Emerson's wealth made holding that view unproblematic.) As late as the 1850s New York's Knickerbockers, led by Washington Irving, conceived of themselves as "gentlemen who wrote, not writers" (Bender 1987: 131). Yet all of these men and women were deeply embedded in the literary marketplace: all of them sold their work to magazine and book publishers.

The Development of Copyright Law in Britain and America

Deeply entwined with cultural conceptions of authorship were laws concerning literary property and the interpretations of those laws. The notion of any right to "copy" a text was originally rooted in the act of printing and selling copies, not in the act of creation by a writer. After the printing press was introduced to England in 1476 by William Caxton, the British Crown held a monopoly over printing and distributing books; it granted printing privileges, exclusive rights to print a specified work for a limited period of time, mostly to printers but occasionally to authors (Rose 1993). In 1557 the Company of Stationers was chartered to regulate the book trade and its members were granted sole authority to print books entered in the company's register. From 1641 to 1694 a series of licensing statutes maintained the stationers' monopoly and continued the conception of copyright centered around the act of printing and the necessity of state censorship.

After losing their monopoly, the stationers lobbied for statutory protection (Feather 1980; Saunders 1992; Deazley 2004). In 1710 they finally got what they wanted: the first parliamentary copyright law, the Statute of Anne, after which copyright gradually came to mean the right of a publisher or author to the exclusive publication of a work in order to prevent literary piracy (Abrams 1953; Patterson 1968; Rose 1993). The more modern idea that literary works were the property of their authors because they were embodiments of authors as individuals was instantiated in the landmark *Millar v. Taylor* decision of 1769 by the Court of King's Bench. This decision set the course for subsequent legal treatment of copyright as foremost a matter of authors' rights (Patterson 1968; Abrams 1983; Saunders 1992; Rose 1993). This development was not, however, without setbacks: the *Donaldson v. Becket* case in 1774, also settled by the Court of King's Bench, limited authors' ownership of copyright to a finite term after first publication. Yet *Donaldson*, like *Millar* before it, made clear that the starting point for the legal treatment of copyright was the rights of the author.

In colonial America copyright law was virtually nonexistent. The few copy privileges granted by colonial authorities pertained to individual publications, and only one of these (the William Billings Privilege, granted in Massachusetts in 1772) was to an author rather than a publisher and it was never enforced (Bracha 2008b). In the absence of general copyright statutes, British law provided the template for legal consideration of literary property rights. Although British legislators and jurists slowly engendered legal protections for British authors, these ideas were never tested in American courts, so they did not create any meaningful protection for American authors before the Revolution (Bugbee 1967; Patterson 1968; Everton 2005).

After the Revolution all states except Delaware passed copyright laws. State legislators were pushed by American authors, such as spelling textbook author Noah Webster and poet Joel Barlow, who argued that their writing deserved protection because it would unite the new nation and promote a national cultural identity; they also claimed that copyright law was needed if the United States was to reach cultural parity with European powers (Barlow 1783; Webster 1843; Charvat 1968; Bracha 2008a, 2010; Pelanda 2011). Although this shows how cultural conceptions of authors shaped copyright law, these copyright laws had no effect on the market for literature, as these state statutes were never tested or interpreted by the courts (Patterson 1968).

In 1787 the Constitutional Convention adopted without debate the Copyright Clause of the US Constitution, granting Congress the power to "promote the Progress of Science and useful Arts, by securing for limited Times to Authors and Inventors the exclusive Rights to their Writings and Discoveries" (US Constitution 1787, article 1, section 8, paragraph 8). In 1790, Congress passed the first federal copyright act "for the encouragement of learning, by securing the copies of maps, charts, and books to the authors and proprietors of such copies" (US Congress 1790a) for fourteen years with the possibility of an extension of fourteen more. Thus American copyright law, like its British role model, balanced authors' ownership rights and society's need to promote innovation. To secure copyright, authors or proprietors had to comply with onerous statutory requirements: pay a fee, deposit a copy of the title of the work in their local district court, publish a copy of the record in a newspaper for four weeks, and file a copyright claim with the secretary of state (US Congress 1790a, sections 3–4). Thus, American copyright law came to recognize that economic rights in literary property did not differ from rights in any other sort of property (Patterson 1968; Rose 1993; Khan and Sokoloff 2001).

There was one glaring omission in American copyright law: works by foreign authors were not protected. Indeed, the Copyright Act of 1790 explicitly excluded foreign works by specifying that "nothing in this Act shall be construed to extent to prohibit the importation or vending, reprinting, or publishing within the United States, of any map, chart, book or books ... by any person not a citizen of the United States, in foreign parts or places without the jurisdiction of the United States" (US Congress 1790a, section 5). This situation was reinforced by the first major revision of federal copyright law in 1831, which explicitly barred foreign authors from copyright protection. In the 1840s and '50s, large American publishing houses observed a pale, informal imitation of copyright law—"courtesy of the trade" (Spoo 2013). Publishers paid foreign writers for advance sheets of their work and, by informal agreement, received exclusive rights to reprint that work, but such payment was still far below the real economic value of foreign work (Charvat 1968; Barnes 1974; Khan 2005; Spoo 2013). Moreover, although the large publishing houses cooperated to develop this system of de facto copyright, many less prestigious publishers reprinted foreign work without making any payment at all (Charvat 1968). This situation benefited American publishers, booksellers, and readers to the detriment of authors everywhere: foreign authors received at most very small royalties and American authors could not compete in price with cheap foreign prose and poetry (Griswold 1981).

The Impact of Copyright Law and Cultural Conceptions of Authorship on Magazines

Magazines Not Protected by Copyright Law

Copyright law was seldom applied to magazines before the Civil War for two reasons: few publishers assumed that American literary property was commercially valuable until well into the 1820s (Charvat 1968) and the onerous procedural requirements for securing copyright constituted a practical obstacle throughout this period (Sprigman 2004). Therefore, very few magazines in this era copyrighted their contents.[15] Moreover, there were no federal court decisions concerning magazines and copyright between 1790 and 1850 (Ginsburg 1990; Brauneis 2008), and litigation over copyright remained quite rare even after 1850. Searches of legal databases revealed only seventeen copyright-infringement actions in federal courts between 1850 and 1860; none pertained to magazines.

There is evidence, however, that the law was constitutive of magazines' practices and conceptions of intellectual property, as sociolegal scholars would predict (Gordon 1984; Edelman and Suchman 1997), arguing that legal relations between economic actors, such as writers and publishers, shapes their interests and goals. A few publishers invoked copyright to secure a monopoly over their magazines. Between 1790 and 1825, forty magazines (7.4 percent of those in the archives) printed copyright notices in early issues. A few others claimed intellectual property rights in editorial statements. For example, Noah Webster, the founder-editor of the *American Magazine*, claimed copy-

[15] In this, magazines were similar to books: the vast majority of books published between 1790 and 1820 were also not copyrighted (Starr 2004; Khan 2005).

right over his periodical, forbade the reprinting of its contents, and threatened lawsuits against those who continued reprinting: "Printers throughout the United States are requested to observe, that this publication circulates as the Editor's property. . . . Several trespasses upon the property of the Editor, in different parts of the country, have been already committed—and will be passed without further notice. But a repetition of the injuries, will call, before the proper tribunal, a legal question of considerable importance; and produce some trouble and expense, which every man of a specific disposition would wish to prevent" (Webster 1788: 2). Still, the vast majority of magazines never invoked copyright law, and no lawsuits involving magazines and copyright were ever recorded.

Magazines Reprint Material Published Elsewhere

The effective lack of legal protection for literary property both benefited and hindered magazines. The primary benefit was that a "culture of reprinting" (McGill 2003) prevailed that created a "literary commons" (Tomc 2012) in which all could share. Without explicit recognition and use of copyright law, magazine publishers could—and often did—reprint material previously published in domestically published books, newspapers, and other magazines without fear of lawsuit (McGill 2003; Haveman 2004).[16]

Postal regulations explicitly supported the practice of reprinting (Kielbowicz 1989). Under the 1792 Postal Act, newspaper printers could "send one paper to . . . every other printer of newspapers within the United States, free of postage" (US Congress 1792: section 21), which encouraged newspapers to reprint the contents of other papers (Smith, Cordell, and Dillon 2013). Since many magazine publishers had previously published newspapers, as chapter 4 will reveal, it is not surprising that the culture of reprinting spread from newspapers to magazines. Like newspapers, magazines were frequently exchanged by publishers, even though, unlike newspapers, magazines had to pay for postage (Mott 1930; Kielbowicz 1989; Jackson 2008). For example, at the end of its first volume, the *Southern Journal of the Medical and Physical Sciences* (1853–57) listed over thirty magazines that it received in exchange. Similarly, the *Southern Cotton Planter* (1853–61) described seven new magazines that it received in exchange and explained, "We cannot name here our several weekly exchanges; our limited space does not permit it; but we cannot forgo the pleasure it affords us to acknowledge their favorable and kind notices and efforts on our

---

[16] This tactic continues even today. *Reader's Digest* began in 1922 by publishing condensed versions of articles from a variety of mass-market magazines, while the *Utne Reader* selects its contents from the pages of "alternative" and independent-press periodicals. Of course, modern print magazines, unlike many of their eighteenth- and nineteenth-century counterparts, pay for this privilege. In contrast, online news aggregators like the *Huffington Post* and the *Drudge Report* republish material that first appeared in other sources—and, like their predecessors in the eighteenth- and nineteenth-century magazine industry, they do so without compensating those sources.

behalf" (Cloud 1853: 371). This system of exchange bound "the printers themselves into a national network" (Gardner 2012: 99).

The practice of reprinting was welcome, sometimes even solicited. For example, the founder of the *Farmer's and Planter's Friend* (1821) requested that other periodicals reprint the original essays he published, noting, "The writer respectfully requests that the printers of news-papers throughout the United States who are devoted to the general welfare of the nature, but particularly to the interests of the farmers and planters, will insert the above" (Guatimozin 1821: 5). Some authors also appreciated this practice. For example, Poe (1835) observed that when literary works were widely reprinted in magazines, "taking hold upon the public mind they augment the reputation of the source where they originated."

Reprinting was widespread and often unacknowledged. For example, the *Balance and Columbian Repository* (1801–11), published in Hudson, New York, exchanged much material with the New York City–based *Impartial Gazetteer* (1788–17). Of the 210 articles published in the first three volumes of the *Balance*, 50 were published in both magazines—17 first in the *Gazetteer* and then in the *Balance*; 30 first in the *Balance* and then in the *Gazetteer*; and 3 first in the *Gazetteer*, then in the *Balance*, and then again in the *Gazetteer* (Pitcher 2000: 151–81). Another 48 articles printed in the first three volumes of the *Balance* came from other periodicals or books. For its part the *Gazetteer* exchanged much material with the *Philadelphia Repository* (1800–1805): some 400 articles appeared in both journals, 90 percent within one year of their first appearance (Pitcher 2000: 183–205).

The high volume of borrowing indicates that most magazines ascribed to an informal norm that allowed the sharing of contents (McGill 2003). They did not mind other magazines lifting material from their pages because they did the same thing. Most viewed this practice as existing outside of any market. Some, like the *Farmer's and Planter's Friend*, even printed notices in their periodicals, explicitly offering to exchange material with other magazines. Such cooperation may have been sustained by a belief that magazines' subscriber bases did not overlap very much, if at all, because of geographic limits on magazine distribution, so reprinting material from one magazine in another would not undermine either's readership (Mott 1930).

Many magazines stated explicitly that they would reprint ("select" or "extract") material from books and other periodicals. Among magazines published from 1741 to 1825 for which prospectuses or editorial statements are available, over half (245 of 478) expressed the intent to reprint material from other sources. For example, one stated that "such articles and documents of various kinds and upon all proper subjects, will be selected, as shall be thought most worthy of preservation" (Sampson, Chittenden, and Croswell 1802: 1). Another declared that "it is our aim . . . to be *useful* rather than original and . . . we shall not hesitate to select from worthy sources" (Foote 1824: 13; emphasis in the original). This happened even with religious, professional, and scientific journals: one religious weekly avowed announced its "leading object [is] to republish from other Magazines such productions as shall appear best calculated to promote useful knowledge, sound morality and vital piety" (*Religious Instructor* 1810: 3).

American magazines also benefited from the lack of copyright protection for foreign authors. For example, *New York Magazine* (1790–97) reprinted eighty-six articles from the venerable *Edinburgh Magazine*, including travel stories, articles about new inventions, essays on morality and science, short stories, and biographies (Pitcher 2000: 129–49). American magazines were not shy about taking advantage of this situation. Dozens explicitly signaled their intention to reprint work from foreign sources by mentioning in their titles or subtitles "foreign publications" or "foreign masters" or explicitly stating the source countries. Many more laid out their intentions to reprint foreign work in prospectuses or editorial statements. For example, *American Mercury* (1784–1829) promised to publish "regular extracts from Cook's last voyage (published by Authority in London, and lately come to hand)" (Barlow and Babcock 1784). The *Philadelphia Magazine and Review* (1799), noting the "extreme folly" of those who did not reprint material from European publications out of a sense of American nationalism, promised to avoid that mistake and publish selections from European publications (*Philadelphia Magazine and Review* 1799: ii). Fifty years later another magazine pledged to "present to the public ... the best of those works in popular literature" from Europe (*International Weekly Miscellany* 1850: 1). Perhaps most brazen was the *Corsair*, launched in 1839 by poet, playwright, and travel writer Nathaniel Parker Willis, who announced it would "take advantage ... of the privilege assured to us by our piratical law of copyright; and in the name of American authors (for our own benefit) 'convey' to our columns ... the cream and spirit of everything that ventures to light in France, England, and Germany" (quoted in Beers 1885: 240). Willis started this periodical because he felt harmed by the lack of international copyright law: "People will say, 'Why, damme, Willis can't get paid for his books because the law won't protect him, so he has hauled his wind, and joined the people that robbed him.'" (quoted in Beers 1885: 241).

Expressed motivations for reprinting varied. Some repeated the stated goal of the *Balance* to preserve worthy material for the future. Others, like the founder-editor of the *Belles-Lettres Repository* (1819), reasoned that reprinting material from other publications was a sounder strategy than relying on original contributions. "To give the public confidence in the stability and permanence of this work, the editors announce it as their intention to assume as the basis of their publication, the selecting and arranging from foreign periodical publications, such matters as comport with the plan of this work, thereby securing an inexhaustible fund of the most entertaining articles from those sources, and superseding the necessity of a steady reliance on the tardiness of paucity of editors and contributors, and also enabling the publishers to appear with the utmost punctuality at the stated day of publication" (Goodrich 1819: 1). Still others claimed to save readers money by making it unnecessary for them to subscribe to many foreign magazines, averring that much of what was published in foreign magazines was not of interest to Americans and that they would sift out the most interesting articles on behalf of their readers.

A Dearth of Original Material

The reprinting of material published elsewhere also hampered the magazine industry: authors could neither be sure they would reap the economic or reputational benefits of publication nor maintain control over the integrity of their words, so they were reluctant to contribute original material to magazines (Haveman 2004). In this, law provided a significant technical constraint on the market for literature. For instance, Robert Aitken and Thomas Paine bemoaned the fact that few Americans had the time or interest to contribute original materials to their *Pennsylvania Magazine* (1775–76), and a later editor lamented,

> The trade of literature is but young in this country: it is not here as in England, where the market is constantly so overstocked with the commodity of authorship, and the dealers in it are so numerous and eager to sell, that any one who wants a small quantity may go to the next shop and purchase by retail. Most of the leading literary characters in America are professional gentlemen, who write for amusement only; while the few who follow it as an exclusive business are generally employed in a way that forbids their undertaking so inconsiderable an office as that of writing a few pages once a month. (*Mirror of Taste and Dramatic Censor* 1810: vi)

Only men with independent means or sinecures that were remunerative but not strenuous could indulge in writing in eighteenth- and early nineteenth-century America; as one humorous anecdote explained, "Secure yourself . . . a livelihood independent of literary successes; and put into this lottery only the overplus of your time: for wo [*sic*] to him who depends only on his pen!—nothing is more casual. The man who makes shoes, is sure of his wages; but the man who writes a book is never sure of any thing" (*Port-Folio* 1815: 201). If an American writer's income was less certain than that of a cobbler, then it is no wonder that magazine editors struggled to find original material with which to engage their readers.

When early magazine editors did manage to persuade writers to contribute original material, authors often demanded anonymity in an effort to preserve their dignity and privacy (Charvat 1968).[17] An article in the *Literary Tablet* (1833–34) explains why this practice was so common:

> It is the characteristic of genius to sequestrate itself from the impudent gaze and slanderous tongue of the noisy throng: nor with less horror has it

---

[17] The practice of anonymous and pseudonymous authorship was not limited to magazines. Books were also published anonymously or under pseudonyms. For instance, James Fenimore Cooper and Washington Irving kept their names off the title pages of their books until the early 1840s.

usually risked exposure to the envenomed shaft of the critic, whose name carries a greater dread, even, than the vociferous rabble, since it is his *profession* . . . to spy out every blemish, while he ingeniously conceals his beauty. . . . It is from a deference to this feeling of modesty and distrust, so often a constituent in the character of the man of genius, that anonymous publications lay a strong claim to our candor. (*Literary Tablet* 1833: 188; emphasis in the original)

Even many of those running magazines preferred to cloak their identities. For instance, the *Lady's Magazine and Repository of Entertaining Knowledge* (1792–93) was edited by "a literary society"; the *Aeronaut* (1816–22) was edited by "an association of gentlemen"; and the *Baltimore Literary Magazine* (1807) was edited by "a gentleman of known literary abilities"—although these abilities could not really be "known" if this gentleman remained anonymous! Others involved with early magazines hid their identities behind pseudonyms. For example, "Robert Rusticoat" was the founder, editor, and publisher of the *Wasp* (1802–3), while the eminent firm of "Goggles, Spectacles, and Co." edited the *Charleston Spectator and Ladies' Literary Port Folio* (1805–6), "Henry Homespun, Jr." edited *Plough Boy* (1819–20), and "An American Patriot" edited *Periodical Sketches* (1820).

The practice of hiding magazine editors' and publishers' identities was most common in the first two decades of the nineteenth century, as figure 3.9 shows. Among magazines founded in the 1800s, 18 percent (37 of 206) had anonymous or pseudonymous founders, editors, or publishers, as did 15 percent of those founded in the 1820s (44 of 285). Anonymity and pseudonymity later declined dramatically, to 4.7 percent (33 of 709) of magazines founded in the 1830s, 3.4 percent (46 of 1,409) of those founded in the 1840s, and just 2.4 percent of those founded in the 1850s. But some magazines continued to hide the names of their contributors until the mid-nineteenth century. For instance, Nathaniel Hawthorne and his sister were the unnamed authors of all material in the *American Magazine of Useful and Entertaining Knowledge* during 1836, and Henry Wadsworth Longfellow objected to the use of his name on the mastheads of the magazines for which he wrote in the 1840s.

Magazine editors' ability to procure original material—especially signed work—for their ventures varied greatly not just over time but also across genres. Until at least the 1830s, general-interest, literary, and political journals found it more difficult than professional and scientific magazines did to persuade writers to submit original material under their own names. For original material they had to rely on their editors and their editors' friends, many of whom demanded anonymity. For example, Charles Brockden Brown wrote almost everything original that appeared in his first magazine, the general-interest *Literary Magazine and American Register* (1803–7), mostly under pseudonyms, as did Joseph Tinker Buckingham for his theatrical and literary review *Polyanthos* (1805–14). Other magazines sought contributors among the members of affiliated literary clubs or gentlemen's societies. The *Monthly Magazine*

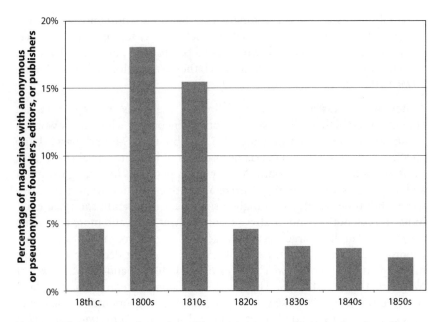

Figure 3.9. The percentage of magazines with anonymous or pseudonymous founders, editors, or publishers, by period.

and *American Review* (1799–1800) and the *American Review and Literary Journal* (1801–2), for example, were both affiliated with the New York Friendly Club, while the *Monthly Anthology* (1803–11) was launched by the Anthology Club, *Port-Folio* (1801–27) was sponsored by the Tuesday Club, and the satirical *Red Book* (1819–21) was published by the Delphian Society. Early in the nineteenth century literary magazines that were affiliated with the burgeoning number of colleges began to appear, which depended on students and faculty for original prose and poetry.

Paying Authors for Contributions

The slow cultural-cognitive shift from author as gentleman-scholar to author as professional was impelled by and reflected in an economic innovation by magazine publishers: in 1819, the *Christian Spectator* (1819–38) pioneered the practice of paying contributors, offering one dollar per page (Mott 1930). The founders of this religious magazine argued the necessity of this innovation:

It has been the misfortune of our country that the efforts made to establish and conduct periodical publications, especially those of a religious character, have been divided. These publications have, therefore, received but a partial support, have been of circumscribed usefulness, and of short continuance. To avoid these evils, an attempt will now be made to attain a concentration of labors. A method in which it is supposed this object may be effected is to allow a compensation to those who contribute to the pages of the proposed work. To make such compensation, is not only necessary, but just. Those who will thus labour for the public good, are not rich, and will need the reward to which they are entitled. (*Christian Spectator* 1819: iii)

Although this was a cultural breakthrough, the sums involved were not enough to earn a living. The average monthly income of white-collar workers in the Northeast between 1821 and 1825 was about thirty-four dollars (Margo 2000); to earn at this level a magazine writer would need to be paid for at least thirty pages of text each month. At sixty pages per issue, including the index and news items, the monthly *Christian Spectator* could not support even two writers full-time. Yet this seemingly insignificant innovation soon had enormous impact, both economically and culturally, as more and more magazines adopted it. The first large-circulation general-interest magazine to pay contributors was *Atlantic Magazine* (1824–25); over the next decade many others followed suit—notably, *Godey's Lady's Book* (1830–98) and *Knickerbocker, or New York Monthly Magazine* (1833–65). Even august literary reviews, whose contributors were most likely to view themselves as gentlemen-scholars and thus most likely to avoid publicity, followed suit: the *North American Review* (1815–1940, 1964–) adopted this market-oriented practice in the mid-1820s.

As this economic innovation spread, magazines began to compete intensely for essays, poems, and especially fiction. For example, the proprietors of *Brother Jonathan* (1839–45) complained that their rivals at the *New World* (1840–45) not only bribed the boys who sold periodicals on the streets of New York City to place the *World* at the top of their piles, filled these boys with alcohol to celebrate the new year, and exhorted them to break the windows of the shop that housed *Brother Jonathan*, but—worst of all—conspired with a local book publisher to print Edward Bulwer-Lytton's new novel *Zanoni* in a special edition, stealing it from *Brother Jonathan*. As they explain, this theft did not succeed:

We do not like to impute motives; but presume that the intention of the gentlemen was partly to annoy the *Jonathan*, and principally to advertise their own edition . . . the *World* came in with the intention to cheat us . . .— *and failed.* That *Zanoni* is ordered, and will be issued from this office with all possible expedition, and the servile copyists and plagiarists of the other paper immediately fall in, and will *fail again.* They may glean after us, as heretofore, but they must keep their place in the rear, and stick to their vocation of plundering the baggage. . . . Many who were cheated into the purchase of the *New World* last week, to read *Zanoni*, and *did not find it*, will not soon forget it. (*Brother Jonathan* 1842: 353–54; emphasis in the original)

After 1830 strident competition over content pushed up prices for short stories and serialized novels—especially those from the pens of established authors. For example, in 1840 Longfellow was paid by the large-circulation *Burton's* (later *Graham's*) *Gentleman's Magazine* (1840–58) $15 to $20 for each poem; by 1843, his price per poem had risen to $50 (Mott 1930; Charvat 1968). This magazine's prices for essays and fiction ranged from $4 to $20 per printed page over the same time period, which translated to $20 to $100 for a 5,000-word article. Similarly, the publishing house of Carey and Lea paid William Leggett $60 for a short story in their 1828 Christmas annual (*Ariel* 1828: 124). To put these prices in perspective, average wages for white-collar workers were about $35 in the late 1820s and about $43 in early 1840s (Margo 2000); thus, Leggett's short story netted him almost two months' worth of an average white-collar income, while by 1843 Longfellow could earn an above-average income by selling a single poem per month and *Graham's* prose writers could do the same by selling one essay or short story every two months.

As competition for literary submissions intensified, a significant cognitive-linguistic shift became apparent: magazines were increasingly likely to view their activities in market terms (Haveman 2004). As the editor of this era's most prominent literary review commented on this nascent market, "Literature begins to assume the aspect and undergo the mutations of trade. The author's profession is becoming as mechanical as that of the printer and the bookseller, being created by the same causes and subject to the same laws.... The publisher in the name of his customers calls for a particular kind of authorship just as he would bespeak a dinner at a restaurant" (Bowen 1843: 110). Similarly, a book review compared the business of literature to that of commercial enterprises, noting, "Both must be regulated, to some extent, by the vulgar law of supply and demand, and their profits, by the same law, cannot be forced beyond the natural level of cost and competition" (*Putnam's Monthly Magazine* 1853: 24).

Even authors who had earlier opposed this market turn benefited from the rising prices paid by magazines. For example, in 1857 Ralph Waldo Emerson was paid $50 for a poem ($1,300 in 2014 dollars) by the *Atlantic Monthly* (Bradsher 1929). With prices like these writers could supplement what little they earned from publishing books by selling stories and poems to magazines. The rising value of literary property also led magazines to trumpet their most popular authors, sometimes over the authors' own objections (Charvat 1968: 292). The marketing of literary property finally laid to rest the custom of literary anonymity. As figure 3.9 shows, in the 1840s and '50s less than 3 percent of new magazines had anonymous or pseudonymous editors or publishers. In addition, virtually all contributions to magazines, except very short items, were signed.

A new occupation—as *magazinist*, a term coined by Edgar Allan Poe—emerged as the practice of paying writers spread and as the idea of author as professional displaced the earlier conception of author as gentleman-scholar. By the early 1840s this occupation had achieved considerable acceptance; its legitimacy is evident in Horace Greeley's advice in 1843 to Henry David Thoreau, urging him to publish his work in mass-market magazines rather than just in small-circulation periodicals, such as the Transcendentalist organ *Dial* (1840–44). "This is the best kind of advertisement for you," Greeley wrote. "Though you may write with an angel's pen yet your work will have no mercantile value unless you are known as an author. Emerson would be twice as well known if he had written for the magazines a little just to let common people know of his existence" (quoted in Wood 1949: 60). Following this prompting, Greeley helped Thoreau place essays in several large-circulation magazines, including *Graham's, Putnam's Monthly Magazine* (1853–57), and the *Union Magazine of Literature and Art* (1847–52).

The slow development of a market for American books also benefited magazines. Because few American authors could earn a living by publishing essays, novels, or poetry in book form, many turned to writing poetry, short stories, serialized novels, and essays for magazines (Wroth and Silver 1951: 113). The career of Edgar Allan Poe exemplifies this dynamic; although Poe was "book-minded" in that he valorized publishing in book form over in periodicals (Charvat 1968: 86–91), he earned much of his meager living by writing for and editing magazines; he worked as editor of six and sought to launch two others but was unsuccessful.[18] His writings also appeared in scores of magazines, ranging from mass-market weeklies like the *New York Mirror and Ladies' Literary Gazette* (1823–42) to highly respected literary quarterlies like the *New York Review* (1837–42). Many other aspiring writers depended on magazines for their livelihoods, including America's first professional novelist, Charles Brockden Brown, and the most popular author of this era, Timothy Shay Arthur. Thus, as with improvements in the material supports for magazines—printing, papermaking, and engraving technologies—the expansion of the magazine industry spurred development of a cadre of professional writers, which helped usher in the first golden age from 1825 to 1850 (Mott 1930; Tebbel and Zuckerman 1991).

Magazines Grapple with Intellectual Property Rights

The practice of paying contributors, which began in 1819 and had become a widely accepted norm by the 1840s, compelled a shift in magazine publishers' views about literary property rights. As noted above, competition among large-circulation magazines over original essays, poetry, sketches, short stories, and serialized novels drove up prices for literary property, especially for work from the pens of established authors. To defend such increasingly expensive property, a few magazines began to copyright their contents—but none litigated to protect this expressed right. Although claiming copyright may have discouraged reprinting by direct rivals in the largest cities, until at least the

[18] Poe worked for *Broadway Journal* (1845–46), *Southern Literary Messenger* (1834–64; Poe's term ran 1835–37), [*Burton's*] *Gentleman's Magazine* (1837–40; Poe's term ran 1839–40), *Alexander's Weekly Messenger* (1837–48; Poe's term ran 1839–40), and *Graham's Magazine* (1841–58; Poe's term ran 1841–42). The magazines he tried to start were to be titled *Penn Magazine* and *Stylus*; all that remains of them is their prospectuses.

late 1840s it curbed but did not end literary larceny among magazines, as small-circulation regional publications continued to reprint material from New York's and Philadelphia's mass-market publications. More effectively, leading large-circulation magazines began to demand exclusive rights to "their" authors' works; for example, *Graham's* demanded exclusive access to Longfellow's work (Charvat 1968; Barnes 1974).

Macroeconomic conditions also hindered the use of copyright to protect magazine contents. The Panic of 1837 and the depression of 1840–43 forced many book publishers out of business. During this period of flux, cheap weekly magazines—most notably the *New World* (1840–48) and *Brother Jonathan* (1839–45)—found it easy to reprint material from books and other magazines without fear of lawsuit from authors or publishers (Charvat 1968; Barnes 1974). Not until after the depression ended did copyright law again offer book and magazine publishers leverage to effectively punish, or at least intimidate, "borrowing" by rival periodicals; a good example is the *American Agriculturist*, which began to be copyrighted in 1858 (Marti 1979). But even then magazines took advantage of the lack of copyright protection for foreign authors—most notably *Harper's Monthly Magazine* (1850–) and *Harper's Weekly* (1857–1916). They used this loophole to reprint British novels in serial form before American publishers issued them as books. And, as was explained above, only a few large publishers (including Harper and Brothers) paid anything for these works.

In sum, two related trends—increasingly professional and market-based conceptions of what it meant to be an author and the development of copyright law—were both enabling and disabling social devices. As enabling social devices they generated an increasing supply of original material for the pages of magazines, but as disabling devices they greatly increased the cost of this material. These changes were further encouraged by the development of two new norms: paying authors for their contributions and using copyright law to protect increasingly expensive literary property. The result was a growing cadre of professional magazine contributors who penned a burgeoning supply of original material that fueled the expansion of the magazine industry. Notably, this trend also increased costs for original articles, which raised barriers to entry into the industry.

CONCLUSION

The material and cultural resources required to publish magazines became increasingly available between 1741 and 1860. At the same time, both the demand for magazines and the supply of original material to publish in them increased. Because of these developments there is a sharp contrast between the struggles of the earliest magazines and the ease with which magazines were launched and managed less than a century later. The very earliest American magazines were written for a tiny, urban, socioeconomic elite and they la-

bored to attract readers and contributors. Very few people in the sparsely settled North American colonies lived near enough to the places where magazines were published, had enough spare cash to purchase magazines, and had
adequate leisure time and illumination to read magazines at night. Over the
course of the eighteenth century urban areas grew, rural areas were better
served by the mails, magazine prices declined, and cash incomes rose; as a result, a somewhat larger swath of the growing American population had access
to magazines. But even in 1800 the potential audience was still quite a small
fraction of the populace. Throughout the eighteenth century, magazine editors had to harangue their friends and gentlemen-scholars to contribute material or else scrounge material from other publications. Even when they had
enough to fill the pages of their magazines, they found potential subscribers
to be scarce and often deaf to the virtues of their products because those products lacked original content. For their part publishers had to negotiate with
local postmasters to distribute magazines and pay high rates relative to newspapers. They also had to limit their products' size and frequency because the
costs of printing and paper were so high.

By the middle of the nineteenth century the situation had improved dramatically. Distribution through the mails was now guaranteed by law and
postal rates for magazines were almost as low as for newspapers. There were
many eager readers who had cash to spend on magazines—especially those
that catered to members of a particular congregation; reform association; racial, ethnic, or linguistic group; or occupation. In addition to being more
populous the country was far more urbanized and better educated. Even those
who lived in rural areas could receive magazines through the faster, more reliable, and more extensive mail service. Americans were also increasingly willing to buy and read magazines. The development of the norm of paying authors for their contributions meant that magazines became a primary channel
for original essays, stories, and poetry (Cairns [1898] 1971; Charvat 1968;
Sedgwick 2000; McGill 2003; Okker 2003; Jackson 2008; Gardner 2012; Spoo
2013). The members of a newly formed occupation, that of the professional
magazine writer, were eager to contribute original material in exchange for
payment even though copyright law was not used by magazine publishers to
safeguard their investment in literary property. The resulting proliferation of
original material made magazines more desirable to readers and in 1825 the
industry entered its first golden age (Mott 1930, 1938a; Tebbel and Zuckerman 1991). In this period magazines became the preeminent means of disseminating literature.

The development of the postal system spurred the spatial stratification of
the magazine industry into a core (in Boston, New York, and Philadelphia)
and a periphery (all other locations). At the core, mass-market magazines
trumpeted their universalistic appeal with national toponyms and sought
readers across the country. In contrast, on the periphery, magazines of smaller
circulation distinguished themselves by appealing to localistic preferences
through the adoption of local toponyms. In addition, the magazine industry

became highly differentiated as dozens of types of specialist magazines arose to serve the members of particular occupations, adherents to many different faiths, advocates of over two dozen reform movements, members of fraternal associations, and lovers of literature and the arts, as well as targeting women and children and members of particular racial, ethnic, or linguistic groups. In this way magazines supported the creation of many modern, translocal communities.

The development of material and cultural supports for magazine publishing were not exogenous to the magazine industry but were instead bound up in the expansion of the industry itself. Magazines, like newspapers, provided a more reliable source of income for printers than did either books or government documents, and it was this income that spurred efforts to improve printing presses and papermaking machines and helped spread these technologies across the continent (Febvre and Martin [1976] 1990: 211). For its part the reading public showed greater interest in becoming literate when there was more to read (Watt [1975] 2001; Schudson 1978). Most basically, magazines helped spread literacy by conveying educational techniques to those who taught day and Sunday schools and by offering a platform for edifying and entertaining material that aimed to engage young minds. Magazines also supported higher education by providing platforms for philosophical, scientific, and literary debates among college faculty and students. Finally, the development of copyright law and the profession of magazine writer were intimately entwined with the growth of the magazine industry. Only when magazine subscription rolls had become very large, showing that original literary products had mass appeal, could writers earn enough from selling their work to make a decent living (Charvat 1968; Dauber 1990).

Chapter 4 probes more intimately the evolution of magazines in America and shows who launched magazines and how magazines' internal operations evolved to take advantage of the increasingly munificent material and cultural resources described in this chapter.

CHAPTER 4

Launching Magazines

*B*ecause magazines in America had such a perilous start, I will begin this chapter by analyzing early magazine founders to determine who launched these publications and why they did so. Given the profound changes in magazine publishing that occurred during the nineteenth century, I will also investigate how later magazine founders differed from their predecessors and how founders' motivations changed over time. I will then investigate what magazine founders said they hoped to accomplish with their publishing ventures—their espoused motivations and goals for their magazines. I end by detailing the strategies magazine founders used to secure public support for their magazines.

WHO FOUNDED AMERICAN MAGAZINES?

In answering this question, I focus on entrepreneurs' social positions—their status, meaning their relative positions in a social hierarchy—which afford them access to the resources they need to start new ventures.[1] There are multiple forms and sources of status (Weber [1968] 1978; Bourdieu [1979] 1984): gender, race, ethnicity, age, family background, educational attainment, income and wealth, occupation, acquired and embodied cultural knowledge, celebrity, and so on. These multiple forms and sources of status have important implications for this analysis. If different forms of status provide access to different types of resources needed to attract readers and inputs, then there may be multiple pathways into the emerging magazine industry. Moreover, changes in material and cultural conditions may alter the value of different status markers and the utility of their attendant resources. This, in turn, may transform access to the industry and change the type of people who are able to launch new ventures.

The many forms and sources of status can be divided along three dimensions: relational (Podolny 1993), demographic (Blau 1977), and cultural (Mohr 1998). My conception encompasses all three; I define status as *any observable distinction between people that stratifies their access to resources.* According to this definition status can be conferred by ties to people and institutions, by mem-

---

[1] This analysis is condensed from the article "How Entrepreneurship Evolves: The Founders of New Magazines in America, 1741–1860" (Haveman, Habinek, and Goodman 2012).

bership in demographic groups, and through use of cultural schemas (widely shared understandings of norms, values, and expectations). Economic resources derived from people's social positions can support the launch of new magazines, but cultural resources (e.g., formal certification) and social resources (e.g., relationships with others) can also help people gain access to productive assets and attract readers.

Sociological theories of industry evolution suggest two opposing predictions about who (which people in which status positions) would have access to the resources needed to launch magazines and how the status of those who founded magazines would change over time as the industry developed. First, if as industries develop it becomes increasingly easy to acquire resources and launch new ventures, then the earliest entrepreneurs would be socioeconomic elites and in occupations related to the industry,[2] while later entrepreneurs would be less elite and include more industry outsiders. Second, if as industries develop it becomes increasingly difficult to acquire resources and launch new ventures, then the earliest entrepreneurs would be nonelites and work in any industry, while later entrepreneurs would be more elite and include more industry insiders. Below, I consider each of these predictions in turn.

Competition and Exclusion from Resource Acquisition

The entrepreneurial task may become more formidable as industries develop. In new industries most organizations are young and small and relations among them are fluid. But as industries develop they often come to be dominated by a few very large and old organizations that have forged strong ties to suppliers and distributors. Because the firms in new industries are young and small, and therefore little known and resource-poor, their presence does not create barriers to entry for other new ventures. But because the large, established firms that dominate older industries are both widely recognized and resource-rich, they are powerful competitors whose presence may make it hard for anyone to launch new enterprises (Hannan and Freeman 1989). This idea harks back to Adam Smith ([1776] 1981) and Karl Marx ([1867] 1977), who argued that small businesses find it hard to compete against large incumbents because the latter benefit from economies of scale and so can pursue technological innovations and aggressive pricing strategies that small enterprises cannot afford.

Another consideration is that the magazine industry's growth and increasing legitimacy created stable webs of relations between industry participants and their suppliers and distributors. In such highly structured interorganizational fields (DiMaggio and Powell 1983), status orderings emerge (Fligstein and McAdam 2012). It is more difficult for outsiders to penetrate the

---

[2] By "socioeconomic elite" I mean simply people in high-status positions—those who have wealth or high levels of education and the skills, knowledge, and social connections that education fosters.

settled social relations that characterize long established industries than the fluid situations that prevail in new industries (Fligstein 2001). In sum, as industries develop, entrepreneurs may have more difficulty acquiring the resources they need to launch new businesses. If so, entrepreneurs will increasingly be either industry insiders or outsiders with considerable wealth or other resources, as only insiders and socioeconomic elites have the resources needed to scale rising barriers to entry. Outsiders without wealth, connections, or reputations will be increasingly excluded.

The history of American magazines suggests that this prediction of competitive exclusion is reasonable. All magazines in the eighteenth century were small ventures, but by the mid-nineteenth century large publishing houses operating industrial presses issued many magazines with print runs in the tens of thousands. For instance, Harper and Brothers, the largest publishing house in the world before the Civil War (Schlesinger 2000) launched eponymous weekly and monthly magazines in the early 1850s that grew to have circulations greater than 50,000. The enormous revenues derived from their large subscription bases allowed mass-market magazine publishers to pay popular authors like James Fenimore Cooper and Nathaniel Hawthorne for original poetry and prose. The presence of these large firms intensified competition and limited potential magazines founders' access to resources and readers. And because these large publishing houses arose in the industry centers, while smaller magazine publishing ventures proliferated everywhere, including on the periphery, the larger publishers' founders might be expected to come from higher-status positions than those elsewhere.

Legitimacy and Easier Access to Resources

In other respects, however, launching new ventures may be harder in newer industries than in older ones. In new industries customers and suppliers are uncertain, even skeptical (Stinchcombe 1965; Aldrich and Fiol 1994), so entrepreneurs must struggle to define opportunities, identify resources, and pry resources away from existing organizations (Rao 1998). Given this difficulty, entrepreneurs in new industries depend greatly on personal and social resources, such as personal reputations and connections to prominent others, which substitute for direct measurement of worth by customers and suppliers alike (DiMaggio 1982; Granovetter and McGuire 1998). Such relationships create halos that instill entrepreneurs' activities with normative and pragmatic legitimacy (Crane 1965; Merton 1968; David, Sine, and Haveman 2013).

As industries develop and expand, they become increasingly legitimate (Hannan and Freeman 1989), which makes it easier for entrepreneurs to recruit employees, acquire funding and equipment, and solicit sales (Aldrich and Fiol 1994). In addition, as industries expand, deep pools of industry-specific resources build up (Hannan and Freeman 1989), paving the path toward entrepreneurship. Moreover, as industries develop, entrepreneurs learn what to do—and *not* do—from observing their predecessors (Aldrich and

Fiol 1994). In sum, acquiring and deploying the resources needed to launch new ventures may become easier as industries develop. If so, entrepreneurs in older industries will have less need for great wealth, high personal standing, or prominent friends than their counterparts in younger industries.

The history of American magazines suggests that this prediction of increased legitimacy and easier access to resources is also reasonable. Many practical challenges to publishing magazines declined dramatically between the eighteenth and mid-nineteenth centuries as key resources like printing presses, paper, postal distribution, and original content all became more readily available. Moreover, demand increased as the industry expanded and magazines became legitimate cultural products and as new audiences emerged for specialized religious, reform, agricultural, and occupational magazines.[3] Therefore, it may have been increasingly easy for anyone—not just industry insiders and socioeconomic elites—to found magazines.

The Importance of Social Position: Occupation, Education, and Location

The likelihood of anyone becoming an entrepreneur depends on social structure and the potential entrepreneur's position within it (Stinchcombe 1965: 147). At any point in time, people in occupations related to an industry or high-status occupations, with high levels of education, and in central locations will have easier access to the resources needed to found new organizations than people in unrelated or low-status occupations, with little education, and in peripheral locations. Below I consider each marker of social position in turn.

Occupation is a general indicator of economic, social, and cultural resources. Prior experience in an industry—or, for new industries, in a related one—gives entrepreneurs knowledge and skills that will help their ventures thrive; it also signals the legitimacy of the new venture to resource providers (Spence 1973; Freeman 1986; Burton, Sørensen, and Beckman 2002). Through their prior work experience, entrepreneurs also forge ties to resource providers (Freeman 1986; Shane and Khurana 2003). For all these reasons, people in occupations related to an industry have better access to the resources they need to launch new ventures than people in other, unrelated occupations. In addition, people in high-status occupations, due to their claims to specialized expertise, which are often sanctioned by state authorities, have better access to economic and cultural resources than do people in low-status occupations (Zhou 1993, 2005; Weeden 2002).

Education both affects and reflects access to economic, social, and cultural resources. Most prosaically, education provides entrepreneurs with valuable

---

[3] I am not claiming that early in their history American magazines were illegitimate—that is, derided as being counter to prevailing social mores. Rather, they were not very legitimate—although they were understood as similar to their European forebears, they were not accepted as "normal" or "useful," much less economically viable.

knowledge and with ties to fellow students. It also signals entrepreneurs' knowledge and social ties to customers and resource providers alike (Spence 1973; Lazear 1977); such signals are especially important in the context of entrepreneurship because of the great uncertainty surrounding new ventures (Backes-Gellner and Werner 2007). Signals of cultural competence based on education may be especially important in an industry like magazine publishing that produces cultural goods whose use value is at least partly symbolic. For magazines, cultural competence entails knowledge of what others might want to read, which is based on the erudition developed through education. Overall, then, people with better educational credentials may find it easier to acquire resources to launch new ventures, especially in cultural industries.

Finally, *location* stratifies access to a variety of resources, as was explained in chapter 3. Many of the resources needed to start any organization are rooted in place, as is demand for products. As a result, industry knowledge and sustained attention from customers are concentrated around locations with many organizations, and entrepreneurs in such locations may find it easier to acquire resources to launch new ventures.

The Evolving Value of Occupation, Education, and Location

Although people in related or high-status occupations, with high levels of education, and in central locations may have superior access to the resources needed to found organizations, resource access will change as occupational status, educational stratification, and locational attractiveness evolve in response to industry development and trends in society at large. Among the magazine founders I studied, four out of five belonged to one of three occupational groups: the publishing trades (printers, publishers, editors, booksellers, bookbinders, and engravers); writers; and the traditional learned professions (physicians, ministers, and lawyers).[4] I will discuss historical trends in each occupational group in turn.

In the eighteenth century printing presses were rare and difficult to operate, and thus *printers* were highly skilled craftspeople, "handicraftsmen, entrepreneurs, and cultural leaders" who were "second in importance only to the clergy as leaders of opinion and public educators" (Bailyn 1960: 93, 95). Although few printers received much formal education, many had ties to political elites because they published official documents for state authorities and often served as postmasters. Moreover, after the Revolution skilled artisans like printers were similar in wealth, income, and lifestyle to merchants and others with nonmanual occupations (Marx [1867] 1977; Bailyn 1960; Botein 1981). Because print shops served as post offices, publishing houses, and bookstores, they were focal points for the exchange of news and intellectual engagement, serving the same civic function as English coffeehouses, French sa-

---

[4] The other magazine founders in the group I studied were music composers and/or publishers, merchants, manufacturers, engineers, state officials, and teachers.

lons, and German *Tischgesellschaften* (Wroth 1931; Everton 2005; Gardner 2012). As the landlords of the eighteenth-century American public sphere, printers were well positioned to acquire content, oversee production, gain access to distribution channels, and attract audiences.

During the nineteenth century, however, the social, cultural, and economic resources associated with printing declined. Printing became industrialized (Lehmann-Haupt 1951; Blumin 1989) and printers were deskilled as printing presses became easier to use (Stott 1990). Technological improvements, driven in part by demand from the growing magazine and newspaper industries, reduced printers' roles from proprietors of small businesses to mere employees of large publishing houses. Thus printers, like other skilled manual workers, saw their incomes, social status, and work autonomy decline (Commons et al. 1918; Stott 1990). The impact on magazine entrepreneurship is clear: by the mid-nineteenth century magazine publishers could easily hire printers; they did not have to be printers themselves. These technological and economic changes also lessened magazine editors' dependence on printers, which made it more difficult for printers to acquire content.

In contrast, people with *other publishing industry occupations* (publishers, editors, and booksellers) continued to provide access to many resources needed to launch magazines. Their focus on the written word always demanded deep knowledge and possession of considerable cultural resources. Moreover, as publishing industry insiders, they had ready access to persistently valuable social resources such as ties to writers and to publishing houses. Therefore, as the cadre of professional writers grew and printing became industrialized, members of other publishing trades remained well placed to acquire original articles and poems for their new magazines and to hire printing presses to produce them.

Eighteenth-century *writers* were almost all patricians: gentlemen-scholars who wrote for their own amusement and for the edification of others (Charvat 1968; Dauber 1990). They possessed the funds to support lives of leisure and the cultivation to write with style, and thus had immediate access to both financial support and content. By contrast, mid-nineteenth-century writers were more heterogeneous: although some were members of the social and economic elite, an increasing number earned their living by writing. Mid-nineteenth century writers included not only belletrists but also hack journalists, technical writers, and bohemians; thus, their economic, social, and cultural resources varied considerably. This means that writers became generally less likely to possess independent wealth or useful social connections and more likely to be restricted in their cultural resources to narrower areas of practical expertise.

Like that of writers, the status of *professionals* underwent a dramatic shift. In the eighteenth century, most professionals were members of the educated elite. Lawyers occupied the apex of colonial society; they were highly educated and well remunerated, and many were directly involved in colonial politics (Tocqueville [1848] 2000; Ferguson 1984; Haber 1991). Many of the eighteenth century's most accomplished gentleman-authors were lawyers (Ferguson 1984). Ministers, too, were well educated and in nine of thirteen colonies they were supported by official, state-sanctioned churches (Ahlstrom 1972; Haber 1991). Although physicians were not quite so distinguished as lawyers or doctors, in part because they competed with low-status barbers, midwives, and lay practitioners, medicine was still an acceptable occupation for younger sons of well-to-do families (Haber 1991; Starr 1982).

Throughout the early and middle parts of the nineteenth century, however, all three professions became contested and their status declined. As the legal profession expanded, self-directed study or apprenticeship became a common pathway into the legal profession and lawyers became more diverse in class, training, and credentials (Larson 1977; Haber 1991) and thus, on average, of lower social status. State licensing laws for legal practice were repealed in most states, eliminating formal state authorization of lawyers and further reducing their status, regardless of their educational credentials (Haber 1991). The status of ministers declined as disestablishment severed their direct relationship to the state, isolated them from political elites, and made them economically dependent on their local congregations (Douglas 1977; Haber 1991). Moreover, interdenominational disputes about theology and church organization undermined ministers' claims to authority, which called into question the status of even those in mainline Protestant denominations (Ahlstrom 1972; Hatch 1989). Physicians faced increasing challenges from homeopaths, mesmerists, phrenologists, Thomsonians, and eclectics who called into question their authority and reduced their social standing (Larson 1977; Starr 1982; Whooley 2013).[5] The licensing laws that distinguished rightful from wrongful medical practitioners and conferred authority on them were repealed starting in the 1830s (Haber 1991; Whooley 2013). Physicians' income levels fell and many had to supplement their medical practices with farming, ministerial work, or trade (Haber 1991). A final challenge to all professions developed as the populist politics of the Jacksonian era reinforced hostility to explicit marks of distinction. In sum, by the mid-nineteenth century, membership in the legal, medical, and ministerial professions implied little of the wealth, power, or prestige that had distinguished them during the eighteenth century, although lawyers' high incomes gave them higher status than doctors or ministers.

Education was always a marker of high status in this era. College graduates were from wealthy families and college education was rare: in 1800 there were a mere 2.7 college students per 10,000 Americans; in 1859, there were still only 10.4 per 10,000 (Burke 1973: 22, table 2.3). Because of the erudition acquired in college and the relationships forged there, college graduates also possessed substantial cultural and social resources. Collegiate life in this era

[5] The experience of the medical and clerical professions in the nineteenth century was the inverse of that of the economics profession in the twentieth century: economics overcame internal competition when neoclassical mathematical theorists made totalizing claims that strengthened the profession's autonomy and authority (Fourcade 2009).

emphasized the classics (Snow 1907), although some colleges began to focus more on modern languages. Regardless of curriculum, the emphasis on literature and debate fostered the skills needed to compose the poetry and belletristic essays that were standard features of most magazines throughout this period. It is not surprising, then, that students at several colleges even launched their own magazines, such as the *University of North Carolina Magazine* (1844–1948) and the *Kenyon Collegian* (1856–).

Finally, *location* stratified access to a variety of material and cultural resources associated with publishing. Most basic was access to printing presses. The first print shops in the colonies were in Boston, New York, and Philadelphia; in the late eighteenth century, printing spread to the backwoods (Wroth and Silver 1951: 69–70) as journeyman printers moved to find clients (Silver 1967). And a series of technological innovations between 1800 and 1832 made printing presses increasingly easy to operate (Berry and Poole 1966; Moran 1973). Thus, location-based differences in access to this resource declined markedly in the wake of early nineteenth-century technological improvements.

Countering this trend is the fact that publishing remained concentrated in Boston, New York, and Philadelphia. These three cities were also home to most of the mass-market magazines published before the Civil War. Because they were the centers of the magazine industry, entrepreneurs located in these cities had access to deeper pools of industry-relevant human and financial resources and to superior information about their industry than did entrepreneurs located elsewhere. Moreover, residence in any one of these cities—the largest in the nation and the centers of commerce and culture—put potential magazine founders close to peerless cultural and economic resources. Thus, people in Boston, New York, and Philadelphia continued to have advantages over people in other locations, at least when it came to publishing magazines (Stott 1990: 23–25). But entrepreneurs in these cities also had to overcome strong competition from nearby incumbents—the large publishing houses that clustered in the industry centers.

The value of occupation, education, and location—embodied in the economic, cultural, and social resources associated with them—changed between the mid-eighteenth century and the mid-nineteenth. Printers' status and access to resources declined, while those of other publishing occupations remained strong. Writers became less patrician and more heterogeneous, so their access to resources generally declined, although their access to resources specific to publishing remained valuable. Professionals were initially members of cultivated elite, but during the nineteenth century their knowledge and credentials became contested and new practitioners without the education, social ties, or wealth of their predecessors came to predominate—although lawyers' consistently high incomes may have buffered them from this trend. College education always indicated high status and was a consistently valuable source of

TABLE 4.1.
Temporal Changes in the Status of Social Positions and Predictions about the
Prevalence of Magazine Founders from Those Positions

Social position	Status in the 18th century	Status in the mid-19th century	Change in the likelihood of magazine founders, 18th to mid-19th centuries	
			Theoretical model	
			Competitive exclusion	Industry legitimation
Occupation				
Printer	High	Low	↓	—
Other publishing trades	High	High	↑	↓
Writer	High	Mixed	↓	↑
Professional minister	High	Contested/ mixed	↓	↑
Professional doctor	High	Contested/ mixed	↓	↑
Professional lawyer	High	Contested/ mixed	↓	↑
College education	High	High	↑	↓
Location in Boston, New York, or Philadelphia	High	High	↑	↓

Note: ↑ indicates that magazine founders were more likely to be in this social position in the mid-nineteenth century than in the eighteenth century; ↓ indicates that magazine founders were less likely to be in this social position. We make no legitimacy-based prediction about the change in the likelihood of printers being magazine founders.

cultural and social resources. Finally, although access to printing presses became widespread, many communities grew into urban areas, and the postal network linked people across the nation, a publisher's location in Boston, New York, and Philadelphia retained considerable economic and cultural value. The first and second columns in table 4.1 summarize these trends.

Predictions: Who Were the Entrepreneurs?

The third and fourth columns in table 4.1 show the predictions generated by combining the two perspectives on industry evolution with historical knowledge about how access to resources evolved for people in different occupations, with different levels of education, and in different locations. On the one hand, if the rise of mass publishers and the increasing cost of original content raised barriers to entry and made it increasingly difficult to acquire the resources needed to launch new magazines, we would expect magazine entrepreneurship to become confined to people in social positions that gave them good access to these resources. Concretely, this competitive-exclusion model suggests that members of publishing trades (other than printers) should have been increasingly common among magazine founders, as people in these occupations could tap into ever more valuable industry networks. By the same token, industry outsiders, printers, writers, and professionals should have become less common because people in these occupations had declining access to resources. College education should have become more common among magazine founders because in this era it was always reserved for the socioeconomic elite and provided access to great cultural and social resources. Finally, more new magazines, especially those founded by industry outsiders, should have been located in Boston, New York, and Philadelphia, as entrepreneurs in those cities always had access to superior economic and cultural resources.

On the other hand, if the legitimation of magazines and the development of deep pools of industry-specific resources made it easier to acquire the resources needed to found magazines, we would expect the opposite: magazine entrepreneurship should be more open to people in all social positions, even those that afforded little access to cultural, economic, or social resources. Concretely, this industry-legitimation model means that professionals and other industry outsiders should become more common among magazine founders, as should writers, while members of publishing trades (other than printers) should become less common.[6] In addition, college graduates should become less common among magazine founders because the economic, cultural, and social resources associated with college education became less important over time. Finally, more magazines should be published outside Boston, New York, and Philadelphia because access to the economic and cultural resources concentrated in those large cities became less important.

Empirical Evidence

To determine who launched magazines from the mid-eighteenth to the mid-nineteenth centuries, I worked with Jacob Habinek and Leo Goodman to analyze the backgrounds of magazine founders in two time periods: from 1741 to 1800, during which time American magazines were few in number and poorly understood, and from 1841 to 1860, when American magazines were commonly accepted means of communication and many reached mass audiences. We limited the analysis to these periods to maximize the temporal contrast between the early years of this industry's history and the period in which it was well established. We sought background information on the founders of all 148 magazines launched between 1741 and 1800, and on the founders of a random sample of 150 magazines from the 2,678 founded between 1841 and 1860. (Appendix 1 describes the samples and the availability of data on each;

---

[6] I make no prediction about printers because there are conflicting trends. Printers' access to economic and cultural resources declined as they moved from being proprietors of the public sphere to mere employees of publishing houses; thus they may have become less likely to found magazines. But access to resources became less important; therefore, printers' likelihood of founding magazines may have remained constant.

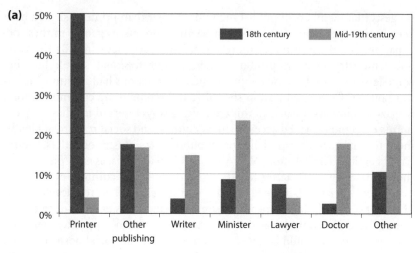

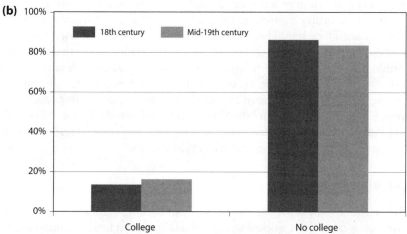

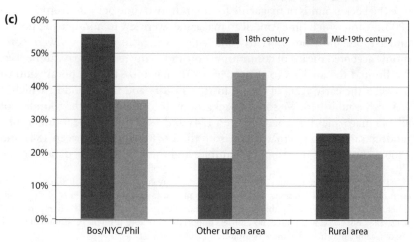

appendix 2 shows the details of this quantitative analysis.) Figures 4.1a–c chart the results of this analysis. Figure 4.1a focuses on occupation, 4.1b on education, and 4.1c on location.

The Eighteenth Century

The earliest magazines were nurtured by men who either had long-standing connections to publishing or were members of the learned elite. For the years 1741–1800, we identified 165 men (but no women) who founded 139 of the 148 magazines launched during those years; data were available on occupation and education for 162 of them. Strikingly, two-thirds of eighteenth-century magazine founders with data on primary occupations were in publishing: 50 percent (81 of 162) were printers and 17 percent (28 of 162) were members of other publishing trades, as figure 4.1a shows. Among these was printer Isaiah Thomas, one of the most respected businessmen of his time (Wroth 1931). The other eighteenth-century magazine founders were for the most part ministers (9 percent), lawyers (7 percent), doctors (4 percent), and writers (4 percent). The clergy included the prominent Boston minister, linguist, and historian Thomas Prince, and the first and second bishops of the Methodist Church in America, Thomas Coke and Francis Asbury. Of the lawyers, two were also clergymen, two were also poets, one was also a printer, and one (Charles Brockden Brown) was also a novelist. The prevalence of lawyers is not surprising given the many contributions lawyers made to American letters (Ferguson 1984). Among the physicians, three-fourths were part of the socioeconomic elite: two were professors at Columbia University's medical school and one was a protégé of Yale University president Timothy Dwight. When one takes into consideration the number of professionals in the population at large in the eighteenth century, magazine founders were sixty-four times more likely to be professionals than was the average American. Finally,

Figure 4.1. (a) Changes over time in magazine founders' occupations.
Note: This figure analyzes 162 magazine founders in the eighteenth century and 103 in the nineteenth century. Each founder's occupation is assessed before he/she founded his/her first magazine. The nineteenth-century sample omits one magazine founder, William August Munsell, who was eight years old when he started his magazine (and so had no occupation before he founded his magazine). We analyzed each occupation independently by comparing the number of founders in the focal occupation to the number of founders in all other occupations. For all χ^2 tests, $df = 1$ and * indicates $p < .05$, ** $p < .01$, *** $p < .001$
(b) Changes over time in magazine founders' education levels.
Note: This figure analyzes 162 founders in the eighteenth century and 104 in the nineteenth century. According to the χ^2 test, there is no association between education and time period: $\chi^2 = 0.39, df = 1, p > .10$.
(c) Changes over time in magazine founders' locations.
Note: This figure analyzes all magazines for which municipal location is known: 147 magazines in both time periods. According to the χ^2 test, the association between location and time is highly significant: $\chi^2 = 23.1, df = 2, p < .001$.

the writers were also quite elite: Jefferson's protégé John B. Colvin and patricians Samuel Harrison Smith, John Lathrop Jr., and Philip Freneau.

Figure 4.1b shows that many eighteenth-century magazine founders were highly educated. Five graduated from Harvard University and six from Yale; others graduated from Edinburgh, Halle, Middle Temple, Oxford, and Princeton Universities, the University of Pennsylvania, and an unidentified Scottish college. In total, 14 percent had attended college, which was more than five hundred times the percentage of Americans enrolled in college in 1800.[7] In addition, several eighteenth-century magazine founders worked in higher education: two taught at Harvard, one at Yale, two at Columbia, and one at the University of Vermont. Several others were renowned for their erudition. For example, Rev. Samuel Williams, who launched an eclectic magazine with a heavy literary component, was commonly called "the most learned man in Vermont"; John M'Culloch, who founded a religious monthly, compiled the first American history textbooks; and Lewis Nicola, who started a general-interest magazine, was a prominent engineer and founder of an early circulating library.

Figure 4.1c shows that eighteenth-century magazine publishing was confined almost exclusively to the Northeast. Boston, New York, and Philadelphia—which were both the largest cities and the commercial and cultural centers—were the locations for over half of all magazine founding, even though they contained only 3.0 percent of the population in 1770, the middle of this time period. Magazine founders were eighteen times more likely to be in those cities than was the typical American. Other, smaller urban areas (those with at least 2,500 inhabitants) were also home to 20 percent of magazines. Magazine founders were five times more likely to be in these smaller urban areas than was the typical American. Notwithstanding this concentration in urban areas, the rural Northeast was also host to many eighteenth-century magazines: almost one-fourth were published in northeastern towns with fewer than 2,500 inhabitants. In contrast, only nine magazines were founded in the South; of these, four were launched in Charleston, South Carolina, and two in Richmond, Virginia—both urban centers.

Together, figures 4.1a–c show that the pool of eighteenth-century magazine founders disproportionately comprised industry insiders and those with high-status positions. Two segments of the elite were predominant: the well educated, and printers and allied tradespeople (the landlords of the public sphere). Most of these men lived in one of the three major northeastern cities.

Not surprisingly given the small population base—barely 900,000 in 1740, rising to 5.3 million by 1800—many eighteenth-century magazine founders were closely connected to people in publishing and to members of the cultural, political, and economic elite. Among them were a nephew of Andrew

---

[7] It would be preferable to compare the percentage of magazine founders and Americans who were college graduates, but the latter number is not available, so we used the next best indicator, the percentage of Americans who were in college.

Bradford (William Bradford, a printer, newspaper publisher, and founder of a prominent American coffeehouse) and a host of men who had close relationships with Benjamin Franklin: his friend James Parker, a prominent colonial-era printer; a nephew, Benjamin Mecom; his business partner Anthony Ambruster; his protégé Mathew Carey; and his former apprentice Enoch Story. The illustrious printer-cum-publisher Isaiah Thomas was followed into magazine publishing by a former partner (Elisha Waldo), a close friend (Colonel John Fellows), and six former apprentices. David Austin, a protégé of the great evangelical theologian Jonathan Edwards, launched two religious magazines, as did William Weyman, son of the prominent Episcopal minister Robert Weyman. Samuel Harrison Smith, the son of Revolutionary-era politician Jonathan Bayard Smith, founded a highly regarded literary review.

The Mid-Nineteenth Century

The contrast between mid-nineteenth-century magazine entrepreneurs and their eighteenth-century predecessors is in some ways quite stark. As figures 4.1a and 4.1b show, professionals and those with a college education continued to make up a large share of founders, but many were members of the growing middle class. Indeed, so ordinary were these people that among the 125 founders identified by name, no background information were available on twenty-one (17 percent). The fraction of founders with no biographical data quadrupled between the two time periods—a statistically significant increase. Although even the most thorough searches are doomed to be incomplete, given the often scattered records available, the contrast between the general notoriety and full archival coverage of eighteenth-century founders and the greater obscurity and sparser archival coverage of their mid-nineteenth-century successors is striking.

Magazine entrepreneurs' social positions became more heterogeneous from the eighteenth century to the mid-nineteenth. Of those whose primary occupation we could pinpoint, there were far fewer printers among the nineteenth-century founders: only 3.9 percent (4 of 103).[8] This decline may stem from printers' shift in status from proprietors to employees; it also suggests the declining importance of controlling the means of production as those means diffused widely. In contrast, the fraction of magazine founders in other publishing trades remained constant at 17 percent, which demonstrates that the resources possessed by other industry insiders remained valuable. In addition, the fraction of magazine founders who produced content increased significantly: 15 percent made writing their primary occupation, which reflects the professionalization of authorship in America (Charvat 1968; Dauber 1990). By the mid-nineteenth century much (but certainly not all) literature was produced by people who earned a living from their writing, selling to

---

[8] One founder was a child, as is detailed later in this section, and was thus excluded from the analysis of occupation.

book and magazine publishers who in turn sought to earn profits by selling to mass audiences. Some of these professional writers appear to have removed the middlemen by launching their own magazines.

The fraction of doctors and ministers—the two professions whose status was the most contested—increased substantially, and the fraction of lawyers decreased by almost half. Even after taking into account the differing prevalence of professionals between the two time periods, the representation of professionals among magazine founders rose: mid-nineteenth-century magazine founders were 115 times more likely to be professionals than was the average American, compared to sixty-four times for eighteenth-century founders. These trends indicate that members of the increasingly contested medical and clerical professions used magazines to support themselves financially, to defend their intellectual or denominational positions, and to build communities of like-minded associates.

This conclusion is bolstered by the striking variety among doctors and ministers in the mid-nineteenth-century sample. Among doctor-founders, college-educated allopaths ("regular" physicians) vied with a variety of less formally educated Thomsonians, botanists, reformed physicians, and eclectics; homeopaths-cum-pharmacists; hydropaths; mesmerists; phrenologists and magnetists; and an assortment of Grahamites, vegetarians, and physical culture advocates. A full 70 percent of these mid-nineteenth-century doctor-founders were affiliated with medical specialties like dentistry that had low status, or they were members of upstart medical sects that were highly contested by the more prestigious "regular" physicians. For their part the minister-founders represented a wide array of faiths: Presbyterian, United Church of Christ, Baptist, German Reformed, Methodist, Universalist, Moravian, Christian Congregation, Seventh-Day Adventist, Norwegian and German Lutheran, Jewish, and spiritualist. Almost three-fourths were members of upstart faiths. In addition, a quarter of they magazines they founded were published in languages other than English, which indicates that they served low-status immigrant communities. This is more than double the faction of all magazines founded between 1841 and 1860 that were published in languages other than English, which suggests that minister-founders were more than twice as likely as other magazine founders in this period to cater to immigrant communities.

Evidence that magazine founders came from an increasingly broad array of social positions is partly reinforced by the analysis of education. While the number of colleges increased more than sixfold and college enrollments quadrupled between 1800 and 1850, the proportion of college-educated founders remained almost constant (14 percent in the eighteenth century, 16 percent in the mid-nineteenth century). Although mid-nineteenth-century magazine founders were 161 times more likely than the average American to have attended college, that ratio was 70 percent lower than in the eighteenth century, which is a statistically significant difference. This suggests that as the magazine industry developed, high socioeconomic status, cultural refinement, and social connections, although still quite valuable, became somewhat less important for launching magazines. Combined with the occupation trends discussed above, this indicates that magazine entrepreneurship spread beyond industry insiders and socioeconomic elites.

Figure 4.1c shows that the fraction of magazines founded in the three largest cities declined substantially, from 56 percent in the eighteenth century to 36 percent in the mid-nineteenth century, even though these cities' populations rose from 3.0 percent of Americans in 1770 to 4.4 percent in 1850. Although magazine founders in the mid-nineteenth century were over eight times more likely to be in the three biggest cities than the typical American, this is a big drop from the eighteenth century, when magazine founders were eighteen times more likely to be in these cities than the typical American. Thus these cities remained at the center of the industry, with many of the largest-circulation publications located there. Smaller urban areas (those with populations of at least 2,500) like Fort Wayne, Indiana, and Galveston, Texas, saw the greatest increase in magazine publishing, from 18 percent to 44 percent, while rural areas (those with populations below 2,500) saw a slight decrease, from 26 percent to 20 percent. The increase in foundings of magazines in small urban areas was due entirely to the rapid urbanization that began in the 1820s and the spread of printing presses across the nation. Although the number of urban areas (outside the three largest cities) grew from nineteen in 1770 to 283 in 1850, in both periods magazine founders were five times more likely than the typical American to be in small urban areas. Taken together, the results on location indicate that even as large publishing firms appeared in Boston, New York, and Philadelphia, people in smaller urban communities, which were often located far from the commercial centers, were increasingly likely to found magazines because there were more of those communities and because printing presses were more widely available.

Together figures 4.1a–c suggest that magazine entrepreneurship spread beyond industry insiders and socioeconomic elites. This conclusion is bolstered by the fact that many mid-nineteenth-century magazine founders came from modest backgrounds and made their reputations and fortunes through their periodicals. For instance, Thomas Hamilton, an African American whose father was a carpenter and who received little formal education, founded the *Anglo-African Magazine* (1859–60), which made him a leading voice among antislavery advocates. Similarly, Timothy Shay Arthur, a miller's son who worked as a clerk for wholesale and insurance companies before he began to write fiction, published *Arthur's Home Gazette* (1850–54) and several other eponymous periodicals that showcased his work. Arthur was "the most published American fiction writer in the century" and "his sales of more than a million copies indicate that he was also one of the most popular American authors of his time" (*American National Biography* 2000). It had become so easy to acquire the resources needed to launch a magazine that a child managed to do so: the sample of mid-nineteenth-century magazine entrepreneurs included an eight-year-old boy, William August Munsell, who launched the

Bee (1844–45) in Albany, New York, and continued to publish it until he came down with whooping cough.[9] The fact that many mid-nineteenth-century magazine founders had limited access to social, cultural, or economic resources is a turnaround from the situation prevailing in the eighteenth century, when magazine founders relied on such resources as printers or professionals, or their wealth and reputations as learned men, to sustain their periodicals.

Yet as the analysis of education shows, there were still many members of the socioeconomic elite among mid-nineteenth-century magazine founders. Theodore Dwight Jr., a Yale graduate and the son of Theodore Dwight Sr., the nephew of both Aaron Burr and Yale president Timothy Dwight, the and author of many popular books and prominent journalist, launched his eponymous *Dwight's American Magazine and Penny Paper* (1845–51) as a vehicle for his own writing. Ormsby Macknight Mitchel, a West Point Military Academy graduate, astronomer, professor at Cincinnati College, and member of the American Academy of Arts and Sciences and the literary Semicolon Society, published the *Sidereal Messenger* (1846–48), the first scientific astronomy journal. Alexander Lyman Holley, metallurgical engineer and son of the governor of Connecticut, partnered with Zerah Colburn, a mechanical prodigy who published a standard textbook on steam locomotive design at the age of twenty-two, to launch *American Engineer* (1857).

Comparing the eighteenth- and mid-nineteenth-century samples of magazine founders, two trends are evident. First, magazine founders were drawn from increasingly broad swaths of American society: fewer people from inside publishing, more from the increasingly contested medical and ministerial professions, fewer with college educations, and more from outside the three biggest cities. Yet among mid-nineteenth-century magazine founders the number of professionals and those college educated were still far larger than their representation in the population at large, and far more magazine founders were in the three largest cities than was the typical American. Moreover, the qualitative evidence indicates that many nineteenth-century magazine founders had strong ties to industry insiders and socioeconomic elites. Thus, the preponderance of evidence suggests the development of the magazine industry from the eighteenth to the mid-nineteenth century widened rather than narrowed the range of social positions from which entrepreneurs were drawn.

---

[9] His father was Joel Munsell, a printer and serial magazine founder-publisher (the *Albany Minerva*, founded 1828, was his first). It appears that little William was able to cajole his father into letting him have access to the printing press. Despite his close connection to a prominent industry insider, it is still remarkable that a child was able to found a magazine in this time period. A total of ten other magazines were founded by those under the age of eighteen (most twelve or younger) in the 1840s and '50s, compared to none in the eighteenth century, two in the period 1800–1819, and eight in the 1820s and '30s. As far as I have been able to discern, few of them had ties to industry insiders.

This ambiguity is reinforced by analyzing trends in magazines launched by organizations. Seventeen of the 150 mid-nineteenth-century magazines we studied were affiliated with formal organizations: the New Jersey Historical Society; the Cherokee Georgia Baptist Convention; the Association of Working Women and Men; the faculty of the Reformed Medical College of Macon, Georgia; the Sons of Temperance; and two teachers' associations, two literary societies, and eight groups of college students. This was a statistically significant increase from the eighteenth century, when four out of 148 magazines were launched by organizations. The surge in the number of organizations founding magazines can be attributed to the growing reliance on formal organizations in all realms of social life, education, science, work, the arts, and leisure; this created a modern "society of organizations" (Perrow 1991) or "organizing society" (Meyer and Bromley 2013) in which formal organizations were powerful actors. Nearly all of the organizations that sponsored magazines were populated by socioeconomic elites—specifically, by the highly educated. Only three of them—the labor union, the botanical medical college, and the frontier Baptist group—suggest access by nonelites to the resources needed to launch magazines.

Interactions among Occupation, Education, and Location

To resolve ambiguities about trends in the social positions from which magazine entrepreneurs were drawn, we analyzed temporal variation in the frequency of magazines with different combinations of founder occupations, education, and location. This allowed us to consider not only the change in the *prevalence* of founders from each social position but also changes in *relationships among* those social positions and thus to clarify the ambiguous relationships discussed above. (For more details on this analysis, see appendix 2.) This analysis showed strong interactions among these three dimensions of status. First, from the eighteenth century to the mid-nineteenth, it became more common for magazines to have both professional founders *and* founders who were in the publishing trades. This suggests that the resources attached to these two occupations became increasingly complementary. Second, it became more common for magazines to have founders who were not college-educated *and* founders who were professionals, as well as to have founders who were not college-educated *and* founders who were in the publishing trades. This indicates that magazine founders without a college education were the most rapidly expanding group within these two occupations. Finally, it became more common to have founders who were professionals *and* who were located outside the three largest cities. This indicates that magazines with professionals among their founders became more geographically dispersed, while magazines with members of the publishing trades and the college educated remained just as concentrated in the major urban centers.

General-Interest versus Specialist Magazines

The push and pull of increasing competition in the three largest cities (the magazine industry centers), which meant that only industry insiders and those with higher status positions (in terms of occupation and education) could found magazines there, as well as expanding legitimacy and opportunity in the industry periphery, which meant that industry outsiders and those in lower-status positions could found magazines there, may have played out differently among general-interest magazines than among magazines devoted to specialized topics (e.g., religion, social reform, or literature) or to particular audiences (e.g., women, Freemasons, or botanic physicians). Specifically, increasing competition in the industry centers may have had stronger effects on general-interest magazines, while increasing legitimacy may have had stronger effects on specialist magazines. Table 4.2 displays this analysis. Some trends are similar for both types of magazine; from the eighteenth century to the mid-nineteenth, both types were significantly less likely to be founded by printers and more likely to be founded by writers or physicians. In addition, both types showed no significant change over time in the likelihood of founders being ministers, lawyers, in other publishing trades, or in having college-educated founders. (In this regard, the disaggregated analysis differs from the analysis shown in figure 4.1a: there the trend for physicians was statistically significant; here it is not, due in part to smaller sample sizes that result from separating general-interest and specialist magazines.)

But, as expected, these two types of magazines had very different temporal trends with regard to location. While over time both types were less likely to be founded in the industry centers, specialist magazines were more likely to be founded in other urban areas and much less likely to be founded in rural areas, and general-interest magazines were equally likely to be founded in other urban areas and more likely to be founded in rural areas. Analysis of interactions between location and founder occupation, and location and founder education, shows that from the eighteenth to the mid-nineteenth centuries specialized religious and medical magazines became more likely to be founded in other urban areas by ministers and doctors who were not college educated. Indeed, among the mid-nineteenth-century magazines that were founded by professionals who were not college educated, almost 90 percent (25 of 28) were religious or medical journals, and three-fourths of these (18 of 25) were located outside the industry centers.

Summary

As the first mass-market magazines appeared, people from increasingly broad swaths of American society were able to launch new magazines because magazines became legitimate cultural products and industry-specific resources became widespread. Therefore magazine founders from many social positions,

TABLE 4.2.
Trends in Magazine Founders' Social Positions:
General-Interest versus Special-Interest Magazines

Social position	18th century		Mid-19th century		χ^2
	Number	Percentage	Number	Percentage	
General-interest magazines					
Printer	67	58%	2	10%	15.9***
Other publishing	25	22%	6	30%	0.66
Writer	6	5%	4	20%	5.42*
Minister	3	3%	2	10%	2.60
Lawyer	8	7%	1	5%	0.10
Doctor	2	2%	3	15%	8.40*
Other	4	3%	2	10%	1.71
College education	13	11%	2	10%	0.003
Boston/New York/ Philadelphia	47	55%	14	38%	3.13
Other urban area	18	21%	8	22%	
Rural area	21	24%	14	38%	
Special-interest magazines					
Printer	27	36%	1	1%	32.7***
Other publishing	17	23%	14	17%	0.84
Writer	0	0%	9	11%	8.84**
Minister	13	17%	23	28%	2.41
Lawyer	3	4%	2	2%	0.33
Doctor	3	4%	15	18%	7.73**
Other	12	16%	19	23%	1.18
College education	14	19%	14	17%	0.09
Boston/New York/ Philadelphia	37	64%	44	39%	8.09***
Other urban area	9	16%	53	47%	
Rural area	12	21%	17	15%	

Note: For occupations, this table analyzes 162 magazine founders in the eighteenth century and 103 in the nineteenth century. The nineteenth-century sample omits one magazine founder: William August Munsell, who was eight years old when he started his magazine. Each founder's occupation is assessed before he/she founded his/her first magazine. I analyzed each occupation independently by comparing the number of founders in the focal occupation to the number of founders in all other occupations, so $df = 1$. For college education, this table analyzes 162 founders in the eighteenth century and 104 in the nineteenth century and $df = 1$. For location, this table analyzes all magazines for which location is known (147 magazines in both the eighteenth century and the mid-nineteenth) and $df = 2$. * indicates $p < 0.05$; ** $p < 0.01$; *** $p < 0.001$. For tables that contain cells with fewer than five observations, p values are based on the Fisher's exact test instead of the χ^2 test.

not just the socioeconomic elite or industry insiders, could acquire the resources needed to launch new ventures. This occurred even in the face of intense competition from powerful mass-market magazines published in Boston, New York, and Philadelphia.

In the eighteenth century, when magazines were novel cultural products, finding skilled printers, obtaining original content, securing distribution, and attracting readers demanded heavy investment of economic, cultural, and social resources. Thus, most early magazine founders were printers or other members of the publishing trades—men who had the experience and connections necessary to secure scarce and hard-to-manage production resources. As the landlords of the eighteenth-century American public sphere (Wroth 1931; Everton 2005; Gardner 2012), these men were also cultural arbiters, so they were well positioned to acquire content, gain access to distribution channels, and attract audiences. Patrician professionals and men of letters were also common among magazine entrepreneurs: they possessed the knowledge and cultivation necessary to provide content and attract audiences and the economic resources needed to underwrite such risky ventures. Skeptics could be persuaded of the merits of these unusual new products by judging not the legitimacy of the products themselves but instead the stature of the men who created them. In this regard, magazines were similar to new types of arts, infrastructure, and professional service organizations founded in the late nineteenth and twentieth centuries (DiMaggio 1982; Granovetter and McGuire 1998; David, Sine, and Haveman 2013).

By the mid-nineteenth century, the greater legitimacy accorded to magazines and the development of industry-specific resources made it easier to launch and run magazines. Distribution through the mail was guaranteed by law, and postage rates for magazines were almost as low as for newspapers. Printing presses had become ubiquitous, and printing had been transformed from a skilled craft performed by business owners into factory work performed by paid laborers. Professional writers were eager to contribute original material for pay, and copyright law was used by publishers to safeguard their investment in literary property. Moreover, accumulated experience with magazines had reduced challenges for founders: potential subscribers, writers and illustrators, financial backers, and government officials all accepted magazines as valued cultural products. As a result, access to necessary resources was easier, which meant that barriers to entry were lower in the mid-nineteenth century. That is why people from more varied backgrounds could launch new magazines.

Professionals—especially small-town doctors and ministers—were most likely to take advantage of these opportunities. The publishing activities of these two groups underwent "antagonistic expansion" (Starr 2004: 26) as rival religious denominations and medical factions launched competing publications to criticize each other and tie their community members closer together (Hatch 1989; see also chapter 5). Because magazines became increasingly legitimate cultural goods they became an increasingly valuable venue for these religious and professional struggles. Beyond these two groups many men and women without industry connections or economic, political, or cultural distinction founded magazines in the mid-nineteenth century.

But it was not easy for potential magazine entrepreneurs in all locations to acquire the resources their new ventures needed. Instead the rise of large and powerful publishing houses in the three biggest cities—Boston, New York, and Philadelphia—meant that industry insiders (writers and members of the publishing trades) were far more likely to launch magazines in those locations. Magazine founders outside the publishing industry often worked outside these three cities; thus, any analysis that ignored location and focused exclusively on occupation and education would yield a false picture of how access to the magazine industry evolved. The rise of large publishing houses in Boston, New York, and Philadelphia may have excluded some people from launching new magazines; indeed, magazines founded in these cities in the mid-nineteenth century were likely to have worked in publishing or be college educated. But such competitive exclusion appears to have been limited in its geographic reach: in the mid-nineteenth century far more magazines were founded by publishing industry outsiders working far from these centers than by publishing industry insiders within them. Magazines with professionals among their founders were less likely to be located in these three cities in the mid-nineteenth century than in the eighteenth century. This was especially true for magazines founded by clergy: in the mid-nineteenth century magazines founded by clergy constituted 24 percent of the sample we analyzed, but only 5 percent of those were located in these three cities. All of this suggests that the greater legitimacy afforded to magazine publishing by the mid-nineteenth century allowed founders with few social, cultural, or economic resources to launch magazines more easily than they could have in the eighteenth century.

WHY WERE MAGAZINES FOUNDED?

Knowing who founded magazines at different points in history begs the question of why magazines were founded in the first place—what their founders hoped to accomplish. To answer this question I assess the espoused motivations and goals of magazine founders as written in the pages of their periodicals.

Joseph Schumpeter ([1934] 1983) argued that entrepreneurs were motivated by the dream of founding a private kingdom, the will to conquer, and the joy of creating. This argument implies the desire for power and independence, the drive to succeed, and the satisfaction of getting things done; it also implies that money per se does not motivate entrepreneurs. Much research confirms this argument: some entrepreneurs are motivated by money, others by technical or aesthetic challenges, and still others by a desire to help a particular subgroup or society at large. For instance, the motivations of American alternative energy entrepreneurs ranged from seeking profits to solving social problems by producing "green" energy (Sine, Haveman, and Tolbert 2005), while those of California winery founders focused on either money or love of their products (Scott-Morton and Podolny 2002). The founders of European sporting goods manufacturing concerns were similarly diverse in their motivations: some focused on their own economic self-interest, others viewed their organizations as supporting and being supported by a particular community, and still others viewed their organizations as benefiting society at large (Fauchart and Gruber 2011).

That entrepreneurs are often motivated by more than narrow economic self-interest should not be surprising. Research on twentieth-century firms shows that most fail quickly: 34 percent of all new ventures with employees failed after two years, 50 percent after four years, and 60 percent after six years (Headd 2001). Given these dismal figures, people who are primarily motivated by money may choose to forgo entrepreneurship and work in established firms, which have far lower failure rates. The situation facing magazine entrepreneurs from the mid-eighteenth century to the mid-nineteenth was no different from that facing other firms founded later. Magazines' median life span was short: only 0.7 years for magazines founded from the 1740s to the 1770s and a paltry 1.9 years for magazines founded in the 1840s and '50s, when the industry was thriving. Among magazines founded during this latter period, 30 percent failed in their first year and an additional 21 percent failed between their first and second year; only 28 percent survived more than five years.

Entrepreneurs' motivations—especially their public expressions of those motivations—are strongly affected by prevailing cultural mores (Mills 1939, 1940; Scott and Lyman 1968; Blum and McHugh 1936). The types of organizations that can be founded at any point in time, and the goals their founders seek to meet through these organizations, depend on the social technology available at that point in time, including cultural conceptions of what organizations can and cannot do (Stinchcombe 1965: 153). Moreover, entrepreneurs' goals for their ventures are constrained by the master rules of society—broadly accepted norms, values, and belief systems (Meyer and Rowan 1977). This suggests that the goals espoused by magazine founders will vary over time.

Tapping into Magazine Founders' Motivations

Although we have a lot of evidence about how entrepreneurs' goals vary *at any point in time*, we know little about how they vary *over time*, which is the focus of my analysis. Magazines often record their founders' motivations in the form of prospectuses and editorial statements. These documents were prepared for specific audiences—potential subscribers and contributors. The founder of one nineteenth-century magazine explained its purpose clearly, writing, "The first number of every periodical work is supposed to demand a prospectus or preface; in which the Editor is bound to explain the motives that have induced him to solicit a share of public patronage, and to unfold the general principles on which he proposes to conduct the publication" (Richards 1811: 1).

Thus, prospectuses and editorial statements reveal founders' espoused goals for their publishing ventures. They were justifications for action (Mills 1940; Scott and Lyman 1968; Swidler 2001) more than motivations to act (Vaisey 2009). Analyzing them allows me to trace magazine founders' vocabularies of motive—the language they used to explain their actions to potential readers and contributors (Mills 1940), their "institutional and political co-ordinates" (Mills 1939: 677)—and see how espoused motivations evolved over time and varied across social sectors. Appendix 2 explains the pros and cons of analyzing these documents and the method of analysis.

Despite their obvious advantages, these documents may have been biased toward expressing socially desirable goals and they may have promised more than their authors could deliver. I therefore do not assume that these documents accurately portrayed magazines' contents or their benefits for readers and contributors. Neither magazine founders nor their readers took these statements at face value. For instance, the founders of one literary monthly noted sardonically,

> The reasons . . . for publishing may be divided into three classes; first, those that are proper to be held out to the world; secondly, those which actually influence the editor; and thirdly, those that arise from the real benefit done to the community. Of the first class are those to be found in every introductory address—that the paper is intended to improve the morals, reform the manners and enlarge the understandings of its readers. Secondly, the motives of the editor are in general two, 1st, that he is too extraordinary a genius to be able to do any one thing that is useful, and 2d, that of all the various contrivances for getting people's money this is the most easily executed. 3dly, the benefit to the community consists in supplying the multiplied demand that must necessarily exist in all refined and civilized societies— for waste paper. (Prescott et al. 1820: 3–4)

Similarly, Isaiah Thomas, founder of the *Worcester Intelligencer* (1794–95), averred that magazine founders promised much but delivered little, noting that "promises of what the Editors *intend* to do, are very freely and brilliantly made, but too often fall short of performance" (Thomas 1794: 1; emphasis in the original). For this reason some magazine founders disdained showy declarations of intent.

Variation in Founders' General Motivations

I coded motivations in three general categories: to serve society at large, to serve a particular community, or to earn a profit or otherwise benefit founders. The analysis is limited to magazines founded from 1741 to 1825 because that is when these documents were available for a large fraction of magazines.

Fifty-five percent of magazines analyzed aimed to serve society, 42 percent aimed to serve a particular community, and only 5.3 percent admitted to wanting to earn a profit or otherwise benefit their founders.[10] A good example of a magazine claiming to serve society at large was the *Time Piece and Literary Companion* (1797–98), founded by Philip Freneau, who wrote that "of all modes of disseminating useful knowledge, that of periodical publications, judiciously managed, has the fairest chance to ameliorate the public mind, advance the happiness of the social State, influence the cause of virtue, obviate the intrigues of ambition; and gradually, among other progressive causes, render man that exalted character, and give him that real pre-eminence which he was evidently designed to hold on the scale of animated nature" (Freneau 1797: 1). In the same vein, Noah Webster, one of the founders of *New York Magazine* (1790–97), informed his readers that "We plead the cause of Science" and hoped by doing so to "render an essential service to society" and to "contribute greatly to diffuse knowledge throughout a community and to create in that community a taste for literature" (Webster 1790: 195–98). The founders of the first medical journal in America, the *Medical Repository* (1797–1824), were seized by the same motivation, "to enlighten our fellow-men and render them more happy" (Elihu Hubbard Smith, quoted in Bender 1987: 32). More modestly, Timothy Kennard, founder of the weekly general-interest magazine *Omnium Gatherum* (1809–10) declared his intent to attract readers of all stripes, "the old and the young, the serious and the lively, the dull or speculative reader, will here find an ample field, for both amusement and improvement" (Kennard 1809: 1).

Among those who claimed to serve a particular community were Methodist bishops Thomas Coke and Francis Asbury, who told readers of their *Arminian Magazine* (1789–90), "What we aim at is the benefit and instruction of those for whom we write and publish—the members of our own society" (Coke and Asbury 1789: iv). Similarly, Alexander Ming, founder of the *Weekly Visitor and Ladies' Museum* (1817–23), declared his intention to benefit "the ladies", as he sought to "portray the beauties of virtue and expose the hideous deformities of vice; to preserve the morals, improve the mind, and divert the leisure hours of the female portion of society" (Ming 1817: 16). Finally, the founder-publisher of the *American Museum and Repository of Arts and Sciences* (1822–23) announced that his magazine "will be peculiarly well adapted for patentees and inventors, to make known their discoveries and improvements" (Milligan 1822: 1).

The first founder to explicitly mention seeking to profit from his magazine was Ezekiel Russell, publisher of the *Censor* (1771–72), who stated plainly that "the common motive of a printer [is] that of procuring an honest support" (Russell 1771: 1). Similarly, the founders of the *Massachusetts*

[10] For a tiny fraction of magazines (2.5 percent), I was unable to assign motivations to any of these categories. For a few magazines (5.7 percent), these documents indicated two motivations—usually profit plus service to society at large or to a particular community.

Magazine (1789–96) listed both financial and reputational benefits as reasons for launching their periodical "by this means to aid ourselves in getting an honest living, with a hope of procuring, in proper time, some reputation in the way of our profession" (Thomas, Andrews, and Sprague 1788: 8). Such a declaration of self-interest did not hurt them—their magazine survived seven full years. A quarter century later, Methodist minister Saul Henkle described the "pecuniary, moral, and intellectual benefit"(1823: 1) he hoped to derive from his *Gospel Trumpet.* It is notable that this statement appeared in the first sentence of his magazine, even before he described its benefits for his fellow congregants.

Magazine founders' general reluctance to discuss self-interested motivations like earning money or cultivating a reputation is not surprising, since these were still relatively new and little-known cultural products. Downplaying selfishness and displaying selflessness instead can help founders of new kinds of organizations, like magazines in the eighteenth and early nineteenth centuries, overcome the risk of being seen as disingenuous, which would lead others to shun their ventures as morally suspect (Fligstein 2001; David, Sine, and Haveman 2013). To avoid the "self-promoter's paradox" (Ashforth and Gibbs 1990; Suchman 1995), founders of new kinds of organizations must appeal to the greater good or place society's or customers' interests above their own. Doing so imparts "normative dignity" (Berger and Luckmann 1967: 93; Fligstein 2001) or "moral legitimacy" (Suchman 1995) by demonstrating that entrepreneurs' actions are undergirded by a prosocial logic and a rejection of narrow self-interest. This tendency is exemplified by Philip Freneau, founder-editor of the *Time Piece and Literary Companion* (1797–1798), who noted that "the editor has determined to undertake his proposed work, not with partial, mercenary, or altogether selfish views but from a conviction that of all modes of disseminating useful knowledge, that of periodical publications, judiciously managed, has the fairest chance to ameliorate the public mind, advance the happiness of the social State, influence the cause of virtue, obviate the intrigues of ambition; and gradually, . . . render man that exalted character, and give him that real preeminence which he was evidently designed to hold on the scale of animated nature" (Freneau 1797: 1). A few entrepreneurs (4.0 percent) sought to convincingly demonstrate selflessness by promising that any profits their magazines earned would go to good causes. For example, as the founders of the *Arminian Magazine* announced, "We do assure the subscribers that the work is undertaken purely to promote the glory of God, and their edification. The profits arising therefrom shall be applied as the wisdom of the [Methodist] Conference shall direct; in carrying on, for instance, our plan of Christian education, or in sending missionaries among the Indians and opening schools for their children" (Coke and Asbury 1789: vi).

The desire to appear selfless led magazine founders to communicate pecuniary concerns to readers indirectly. Most frequently they mentioned the need to have enough subscribers to cover production costs and to have those subscribers pay on time. For example, Joseph Dennie, founder-editor of the *Port-Folio* (1801–27), went on at length about the necessity of putting a magazine on sound financial footing:

> A paper to be advantageously edited, must be liberally supported. The compositor *must* be requited for his mechanical toil, the publisher *must* be compensated for his cares and risque; and the conductor, if competent to his highly responsible duties, has a claim to what an ancient author, who well knew the value of literary service calls the 'quiddam honorarium', the generous stipend for mental efforts, not the paltry wages of a vulgar hireling. If an industrious and high minded man thus situated, received only a servant's price of labour, he will quickly sink to the level of the mercenary fugitive in the gospel. He will flee from or neglect his duty, because he is an *hireling*. Literary industry, usefully employed, has a sort of draught upon the bank of opulence, and has the right of entry into the mansion of every Mæcenas [Roman patron of the arts]. (Dennie 1801: n. 5; emphasis in the original)

Similarly, Richard Henry Dana, founder of the *Idle Man* (1821–22) explained, "I am not rich enough to write for mere amusement; so that if not paid for what I do, I must stop" (Dana 1821: 8). Thus, although magazine founders may have seldom stated their desire to earn profits from their ventures, they were very often explicit in their concerns about magazine finances.

Temporal Shifts in Founders' Motivations

Figure 4.2 shows trends over time. The data are grouped into five periods: 1741–83 (the colonial and Revolutionary eras), 1784–1800 (the early republic), 1801–10, 1811–20, and 1821–25. The fraction of magazine founders espousing to serve society at large fell by more than half, from 82 percent during the years 1741–83 to 38 percent during the years 1821–25. Over the same span of time the fraction of magazine founders espousing to serve a particular community trebled, from 18 percent to 61 percent. Finally, the fraction admitting to being motivated by profit or other forms of self-interest fluctuated between 3 percent and 9 percent, with no obvious time trend.

Figure 4.3 shows the distribution of types of communities magazines claimed to serve between 1741 and 1825, while figure 4.4 shows trends over time for each type of community. Most common was a geographic community (ranging in scope from all of America to a single town), which 15 percent of magazines claimed to serve. Almost as common was a religious community, which 14 percent of magazines claimed to serve. Less common community types were demographic, meaning children, students, women, or members of racial, ethnic, or linguistic groups (7.4 percent); occupational (5.5 percent); and political (2.5 percent), including both organized political parties and informal factions).[11] Finally, 1.9 percent of magazines claimed to serve

---

[11] The paucity of political magazines is likely due to the fact that partisan newspapers were available to discuss politics and public policy. Also, most social reform magazines had politi-

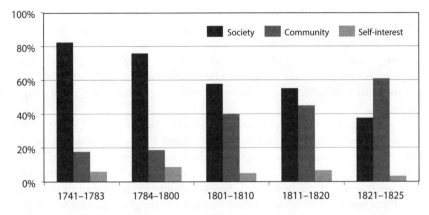

Figure 4.2. Trends in magazine founders' motivations, 1741–1825, by period.

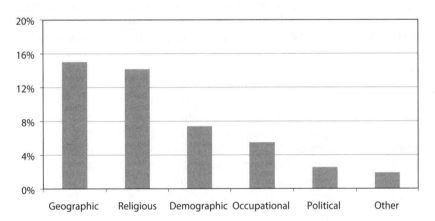

Figure 4.3. Type of community served by magazines founded 1741–1825.

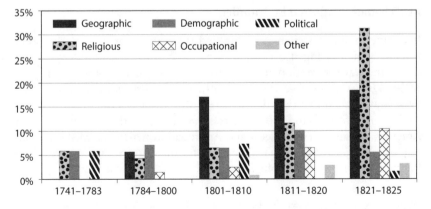

Figure 4.4. Trends in type of community served by magazines founded 1741–1825, by period.

members of a particular organization—usually a fraternal order or a social reform society. Although almost equal fractions of magazines claimed to serve particular geographic and religious communities, and both types of claim became more common as time passed, claims of service to particular geographic communities outnumbered claims of service to particular religious groups until 1820, after which claims of service to particular religious groups exploded.

Taken together these figures suggest that magazines started out as symbols of the unification of the thirteen colonies (later, states) into a single society but later came to reflect divisions in this society along geographic, religious, demographic, occupational, and political grounds. They also suggest that religion became an increasingly salient axis of difference in American society, a trend that was driven and supported by the increasingly broad array of faiths in the field of American religion, which I will discuss in chapter 5. These figures also reflect the appearance of specialized magazines serving members of the nation's increasingly complex occupational structure, which I will probe in chapter 7. More generally these figures reveal the many different types of modern, translocal communities that were fostered by magazines, as well as the regional (and often traditionalistic) communities of place that were sustained by magazines.

The shift to serving particular communities complemented magazines' original unifying function, rather than replaced it: there was no clear geographic differentiation between general-interest and specialist magazines. These types of magazines were equally likely to be published in the industry's geographic core (Boston, New York, and Philadelphia) as within the industry's periphery: a cross-tabulation of generalist/specialist genre and core/peripheral location showed no significant pattern ($\chi^2 = .438, p = .508$). Thus, the members of many different religious communities, whose internal bonds were reinforced by magazines targeting their particular denominations, might still find common ground in their reading of the same general-interest magazines.

Key Themes Explicated by Founders

Magazine founders' statements addressed many different themes, the prevalence of which changed over time. Some early magazine founders had observed the warm reception accorded to British magazines—for example, the *Tatler* (1709–11), the *Spectator* (1711–14), and *Gentleman's Magazine* (1731–1914)—and stated that they desired to emulate those examples. For instance, Andrew Bradford, founder of the *American Magazine*, the first published in America, declared, "The Success and Approbation which the MAGAZINES, published in *Great-Britain*, have met with for many Years past, among all the Ranks and Degrees of People, *Encouraged* us to Attempt a Work of the like

---

cal overtones, so many debates about politics and public policy were carried in social reform magazines.

Nature in *America*" (Bradford 1740: 1; emphasis in the original). Such a strong connection to the British press should not be surprising, for these Americans were originally British subjects and most were descended from British subjects; they took pride in their heritage and admired their mother country's culture (Fischer 1989). As Benjamin Davies, founder of the *Philadelphia Magazine and Review* (1799), explained, "America is, and long must be beholden, in a very considerable degree, to the presses of Great Britain. The literature of the two countries is, indeed, a sort of common stock; but, for one publication of ours, we receive, at least, five hundred in return" (Davies 1799: ii).

While they recognized the value of British publications, some American entrepreneurs averred that British periodicals did not provide adequate coverage of American affairs. William Smith, founder of the *American Magazine and Monthly Chronicle* (1757–58) put this most plainly: "It has long been a matter of just complaint among some of the best friends of our national commerce and safety that the important concerns of these colonies were but little studied and less understood in the mother country ... it is complained that the difficulty of acquiring any tolerable notion of American affairs has been discouraging to many" (Smith 1757: 3). Entrepreneurs like Smith sought to provide locally relevant alternatives to British magazines by publishing local government proceedings, accounts of American religious revivals, essays on local politics, letters from travelers to the frontier, and information about Atlantic and Caribbean trade. Still, the way American magazines covered the politics, economy, religion, and social life in the British colonies and the early republic was similar in all respects to the way British periodicals of that era covered Great Britain. Ironically, as American magazines came over time to focus more on American politics, commerce, and culture, some entrepreneurs were moved to publish magazines, like *Shamrock* (1810–25) and *Albion* (1822–75), that covered affairs in Britain. These divergent trends show the constant push toward and pull away from a common American social center that magazines reflected and supported.

Notwithstanding American magazines' common resemblance to British ones, many American entrepreneurs, even in the colonial era, viewed their periodicals as keystones of political freedom. For instance, the preface to Smith's *American Magazine* proclaimed that "we shall think it our duty to give our readers such an authentic account of every thing relating to their own happiness and safety, as a *free people* have a right to expect" and went on to promise that the essays published would promote "a *love of LIBERTY* and our *excellent constitution*" (Smith 1757: 3–4; emphasis in the original). Similarly, Ezekiel Russell, editor of *The Censor* (1771–72) proclaimed that he himself was "a hearty friend to his country, and as warm a lover of that constitutional liberty which is the birth-right of a British subject" (Russell 1771: 5). Thus from the start, magazines were designed to contribute to the public sphere by strengthening democratic politics. This sentiment only intensified during the Revolution, when magazines emphasized the importance of instilling civic virtues in all citizens. For instance, founder-editor Hugh Henry Brackenridge of the *United States Magazine* (1779) argued that "in these United States, the path to office and preferment lies open to every individual. The mechanic of the city, or the husbandman who ploughs his farm by the river's bank, has it in his power to become, one day, the first magistrate of his respective commonwealth, or to fill a seat in the Continental Congress. This happy circumstance lays an obligation upon every individual to exert a double industry to qualify himself for the great trust which may, one day, be reposed upon him" (Brackenridge 1779b: 9).

During and after the Revolution magazines sought to showcase distinctly American ingenuity and talent and to forge a national identity. One prominent example is Noah Webster's *American Magazine* (1787–88), which he launched to promote a uniquely "American" language and literature, declaring that "America must be as independent in *literature* as she is in *Politics*, as famous for *arts* as for *arms*" (quoted in Warfel 1953: 1–4; emphasis in the original), which echoed Webster's goal, with his spelling and grammar book, "to add superior dignity to this infant Empire" (Webster [1783] 2011: n.p.). Similarly, Brackenridge took his inspiration from Revolutionary War–era essayists and hoped to add to that legacy, writing, "The British officers ... on perusal of our pamphlets in the course of the debate [about American independence], and the essays and dissertations in the newspapers, have been forced to acknowledge, not without chagrin, that the rebels, as they are pleased to call us, had some *damn'd* good writers ... and that we had fought them no less successfully with the pen than with the sword. We hope to convince them yet more fully, that we are able to cultivate the *belles-lettres*, even disconnected with Great-Britain" (Brackenridge 1779a: 3–4; emphasis in the original). Webster and Brackenridge were joined in their quest to promote American literary nationalism by many others—notably, Shepard Kollock and David Austin (both were involved in the *Christian's, Scholar's, and Farmer's Magazine* [1789–91]; Austin also launched *American Preacher* [1791–92]), Charles Brockden Brown (*Monthly Magazine and American Review* [1799–1800], *American Review and Literary Journal* [1801–02], *Literary Magazine and American Register* [1803–7], and *American Register* [1807–10]), Mathew Carey (*Columbian Magazine* [1786–90], *American Museum* [1787–92], and Samuel Harrison Smith (*American Monthly Review* [1795] and *American Universal Magazine* [1797–98]). As the analysis of magazine titles in chapter 3 suggested, such patriotic, unifying goals were often signaled by titles that contained universalistic toponyms like *American* or *Columbian*.

How Did Magazines Gain Public Support?

Having explained who founded American magazines and why, I will now discuss the strategies magazines used as they struggled to overcome an initial dearth of legitimacy.[12] As Noah Webster, founder-editor of the *American Maga-*

---

[12] A portion of this material is revised from "Antebellum Literary Culture and the Evolution of American Magazines" (Haveman 2004).

zine (1787–88) lamented, "The expectation of failure is connected with the very name of a Magazine" (1788: 130). My focus here is on how magazine founders wooed subscribers, their main source of financial support (Mott 1930; Richardson 1931), to overcome this dismal expectation of failure. As with the analysis of magazine founders' motivations, the analysis presented below is based on perusal of magazines founded from 1741 to 1825 because the archives are relatively complete for that period.

Magazines founders sought to increase their chances of success by publishing reading matter that would stand the test of time—or, at least that they believed would do so. For instance, the preface to the *American Magazine and Monthly Chronicle* (1757–58) drew a clear distinction between newspapers and magazines, and characterized magazines as durable publications:

> It is evident, then, that an undertaking calculated to give persons at a distance a just idea of the public state of the American colonies, or to give one colony an idea of the public state of another, must be something executed on a different plan from common gazettes, and which will by no means interfere with their design, nor limit them in their circulation and use. In short, it must be something that is durable in its nature, and convenient for being transmitted and preserved entire, for future as well as present reading. (Smith 1757: 4)

To emphasize the lasting value of their magazines, many publishers offered late-arriving readers the opportunity to purchase back issues. For instance, the cover page of the *American Magazine and Monthly Chronicle* listed the locations where it was for sale and declared, "There may be had compleat SETTS from the Beginning." Similarly, the editor-publishers of the *New Haven Gazette* (1786–89) stated that they would print extra copies of the early issues of the first volume and hold them for late-arriving subscribers (Meigs and Dana 1786: iv). And Benjamin Lundy, founder of the antislavery monthly *Genius of Universal Emancipation* (1821–39), offered subscribers a title page and index for each twelve-issue volume, declaring that "the printing will be neatly executed, that it may be an object to file the numbers and have them bound" (Lundy 1821: 3). Magazine proprietors were not alone in thinking that their publications had lasting value; for example, one subscriber to the *Genesee Farmer* (1831–39) wrote that this magazine "ought to be preserved by every subscriber ... for binding at the close of the volume, thus furnishing every farmer with a cheap and beautiful '*text book*' ... of 416 pages" (Burdick 1838: 173; emphasis in the original).

In addition to publishing material of longer-lasting interest than was available in newspapers, magazines were also physically superior to newspapers—or so their publishers argued. For instance, the *Arminian Magazine* (1789–90) noted in the preface to its second volume that because the binding was of good quality, "this Magazine may serve the next generation" (Asbury 1790: iv). But entrepreneurs often found it difficult to achieve their goals of producing long-lasting publications; for example, although Mathew Carey, editor and publisher of *American Museum* (1787–92), conceived of his magazine as a vehicle whose physical medium would be kept for many years because its contents had lasting value, he complained about the perishable nature of newspaper stock that he was forced to use.

As new kinds of cultural goods, the earliest American magazines were precarious ventures that required considerable explanation and exhortation.[13] Andrew Bradford's *American Magazine*, for example, began with eight pages detailing what it would and would not contain. Similarly, Hugh Henry Brackenridge described the contents of his *United States Magazine* in detail:

> It will contain the writings of the sage historian; it will convey the thoughts, remarks, proposals, theories and reasonings of the politician; it will collect the genuine letters of the hero, or the statesman; it will communicate the observations of the curious traveller; it will unfold the new discoveries of philosophers; it will disclose the avenues of trade and commerce; it will record proceedings in the courts of justice; it will select from late and curious publications; it will comprize [*sic*] the most remarkable events in Europe and America; in short, will comprehend a great variety of matter, on a great variety of subjects. Instruction will appear in every shape of essays, sketches, schemes, tracts, and dissertations. (Brackenridge 1779b: 9–10)

Such lengthy explanations of magazine contents continued in the first decades of the nineteenth century. For instance, Joseph Tinker Buckingham described his literary miscellany *Comet* (1811–12) thus: "As we should not ask a lady or gentleman to take supper with us, without first giving a bill of fare, so we hold it meet to inform the purchaser of this work, that it is intended to contain essays, literary, critical and moral; biographical sketches of eminent characters; interesting anecdotes, aphorisms, and maxims; strictures on the stage, with notices of new plays and performances; notices of other publick amusements; poetry; new publications, &c &c" (Buckingham 1811: 1–2). The even more detailed description of the *Christian Examiner* (1824–69) took up one page of its four-page preface, while that of the *Literary Gazette* (1821) took up two pages of its four-page prospectus. But some nineteenth-century magazine founders perceived that magazines' growing legitimacy reduced, if it did not completely eliminate, the need for such involved introductions. As Rev. Ebenezer Chase, founder of the *Religious Informer* (1819–30) averred, "A lengthy address will be unnecessary at this time. The public are generally convinced of the propriety of circulating Religious Intelligence." (Chase 1819: 6)

Explanation was a simpler matter to resolve than exhortation, however. Because eighteenth-century Americans produced most of what they consumed and purchased little—certainly very little that was designed, like maga-

---

[13] Magazine founders were well aware of the difficulties that faced them. Indeed, many had faced those difficulties in the past, for many were involved with several publishing ventures. For instance, Isaiah Thomas listed, in the first several issues of his *Worcester Magazine*, notices demanding payment from delinquent subscribers to his previous venture, the defunct newspaper *Massachusetts Spy*.

zines, to be of temporary use—the earliest magazines found it difficult to attract and keep subscribers. For example, the introduction to the *American Magazine and Historical Chronicle* (1743–46) stated that the founders "have not as yet such a Number of Subscribers as are sufficient to support [the magazine]" but then declared optimistically that they were "not doubting that if the Design be well executed, further Encouragement will arise hereafter" (Eliot and Blanchard 1743: i–ii). Some entrepreneurs rushed in with only the merest hope of developing a large enough audience to make their publications viable—and admitted this in print. For example, James Parker and William Weyman advertised, below the masthead of the *Instructor* (1755), that their magazine was "To be continued Weekly (*if suitable Encouragement*)" (emphasis in the original). Similarly, the publisher of the *New York Missionary Magazine* (1800–1803) hoped that "a generous public will not permit such an undertaking to be frustrated for want of pecuniary support" (Swords and Swords 1800: 5). And the founding editor of the *Presbyterian Magazine* (1821–22) lamented that "our subscription list is, at present, scarcely sufficient to enable us to defray the necessary expenses of the publication" (Neill 1822: 45) Finally, the editors of the *Boston Journal of Philosophy and the Arts* (1823–26) complained at the end of their first volume that they had too few subscribers to make their publication as interesting or useful as it could be.

Other magazine founders claimed to be optimistic about the fates of their magazines because they believed in their publications' innate usefulness. Consider these statements, both taken from magazines launched in the eighteenth century, when there was immense uncertainty about the value of these novel cultural goods and most survived less than a single year:

> The Editor is very conscious of the difficulties attending the establishment of a publication of this nature. It has frequently been attempted, and notwithstanding the aid of an extensive circulation, they have as frequently been dropt, although some of them may vie with most works of the kind that have been attempted, and have been marked with universal approbation; he, however, is confident, that he enters a field, where there is still abundant room for public favour arising from obvious utility. (Condie 1798: 4–5)

> A Lady paper [magazine for women] is a novelty in this part of the country [Connecticut], and many will predict that it cannot be supported; but I find there is taste enough among the ladies to encourage a work of this kind, and hope there is spirit enough to keep such a work from sinking, if properly conducted. (Beach 1798: 2)

Their optimism was misplaced, as both magazines expired less than a year after founding. Despite magazines' high failure rate, later entrepreneurs were often equally hopeful. For instance, the founder of the *United States Literary Gazette* (1824–26) declared confidently, "We do ... expect success, because we are confident in our ability to make a Literary Gazette, which shall be *highly useful* to the reading public of this country" and stated that "we hope to supply an existing demand" (Parson 1824: 1; emphasis in the original).

A few entrepreneurs—luckier, more risk-averse, or more skillful than those who depended on chance—secured enough subscriptions before launching their periodicals to make a go of it for at least one year. For instance, Cornelius Davis, founding editor of the *Theological Magazine* (1795–99) stated that he was prompted to launch this publication because "many respectable characters" encouraged him and "promised their assistance" (Davis 1796: n.p.). Indeed, some calls for subscriptions greatly exceeded expectations; for instance, the founders of *Christian's, Scholar's, and Farmer's Magazine* (1789–91) declared in the introduction to their first issue, "The Encouragement that hath been given to publish this Magazine, enables the Proprietors to reduce the Price of it from two and one-half Dollars, to two Dollars per Annum" (Kollock and Austin 1789b: n.p.). And Thomas Skillman, founder of the Presbyterian weekly *Western Luminary* (1824–35) trumpeted his base of support, writing, "It affords us hearty pleasure ... to be enabled to announce a considerable and growing patronage to this enterprize [*sic*], from the most respectable portion of the population of our own and several adjoining states" (Skillman 1824: 2).

Many magazine founders claimed legitimacy by printing lists of subscribers. In what was perhaps the most crass attempt to demonstrate legitimacy, Mathew Carey's *American Museum* (1787–92) devoted twelve precious pages (out of eighty-eight) up front (even before the introduction for readers!) to a list of subscribers, starting with president George Washington, his mentor Benjamin Franklin, and Virginia governor Edmond Randolph. His list of 404 subscribers highlighted some forty-two members of the American Philosophical Society, twenty-seven delegates to the Constitutional Convention, twenty-eight other high-ranking government officials (including Thomas Jefferson, US ambassador to France), and nine college professors and high-ranking clergymen. Carey's rather unsubtle plea for legitimacy worked: his magazine was one of the most successful of the eighteenth century (Mott 1930; Charvat 1968), eventually enrolling 1,250 subscribers, more than double the 600 that prominent printer-publisher Isaiah Thomas estimated in 1775 was required for an eighteenth-century periodical to break even (Schlesinger 1958: 304), and producing twelve complete semiannual volumes, thus lasting far longer than other eighteenth-century magazines. This practice of claiming legitimacy by printing lists of subscribers continued into the nineteenth century; for example, the *Ladies' Literary Museum* (1817–25) printed a two-page list of subscribers in its first issue.

Printing subscriber registries had the effect of making observable the "invisible communities" (Park 1940) of subscribers, solidifying the bonds between them and enticing outsiders to join them. Several magazines, including the *Ladies' Literary Museum*, listed the municipality in which each subscriber lived, along with her name, thereby demonstrating the geographic scope of their invisible communities—in this case, from Burlington, New Jersey, to

Richmond, Virginia. Even specialized magazines that targeted the members of a single profession sought to build subscriber lists through this kinds of legitimating tactic: *New York Magazine* (1790–97) highlighted president George Washington and vice president John Adams at the top of its three-page roll call of subscribers in its inaugural issue; the *Monthly Military Repository* (1796–97) recorded subscribers on six pages at the end of its first issue; and the *Medical Repository* (1797–1824) listed subscribers on eight pages at the front of its first issue.

Another common legitimating tactic involved printing letters from luminaries to prove their publications' value. For instance, John Wood, founder of *United States Magazine* (1794), printed "recommendations" from the governor of New Jersey and two prominent Presbyterian ministers, expressing approval and pleasure in the inaugural issue. In a rather obvious attempt to curry favor, the founders of the *Christian's, Scholar's, and Farmer's Magazine* (1789–91), dedicated their periodical to William Livingston, governor of New Jersey, declaring "with great Esteem and Respect, Inscribed By his Excellency's most obedient, and very humble Servants" (Kollock and Austin 1789a: 3); they placed this dedication before the preface explaining their magazine's goals.

The need to legitimate magazines through endorsement by notables continued to be felt in the nineteenth century. For example, the Catholic monthly *Gospel Advocate* (1821–26) printed it its first issue an endorsement signed by eleven prominent clerics; the Congregationalist-Presbyterian journal *Evangelist* (1824–25) listed the names of twenty-two ministers in the Hartford, Connecticut, area who supported it; the Episcopalian *Gospel Messenger and Southern Christian Messenger* (1824–53) was endorsed by the bishops of the church in North and South Carolina; and *Odd Fellows' Magazine* (1825–26) was "recommended" by six prominent members of this fraternal lodge. The *African Repository and Colonial Journal* (1825–92), which was affiliated with the American Colonization Society, trumpeted support from the national governing bodies of the Presbyterian, Baptist, Episcopal, and Methodist churches, seven state legislatures (from New Hampshire south to Georgia and west to Ohio), members of the federal government, and several well-known literary, religious, and political magazines, including the venerable *North American Review* (R. T____x 1825: 6). In the same spirit, the *Journal of Jurisprudence* (1821) printed testimonials from four other magazines in its inaugural issue.

Such endorsement allowed magazine founders to "borrow" status from the prominent people who vouched for them and their publications. Much research has shown that status is contagious: ties to high-status others create halos that imbue entrepreneurs' activities with normative and pragmatic legitimacy (Crane 1965; Merton 1968; Podolny 1993). When readers and contributors assess the value of a new social arrangement, like magazines, they often rely on easily observed signals, such as the status and legitimacy of its affiliates (DiMaggio 1982; Granovetter and McGuire 1998; David, Sine, and Haveman 2013). The testimonials in the inaugural issues of the *African Repository* and *Journal of Jurisprudence* discussed above reveal that by the 1820s the magazine industry had become so accepted that existing magazines could provide meaningful support for new ones.

CONCLUSION

This chapter has shown just who magazine founders were and how the backgrounds from which they were drawn changed as the industry developed. The men who founded magazines in the eighteenth century—when they were a novel cultural product, their audience was uncertain, and production and distribution were difficult,—had high social status. But by the mid-nineteenth century, when magazines were an established part of American cultural and social life, their founders had become much more varied in status, including free blacks, recent immigrants, members of upstart medical sects, backwoods literati, women, and children.

This chapter has also revealed that magazine founders' goals for their new publications were highly varied. Most entrepreneurs asserted that they sought to benefit society at large or support a particular community. Only a tiny fraction admitted that they sought to earn a profit or otherwise benefit themselves. Indeed, some entrepreneurs sought to demonstrate selflessness by promising that any profits their magazines earned would go to a good cause. The founders' motivations shifted over time: magazines started out as symbols of the unification of the colonies (then states) into a single society, but later came to reflect social divisions along geographic, religious, demographic, occupational, and political grounds. Thus magazines increasingly sought to support the highly differentiated subgroups that developed as America modernized.

The chapter concluded by describing the tactics that magazine founders deployed a wide array of tactics to gain legitimacy and support from subscribers. Most commonly, magazine founders described in detail what their publications would contain and made extravagant claims about why their publications would be of enduring value; they also highlighted their ties to prominent others and published endorsements from prominent people, which allowed them and their fledgling publications to "borrow" status. Finally these founders strived for legitimacy by making observable the "invisible communities" (Park 1940) of subscribers by printing their subscription lists.

CHAPTER 5

Religion

*T*his chapter, and the two that follow it, examine the interplay between magazines and three sectors of eighteenth- and nineteenth-century American society—here religion, later social reform and the economy. In all of these chapters my primary focus is on how the growing number and variety of magazines supported and channeled community building in America—especially the translocal communities that were a big part of how this society became more modern. I recognize, however, that magazines both shape their surroundings and are shaped by them; therefore, in all three chapters, I attend to how trends in American society affected magazines.

I begin this chapter by describing how the field of American religion evolved from 1740 to 1860. After that, I discuss the interplay between religious events and institutions, on the one hand, and religious magazines on the other. I conclude by discussing how the proliferation of religious magazines affected the rest of the magazine industry.

The Changing Face of American Religion

The 120 years from 1740 to 1860 saw great tumult and rapid growth in American religion. First and foremost, the number of distinct religious groups increased due to the disestablishment of state religions, several waves of immigration, and three series of religious revivals. Religious diversity spurred larger numbers of people to participate actively in religious services, reducing the ranks of the "unchurched." Such diversity also increased competition among faiths, which involved ideological struggles over theological tenets and organizing principles as well as strategic rivalry over members. Second, in the early nineteenth century the several regional religious fields became increasingly interdependent and formed a single national field. Westward migration and energetic recruitment efforts left many religious communities with growing numbers of increasingly widespread congregations. To bind congregations into strong communities of faith, most religious groups built national organizational structures, often with nested regional and local subunits. Third, despite their centralizing efforts, religious communities also fragmented repeatedly through schisms spurred by evangelic challengers and the debate over slavery. In this section I will first describe increasing religious diversity, and then explain both the centripetal pull toward national religious organizations and centrifugal drives toward many different communities of faith.

The Rise of Religious Diversity

Nine of the thirteen British colonies had established (state-sanctioned and state-supported) churches as of 1776: the Anglican Church in the Carolinas, Georgia, Maryland, New York, and Virginia, and the Congregational Church in Connecticut, Massachusetts, and New Hampshire. The colonies were also home to a wide array of dissenting faiths, which were quite heterogeneous in terms of ethnicity and theology. Their ranks included English Seventh-Day Baptists, Quakers, and Catholics; Scottish and Irish Presbyterians, Quakers, and Catholics; German Lutherans, Mennonites, Dunkers, Moravians, Seventh-Day Baptists, and Schwenckfelders; Dutch and German Reformed; French Huguenots; several kinds of Swiss Protestants; and Sephardic Jews (Ahlstrom 1972). Across the nine colonies with established churches, dissenting congregations constituted over half of the total number (Finke and Stark 1992: 277–88). In Georgia, New York, and North Carolina dissenting congregations outnumbered the established Anglican Church more than five to one. Even in the Massachusetts Bay Colony, which was the closest thing to a theocracy in colonial America, dissenting congregations constituted almost a quarter of the total churches in 1776.

After the Revolution gradual disestablishment, starting with New York in 1777 and ending with Massachusetts in 1833, leveled the playing field in the competition for souls. The Anglican (later Episcopalian) Church was profoundly harmed by losing its position as an established church. Its situation was exacerbated by the loss of most of its priests and missionaries, who returned to England en masse, and tens of thousands of its loyalist adherents, who moved to Upper Canada during and after the Revolution. Even worse, many who remained were viewed with suspicion as British loyalists. Because the Congregational Church also lost its position as an established church, its membership became increasingly nominal (Ahlstrom 1972), but this denomination was better off than the Anglican because Congregational leaders and adherents were identified with the patriots, not the loyalists. More broadly, disestablishment made all denominations voluntary organizations: rather than compel membership they had to entice it (Smith 1962; Ahlstrom 1972; Goen 1985; Finke and Stark 1992). In addition to adjusting to this voluntary status, American churches had to work to construct sovereign religious organizations and dismantle those, like the Anglican, Dutch Reformed, and Moravian churches, that were subordinate to foreign powers. Thus, after 1783 religion became American as it had not been before the Revolution.

Waves of immigration—notably, of Irish Catholics and of German Lutherans, Anabaptists, and Catholics—further increased religious diversity (Niebuhr 1929; Ahlstrom 1972). Perhaps more important were three waves of religious revivals that swept across America in 1738–776, 1790–1845, and 1857–61

(Smith 1957; Ahlstrom 1972; Carwardine 1978, 1993; Hatch 1989; Butler 1990; Long 1998). Revivals, which remain common today, are emotionally charged meetings where fiery preachers thunder at large crowds of believers and potential converts; they take place at both regular church services and specially planned events. In this era they occurred in three stages, commonly called the Great Awakenings.[1] The First Great Awakening began in 1738 with the itinerant preaching of the Methodist George Whitefield in Georgia; he later traveled to New Jersey, New York, Pennsylvania, throughout New England, and as far south as the Carolinas, attracting crowds of up to 20,000. He was succeeded by a host of others—most notably, Presbyterian theologian Jonathan Edwards, Presbyterian preacher Gilbert Tennent, and Congregationalist wild man James Davenport. In the South the First Great Awakening was more a missionary effort involving outreach to the unchurched than a revival of lapsed faith (Ahlstrom 1972: 315); it occurred primarily in the years 1742–43 for the Presbyterians, 1754–76 for the Baptists, and 1763–76 for the Episcopalians and Methodists.

The Second Great Awakening grew out of the first (Ahlstrom 1972: 289). It began in the early 1790s and continued, in different locations, until the mid-1840s. Between 1797 and 1801 it surged in Congregational churches all over New England, then ebbed, only to resurge several times between 1815 and 1831. Charles Grandison Finney led revivals in Congregational and Presbyterian churches in western New York (the "burned-over district") from 1824 to 1832; itinerant preachers of many stripes followed in his wake. In Kentucky, Tennessee, and southern Ohio, revivals started in 1799 and lasted until the late 1830s (in a few places, until the mid-1840s), involving mostly Baptists, Methodists and, to a lesser extent, Presbyterians.

The smaller Third Great Awakening ran from 1857 to 1861 (Smith 1957; Carwardine 1978; Long 1998). Unlike its predecessors it was driven by laypeople rather than clergy and emphasized close connections between personal salvation and "benevolence" (Smith 1957). In 1857 revivals broke out in several cities—Baltimore, Cincinnati, New York, and Providence, Rhode Island—and scores of towns in New England; the next year, revivalist fervor spread throughout the Northeast and the frontier states, and then died down after the Civil War broke out. This wave of revivals involved all major denominations, including the Baptist, Congregationalist, Lutheran, and Methodist.

---

[1] Historians have long debated whether the Great Awakenings were truly coherent phenomena. Some argue that the incidence of revivals was not much higher during the years encompassing these awakenings than during other years; hence, they were not especially pronounced outbursts of religious (re)conversion (e.g., Butler 1982: 1990). For example, the First Great Awakening was preceded by sixty years' worth of revivals in Northampton, Massachusetts (c. 1670 to 1732), and by a series of revivals in Connecticut in 1721. Others recognize the Great Awakenings as social facts and have ascribed their causes to cycles that are deeply rooted in American society (e.g., McLoughlin 1978) or to secular trends (e.g., Smith 1957; Ahlstrom 1972; Lambert 1999). I take no stand in this debate, as I am concerned with specific religious events and institutions: the occurrence of religious revivals and the growth of new religious communities.

 # Colonies/states/territories where revivals occurred each year

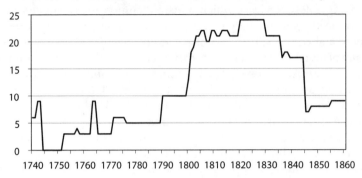

Figure 5.1. Number of colonies/states/territories where revivals occurred, 1740–1860.

Note: These counts are based on readings of a comprehensive history of American religion (Ahlstrom 1972) and several histories of revivals (Beardsley 1912; Smith 1957; Rossel 1970; Carwardine 1978; Hatch 1989; Crawford 1991; Lambert 1999; Hankins 2004).

To show how widespread revivals were, figure 5.1, which is based on several histories of revivals, plots the number of locations (mostly colonies or states, sometimes organized territories) that experienced at least one revival each year from 1740 to 1860. Revivals became increasingly widespread between 1740 and 1743, during the initial stages of the First Great Awakening, and then declined. They resurged in many locations after 1750. The number of colonies experiencing revivals peaked at nine in the early 1740s (concentrated in New England) and again in the 1760s (concentrated in the South). Revivals continued in a few locations through the Revolutionary War and beyond, mostly in the South and on the frontier. Revival activity increased again in 1790 at the start of the Second Great Awakening. The number of locations experiencing revivals peaked in the late 1820s at twenty-one out of twenty-four states, plus three territories; after this date, revival activity declined to a moderate level. This graph shows clearly that revivals had become a standard weapon in the "tool kit" (Swidler 1986) of American religious leaders, one that did not fade from use even after the end of the Second Great Awakening (Miller 1965). Indeed, professional revivalists made careers out of leading these events (Smith 1957: 47–49; Mathews 1969).

The Second Great Awakening saw the emergence of a new form of revival, the camp meeting, an enthusiastic multiday service held outdoors for crowds who ate and slept on the spot because they were far from home. Consider these eyewitness reports of the Cane Ridge camp meeting, held August 6–12, 1801, which served as a template for many later revivals:

The noise was like the roar of Niagara. The vast sea of human beings seemed to be agitated as if by a storm. I counted seven ministers, all preaching at one time, some on stumps, others in wagons and one standing on a tree which had, in falling, lodged against another. ... At one time I saw at least *five hundred* swept down in a moment as if a battery of a thousand guns had been opened upon them, and then immediately followed shrieks and shouts that rent the very heavens. (James B. Finley, quoted in Taylor 1964: 461; emphasis in the original)

Here were collected all the elements calculated to affect the imagination. The spectacle presented at night was one of the wildest grandeur. The glare of the blazing camp-fires falling on a dense assemblage of heads simultaneously bowed in adoration and reflected back from long ranges of tents upon every side; hundreds of candles and lamps suspended among the trees, together with numerous torches flashing to and fro, throwing an uncertain light upon the tremulous foliage, and giving an appearance of dim and indefinite extent to the depth of the forest; the solemn chanting of hymns swelling and falling on the night wind; the impassioned exhortations; the earnest prayers; the sobs, shrieks, or shouts, bursting from persons under intense agitation of mind; the sudden spasms which seized upon scores, and unexpectedly dashed them to the ground—all conspired to invest the scene with terrific interest, and to work up the feelings to the highest pitch of excitement. (M'Nemar 1807: 71)

As these accounts indicate, revivals generated collective effervescence (Durkheim [1912] 1996; see also Sewell 1996), intense shared emotional experiences; their participants perceived revivals as extraordinary events that transcended their individual experience and bonded them into a single community. The crowds at revivals were huge, in sharp contrast to participants' everyday lives in small towns or on isolated farms. At Cane Ridge, for example, attendance was estimated at between 10,000 and 25,000—an astonishing figure given that the population of nearby Lexington, Kentucky's largest town, was just over 2,000 (Ahlstrom 1972: 432–35). Multiple preachers spoke, infecting each other with enthusiasm. Each person's experience was echoed and magnified by others nearby. Celebrants stayed together for extended periods of time—Cane Ridge, for example, lasted over a week—so excitement rose to a crescendo. Revivals often continued late into the night, when the eerie atmosphere created by darkness, pierced only by flickering light from bonfires and torches, lent itself to apprehension of mystery and miracle. The result was an avalanche of religious fervor. Participants entered a liminal state in which ordinary social constraints and hierarchies dissolved; they experienced a profound sense of closeness to God and one another (Turner 1969), often comprehended as a rebirth. In this way revivals engendered and supported a romantic Christianity—a religion of the heart rather than the mind (Miller 1965).

Revivals had cascading effects on the vitality and structure of American religion. First, spurred by intense personal experiences of Christ and fresh interpretations of the Bible that resonated with a growing democratic sensibility, thousands converted to evangelical Christianity and participated actively in religious services (Ahlstrom 1972; Carwardine 1978; Butler 1990).[2] Participation in organized religion more than doubled, from 17 percent in 1776, the earliest year for which comprehensive data are available, to 37 percent in 1860 (Finke and Stark 1992: 15–16; see also Carwardine 1993: 44; Long 1998: 144–50). The intense, emotionally charged nature of people's experiences at revivals created a deep-seated ideology that spanned all religious communities: evangelicalism could redeem mankind by building Christ's kingdom on earth (Miller 1965; Tuveson 1968; Higham 1974; Dolan 1978; Goen 1985; Noll 2002: 187–208). In this way revivals connected Americans together and laid the foundation for a deeply Protestant nation.

Second, the leaders of revivalist movements created new ideologies to guide their converts' building of religious communities that would emulate the purity of early Christianity. Revivals amplified the willingness of Americans in all walks of life to question constituted church authorities (Ahlstrom 1972; Carwardine 1978; Hatch 1989; Long 1998). Revivalists seceded from established religions to found dozens of new sects and full-fledged churches: several different variants of the Baptist and Methodist faiths; assorted Christian, Christian Connection, and Disciples of Christ congregations; the Church of God, the Mennonite Brethren, and the Plymouth Brethren; the Adventist, Christadelphian, and Mormon sects; Methodist-leaning spin-offs from the Lutheran and Mennonite churches; evangelical variants of the Congregational, Episcopal, and Presbyterian churches; and dozens of utopian communities, including Brook Farm, Hopedale, Oneida, the Shakers, and the Society of the Publick Universal Friend (Kanter 1972; Clark 1965). By spurring the creation of new religious communities, revivals in this era fostered pluralism—recognition of and adaptation to religious diversity that led to tolerance—which remains the hallmark of American religion today (Marty 1963; Hatch 1989; Butler 1990) and which requires an essentially modern worldview.

Yet it is notable that many of these offshoots of revivalism were intensely value-rational and emotionally rational in ways that may strike contemporary observers as bizarre. Consider, for example, two prominent examples of religious communities with unusual theologies, both of which survive in some form today: millennialists and Mormons. From the 1830s onward, several closely related groups of millennialists based their theologies on the apocalyptic books of the Bible and urged people to ready themselves for the imminent Second Coming of Christ, at which time the world would end, the final judgment would be handed down, good and evil would fight a final battle, and the faithful would be "raptured" up to heaven (Tuveson 1968; Ahlstrom 1972;

[2] Evangelical Christianity generally involves belief in a trinitarian God, humankind's fall from grace through original sin, salvation through Christ, repentance and faith achieved through acceptance of the Holy Ghost and a personal experience of being "born again," the need to live a moral life, and a final judgment ("the Rapture") that is foretold in Revelations (Ahlstrom 1972; Carwardine 1993).

Carwardine 1993). Although some groups never set a date for this fateful event, their leaders anticipated it would occur within their followers' lifetimes, a gospel they continued to preach throughout the nineteenth century. Other groups—notably, those who followed William Miller—set two dates, first in 1843 and then, after nothing happened, again in 1844; when both prophesied dates passed believers regrouped and their sect was slowly transformed into the Seventh-Day Adventist Church.[3] Similarly offbeat was the Mormon faith, which began when Joseph Smith announced that the angel Moroni appeared to him in a vision and told him where to find golden plates inscribed in "reformed Egyptian" hieroglyphics, along with two seer stones, the Urim and Thummim, to be used in translating the plates' messages into English (Ahlstrom 1972; Hatch 1989). Mormonism's alternative world history and profoundly revolutionary theology (it was intended to stand in relation to Christianity as Christianity did to Judaism) drew numerous converts, but the practices Smith ordained for his followers—notably, polygamy—outraged many Americans.

No matter how common or unusual their theologies and practices, revivalist faith communities provided outlets for democratic republican sentiments (Wiebe 1984: 157–60; Goen 1985: 20–21; Hatch 1989: 9–11). Notably, the Disciples of Christ (also known as the Christians and the Christian Connection), a loose network of religious radicals led by ministers who split from the Baptist, Methodist, and Presbyterian churches, expanded rapidly in the wake of revivals. Between 1790 and 1815 this group coalesced into a single organization under Barton Stone and Alexander Campbell. Its leaders demanded "a new kind of church based on democratic principles, and a new form of biblical authority calling for common people to interpret the New Testament for themselves . . . religion of, by, and for the people" (Hatch 1989: 69).

All new revivalist ideologies were bundled into systems of piety and authority that stood in opposition to those of older religions, as the Disciples of Christ's theology and organizing principles show. Thus, the third consequence of revivals was to engender intense competition among religious ideologies. This accords with religious-economies theory (Finke and Stark 1988, 1992), which argues that religious competition increases with the number of different faiths and with the extent to which those faiths have about the same number of adherents; thus competition increases as religious markets become more pluralistic.[4] Competition from other faiths spurred vigorous mobiliza-

---

[3] Yet a sizable number of contemporary observers, at least in the United States, would not view the millennialist theology as weird. A recent poll conducted by the Pew Research Center found that 41 percent of Americans believe that Christ is likely to return to Earth by 2050, compared to 46 percent who believe it is unlikely to happen or definitely will not happen (Pew 2010). Surprisingly, given the world-changing impact of such an event, 13 percent of Americans would not venture a guess as to its likelihood.

[4] Although the relationship between religious pluralism and competition are debated by sociologists (for recent critiques, see Chaves and Gorski 2001; Voas, Crockett, and Olson 2002), historians agree that revivals and the religious diversity that resulted from them did indeed foster

tion efforts as churches worked to recruit new members and retain existing ones. Competition also played out in ideological struggles over theological tenets and principles of church organization, as churches sought to differentiate themselves from rivals and appeal to a wide range of potential "customers" in the market for faith. Presbyterian minister Timothy Flint charged that "Nine pulpits in ten in our country are occupied chiefly in the denunciation of other sects" (*Western Review*, 1830, quoted in Mott 1930: 369). As Alexander Campbell, Disciples of Christ leader and magazine editor, neatly summarized the situation, "The Presbyterians, Baptists, Methodists, Episcopalians, and Roman Catholics, all stand upon the same footing. Each one under this divine authority, claims the right to wage war upon the rest in defence of their faith; and thus we have five different organized armies, marshalled under different standards, commanded by different officers, and united by different creeds, in active conflict" (Campbell 1826: 324).

Religious competition centered on the right of authorities in the older denominations—specifically, learned theologians and the educational institutions that trained, licensed, and monitored ministers—to determine who should preach, what should be preached, and where and how preaching should occur. Take the dispute between Congregationalist minister Lyman Beecher and itinerant Methodist preacher Lorenzo Dow. In a speech at Yale University, Beecher castigated revivalist preachers as "illiterate men ... utterly unacquainted with theology," said that he feared that their listeners were "exposed to the errors of enthusiastic and false teachers," and asserted that "religious and moral and literary influence ... belongs to the [college-educated] Ministry" (Beecher 1814: 7). In response Dow justified the who, what, where, and how of his ministry by appealing "to two simple criteria: divine evidence in the soul and the effectiveness and power of [his] preaching" (Hatch 1989: 20).

There were clear winners and losers in the battle for souls. Baptists and Methodists gained the most, Presbyterians held their ground, and Congregationalists and Episcopalians suffered the most—not from declines in absolute numbers but rather from growing more slowly than the expanding population base. In 1750, the first year for which good data are available, 32 percent of all American congregations were Congregationalist, 19 percent Episcopalian, 16 percent Presbyterian, and 9 percent Methodist (Gaustad 1962). In 1860, Methodists led with 37 percent of all congregations, followed by Baptists with 22 percent, Presbyterians with 12 percent, Catholics with 5 percent, and Congregationalists, Episcopalians, and Disciples of Christ with 4 percent each (Burke 2006).

As it is today, American religion in this era was divided along regional lines. Figures 5.2a–d trace the evolving religious mix in four regions, New England (5.2a), the mid-Atlantic states (5.2b), the South (5.2c), and the west-

---

competition between faiths (Smith 1962; Ahlstrom 1972; Dolan 1978; Marty 1987; Hatch 1989; Butler 1990).

ern frontier states (5.2d),[5] focusing on the twelve churches with the largest number of congregations across all locations for the entire period 1740–1860.[6] They are listed in descending order, from the Methodists (400,000 congregation-year records, 1740 to 1860) to the Universalists (23,000); all smaller faiths are in the "other" category.

Most American religious communities had strong regional centers. Figure 5.2a shows that New England was always a bastion of the Congregational Church, although that faith dwindled from constituting over 80 percent of congregations in 1740 to only 25 percent in 1860, and Congregationalists' stranglehold was gradually usurped by Baptists, Methodists, and Universalists. Figure 5.2b reveals that the mid-Atlantic states had substantial levels of religious heterogeneity throughout this period, but the mix shifted from Dutch and German Reformed, Lutheran, Presbyterian, and Quaker to Baptist, Methodist, and Presbyterian. Figure 5.2c demonstrates that in the South, the Episcopal Church shrank from constituting almost two-thirds of congregations in 1740 to only 5 percent in 1860, while the Baptists and Methodists grew from less than 1 percent each to 44 percent and 32 percent, respectively. Finally, figure 5.2d shows that the frontier states were transformed from Baptist strongholds in 1780 to a mix of Baptists, Methodists, and Presbyterians, supplemented by a host of other, much smaller faiths led by the Disciples of Christ and the Lutherans. Because of this great regional variation in religious composition, religious conflict in this era was always tinged with regional overtones.

The Development of National Religious Organizations

Figure 5.2d shows that as European settlement pushed westward, many religious communities spread beyond their old regional strongholds—not just the Baptists, Methodists, and Presbyterians but also the Catholics, Disciples of Christ, Lutherans, and Mennonites. Following the Methodists' successful example of circuit riders, Baptist ministerial outreach covered the nation as early as the 1820s; smaller groups like the Disciples of Christ soon followed (Smith 1962; Hatch 1989). As a result, the activities and orientations of many religious communities became increasingly national in scope (Ahlstrom 1972; Goen 1985; Hatch 1989; Newman and Halvorson 2000).

To combat geographic isolation and bind far-flung adherents into a strong community of faith, many churches developed truly national organizational

---

[5] New England includes Connecticut, Maine, Massachusetts, New Hampshire, Rhode Island, and Vermont. The mid-Atlantic states include Delaware, New Jersey, New York, and Pennsylvania. The South includes Alabama, Florida, Georgia, Louisiana, Maryland, Mississippi, North and South Carolina, and Virginia. The West includes all other states that entered the Union by 1860.

[6] Statistics on religious communities' regional "market shares" are based on data I collected on twenty-five denominations, which are described in appendix 1. These data record the number of congregations affiliated with each religious community in each state, for each year, from 1740 to 1860.

(a)

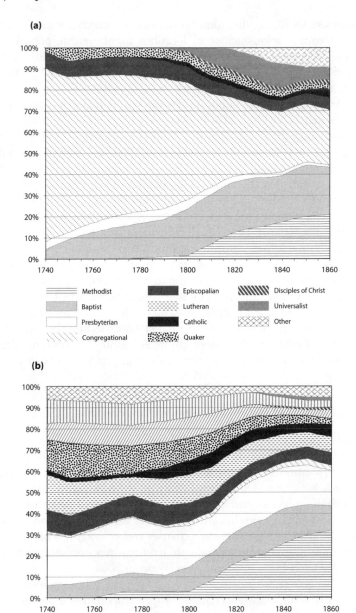

(b)

Figure 5.2. (a) The evolving demography of religious congregations in New England, 1740–1860; (b) the evolving demography of religious congregations in the mid-Atlantic states, 1740–1860;

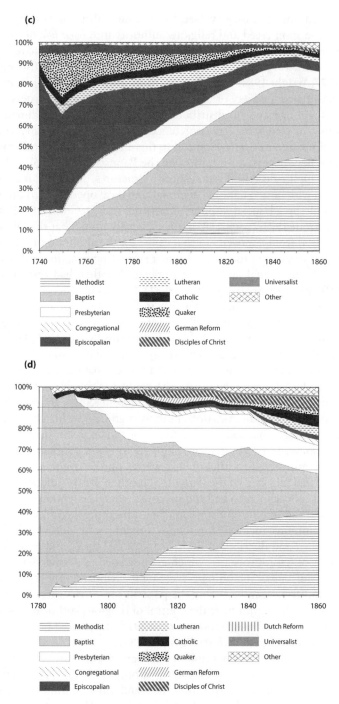

(c) the evolving demography of religious congregations in the South, 1740–1860; (d) the evolving demography of religious congregations in the West, 1780–1860.

structures. In doing so they evolved from loose affiliations of congregations based on common creed and religious authority into *bona fide* organizations that pooled resources from multiple congregations to underwrite nationwide religious marketing efforts (Smith 1962; Mathews 1969; Ahlstrom 1972; Hood 1977; Wright 1984; Goen 1985; Chaves 1993; Nord 2004). These structures coordinated a variety of connective efforts: itinerant ministers and colporteurs (paid agents who distributed religious tracts), the ordination and disciplining of clergy, regular conferences for clergy and/or laity, collective support of missionaries, and—central to this analysis—denominational magazines and newspapers. Even faiths like the Baptists and Disciples of Christ, which had highly decentralized authority structures, developed federated organizations with nested national, regional, and local operations to share information and spread social support (Garrison and DeGroot 1948; Wrather 1968; Ahlstrom 1972; Goen 1985). It is especially ironic that the Disciples of Christ evolved from a movement that called for the abolition of formal organizational restraints on the faithful into a large denomination only by building the kind of formal authority structures that they had once inveighed against (Wrather 1968; Hatch 1989: 68–81). For all churches these formal organizational structures made it possible to forge bonds of affiliation within local residential communities and to promote solidarity and collective identification among geographically dispersed adherents (Smith 1968, 1978).

In building federated organizational structures that spanned the entire nation, American denominations followed a broader pattern in American civic life that developed during the nineteenth century (Schlesinger 1944; Skocpol 1997; Skocpol, Ganz, and Munson 2000; Mazzone 2004). Indeed, the structures that American denominations built were affiliated with a host of formal voluntary societies that sought to achieve four main goals: outreach, education, publishing, and social reform. Domestic missionary societies converted natives and ministered to unchurched whites on the frontier while foreign missionary societies carried the Gospel to "heathen" lands. Educational societies founded colleges, which had at their core theological schools that provided standardized training to ministers, and subsidized theological students. Sunday school unions inculcated religious principles in children. Publishing houses printed and distributed Bibles, educational tracts, and periodicals. Finally, a slew of reform societies, which are discussed in chapter 6, promoted a wide variety of causes, including protecting the Sabbath, suppressing vice, reducing drunkenness, and assisting the poor. In some cases these voluntary associations were brought under the control of religious authorities before the Civil War, but much organizational consolidation occurred late in the nineteenth or early twentieth century (Wright 1984).

Some of the organizational linking mechanisms built by religious groups were massive. For instance, Sydney E. Ahlstrom (1972: 436–37) reported that in 1844 the Methodists had some four thousand itinerant ministers to supplement their almost eight thousand settled ministers. These itinerants were organized into a system of circuits and preaching stations, with the nation di-

Denomination	Collective bodies to ordain & discipline clergy	Conferences for clergy &/or laity	Itinerant clergy	Collective support for misionary societies	Magazines
Adventist		■	■		■
Amish					
Apostolic Christian			■		
Baptist	■	■	■	■	■
Catholic	■	■	■	■	■
Christadelphian	■				■
Church of God	■	■	■	■	■
Congregational	■	■		■	■
Deist/Atheist					■
Disciples of Christ	■	■		■	■
Dunker			■		
Dutch Reformed	■	■		■	■
Episcopalian	■	■		■	■
Evangelical Association	■	■	■	■	■
German Reformed	■	■		■	■
Jewish	■	■			■
Lutheran	■	■		■	■
Mennonite	■				
Methodist	■	■	■	■	■
Morman	■	■	■	■	■
Moravian	■	■		■	■
Presbyterian	■	■		■	■
Plymouth Brethren					■
Quaker	■	■		■	■
(River) Brethren in Christ			■		
Shaker	■				
Spiritualist					■
Swedenborgian	■	■			■
United Brethren in Christ	■	■	■	■	■
Unitarian	■	■		■	■
Universalist	■	■			■
Total	**20**	**23**	**17**	**17**	**28**

Figure 5.3. Building formal structures in American denominations: linking mechanisms.

vided into districts, each managed by a presiding elder. Another striking example comes from the Moravian Church; this tiny denomination, which had fewer than fifty congregations as late as 1860, mounted dozens of domestic missions, starting when the first congregation arrived in America in 1740 and continuing into the twentieth century. Their targets ranged from white settlers along the frontier to the Catawbas in the Carolinas, the Cherokee in Georgia and Alabama, the Dakotas west of the Mississippi, the Iroquois around the Great Lakes, and the Natchez in Mississippi (Hutton 1923). Finally, many religious magazines gained nationwide audiences; for example, the *Christian Advocate* (1826–1956) had 50,000 subscribers in 1860, while the *American Messenger* (1843–1923) boasted 190,000 subscribers in 1848 and over 200,000 by 1852.

Figure 5.3, which is based on dozens of histories of religion, shows which faiths had which structural elements before the Civil War. It includes virtually all independent denominations, but it does not include schismatic groups like the many "flavors" of Baptists and Mennonites. It also includes four formally unorganized groups—Adventists, atheists, deists, and spiritualists.[7] It focuses on five important linking mechanisms: collective bodies based in America to ordain and discipline clergy, conferences for clergy and/or laity, itinerant clergy, missionary societies, and denominational magazines. For each religious group, cells shaded gray indicate that its leaders (or an affiliated voluntary society) had established that linking mechanism before 1860.

Collective bodies to ordain and discipline clergy. Almost two-thirds of religious groups (20 of 32) built formal structures to oversee these functions; those that did not were small (Apostolic Christians, Christadelphians, and River Brethren in Christ), not yet formally organized into denominations (Adventists, atheists, deists, and spiritualists), or opposed on principle to formal hierarchy (the Amish, Mennonites, Plymouth Brethren, and Quakers). When these formal authority structures were erected varied; the earliest denomination imported from Europe to accomplish this was the Lutheran Church, which was already independent of European authorities before the Revolution. The Moravian Church was the last; not until 1857 was the American Moravian Church granted independence from the German one, with a provincial synod to manage church property and govern members (Corwin, Dubbs, and Hamilton 1894; Hutton 1909; Ahlstrom 1972). A few denominations set up formal structures in America but did not become fully independent of European authorities before the Civil War. Most notable of these were the Catholics: although John Carroll was appointed bishop of Baltimore and made responsible for organizing the Catholic Church in America, he was always subordinate to Rome (Ahlstrom 1972; Dolan 1978)

Conferences. Over 70 percent of religious groups (23 of 32) connected their leaders and/or members with conferences. Such gatherings were not limited to large denominations, like the Congregationalists, Episcopalians, and Presbyterians; instead, many small groups, like the Church of God, Swedenborgians, and United Brethren in Christ, also held conferences. Even some groups that did not create formal authority structures—notably, the Adventists, Mennonites, and Quakers—held conferences to bring church leaders and members together.

Itinerant clergy. Traveling ministers were used by over half of all religious groups (17 of 31), both large (Baptist, Congregational, Methodist, and Presbyterian) and small (Apostolic Christian, Church of God, and Shaker). This tactic was necessary to "stretch" the reach of clergy, as there were few preachers to lead the faithful. Donald G. Mathews (1969) estimated that after the Revolution there were only 1,499 clergy to serve some 2.5 million people scattered over 823,000 square miles—only six clergy per 10,000 Americans and less than two per 1,000 square miles. In 1816, one Congregational official calcu-

---

[7] The Adventists were a distinct religious community by the 1840s, but they did not formally organize into a denomination until 1861.

lated that there were only 2,000 "educated" ministers to serve a population of 8.5 million—just 2.4 clergy per 10,000 Americans (Pearson 1816)—but of course this dismal figure ignores those preachers who lacked formal theological training but were instead called to the ministry (e.g., Baptists) or elected by their fellow congregants (e.g., Mennonites). Even as late as 1850, census records indicate that there were only thirteen clergy per 10,000 Americans— just ten per 1,000 square miles (Sobek 2006).

Missionary societies. These either complemented itinerant clergy or substituted for them in just over half of all faiths. Some missionary efforts predated the Revolution. The Society for the Propagation of the Gospel in Foreign Parts was founded in 1701; for the next eighty years, it was the chief means of expanding the Church of England in America. It recruited missionaries, supported clergy in existing parishes, sent itinerant missionaries to organize new parishes, and tried to evangelize Indians and slaves; perhaps most important, it coordinated the far-flung Anglican community (Ahlstrom 1972). Those tireless proselytizers, the Moravians, founded a missionary society in 1745; it fell apart during the Revolution but was resuscitated in 1787 as the Society of the United Brethren for Propagating the Gospel among the Heathen (Hutton 1923). After the Revolution many other faiths sought to organize missionary work within religious authority structures. The German Reformed Church constituted a standing committee on missions in 1813, the Presbyterians founded a board of missions in 1816, the Unitarians launched their eponymous missionary society in 1825, and the Reformed Dutch Church organized a board of domestic missions in 1831. Even small faiths like Philip Otterbein's United Brethren in Christ and Jacob Albright's Evangelical Association organized missionary societies.

Other missionary societies were interdenominational or independent of denominational authorities, but often informally affiliated with one or more denominations. For example, the New York Missionary Society formed in 1796 by members of the Baptist, Presbyterian, and Reformed Dutch churches to convert Native Americans was not under any denomination's control. Similarly, the United Foreign Missionary Society, formed in 1817 by the Associate Reformed, Presbyterian, and Reformed Dutch churches, was managed by laypeople rather than church officials.

Magazines. Finally—yet most central to this analysis—all faiths but three published magazines. One exception was the Amish, who vehemently resisted all trappings of formal organization and the hierarchy that accompanied it. The other two were tiny religious communities: the Apostolic Christians and the River Brethren in Christ. Notably, six groups that did not create any other organizational linking mechanism—Christadelphians, Jews, Plymouth Brethren, atheists, deists, and spiritualists—published magazines to create a sense of collective identity, defend their principles from attacks by rival faiths, or proselytize.

New upstart faiths were especially likely to support magazines because the leadership positions in these new, revivalistic religious communities were fragile. Revivals, no matter how prolonged, are merely brief departures from everyday life. Revivalistic fervor could easily dissipate when converts returned home and immersed themselves in familiar routines. The success of revivals could be measured by "the number of new churches organized which would persist when enthusiasm had died down, and the number of converts who remained in the churches once their emotions had been channeled from public ecstasy into private devotion" (Mathews 1969: 35–36). Success in these terms was by no means assured in this era. As Alexis de Tocqueville astutely observed, America was a society of strangers who lacked the traditional bonds of family and place ([1848] 2000). A paucity of social ties made it difficult for participants in revivals to cohere into stable religious communities and retain converts, much less attract new members (Stark and Bainbridge 1980). In the absence of social ties, repetition was needed to reinforce religious community. Thus, to maintain their status as religious leaders, revivalists had to reinforce their messages, and they very frequently turned to magazines to do so.

For example, both of the offbeat, upstart religious communities described above, millennialism and Mormonism, were supported by magazines, which helped spread their unusual gospels and practices more widely than their small number of clergy could, and which reinforced the lessons learned in religious meetings. The millennialists who offered no specific date for the Rapture published the *Theological and Literary Review* (1848–61), *Millennial Messenger* (1855–56), and *Waymarks in the Wilderness* (1855–57), while the Millerites published *The Literalist* (1840–45) and the *American Millenarian and Prophetic Review* (1842–49). After William Miller's prophesied events failed to occur and the sect began to reorganize itself into what would in 1863 become the Seventh-Day Adventist Church, a series of magazines affiliated with that emerging denomination appeared—most notably the *Second Advent Review and Sabbath Herald* (1850–, under various names) and *Youth's Instructor* (1852–1952). The Mormons published the *Latter Day Saints' Messenger* (1834–38), *Gospel Reflector* (1841), *Voree Herald* (1846), *Olive Branch* (1848–52), *Seer* (1853–54), and *True Latter Day Saints' Herald* (1860–1923)—a prodigious number of publications for a sect that had no more than three congregations at any point during this era and was constantly moving to escape prosecution.

Religious Fragmentation

Even as they became nationally integrated organizations, American churches fragmented in disputes over theology and politics. Schisms were the typical responses to major denominational discord during this era: the remarkable profusion of churches and sects described above was due mostly to the splintering of existing religious communities by disaffected clergy, not the fabrication of entirely new religious groups by laypeople (the birth of the Mormon sect is a rare counterexample that tests this rule). Early internecine conflicts originated in revivals, which made all Americans more willing to engage in theological debates and question church authorities (Ahlstrom 1972; Carwardine 1978; Finke and Stark 1992; Long 1998). Evangelical challengers opened rifts that led to schisms in the Baptist, Congregational, Dutch and German Reformed, Lutheran, Mennonite, Methodist, Plymouth Brethren, Presbyterian, Quaker, River Brethren in Christ, and Universalist churches. Later on, as American churches became increasingly embedded in wider fields of cultural and political contention (Niebuhr 1929), the force behind these schisms shifted to politics. Most prominent in this era was the North–South divide over slavery. Debates unleashed by the antislavery movement became the primary division within many faiths (Young 2006), causing schisms among the Baptists, Methodists, and Presbyterians (Goen 1985).

Throughout this era schisms were driven by disaffected subgroups who mobilized grievances and distinctive identities to create new sects that more closely accorded with their particular beliefs, extrareligious (political) positions, and desire for autonomy from central religious authorities (Liebman, Sutton, and Wuthnow 1988; Bainbridge 1997; Sutton and Chaves 2004). The cumulative result was that American religion became a heterogeneous and contentious institutional field that both expressed and constituted many distinct, and often opposing, subcultures (Hatch 1989). This field was replete with disputes about the nature of faith, which took the form of struggles over meaning, authority, and boundaries. The leaders of schismatic groups created novel symbols (the Bible as a book that anyone could read and understand) and reformulated old practices (open-air services), and used these symbols and practices to reconstitute the meaning of Christianity (a "revived" faith, restored to its "original" state) and Christian identity (believers had to be "born again"). Basing their claims on their own idiosyncratic interpretations of the Bible (or, in the case of the Mormons, on new sacred texts written or discovered by sect leaders), upstart religious leaders asserted that they had discovered a purer authority than that claimed by established theologians. Because these leaders claimed such a pure authority, they sought to displace the dry functionaries in older churches that, the upstart preachers argued, led older churches away from God.

Summary

Between 1740 and 1860 religion became central to American society. Rates of religious participation more than doubled, the number of congregations increased almost fortyfold from 1,350 to 54,000,[8] and the number of distinct

---

[8] It is difficult to determine to what extent the growth of congregations improved Americans' access to organized religious life. On the one hand, because population growth was so explosive, the number of congregations per capita rose only slightly, from fifteen per 10,000 in 1740 to seventeen per 10,000 in 1860. On the other hand, because of rapid urbanization starting in the 1820s, the average size of congregations increased, meaning that a constant number of congregations per capita served a larger number of Americans.

religious groups more than doubled from thirteen to thirty-one.[9] The upshot is that the field of American religion became increasingly heterogeneous and contentious, and schisms shook all religious groups. Moreover, religion became increasingly embedded in broader cultural and political debates—notably, republican politics and social reform causes like the abolition of slavery. Finally, religious groups increasingly created formal organizational structures to combat geographic isolation and bind far-flung adherents into cohesive communities of faith. The question remains as to the role magazines played in the evolution of this field.

THE INTERPLAY BETWEEN RELIGION AND MAGAZINES

Religious magazines facilitate projecting new theological principles and religious identities, and undermining old ones.[10] They allow writers and editors to draw sharp distinctions between the lapsed and the saved, between the true and the fallen church, between sacred practices and debased ones. Moreover, because religious magazines are serial publications, they stabilize those distinctions through repetition. Given their many benefits for religious groups and the centrality of religion in American culture in the years 1741–1860, it is not surprising that religious magazines constituted one-fourth of all magazines founded in this era. Because religious magazines were more successful than those of other genres, they tended to stay in print longer than most other types; as a result, religious magazines constituted 36 percent of annual observations on magazines for that period. Over 90 percent of religious magazines (1,142 of 1,229) proclaimed a doctrinal and/or organizational affiliation with a particular community of faith, a handful were explicitly nondenominational, and the remained focused on attacking a particular subcommunity— Catholics, Jews, or Freemasons—but did not proclaim a particular denominational affiliation.

The first religious magazine was *Christian History*, founded in 1743 by Thomas Prince Sr., a noted historian and minister of the South Church in Boston. This was America's first successful magazine: it not only survived two full years but also reached readers on both sides of the Atlantic who eagerly awaited its reports of religious revivals that were then sweeping through the colonies and Scotland (Lambert 1999: 119–20). Only two other religious magazines were founded before the Revolution (*Ein Geistliches Magazien* in 1764 and the *Royal Spiritual Magazine* in 1771); not until after peace was restored did religious publishing begin to take off. From 1784 to 1800, 20 religious magazines were founded (an average of 1.2 per year); from 1801 to 1825, 242 were founded (9.7 per year). Religious magazine publishing exploded during

[9] This number understates the situation, as it does not count the many distinct groups within some denominations, such as the different types of Baptists, Mennonites, and Presbyterians.

[10] Some of this analysis is condensed from "Pulpit and Press: Denominational Dynamics and the Growth of Religious Magazines" (Goldstein and Haveman 2013).

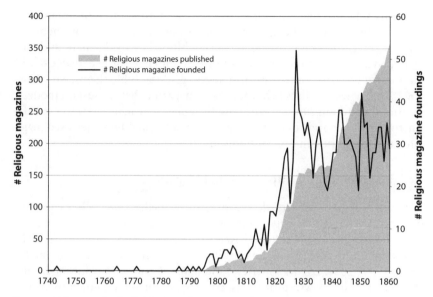

Figure 5.4. The growth of religious magazines, 1740–1860.

the first golden age of magazines, from 1826 to 1850, when 768 religious magazines were founded (30.7 per year). In the last decade before the Civil War, 305 were founded (30.5 per year). Figure 5.4 charts the growth of religious magazines over time. The gray area plots the number of religious magazines published in any given year, and the solid line indicates the number founded.

Most founders of religious magazines were local clergy, while a substantial minority were central or regional religious authorities, including missionary societies; the remainder were laity. Although the data are spotty, those who founded ninety-one religious magazines from 1741 to 1820 could be ascertained from perusal of prospectuses and articles in magazines that were available in central archives. In this sample, 56 percent of founders were local clergy, 24 percent were national or regional authorities, 18 percent were laity, and 1 percent were unknown. For later magazines, many of which were not available in central archives, analysis of a random sample of thirty magazines that came to publication in the 1840s and '50s yielded good data on the founders of twenty-one magazines. Of these, nineteen were founded by ordained ministers or official denominational organizations; only two were founded by laity. Taken together these patterns indicate that religious magazines were published predominantly, although not exclusively, by religious officials.

Religious magazines produced radical changes in the structure of religion in America (Marty et al. 1963; Hatch 1989; Nord 2004). By forging links among the faithful, religious magazines sustained the new religious communities that arose from revivals and propelled their expansion. And by providing a voice for theological reassessment and the restructuring of ecclesiastical authority, religious magazines hastened the transformation of the established churches that were challenged by revivalists and schismatic movements. In doing so magazines built on a tradition established by the Puritans and reinvigorated by revivalist preachers: reading was central to the experience of religion in America, for Americans had always read the Bible themselves (Nord 2004). In the next sections I chronicle how magazines helped sustain modern, translocal communities of faith: how they deployed magazines to craft distinctive identities and compete against other faiths, and how they used magazines to forge bonds among far-flung adherents.

Religious Pluralism, Competition, and Magazines

American religious leaders' devotion to print media, especially magazines, continued a trend that began almost as soon as the printing press was invented. Ever since the Protestant Reformation began in Germany in 1517, "Protestant leaders regarded the printing press as a means of propagating the truth." (Starr 2004: 26). In America, Protestants' devotion to print media also pushed Catholics, Jews, spiritualists, atheists, and deists to launch their own magazines, to defend their beliefs (and, for Catholics and Jews, their ethnic communities) from attacks by other, larger religious groups, and to forge social and emotional bonds among their adherents.

As disestablishment transformed all American churches into voluntary organizations, magazines offered religious authorities platforms to woo new adherents and contest other faiths. As Robert Foster, the editor of the *Christian Herald*, declared in 1823, "Preaching of the gospel is a Divine institution—'printing' no less so.... They are kindred offices. The PULPIT AND THE PRESS are inseparably connected.... The Press, then, is to be regarded with a sacred veneration and supported with religious care. The press must be supported or the pulpit falls" (quoted in Hatch 1989: 142; emphasis in the original). By the 1830s religious magazines had become "the grand engine of a burgeoning religious culture, the primary means of promotion for, and bond of union within, competing religious groups" (Hatch 1989: 125–26). This judgment accords with the editors of the *American Messenger* (1843–1923), who asserted, "In a world where thought is unbound, and inquiry is unrestricted, THE PRESS becomes, perhaps, the most important of human agencies for good or evil. We can neither resist nor disregard its action. We cannot tie up men's purses that they shall not buy, nor seal up their eyes that they shall not read, nor shut up their spirit of inquiry that they shall not investigate. The world has gone to reading, and read they will, for weal or woe." (Nord 2004: 114; emphasis in the original).

This magazine, the organ of the American Tract Society, had considerable influence, as it reached over 100,000 subscribers across the nation. Similarly, the editor of the *New York Evangelist* (1830–1902) concluded that religious periodicals were a power unto themselves:

The mighty power they have gathered to themselves, the controlling sway they exert upon the opinions, faith and conduct of the times, are among the most striking and eventful characteristics of modern society. The whole aspect of our civilization is changed by the fact. A new power truly has arisen, of greater pretensions, more intense activity, with more incessant and penetrating agencies, and more abundant facilities, seeming to have no limits to its scope, no restraints upon its development, and no modesty in its demands. All the discoveries of science only tend to augment its power, and the every day's progress more and more shapes and adapts society to its influences. Where it is to end—whether it is to gain the absolute monopoly of all the intellectual and moral forces of society, and to supplant all other agencies, by which opinion is controlled, sentiment guided, and character built up—are questions pressing sore for an answer.... The real sphere of the press has not yet been fully determined. It is a new power in the world; a brawny, lusty youth, overlaid with undeveloped muscle, and giving promise of gigantic proportions, and power beyond all former example. (Field 1856: n.p.)

Religious groups of all stripes embraced the press because "getting into print became the primary way to prescribe and contest values during the nineteenth century" (Moore 1989: 219). Figure 5.5 charts the number of annual observations on magazines affiliated with each religious community between 1741 and 1860.[11] Religious communities are grouped based on their position in the American religious field; within each group, they are listed in descending order by number of annual observations on affiliated magazines. The three mainline Anglo-Protestant churches (Congregational, Episcopalian, and Presbyterian) accounted for 30 percent of annual observations on religious magazines and 23 percent of religious magazines founded in this time period. Other smaller Protestant denominations with long histories (Dunker, Dutch and German Reformed, Lutheran, Moravian, Mennonite, and Quaker) accounted for 11 percent of annual observations on religious magazines and 12 percent of religious magazine foundings. The two biggest upstart faiths, Baptist and Methodist, published almost as many magazines as the three mainline faiths: 26 percent of annual observations on religious magazines and 29 percent of religious magazine foundings. Other smaller upstart churches and sects (Adventist, Christadelphian, Church of God, Disciples of Christ, Evangelical Association, Mormon, Plymouth Brethren, River Brethren, Shaker, Swedenborgian, Unitarian, United Brethren in Christ, and Universalist) accounted for 23 percent of annual observations on religious magazines and 26 percent of religious magazine foundings. Catholics and Jews accounted for 5 percent of annual observations on religious magazines and 6 percent of religious magazine foundings. Even atheists, deists, and spiritualists, who were not formally organized during this era, published magazines to

[11] Analysis of the number of magazines founded yields a very similar pattern.

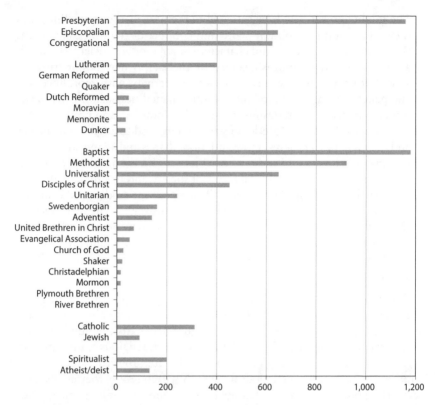

Figure 5.5. The number of religious magazines by faith and faith group.
Note: This figure counts magazine-year observations.

promote their beliefs and support their communities; together these groups accounted for 4 percent of both annual observations and foundings.

Many of the theological and strategic battles between religious groups played out in the pages of religious magazines (Marty et al. 1963; Hatch 1989; Moore 1989; Lambert 1999; Nord 2004). There is ample evidence that religious publishing was driven by competitive threats from other faiths. For instance, the Presbyterian *Christian's Magazine*, founded in 1806 by Rev. Dr. John Mitchell Mason, inveighed against preachers from upstart denominations, like the Baptists, Disciples of Christ, and Methodists, who had no theological training: "The mischiefs arising from these sources are increased by the activity of a 'zeal not according to knowledge,'" Mason wrote. "The duty of Christians is to confront and repel, not abet the enemy, nor admit him into their camp in order to subdue him.... [T]he *Christian's Magazine* will not be backward in strengthening their hands and stirring up their zeal in this contest." (1806: iv–xiv). Magazines affiliated with the Disciples of Christ argued for religious liberty, likening it to the political liberty Americans had won for themselves in the Revolution. For example, Elias Smith launched the *Herald of Gospel Liberty*

(1808–17) and in its inaugural issue trumpeted, "RELIGIOUS LIBERTY, signifies a freedom to believe in God, and to obey him according to the manifestation which he has made to man, in his works, in the scriptures, and by the spirit of truth, the *manifestations* of which is given to every man to profit withal" (Smith 1808: 2; emphasis in the original). This movement's leaders used magazines to disparage all mainline churches, their cool-headed seminary-trained clergy, and their complacent middle-class adherents, arguing,

> When religion became fashionable, the Church became proud and min-
> gled with the world and when adulterated she was no longer satisfied with
> the ministers of the Lord's making [those who felt emotionally called to
> the ministry] in consequence of which she turned her attention to the
> making of ministers for herself in human seminaries polished with gold as
> Aaron made the molten calf and these molten calves she called Clergy: but
> this is not a new testament name; nor is it justly applicable to any true
> gospel minister.... For clear it is, that when a false religion once becomes
> established in the mind, it produces a greater and more confirmed enmity
> against divine truth and genuine religion and constitutes a greater distance
> from God than can exist in the mind of an openly profane worldling ...:
> so that a false religion evidently places a man in a much worse situation,
> and at a much greater distance from God, than he would have been with-
> out any at all. (Sarjent 1807a: xii–xv)

> The corruptions of Theology have laid the foundation for and given birth
> to those imperfections and Tyranny, while they have equally effected a re-
> moval of sound Ethics from the Church.—Thus have the Clergy taken way
> the Key of the divine Empire and all the powers of government from the
> saints. (Sarjent 1807b: 104–5)

Some religious magazines opposed sectarianism and instead sought national religious unity. But their ostensible drive for unity was not their real
goal—most magazines whose editors declared them nondenominational actually favored some religious traditions over others. Most notable among
these "not really nondenominational" magazines were those published to support the Congregationalists and Presbyterians' Plan of Union, which sought
to combine their domestic missionary efforts, recognize each other's ministry
and church organization, and allow newly formed congregations to affiliate
with either a presbytery or a Congregational association and in so doing battle advances by the upstart Baptists and Methodists (Ahlstrom 1972: 456–57).
The Plan of Union was supported by magazines like the *Home Missionary
Magazine and Pastor's Journal* (1828–1909) and the *American Messenger* (1843–
1923), which were distributed nationwide. In response, the Baptist *Christian
Review* (1836–62) explained that the church needed magazines to connect the
faithful and defend its principles, noting, "We see every denomination adher-
ing firmly to its own cherished doctrines and polity, and announcing itself as
occupying that exact spot—that Chinese center—to which all others should

return from their wanderings, to find rest. An invitation to union generally means, that all other Christians ought to renounce their peculiarities, and return to the bosom of the one pure and orthodox church.... We know ... that the Baptists are considered as peculiarly exclusive; and the exhortations to union are commonly meant for their special benefit." (Knowles 1836: 7). Many Congregationalists and Presbyterians were optimistic that they could unite Americans in faith; for instance, Princeton University theologian Charles Hodge claimed that America was becoming one people, "having one language, one literature, essentially one religion, and one common soul" (quoted in Marty 1976: 73). But their optimistic words were drowned out by the contentious tone of most religious discourse.

Some magazines fought direct battles against particular rival faiths. For instance, the Congregational *Panoplist*, founded in Charlestown, Massachusetts, in 1805 by Rev. Jedediah Morse, inveighed against the "poisons" spread by Unitarian magazines. A subsequent Congregational publication, the *Spirit of the Pilgrims*, founded in 1828 by the prominent minister Lyman Beecher, declared that the *Panoplist* "rendered incalculable service to the cause of truth, by compelling Unitarians to leave the concealment, by which they had so long been gaining influence, and in which lay the greater proportion of their strength" (Beecher 1828: 3). Beecher's magazine continued the *Panoplist's* goal of countering the Unitarian movement by debating perceived Unitarian slanders against Congregationalism:

> Misrepresentations, the most palpable and injurious, of the doctrines, preaching, and motives of the orthodox [Congregationalist], have been common for many years; and the continual repetition of them has by no means ceased. The apparent object has been to keep the members of Unitarian congregations from entering the doors of an orthodox church.... There are not a few proofs, however, that these misrepresentations are soon to recoil upon their authors with unexpected violence ... Unitarians have a magazine published here, upon which they spare no labor, and which is constantly employed in promoting their cause. We must have the means of meeting them on this ground.... They have found it necessary to make strenuous efforts to keep up the publication and circulation of their magazine; and surely, with our views of truth and duty, we cannot do less than they. (Beecher 1828: 5–7)

Unitarians responded with magazines like the *Christian Disciple* (1813–23), with which they sought to defend what they saw as religious truth, and the aptly named *Unitarian Defendant* (1822), in which they lamented the attacks on them made by Congregationalists, writing, "A species of persecution has sprung up within a very few years against that class of Christians, who, believing in the strict unity of God, have ventured to conform their worship to this great and impressive doctrine.... It is a truth too notorious to be controverted that on every occasion, without exception, where the Trinitarian controversy has been agitated of late years in this country, the Unitarians have been the party attacked. . . . We consider ourselves forced into the controversy." (Gilman and Hurlbut 1822: 1). In the same vein, Connecticut Episcopalians countered losses to Congregationalists and Presbyterians by launching the *Watchman* in 1819:

> It appears that "an association of gentlemen" has been formed, professedly for the purpose of "inculcating the doctrines which have ever prevailed in the great body of the Congregational and Presbyterian churches,"—but *really*, as one of its members is said to have unwarily voiced, "TO WRITE DOWN THE [EPISCOPAL] CHURCH IN CONNECTICUT!" . . . It cannot be supposed that the friends of the Church will view attacks of this nature with indifference. . . . But it is in their indispensable duty, to defend and explain the principles which they profess, in such a manner, as to repel unfounded imputation, and to turn the weapons of assault back upon their adversaries. This they propose to do in the pages of the *Watchman*. (*Christian Watchman* 1819: 3)

Starting in the late 1820s, Catholicism was increasingly the animus for Protestant mobilizing. Anti-Catholic sentiment was, at its core, nativist; in echoes of contemporary anti-immigrant sentiments, anti-Catholic protesters were motivate by hatred of foreigners who competed with native-born Protestants for jobs and control of government (Billington [1938] 1963; Gorman 1939; Tyler 1944: 363–95). Nativists argued that Catholicism was incompatible with American citizenship and feared Catholic plots to overthrow their democratic government, starting with Catholic control of the Mississippi River Valley (Billington [1938] 1963; Gorman 1939). To expose the moral and political evils of popery, Protestants published numerous anti-Catholic periodicals. One of the most vehement of these was the *Protestant* (1830–32), whose prospectus made clear its singular mission: "The sole objects of this publication are, to inculcate Gospel doctrines against Romish corruptions— to maintain the purity and sufficiency of the Holy Scriptures against Monkish traditions—to exemplify the watchful care of Immanuel over the 'Church of God which he hath purchased with his own blood,' and to defend [the] revealed truth" (Rev. George Bourne, quoted in Billington [1938] 1963: 53). Its contents were to include "Narratives displaying the rise and progress of the Papacy; its spirit and character in former periods; its modern pretensions; and its present enterprising efforts to recover and extend its unholy dominion, especially on the western continent. Biographical notices of Martyrs, Reformers and Popish Persecutors. Essays describing the doctrines, discipline, and ceremonies of the Romish Hierarchy; and its desolating influence upon individual advancement, domestic comfort, and national prosperity" (Bourne, quoted in Billington [1938] 1963: 54). The editor of this violent periodical, Rev. George Bourne, helped launch a formal organization devoted to the persecution of Catholicism in America, the New York Protestant Association, which in 1832 held a series of debates between Catholic priests and Protestant clergy. These debates, widely publicized by the *Protestant*, often ended in riots that further inflamed the anti-Catholic cause and spread it to many cities in the East (Billington [1938] 1963). That magazines were viewed as critical to broadening support for the anti-Catholic movement is evidenced by the fact that a federation of local anti-Catholic societies, the Protestant Reformation Society, made the *American Protestant Vindicator* (1834–45) its official organ soon after the society's formation.

Maryland had since its founding been home to the largest group of Catholics in America, so it is not surprising that Protestant persecution of Catholics had deep roots there. One of the most influential anti-Catholic magazines was the *Baltimore Literary and Religious Magazine* (1835–41). Despite its name, this monthly was first and foremost devoted to persecuting Catholicism; as its editors, Robert J. Breckenridge and Andrew Boyd Cross, explained, "The larger part of our matter must ... be expected to relate to the great contest with the apostate church of Rome ... we should bequeath to our country and our children, the weapons, not carnal but spiritual, of this warfare, against the most corrupt of all superstitions—most debasing of all tyrannies—and most hateful to God, of all apostasies!" (Breckenridge and Cross 1836: 2). This magazine folded when Cross left the editorial team, but the hole it left was immediately by the *Spirit of the XIX Century* (1842–43), in which Breckenridge continued his attacks on Catholicism. Anti-Catholic magazines were joined in their attacks by religious magazines affiliated with many different Protestant denominations. The *New York Observer* (1827–1912), an organ of the Old School Presbyterians; the Regular Baptist *Christian Watchman* (1819–48) of Boston; the *Magazine of the Reformed Dutch Church* (1826–30); the *Lutheran Observer* (1831–1917); and the *Second Advent Review and Sabbath Herald* (1850–) all regularly accused Catholics of idolatry, blasphemy, moral weakness, and anti-Christian sentiment and excoriated the proselytizing efforts of Catholic schools.

As a defense Catholics also turned to magazines. One of the earliest was the *United States Catholic Miscellany* (1822–61), founded by bishop John England, who used this periodical to combat published attacks on his church; for example, shortly after his magazine was launched, he responded vigorously to an essay in the *Gospel Advocate* (Gorman 1939). A notable addition to this literature was the Baltimore-based *United States Catholic Magazine* (1842–49), founded by Rev. Charles Ignatius White. Along with *Brownson's Quarterly Review* (1844–75), this magazine published articles and reviewed books that defended Catholicism in the United States and abroad; they also defended Catholics from organized attempts to convert them to Protestantism (Gorman 1939). Not surprisingly, given that Catholics were a minority until very late in this era and as such needed resources to mobilize in defense of their community, Catholic magazines outnumbered anti-Catholic publications two to one.[12]

---

[12] This comparison is limited because many anti-Catholic books, but few pro-Catholic ones, were published in this era.

Live debates between Protestants and Catholics found a wider audience by being reprinted in magazines and newspapers. One of the most famous debates, an exchange in Philadelphia in 1833 between the Presbyterian minister John Breckenridge and the Catholic priest John Hughes, took the form of a series of letters on the question "Is the Protestant religion the religion of Christ?" that were published over eight months in the *Protestant Magazine* (1833–36) and the *Catholic Herald*, a periodical founded for this express purpose (Billington [1938] 1963). Many religious periodicals reprinted these letters, including the *Episcopal Recorder* and the Presbyterian *New York Observer*. Another famous debate occurred in New York the same year between Dutch Reformed minister W. C. Brownlee and three Catholic priests, John Powers, Thomas C. Levine, and Felix Verela. It also took the form of a series of letters published in Protestant and Catholic magazines. Such debates continued into the 1840s, and most people encountered them in the pages of religious maga zines or anti-Catholic pamphlets.

Jews were also the focus of religious mobilizing in the pages of the religious press, although they were fewer in number than Catholics and so a less frequent target. Three magazines were launched starting in the 1820s with the express purpose of converting Jews to Protestant Christianity. Some of these anti-Jewish activists were motivated by the desire to save souls. For example, the New York–based *Israel's Advocate* (1823–26) may seem, based on its title, to support Judaism, but its true intentions were revealed by its subtitle: *The Restoration of the Jews Contemplated and Urged*. These anti-Jewish magazines, as well as anti-Jewish slights printed in other religious magazines, were countered by eleven magazines founded by and for Jews. For instance, *Israel's Advocate* was countered immediately by Solomon Henry Jackson's *Jew; Being a Defence of Judaism against All Adversaries, and Particularly against the Insidious Attacks of Israel's Advocate* (1823–25).

Magazines Counter Geographic Spread and Isolation

Basic conditions of life in this era made face-to-face communication among religious leaders and direct interaction between leaders and their increasingly far-flung flocks difficult; it also made religious communities increasingly dependent on publications—not just magazines, but also Bibles, educational tracts, and newspapers. People were spread thinly, especially in early years and along the frontier, and travel was slow and arduous, as was described in chapter 3, even after canals were built in the early 1800s and railroads in the 1830s. Moreover, as explained above, there were never enough preachers to lead the burgeoning number of congregations. Given the persistent dearth of clergy, religious groups could not depend solely on local pastors or itinerant preachers to fight their theological battles or inculcate the tenets of their faith in their followers. It is not surprising, then, that religious magazines were a primary platform through which religious groups communicated, energized adherents, and forged distinctive identities (Marty et al.

1963; Hatch 1989; Moore 1989; Lambert 1999; Nord 2004). Although there were several possible antidotes to geographic isolation, including circulating preachers, camp meetings, and sermons reprinted as pamphlets, magazines were particularly useful for reinforcing adherents' shared identities and disseminating information widely among both preachers and laity. As serial publications, magazines could foster reciprocal interactions between editors and their readers and so weave readers together in "imagined communities" (Anderson [1983] 1991) whose members shared not only common conceptions of theology and ritual, but also a collective understanding of moral values.

Figures 5.6a–d trace the evolving mix of religious publishing in the same four regions used in the analysis above of religious congregations: New England (5.6a), the mid-Atlantic states (5.6b), the South (5.6c), and the western frontier states (5.6d). These figures group religious communities according to their place in American religious history: the three mainline Protestant faiths (Congregational, Episcopalian, and Presbyterian), other long-established faiths (Dunker, Dutch and German Reformed, Mennonite, Moravian, and Quaker), the two largest upstart faiths (Baptist and Methodist), other upstart faiths (Adventist, Christadelphian, Church of God, Disciples of Christ, Evangelical Association, Mormon, Plymouth Brethren, River Brethren, Shaker, Unitarian, and Universalist), non-Protestant faiths (Catholic and Jewish), and unorganized religious communities (deist, atheist, and spiritualist). Although religious publishing began in 1743 with the publication of *Christian History* in Boston, it did not flourish until the first decades of the nineteenth century, first in the Northeast, then in the South and West. Before 1800, only twenty religious magazines were launched: four in New England, fifteen in the mid-Atlantic states, and one in the South. Therefore, the figures for New England and the mid-Atlantic states start in 1800, while those for the South and West start in 1820.

The distribution of denominational magazines in some ways mirrors the distribution of religious congregations: both had strong regional centers. But there are also important differences between the two distributions. Although New England was always a bastion of the Congregational Church, figure 5.6a shows that over the six decades covered by this figure, Congregationalist magazines were almost matched in numbers by Baptist ones: 337 magazine-year observations for the former and 322 for the latter. And Episcopalian magazines were outnumbered by Unitarian and Universalist magazines, 180 magazine-year observations to 181 and 304, respectively. Figures 5.6b and 5.6d reveal that the mid-Atlantic states and the West always had a heterogeneous mix of religious magazines. Finally, figure 5.6c demonstrates that, in the South, mainline Protestant (mostly Episcopalian and Presbyterian) magazines were outnumbered by magazines affiliated with upstart faiths before 1830.

Denominational publishing was largely an urban phenomenon. As table 5.1 shows, 36.8 percent of denominational magazines were published in the three largest cities (Boston, New York, and Philadelphia), 46.7 percent in smaller cities and towns (places with populations over 2,500), and only 16.5

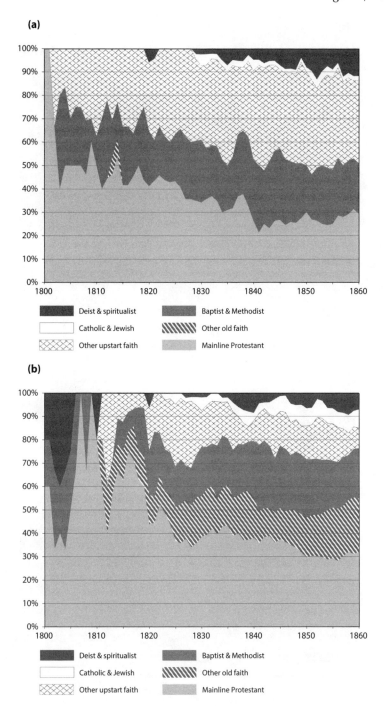

Figure 5.6. (a) The evolving demography of religious magazines in New England, 1800–1860; (b) the evolving demography of religious magazines in the mid-Atlantic states, 1800–1860; (c) the

(figure continues on next page)

(c)

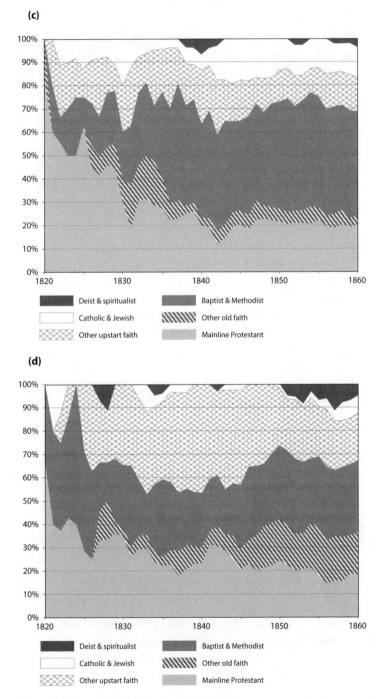

(d)

Figure 5.6. (*continued*) evolving demography of religious magazines in the South, 1820–1860; (d) the evolving demography of religious magazines in the West, 1820–1860.

TABLE 5.1.
The Distribution of Denominational Magazines by
Religious Group and Location Size

Religious group	Boston/ New York/ Philadelphia	Other urban	Rural	US
Mainline	1,076	958	391	2,425
Other older Protestant	207	490	163	860
Baptist and Methodist	682	1,133	284	2,099
Other upstart Protestant	626	811	406	1,843
Catholic and Jewish	181	221	0	402
Unorganized groups	159	103	68	330
Total	2,931	3,716	1,312	7,959

Note: This table is based on several histories of religion in America: Carroll 1893; Smith 1962; Clark 1965; Mathews 1969; Ahlstrom 1972; Hood 1977; Wright 1984; Goen 1985; Mead 1985; Hatch 1989; and Newman and Halvorson 2000. Specific information for several denominations came from denominational histories: Adventist (Olsen 1925; Tyler 1944; Loughborough [1909] 1972); Apostolic Christian (Ruegger 1949); Baptist (Newman 1894); Catholic (Dolan 1978); Church of God (Forney 1914); Disciples of Christ (Garrison and DeGroot 1948; Wrather 1968); Jewish (Ashton 2008; Faber 2008); Mennonite and River Brethren in Christ (Huffman 1920; Smith [1920] 1957); Moravian (Corwin, Dubbs, and Hamilton 1894; Hamilton 1900; Hutton 1909, 1923; Langton 1956); Shaker (Tyler 1944); Swedenborgian (Meyers 1983); and Unitarian and Universalist (Allen and Eddy 1894). Details on itinerant preachers came from Wright 1976.

percent in rural areas. Magazines affiliated with mainline denominations were slightly more likely than those affiliated with upstart groups or other older Protestant faiths to be published in the three biggest cities and slightly less likely to be published in smaller urban areas. Jewish and Catholic magazines were exclusively urban phenomena.

Magazine founders were well aware of the ways the press could be deployed to build community—both locally and translocally. They often touted the ability to connect far-flung adherents as a chief benefit of their publications. For example, the editors of the Baptist *Latter Day Luminary* (1818–25) noted magazines' superiority to Bibles and religious tracts:

The diffusion of Bibles and the publishing of the ever-lasting Gospel are, without doubt, the grand means which the spirit of the Lord will employ for subduing the nations to the dominion of the Son of God; but there are other means which have been succeeded with his blessing, and have conduced [*sic*] to the moral welfare of thousands. . . . Magazines . . . have given rise to a new epoch in the history of intellectual improvement. They come to the purchaser on terms so reasonable, and at periods so regularly distant, as to render the procuring of them a circumstance unattended with inconvenience . . . they portray and transmit characters and events as they daily occur. . . . They convey information through regions which larger publications [Bibles and books] cannot reach. (*Latter Day Luminary* 1818: iv–v)

Similarly, the group of Connecticut-based Episcopalian clergymen who founded the *Churchman's Repository for the Eastern Diocese* (1820) explained, "The want of a religious publication ... serviceable to Episcopalians in this section of the Country, has long been acknowledged by all. ... [Episcopalians] are few in number, are scattered over an extensive territory, and are generally so distant from each other, that some of them are almost exclusively confined to the ministrations of their respective pastors. It is difficult therefore to have those ministerial exchanges which ... benefit their parishes. From these evils are apt to flow much ignorance ... and a great want of union and zeal" (Morss et al. 1820: 3). High levels of geographic dispersion spurred even such committedly decentralized groups as the Baptists and Disciples of Christ to support many periodicals (Garrison and DeGroot 1948; Wrather 1968; Goen 1985: 60). For example, the Baptist *Columbian Star* (1822–29) stated that its principle objective was "to diffuse necessary information and to invigorate the efforts of our brethren" (*Columbian Star* 1822: 3). A later Baptist magazine commented on how well magazines united the faithful of all denominations, noting, "The different denominations are extensively acting on the acknowledged power of the press as an agency of disseminating their views, and of keeping their members united, harmonious, and efficient as sectarians" (*Christian Secretary* 1848: 1).

Many religious magazines sought (or at least, claimed) wide audiences. One-fourth of annual observations on religious magazines made explicit claims about their geographic scope of circulation in their titles or subtitles. Of these, 25 percent claimed to serve the entire nation and 33 percent a multistate region like New England, while 15 percent claimed to serve a single state and 26 percent a single county or municipality. And although subscription data are available for only 4 percent of religious magazines, we know that some had mass followings; for instance, the Episcopal *Churchman's Monthly* had 12,000 subscribers in 1804, the Disciples' *Millennial Harbinger* had 15,000 subscribers throughout the 1850s, and the Methodist *Christian Advocate and Journal* had 28,000 in 1828 and 50,000 in 1860. Bibliographer Gaylord P. Albaugh (1994) estimated that by 1830 religious periodicals had over 400,000 subscribers in total. Many religious magazines were read by more than just their subscribers, a fact that was well known in this era: in a widely reprinted article, one minister complained that "many read ... who do not themselves subscribe ..., they being in the habit of borrowing from their neighbours" (Nevins 1839: 38). Assuming at least five readers per subscription, to allow for the fact that magazines in this era were passed from reader to reader and their contents were discussed in private homes and at social gatherings (Mott 1930; Albaugh 1994), we can conclude that about one-sixth of free Americans read religious magazines at that time. Although aggregate circulation estimates are not available for later years, we can also conclude that many more free Americans read the far larger number of magazines published during the ensuing three decades.

Religious magazines were both instruments for the mobilization of church members and reflections of national church organizations' efforts to pool resources from multiple congregations and share them across locations. Denominational publishing efforts represented one of the earliest instances of "a fundamental characteristic of modern denominationalism: the gathering of local and regional efforts into comprehensive organizational unity" (Smith 1962: 78). The organizational structures that denominations and affiliated voluntary associations built to publish and distribute religious magazines ushered in an organizational revolution: these large bureaucracies (the second example of bureaucracy in America, after the post office and before the railroads) administered operations across the continent and in doing so, pioneered the modern nonprofit corporation (Hall 1998; Nord 2004).

Religious magazines' founders often justified their publications by claiming the need to reach congregations that were located far from their geographic strongholds and thus had few other religious resources to draw on. For instance, explaining their rationale for forming another Congregationalist periodical in New England, the (unknown) editor of the *Christian Monitor* (1814–17) pointed to the need to disseminate cultural resources throughout a large state, Maine, where fellow adherents had few churches they could attend:

> Periodical publications have an extensive influence upon the minds morals and happiness of men. ... But do any of these publications have an extensive circulation in the District of Maine? ... The natural consequences of this state are forgetfulness of God and divine things, ignorance, error, profanity, a disregard of the Sabbath and the institutions of religion, immorality, and impiety. The means by which these evils must be arrested are the preaching of the gospel and the circulation of religious periodicals. The first of these can, at present, be but partially enjoyed. But, by the patronage and exertions of the well-disposed, a religious publication may be widely circulated and have a most beneficial effect upon the morals and religious state of this section of the Union. (*Christian Monitor* 1814: 1–2)

Others, like the minister-founders of the *Virginia Religious Magazine* (1804–7), a Presbyterian organ, justified their magazines by arguing that periodicals published elsewhere seldom reached their community, writing, "In the Eastern States, Religious Magazines are published, and conducted with great propriety, but the distance we are from them, and the difficulty of conveyance, renders it impracticable to obtain them with punctuality; and impossible that their circulation among us should be general" (*Virginia Religious Magazine* 1804: iv). In 1817, the editor of the *Massachusetts Baptist Missionary Magazine* (1803–1945) looked back on fourteen years of publishing and concluded that his periodical had succeeded in uniting his fellow coreligionists across that state: "Through this medium, churches, widely dispersed, have been made acquainted with each other's circumstances, and with the wonderful things which God has been doing in our land" (Baldwin 1817: 3). Given these successes, he expanded his mission to encompass the entire country and changed the name of his magazine to the *American Baptist Magazine and Missionary Intelligencer* to reflect this change.

Magazines Reflect and Support Religious Fragmentation

In this era, magazines were central to the fracturing of denominations as vehicles for contention (Hatch 1989; King and Haveman 2008). Previous research has shown that in the aftermath of schisms that create new sects, competition increases because the number of distinct subgroups increases (Carroll and Huo 1986) and existing groups mobilize to debate schismatic ones (Barnett and Woywode 2004). Schismatic sects are usually more similar to their "parent" faith than they are to other faiths; for instance, the Associate, Cumberland, and Reformed Presbyterian churches were more similar, in terms of theology and membership, to the original Presbyterian Church than to the Baptist, Congregationalist, Episcopalian, or Methodist churches (Ahlstrom 1972). Competition is most intense between ideologically proximate groups: those that are similar enough to occupy the same general resource space but different enough to prevent solidarity and cooperation (Barnett and Woywode 2004; Fligstein and McAdam 2012). Proximate challenges elicit particularly strong countermobilization efforts because they threaten ideological groups' basic identities and domain claims. Internecine religious conflicts are particularly likely to spawn new magazines because magazines are not simply incarnations of alternative moral or political visions but also political instruments in ongoing struggles over claims to truth, purity, and heritage. Such intense competition spurs the publication of magazines to mobilize group members, contest the claims of other groups, and build distinctive group identities.

The history of American religion provides much evidence that schisms increased religious competition in this era, and that increased competition spurred the publication of many religious magazines. Magazines were common weapons in disputes between schismatic sects and parent churches as well as platforms for debates within schismatic sects. For example, the itinerant Baptist preacher John Leland contributed many articles to the monthly *Reformer* (1820–35) opposing the tendencies of Regular Baptists to emulate mainline denominations by founding missions, creating a clerical hierarchy supported by theological seminaries, and establishing formal creeds such as Sabbatarianism (Hatch 1989: 95–101). Similarly, the semimonthly *Mutual Rights and Christian Intelligencer* (1828–30) championed revivalism and evangelism, which members of the schismatic Methodist Protestant sect felt were imperiled by the "creeping respectability" of the Methodist Church (Hatch 1989: 201–206).

Starting in the 1830s these debates became tinged with political overtones as denominations became enmeshed in wider fields of cultural and political contention (Niebuhr 1929). As explained above, the North–South divide was reflected in the sundering of several denominations. As a result there was a sharp increase in the number of magazines with the word *Southern* in their title, such as the *Southern Methodist Quarterly Review*, founded 1847, which cast itself as a proslavery alternative to the established antislavery *Methodist Quarterly Review*. From 1815 until the American Anti-Slavery Society was founded in 1833 to coordinate the abolitionist movement across the nation, only 1.1 "southern" religious magazines were published per year on average; the number rose to 6.6 per year in the remainder of the 1830s, then to 8.0 per year in the 1840s and 10.0 per year in the 1850s.

The Joint Impact of Religious Institutions on Magazine Publishing

Thus far I have considered several fundamental shifts in American religion separately—the rise of a pluralistic, nationwide field of religion, the competition engendered by pluralism, the rise of internal competition from schismatic groups, and the development of national infrastructures. But the historical record shows that these trends were causally related: revivals created a pluralistic field and pushed denominations to proselytize across the growing nation; revivals were also the cause of many movements that split denominations into competing subgroups; and both competition and geographic expansion pushed denominations to create national infrastructures.[13] The question remains as to whether these trends had independent or interdependent effects on the growth of religious magazines, a key part of denominations' organizational infrastructures. To answer this question I now report a dynamic statistical analysis done with Adam Goldstein of the growth of religious magazines that were formally affiliated with a particular denomination. This analysis starts in 1790 because that is the first year for which good data are available on many explanatory factors. Only five religious magazines were published before this date, so this analysis covers virtually the entire history of this religious resource. This analysis includes all twenty-two denominations founded before 1860 for which good data on the number and location of their congregations exist: Adventist, Baptist, Catholic, Church of God, Congregational, Disciples of Christ, Dunker, Dutch Reformed, Episcopalian, German Reformed, Jewish, Lutheran, Mennonite, Methodist, Moravian, Mormon, Presbyterian, Quaker, Shaker, Swedenborgian, Unitarian, and Universalist. Together these groups accounted for 94.3 percent of all religious congregations in the United States in 1776, 98.8 percent in 1850, and 99.6 percent in 1860 (the only years for which reliable national counts of religious organizations are available), so these data quite accurately represent the field of American religion.

---

[13] For the sake of brevity, in this section I use the word *denomination* to refer to both long-established, stable groups like the Presbyterians and newer, often unstable fringe groups like the Adventists and Mormons of this era, which are often labeled sects or movements.

To explain the growth of denominational magazines, we build on religious-economies theory, which views religious organizations as similar to for-profit firms that compete for customers. This theory holds that competition (measured as religious pluralism, using the complement of the economic index of market concentration) forces churches to work harder to recruit and retain members, which results in more vigorous mobilization efforts (Finke and Stark 1988, 1992; Iannaccone 1994), including publishing more magazines to energize adherents, reach out to the unchurched, and woo members of other faiths. The roots of this competitive-mobilization thesis extend back to Adam Smith, who argued in book 5 of *The Wealth of Nations* that monopolistic religions tend to produce indolent clergy who expend little effort to excite or maintain their adherents' faith; he implied that competition in the market for souls would stimulate more energetic efforts. Max Weber echoed Smith's argument in regard to the United States, where he was struck by the vigorous mobilizing efforts he observed among competing religious groups (Scaff 2011).

Although religious-economies theory's central prediction—that religious diversity engenders competition—accords with the historical record, its value for explaining the dynamics of religious magazines in this era is hampered by its narrow conceptions of religious organizations and the contexts in which they interact. It treats religious organizations as unitary entities, similar to single-establishment firms competing in local markets.[14] Accordingly it has been tested by examining whether the association between competitive intensity and mobilizing efforts within a given geographic unit is positive or negative. This approach assumes, either by theoretical premise or methodological fiat, that the factors driving religious mobilization are localized, that religious mobilization is locally oriented, and that religious organizations' activities in different localities are independent of one another. Such assumptions ignore the history of American religious organizations: they have long had congregations in multiple locations and as early as the nineteenth century they oriented their actions toward a national field rather than purely local markets (Smith 1962; Ahlstrom 1972; Goen 1985; Finke and Stark 1992). More generally, such assumptions do not reflect the complex multiunit nature of religious organizations, whose members are connected horizontally through worship services and Sunday schools and vertically through religious authority and agency structures (Chaves 1993; Stout and Cormode 1998). Past studies of religious mobilization have thereby conflated the (hotly contested) question of whether religious organizations mobilize in response to competitive pressures with the (usually unexamined) presumption that such mobilization is organized in a manner akin to independent firms competing in unrelated local markets.

[14] Recent theoretical restatements recognize denominations as multilevel entities with core-versus-periphery structures (Stark and Finke 2000: 162–65). But the analytic strategies developed to test this theory still treat religious organizations as if they were atomized entities.

There are two additional concerns. First, both proponents and critics of this theory have focused attention on the ostensible incentives to mobilize (competition) and have ignored what social movement scholars have long known—namely. that the capacity to do so (resource availability) is critical (McCarthy and Zald 1977; Edwards and McCarthy 2004). Second, debates have focused on competition *among* denominations and have given little consideration to competition *within* them from movements of schismatic subgroups, despite the central role of fragmentation in American religion (Liebman, Sutton, and Wuthnow 1988; for a notable exception, see Wilde 2007). To explain the effect of such oppositional movements, social movement scholars point to situations where conflict internal to a group reflects larger social cleavages and argue that each side in the conflict responds to the other's mobilizing activities (Zald and Useem 1987; Meyer and Staggenborg 1996; Kim and Pfaff 2012).

We develop an alternative account of religious competition by incorporating insights from social movement theories of mobilization, coupled with a more sociologically grounded conception of religious denominations as multilevel, translocal organizations operating within national fields. We accept the premise that religious organizations *do* compete: they woo people away from other faiths, strive to retain the adherents they already have, and reach out to the unchurched.[15] But we move beyond the microeconomic assumptions of religious-economies theory to generate a more compelling explanation of the patterns by which religious organizations mobilize their adherents. First, we build on historical accounts of American religion (e.g., Goen 1985) and theories of churches as organizations (e.g., Chaves 1993) to consider the translocal dynamics of competitive mobilization. Second, we build on resource-mobilization theory in the social movement literature (McCarthy and Zald 1977; Edwards and McCarthy 2004) to examine how mobilizing efforts reflect variations in religious organizations' capacities as well as their leaders' motivations. Finally, we analyze how patterns of religious mobilization resulted from fragmentation within denominations as well as competition between them. The result is a series of more nuanced arguments about religious mobilization that go far beyond—and in some cases directly oppose—religious-economies theory.

Theory. Most research in this tradition has conceived of religious organizations as similar to single-market firms that compete in local religious markets because religious "consumers" choose which church to attend within their local community (Finke, Guest, and Stark 1996). Because consumers' actions are geographically localized, religious suppliers compete for them locally. As I have explained above, however, American denominations in this era were multiunit entities that competed in interdependent religious markets embed-

---

[15] We leave aside the issue of the commitment displayed by adherents, which is theoretically and empirically distinct from efforts to recruit and retain them.

ded in a national field. Accordingly, although we test for the effects of local competition and local resources to support competitive mobilization, we also assess the effects of competition at the national level and investigate how denominations' magazine publishing activities in local markets were affected by their positions in other markets.

Let us start with predictions about local (state) markets for religion. Religious mobilization should be greater when and where a denomination experiences more intense local competition. Competition is a function of local market structure: it increases with the number of denominations in a local market and with the equality of denominations' market shares (their numbers of adherents)—that is, as religious markets become less monopolistic and more pluralistic. Therefore, denominations will need more mobilization tools, such as magazines, in more pluralistic religious markets. Moreover, as religious markets become more pluralistic, denominations must work harder to distinguish themselves from other faiths and demarcate their own niches, answering the questions "Who are we?" and "What makes us unique?" Because magazines are ideal instruments to define denominations' distinctive identities, they should publish more of them as pluralism increases.

The intensity of competition a denomination experiences should also depend on its position within its local market. Denominations should publish more magazines when and where they have more resources to do so—that is, in their core strongholds, the locations where their market share is higher (Chaves 1993). Because magazines, even in the eighteenth century, were often distributed far beyond their sites of production, denominations could use magazines to support adherents' faith in locations where adherents were socially isolated and resources were scarce—that is, in locations where the focal denomination's share of the local religious market (number of adherents or congregations) was low. In such locations adherents have fewer opportunities to interact with coreligionists (Olson 1998; Perl and Olson 2000), and so will be more vulnerable to overtures from proselytizers in rival denominations. But the resources needed to support magazines (clergy to contribute sermons and educational articles, and laity to pay subscription fees and contribute letters, poetry, and stories) are also lower in such locations. Thus, denominational magazine production should be concentrated in areas where denominations have the most slack resources (where their market share is highest) and distributed to areas where they have the greatest need (where their market share is lowest). Moreover, denominations should be more likely to mobilize against competition when and where they experience more competition *and* have more resources to respond to that competition. This suggests that the positive effect of local market share should be strongest in markets that are highly pluralistic.

As American denominations expanded across the nation, religious competition became delocalized, unmoored from any single location. Instead, rivalries between denominations played out simultaneously in multiple local markets, and their actions in one market were shaped by their relations with rivals in others. In such circumstances, denominations' actions in one local market should be shaped by their relations with rivals in others. If so, the competitive impetus to mobilize in one local market would depend not only on that market's attributes but also on its position vis-à-vis other markets in the national field. In particular, denominations should be more likely to mobilize in a given location when their interactions with rivals are more concentrated in that location. The more denominations encounter their rivals across multiple markets, the more geographically dispersed and less localized their rivalries become. This should prompt them to consolidate their mobilizing efforts. Therefore, the impetus to engage in separate mobilization efforts in any single market should decline with the extent to which religious organizations encounter rivals in multiple local markets.

Now consider how competitive dynamics played out across the national level in this era. There are three parts of this dynamic process. First, while dominant churches can afford to be complacent, embattled minority churches must work hard to recruit and retain members, so they must mobilize their small pools of resources intensively (Finke and Stark 1992; Stark and McCann 1993). Therefore, the number of denominational magazines published should be negatively correlated with a denomination's share of the national market. Thinking dynamically leads to the conclusion that competition is a function of *trends* in market share more than *levels*, as weakening competitive positions (declining market shares) should spur leaders of even dominant groups to take action, while stable competitive positions should make leaders of even minority faiths less inclined to aggressive mobilization (Wilde 2007). For example, in early nineteenth-century New England, when Congregationalists were losing market share to the Baptists and Methodists (although they remained numerically dominant), prominent Congregationalist minister Lyman Beecher pushed his fellow clergymen to more vigorous mobilization efforts (Finke and Stark 1992: 98).

Second, competition from other faiths in a national field may drive denominations to integrate their adherents into a cohesive community by forging strong bonds between them. If so, the growth of denominational magazines would be an integrative response to the dispersion of adherents across ever-broader swaths of space. The geographic dispersion of a faith's congregations should increase demand for magazines because magazines, like other media, forge bonds among readers, especially for those who are far apart and unlikely to meet face-to-face. Magazines supplement purely ritualistic bases of collective identification, allowing far-flung adherents and members of the collective to discuss and reinforce shared beliefs (Park 1940; Anderson [1983] 1991; Calhoun 1991: 1998). This logic suggests that operating across more locations should necessitate publishing more magazines to bind coreligionists together.

Third, in this era, much competition occurred *within* denominations— among conflicting subgroups. Denominations were embedded in wider fields of cultural and political contention (Niebuhr 1929) and internalized cultural divisions from society at large that often erupted into divisive conflicts that split denominations into competing factions. Schisms should spur the launch of new magazines because they increase the number of distinctive subgroups and because they mobilize existing subgroups. Moreover, research on newspapers has shown that competitive mobilization through media is most intense between ideologically proximate groups: those that are similar enough to occupy the same general resource space but different enough to prevent solidarity and cooperation (Barnett and Woywode 2004). Proximate challenges elicit particularly strong countermobilization efforts because they threaten basic identities and domain claims. Internecine religious conflicts are particularly likely to spawn new media like magazines because media are not only incarnations of alternative moral visions but also political instruments in ongoing struggles over claims to truth, purity, and heritage. Taken together, these ideas imply that the number of magazines denominations publish should increase during and after schisms.

Empirical analysis. We analyzed the number of magazines affiliated with a given denomination in a given year, either in a given state or across the nation. We defined a denominational magazine as one that proclaimed a doctrinal and/or organizational affiliation with a particular denomination. The analysis excluded nondenominational religious magazines (113 magazines, 625 annual observations on magazines) and magazines whose affiliated denomination we could not pinpoint (81 magazines, 215 annual observations; appendix 2 describes the statistical analyses in detail.) In these analyses we controlled for other factors, besides the ones we were interested in, in order to rule out alternative explanations. And because, as appendix 2 explains, our analysis included the lagged (prior-year) dependent variable, the estimated coefficients on other variables can be interpreted as dynamic effects—that is, the estimated effect of a change in one variable on an increase or decrease in the number of denominational magazines published between that year and the prior year.

At the state level the statistical analysis shows that, net of other explanatory variables and control variables, the number of denominational magazines published in a local market increased with the level of pluralism in that market, consistent with religious-economies theory. The number of denominational magazines published in a local market also increased with two different measures of local market share—the percentage of congregations in the focal market that were affiliated with the focal denomination and the fraction of the denomination's congregations that were in the focal market. These results indicate that magazine publishing occurred when and where denominations possessed a growing concentration of resources. Interactions between both measures of market share, on the one hand, and pluralism, on the other, were also positive—as expected. This pattern of results indicates that the impetus to mobilize (stronger in more pluralistic local markets) and the capacity to do so (stronger in markets where the focal denomination's market share was larger) accentuated each other's effects. Finally, as expected, multimarket contact retarded the growth of denominational magazines, suggesting that the delocal-

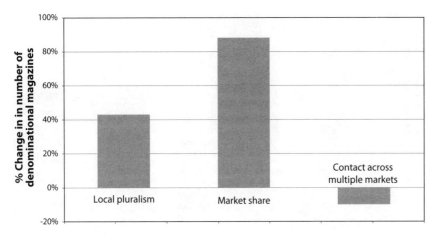

Figure 5.7. State-level denominational magazine growth: standardized coefficients for statistically significant theoretical variables.

ization of competition led denominations to geographically concentrate their magazine publishing efforts in their core strongholds.

How big are these effects? Figure 5.7 depicts standardized coefficients for all main effects and controls.[16] The height of each bar corresponds to the factor by which the number of denominational magazines is expected to increase if the level of the focal variable increases by one standard deviation, holding all other variables constant. A one-standard-deviation increase in local pluralism increased the expected number of denominational magazines published by 43 percent, while a one-standard-deviation increase in local market share increased the expected number of magazines by double that amount, 88 percent. The negative effect of contact with rivals across multiple locations was much smaller: a one-standard-deviation increase in the extent to which denominations met local rivals across multiple other markets reduced the expected number of magazines by 10 percent.

At the national level the statistical analysis showed that, net of other explanatory variables and control variables, denominational market share had a significant negative effect, as expected. This finding suggests that weakening national competitive positions mobilized denominations to publish more magazines, whereas strengthening competitive positions made them less apt to expand their publishing efforts. The effect of spatial scale was positive and significant, which supports the claim that denominational magazines grew in response to the challenges of organizing the faithful across ever larger geographic areas. The positive effect of spatial scale is independent of the effect of denomination size (number of congregations), which suggests that spatial

[16] These estimates are derived from a model that included all main effects but did not include the interactions between market share and local pluralism. Thus all bars, including those for market share and local pluralism, represent average effects.

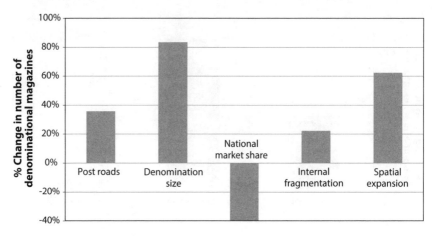

Figure 5.8. National-level denominational magazine growth: standardized beta coefficients for all statistically significant variables.

scale taps into geographic expansion in particular, not denominational growth in general. Finally, the number of denominational magazines increased with the cumulative number of schisms within the focal denomination. This suggests that denominations that experienced more internal discord published more magazines, as both splinter groups and established groups sought to mobilize supporters.

Figure 5.8 charts standardized coefficient estimates for all statistically significant effects in the national-level analysis. The height of each bar represents the expected percentage change per year in the number of magazines published, given a one-standard-deviation increase in the corresponding variable and holding all other variables constant. Not surprisingly, expansion of the postal system (0.36) and increasing denominational size (0.83) were both associated with substantial growth of denominations' publishing infrastructures. Yet the effects of a denomination's geographic expansion (0.62) and market share (−0.40) were similar orders of magnitude. Increasing internal fragmentation due to schisms had a smaller standardized effect (0.22), which is due in part to the low variance of that variable.

CONCLUSION

Starting in 1743, when the first religious magazine was launched, American religious communities depended ever more heavily on magazines to project their theological principles and cultural identities, to forge enduring bonds between members, and to compete with other faiths in the marketplace for souls. The flourishing of religious magazines was one instantiation of the modern organization of American religion on a national scale, as churches

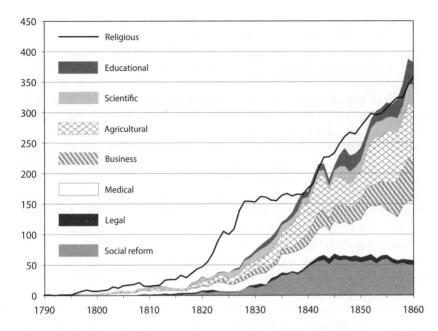

Figure 5.9. The growth of religious magazines versus other specialized magazines, 1790–1860.

expanded across the continent and used magazines to connect their far-flung flocks. Statistical analysis showed that religious groups competed both locally and nationally by publishing magazines to recruit and retain adherents. It also showed that local competitive mobilization through magazines depended on the extent to which rivalries between faiths played out simultaneously in multiple markets. Three related trends in the history of American religion—the development of a pluralistic nationwide field of religion, the competition engendered by pluralism, and the rise of internal competition from schismatic groups—had independent effects on the growth of denominational magazine publishing. But there is also evidence that denominations' magazine publishing efforts grew faster when and where both competition (pluralism) and resources (market share) were high. Thus the impetus to mobilize in the face of competition drove religious groups to act only when and where their resource capacity to mobilize was strong.

Religious events and institutions both supported religious magazines and were supported by them. But the burgeoning number of religious magazines had widespread effects far beyond the field of religion: they changed the nature of the magazine industry as a whole. Religious magazines were the first specialized genre to proliferate; they were followed by magazines devoted to several very different social causes and communities: social reform, professions, agriculture, education, and science and engineering. Figure 5.9 compares the growth of religious magazines with magazines devoted to those other social causes and communities from 1790 to 1860. (Only five religious magazines were published before that date, and no magazines were published before that date in any of the other genres shown here.) This figure shows that in most years more religious magazines were published than magazines in all other genres combined; not until the 1850s did these other genres, collectively, come to outnumber religious magazines.

Their large numbers and mass appeal gave religious magazines great legitimacy. Because religion became central to American culture in this era, religious magazines could also "borrow" legitimacy from the denominations with which they were affiliated. Moreover, the use of magazines by virtually all religious groups—including upstart faiths and immigrant religious communities whose members spoke languages other than English—demonstrated that magazines were powerful tools for many people, and not just those with high social status (in terms of education and occupation); this finding echoes the conclusion drawn from the analysis of magazine founders in chapter 4. In the wake of the growth of magazines affiliated with so many different denominations, magazines came to be seen as a cultural product that could be deployed by anyone for almost any purpose—cultural, economic, or political.

The flourishing of religious magazines was both directly and indirectly responsible for the growth of magazines devoted to social reform efforts: directly, religious magazines served as organizing templates and infrastructures for magazines devoted to reform movements; indirectly, the flourishing of religious magazines legitimated the use of magazines to agitate for social reform causes. The flourishing of religious magazines also legitimated the use of magazines to build community among members of emerging professions and other specialized occupations and to support modernizing efforts in agriculture, education, and science and engineering. In short, as magazines were shown to be useful platforms for religious debate and community building, the leaders of other kinds of communities came to see their value. Thus the largely Protestant American faiths were modernizing forces (Bellah 1968), as they pioneered the development of translocal communities. This conclusion is reinforced by studying the Sunday school movement, which was a highly organized impulse on the part of many denominations to educate the young and thus represents a second outcropping of the modernizing temperament of religion in this era. To see how modernization played out in other arenas of social life, chapters 6 and 7 analyze the growth of magazines devoted to social reform and the economy, respectively.

CHAPTER 6

Social Reform

hapter 5 outlined the connection between religion and magazines. In this chapter I analyze the "benevolent empire" (Foster 1960; Griffin 1960), an interorganizational field (DiMaggio and Powell 1983) that consisted of a wide array of voluntary social reform associations, the religious structures that supported them, and the magazines that both supported organized reform efforts and were supported by them. I begin by describing the history of reform movements, noting connections among successive movements and detailing the formal organizations that supported them. I then examine the religious roots of social reform. Next I describe the specialized magazines that reform leaders launched to broadcast their views and show how many distinct communities—some directly opposing others, some supporting each other—were sustained by these publications. I also analyze how often the many different social reform movements were covered across all magazine genres. I conclude with an in-depth analysis of the antislavery movement and its relationship with both religion and magazines.

THE EVOLUTION OF SOCIAL REFORM MOVEMENTS

In the eighteenth and nineteenth centuries, the most prominent social reform movements were those of abolition, temperance, and Sabbatarianism.[1] But reformers in this era also agitated to eradicate an amazingly wide (and sometimes bizarre) array of other social ills: reforming prostitutes and seamen; promoting the rights of women and workers; helping the blind, the deaf and dumb, the insane, debtors, paupers, orphans, widows, Indians, and free blacks; advocating free love, nonviolence, prison reform, phonetic spelling, dress reform, more frequent bathing, manual labor for seminarians, and vegetarianism; and crusading against war, capital punishment, dueling, cock-

---

[1] Chapter 5 briefly discussed movements that were often under the direct control of religious authorities: the movements to distribute Bibles and religious tracts, and the home and foreign missionary movements. Here, in an effort to broaden the discussion and assess more purely cultural connections between religion and reform, I focus on reform movements that were less formally connected to religious authorities. I am ignoring the first successful social movement on American soil—the popular mobilization against colonial rule from 1765 to 1776, which culminated in the Revolution (Tarrow 1998)—because that movement occurred when American magazines were in their infancy, so magazines' impact was minimal.

fighting, bullbaiting, swearing, tobacco, tea and coffee, novels, theater, card playing, and gambling. In this section I first trace the temporal arc of the three biggest movements, then discuss several smaller movements together under the rubric of humanitarian reform, and end by discussing the early women's rights movement. I show how movements built on each other by using similar rhetorical arguments that emphasized individual rights and the need to improve the moral condition of humanity (Tyler 1944; Rendall 1984; Mintz 1995). For example, the first wave of the Sabbatarian movement created tactics used by subsequent movements, while the temperance movement's tactics were imitated in the second wave of the Sabbatarian movement. I also reveal how these movements became "modern," mobilizing to sustain efforts that were formally organized, transcended regional boundaries, and aimed at distant targets—often, but not always, the state (Hobsbawm 1959; Rudé 1981; Tilly 1986, 1995; Calhoun 1993; Tarrow 1998). And I highlight the role that formal organizations played in modernizing these movements by supporting their efforts to mobilize supporters across the expanding nation (Cairns [1898] 1971; Staudenraus [1961] 1980; Abzug 1994; Stewart 1997; Fanuzzi 2003; Nord 2004).

Sabbatarianism

Sunday mail was the first target for widespread grassroots protests in the early republic. Sabbatarians mounted two massive waves of protest, the first from 1810 to 1817, the second from 1826 to 1831; smaller-scale protests continued for decades afterward. The first protests were spurred by an act of Congress in 1810 requiring local postmasters to deliver on demand any item they received on any day of the week and to open their offices to the public every day the mail arrived. Sunday mail had been a standard feature of the postal service since before the Revolution, but it had never before been explicitly mandated. The Postal Act of 1810 brought the federal government into everyday contact with ordinary people and energized many of them to vent their anger at what they viewed as the government's violation of theological tenets about Sabbath keeping and its running roughshod over local and state laws governing the Sabbath (John 1990, 1995). Thus, beyond the issue of moral conduct, Sabbatarian protests raised a serious question of sovereignty.

The second wave of Sabbatarian protests was unleashed by a 1825 postal law that reenacted the 1810 regulations. Large-scale protest was catalyzed by the formation of a formal association—the General Union for Promoting the Observance of the Christian Sabbath—in May 1828. William Lloyd Garrison declared it "the most efficient instrument in the cause of religion and public morality every put into practice in any age and country" (quoted in John 1995: 180). The union asked its members to take a pledge to uphold the Sabbath by refraining from working, traveling, and playing, and to boycott transportation companies that operated on Sunday. In some places, local chapters urged members to withhold their trade from commercial enterprises that were open on Sundays. The union also distributed to local chapters templates for petitions to the US Congress to end Sunday mail service (John 1990, 1995).

There was opposition to Sabbatarianism, mostly during the second wave of protests. A countermovement was first formally organized in New York in 1828; other anti-Sabbatarian groups sprang up in cities throughout the country (Wyatt-Brown 1971). Anti-Sabbatarian support was strongest in cities that were geographically distant from the nation's commercial centers, like Cincinnati, New Orleans, and Rochester, New York. Anti-Sabbatarians were a diverse group, including both merchants and laborers (Johnson 1978; Roth 1987). This countermovement's strength, and its alignment with the interests of federal authorities, who defended Sunday mail on economic and national defense grounds, ultimately persuaded Sabbatarian leaders that their cause was doomed, and they disbanded their organization in May 1832.[2]

Although it failed in its quest to end Sunday mail service, the Sabbatarian movement is notable for pioneering two tactics that were adopted by many later movements: the petition and the boycott (Wyatt-Brown 1971; John 1995). Participation in this movement also led many to embrace the cause of abolition (Wyatt-Brown 1971), as I discuss below.

Temperance

The temperance movement began shortly after the Revolution as small groups of individuals took sobriety pledges. In 1808, the members of the Moreau Society, the first American temperance association, pledged to not drink distilled spirits, although they could still consume wine, beer, and cider (Hay 1855). Before that time the effort to promote temperance had enjoyed little support; it consisted primarily of proselytizing by individuals who, like the members of the Moreau Society, had vowed to abstain from hard liquor. The movement was limited by geography to the Northeast and by class to clergy and other elites, so it did not grow much until after 1825, when many faiths officially disavowed hard liquor. The proliferation of asylums during the first half of the nineteenth century also served as a catalyst to temperance activists, who often pointed out how drink contributed to deviance and argued that temperance was a means of promoting self-discipline (Tyrrell 1979a). An even more important catalyst was the formation of the first nationwide temperance association, the American Society for the Promotion of Temperance (later known as the American Temperance Society), in 1826. Its nested arrangement of national, regional, and local organizations reduced mobilization and coordination costs by providing templates for organizing and ways to link local

[2] Although another Sabbatarian organization, the American Foreign and Sabbath Union, was active in the 1840s, it never grew very strong.

groups to a nationwide effort to shape public opinion and influence federal and state legislators (Schlesinger 1944; Skocpol 1997; Skocpol, Ganz, and Munson 2000). This militant organization used revivalistic methods, sent lecturers throughout the country, and published pamphlets and magazines. By 1835 it boasted over 1.5 million followers (American Temperance Society 1835). It also had considerable impact on Americans' behavior: Alexis de Tocqueville, during his tour of America, remarked that the effect of temperance societies was one of the most noticeable things in the country, as "a hundred thousand men publicly engaged not to make use of strong liquors" ([1848] 2000: 492). Its success led imitators in other movements, such as those for abolition and peace, to emulate its structure; such strategic imitation resolved uncertainty around the best way to organization and boosted legitimacy by adopting a recognized template (Meyer and Rowan 1977; DiMaggio and Powell 1983).

To unite local and regional temperance groups that were not affiliated with the American Temperance Society, the American Temperance Union (originally named the United States Temperance Union) was formed in 1833. But with its formation the movement began to factionalize, largely over debates between those who preferred to ban hard liquor but not beer, wine, or cider (as the American Temperance Society originally advocated) and those who demanded complete abstinence from all alcoholic beverages, as called for in the American Temperance Union's charter (Tyrrell 1979a). Partly as a result of the Union's more radical stance, the movement declined precipitously (Tyler 1944: 329). Identification of the temperance movement with abolition furthered its decline (Tyler 1944; De Benedetti 1980).

In the wake of this decline, three competing national temperance associations were established—the Washington Temperance Society (1841), the Sons of Temperance (1842), and the Independent Order of Good Templars (1851)—to promote three very different agendas. The Washingtonians were a congeries of working-class clubs whose members helped each other keep temperance pledges through self-organized narrations of life histories, presaging the system used by Alcoholics Anonymous today. The Sons of Temperance were more prosperous than the Washingtonians; they sought social benevolence along with temperance. The Templars offered wide-ranging fraternity, welcoming women and blacks as well as white men. These organizations reinvigorated the crusade against drunkenness: the Washingtonians peaked at 600,000 members, the Sons of Temperance at almost 250,000, and the Templars at 60,000 (Hodges 1877; Skocpol 1999). Despite their many differences, these organizations were quite effective: between 1846 and 1855 they helped pass laws prohibiting alcohol sales in fourteen of thirty states. Annual consumption of distilled spirits among people fifteen years of age or older declined from 8.7 gallons per capita in 1810 to 3.6 gallons in 1850 (Rorabaugh 1979: 233). But class-based conflicts between the proletarian Washingtonians and the more elite Templars and Sons of Temperance weakened the temperance movement in the 1850s.

Abolition

The roots of this movement run deep in American history. As early as 1688, Quakers mounted sporadic campaigns to abolish slavery through manumission. In 1758, after considerable discussion and infighting, most New Jersey and Pennsylvania Quakers adopted a policy "to put a stop to the increase of the practice of importing, buying, selling, or keeping slaves for the term of life" (Zilversmit 1967: 74). Opposition to slavery spread slowly among other faiths in the late eighteenth century, but it had little impact on society at large.

The organized antislavery movement began in 1775, when the first antislavery association, the Pennsylvania Abolition Society, was founded. For the next half century, the movement attracted political and economic elites who used judicial appeals and state-oriented institutional pressure to push for manumission of slaves, legal aid for free and enslaved blacks, and compliance within existing laws for the protection, supervision, and education of slaves. But widespread support was slow to develop as the concern for human rights faded in the early nineteenth century and political debates shifted to foreign relations (Tyler 1944; Newman 2002). The question of whether Missouri would be admitted to the Union as a slave or free state brought the issue of slavery to a boil, but only temporarily. The movement did not take off until 1833, when it was catalyzed by the formation of a federated organization, the American Anti-Slavery Society, which was patterned on the American Temperance Society and knit local groups into a cohesive, nationwide effort (Schlesinger 1944; Skocpol 1997; Skocpol et al. 2000).[3] The forty-seven antislavery societies operating in 1830 exploded to over four hundred in 1835 and then to over 1,600 with 90,000 members in 1839 (American Anti-Slavery Society 1834–40).

As it grew the antislavery movement was transformed into a radical grassroots campaign that emphasized moral suasion and individual conversion tactics. It became formally political in 1839 when the Liberty Party, the first antislavery party, held its first convention (McKivigan 1984). But in 1840 the movement fragmented over what role women should play and whether it should engage in political action or restrict its activities to moral suasion. Notwithstanding this division, abolitionists' efforts continued unchecked and this movement remained a vibrant part of the American political scene, with supporters from all walks of life scattered from California to Maine. To coordinate these far-flung activists, national conventions were held in 1853 and 1855.

A collective effort to oppose abolition, the African colonization movement, was conducted largely by slave owners from border states (i.e., slave states that did not join the confederacy: Delaware, Kentucky, Maryland, and

---

[3] This was a deliberate imitation: an article in the *Genius of Temperance* (1829–33), reprinted in the *Genius of Universal Emancipation*, called for the formation of an abolition society with the same federated structure as the temperance society (Humanitas 1831: 112).

Missouri) who found that slavery was no longer profitable (Tyler 1944; Fuller 1986). This countermovement was premised on slaveholders' belief in blacks' inferiority to whites and on their fears that free blacks might instigate race wars if their numbers became large enough. Colonization advocates raised funds to remunerate slave owners who voluntarily emancipated their slaves and "repatriated" free blacks to Africa to reduce their numbers in America. The American Colonization Society was founded in 1816 to coordinate the efforts, and although the movement persisted in trying to send free blacks to Africa long after the Civil War, it was a failure on both ideological and practical grounds (Tyler 1944; Staudenraus [1961] 1980; Miller 1975). Ideologically, it diverted attention from the evils of slavery by embracing the idea of black inferiority; practically, it effected very few incidents of manumission and transported very few free blacks to Liberia—only fifteen thousand according to the society's own records (Staudenraus [1961] 1980: 251), but a quarter of that number by other estimates (Tyler 1944). Many of those emigrants were blacks born free, not manumitted slaves, and a large fraction of them were stricken by disease and harassed by nearby natives.

Humanitarian Reform

Many efforts to assist the downtrodden were organized between the Revolution and the Civil War: reforming prostitutes and seamen; helping the blind, deaf and dumb, insane, debtors, paupers, orphans, widows, and free blacks; advocating prison reform and crusading against capital punishment. These causes were united by a desire to provide material aid and moral guidance to the downtrodden, whose numbers were growing rapidly as the nation urbanized. In increasingly crowded cities, the emerging middle class could not avoid seeing the wretched condition of the poor. As the number of urban areas exploded from ninety in 1830 to almost four hundred in 1860, the social inequality first seen in Boston, New York, and Philadelphia became apparent in many other parts of the country. Reformers sought to maintain social stability by instilling morality in the fallen and providing relief to the destitute (Foster 1960; Rothman 1971; Boyer 1978). They petitioned legislatures to keep minor debtors and the insane out of prison, pushed for changes in legal codes to shift the emphasis from corporal punishment (hanging, whipping, confinement in the stocks, banishment) to rehabilitation, pressed to make seduction and adultery crimes, and lobbied for financial support for custodial institutions and for improved prisons.

Many of these efforts were organized by voluntary societies. Two waves of humanitarian reform societies emerged, the first soon after the Revolution, the second after the War of 1812 (Foster 1960; Griffin 1960; Smith-Rosenberg 1971; Boyer 1978). But unlike the Sabbatarian and abolition movements, no nationwide federated organization appeared to catalyze and coordinate humanitarian causes. Other reformers' efforts revolved around custodial institutions (as opposed to voluntary societies) that housed and educated the downtrodden. These institutions took highly varied forms, depending on the group being served: there were houses of refuge, which combined the functions of shelters with those of Sunday schools and vocational training institutions, for destitute widows, free blacks, juvenile delinquents, and prostitutes; halfway houses for former prisoners; asylums for orphans and the insane; hospitals and dispensaries for poor women and children; and residential schools for the blind and the deaf and dumb (Rothman 1971).

Many humanitarian societies and custodial institutions were founded and run by women (Boyer 1978; Berg 1980; Scott 1991). Women's work in these societies led them to embrace a consciousness that women of all classes shared legal disabilities that were distinct from those of men (Rossi 1973; Melder 1977; Berg 1980; Mintz 1995; Marilley 1997).

Women's Rights

The first efforts to improve women's position focused on female education. Many writers, including prominent physician Benjamin Rush, lamented the ornamental and superficial nature of female education that had prevailed throughout the eighteenth century and argued that one of women's most important tasks was to educate their children and socialize them to be good citizens (Welter 1966). Reformers called for more rigorous education for girls, involving academic subjects as well as instruction in practical tasks, stressing both intellectual improvement and moral character development. As education moved out of the home and into formal institutions (Cremin 1970; Kaestle 1983), the female education movement's emphasis shifted from preparing women to teach their children to preparing women for the labor market through general education and specific skills training (Cott [1977] 1997; Rendall 1984). This led to the founding of many schools and colleges to train women as teachers; some of these "normal schools" developed into full-fledged colleges.

In the 1830s the focus expanded to include reform of marriage laws. Activists identified the legal and economic framework of marriage as a deeply oppressive remnant of the feudal system and worked to modernize this institution (Basch 1982; Rendall 1984; Flexner and Fitzpatrick 1996; Marilley 1997). By 1850, reformers had pushed most states to pass laws permitting married women to own property; however, husbands retained legal rights to their wives' earnings and custody of their children after divorce (Flexner and Fitzpatrick 1996; Friedman 2005). In the late 1840s the focus shifted again to female suffrage, which came to be seen as necessary for the achievement of all other goals, including further reform of marriage laws (Rendall 1984: 302). The movement's first convention was held in 1848 in Seneca Falls, New York. The first national convention followed two years later in Salem, Ohio, and became an annual event. The temperance and women's rights movements became interdependent: women's rights crusaders viewed female suffrage and reform of marriage laws as necessary to safeguard wives and children from the depredations of drunken husbands and to secure passage of stricter liquor laws (Rendall 1984; Flexner and Fitzpatrick 1996). In this spirit the Washingtonians and Sons of Temperance established women's auxiliaries.

The women's rights movement was the daughter of earlier reform movements in three respects. First, women often led humanitarian and antislavery societies (Berg 1980), where they learned valuable management skills and developed self-confidence in their ability to effect social change, as well as a strong sense of sisterhood, a consciousness that women of all classes shared legal disabilities that were distinct from those of men (Rossi 1973; Melder 1977; Berg 1980; Mintz 1995; Marilley 1997). Second, women's rights developed into a collective goal within earlier movements (Berg 1980; Rendall 1984; Abzug 1994; Flexner and Fitzpatrick 1996; Marilley 1997). Third, earlier movements provided this movement with organizational structures, members, strategy (both the abolition and women's rights movements agitated for total suffrage), and ideology (to justify their existence, all three movements invoked the notion of human rights; Berg 1980; Phillips 1985; Rosenthal et al. 1985).

The Modernization of Social Movements

Whereas social protests in the early eighteenth century tended to be short-lived outbursts mounted by loosely connected groups that were regionally rooted and emphasized local demands, a century later social protests were sustained and formally organized, transcended neighborhoods, and were aimed at distant targets—often, but not always, the state (Hobsbawm 1959; Rudé 1981; Tilly 1986, 1995; Calhoun 1993; Tarrow 1993, 1998). In this way the movements became modern. The birth of modern movements was due to a shift in the repertoires of contention—the set of actions activists used to assert their claims—from parochial, bifurcated, and particular to cosmopolitan (focused on national targets), modular (flexibly adaptable), and autonomous (independently useful; Tarrow 1993; Tilly 1995). Modern movement tactics included mass-signed petitions submitted to elected officials, boycotts of business concerns that acted contrary to movement principles, paid agents who traveled across the country lecturing and mobilizing support, and specialized magazines proclaiming movement principles. These new repertoires of contention were promulgated widely by social movement organizations, which forged extensive, often nationwide, networks of reformers and developed flexible routines that facilitated sustained mobilization and protest (Tarrow 1998).

The prototypical example of the modernization of social reform movements is the antislavery movement. In some respects early antislavery societies supported a premodern social movement, one that depended on the peculiarities of local resources and whose targets were often local slave owners. But in many other respects, they formed the basis of an almost modern social movement: they were formal organizations that repeatedly used modular tactics—petitions and lawsuits—over extended periods of time and aimed these tactics at state authorities (Newman 2002). The antislavery movement became fully modern when the American Anti-Slavery Society was founded in 1833. This organization not only catalyzed others but also transformed politics: after 1830, the use of magazines, grassroots organizing, and graphic images—all tactics antislavery advocates helped pioneer—came to define American politics (Newman 2002). Rather than having prominent citizens sign petitions or bring lawsuits, the American Anti-Slavery Society sought to build widespread support to end slavery through a moral transformation that would turn the entire populace into abolitionists. To that end it relied on traveling agents, the propagation of literature, and the formation of local societies.

Many other movements were transformed by the formation of federated organizations that made possible coordinated action across the nation, including Sabbatarianism, temperance, and peace. The federated structures gave these movements' formal organizations great flexibility: they could interact with local communities as easily as they could with state officials or the federal government, and they could pursue social as well as political change (Skocpol 1999; Skocpol et al. 2000). The power of federated organizations to push for reform on multiple levels quickly became obvious to contemporaries. Most famously, Alexis de Tocqueville remarked, "Americans of all ages, all conditions, and all minds constantly unite. Not only do they have commercial and industrial associations in which all take part, but they also have a thousand other kinds: religious, moral, grave, futile, very general and very particular, immense and very small ... if it is a question of bringing to light a truth or developing a sentiment with the support of a great example, they associate" (Tocqueville [1848] 2000: 489). Similarly, prominent Unitarian clergyman William Ellery Channing noted that "one of the most remarkable circumstances or features of our age, is the energy with which the principle of combination, or of action by joint forces, by associated numbers, is manifesting itself. It may be said, without much exaggeration, that every thing is now done by societies. . . . Men, it is justly said, can do jointly, what they cannot do singly. The union of minds and hands works wonders. Men grow efficient by concentrating their powers" (Channing 1872: 282). But Channing also cautioned against the dangers of these organizations, explaining that they were able to create "disciplined armies" that could change society for the worse, as well as for the better. "So extensive have coalitions become," he wrote, "and so various and rapid are the means of communication, that when a few leaders have agreed on an object, an impulse may be given in a month to the whole country. Whole States may be deluged with tracts and other publications, and a voice like that of many waters, be called forth from immense and widely separated multitudes. Here is a great new power brought to bear on society, and it is a great moral question, how it ought to be viewed, and what duties it imposes" (Channing 1872: 283–84).

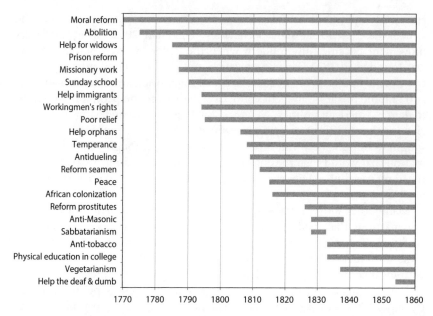

Figure 6.1. Timeline for the establishment of the first formal organization to support each social reform movement.

Figure 6.1 chronicles organizational developments for all social reform movements that had at least one formally organized voluntary society founded during this era. For each movement, this figure notes the year in which the first organization was founded. The figure reveals that associations were created to support many social movements—not just the large ones, like the antislavery, temperance, and missionary movements, but also many small and obscure movements including the drive to outlaw dueling and the crusade against tobacco.

The creation of reform associations was made easier by passage of laws that allowed general incorporation of nonprofit organizations. Prior to passage of these laws, each individual organization had to appeal to state legislators for a special corporate charter. Because these charters involved special privileges, founders had to demonstrate that their organizations would serve the public interest; general incorporation laws obviated such efforts (Kaufman 2008).[4] In turn these formal organizations created a field of social reform in which individuals, informal groups, and the organizations themselves sometimes cooperated and other times competed over material and symbolic resources (DiMaggio and Powell 1983; Calhoun 1993; Fligstein and McAdam 2012).

[4] In turn, passage of these laws was spurred by the increasing legitimacy of formal organizations, which was due to the positive experiences many Americans had with reform societies (Seavoy 1978: 78; Creighton 1996).

RELIGION AND REFORM: THE MORAL IMPULSE

In this era, as in later periods, there were two deep connections between religion and reform. The first was in theological principles—notably, the doctrine of disinterested benevolence and the energy of religious revivalism. As Sydney E. Ahlstrom explained so eloquently, "The historical roots of humanitarian reform lay, first of all, in the Puritan's basic confidence that the world could be constrained and re-formed in accordance with God's revealed will. Revivalism intensified the nation's sense of millennial expectancy, and a doctrine of 'disinterested benevolence' of Edwardsean lineage informed the Second Awakening's manifold activities, giving rise to the evangelical vision of a great Christian republic stretching westward beyond the Appalachians as a beacon and example for the whole world" (1972: 637–38). The second connection between religion and reform was religious institutions' formal organizational structures, personnel, and proselytizing practices. I will discuss each in turn.

Theological Principles Supporting Reform

Because theologies frame peoples' beliefs about what society should be, they shape people's cognitive dispositions toward mobilizing efforts (Wood 1999). In the era under examination, as in the contemporary era, churches' support for many social movements was impelled by their central concern for morality and community. (See Tocqueville [1848] 2000: 278–82, Smith 1957, Tuveson 1968, Abzug 1994, Mintz 1995, and Hirrel 1998 on the eighteenth and early nineteenth centuries; see Morris 1984, Smith 1996, McAdam 2003, and Bail 2015 on the twentieth and twenty-first centuries). Because religious culture is by its very nature congruent with the ideals of many reform movements, activists can easily link movement ideals to religious beliefs, so churches are extremely effective mobilizing structures. Churches bring people together to demonstrate their shared commitment to values, symbols, and rituals, so they strengthen adherents' social bonds, making it easier for them to band together to fight social evils. To the extent that churchgoers espouse values congruent with those of movements, they are a receptive audience and are easily brought into movements (Freeman 1973; Wood 1999). For example, because Sabbatarians framed Sunday mail service as a violation of the Lord's day, they received broad support from authorities in many Protestant denominations: Baptist, Congregationalist, Dutch and German Reformed, Episcopalian, Lutheran, Methodist, Presbyterian, and Unitarian.

There was early support for some reform movements by authorities in Calvinist faiths (Congregational, Dutch Reformed, and Presbyterian), especially in New England. Support was rooted in the eighteenth-century theology of disinterested benevolence articulated by Congregational minister Samuel

Hopkins in his *System of Doctrines Contained in Divine Revelation*, published in 1793. Hopkins, who was a student of Jonathan Edwards and the most prominent Calvinist theologian in America at that time, taught that God had a self-less or "disinterested" love for his creatures, and that the elect shared this disposition (Haroutunian 1970). Similar ideals were promulgated by several Quaker theologians and by John Wesley and George Whitefield, the cofounders of the Methodist Church (Miller 1965). This "practical religion" had great social utility (Tyler 1944: 489; Staudenraus [1961] 1980: 13) as such reformers as Lyman Beecher thundered against social ills like dueling and intemperance and argued for organized moral reform campaigns (Beecher 1803, 1809, 1827; Boyer 1978; Abzug 1994; Hirrel 1998).[5]

Movements ranging from abolition to moral reform to assistance for distressed groups and crusades against public vices were motivated by humanitarian concerns central to the doctrine of disinterested benevolence. Activists in many movements emphasized the need to improve humanity's moral condition. For instance, abolitionists conceived of slaveholding as sinful and slave owners as sinners, and viewed the enslavement of blacks as contrary to Christianity. As one article noted, "The doom of the children of Africa is fixed: their lot is dreadful bondage! O Christianity! Thou whose mild teacher taught self-denial to the world ... can thy professors make captive and destroy their brethren?" (*American Museum*, quoted in Zilversmit 1967: 171).

Key to the antislavery movement was William Lloyd Garrison's drawing a connection between it and the idea of a national sin (Abzug 1994: 135). The close connection between religion and temperance is evident in the guiding statement of the American Temperance Society (1835): "Alcohol, when used as a beverage, causes death to the bodies and souls of men." For their part, Sabbatarians argued that prohibiting Sunday mails would "restore Godly order to a fallen community" (Abzug 1994: 114). And the Society for Alleviating the Miseries of Public Prisons declared that "the obligations of benevolence, which are founded in the precepts and examples of the Author of Christianity, are not canceled by the follies or crimes of our fellow creatures" (quoted in Tyler 1944: 267). For the women's rights movement, evangelical religion provided a powerful imagery that embodied and gave strength to the particular qualities of womanhood (Rendall 1984: 323).

The proliferation of reform movements increasingly reflected the democratization of Christianity through religious revivals, which broadened the base of reformers beyond New England Calvinists (Hatch 1989). In this way religious movements spurred reform movements (Calhoun 1993). Many who were touched by revivals rejected Calvinist notions of original sin and predestination and instead embraced the Arminian notion of human perfectibility (Mintz 1995). Revivals instilled a sense of moral obligation to transform one-

[5] Of course, these movements also revealed the Puritan impulse to dictate to others how they should conduct themselves (Griffin 1957, 1960; Foster 1960).

self and the world in God's image. As prominent revivalist Rev. Mark Tucker declared, revivalism pushed Americans to "begin to live, *for a time*, as they ought *always* to live" (1833: 129; emphasis in the original) and to make America a more perfect society by improving themselves and showing benevolence toward the less fortunate (Tuveson 1968; McLoughlin 1978; Hatch 1989; Butler 1990; Abzug 1994; Mintz 1995; McCarthy 2003). Accordingly, many reformers tried to solve personal and social problems by adopting strategies of action used in revivals: enthusiastic evangelical rituals such as public lectures, pledges, and testimonies. The antislavery and temperance movements emphasized public confessions and personal repudiations of sin. For their pronounced revivalist hue, Michael P. Young dubbed them "confessional protests" and argued that a combination of "the evangelical schemas of public confession and the special sins of the nation mobilized support for these movements within a national infrastructure of Protestant institutions" (2002: 661). Sabbatarian and temperance pledges, along with vows to free one's slaves, became "sacred invocations" within those movements (Abzug 1994: 93).

Most notable is the case of abolitionism. Several theological tenets spread by revivalists were congruent with this movement (McKivigan 1984: 19–20; Mintz 1995; Stewart 1997; Hirrel 1998). Most important was the Arminian doctrine that every human being possessed free will, which was highly conducive to antislavery efforts. Revivalists also emphasized the need for people to repent their sins and take personal responsibility for their salvation: immediate repentance for wrongdoing and cessation of evil actions—like owning slaves—was required for redemption. The doctrine of perfectionism, which sought the moral perfection of not just oneself but society at large, also supported the drive for emancipation of the slaves. The doctrine of disinterested benevolence, which was spread far beyond New England by revivalists like Charles Grandison Finney, taught people that to prove their love of God, they had to overcome self-interest and show benevolence to all humankind. This doctrine stimulated some to free their own slaves and others to call for the emancipation of other people's slaves; it also led to widespread efforts to reform the morals of fallen women and seamen and to help the downtrodden (Stewart 1997; Hirrel 1998).

Many reformers relied on the Bible to support their positions. For example, Theodore Dwight Weld published a pamphlet titled *The Bible against Slavery*. Antislavery arguments were countered by proslavery advocates with their own interpretations of the Bible (Noll 2002), like Virginia Baptist minister Thornton Stringfellow's tract titled *A Brief Examination of Scripture Testimony on the Institution of Slavery*. Debates over temperance also often invoked the Bible (Murphy 2008). Those who pushed for total abstinence developed the "two-wine" theory that distinguished between "good" beverages mentioned in the Bible (consisting, they claimed, of unfermented grape juice) and "bad" ones (fermented grape juice; Tyrrell 1979a; Murphy 2008); they also used biblical arguments to condemn drinking—notably, Paul's warning in Ephesians

5:18 ("be not drunk with wine") and the condemnation of Noah's drunkenness in Genesis. For their part, crusaders for women's rights invoked the Bible when pleading for political equality and their right to speak in public: "Did St. Paul but know of our wrongs and deprivations, I presume he would make no objections to our pleading in public for our rights. Again; holy women ministered unto Christ and the apostles; and women of refinement in all ages, more or less, had had a voice in moral, religious, and political subjects" (Maria Stewart, 1833, quoted in Rendall 1984: 248).

Religious Organizations Provided Resources for Reform

In addition to ideals that motivate reform efforts, churches offer organizing templates, based on their formal structures, that reformers can adopt. Use of such well-established forms reduces the costs of launching and running reform associations by simplifying organizational design decisions and providing proven leaders; by making reform associations seem familiar, it also helps reform associations acquire constitutive legitimacy (Meyer and Rowan 1977; DiMaggio and Powell 1983). In this way churches offer concrete analogies for movements—cultural tools that can be used in many contexts to legitimate movements and ease their expansion (Douglas 1986: 45–53; Swidler 1986). Churches also provide funding and infrastructural support in the form of practices, like revivalistic confessions, that reinforce bonds among activists.

In the contemporary era, the clearest example of the organizational dependence of reform on religious institutions is the Southern Christian Leadership Conference, which was literally built on the infrastructure of and with resources derived from African American churches (Morris 1984; McAdam 2003). The same pattern can be seen in the eighteenth and early nineteenth centuries, as many reformers used religious organizational templates to build reform societies (Skocpol et al. 2000). For example, the American Temperance Society was explicitly modeled on the American Board of Commissioners for Foreign Missions, an organizational outgrowth of the Presbyterian Church (Murphy 2008: 95–112). Many reform movements in this era relied on churches' human and financial resources. Most notably, clergy often founded or led reform movements and societies; such positions were often necessary additions to the meager stipends ministers received from their congregations (Foster 1960: 143). For example, the American Temperance Society was founded by three clergy, and two out of five members of its first executive committee were clergy. In the same vein, Presbyterian authorities led the Sabbatarian crusade, distributing blank petition forms to every one of its congregations and urging every minister to preach in support of the movement; they also pushed Congregationalists to mount petition drives (John 1990).

Reformers deployed a host of proven religious mobilization tactics. In using traveling agents to lecture the public and set up local societies, the American

Temperance Society imitated churches' use of itinerant ministers (Tyrrell 1979a; Abzug 1994) and missionaries (Murphy 2008), both of which had proven to be successful in proselytizing; in turn, later reform efforts—most notably, humanitarian reform movements—followed the path forged by the American Temperance Society by relying heavily on traveling agents (Rendall 1984). And reformers of all stripes followed churches in using magazines to spread the gospel of reform and sustain the faithful in the cause.

MAGAZINES AND REFORM

The Rise of Social Reform Magazines

Reformers in this era launched over three hundred magazines specifically devoted to particular reform causes and wrote many articles that appeared in religious and general-interest magazines. Prominent examples of such specialized reform magazines include the American Peace Society's *Harbinger of Peace* (1828–1939; after 1831, its name changed several times), the American Temperance Society's *Journal of Humanity* (1829–33), the New York State Temperance Society's *Temperance Recorder* (1832–43), the American Anti-Slavery Society's *Anti-Slavery Record* (1835–37) and *Anti-Slavery Examiner* (1836–45), the New York Female Moral Reform Society's *Advocate of Moral Reform* (1835–1941), the Pennsylvania Prison Society's *Journal of Prison Discipline* (1845–1919), and the National Women's Rights Convention's *Una* (1853–55).

These magazines allowed reform advocates to present opposing viewpoints on social causes. Abolitionist magazines thundered against slavery while southern magazines, such as the influential *DeBow's Review* (1846–80), replied with vigorous defenses of the "peculiar institution" on which the plantation economy depended. For its part, the African colonization countermovement benefited from publishing a magazine, the *African Repository and Colonial Journal*, which it launched in 1825 and which helped it build a truly national membership (Staudenraus [1961] 1980). Advocates of African colonization also debated abolitionists in the pages of specialized social reform magazines, general-interest magazines, and other specialized magazines (medical, literary, educational, etc.). Among abolitionists, gradualists were arrayed against immediatists, and both sides argued the merits of their agendas in the press. Such internal dissension was not limited to the abolition movement. Temperance advocates also argued among themselves, debating the virtues of total abstinence versus less-stringent temperance. Pacifists all agreed that offensive wars were wicked, but among themselves disputed the morality of defensive wars. Women's rights advocates battled those who advocated narrow, family-based spheres of influence for women. Finally, prison reformers debated both tactics and the details of prison design (physical layout and workflow).

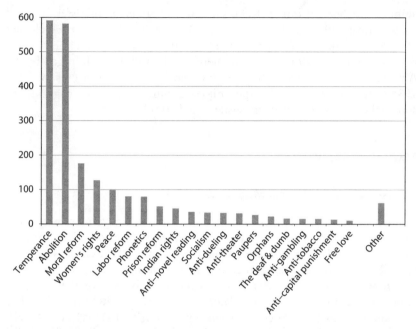

Figure 6.2. Social movement targets in specialized magazines, 1741–1860.

To assess how much specialized social reform magazines focused on various causes, figure 6.2 plots the number of annual observations on specialized social reform magazines published between 1741 and 1860 for each reform target. Abolition and temperance were by far the most common social reform topics in these magazines, with 530 and 452 annual observations, respectively. Women's rights and pacifism were also quite common, with 128 and 104 annual observations, respectively. But many other reform efforts were also prominently covered by these magazines, including the drive to simplify language through adoption of phonetic spelling, campaigns for workers' and Indian rights, and the prison reform movement. Among social vices, dueling, novel reading, and theatergoing were the most frequently targeted by specialized reform magazines.

Almost one-fourth of other magazines—both general-interest magazines and specialized nonreform periodicals like religious magazines—covered a wide array of reform causes. For example, describing the hypocrisy subscribing to the Declaration of Independence while holding slaves, an abolitionist writing in a general-interest periodical lamented, "If . . . we persevered in this wicked practice . . . , when we have done so much to rescue ourselves from the hands of oppression, will not the world call us liars and hypocrites? Was it for this . . . that half the world was agitated with an eight years' war? Was it for this that a hundred thousand men were killed?" (*American Museum*, 1797, 1:210, quoted in Zilversmit 1967: 170).

Joseph Dennie's influential political and literary journal *Port-Folio* (1801–27) was a platform for articles cautioning against the consumption of whiskey, while one of the most important literary journal of this era, the *US Magazine and Democratic Review* (1837–1959), was strongly protemperance. Popular medical journals supported the temperance cause by decrying the deleterious physical consequences of drinking spirits; for instance, the prospectus of the *Journal of Health* (1829–33), the nation's first popular health magazine, claimed it was devoted to "the value of dietetic rules" and "the blessings of temperance" (*Journal of Health* 1829: 1). The *Advocate of Peace*, the organ of the American Peace Society, reported that two dozen religious periodicals had published articles in support of that movement (Beckwith 1837: 32–33; *Advocate of Peace* 1838: 13). Early women's rights activist Judith Sargent Murray wrote a series of essays titled "The Gleaner" that were published in the general-interest *Massachusetts Magazine* (1792–96), arguing that the future implied real equality between men and women and advocating a liberal, wide-ranging education for women so that their reasoning and judgment would be as good as men's.

To chart the importance of *all* magazines—not just specialized social reform periodicals—to reform movements, I counted the number of articles about each movement in the American Periodical Series Online between 1741 and 1860. Although this archive does not include all magazines, it has the great benefit of allowing electronic searches for key words. (Appendix 2 shows how I conducted these searches, and lists the key words used in the search for magazine articles about each movement.) Figures 6.3a–c chart the results of this search: figure 6.3a examines the major social movements, 6.3b the humanitarian movements that sought to help others, and 6.3c other social movements.

Figure 6.3a shows that the antislavery movement garnered the lion's share of press, with over 100,000 articles and letters to the editor published in magazines. This count dwarfs the 15,000 published pieces about the countermovement for African colonization. Coverage of the temperance, mission, and peace movements was also quite extensive, with 57,000, 37,000, and 23,000 articles and letters, respectively. The Sabbatarian movement (and the anti-Sabbatarian countermovement) also received extensive coverage in magazines, but the total number of pieces written was far lower (7,000) because this movement was active for a much briefer period than the other major movements. Figure 6.3b shows that among the many movements launched to help the less fortunate, "fallen women" got the most coverage, with 37,000 articles and letters. Other humanitarian movements were discussed far less often in magazines, as were the other smaller social movements shown in figure 6.3c. For example, there were 13,000 articles and letters about helping widows and the blind, but fewer than 8,000 about the deaf and dumb. Not surprisingly, movements that began late in this era, such as those advocating vegetarianism and phonetic spelling reform, received very little coverage: only 321 articles and letters about the former and 294 about the latter.

(a)

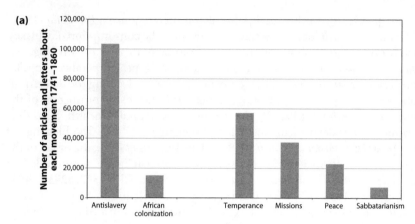

(b)

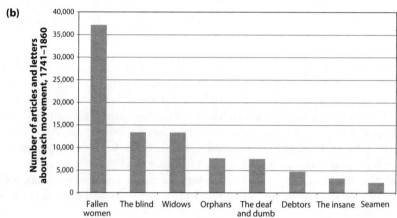

(c)

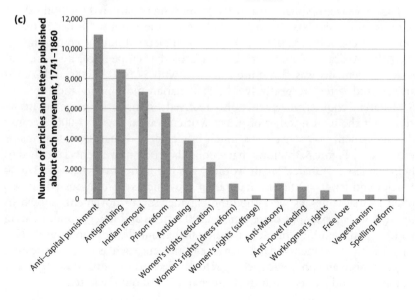

The Interplay between Magazines and Social Reform

Magazines supported social reform movements in several different ways: they provided publicity, catalyzed action, theorized movements and framed their goals for the general public, and bound far-flung activists into modern, translocal communities of purpose. I will discuss each of these benefits in turn. I conclude by considering the reverse causal relationship—the impact of reform associations on magazines.

As with the religious organizations studied in chapter 5, there were several other social "glues" that reform organizations could use to create modern, translocal communities of purpose: books and pamphlets, religious organizations, and federated reform societies. For reform societies, magazines were more useful social glues than books and pamphlets because magazines generally saw wider circulation. Analysis of the few reform magazines for which circulation data are available shows that six had circulations over 20,000, and two (*Temperance Recorder* and *Slave's Friend*) had circulations over 100,000. In contrast, by far the best-selling book in this era was *Uncle Tom's Cabin*, which sold 310,000 copies(Zboray 1993: 122); most books sold far fewer than 100,000 copies (Hart [1950] 1963; Winship 2001). These mass-circulation magazines provided antidotes to far-flung reformers' geographic isolation and disseminated information widely. Moreover, magazines are serial publications, which allows them to develop rich reciprocal interactions between editors and their readers, something that books and pamphlets cannot. In the era under study their serial nature made it possible for reform magazines to weave readers together in cohesive communities whose members shared a collective understanding of moral values and purpose-driven identities. As explained above, religious and reform organizations provided leadership to get movements underway and supportive cultural schemas. But magazines had the great advantage of being able to turn reform advocates into active participants by soliciting news about protest events at home and abroad, updates on the growth of local reform societies, information about institutions for the downtrodden, details of legal advances pushed by reformers, extracts from stirring speeches made to reform societies and legislatures, lurid reports of injustices and degradation, queries and quibbles to be answered by the editors or other readers, poetry and stories, and interesting articles from other magazines and newspapers. Finally, magazines served as important reinforcements to formal religious authorities, as ministers were always scarce during this era: as late as 1850, there were only thirteen clergy per ten thousand Americans (Sobek 2006).

Figure 6.3. (a) The number of articles and letters in magazines about major social reform movements, 1741–1860; (b) the number of articles and letters in magazines about social reform movements to help the less fortunate, 1741–1860; (c) the number of articles and letters in magazines about other social reform movements, 1741–1860. Source for all figures: American Periodicals Series Online.

Garnering Publicity for Reform Movements

Sociological theory holds that there are strong reciprocal relationships between social movements and magazines. Most basically, social movements
need media coverage to ensure that the state and the general public pay attention to what activists do (Lipsky 1968). This is precisely what nineteenth-
century magazines did for reform movements. One contributor to the *Harbinger* (founded in 1845 by poet Charles A. Dana to support Fourierism, abolition,
and free love) reported that it had gained support throughout the city's largest
metropolis, writing, "I have the greatest pleasure in assuring you that the HAR-
BINGER is received with great and increasing favor in New York, that its circle
of readers ... is weekly widening and deepening; for it is beginning to make
its way among different *strata* of population from its own. ... Already I see the
good effects ... in the conversations of literary societies, and even in fashion-
able society. At the theatre, in hotels, on steamboats, in the picture-gallery,
common-place conversation is often interrupted by a discursive discussion of
some topic in the Harbinger" (*Harbinger* 1845: 134).

Similarly, a reader of the *Phalanx* (1843–45), which was devoted to spreading Charles Fourier's utopian socialist principles and his goal of reorganizing
society into small, self-sufficient "associations" declared that "the wide circulation of your journal enables you to give extensive publicity to the history and
present condition of the young and vigorous [local] Association" (Brown
1844: 100). In the same vein, an upstate New York subscriber to *Young America*
(1845–49), which sought broad social and political reform, wrote, "I have circulated your papers as far as I could, some to Dutchess county and some to
Erie county, and I think they will yield some sixty and some an hundred fold.
I have heard from Tompkins county. The fire of reform is kindling there, and
I will send papers there as soon as I get them" (A Female 1845: 4). Some enthusiastic subscribers even paid for additional copies of magazines, which they
gave to their neighbors to recruit them to the cause. For instance:

> I propose to send enclosed in this three dollars, for which you may send
> one paper of the first volume ..., for I want to have them bound so that I
> can lend it to my neighbors: and for the balance you may send me some
> back papers to sew together to lend around. ... I can spare this to help suf-
> fering humanity. (A.E. 1845: 1)

> I ... hope you will meet with sufficient support in so great and good an
> undertaking. I have this day obtained three subscriptions, and shall con-
> tinue my attention, and procure as many as I possibly can. (*Genius of Uni-
> versal Emancipation* 1821: 50)

Readers cared so much about reform magazines that they often suggested
new topics for discussion. For example, one reader of the *Genius of Universal
Emancipation* asked that the editors and other readers debate a series of questions about the inconsistent ethics espoused by slave owners and develop re-

sponses to their objections to abolition (Enquirer 1821: 21). One highly involved reader of the *Hangman* (1845–67), which opposed capital punishment and espoused prison reform, even suggested a new title, to broaden that magazine's reception and hone its message: "The *name* I like very much; but as very much depends upon the Abolition of Capital Punishment, would it not be well to append a running title under it, as 'The Prisoner's Friend, Devoted to the Abolition of Capital Punishment, and the Improvement of Prison Discipline.' Or something like this" (Upham 1846: 6). By the time this letter was printed, the magazine in question had indeed taken the suggestion and changed its name.

Some reform magazines had mass followings and so could effectively publicize reform movements across the nation. The *Temperance Recorder*, the organ of the New York State Temperance Society, was one of the highest-circulation journals of this era, with over 200,000 subscribers from its inception in 1832 to its last year of operation in 1843 (Cairns [1898] 1971). The *Slave's Friend*, a children's abolition magazine published by the American Anti-Slavery Society, had 131,500 subscribers in 1837. The abstinence-promoting *Water-Cure Journal* had 50,000 subscribers in 1850; while the *Youth's Temperance Advocate*, the *Harbinger of Peace*, and the *Advocate of Moral Reform* all had over 20,000 subscribers; and the *Cold Water Army and Youth's Picnic* had 15,000. Activists themselves recognized the great power of reform magazines—even those with smaller circulations. For example, abolitionist William Lloyd Garrison declared that there were a "multitude of journals ... scattered over the land, thicker than raindrops, and as nourishing to the soil of freedom" (quoted in Fanuzzi 2003: xi).

One common and powerful method magazines in this era used to helped movements reach and energize large audiences was the republishing of speeches given by movement activists and articles written by them. For instance, Sojourner Truth's speech at the 1851 national women's convention, "Ain't I a Woman?," was published in the *Anti-Slavery Bugle* immediately after the convention ended; it was reprinted dozens of times in the ensuing decade. Similarly, Dr. Benjamin Rush's essay "Thoughts upon Female Education" was reprinted several times in the decade after its first appearance in 1790 in the *Universal Asylum and Columbian Magazine*. Magazines also published some articles that sparked great controversy, such as Margaret Fuller's "The Great Lawsuit: Man *versus* Men. Woman *versus* Women." This fiery feminist essay was first published in 1843 in the *Dial*, the organ of transcendentalism, which Fuller edited, before an expanded version was printed in book form as *Woman in the Nineteenth Century* (Fuller 1845)—a foundational work in feminist theory. Magazines also published fiction that vividly captured the plight of the unfortunate and drummed up support for social movements. Perhaps the most famous example is Harriet Beecher Stowe's novel, *Uncle Tom's Cabin*, which was published serially in the *National Era* 6 May–6 June 1851, before it was issued in book form. Such rich, emotion-laden material engaged readers and drew them to the cause, just as emotionally charged statements by civil-society organizations in the twenty-first century swayed Americans' attitudes about Islam in the wake of the September 11, 2001, attacks (Bail 2015).

Success in publicizing reform movements was sometimes seen in the strident opposition that magazines encountered. One letter in Benjamin Lundy's *Genius of Universal Emancipation* (1821–39) from a reader in South Carolina reported that his neighbors "call it a dangerous publication, and affect to dread its circulation as they would the application of a match to a magazine of powder" (*Genius of Universal Emancipation* 1827: 2). In the same vein, a letter in *Subterranean* (1843–47), the organ of the National Workingmen's Association, stated, "The appearance of your incorruptible paper has spread terror and dismay among the thieves, public robbers, and old hunkers [conservatives] of Brooklyn, the hypocritical city of churches. The lazy officials are horrified—whose occupation, like Othello's, is nearly gone. They can no longer swear, lie, steal, or commit perjury, with impunity, since you have reappeared to expose them" ("The Ghost of Jacob Patchen" 1845: 2).[6] By the same token, a letter in the *Hangman* celebrated the hostility that the magazine provoked in those who supported capital punishment: "I am glad you have started the Hangman.... The stir already raised against it by those whose cry is for blood, is evidence that it is doing good" (Davis 1845: 31).

Framing and Theorizing Reform Movements

Beyond publicity, social movements need magazines to transmit images and information that push the state and the public to codify what activists do as legitimate protests rather than criminal disturbances (Turner 1969). Movements accomplish these ends by framing their goals and tactics as compatible with prevailing cultural elements (Snow et al. 1986; Snow and Benford 1992). When magazines pick up these frames and transmit them, the potential for mass recruitment materializes. In this way magazines help theorize movements: they make sense of the principles on which movements are built and so make their goals appear both appropriate and acceptable (Strang and Meyer 1993). This clearly was the result for one reader of *Young America*, who wrote, "Having seen your valuable paper a few times, (which I now constantly read,) I was forcibly struck by the principles I saw there promulgated" (A.K.K. 1845: 4). Beyond simply persuading readers that the causes espoused by magazines were acceptable, some reported that reading reform magazines had reversed their views. For example, as one reader wrote, "Having recently perused the second no. of 'THE ABOLITIONIST,' containing extracts from the Report of the New-England Anti-Slavery Society ... I have been led into an entirely new series of reflections on the subject of slavery. Although, for several years, I have sustained the African Colonization Society, by membership, publicly advocating its claims, and taking contributions in its support; and although it is yet

---

[6] This author's pseudonym referred to a local antidevelopment activist who had died in 1840.

sustained by so many of our philanthropists of the north; with my present views of the subject, I can stand by it no longer" (H.J. 1833: 60).

In a perfect inversion of this process, one letter writer to an African colonization journal reported changing his views, too, as a result of reading the journal:

> About a year since an Agent of the Colonization Society, Mr. Tracy, called on me to solicit aid for said Society, but finding me somewhat prejudiced against it, he promised me the use of the African Repository for *one year* if I would pay the postage. This I consented to do and have received it for one year. And now I confess that my feelings and views are very different in regard to colonization than they were a year ago. I now regard it as a great and good enterprise, yea one of the greatest and best enterprises of the age, one worthy the cordial support of every philanthropist and christian.... I design in future to give it my cordial support and I believe all would come to a like conclusion who would give the subject a candid and careful examination. (Halbert 1850: 144)

Like sociologists, media scholars have long recognized the impact that media, including magazines, have on how movements are framed. Media are "a site on which various social groups, institutions, and ideologies struggle over the definition and construction of social reality" (Gurevich and Levy 1985: 19). They are "a significant social force in the forming and delimiting of public assumptions, attitudes, and moods—of ideology, in short" (Gitlin 1980: 9). For example, the *Advocate of Moral Reform* became a platform for discussion of an emergent feminist sensibility that connected its readers across class lines, throughout the nation: "The paper is ... needed to afford a channel of communication, in which the thoughts and feelings of females throughout the country may more freely mingle than they could do in any other way. It will be obvious to all, that this can only be accomplished ... in a paper conducted exclusively by ladies, and devoted to their interests" (*Advocate of Moral Reform*, 1837, 265, quoted in Berg 1980: 193).

Interpretive work done by movement organizers, magazines, and their readers may result in a series of transformations and reinterpretations of the messages sent by activists and organizers (Gamson et al. 1992; Gamson and Wolfsfeld 1993). Thus, magazines reflect as well as create cultural frames around social structures and the ways they might be reformed. Two magazines for women present an excellent contrast in this regard. Sara Josepha Hale's *Godey's Lady's Book*, a large-circulation general-interest magazine, advocated a moral influence for women at home but rejected all claims to female suffrage; thus, this magazine framed women's moral compass as being limited to domestic matters. In contrast—and in explicit opposition to Hale—Paulina Wright Davis's *Una*, a women's rights magazine, embraced both a domestic moral agenda for women and their right to participate in national politics (specifically, suffrage and temperance), which she argued was essential to safeguarding women and children at home; thus she framed women's moral role as one that involved the public sphere as well as the domestic one. In the last decade before the Civil War, advocates for women's rights made the same claims as they made for blacks based on a frame of essential similarity for all human beings: just as blacks and whites are all human beings and should be treated the same, women and men are human beings and should be treated the same (Tonn 1991; Marx Ferree 2012).

Specialized magazines—those that focus on social reform—are especially important to social reform movements because they create and sustain collective movement identities. For example, by publishing articles that challenged women's traditional role in society, the *Advocate of Moral Reform* and the nationwide moral reform movement with which it was affiliated gradually evolved from detailing the plight of "fallen women" to expressing protofeminist sentiments about a community of women across class lines who were united by their shared interests in economic and social equality with men (Berg 1980). Specialized outlets like the *Advocate of Moral Reform* are powerful not just because of their targeted focus (Corzine 1981) but also because they are more likely than mass media (or other specialized media not affiliated with movements) to frame movement ideals and actions in a way that is consistent with the views of movement adherents (Fine and Kleinman 1981). Specialized reform magazines work from inside movements, while mass-market and unaffiliated specialized magazines work from outside, "translating" movements to the general public. There is always a good chance that meaning will be lost in translation.

Building Modern, Translocal Communities of Purpose

Media scholars have long held that magazines, like other print media, allow people to interact despite spatial and temporal distance and so engender social interactions that transcend space and time (Thompson 1995)—the essential pattern for modernity. In America in the nineteenth century, magazines made possible the development of modern social movements whose protests were sustained, formally organized, transcended neighborhoods, and aimed at distant targets such as the state (Tilly 1986, 1995; Tarrow 1998). For example, the *Genius of Universal Emancipation* proclaimed that "important information from every part of the country, contained in numerous publications, will be collected for this paper, and presented to its readers" (Lundy 1821: 2) with the aim of building a nationwide community of activists. More concretely, the *Advocate of Moral Reform* helped its sponsor, the New York Female Moral Reform Society, build a network of 555 auxiliary societies and become a truly national organization; to reflect its growing base, the organization's name was changed to the American Female Moral Reform Society (Berg 1980: 191). Letters from readers often reported on local associations, which highlighted the strength of nationwide reform efforts; such letters were staples in magazines devoted to abolition and African colonization, peace, temperance, various humanitarian reform efforts, efforts to support women and working men, and those promoting socialist and utopian principles. Reform magazines of this era literally incorporated their readers by printing not just letters to the editor but also reader-contributed poems, stories, essays, and news items.

One way that magazines promoted modern, translocal activism was by facilitating the distribution of petitions that readers could fill in and send to political representatives. One prominent example involved the *Advocate of Moral Reform* (1835–1941), the organ of the New York Female Moral Reform Society (Robertson 2006). In 1838 this magazine printed a blank petition for a law against seduction, and called on the society's 361 local affiliates to petition the state legislature. In response to this campaign the legislature received over 20,000 petitions, which resulted in that body debating (but, alas, not passing) such a bill. It took another eight years, but the society's campaign, always supported by its magazine, finally succeeded: not one bill but two were passed. The first focused on seduction, the second on the related issue of abduction. In coordinating such petition campaigns nineteenth-century magazines were pioneers of the tactics central to contemporary Internet-based movement organizations, such as Moveon.org, Ultraviolet, and ColorofChange.org,[7] which e-mail subscribers petitions to sign and deliver them electronically to government authorities and corporations.

For some readers reform magazines were lifelines, essential ties to their geographically distant fellow activists. One subscriber to *Harbinger* pleaded, "Please continue to send me 'The Harbinger.' I cannot do very well without its weekly visits for it is the only *kindred* in the Faith and Spirit that I now have communion with" (*Harbinger* 1846: 18). As a reader of the perfectionist *Circular* (1851–76), the organ of the Oneida community, effused, "The reading has been a cordial to my soul, and a lamp to my feet. It has been the means of inducing self-examination, which has profited me much" (Grenell 1845: 36). Other readers were so committed that they pledged their time and money to support the causes espoused by these magazines—and the magazines themselves. For instance, one minister wrote about the prison reform magazine to which he subscribed, "I have received regularly the numbers of 'THE HANGMAN' up to the present date, and am much pleased by both its character and spirit. . . . I have long been opposed to Capital Punishment, and will do all I can in my feeble way to assist you" (Quimby 1845: 31).

Reform Causes Also Benefited the Magazine Industry

It is important to recognize that as much as magazines supported reform movements, these movements also supported magazines. Paraphrasing Alexis de Tocqueville ([1848] 2000: 494), magazines made social reform associations, and social reform associations made magazines. As mentioned above, many social reform magazines were formally affiliated with reform associations;

---

[7] See http://www.moveon.org, http://www.weareultraviolet.org, and http://www.colorofchange .org.

these affiliations enhanced the impact of both the magazines and the associations. Most notably, reform movements provided provocative images and engrossing and entertaining reading material for the pages of magazines: reports of local protest events and reform efforts, lurid tales of deprivation and degradation, moving poetry, and passionate essays. By engaging audiences, such rich material encouraged sales and helped magazines thrive. Perhaps the most stirring material published in any reform magazine was *Uncle Tom's Cabin* which, as was mentioned earlier, was published in serial form in the *National Era* in 1851 before it appeared in book form. The appeal of emotionally charged material about reform causes to the editors and readers of nineteenth-century magazines continues today (see Jasper 2011 for a review). Reform movements also developed captive audiences for magazines from their memberships; moreover, many members of these captive audiences contributed to reform magazines, making their production easier. In all these ways reform movements, like religious movements before them, helped stimulate demand for magazines.

The Press, the Pulpit, and the Antislavery Movement

The two sections above revealed the connections between social reform movements and religion on the one hand, and social reform movements and magazines on the other. In this section I use the antislavery movement as a strategic case to analyze the interplay among religious organizations, organized social reform movements, and magazines. This case is strategic in two respects: it is one of the most important reforms of this era and there is an abundance of good data on antislavery societies and magazines. Analyzing this strategic case resolves an important causal ambiguity by calculating *independent* effects of religion and magazines on social movement organizing, and effects of magazines *net of* their support from social reform organizations. Based on joint work with Marissa King,[8] I show that the development of magazines was a cause, not merely a consequence or companion, of the growth of antislavery organizations. This analysis also extends our thinking about the relationship between religion and reform from a narrow focus on the *strength* of religious beliefs to include their *content*. Theology—specifically, an orientation toward this world or heaven—determined whether religious resources were available to antislavery organizations: this-worldly religions supported antislavery organizing, while otherworldly religions undermined it.

Historical accounts of the antislavery movement have typically focused on either the role of the media (Savage 1938; Newman, Rael, and Lapsansky 2000; Newman 2002; Fanuzzi 2003; Nord 2004) or religion (Smith 1957; Barnes 1964; Bolt and Drescher 1980; McKivigan 1984; Abzug 1994; Mintz

[8] This section is based on "Antislavery in America: The Press, the Pulpit, and the Rise of Antislavery Societies" (King and Haveman 2008).

1995; Stewart 1997; Young 2006). Very few studies have given equal attention to both causal forces, perhaps because the situation is complicated—first by reciprocal interdependence between media and social movement organizations, and second by church support for both media and social movement organizations. This complex system of causal relations makes it impossible to determine, using qualitative historical methods, the answers to two questions: Did media have any independent influence on eighteenth- and nineteenth-century social movements—that is, influence that was separate from the influence that churches exerted through the media they published? And, to what extent did churches have direct effects on social movements in this era, separate from their indirect effects through church-supported media?

Sociological research on contemporary social movements has shown that movements are supported by both media and religious organizations. Media can support the growth and goals of social movements (see, e.g., Halloren, Elliott, and Murdock 1969; Molotch 1973; Gitlin 1980; Gamson and Wolfsfeld 1993; Roscigno and Danaher 2001; Andrews and Biggs 2006). Religious organizations provide a foundation for many social reforms (Morris 1984; Smith 1996; Wood 1999; McAdam 2003). But most previous studies have failed to disentangle the impact of these two causal factors. The situation is complicated by the fact that social movements launch their own newspapers, magazines, and websites, and provide other (nonaffiliated) media outlets with material that may attract a wide audience (Gitlin 1980; Gamson and Wolfsfeld 1993).

Sociological research on contemporary social movements has also emphasized the importance of the effects of religious belief *strength* (e.g., Morris 1984; Smith 1996), arguing that social movement organizations are often built on the institutional infrastructure of religious organizations and that movements thrive when they are underpinned by fervent religious beliefs. But it is important to understand not just how strongly activists are connected to religious institutions but also *which* religious ideals activists draw on to support their mobilization efforts (Wood 1999).[9] As Doug McAdam (2003: 290) concluded, "Prior organization and all the resources in the world matter little if their use is not governed by shared meanings and identities legitimating contention." To bring shared meanings and identities into the analysis of the antislavery movement, it is essential to assess the theologies espoused by religious organizations, which I do in the next section.

Theology and Support for Social Reform Movements

Not all religious organizations support social movement organizing; instead, they vary in the degree to which their theologies are congruent with the idea

---

[9] This is not to say that religious ideals are always harnessed to action: rather than *making* church members join or oppose social movements, a theology creates the *potential* for action by making adherents more or less likely to conceive of serving or opposing reform as being consistent with their religious beliefs. Like other cultural schemas, theologies can thus motivate future action as well as justify past action (Vaisey 2009).

that improving society is a moral act (White and Hopkins 1976; Wood 1999). The extent to which churches' resources will be deployed for reform depends on their theological orientations—notably. whether they are this-worldly or otherworldly (Weber [1922] 1993: 166–83; Tuveson 1968).

This-Worldly Religions

These faiths embrace participation in the institutions of the secular world. The faithful are urged to improve the world, to transform it in line with the tenets of their faith, especially by showing benevolence toward the less fortunate. This-worldly theologies are consistent with the ideals of most social movements—in particular with the belief that improving society is a moral act. As Talcott Parsons ([1922] 1963: lxii) explained, every adherent to this-worldly theologies "seeks mastery over the worldly component of his individual personality, and seeks in principle to extend this mastery to all aspects of the human condition. His goal is to attain mastery over the human condition as a whole." In other words, this-worldly churchgoers regard the world as amenable to Christian discipline. Because members of this-worldly churches think like activists, they are predisposed to join social movements.

In the eighteenth and nineteenth centuries this-worldly theologies were undergirded by a principle of disinterested benevolence—the faithful have a moral responsibility to reform society as a whole—that pushed their adherents to engage in social reform efforts (Tuveson 1968; Butler 1990; Carwardine 1993). The leaders of this-worldly churches sought to rid the country of sin because they believed that the American community had a collective covenant with God to act as "a city on a hill," a pure community that would withstand scrutiny by all observers and serve as a model for the rest of the world—in other words, a "redeemer nation" (Tuveson 1968). Only in this way would God's will be enacted. Their determination to reform society was strengthened by their belief that they were but instruments in God's plan for reordering human society. In particular, this-worldly theologies made it possible for adherents of these faiths to visualize the abolition of slavery as a step toward the creation of a purer Christian community. The key to the antislavery movement may have been Garrison's drawing a connection between antislavery sentiment and the this-worldly idea of a national sin (Abzug 1994: 135).[10]

The two largest this-worldly churches of the eighteenth and early nineteenth centuries, the Congregational and Presbyterian, merit special attention. Members of these faiths "saw no lines of division between an individual's responsibilities to himself, his church, and the wider world, and recognized the importance of political engagement" (Carwardine 1993: 123). Because they believed the faithful have a moral responsibility to reform society, these faiths deployed church resources to promote widespread social change—no-

---

[10] Even though he was nominally a Baptist, abolitionist William Lloyd Garrison strongly endorsed clerical influences on the secular world (Abzug 1994: 137).

tably, by establishing benevolent societies such as the American Sunday School Union and the New York Association for Improving the Condition of the Poor that aimed to correct peoples' failings by propagating religious values and so purifying the nation of its collective evils (McLoughlin 1978; Butler 1990; Carwardine 1993; Hirrel 1998). Many of these church-sponsored benevolent societies shaded into reform associations because their underlying principles could be applied to reform efforts like abolition and temperance; after all, if true virtue consists of promoting the greatest good for all human beings, then slaveholding and drunkenness must be seen as violating moral principles (Hirrel 1998).

These benevolent societies reflected the "genteel orthodoxy" of the Congregationalists and Presbyterians (Young 2006: 6): many of them were members of the social and economic elite. Their vast resources allowed these churches to direct massive publishing campaigns, raise enormous sums of money, and develop a nationwide network of auxiliaries. Between 1811 and 1830, Congregationalists and Presbyterians raised over $2.81 million for their benevolent societies (Young 2006: 73). To put this in perspective, that sum was almost 80 percent of the $3.59 million the federal government spent on internal improvements between the Revolution and 1830 (Sellers 1991). The combination of a particular this-worldly ideology of disinterested benevolence and the organizational resources of this-worldly churches created a powder keg of reform activism.

The principle of disinterested benevolence that undergirded this-worldly religions was often directed toward the abolition of slavery. By 1837, fully one-third of Congregational ministers in Massachusetts were members of antislavery societies (Dorchester 1888: 460). As an editorial in the *Congregational Quarterly* put it, "it should be remembered that leading Garrisonians ... imbibed their antislavery sentiments ... from Congregational sources" (quoted in Dorchester 1888: 461). In 1817 the Presbyterian Church's General Assembly unanimously approved a declaration condemning slavery as "a gross violation of the most precious and sacred rights of nature" and "utterly inconsistent with the law of God" (quoted in Abzug 1994: 132), although the church later split, due partly to tensions around slavery.

Otherworldly Religions

These faiths require followers to disdain participation in the secular world and to attend instead to perfecting their souls and developing personal relationships with God. Otherworldly theologies hold that Christians should withdraw as far as possible from all civic and social concerns (Ahlstrom 1972: 231). Connection to the world is regarded as acceptance of the world, which is perilous because it alienates congregants from God. Because otherworldly theologies contend that congregants should focus on saving their own souls rather than reforming society, these faiths push congregants to abstain from, and even oppose, social reform movements. Thus, otherworldly theologies would discourage such meddling in the secular world. The only exceptions are movements that push for personal, rather than societal, reform, as the temperance movement did in the 1830s and the virginity pledge movement does today.

In the era under examination the essentially individualistic nature of otherworldly theologies was at odds with Puritan campaigns against public sin. Otherworldly churches held that moral transformation would come about through personal conversion and confession rather than large-scale organizing. Leaders of otherworldly churches viewed the benevolent organizations supported by this-worldly churches as elitist and condescending (Miller 1965; Butler 1990; Carwardine 1993). This rejection of organized reform movements was in keeping with otherworldly churches' populist nature: their members tended to be poor farmers and artisans rather than the wealthy businesspeople who were the backbone of this-worldly churches. Most otherworldly churches had fewer material resources than this-worldly churches, so they had little to offer social movements even if they had been inclined toward reform. For all these reasons the adherents of otherworldly faiths were unlikely to participate in most organized social reform movements; if anything, they were likely to oppose reform efforts as threatening to pollute their souls.

The biggest otherworldly churches of this era were the Baptist and the Methodist. Their official stance toward slavery was neutral. They held that slavery was primarily a political and economic problem, not a moral one, so they concluded that slavery was not within the purview of the church (Loveland 1966; Butler 1990). For example, although the Methodist General Conference of 1836 recognized the immorality of slavery, it also forcefully denounced "modern abolitionism," meaning the actions of the American Anti-Slavery Society and its affiliates (Ahlstrom 1972: 661). In the end, this church's unity depended on its being neutral toward slavery (Ahlstrom 1972: 662). This is not to say that all Baptists and Methodists were neutral toward or supported slavery. Before the mid-1820s many spoke against it, even in the slave-dependent southern states (Butler 1990; Abzug 1994). But this antipathy did not translate into support for abolition societies; instead, antislavery sentiment was manifested in slave owners' personal pledges to free their slaves, often when they died (Butler 1990; Abzug 1994; Newman 2002). Methodist and Baptist officials eventually found that the slave question could not be suppressed; both churches cleaved into two parts (the Methodist Church in 1844 and the Baptist Church in 1845)—one part northern and antislavery, the other part southern and proslavery.

Building on this logic, figure 6.4 summarizes the complex interplay of factors that contributed to the rise of the antislavery movement. Antislavery society foundings were promoted by print media (newspapers and magazines) and this-worldly churchgoers, while otherworldly churchgoers either undermined antislavery organizing or had no impact on it. Thus religious culture moderated the effect of religious resources, which were differentially distributed

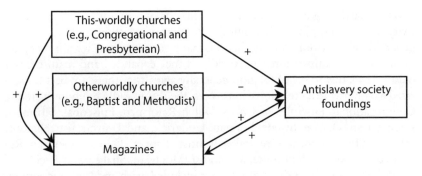

Figure 6.4. The causal model: churches, print media, and antislavery societies

among churches. Further complicating the situation was the fact that churches were also "pioneers of print" (Nord 2004) and contributed significantly to the development of print media. In addition, the relationship between the media and antislavery organizing is endogenous: antislavery societies were both supported by and supportive of the media. Antislavery societies supported the media directly by publishing periodicals of their own and indirectly by creating engaging material to fill the pages of unaffiliated periodicals.

Empirical Analysis

To test the predictions depicted in figure 6.4 we analyzed the number of antislavery societies founded in each state in each calendar year. We defined an antislavery society as any organization that worked to limit the spread of slavery to new states and territories or any organization that advocated or worked for manumission, emancipation, or abolition. We excluded African colonization societies from this analysis because they had very different ideological dispositions, objectives, and constituencies than antislavery societies. (Appendix 1 explains the sources of data on the 1,534 antislavery societies we analyzed, while appendix 2 explains the methods of analysis.) Our analysis spans the rise of the antislavery movement; it ends just as the movement began to splinter in 1840. This choice of time frame was driven by historical considerations and by limitations on the availability and reliability of data. Only eight antislavery societies were founded before 1790, and data on some explanatory factors are impossible to obtain before that date, while accurate data on antislavery societies becomes increasingly difficult to find after 1840 because the movement fractured into competing camps. This analysis includes all twenty-six states that achieved statehood before 1840. The original thirteen colonies were included in the analysis for 1790–1840; newer states were included from the year they achieved statehood to 1840.

Data and method of analysis. We aggregated data on religious congregations into two categories: this-worldly and otherworldly religions, based on readings of Weber ([1922] 1993), Tuveson (1968), Ahlstrom (1972), and Hatch

(1989). Classifying any faith as this-worldly or otherworldly requires sensitivity to time and place. Although the Baptist and Methodist churches were generally otherworldly during this era, many congregations within these denominations became more this-worldly as they expanded and matured. But before 1840, historians of religion generally agree that these are best categorized as otherworldly religions. In this era, the this-worldly religions were the Congregational, Disciples of Christ, Dutch Reformed, Episcopal, Mormon, Presbyterian, Quaker, Swedenborgian, Unitarian, and Universalist religions; otherworldly religions were the Adventist, Baptist, Dunker, German Reformed, Lutheran, Mennonite, Methodist, Moravian, Shaker, and Society of the Publick Universal Friend. We did not include Jewish and Catholic congregations in the analysis, as both faiths had very small presences before 1840 and their theologies did not fit neatly into the this-worldly versus otherworldly classification.

To assess whether magazines were a cause, a correlate, or a consequence of the organized antislavery movement we used the instrumental-variable technique, which separates the endogenous and exogenous components of magazines in the causal system depicted in figure 6.4. (Appendix 2 explains this procedure.) The upshot is that, after taking endogeneity into account, we can see the effect of magazines on antislavery organizing *net of* the effect of antislavery societies and churches on magazines.

Results. Figures 6.5a–b show the effects of the variables of central interest on the number of antislavery societies founded in a focal state in a focal year. These effects are net of controls for the size of the free and slave population, urbanization, and exports in that state and year, plus a dummy to mark the period after the American Anti-Slavery Society was founded in 1833. (Appendix 2 shows detailed results.) Figure 6.5a shows the results of the analysis including all magazines genres; figure 6.5b shows the results of the analysis including only those magazines that were devoted to social reform causes. In both figures, the light gray bars show the results from statistical models that *do not* take into consideration either the reciprocal relationship between magazines and antislavery societies or the impact of churches on magazines. The dark gray bars show the results from statistical models that *do* take these complex causal links into consideration. Thus these figures reveal how correcting for endogeneity affects the results.

In figure 6.5a the effects of all magazines are about the same magnitude in both analyses. But in the analysis that takes into consideration the endogeneity of magazines, the (net) effects of both kinds of churches are far larger: 10 times as large for this-worldly churches, 3.5 times as large for otherworldly churches. Figure 6.5b shows similar patterns: the effect of social reform magazines is only slightly larger (25 percent) in the analysis that takes into consideration the endogeneity of magazines, while the effect of this-worldly churches is 2.5 times as large and that of otherworldly churches is 4.5 times as large. These greatly increased effect magnitudes demonstrate that much of the impact of churches is obscured when the endogeneity of magazines is not taken

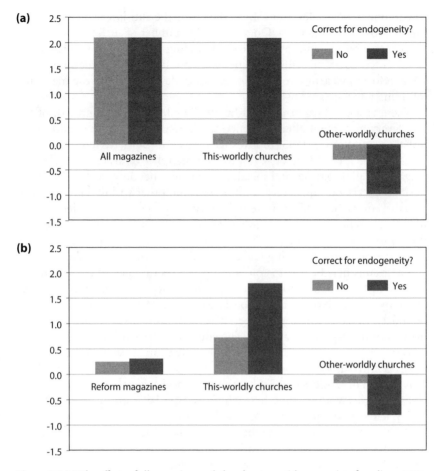

Figure 6.5. (a) The effects of all magazines and churches on antislavery society foundings, 1790–1840; (b) the effects of reform magazines and churches on antislavery society foundings, 1790–1840.

into account—that is, when the statistical analysis conflates the effect of magazines on reform movements with the effect of churches and reform movements on magazines.

Both kinds of churches had substantial impacts on antislavery organizing. On average, increasing the number of this-worldly churches by one standard deviation above the mean more than doubled the number of antislavery societies founded, while increasing the number of otherworldly churches by one standard deviation above the mean decreased the number of antislavery societies founded by 99 percent. These results also indicate show that social reform magazines had greater power than other types of magazines to support antislavery societies. On average, across all genres, magazines increased the antislavery society founding rate by 22 percent. If the number of magazines rose to one standard deviation above the mean, the antislavery society founding rate rose by 150 percent. On average, the number of social reform magazines increased the antislavery society founding rate by only 8 percent, because so few social reform magazines were published. But if the number of social reform magazines rose by one standard deviation above the mean, the founding rate increased fivefold.

These empirical patterns could be attributed to the rapid growth of the antislavery movement after the American Anti-Slavery Society became a national organization in 1833. To investigate this possibility, we redid the analysis using data for 1834–40 only. In this truncated slice of history, the effects of magazines (all magazines and social reform magazines only) had the expected positive effects on antislavery foundings while otherworldly churches had negative effects. Both effects were in line with expectations. The effect of this-worldly churches was unexpectedly negative; however, these effects were tiny: if the number of this-worldly churches increased by one standard deviation above the mean, the founding rate decreased by less than 0.02 percent.

The results may be due to conflating processes that played out differently in the North and South. To assess this possibility we reanalyzed the data separately by region: North versus South, using the Mason-Dixon Line as the boundary. In both subsamples the effects for most variables of interest remained in the expected direction. The effects of otherworldly churches were consistently negative. The effects of this-worldly churches were always positive in the South but sometimes positive and sometimes negative in the North. This pattern of results suggests that the reciprocal association between magazines and this-worldly churches, which is especially strong in the North ($r = .87$), may have operated primarily through the discursive potential of the media, which this-worldly churches were crucial in developing. The effects of magazines were consistently positive, but they were strongest in the North, which accords with the historical record: there was a considerable state-supported effort in the South to suppress abolitionist literature, including attempts to outlaw the distribution of abolitionist magazines in the mails and the burning of those magazines at post offices.

Summary. This era saw an efflorescence of reform associations and the birth of the modern social reform movement. A growing body of scholarship has examined the burgeoning of associationalism, including organized social reform efforts, in this era. This analysis contributes to this work by using a powerful case to statistically assess explanations derived from theory and qualitative historical studies. Consistent with arguments advanced by scholars of social movements and civic associations (Tilly 1986; Tarrow 1998; Skocpol 1997; Skocpol et al. 2000), both churches and magazines influenced the development of antislavery societies. And consistent with Weberian analyses of the impact of religious tradition on civic and political engagement (Hirrel 1998; Wuthnow 1999; Wood 1999; Beyerlein and Hipp 2006), churches with different theological orientations had different relationships to antislavery societies: this-worldly churches supported them, while otherworldly churches undermined them.

This analysis resolves persistent ambiguities in causal reasoning about the role of the media in the antislavery movement. Although historians have long recognized the importance of the state, religious institutions, and the media for the development of the antislavery movement, historical analyses have struggled with the complex interplay between these factors. This analysis disentangled reciprocal causation to determine whether print media are a cause, a consequence, or merely a companion of the formation of social movement organizations. Before we partialed out reciprocal causation, it seemed that both this-worldly churches and mass media supported antislavery organizing, while otherworldly churches undermined it. But after we partialed out reciprocal causation, the effects of churches became stronger while the effect of magazines remained about the same.

CONCLUSION

This chapter has traced the emergence of social reform movements from the mid-eighteenth century to the mid-nineteenth, probed the tight connection between reform and religion during this era, and demonstrated the reciprocal impact of reform on magazines and magazines on reform. Many reform efforts in this era hinged on magazines, which allowed social reform movements to become in and of themselves modern—to transmit news about social wrongs and protest efforts over great distances and to spur and coordinate protests in many locations; in doing so magazines knit together communities of reformers that spanned the nation. Through this transformation these movements also helped modernize American society at large by supporting translocal groups that were united by their religious ideals and their political goals.

Reformers of this era built on the foundations of formal organization laid by religious institutions and affiliated religious publishing and missionary societies to create bureaucratic organizations to oversee criminal justice and social welfare. These organizations developed and routinized powerful practices, such as confessional protests, that energized activists and caught the eye of the public. In launching hundreds of voluntary societies, most of which were legally incorporated, reformers created a very modern nonprofit sector in the United States long before the railroads created the first large for-profit corporations (Hall 1984, 1992). Indeed, many states passed general laws of incorporation for benevolent, charitable, scientific, and missionary societies long before they passed such laws for business concerns; for example, New York allowed the general incorporation of nonprofit organizations in 1784, and of for-profit corporations in 1846 (Baldwin 1901). Passage of laws allowing general incorporation was made possible by the increasing legitimacy of the corporate organizational form, which was due to the positive experiences many Americans had with incorporated reform societies (Seavoy 1978: 78; Creighton 1990). These formal organizations made it possible for nineteenth-century social reform movements to mount what scholars have described as quintessentially modern movement repertoires of contention: sustained protests that transcended neighborhoods and that were aimed at distant targets—often, but not always, the state (Hobsbawm 1959; Rudé 1981; Tilly 1986, 1995; Tarrow 1998).

Reformers of this era were well aware of the modernizing temper of their movements and affiliated voluntary societies. For example, Jeremiah Evarts, an official in the General Union for Promoting the Observance of the Christian Sabbath, said that his organization was transforming philanthropy into "the science of doing good" (Tracy 1845: 64). This modernistic tone is ironic, considering that this organization's goal was highly traditional (derived as it was from biblical literalism), not modern, in nature. Similarly, the temperance movement relied heavily on statistics to motivate support; by combining statistics with research on the physiology of drinking, the temperance movement was able to create a "scientific" picture of this social ill (Abzug 1994: 93–95). Moreover, the temperance movement was an alliance between economic modernizers (entrepreneurs in northern cities and farmers who favored new "scientific" agricultural techniques) and Calvinist clergy; thus, the temperance movement was an early step on the path toward the emergence of modern industrial society (Tyrrell 1979b).

More generally, social reform movements of this era were modernizing forces because they expanded the basis for authority from the ministry to the laity (Abzug 1994; Boyer 1978). Although ministers often led reform movements, these movements also gave power to many laypeople—notably, women in the emerging middle classes, businessmen, and working-class people. Few movement organizations (apart from some tract, Bible, Sunday school, and missionary societies) were under the control of central or regional religious authorities. Women like Catherine Beecher and sisters Sarah Moore Grimké and Angelina Emily Grimké were prominent in antislavery, moral reform, and humanitarian societies; businessmen like Arthur and Lewis Tappan led the second phase of the Sabbatarian movement and later were involved in the antislavery movement; and many nameless members of the working classes pushed for their own economic rights and created their own temperance societies. Perhaps most notable in this regard are the working-class Washingtonians, who eschewed any overt connection to religious institutions and instead focused on members' abstinence pledges and the social support they derived from meetings with fellow members.

We must recognize the complexity of the interplay between reform and modernization: although social reform movements of this era created enduring and very modern institutions in the shape of formal organizations that linked reformers across the growing nation, these movements were also driven by the consequences of economic modernization itself (Abzug 1994; Mintz

1995). For example, the early labor movement was driven by the decline of the apprenticeship system and the rise of paid wage labor (Foner 1947); the women's rights movement responded to changes in home life wrought by the shift of economic production outside the family circle (Douglas 1977; Rendall 1984; Flexner and Fitzpatrick 1996); and several moral reform and humanitarian movements, including the reform of prostitutes and juvenile delinquents, and aid to widows and children, were impelled by the many vices that bedeviled the burgeoning cities (Griffin 1960; Rothman 1971; Boyer 1978; Katz 1986).

And we must also recognize that not all social reform movements or their affiliated magazines—modern as they may seem to us today—were successful, even when supported by magazines. Among social reform movements, Americans came together to advocate such idiosyncratic reforms as free love, phonetic spelling, dress reform, vegetarianism, and abstaining from tea and coffee. Well known is Amelia Bloomer and her eponymous outfit, which freed women from the constraints of corsets and skirts and which she promoted in the *Lily* (1849–59), the women's rights magazine she founded after attending the 1845 Seneca Falls Women's Convention. From the perspective of the twenty-first century, this certainly seems modern, but it was clearly counter to the nineteenth-century American zeitgeist; even Bloomer herself eventually abandoned this style of dress. Two other notably modern-seeming but offbeat causes were spelling reform and vegetarianism. The former sought radical changes in orthography—specifically, to promote phonetic spelling—that activists argued were "modern" but that were roundly rejected by people outside this small movement. For their part, vegetarians argued that animal-based diets were archaic and harmful. To support their cause, spelling reformers published *Comstock's Phonetic Magazine* (1846–51), the *Fonetic Advocate* (1848–59; after 1854 titled *Tip of the Timz*), the *Fonetic Propagandist* (1851–52), the *American Phonetic Journal* (1855–59), *Graham's Phonetic Quarterly* (1856), and the *Literary Locomotive and Phonetic Paragon* (1858–59). Similarly, advocates of vegetarianism published the *Graham Journal of Health and Longevity* (1837–39, founded by Sylvester Graham, of the eponymous cracker), the *Health Journal and Advocate of Physiological Reform* (1840–42), and the *American Vegetarian and Health Journal* (1850–54). Yet neither of these seemingly modern reforms gained traction in American society at large.

Chapter 7 continues to probe the modernization of American society, focusing on more purely economic issues: industrialization and the decline of household manufacturing, the replacement of barter by monetary exchange and the rise of commerce, the turn toward rational science as a basis for claims about the material world, and the rise of "scientific" agriculture.

CHAPTER 7

The Economy

*A*fter discussing the modernizing temper of social reformers in chapter 6, I now survey the economy and tell another part of the story of how America became modern. I begin by describing the shift from an economy that was largely based on agriculture and barter to one that was based much more on the monetary exchange of services and industrially produced goods, although agriculture remained the largest sector of the economy. Next, I discuss money-based commerce and the role magazines played in this rapidly growing part of the economy. I then turn to examine rise of rationality and "science" in America, which was part and parcel of economic modernization. After that, I resume my focus on magazines as a technology for social connection that promoted modernization by demonstrating how they shaped modern, translocal agricultural communities of practice and fostered the development of scientific agriculture. But my analysis also reveals several ways in which agricultural magazines supported communities of practice that had a distinctly traditional, antimodern cast.

ECONOMIC DEVELOPMENT

General Trends

The story of the 120 years from 1740 to 1860 is one of a turbulent, but generally expanding, economy (North 1961). The severe depression that set in before the Revolutionary War, caused by the British blockade of American seaports, ended around 1793. After that, economic output rose. Figure 7.1 tracks the best measure of local economic output, gross domestic product (GDP), the total value of goods and services produced within a territory. It shows that GDP, measured in constant dollars, grew a hundredfold between 1740 and 1860 while GDP per capita, also measured in constant dollars, almost trebled. There were, however, many rough spots on the road to increased prosperity (Smith and Cole 1935s). During the wartime depression of 1778–81 the economy shrank by 14 percent.[1] The young republic grew very slowly until 1790,

---

[1] All calculations of economic growth and contraction from this point on are measured in constant dollars and are assessed per capita.

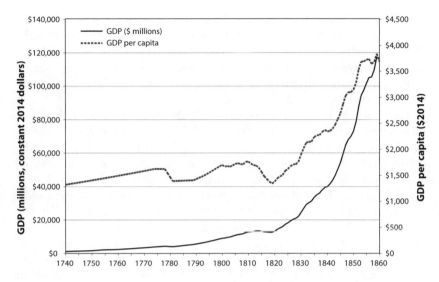

Figure 7.1. Economic growth, 1740–1860. Sources: Sutch (2006); McCusker (2000, 2001).

just 0.14 percent per year on average; after that point, economic growth ac-celerated, reaching almost 2 percent per year by the end of the eighteenth century despite the disruption wrought by the financial panic of 1797. The first two decades of the nineteenth century were extremely turbulent, with the embargo of 1808–10, the recession brought about by the War of 1812, and the financial panic of 1819 marking economic nadirs. The next four decades were more placid, although economic growth was interrupted by financial panics in 1837 and 1857 as well as depressions in the 1820s and early 1840s.

Economic development was uneven across regions. In the colonial era, set-tlers in the southern colonies were wealthier than those in the North (Jones 1980; Burnard 2001). After the Revolution, standards of living in the mid-Atlantic states and southern New England rose above those in the South. Economic expansion in the Northeast was driven by industrialization, as many small manufacturing concerns sprang up there beginning in the 1830s. The South always grew marketable crops. During the colonial era, tobacco was grown in Maryland and Virginia and rice in South Carolina. After the Revolution, cotton was grown throughout the South; sugarcane in Louisiana; and flax, grain to make whiskey, and hemp in Kentucky and Tennessee. The economy of the South was therefore always more market-oriented than that of the North. There was, however, scant evidence of industrialization in the South before the Civil War.[2] The West industrialized more slowly than the

[2] This lack of industrial activity does not mean that the southern economy was not capi-talistic—it definitely was, as it was increasingly entwined in national and international market exchanges (Shore 1986; Fogel 1989; Fogel and Engerman 1995; Larson 2010). But the South's

Northeast but faster than the South. Industrialization in the West followed a similar pattern as in New England, as small-scale factories sprang up in the 1840s and '50s to manufacture farm equipment. The largest industrial concerns in the West were the meatpacking plants that slaughtered hogs driven from western farms, dressed their carcasses, and cured meat and fat for shipment to New Orleans and the Northeast.

The American economy always depended greatly on international trade—mainly with the West Indies and Europe, to a lesser extent with Latin America and Africa, and later with Asia. Demand for American exports grew as the colonies became more tightly enmeshed in an expanding commercial empire; as a result, by the mid-eighteenth century the standard of living in the American colonies had risen above that of most European countries (North 1961; McCusker and Menard 1991). Regional variations in exports abounded. The Northern colonies exported ships, naval stores, dried codfish, pine masts, shoe leather, fattened livestock, and beaver furs to the West Indies and Europe; in the late colonial era they also exported wheat, horses, beef, pork, and flaxseed (North 1961; Schumacher 1975; McCusker and Menard 1991). The southern colonies, of course, exported tobacco, rice, and indigo. Exports boomed after the British blockade was lifted in 1793 because the great wars in Europe between the British-led coalition and the French-led alliance disrupted European economies and opened up large markets for Americans' increasing output (North 1961; Sellers 1991). The embargo of 1808–10 and the War of 1812 diminished, but did not completely cease, American exports to Europe and the West Indies (North 1961). Over time cotton began to eclipse other large export commodities; by the 1830s the value of cotton exports was greater than that of all other exported commodities combined (North 1961).

Agriculture

In America, as in Europe, economic modernization had its roots in agriculture (Jones 1968; Clark 1990; Rothenberg 1992; Appleby 2010). Agriculture was by far the largest sector of the economy in the colonial era and it remained the largest throughout the era under study. In 1740, 95 percent of Americans lived in rural areas (those with fewer than 2,500 inhabitants) and the vast majority of those worked full-time on farms. Only a small minority of rural Americans were town-dwelling doctors, ministers, lawyers, shopkeepers, or artisans, and many of those farmed part-time, cultivating small plots of land and raising some livestock. Notwithstanding agriculture's central role in the American economy throughout this period, the percentage of the labor force who were working in farming full-time declined from 74 percent in 1800, the first year for which data are available, to 53 percent in 1860 (Leber-

---

reliance on slave labor gave rise to a premodern, hierarchical, and paternalistic society based on nonmarket relations between master and slave (Fox-Genovese and Genovese 1983; Egerton 1996). Thus, economic development in the South was both modernizing and antimodernizing.

gott 1964: table A-1), while the percentage of Americans living in rural areas declined from 93 percent in 1800 to 80 percent in 1860 (Purvis 1995; Moffat 1992, 1996; US Census Bureau 1998).[3] Not only did fewer Americans work on farms, but fewer rural dwellers did so as well: 66 percent of rural residents worked full-time on farms in 1860, compared to 80 percent in 1800.

Throughout the eighteenth and early nineteenth centuries rural households were the primary economic units. In the eighteenth century they raised animals and plants for food; harvested lumber for buildings, tools, and fuel; processed and preserved food; made candles and soap; spun wool, cotton, and linen into thread and wove thread into cloth; sewed clothing and pieced together quilts and rugs from rags; cobbled rough shoes and boots; and fashioned wooden farm implements, kitchen utensils, and tableware (Tryon 1917). Notwithstanding their capacity for making a wide array of necessary objects in-house, many rural households had by the mid-eighteenth century begun to participate in market exchanges; due to the persistent shortage of currency, they usually bartered farm products for other goods. For example, in 1740, 80 percent of farmers in southern Pennsylvania sold what they produced in the market, and these market transactions averaged 40 percent of their total production (Lemon 1967). At the same time, exports of tobacco to Great Britain dominated the economies of Virginia and Maryland (Price 1964). Even in areas that lacked easy access to urban markets or overseas trade routes, such as central Connecticut and western Massachusetts, farmers in the mid-eighteenth century sold some of what they produced to merchants in coastal port towns (Martin 1939; Pabst 1940–41).

By the late eighteenth century farmers throughout Massachusetts were engaged in commercial agriculture, and a coordinated market for farm labor, increasingly differentiated agricultural products, and manufactured goods developed along the Eastern Seaboard, linking farmers in Massachusetts to merchants, manufacturers, and consumers throughout New York and Pennsylvania (Rothenberg 1992). At this time farmers in the mid-Atlantic states sold provisions to merchants serving the burgeoning number of iron works (Doerflinger 2002), while frontier farmers in Illinois, Indiana, Kentucky, and Ohio bartered farm produce to merchants and itinerant peddlers in exchange for cloth, ironware, sugar, wine and spirits, and coffee and tea (Loehr 1952). In the early 1800s, farmers everywhere, from Vermont to Virginia to Ohio, joined the craze for merino sheep, which produced finer wool than common sheep; as a result, their interests became increasingly tied to those of textile manufacturers, and the rudiments of industrialism and markets developed in most rural areas (Stoll 2002).

---

[3] The labor force included those who were ten years or older, both free and slave. Those living in rural areas who did not work on farms included not just those under ten years of age but also those who worked in forestry and fishing; in the medical, legal, and clerical professions; in small local manufactories (e.g., in grain mills and distilleries, as blacksmiths and coopers); and in retail and wholesale trade.

Eighteenth- and early nineteenth-century farmers sold to merchants in nearby towns a wide array of farm products: grain and hay, meat and livestock, butter and cheese, potatoes, apples and cider, wool and flax, potash and dung, and timber and wood products like barrels and shingles (Tryon 1917; Rothenberg 1992). Moving from the North to the South, farm sales tilted away from meat, livestock, dairy products, apples, potatoes, and wood products and toward tobacco, corn, flax, hemp, rice, indigo, and cotton. Farmers everywhere used the funds they earned from sales to purchase the things they could not produce themselves: salt, flour and meal, molasses and sugar, tea and coffee, rum, dry goods and notions, lime, bricks, and iron (Rothenberg 1992).

Figures 7.2a–b chart the growing commercial market for agricultural products from 1800 to 1860. Because this analysis excludes bartered exchanges, it reflects two aspects of economic modernization: the expansion of markets and the replacement of barter by monetary exchange. Figure 7.2a charts the dollar volume of sales of livestock and crops (in constant 2014 dollars); it shows generally accelerating growth of the commercial market for farm products. After adjusting for inflation, total sales of livestock and crops increased by 164 percent from 1800 to 1830, the midpoint of this time series, and by another 282 percent from 1830 to 1860. To reflect the fact that the farm population expanded greatly during this period, from 4.3 million to 20.1 million, figure 7.2b charts sales per capita based on estimates of the farm population; it shows more muted, but still accelerating, growth. Total sales per capita increased by 16 percent from 1800 to 1830, and by another 86 percent from 1830 to 1860. Scaling farm sales by the number of farmworkers, rather than the total farm population, shows almost identical patterns.

As mentioned above, there was great regional variation in the nature and developmental trajectory of commercial agriculture (Bushman 1998). In the colonial era, New England farmers mostly grew what they needed; they also fished the rivers and lakes and gathered berries, nuts, and mushrooms from the forests; and they sold production that was surplus to their households' needs in markets located in nearby coastal towns. After the Revolution, New England agriculture became increasingly commercial and distribution expanded from nearby towns all the way to the southern states (Marin 1938–39; Pabst 1940–41; Danhof 1969; Rothenberg 1992). Similarly, in the colonial era, New York and New Jersey farmers shipped food products to both New York City and Philadelphia. In the early republic, agriculture in this region became even more commercialized, as many new urban areas in New York State, such as Albany, Hudson, Rochester, and Troy, sprang up.

Pennsylvania in the colonial era was populated by small landowners who engaged in mixed farming. Pennsylvania "Dutch" (actually German) farmers carefully conserved their land by rotating crops, sowing cover crops like red clover and timothy grass, and fertilizing with lime, gypsum, and manure (Gates 1960)—all practices that the agricultural reformers I discuss below sought to promulgate across the nation in the nineteenth century. Like their

(a)

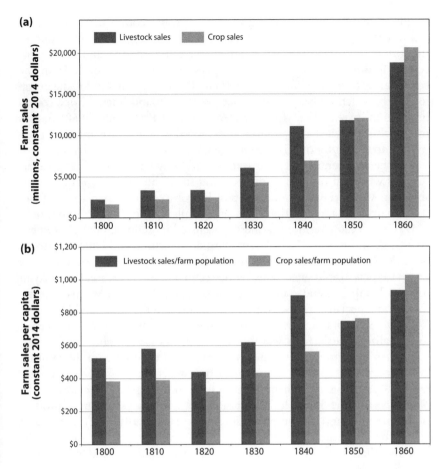

(b)

Figure 7.2. (a) The growing market for farm products, 1800–1860; (b) the growing market for farm products, 1800–1860, relative to the farm population. Sources for both figures: Towne and Rasmussen (copyright 1960, Princeton University Press: table 1, pp. 265–66); McCusker (2001).

counterparts in New England, Pennsylvania farmers in the colonial and Revolutionary eras sold surplus production to urban markets (Lemon 1967). In the young republic the commercialization of agriculture continued as the major urban market for agricultural products, Philadelphia, expanded rapidly.

From the mid-eighteenth century onward tobacco farming in Maryland, North Carolina, and Virginia relied increasingly on slave labor and the average size of plantations increased as small holdings were absorbed into larger ones (Wertenbaker 1922; Gates 1960; McCusker and Menard 1991). After soil had been depleted by year-after-year tobacco crops, first wheat and then corn and mixed farming replaced tobacco, and cultivation of tobacco moved ever westward from the coastal plain to the Piedmont (Craven [1925] 2007). South Carolina in the colonial era grew rice in the tidewater area; this crop was supplemented by indigo starting in the 1750s and cotton in the late eighteenth century (Gray 1933; McCusker and Menard 1991). The invention of the cotton gin in 1793 mechanized the harvest of both long- and short-staple cotton, leading to a boom in cotton planting across the South, from the coastal areas to the Piedmont (Gates 1960). Driven by demand for cheap cotton cloth, which replaced more expensive woolen and linen fabrics, cotton production increased sixtyfold between 1790 and 1815 (Gates 1960). As this monoculture exhausted the soil, farmers moved west and brought cotton cultivation to the southern Mississippi Valley.

On the frontier, advances in transportation systems—specifically, canals that cut westward from the Northeast and steamships that plied the Mississippi and Missouri Rivers—made it possible for western farmers to ship foodstuffs to urban markets in the Northeast and plantations in the South (Loehr 1952; Gates 1960). Vermont farmers specialized in grain and dairy products, New York and western Pennsylvania farmers in wheat, and Ohio farmers in hogs (Rothenberg 1992: 113). In the newer regions of the South, Louisiana began to specialize in sugar cane, Tennessee in flax and corn, and Kentucky in tobacco, hemp, flax, and grain to make whiskey (Gates 1960). As canals, steamships, and especially railroads opened up markets in the South and Northeast (Fishlow 1965), prairie farmers in Illinois, Indiana, Iowa, and Missouri began to specialize in cattle, hogs, wheat, and corn (Gates 1960; Bogue 1963).

As these descriptions indicate, the agricultural economies of different regions became increasingly interdependent. Canals and steamships, and later railroads, eased the movement of agricultural products from the West to the Northeast and the South, knitting together a nationwide system of production, marketing, and consumption. Shipment of foodstuffs from the West also led to the stagnation of agriculture in New England, and the focus of the economy there shifted to industry, with manufacturing powered by the abundant riverways.

Agriculture not only constituted the largest portion of the economy before the Civil War but also was fundamental to economic development in one other way: the earliest American manufactures produced goods that could be sold in quantity to farmers (Lebergott 1966). In the colonial era, farmers bought nails, window glass, tinware, horseshoes, and shoes from local manufacturers. In the early republic they added to this list clocks and watches, food mills, stoves and oil lamps, wagons and buggies, and a host of iron and steel agricultural implements: ploughs, seed drills, cotton gins, seeding machines, and reaping machines (Ardrey 1894; Tryon 1917). American inventors and manufacturers continued to cater largely to farmers in the last decades before the Civil War, most notably with Cyrus McCormick's mechanical reaper (invented in 1831 but not perfected until 1845), John Avery and Hiram Abial Pitts's steam-powered mechanical thresher (invented in 1834), John Deere's self-scouring steel plough (1837), G. Page's harrow (1847), John Manny's combined reaper and mower (1851), and C. W. and W. W. Marsh's harvester (1858).

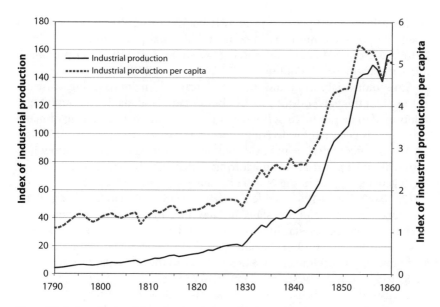

Figure 7.3. Index of industrial production, 1790–1860. Source: Davis (2004). Used with permission of Oxford University Press.

Manufacturing

Trends in agriculture and manufacturing are intimately related. As agriculture's share of GDP declined, manufacturing's share rose, as figure 7.3 shows. It charts an index of industrial production,[4] and shows an increase of 400 percent from 1790, the first year for which data are available, to 1860. Moreover, as agriculture became oriented toward commercial markets, small artisanal shops and industrial factories of varying sizes sprung up to produce goods for farm households, including meal and flour, beer and spirits, lumber, textiles and apparel, shoes and boots, hats, baskets and barrels, pots, tinware and copperware, and firearms (Tryon 1917; Hindle and Lubar 1986). Many of the earliest factories were textile mills, which were not fully vertically integrated; instead they produced yarn that was woven into cloth by people working in their homes, according to the putting-out system of subcontracting. By 1860, most demand for manufactured goods was supplied by producers outside the home, except in the newest frontier regions and on some of the larger southern plantations (Tryon 1917). The value of household manufacturing

[4] This index includes goods produced in large factories, smaller artisanal shops, and in households through the putting-out contract system. It excludes goods for which there was no information on the value of production—mostly alcohol and tobacco—which James H. Davis (2004) estimates would have amounted to 5 percent of the total. The base year is 1849–50, when this index was set to 100.

declined from $4.80 per person in 1810 to $2.13 in 1840 and just $1.02 in 1860.[5] To put these numbers in context, industrial production for the year 1809 was estimated at approximately $147 million, or $20.88 per person; in 1859, it was almost $2.4 billion, or $78.28 per person (Poulson 1969).

Still, industrialization did not transform all manufacturing; instead, throughout this era foodstuffs such as butter, cider, and maple syrup and sugar continued to be produced at home while household manufacturing of many other goods persisted for decades in out-of-the-way places (Tryon 1917; Hayter 1968). Rates of decline in household manufacturing and rates of growth in artisanal and industrial manufacturing varied greatly across regions—they were generally faster in the North and slower in the West and South (Tryon 1917: 308–9; North 1961). Table 7.1 charts household manufacturing by region and, within region, by state. In New England the value of household manufacturing per capita (in constant 2014 dollars) declined from $2.58 in 1840 to $0.46 in 1860. Over the same period the value of household manufacturing per capita declined from $1.69 to $0.22 in the mid-Atlantic states, from $2.83 to $1.25 in the West, and from $2.16 to $1.67 in the South.[6]

Industrialization began first in New England, where farming had always been a struggle and water power was readily available to be harnessed for manufacturing. For example, in Massachusetts, the towns of Waltham and Lowell began to specialize in textiles, increasingly so after the water-powered loom was invented in 1815; indeed, in the 1820s, the Lowell textile mills became the first modern American factories. Industrial products such as textiles, shoes and boots, firearms, and clocks and watches were shipped from New England to markets across the nation. Industrialization turned many small New England settlements into sizable urban areas whose growing populations needed to be fed. This increasing urban demand for foodstuffs and other farm products allowed New England farmers to sell more of their output to urban markets. In turn, the ever larger flow of payments for agricultural products from urban areas to rural ones sparked demand for manufactured goods on farms. Industrialization also created demand for semiskilled factory workers; the promise of good wages encouraged young women in particular to leave farms and work in factories (Kulikoff 1992: 28). In Massachusetts, the leader in industrialization, a capital market in the region around Boston

[5] Household manufacturing includes articles "made in the home and on the plantation by members of the family or plantation household from raw material produced largely on the farm where the manufacturing was done" (Tryon 1917: 1). It excludes goods produced for sale (as handicrafts) and things made from materials obtained from external sources (as in the putting-out system). The amount recorded for 1810 may slightly understate the value of household manufactures because it excluded items made mostly but not exclusively outside the household such as shoes, candles and soap, beer, and spirits. All estimates of the value of household manufactures are given in constant (2014) dollars.

[6] New England includes Connecticut, Maine, Massachusetts, New Hampshire, Rhode Island, and Vermont. The mid-Atlantic states include Delaware, New Jersey, New York, and Pennsylvania. The South includes Alabama, Florida, Georgia, Louisiana, Maryland, Mississippi, North and South Carolina, and Virginia. The West includes all other states that entered the Union by 1860.

TABLE 7.1.
The Decline in Household Manufacturing, 1840–1860, by Region and State

		Constant $ (2014)			Constant $ (2014), per capita		
	State	1840	1850	1860	1840	1850	1860
New England		$5,775,883	$2,226,927	$1,442,333	$2.58	$0.82	$0.46
	CT	$283,124	$266,277	$63,735	$0.91	$0.72	$0.14
	MA	$2,903,372	$284,394	$320,128	$3.94	$0.29	$0.26
	ME	$1,006,994	$711,355	$638,972	$2.01	$1.22	$1.02
	NH	$673,881	$544,951	$326,854	$2.37	$1.71	$1.00
	RI	$64,070	$36,697	$10,186	$0.59	$0.25	$0.06
	VT	$844,441	$383,254	$82,457	$2.89	$1.22	$0.26
Mid-Atlantic states		$7,765,780	$3,019,894	$1,702,680	$1.69	$0.50	$0.22
	DE	$77,761	$52,799	$22,902	$1.00	$0.58	$0.20
	NJ	$252,407	$156,206	$35,918	$0.68	$0.32	$0.05
	NY	$5,804,320	$1,773,312	$934,658	$2.39	$0.57	$0.24
	PA	$1,631,293	$1,037,577	$709,202	$0.95	$0.45	$0.24
South		$11,083,686	$14,426,721	$12,629,512	$2.16	$2.24	$1.65
	AL	$2,073,233	$2,678,832	$2,366,297	$3.51	$3.47	$2.45
	FL	$25,294	$104,684	$82,359	$0.46	$1.20	$0.59
	GA	$1,837,271	$2,547,043	$1,863,610	$2.66	$2.81	$1.76

TABLE 7.1. (*Continued*)

	Constant $ (2014)			Constant $ (2014), per capita		
State	1840	1850	1860	1840	1850	1860
LA	$81,609	$192,842	$653,703	$0.23	$0.37	$0.92
MD	$220,390	$154,886	$87,234	$0.47	$0.27	$0.13
MS	$854,953	$1,612,214	$1,799,464	$2.28	$2.66	$2.27
NC	$1,769,185	$2,889,915	$2,662,946	$2.35	$3.33	$2.68
SC	$1,165,112	$1,259,728	$1,061,231	$1.96	$1.88	$1.51
VA	$3,056,638	$2,986,577	$2,052,669	$2.47	$2.10	$1.29
West						
AR	$613,100	$883,956	$1,326,986	$6.28	$4.21	$3.05
CA		$9,695	$332,844		$0.10	$0.88
IA	$32,506	$306,498	$413,612	$0.75	$1.59	$0.61
IL	$1,243,809	$1,600,970	$1,201,974	$2.61	$1.88	$0.70
IN	$1,614,655	$2,259,053	$1,284,222	$2.35	$2.29	$0.95
KY	$3,282,962	$3,405,989	$2,728,311	$4.21	$3.47	$2.36
MI	$142,656	$472,225	$185,859	$0.67	$1.19	$0.25
MN			$10,391			$0.06
MO	$1,439,071	$2,319,532	$2,583,384	$3.75	$3.40	$2.19
OH	$2,320,874	$2,371,459	$741,059	$1.53	$1.20	$0.32
OR			$60,251			$1.15
TN	$3,613,703	$4,345,963	$4,133,620	$4.36	$4.33	$3.72
TX		$369,783	$760,614		$1.74	$1.26
WI	$15,732	$60,421	$166,638	$0.51	$0.20	$0.21

Source: Household manufacturing statistics come from Tryon 1917, tables XI (p. 166) and XVII (pp. 308–9).

emerged by 1838 to channel farmers' savings into new types of investments in industrial enterprises (Rothenberg 1992).

The other regions of the country followed the path blazed by New England. In the mid-Atlantic states, especially New York and Pennsylvania, many manufacturing concerns sprung up in the early nineteenth century—notably, iron works—but most of these enterprises were smaller than those in New England. The frontier regions industrialized much more slowly than the Northeast and by 1860 had reached a much lower level of industrial output than the Northeast. Apart from meatpacking and milling of wheat and corn, most industrial concerns in the West produced goods, like farm implements, for sale in local markets. Finally, the South was even less industrialized than most frontier states, despite some mobilizing by visionaries like magazine editor James D. B. DeBow to introduce manufacturing in the form of cotton mills (Coulter 1930).

A national system of cities developed between 1820 and 1860 (Pred 1973, 1980) as what had been scattered villages and farms were folded into a network of regional commercial and manufacturing centers (Warner 1972). The largest cities—not just Boston, New York, and Philadelphia but also regional hubs such as Baltimore, Chicago, Cincinnati, New Orleans, and St. Louis—came to dominate the economy. These cities produced goods, including magazines, that were distributed widely to smaller settlements; in exchange they absorbed an increasing fraction of agricultural production. In their banks, insurance companies, and merchant houses, these cities also accumulated the capital that fueled the growing industrial concerns, including large publishing houses such as Frank Leslie and Harper and Brothers; these cities were also home to most of the joint-stock companies that pooled individuals' savings to launch large, capital-intensive manufacturing concerns such as textile mills, foundries, and machine shops and transportation facilities such as turnpikes, bridges, canals, and railroads (Cochran 1981; Seavoy 1982).

A Novel Social and Economic Device: The Corporation

Industrialization brought with it tremendous changes in the way economic activity was administered outside agriculture. In manufacturing, farm households and small artisanal shops where owner-masters trained apprentices and journeymen in their crafts gave way to larger industrial enterprises overseen by hired managers rather than owners, often with geographically dispersed subunits (Bendix 1956; Chandler 1977). The capacity to lend money and manage risk grew with the number of banks and insurance firms, some with geographically dispersed subunits (Lamoreaux 1994; Bodenhorn 2000). Transportation of goods between sites of production and sites of sale and consumption was facilitated by for-profit businesses devoted to infrastructure development: canals and waterways; bridges and tunnels; plank roads and turnpikes; dams and dikes; docks, wharves, piers, and harbors; and railroads.

TABLE 7.2.
The Distribution of Corporations Created by Special Charter,
by Period and Business Type

Type	Period 1770–1800	1801–20	1821–40	1841–60	Total
Manufacturing	7	362	1,504	2,049	3,922
Mining	1	29	427	1,051	1,508
Banking	28	351	790	1,295	2,464
Insurance	32	143	689	1,274	2,138
Utility	30	68	175	648	921
Bridge	72	274	512	573	1,431
Turnpike	70	881	1,008	1,990	3,949
Plank road	0	1	0	1,101	1,102
Other infrastructure	68	174	489	440	1,171
Railroad	0	1	883	1,875	2,759
Other	2	114	641	1,387	2,144
Total Corporations	308	2,350	6,840	12,943	22,441

Note: Business type is from Wright's data set (2014). "Other infrastructure" includes boom, canal, dam, dike, dock, drainage, harbor, pier, tunnel, waterway improvement, and wharf companies. "Other" includes agriculture, cemetery, construction, education, entertainment, exchange/guarantee, ferry/navigation/transportation, fire protection, fishery, hospital, hotel/spa, land development, library, livery, market/mercantile, milling, museum, newspaper/printing, park, salvage, scientific, telegraph, and warehouse companies. Business types are not mutually exclusive, as corporations could be involved in multiple business lines; for example, railroad and canal.

Driving growth in all these sectors of the economy was a legal innovation: the corporation. In the eighteenth century, special charters created over three hundred corporations to develop transportation infrastructure or municipal services (mostly water utilities), insurance companies, and banks (Davis 1917: 26; Wright 2014). The number of corporations created by special charter increased dramatically from the late eighteenth century to the eve of the Civil War, as table 7.2 shows: 2,350 were founded between 1801 and 1820, 6,840 between 1821 and 1840, and 12,943 between 1841 and 1860. Over these six decades corporations evolved from quasipublic entities chartered by governments to accomplish tasks that were in the public good to private entities routinely created to undertake for-profit enterprise (Roy 1997; Perrow 2002).

Most numerous among these corporations were infrastructure companies: 3,949 companies running turnpikes; 1,431 bridges; 1,102 plank roads; and 1,171 other infrastructure systems. In addition, there were 2,759 specially chartered railroad companies and 921 utilities. Some 3,922 corporations created by special charter were involved in manufacturing. Although they were fewer in number than manufacturing corporations, at 2,464, incorporated banks were among the pioneers of this form: the Bank of North America received the first wholly American corporate charter in 1781 from the Continental Congress

(Roy 1997). There were also 2,138 insurance companies and 1,508 mining concerns. Finally, 2,144 corporations were responsible for a host of other activities: cemeteries, construction and land development firms, hospitals, hotels and spas, ferries and transportation companies, fire protection services, libraries, livery services, markets and mercantile houses, mills, printing houses and newspaper companies, salvage operations, telegraphs, and warehouses.

This legal innovation made possible much larger business concerns because incorporated joint-stock companies could pool the savings of many individuals in large, capital-intensive manufacturing facilities, transportation infrastructure, financial-services firms, and mining operations. Corporations were designed to survive the turnover of investors, which unincorporated organizations could not, and so had potentially infinite life spans (Cochran 1981; Seavoy 1982; Sellers 1991; Perrow 2002).

Forming corporations was made easier by passage of general incorporation laws, starting with Connecticut in 1837, which allowed founders to simply register corporations rather than requesting special charters (Kaufman 2008). In turn, passage of these laws was facilitated by the growing recognition that nonprofit corporations such as reform societies were efficient and effective means of solving large-scale social problems (Seavoy 1982; Creighton 1996). These legal initiatives were also driven in part by the widespread failure of public corporations during the panic of 1837 and depressions in the early 1840s (Roy 1997). We have only rough estimates, but recent research indicates that thousands of corporations were created by general incorporation, although their numbers were fewer than those of special-charter corporations (Wright 2012).

In the largest corporations, ownership was separated from day-to-day management (Berle and Means 1932; Cochran 1981; Perrow 2002); indeed, many owners did not live near them, instead delegating the authority to supervise workers to foremen or managers on-site. The rise of the corporate form of industrial and commercial organization fundamentally transformed working conditions: on the eve of the Civil War, workers were less likely to work for themselves on their own farms (whether they owned the land or rented it) or in their own craft shops and more likely to be employees of others in manufacturing, mining, financial, construction, or commercial operations (Gordon, Edwards, and Reich 1982; Prude 1983 [1999]; Perrow 1991, 2002). In the burgeoning number of factories, many different production processes were integrated and located under one roof. These integrated operations developed elaborate divisions of labor, with foremen centrally placed to tend machinery, select workers and assign them to tasks, and oversee their work. This administrative system was far more complex than that prevailing in earlier factories, such as shoe factories and textile mills prior to the introduction of water-powered looms, which relied on networks of home producers.[7]

[7] Yet integrated factories were not, as many have reported, the first organizations to develop such complex administrative systems. Similarly complex administrative systems had already been

Summary

Over 120 years the American economy expanded greatly, propelled by the shift from a mostly traditional agricultural and trading economy toward a modern mixture of commerce, manufacturing, and agriculture. Notwithstanding its growth the economy was highly turbulent; growth was frequently retarded by wars, embargoes, recessions, and financial panics. Agriculture was always the largest sector of the economy, but it slowly became less dominant and became increasingly intertwined with commercial markets in urban areas and with industrial manufacturing. Industrialization proceeded steadily but unevenly—first and fastest in the Northeast, later in the West, and very haltingly in the South. The rise of large business concerns was made possible by a legal innovation: the corporation.

COMMERCE AND MAGAZINES

The Currency Problem

The development of a national market for agricultural products and the rise of artisanal and industrial manufacturing to produce goods for personal and farm use was accompanied by a rise in long-distance commercial exchange— a "market revolution" (Sellers 1991; Larson 2010) that was part and parcel of modernization. But commercial transactions were hindered by the lack of a single, stable currency.[8] In the colonial era, specie (gold and silver coins) was always scarce because the balance of trade with Britain drained specie from the colonies and, acting under mercantilist principles, British authorities forbade the export of specie and the establishment of mints in the colonies. Although colonial authorities printed paper bills of credit, they were poor substitutes for official money because they were so unstandardized and they were often overissued, leading to inflation (Nussbaum 1957). After the Revolution the only legal tender was specie issued by the federal government; reacting to the devaluation of paper currency issued during the Revolution, the Constitution forbade state governments to coin specie or issue bills of credit (US Constitution 1787: article 1, section 10, paragraph 1; Nussbaum 1957; Hurst 1973);

---

developed for the largest employing organization in this era, the US Post Office, which had to oversee and coordinate the efforts of a far-flung workforce (Cochran 1981; John 1995). And several national social reform organizations were also pioneers in the development of complex administrative systems (Hall 1984, 1992).

[8] Although I focus here on the commercial problems caused by the currency shortage, this was also a political issue. For example, Shays' Rebellion in Massachusetts in 1786–87 was brought about in part because of the misery suffered by the rural population due to the scarcity of specie and paper money and the dramatic devaluation of continental bills—bills of credit issued by the United Colonies to finance the Revolution—and paper notes issued by Massachusetts (Szatmary 1980).

it reserved the power to coin specie for the federal government, but even there did not explicitly allow the issuing of paper currency (US Constitution 1787: article 1, section 8, paragraph 5). Although much foreign currency circulated in the new nation, it did not make up for the dearth of American coins. Since specie was scarce, people used paper notes in everyday transactions. In the colonial and revolutionary eras these notes were issued by government authorities; in the new nation, most notes were issued by banks, although some were also issued by other types of corporations, tradespeople, and merchants—even churches (Hepburn 1903; Nussbaum 1957).

The banking system in the new nation was highly decentralized, with all bank charters issued by the states except those of the First and Second Banks of the United States. Two banks operated in 1784; their number grew to twenty-eight in 1800, 327 in 1820, and 713 in 1836 (Bodenhorn and White 2006; Bodenhorn 2006). These counts do not equal the number of state-chartered banks *founded*, as many state-chartered banks failed during this era; for example, 165 failed between 1811 and 1830 (Hepburn 1903: 91). The charter of the Second Bank of the United States expired in 1836 after president Andrew Jackson vetoed the bill to renew its charter. The number of state-chartered banks more than doubled over the next twenty-five years, reaching 1,562 in 1860 (Bodenhorn 2006). This proliferation was facilitated by state laws granting banks charters after their founders complied with a few simple requirements; before then, banks required special charters from state legislatures.

All of these many banks issued paper notes that were their main source of income (Hepburn 1903). Bank notes of this era were signed by bank presidents as guarantees that banks would redeem notes for the amount of specie indicated on them—their face value. As notes passed from their original purchasers to chains of others in series of commercial transactions, these personal guarantees became impersonal, institutional ones—a thoroughly modern development. Although their original function was as promissory notes, through these chains of exchange paper bank notes took on a new role: they were increasingly used as money, as substitutes for specie. The notes therefore increasingly facilitated the expansion of commerce (Bodenhorn 2000; Mihm 2007). But banks often issued more notes than they had specie to redeem, in large part because banking in this era was highly speculative; as a result, many notes were not worth their face value. As John Kenneth Galbraith commented, this monetary system was "without rival, the most confusing in the long history of commerce" (1975: 88–89). This situation created serious obstacles to commerce, especially long-distance exchange, and in this way impeded the development of a modern, nationwide commercial culture (on how a unified national monetary system can engender a common commercial culture, see Helleiner 1999). Although paper bank notes had the potential to assign standardized value to goods and services—and thus help dissolve traditional, concrete, and personal relations and replace them with modern, abstract, and impersonal ones (Marx [1846] 1947; Simmel [1900] 1990)—their sheer variety made this impossible.

The biggest impediment to the development of long-distance commerce and a modern commercial culture was the fact that bank notes were not universally convertible into specie.[9] Local notes were usually convertible at face value if the issuing bank was deemed sound, but notes issued by nonlocal banks were discounted because of uncertainty about their solvency and the often substantial costs associated with returning notes to them for conversion into specie. All economic transactions required estimating the value of the notes being exchanged—which in turn required estimating how much trust to place in the issuing banks. The editor of a business newspaper explained this situation:

> Go to your fish woman on Market street wharf and offer to her a one dollar note of the Berks County Bank. "Sir," she will tell you, "notes of that bank will not pass now." Display to her then the contents of your pocket book, and let her have her choice of Indiana, or Illinois, or Alabama, or Georgia paper. "Sir," she will say, "I know nothing about the notes of those distant banks. Please to give me a city note." You offer to her a Moyamensing note, or peradventure, a Penn Township. "Sir," she will tell, "you those notes were very good a short time ago but they are now below par. Please to give me a note on one of the other city banks." (Gouge 1842: 306)

As this anecdote reveals, currency in this era was deeply socially embedded: if even a single official currency can take on multiple social meanings and embed economic exchange in webs of particular social relations, as Viviana Zelizer (1994) has demonstrated, the great variety of notes in circulation in this era only intensified that dynamic. More fundamentally, uncertainty surrounding bank notes called into question the foundations of the developing capitalist system; in this way it undermined the trust—the faith or confidence that a note was worth what it said on its face—that was essential for modern commerce to flourish (Simmel [1900] 1990; Mihm 2007). This sentiment was reflected in the comments of one contributor to *Merchants' Magazine*, who wrote, "The only way to give value to these State bank notes is to induce the community, and the world at large, to believe they have equal value to gold, or to beget *confidence* in them, for without confidence ... there is no real value in anything" (*Merchants' Magazine* 1852: 616; emphasis in the original).

The confusion and uncertainty created by the proliferation of bank notes was exacerbated by counterfeiting: as much as 40 percent of all notes in circulation before the Civil War were counterfeit (Mihm 2007). There were several types of bogus notes (Dillistin 1949; Mihm 2007): counterfeit notes were cop-

---

[9] Private (nonchartered) banks also issued notes that functioned similarly to chartered bank notes (Sylla 1976). The situation was exacerbated by the fact that paper notes were also issued by nonbank corporations and tradesmen (Nussbaum 1957); one historian concluded that "it appears marvellous that, when nearly every citizen regarded it as his constitutional right to issue money, successful trade was possible at all" (Hepburn 1903: 90).

ied from genuine ones, closely resembling them in terms of size, shape, and engraving; spurious notes did not resemble any legitimate note and often bore the names of fictitious banks; altered notes had the name and location of suspended banks replaced by those of reputable banks; and raised notes were genuine notes changed to indicate higher denominations. In addition, notes from banks that had suspended operations continued to circulate even though they could never be redeemed. Bogus notes of all kinds became easier to pass as the number of note-issuing banks grew because no one could be familiar with the wide array of genuine notes in circulation, which numbered over 10,000 by the 1850s (Mihm 2007). In 1856, two-thirds of banks (946 of 1,409) had their notes counterfeited or altered, and there were 1,462 distinct kinds of counterfeited notes; 1,119 kinds of altered notes; and 224 kinds of spurious notes (Hepburn 1903: 160). People in this era were well aware of this problem; for example, one magazine article described "an alarming crisis" of counterfeiting and complained that "it is not on the wealthy that the effects of this iniquity fall . . . it is the poor who are the least qualified to judge [bank notes]" (*Masonic Mirror and Mechanics' Intelligencer* 1825: 2), while the *Bankers' Magazine* (1846–1903) published dozens of articles on the topic. Even general-interest, religious, social reform, and literary magazines published articles lamenting counterfeiting.

Bank Note Reporters and Counterfeit Detectors

Responding to the immense uncertainty and confusion wrought by the proliferation of state bank notes, some forty-three bank note reporters and counterfeit detectors were published beginning in 1826. Given their general value, it is not surprising that several had large circulations: *Thompson's Bank Note and Commercial Reporter* (1836–) had 80,000 subscribers in 1853 and 100,000 in 1855, while *Leonori's New York Bank Note Reporter, Counterfeit Detector, Wholesale Prices Current, and Commercial Journal* (1850–57), had 45,000 subscribers in 1856. These specialized periodicals helped bankers, merchants, farmers, artisans, manufacturers, tradespeople, and consumers assess the quality of the bewildering array of bank notes they were offered, most of which were issued by the hundreds of state-chartered banks and which were easily copied or forged (Dillistin 1949; Mihm 2007). In this regard, this subgenre was similar to the lists of stolen credit card numbers used by twentieth-century merchants before the advent of credit-card scanners (Henkin 1998).

Before the first bank note reporters and counterfeit detectors were launched, the main source of information about the value of notes issued by distant banks and descriptions of counterfeit notes was newspapers; a few occasional pamphlets devoted to this topic were also published. But as the number of note-issuing banks grew, newspapers could not cover them all, much less report in detail on counterfeiting operations, while pamphlets issued at a single point in time soon lost their value as new banks opened, new notes were printed, and new instances of counterfeiting were discovered. Thus, bank note reporters and counterfeit detectors filled an urgent need: because they were devoted to currency, these magazines offered more complete coverage than newspapers; and because they were periodicals, they were frequently updated, unlike pamphlets. Different types of readers used these magazines in different ways: bankers and large merchants, for example, needed more up-to-date information than did artisans and farmers. To accommodate the varied needs of their readers several of these magazines were published in different formats; for example, *Sheldon's North American Bank Note Detector and Commercial Reporter*, published in Chicago from 1853 to 1865, was available in semiweekly, weekly, semimonthly, and monthly formats for subscription prices that ranged from one to four dollars per year (Dillistin 1949).

These magazines facilitated commerce by assuring economic actors—bankers, merchants, artisans, manufacturers, farmers, tradespeople, and consumers alike—that their collective expectations of the value of paper currency were true (Weber [1968] 1978; Simmel [1900] 1990). In this way bank note reporters sustained commercial communities, webs of relations among many different types of economic actors that often covered large territories and thus created a widespread commercial public culture. Commercial exchanges were only made possible by people's beliefs about other people's beliefs—both you and I believe this bank note is worth two dollars, so we can use it to trade goods and services, and to store value for future exchanges—and such shared beliefs were fostered by bank note reporters. By creating common understandings of the value of bank notes, these magazines made it possible for commercial exchange to be embedded in larger communities, which transcended specific times, places, and social relations (Zelizer 1994; Giddens 1990). These magazines also enhanced calculability and rationality in the economy, congruent with Max Weber's ([1968] 1978: 81, 86) argument, by making it possible for people in many walks of life to forecast their financial situation and meet long-term goals, thus facilitating modernization.

The value of these magazines was recognized by both contemporaries and later observers alike. For example, one newspaper editorial declared, "We recommend this periodical to every person who wants an accurate guide to the value of all sorts of bank note currency" (*New York Herald* 1842), and another said that such publications "should be a regular visitor at the offices and stores of every merchant and business man" (*Evangelical Magazine and Gospel Advocate* 1843: 287). As Robert Adams, a congressman from Pennsylvania, testified to their importance three decades after these periodicals flourished, "In conversations with my father, who was one of the old-time merchants of Philadelphia, I have heard him say that it was absolutely necessary for every merchant and storekeeper from one end of the land to the other to subscribe for these detectors in order that he might know the rate of discount on the money which he took over his counter" (Adams 1894: 5790–92). A final indicator of their importance is the fact that information from bank note reporters and counterfeit detectors was routinely reprinted in many other magazines, ranging from general-interest periodicals to religious and reform magazines.

Despite this positive reception, bank note reporters and counterfeit detectors were also subject to severe criticism (Dillistin 1949; Henkin 1998; Mihm 2007). One critic charged that a counterfeit detector "only announces the extent of the evil; it does not cure it ... nobody can tell the good from the bad" (Benton 1834: 255). Some castigated these magazines for "puffing" (inflating) the value of notes issued by particular banks, whose directors compensated publishers for their services, or for deflating the value of notes issued by rival banks. Others complained that they reported bogus notes too late and so lulled their readers into a false sense of security. Still others argued that counterfeiters could "game" the system created by these magazines by first producing notes with obvious faults that would be easily detected and described, and later print faultless notes that would pass for genuine. Others grumbled, calling into question legitimate notes issued by sound banks, and in so doing undermined the entire system of paper notes. Thus, these magazines in some ways hindered rather than helped commerce. In the end this particular manifestation of print culture (bank note reporters) could not solve the problems caused by another manifestation of that culture (paper notes; Henkin 1998). Indeed, even bank note reporters themselves could be counterfeited.

Business Magazines and Economic Modernization

In addition to bank note reporters, some 123 business magazines were published before the Civil War. The first, *Le Niveau de l'Europe and l'Amerique Septentrionale* (1794–96), was founded by Pierre Egron in Philadelphia, the largest city at that time; this pioneering periodical, which as its title suggested was published in French and targeted French readers, recorded the amount and contents of exports into and out of North American and European ports, described manufacturing facilities in the young republic, and reported American meteorological observations to facilitate business planning (Marino 1962). Not until 1815 was another business magazine—the *General Shipping and Commercial List* (1815–94)—launched, this time in New York City, which had displaced Philadelphia as the largest commercial center. This genre began to proliferate in the 1820s and '30s, and the number of magazines devoted to business rose from one in 1820, to fifteen in 1840, and to fifty-two by 1860. One of the most famous business magazine of this era was Freeman Hunt's *Merchant's Magazine and Commercial Review* (1839–70), which was published in New York. This monthly published articles on business law, currency, insurance and banking, and international treaties; it also reviewed books on business and the biographies of successful merchants. In the South, James D. B. DeBow published the influential *Commercial Review of the South and West* (1846–80; later called *DeBow's Review*), which sought to foster the development of transportation, commerce, and manufacturing in the South and West.

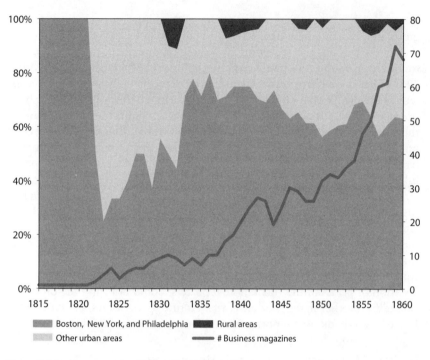

Figure 7.4. Business magazines by location, 1815–1860.

More than most genres, the vast majority of business magazines (92 percent of annual observations) were concentrated in the ten largest cities. Figure
7.4 plots business magazine publishing overall and by location from 1815 to
1860. (Just three publications of this genre came before 1815.) For each year
the line traces the number published; the dark area, the percentage in the
three largest cities (Boston, New York, and Philadelphia); the light area, the
percentage in other urban areas (locations with over 2,500 inhabitants), and
the medium-dark area, the percentage in rural areas. Over 60 percent of annual observations on business magazines were in the three biggest cities, another 35 percent in other urban areas, and only 1 percent in rural areas. New
York City alone was home to almost half of annual observations on business
magazines. This geographic distribution reflects the generally urban nature of
business in this era.

Most business magazines were devoted to particular industries or specialized occupations: bookselling, shoe and leather manufacturing, harness and
carriage making, tailoring and drapery, telegraphy, railroading, dry good
wholesaling and retailing, the wine trade, finance and banking, insurance, investment securities, domestic corn and grain markets, and export markets.
There was even an early, albeit short-lived, magazine for consumers, the *Rox-
bury Index* (1853), which, its subtitle indicated, sought to direct its readers "to
the proper places to make their purchases." Because they targeted narrow audi-

ences, many business magazines were similar to contemporary trade magazines in that their contents were of interest only to people in specialized trades; they therefore had limited circulation.

With the exception of the bank note reporters described above, most business magazines had limited impact on the economy. Specialized, business-oriented newspapers, most published daily, listing price currents, foreign exchange rate currents, stock exchange currents, bills of entry, and marine lists, and papers that combined two or more of these functions, were far more numerous and far more important than business magazines (Cochran 1961: 119; McCusker 2005). These specialized papers improved the profitability of American business concerns by expanding their stock of up-to-date information about domestic and international markets and so reducing the risks they bore; their impact reflects Benjamin Franklin's adage "Time is money."

In addition to business magazines, a growing number of technical and scientific magazines supported industry. Like many of the agricultural magazines described below, these publications reflected a profound shift in Americans' understandings of science, from arid empiricism to theory-driven tinkering, which facilitated the accumulation of knowledge (Bender 1987); most prominent among these were the *Franklin Journal and American Mechanics Magazine* (1826–1931) and the *Mechanics' Magazine* (1833–38). These periodicals diffused information about new inventions, serving as repositories of science and engineering. One of the most useful was the *Franklin Journal*'s descriptions of all patents issued, which it published from its founding up to 1843, when the US Patent Office began to publish those descriptions directly. In addition, there were a few magazines devoted to basic science; the most influential of these was *Scientific American* (1846–), which has been touted as "perhaps the greatest advocacy periodical of the [antebellum era]" (Hindle and Lubar 1986: 92) because it promoted the idea that progress could best be achieved through innovation and because it had wide circulation (estimated at thirty thousand from 1853 to 1860).

Summary

Magazines provided limited support to economic modernization. The biggest impact they had was to support commerce and overcome the shortcomings of this era's decentralized and confusing monetary system, although their record on that was mixed. The benefits of magazines for the economy would not be strongly felt until long after the Civil War.

RATIONALITY AND "SCIENCE" IN AMERICA

One of the hallmarks of modernity is that action is instrumentally rational (*zweckrational*) rather than traditional—that is, action is guided by calculations of costs and benefits as they relate to long-term goals rather than by custom or habit (Weber [1968] 1978).[10] Because science is one of the most rational, goal-oriented pursuits in modern societies, we must situate it historically before we try to understand scientific trends in this era.

The term *science* has a particular meaning that is itself essentially modern.[11] Echoing Max Weber's remarks about rationality versus tradition, twentieth-century philosophers of science distinguished between *common sense*, meaning the wisdom that accumulates over time, and *science*, meaning a specific set of methods developed to achieve the goal of advancing knowledge through empirical inquiry. As Karl R. Popper explained, "the work of the scientist consists in putting forward and testing theories" ([1934] 1968: 31). Ernest Nagel expanded on this point, noting, "The sciences seek to discover and to formulate in general terms the conditions under which events of various sorts occur.... The distinctive aim of the scientific enterprise is to provide systematic and responsibly supported explanations" (Nagel [1961] 1979: 4, 15).

"Systematic and responsibly supported explanations" require the use of codified and public methods to generate and analyze data. These methods make it possible to assess the validity and reliability of data and the adequacy of the analytical techniques used on data and thus the quality of the inferences drawn from them. Therefore, the content of science is primarily the methods used, not the particular subject matter under investigation. Furthermore, because uncertainty is a central aspect of all scientific research, inferences without estimates of uncertainty are not scientific (Popper [1934] 1968). To be valid, therefore, scientific research must adhere to rules of inference, which compare the samples under study to the populations from which they are drawn and allow scientists "to make reliable predictions of events yet unknown" (Braithwaite 1950: 1).

In describing the development of science in this era, I place the word "scientific" in quotation marks for three reasons. First, development of the design of experiments, the basic scientific method, did not begin until after the Civil War, when Charles Sanders Peirce published "Illustrations of the Logic of Science" in 1877 and "A Theory of Probable Inference" in 1883. Before this, the word *experiment* meant any observation in which some circumstances were under control of the observer—no comparison of *experimental* and *control* conditions was required. Second, probability theory, which is necessary for calculating uncertainty, was in its infancy before the Civil War, and statistical theory, which is necessary for applying estimates of uncertainty to observed

[10] Weber discussed two other ideal-typical modes of behavior: *wertrational* (rational means to irrational ends) and *affektual* (guided by emotion). But the contrast between *zweckrational* and traditional behavior is most relevant to understanding how science is modern.

[11] I do not mean to imply that the definition of science is not a social construction (Taylor 1996); I merely seek to shed light on important differences between what "scientists" in the eighteenth and nineteenth centuries did and what their successors have been doing in the past eight decades.

data, was not yet developed (much less integrated with probability theory) until long after the Civil War (Porter 1986; Stigler 1986). Third, the integration of statistics with experimental design, the bedrock of the scientific method, did not begin until Ronald A. Fisher published *Design of Experiments* in 1935 (Porter 1986).

Even though the basic tools of scientific research had not yet been developed, there is ample evidence that during the early decades of the nineteenth century Americans began to devise and test new methods to reduce the costs and enhance the benefits of action oriented toward their diverse goals: new pedagogical techniques; new ways of administering enterprises and managing financial transactions; new ways of investigating biological, chemical, physical, and geological phenomena; new approaches to harnessing the power of oxen, horses, water, steam, and coal to improve agriculture, manufacturing, and transportation; new medicines and medical procedures; and new techniques for husbanding land, crops, and livestock. All of this tinkering could best be described as "protoscience" because although it did not follow scientific methods as they are understood today it did follow the spirit of scientific research. Nineteenth-century tinkerers gathered empirical evidence, mostly through experiments, albeit without the controls and pretests that are the core of the experimental method. Moreover, because nineteenth-century tinkerers sought to improve current practice, they were guided by instrumentally rational goals. The development of protoscience during this period required a dramatic shift in epistemology, a reformulation of what knowledge *is* and how it is to be obtained—by experimentation rather than by tradition. Yet, because it was not fully scientific—tinkerers in this era had an abundance of empirical evidence but a paucity of theories that convincingly explained that evidence and no statistical theory to inform sampling techniques or to guide them in generalizing from their samples to the populations from which those samples had been drawn—the results of this tinkering usually fell far short of what was hoped for.

"Practical Science"

Surveying America in 1830, Alexis de Tocqueville declared that Americans were addicted to "practical science." Rather than selling their products "very dear to some," as was the pattern among artisans in aristocracies, Americans sought to "sell them cheaply to all." He added, "There are only two manners of lowering the price of merchandise. The first is to find better means—shorter and more skillful—of producing it. The second is to manufacture a greater quantity of objects, nearly alike, but of less value ... all the intellectual faculties of the worker are directed toward these two points. He strives to invent processes that permit him to work not only better, but more quickly and with less cost" (Tocqueville [1848] 2000: 440–41). Based on such "practice science," industrialization was inherently modern because it required mechanical and social innovations, and thus required a modern willingness to experiment and take risks.

To index the development of practical science, harnessed as it was to improve manufacturing and make possible the production of large quantities of goods at low prices, we can use data on patents. The Patent Act of 1790, the first such act passed, gave inventors a fourteen-year monopoly on their patented products and authorized the creation of an institutional infrastructure to oversee those monopolies—the US Patent Office. The act required a careful examination of every patent application. It defined as patentable "Any useful art, manufacture, engine, machine, or device, or any improvement therein not before known or used" (US Congress 1790b: section 1). Patent inspectors also demanded that patented inventions be original (Hindle and Lubar 1986). The Act called for detailed specifications, drawings and, where feasible, a physical model. In 1793 a new patent law eliminated the requirement that all patent applications be examined; instead, patents were merely registered, and patent infringement claims were left to be worked out in the courts (Hindle and Lubar 1986). This unsatisfactory situation remained unresolved until 1836, when a third patent act was passed. This act mandated a corps of patent examiners who would assess the originality, novelty, and utility of all inventions submitted for review.

Figure 7.5 charts the pace of patent activity from 1790 to 1860. The solid line charts the number of patents issued; the dotted line, the number per capita (scaled by one million Americans to make it easier to understand). The number of patents issued increased slowly but unevenly, from three in 1790 to 752 in 1835. Patent activity then declined until the late 1840s, when it picked up and began to surpass the pace of the early 1830s. From 1849 to 1853, about a thousand patents were issued each year. Starting in 1854, patent activity increased dramatically, and the number of patents peaked at 4,588 in 1860. Looking at patents issued per capita reveals similar trends: a slow and unsteady rise from 1790 to 1835, a decline until the late 1840s, and a very steep rise in the 1850s.

Not all advances in practical science were patented or even patentable. Most notable among unpatented innovations are two that were essential for industrial-scale manufacturing: interchangeable parts and assembly lines. The first known instance of an American manufactured product made with interchangeable parts was Eli Terry's clocks, which came into production in 1816 and had wooden mechanisms (Muir 2000). Perhaps more important were interchangeable *metal* parts, which, along with assembly lines, were first used together in America in Simeon North's and John Hall's Connecticut factories around 1820 to accelerate the production of muskets and rifles (Hounshell 1984; Gordon 1989). In the three decades before the Civil War, both innovations diffused widely to factories across New England, which turned out ever greater numbers of wooden and brass clocks and watches, linen and woolen textiles, leather shoes, iron and steel farm machinery, and sewing machines.

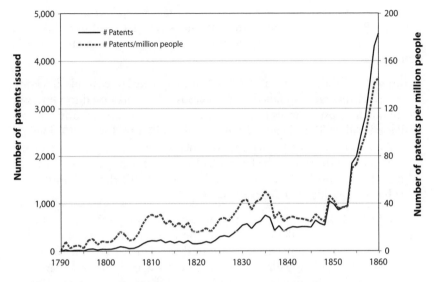

Figure 7.5. Patent activity, 1790–1860. Source: US Census Bureau (2001).

"Scientific" Agriculture

Agricultural reformers of this era conducted myriad experiments with plants, animals, tools, techniques, and fertilizers and soil amendments. As with other scientific activities, agricultural reform required a dramatic shift in epistemology, a sweeping reformulation of conceptions of what farming knowledge was and how it should be obtained: experimentation had to replace tradition. Despite this modernizing trend, scientific agriculture did not fully deliver on its promises. For example, shortly after the Civil War ended, James S. Gould, president of the New York State Agricultural Society, lamented the lack of rigor in many agricultural experiments. "We have theories of agriculture without end, propounded for our consideration," he noted; "innumerable guesses have been hazarded upon every conceivable topic; inconclusive experiments which no man can number have been made, and yet to our shame be it spoken there is scarcely a single question which has been mooted in American agriculture than tan be said to be settled on the sure basis of reliable experiments" (*New York State Agricultural Society Annual Report* 1866, 158, quoted in Danhof 1969: 70).

Nineteenth-century agricultural experiments were marred by a lack of control conditions and by the inclusion of too many variables, which made them vulnerable to confounding effects. Even Orange Judd, the most successful agricultural magazine editor of the 1850s, who had trained at Yale University under an eminent agricultural chemist, John Pitkin Norton, recognized in 1861 that "much of the *so-called agricultural science* is yet unreliable" (*American*

Agriculturist, January 1861, 1, quoted in Marti 1980: 36, n.28; emphasis added).
Margaret Rossiter has explained the difficulties facing agricultural tinkers of
this era clearly, focusing on soil chemistry, which was in its infancy in that
time period:

> Just what ... did a given "success" or "failure" prove? For example, if a farm-
> er's experimental crop failed, was it because (1) he had used too little (or
> too much) gypsum or his technique was otherwise faulty; (2) other factors
> like rainfall, field drainage, or type of soil had entered in; or (3) Liebig's
> explanation [he was a pioneering soil chemist] was wrong or inadequate?
> ... If, on the other hand, the farmer had a successful crop ..., which of the
> many factors involved was the true reason—this year's charcoal or the lime
> he had been using all along? (1975: 30)

The work of Edmund Ruffin, a prominent agricultural reformer from Virginia, provides an excellent example of how "scientific" agriculture often
failed to achieve its noble aims. Ruffin pushed southern farmers to amend
their soil with marl (fossilized calcium carbonate, or limestone, harvested
from ancient seabeds) to lower soil acidity and enhance plant growth. But his
campaign downplayed the necessity of adding organic matter to depleted
soils by dressing them with manure, which limited the benefits of marl (Stoll
2002). In addition, many southern farmers who copied Ruffin's experiments
failed dismally because soils varied greatly across the South, a fact that Ruffin
did not recognize because his knowledge of geology and soil chemistry was
quite limited. Across the United States, no one fully understood the complexly interrelated effects of organic and inorganic materials on soil and plants
(Rossiter 1975). Similar evidence of the failures of other protoscientific efforts
can be found in the history of medicine, geology, and mechanics (Davies 1955;
Cassedy 1969, 1984; Rossiter 1975; Brown 1976; Oleson and Brown 1976;
Hindle and Lubar 1986; Bynum 1994; Haller 2005).

Armed with a historically sensitive understanding of what science meant
in America before the Civil War, we can now focus on agriculture as the locus
of protoscientific tinkering. The next section describes the development of
innovative, modernistic agricultural techniques and then assesses the roles
magazines played in building protoscientific agricultural communities.

A NEW AMERICAN REVOLUTION: AGRICULTURE BECOMES "SCIENTIFIC"

Agricultural Practices

Notwithstanding the impact of agriculture on the development of industry
and thus on the modernization of America, agriculture itself became modern
and scientific only gradually, starting in the first decades of the nineteenth
century. At that time observers, both natives and visitors from England, la-

mented Americans' slovenly and predatory farm practices (e.g., Strickland 1801; Weld 1807; Jeffreys 1819; Taylor [1813] 1977; Dwight 1822). John Taylor ([1813] 1977), a Virginia planter and author of *Arator*, a collection of essays, declared, "Let us boldly face the fact. Our country is nearly ruined." Similarly, George W. Jeffreys (1819) of North Carolina described "a land-killing system" that had to be reformed to avoid "want, misery and depopulation."

Before 1815, American farmers knew virtually nothing about the principles of plant and animal breeding, soil chemistry, or botany; they were not motivated to learn these things because there was far more land than they could cultivate. As George Washington observed in 1791, "The aim of the farmers in this country (if they can be called farmers) is, not to make the most from the land, which is or has been cheap, but the most of the labour, which is dear: the consequence of which has been, much ground has been scratched over, and none cultivated or improved as it ought to have been" (quoted in Blodget [1806] 1964: 91).

As a result, most farmland in the long-settled coastal areas was overcropped, livestock were poorly fed, and farm buildings were dilapidated; moreover, farmers seldom applied calcium fertilizers or manure, few rotated crops to avoid exhausting their land, and most ploughed in ways that rapidly eroded the precious topsoil (Gates 1960; Jones 1974; Cochran 1981; Stoll 2002). Rather than investing in the land they already owned by tending it better or buying better machinery, farmers bought new land to speculate on price appreciation even though they had insufficient resources to cultivate that land sustainably. They planted whatever crop was most easily marketable and most suitable for their farm's climate and topography; when the resulting monoculture exhausted the land, they sold the land and moved west, or stopped cultivating the land and let it revert to scrub forest (Danhof 1969; Jones 1974). One article summarized the situation neatly, noting that "our policy has been, by the prodigal management of our public domain, to set in motion a constant current of emigration, which has not only carried off from the sea-board, all accessions of labor and capital from Europe, but which has drained the old states of their most active and vigorous population" (*American Farmer* 1839: 33).

Agriculture was not only unscientific in the early nineteenth century but was in some ways *antiscientific* as many farmers, guided by ancient superstitions, used the phases of the moon to determine when to spread manure, plant seed, sow root vegetables, reap crops, shear sheep, breed and slaughter livestock, smoke bacon, fell timber, draw sap for maple syrup, and set out, prune, and graft fruit trees (Nettles 1938: 494–95; Hayter 1968).

Three related trends impelled the protoscientific reform of American agriculture: (1) farmworkers began to leave rural areas for jobs in the growing urban areas and to develop their own farms in the trans-Appalachian regions that opened up after the War of 1812 ended; (2) demand increased for food and other farm products—such as wool, flax, pearl ash, and wood products—in the growing urban areas, which spurred farmers to improve yields; and (3) the development of transportation systems made it easier to deliver farm products to urban markets, which also spurred farmers to improve yields (Gates 1960; Danhof 1969; Cochran 1981). To cope with the scarcity of farmworkers and with rising wages for those who remained behind, farmers turned to mechanized equipment that rendered planting and harvesting less labor-intensive, tried new plant and animal breeds that promised to superior results, and experimented with new techniques that might improve crop and livestock quality and yields.

The upshot of these developments is that after about 1815, American farmers began to practice what they proclaimed as scientific agriculture (see, e.g., Gray 1842; Ruffin 1852; Norton 1855). They systematically rotated crops and fertilized them with manure, amending their soil with lime, gypsum, and guano (bird dung) to reduce its acidity. They tilled hilly fields in horizontal patterns to reduce the erosion of precious topsoil and tiled swampy fields to improve drainage while preserving topsoil. They invested in new mechanical equipment like rakes and reapers that accelerated the pace of farmwork and greatly reduced the need for hired labor.[12] They planted red clover, grasses such as timothy and Bermuda, and legumes such as cowslip and alfalfa to enrich the soil while producing valuable feed for cattle, hogs, and sheep that would, in turn, produce manure. They imported new plant and animal breeds from abroad, such as Spanish merino sheep, English shorthorn cattle, Shanghai chickens, Mexican cotton, and Peruvian lima beans. They carefully bred better plants and animals (for example, crossing the purple Chile potato with existing species to create disease-resistant hybrids), and fed their animals better (for example, feeding hogs corn rather than letting them scavenge in the woods). And they devoured the dry academic writings of German and British chemists and geologists, along with the more accessible translations of these ideas by Americans who had studied in Europe.

Countering this trend toward a modern science were many weird agricultural crazes that failed the logic of even a protoscience (Gates 1960; Rossiter 1975). Most notable among these was the silkworm craze of the 1830s and '40s. As one editor put it in 1835, "We hope and believe that the culture of Silk . . . will eventually become the employment of a portion of the family of every farmer; and not only be made a source of considerable profit to the individuals engaged in this *fine art* but a great national benefit; not only save *millions* to the United States now being sent out of the country for the *importation* of this useful as well as elegant article, but become a great source of national income by its *exportations*" (Barrett 1835: 1; emphasis in the original). Although the hope that the mulberry trees on which silkworms feed could be successfully grown in many parts of the United States proved false, it faded very slowly; indeed, this sunny forecast was not completely eclipsed by harsh reality until long after the Civil War. The objects of other farming fads in-

---

[12] Not all areas benefited from mechanization: the land was too poor and the climate too cold in northern New England, and the terrain was too hilly and the soil too thin in Appalachia.

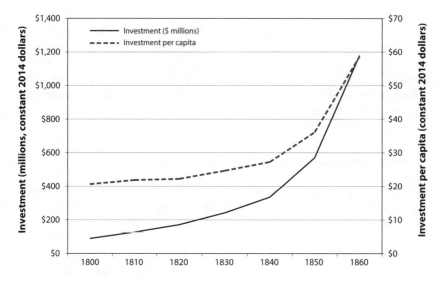

Figure 7.6. The growth of investments in farm implements and machinery, 1800–1860. Sources: Towne and Rasmussen (copyright 1960, Princeton University Press: table 4, p. 276); McCusker (2001); US Census Bureau (2001).

cluded charcoal as a soil additive, Wyandott corn, Iverson's fescue grass seed, sugar beets, mangel-wurzels,[13] Chinese sugar cane, Osage orange hedges, African Rohan potatoes, Dorking poultry, and Leghorn cattle. Virtually all efforts to introduce these new plant and animal species ended in failure.

Notwithstanding the failure of these often irrational fads and the great economic toll they exacted, farmers who embraced scientific agriculture dramatically increased their output, which allowed them to sell far more of their production in commercial markets. By some estimates the fraction of Northern farm output sold in commercial markets doubled between 1820 and 1870 (Danhof 1969). A less significant increase was evident in the South, however—in part because farmers there had long produced marketable crops like tobacco, cotton, rice, and indigo (Gates 1960).

To track the rise of "scientific" agriculture, figure 7.6 charts the value of investments in farm implements and machinery each decade from 1800 to 1860, measured in constant 2014 dollars.[14] From 1800 to 1840, investments in farm machinery increased steadily by 40 percent per decade, on average. From 1840 to 1850, these investments increased more rapidly, by 70 percent. Finally, from 1850 to 1860, these investments more than doubled. The dotted line on this figure plots investments per capita (based on estimates of farm populations), to take into account the country's rapid growth. It shows a similar, al-

[13] Mangel-wurzels are large beets that can be used as fodder for livestock.
[14] This is only a partial index of scientific agriculture, for it ignores many important reforms that did not involve mechanical equipment, such as rotating crops, fertilizing and amending soils, and tiling swampy fields (Gates 1960; Stoll 2002), which cannot easily be quantified.

though less pronounced, pattern: investments per farm resident increased by an average of 7 percent from 1800 to 1840; they rose dramatically (by 33 percent) from 1840 to 1850, and even more dramatically (by 63 percent) from 1850 to 1860. Such investments often brought great benefits to farmers. For example, cotton cultivation spread across the southern states after the widespread adoption of the cotton gin, which eliminated serious labor bottlenecks and boosted productivity: no longer was it necessary to laboriously separate cotton fibers from seed by hand.

Magazines Promote Scientific Agriculture

Before 1815 there were almost no locally published resources to help farmers improve their practices and increase the quality and quantity of their output. Fewer than a dozen agricultural treatises had been published in America, so farmers were forced to rely on British books, whose advice was often ill suited to American soils and climates (Demaree 1941; Danhof 1969). Local agricultural societies tried to fill the gap by publishing proceedings of their meetings, but those dry treatises, written by educated elites, had little appeal for practicing farmers (Demaree 1941; Bardolph 1948; Marti 1979, 1980; McClelland 1997). More relevant were almanacs, which provided useful meteorological forecasts and guides for seasonally appropriate farmwork; however, their focus on astronomical events rendered their agricultural advice of dubious utility (Woodward 1927). Newspapers contained occasional articles about farming, but apart from regular columns on agriculture, which began to appear toward the end of the eighteenth century, their focus was on current events; still, they were the chief medium to promote new agricultural ideas up to 1815 (Woodward 1927). Finally, country fairs, often sponsored by local agricultural societies, proved to be effective but time-limited ways to reach practicing farmers (Gates 1960; Marti 1979; McClelland 1997).

The situation improved when American agricultural magazines began to appear, starting with the *Agricultural Museum* (1810–12). Because they were written by and for farmers—most subscribers were working farmers, not tradespeople or professionals (McMurry 1989)—and because their contents were prosaic and practical, unlike the highbrow and theoretical proceedings of agricultural societies, agricultural magazines proved to be the most powerful medium for diffusing knowledge of protoscientific agricultural practices and news about agricultural innovations that promised to boost production and keep previously cleared farmland in use (Gates 1960; Towne and Rasmussen 1960; Danhof 1969; Rossiter 1975). The *Agricultural Museum* clearly laid out the reasons why agricultural magazines were superior to the alternatives:

> The mass of common farmers are slow in changing their mode of agriculture—To dissipate their prejudices, they want information, as well as the successful examples of their more enlightened neighbors. The institution of Agricultural Societies . . . may be expected to produce, ultimately, the

most important results. But, without a free communication of ideas . . . their operation must necessarily be retarded, and their influence on the community be circumscribed within narrow limits. The man of Science may have access to the books of other countries—he may be able to derive important instruction from them, by a proper selection of such articles as are applicable to the soil and climate of his own country. But such books are not within the reach of every one; and if they were, a judicious and profitable use of them could not be expected—The common Newspapers are so engrossed by politics, and so devoted to party purposes as . . . to preclude their utility in this respect. The [general-interest] Magazines, Museums, and other periodical Works, which have heretofore been published in this country, have embraced so wide a range, and been so appropriated to other sciences and pursuits, as to render them of little service to the Agriculturist. (Wiley 1810: 2)

Agricultural magazines published articles about British and German advances in chemistry, geology, and agricultural science, as well as the writings of American experts; they advertised and excerpted lectures given to agricultural societies; they printed many articles contributed by working farmers about new methods and materials; and they touted innovative farm implements, novel breeds of plants and livestock, inventive techniques, and new types of soil amendments. In addition to practical advice and information, many agricultural magazines offered farmers and their families an eclectic array of refined entertainment, the inclusion of which reflected the commonly held sentiment that farming was the noblest of all occupations. For example, the popular *Country Gentleman* (1852–1955) was subtitled *A Journal for the Farm, the Garden, and the Fireside; Devoted to Improvements in Agriculture, Horticulture, and Rural Taste; to Elevation in Mental, Moral, and Social Character and the Spread of Useful Knowledge, and Current News.*

This genre grew slowly at first: by 1820 there were only six agricultural magazines in print; by 1830 there were still only ten. After that date, agricultural magazines began to proliferate rapidly: in 1840, fifty agricultural magazines were published and by 1860, there were eighty-seven, spread across the nation. Tables 7.3a–b show how the geographic distribution of these publications evolved over time. Table 7.3a compares the number of annual observations on magazines in New England, the mid-Atlantic states, the South, and the West, while table 7.3b compares the number of annual observations in the three magazine industry centers (Boston, New York, and Philadelphia), in other urban areas (locations with over 2,500 inhabitants), and in rural areas. Throughout this era almost four hundred different agricultural magazines were launched. Although most were published in New England and the mid-Atlantic states, as table 7.3a shows, after 1830 increasing numbers were published in the South and West. Indeed, in the last decade before the Civil War, western agricultural magazines (33 percent of magazine-year observations in that period) outnumbered those in New England (21 percent) and the mid-

TABLE 7.3A.
The Distribution of Agricultural Magazines by Time Period and Region

Region	Period			Total
	1810–29	1830–49	1850–60	
New England	58	192	175	425
Mid-Atlantic states	23	203	242	468
South	16	158	139	313
West	11	220	271	502
Total	108	773	827	1,708

TABLE 7.3B.
The Distribution of Agricultural Magazines by Time Period and Location Size

Location	1810–29	1830–49	1850–60	Total
Boston/New York/Philadelphia	34	164	182	380
Other urban	35	387	535	957
Rural	39	222	110	371
US total	108	773	827	1,708

Atlantic states (29 percent). Table 7.3b shows that agricultural magazines published outside the three magazine industry centers (Boston, New York, and Philadelphia) outnumbered those published in them by three to one. More agricultural magazines were published in urban areas outside the three magazine industry centers (56 percent) than in rural areas (21 percent). This geographic distribution indicates two things: magazines were published in urban areas and distributed to rural ones, along the postal network that radiated outward from urban areas; and they were published all over, which made it possible for them to help with region-specific farming issues.

In addition to general farm magazines, dozens of highly specialized magazines were launched to meet the needs of the increasing number of farmers who focused on particular crops and specific types of livestock. There were magazines targeting silk growers, cotton planters, fruit orchardists, tobacco growers, rice planters, viticulturists, beekeepers, horse breeders, wool growers, dairymen, and other specialized livestock breeders—even magazines that sought to appeal to gardeners in urban areas. For example, seven magazines devoted to silk production were founded during that fad's brief heyday: the *American Silk Grower and Agriculturist* (1836–39); the *Silk Culturist and Farmer's Manual* (1835–39); *Fessenden's Silk Manual and Practical Farmer* (1835–37); the *Journal of the American Silk Society* (1839–41); the *Silk-Grower and Farmer's Manual* (1838–39); and the *Southern Silk Manual and Farmer's Magazine* (1838–39). The *Silk Grower and Farmer's Manual* claimed a circulation of over ten thousand in 1839. To the extent that these magazines were successful (had reasonable circulations and long lives), they promoted highly differentiated communities of practice that were part and parcel of the modernization of agriculture.

Over two dozen agricultural magazines of this era have been described by historians as highly influential (see, e.g., Demaree 1941: 12–19; Bardolph 1948: 94; Lemmer 1957; Gates 1960: 341–343; Marti 1979). In the North these were the *American Farmer* (1819–34), *Plough Boy* (1819–23), *New England Farmer* (1822–46), *Genesee Farmer* (1831–39), *Cultivator* (1834–65), *Farmers' Monthly Visitor* (1839–53), *American Agriculturist* (1842–), *Horticulturist and Journal of Rural Art and Taste* (1846–75), *Rural New Yorker* (1849–64), *Working Farmer* (1849–75), and *Country Gentleman* (1852–1955). In the South the influential magazines included the *Southern Agriculturist* (1828–46), *Farmer's Register* (1833–43), *Southern Planter* (1841–1969), *Southern Cultivator* (1843–1935), and *American Cotton Planter* (1853–61). In the West the influential magazines included the *Western Farmer and Gardener* (1839–45), *Prairie Farmer* (1840–58; originally titled *Union Agriculturist and Western Prairie Farmer*), *Agriculturist* (1840–45), *Michigan Farmer* (1843–62), *Ohio Cultivator* (1845–64), *Valley Farmer* (1848–1916), *Wisconsin Farmer* (1849–74), *Ohio Farmer* (1851–62), *California Farmer* (1854–89), *Northwestern Farmer and Horticultural Review* (1856–1929), and *Oregon Farmer* (1858–62).

Agricultural magazines created widespread communities of practice as they forged strong bonds between editors and readers as well as close connections among the editors of different magazines (Demaree 1941). For example, the editor of the pioneering *Agricultural Museum* stated in its first issue that his publication would be "the means of free communication of sentiment, and general interchange of ideas on the important subject of their occupations" (Wiley 1810: 2–3). Similarly, the founders of the *New England Farmer and Horticultural Register* sought to create "a vehicle of 'reciprocal communications'" (Shepherd and Fessenden 1822b: 6). These were no idle boasts: agricultural magazines often achieved their goal of fostering interactions among their readers and in doing so created a strong public culture centered on agricultural reform. As early as 1826 the *American Farmer* had correspondents in most of the eastern states and from states as far west as Missouri as well as subscribers across the country (Pinkett 1950; Lemmer 1957). In the 1840s and '50s the four great New York–based agricultural magazines—the *Cultivator* (Albany), *American Agriculturist* (New York City), *Rural New Yorker* (Rochester), and *Country Gentleman* (Albany)—each had hundreds of correspondents and subscribers throughout the country. Correspondence was facilitated by reductions in postage on letters in 1845 (from twenty-five cents to ten) and 1851 (to three cents), which dramatically increased the volume of letters in the mail (the number letters mailed per capita rose from two to almost six between 1844 and 1860) and engendered a culture of long-distance communication and inquiry (Henkin 2006). Exchanges among subscribers, brokered by agricultural magazines, were critical in cultivating (pun intended) protoscientific agriculture and supporting translocal communities of practice.[15] As one correspondent to the *New York Farmer* (1828–37) explained, "many of your readers are well qualified" to provide information about the experiments they conducted, adding that "such investigations, should they be published in your paper, might be the means of leading into far more valuable insight into this business [peach-tree cultivation], than the most extensive or scientific labors of any single individual" (Wilson 1831: 34).

Many of the most influential agricultural magazines had large circulations (Jordan 1957; Danhof 1969; Marti 1980), so the communities of practice they created were quite substantial. The *Cultivator* reached 15,000 subscribers in 1834, its first year of operation; its circulation rose steadily after that, reaching 20,000 in 1839 and 21,000 in the 1850s. The *Country Gentleman* had over 20,000 subscribers every year between its founding in 1852 and the Civil War. The *Genesee Farmer* had 10,000 subscribers in 1839, the *Iowa Cultivator* had 10,000 soon after it was founded in 1845 and over 12,000 by 1859, the *New England Farmer* (1846–64) had 16,000 in 1854, the *Michigan Farmer* had 12,000 in 1857, the *American Cotton Planter* had 10,000 in 1858, the *Working Farmer* had 30,000 in 1860, and the *Illinois Farmer* had 10,000 that same year. The two largest-circulation agricultural magazines, the *Rural New Yorker* and *American Agriculturist*, reached 70,000 and 80,000 subscribers, respectively, just before the Civil War. Even if these numbers are higher than actual circulation figures (they were self-reports, and magazine publishers and editors had incentives to puff up their sales numbers), they are quite impressive.

Collectively, agricultural magazines garnered a large audience. One historian estimated that the combined circulation of agricultural magazines in 1830 was over 100,000 and that in 1860 it was between 250,000 and 350,000 (Gates 1960: 343; for confirmation of these estimates, see Danhof 1969: 56). Assuming that, like religious magazines, agricultural magazines were passed around and read by an average of five people,[16] this means that in 1830, a half million Americans out of the 3.02 million people in the nonslave farm labor force (Lebergott 1964) read agricultural magazines—or one in six members of the nonslave farm labor force. Agricultural magazines increased their penetration over time: in 1860, about 1.5 million people read magazines out of the 8.77 million members of the nonslave farm labor force—slightly more than one in six.

The most influential editors of agricultural magazines traveled widely, giving lectures and visiting farms and fairs, which bolstered the translocal com-

[15] In their propensity to publish reader-contributed articles, agricultural magazines were similar to newspapers in the same era, which contained reader-to-reader communications, mostly offering advice rather than opinion (Schudson 1995).

[16] This estimate of the number of people who read each issue of agricultural magazines may be low. For example, the *New England Farmer* discussed "the hundred thousand who compose our conversation Club" (*New England Farmer* 1852: 1). If its actual circulation that year was 14,000 to 15,000 copies (circulation was reported at 16,000 in 1854), then each copy was read by seven people, not five.

munities of practice their magazines had created. For example, Solon Robinson, a roving correspondent for the *American Agriculturist*, the *Cultivator*, and the *Prairie Farmer*, traveled throughout the United States and into Canada, while Daniel Lee, editor of the *Genesee Farmer*, lectured across New York State. Starting in the 1840s many of the most influential contributors to agricultural magazines were affiliated with colleges and used magazines as platforms to spread their knowledge of chemistry and biology. Perhaps the most prominent was John Pitkin Norton, a frequent correspondent with the *Cultivator* and the *American Agriculturist*, and a Yale University professor who had studied agricultural chemistry in Scotland. Norton's letters describing his research created a craze for the chemical analysis of soil, plants, and fertilizers in the 1840s and '50s (Rossiter 1975: 91–124). After his unexpected death Norton was followed by Samuel W. Johnson, first of the New York State Normal School and then of Yale University, who wrote a series of articles about the nature and use of science in the *Country Gentleman* (Rossiter 1975: 128–48). Even smaller publications in the West and South touted the scientific credentials of their contributors. For example, the founder of the St. Louis–based *Valley Farmer* (1849–1916) described in detail the bona fides of his editorial associate, Dr. H. Gates, "a thorough practical and theoretical Agriculturist, Chemist, and Botanist" (Abbott 1849: 1).

Many editors of agricultural magazines were active in agricultural societies, and these affiliations enhanced the impact of both magazines and societies. For example, John Skinner, founder-editor of the *American Farmer*, was a member of the Maryland Agricultural Society; Jesse Buel, editor of the *Cultivator*, helped found the New York State Agricultural Society, while Luther Tucker, founder-editor of the *Genesee Farmer*, served as the society's secretary and treasurer; and John A Kennicott, editor of the *Prairie Farmer*, founded the Northwestern Fruit Growers' Association. Even editors of the lesser-known, smaller-circulation magazines were often connected to their local agricultural societies: Tolbert Fanning, editor of the Nashville *Agriculturist*, was a leader of the State Agricultural Society of Tennessee, while Norman J. Colman, publisher of the St. Louis–based *Valley Farmer*, was the first secretary of agriculture for Missouri. Some ties between agricultural magazines and agricultural societies were formal, as some magazines were the official organs of those societies: the Nashville *Agriculturist* came to be sponsored by the State Agricultural Society of Tennessee, the *Prairie Farmer* was from its inception sponsored by the Union Agricultural Society, the *Cultivator* sponsored by the New York State Agricultural Society, the *Farmer's Cabinet* by the Philadelphia Agricultural Society, and the *New England Farmer* by the Rhode Island Society for the Encouragement of Domestic Industry. Agricultural societies recognized the benefits of these affiliations, as one article attests:

The great interests of agriculture, like those of commerce, require the general diffusion of information, not only in regard to modes of cultivation, but also to the progress of crops . . . : the weather for culture and harvesting, and the prices for commodities. To these purposes, the Agricultural Societies of England and Scotland give particular attention, and their reports are made monthly or quarterly to the agricultural journals of these countries; and the prices and consumption are regulated in a very great degree by the accurate information through these channels.... We would now propose ... to the Agricultural Societies of the Southern States ... to imitate the European societies ... and to make your periodical the channel for communicating to the public their reports. (*Southern Agriculturist and Register of Rural Affairs* 1836: 19)

Agricultural magazines were influential because they provided farmers with knowledge of experiments conducted nearby and far away—many more experiments than any single farmer could have conducted himself. For example, in 1819 in the prospectus of his *American Farmer*, the first prominent agricultural magazine, John Skinner announced that he would collect in its pages "information from every available source on every branch of husbandry" (Skinner 1819: 1). His goal was to allow subscribers to study many systems of farming and adopt those that experience had proven were the best. In the same vein the founders of the *New England Farmer* (1822–46) noted that the "science of agriculture is to a great degree founded on experience," so "every farmer should know what has been done, and what is doing by others ... and he should impart to others the fruits of his knowledge and experiments" (Shepherd and Fessenden 1822a: 1); this magazine's motto proudly proclaimed that it sought "to improve the soil and the mind." Meanwhile, the *Southern Cultivator* (1843–1935) announced that its purpose was "to introduce an enlightened system of agriculture" (Jones and Jones 1843: 6), and the *Southern Planter* (1841–1969) argued, "Farmers must ... apply science to agriculture ... by becoming thoroughly versed in ... mechanical principles" (Botts 1841: 91).

Magazines advanced scientific agriculture by reviewing the books their editors deemed useful to working farmers, both foreign and domestic. Editors also encouraged farmers facing problems to submit questions for publication, which were answered in print by the editors themselves or other readers. In this way agricultural magazines served as clearinghouses of agricultural facts, opinions, and problems; reading these magazines enhanced farmers' ability to learn about and evaluate a multitude of new practices, animal and plant breeds, equipment, feed, and soil amendments; reading, discussing, and contributing to these magazines created a public culture devoted to agricultural improvement. Agricultural magazines had the great advantage that they could be saved up and read at leisure—for example, in the winter months, when farmers could plan their next year's activities in advance. They also provided information about market prices, which was critical for the transition to commercial farming because it guided the most profitable choice of animals to raise and plants to cultivate.

Agricultural magazines' main function was educational; for example, recall the subscriber to the *Genesee Farmer* (1831–39) who was quoted in chapter 4, arguing that this periodical's issues, when collected together and bound, would serve farmers as a "cheap and beautiful '*text book*'" (Burdick 1838: 173; emphasis in the original). Similarly, the editors of the *American Agriculturist* stated, "We intend to give a series of volumes that will not only provide matter for present entertainment, but contain such information as will justify being bound, and having their appropriate place hereafter in the library, as a work for future reference and perusal" (Allen and Allen 1842: 2).

To fulfill their educational mission, agricultural magazines provided systematic instruction in the fundamentals of the protoscientific theories of agriculture: plant and animal physiology, animal breeding, plant and animal growth, and soil fertility. They also provided instruction in farming practices. As patented—and therefore expensive—innovations in farm equipment multiplied, agricultural magazines advised farmers on which ones would be most worthwhile; they printed detailed descriptions and drawings to clarify the construction and working principles of new machines. In this way agricultural magazines of this era compared equipment to guide their readers' purchases, just as contemporary magazines like *Consumer Reports* and *PC Magazine* do today. In addition, agricultural magazines of this era exhorted farmers to build sheds and barns to shelter their livestock and their expensive machinery from the ravages of the weather.

Many articles in agricultural magazines were devoted to persuading farmers that their current methods were ruinous, wasteful, and unscientific. For example, James Madison's speech to his local agricultural society in 1818, in which he enumerated "errors of husbandry" and provided guidance for how to cultivate sustainably, was reprinted in the *American Farmer* over three issues (20 August, 27 August, and 3 September 1819; Stoll 2002: 37–41); the speech later reappeared in dozens of agricultural magazines. To give another example, Edmund Ruffin's campaign in the pages of his *Farmers' Register* (1833–43) to improve southern soil by spreading marl (limestone) changed farming practices throughout the South even though his journal (which was quite expensive, at $5.00 per year) never had more than fifteen hundred subscribers. As George F. Lemmer has explained, "between 1838 and 1850 the value of land in the tidewater region of Virginia had risen by more than $17,000,000 as a result of the use of marl and other forms of lime. . . . This rise in value had resulted from the application of marl and lime to about one-twentieth of the cultivated land in the tidewater region" (Lemmer 1957: 14). For its part, the *American Cotton Planter* (1853–61) reprinted an article from the *National Intelligencer* declaring baldly that "American agriculture is distinguished by two prominent features—its productiveness of crops and destructiveness of soils" (*American Cotton Planter* 1853: 172).

It is no exaggeration to say that agricultural magazines preached the gospel of scientific agriculture. For example, the *American Agriculturist* explicitly stated that its target audience was "the more advanced and scientific Farmer and Planter" (Allen and Allen 1842: 1), while the *American Cotton Planter* (1853–61) claimed "every department of the great business of farming is . . .

that Agriculture is a Science" (Cloud 1857: 372). Similarly, the *Western Plough-boy* (1831–32), the first agricultural magazine in Illinois and the second west of the Alleghenies, declared its allegiance to science: "There is no class of people whose business is susceptible of being more benefitted by an advantageous application of scientific principles to practical operations than that of the farmer" (Sawyer 1831: 4).

Agricultural magazines urged readers to study science—especially soil chemistry and veterinary science. For example, the *Cultivator* had special columns targeted to farm youth in which the editors laid out the fundamentals of science; the magazine also published excerpts from (mostly European) scientific treatises. In the service of science, agricultural magazines made available to American farmers cutting-edge scientific findings from Europe, even before books written in German and French were translated into English; for example, the influential German soil chemist Justus von Liebig's text on soil chemistry was not published in English until 1840, but excerpts and interpretations of the British soil scientist Sir Humphrey Davy's 1813 text *Elements of Agricultural Chemistry* and translations of the writings of other German soil chemists were published in the *Cultivator* in the 1830s (Rossiter 1975: 9–11).

To augment their own efforts to develop and diffuse the principles of scientific agriculture, many magazines called for the establishment of state agricultural societies and county-level educational institutions. Agricultural schools, they argued, would train farmers in scientific principles: they would be places "where our sons may acquire every branch of practical knowledge" (Abbott 1852: 2). Only specialized agricultural schools could provide "opportunities of serving an apprenticeship to this complicated, scientific, and mechanical ... profession" (Botts 1841: 92).

Agricultural magazines were especially valuable in the trans-Appalachian West, where the soil and climate were very different from those in the East. In this region agricultural editors explained to newcomers how to break the tough prairie sod and plough its deep soil; how to mulch crops in dry areas, tile them in swampy areas, and fertilize them everywhere; how to select and breed superior livestock and plants; how and what to feed livestock; and what kinds of agricultural products were most marketable. Western editors also instructed farmers to build windmills to power grain grinding machines in place of scarce water power. In this way agricultural magazines were instrumental in developing communities of practice that were firmly rooted in their particular locations—communities of place.

Yet the editors of these periodicals often fought an uphill battle, as many farmers were skeptical about "book farming" and were reluctant to subscribe to magazines. This reluctance reflected a tension that is inherent in all social change. Although farming was a slow way of earning a living, it was also a safe and certain way. Many nineteenth-century farmers were unwilling to deviate from what they viewed as tried-and-true agricultural methods. For example, one contributor to Jesse Buel's *Cultivator* wrote that many farmers resisted agricultural reform because their traditions, "venerated only for their antiquity," remained widespread (Walsh 1840: 34). Thomas Green Fessenden, editor of the *New England Farmer*, said that innovations in farm machinery were ignored by farmers who "very absurdly retain their old implements, though convinced of their inferiority" (1839: 330). Similarly, in the pages of the *American Farmer*, Richard Bruckner complained about "the great prejudice ... against the most improved systems of cultivation" (quoted in Stoll 2002: 62). In 1823 the august Levi Lincoln Jr., who was later elected governor of Massachusetts, argued in the *New England Farmer* that farmers were prone to follow traditional routines and unlikely to experiment with agricultural reforms:

> *Habit and Prejudice* are powerful opponents of improvement, and they are in a great measure incident to the business of Agriculture. The cultivation of the earth, is a *practical* lesson, taught to the Husbandman in earliest life. He is instructed in the way of his fathers, and the *mode* which experience has approved as safe, will be reluctantly yielded to the mere promise of experiment. Hence, from generation to generation, men pass on in the track of their predecessors: believing that the path which is explored, is in the only direction to their object, and those who deviate, wander to their destruction. (Lincoln 1823: 180; emphasis in the original)

Resistance to agricultural reform was greatest in the South, where cotton was king and there was little economic incentive to allocate acreage to cattle grazing and the forage crops that were needed to produce manure, much less to spare the labor of slaves who would otherwise have been tending cotton (Hall 1940; Stoll 2002).

Traditionalist attitudes toward farming were expressed in hostility toward "book farming." If a farmer discovered something for himself and told his neighbors, they would quickly adopt the innovation, but "if this man, desirous of benefiting a whole community by his experience ... shall write out his experiment, and cause it to be printed in a book or periodical, that moment it becomes part of book-farming, and ceases to have virtue in the eyes of many. There is a magic in types, it would seem, that converts what is wisdom when spoken into folly when printed" (*Cultivator* 1853: 353). Another editor lamented, "Too many farmers still think that reading, reflection, reasoning ... is of no use to them. They laugh at science; call it book farming with a sneer, if some neighbor tries to pry into the secrets of the trade, or sends his son to an agricultural school. The farmer, they think, need not know much" (Francis 1857: 76).

In a reaction against traditionalists, reform-oriented magazine editors sought to vindicate "book farming." In 1841 the inaugural issue of the *Union Agriculturist and Western Prairie Farmer* expressed pity and contempt "for the man who thinks that if we used books, we must close our eyes against the light that is beaming upon is from other sources; or that we must become mere theorisers, and the victims of ruinous experiments" (Putnam 1841: 3). In the same vein, the magazine's editors argued, "Agriculture will be successfully promoted, only in proportion as men are acquainted with the best modes and seasons of culture, the laws of vegetable and animal physiology, and the probable existence of that demand which it will be most profitable to supply" (Wayland 1841: 3). Eight years later, the same magazine, now titled simply *Prairie Farmer*, took up the debate again, commenting, "Where there is reading, there must be some thinking; and where there is thinking applied to any branch of labor, that labor is at once lifted from the catalogue of servile drudgeries, and made to that extent, and ennobling occupation.... It is only as the mind works with the hands that labor becomes ennobled" (Wright and Wright 1849: 36).

It was not, however, entirely unreasonable for farmers to be skeptical of the many newfangled farm implements and practices, as many promised far more than they delivered. Most famously, Cyrus McCormick admitted that his reaper, invented in 1831 and patented in 1834, had little practical value until his second patent in 1845 (McClelland 1997: 152–54). In addition, many farmers' experiences with and indirect knowledge of the dozens of agricultural crazes that diffused during this era, most of which failed badly, only strengthened their conviction that the tried-and-true methods were the best.

Not all of what was published in agricultural magazines promoted modern, protoscientific agriculture. Indeed, they often promoted novelties and fads, like silk cultivation, broom corn, and Chinese tree corn (Gates 1960; Bogue 1963), that ran counter to protoscientific efforts to reform agricultural practices. More critical is that many articles were oriented toward a mythical, traditional past: they defended farming as the most fundamental of occupations and, with great sentimentality, celebrated its independence, security, and closeness to nature (Hofstadter 1955; Hayter 1968; Danhof 1969). Even the most reform-oriented magazine editors reminded readers that farming was a noble occupation: the farmer was independent, God-fearing, the backbone of American society, and deserving of recognition and praise from other Americans (Abbott 1968; Kulikoff 1992). For example, the editor of the *Plough Boy* asserted that agriculture was "that art which forms the basis of all others, and of civilized society" and said of farmers "theirs ... is the true republican party; ... theirs is the party whose first leaders were the patriarchs of the human race"; he also called for his readers to "VENERATE THE PLOUGH!" (Southwick 1819: 1–2; emphasis in the original). In the same vein, the masthead of the *American Agriculturist* quoted George Washington: "Agriculture is the most healthy, the most useful, and the most noble employment of Man"; and the editor of *The Plough, the Loom and the Anvil* (1848–59) praised agriculture as "the heaven-appointed calling for two-thirds of the human race" (Skinner 1857: 1). A contributor to the *Cultivator* lauded agriculture among occupations as "the most indispensible [*sic*], the best preserver of health, of morality, of virtue, and of religion" (Walsh 1840: 34). Finally, the *Genesee Farmer* proclaimed that its "grand object" was "the improvement of the practice of agriculture, by the diffusion of agricultural knowledge, and the inculcation of what may be denominated the agricultural virtues—INDUSTRY, PRUDENCE, and

ECONOMY" (Tucker and Stevens 1831: 2; emphasis in the original). This attitude was reactionary, if not regressive, as it was often a response to an antifarm sentiment that valorized urban occupations as "modern" and denigrated farming as "traditional" or "old-fashioned" (Abbott 1968; Chaplin 1993; McClelland 1997). It represented an effort to defend a particular occupational community and to build a cohesive identity for farmers in the face of industrialization. Thus the magazines supported antimodern communities of practice as well as modern, protoscientific ones. In this regard they were similar to religious and reform magazines.

Readers sincerely appreciated agricultural magazines. Consider this example, from a subscriber to the *American Farmer* (1839–97): "Please accept my best wishes for your personal welfare and the success of your ably conducted journal, which greets us promptly each month, filled with such interesting and useful matter" (Shriver 1860: 24). Speaking for farm wives, another reader praised that same magazine: "every housekeeper who devotes a short time, each month, to reading your journal, is not only much improved by it, but entertained as well as enlightened" (*American Farmer* 1860: 210). Writing about an earlier magazine with the same name, an anonymous planter declared, "Thou must be assured I am gratified with thy publication—it amuses, and at the same time may correct evil habits where they exist" (*American Farmer* 1825: 165). One subscriber to the *Southern Agriculturist and Register of Rural Affairs* (1829–46) stated bluntly, "A *farmer*, if he takes but one publication, that surely ought to be on agriculture" (M'Donald 1836: 411; emphasis in the original). And a contributor to the *Genesee Farmer* (1831–39) concurred, writing, "There should be papers printed, in different sections of our country, on those important subjects, agriculture and horticulture, that the most numerous and important part of the population of our country, (I mean the farmers,) have a regular channel for the interchange of opinions on those subjects in which they are engaged" (Greiggs 1833: 46).

Still another, writing about the *Farmer's Register* (1833–43), lauded

the transforming influence your valuable periodical has exerted and is still exerting hereabouts, in the improving of our farms, our stocks, and all that pertains to our advancement in agriculture. In this small neighborhood it has been the means of adding thousands of dollars to the value of our farms. . . . It has changed the old practice in farming, introduced a love of system, order and science, and excited a laudable emulation and competition in the cultivators of the soil. . . . [Because of the *Farmer's Register*] agricultural topics became subjects of discussion in all that neighborhood, and all suitable occasions were employed to diffuse the principles of the new system. (*Farmer's Register* 1843: 157)

Yet another praised agricultural magazines in general, writing, "It is to our agricultural papers, most emphatically, that we owe the *awakening* which has taken place in this State, on the subject of agricultural improvement. Without them, nothing of this kind could even be effected. There is no feasible substitute for them" (Randall 1844: 3).

Of course, readers' comments were not uniformly positive. For example, one reader requested that editors include more articles written by "practical farmers" rather than "flowery theorists" (Kimball 1845: 213). Most complaints, however, involved criticism of others' contributions; indeed, some exchanges between contributors became quite heated.

Summary

The rise of scientific agriculture required a two-part shift in cultural values. The first part involved the development of a new mind-set, "an acceptance of agriculture as market-focused, profit-motivated, and characterized by a rational approach to technology; that is, of agriculture as business" (Danhof 1969: 22; see also Clark 1990; McClelland 1997). Farmers had to experiment, take risks, and flexibly adapt to changing circumstances—as one historian put it, they had to ask "Is there a better way?" (McClelland 1997: x). They had to weigh costs and benefits in the light of their long-term goals. They had to pay attention to conditions in urban markets far away from their homes. And they had to deal with market intermediaries, such as meatpackers, wool dealers, egg and dairy wholesalers, and cattle drivers. The second part of this cultural shift required systematic consideration of cause and effect: farmers had to recognize that their own actions could harm or improve the soil. In turn, this required farmers to take responsibility as purposively rational individuals (Stott 2002) in the spirit of agricultural reformer Jesse Buel: "Individuals, it is true, are but units—yet the aggregation of units makes millions, and the aggregation of individuals constitutes nations. We should all act as though individual example had an imposing influence upon the whole" (*Cultivator*, March 1838, quoted in Stoll 2002: 23).

The development of scientific agriculture had an important but unanticipated impact on community in rural areas. To the extent that scientific agriculture restored and preserved the fertility of farmland, farm families were able to stay in one place rather than migrate to new land. Thus the adoption of scientific agriculture rendered rural communities more stable and more cohesive (Stoll 2002) and strengthened communities of place. In addition, by paying attention to the specific needs of farmers given a particular region's soil type, temperature, precipitation, and topography, regionally focused agricultural magazines both reflected and reinforced bonds among farmers in that region. Both the development of scientific agriculture and its promulgation by agricultural magazines were expressions of a desire to persist, to claim a stake in a particular local farming community.

Agricultural magazines were by far the most influential medium for spreading the principles and practices of scientific agriculture (Demaree 1941; Lemmer 1957; Gates 1960). By 1860, improved agricultural methods had spread throughout the North and West (Gates 1960; Danhof 1969; Stoll 2002).

Although progress was slower in the South, many farmers there, especially in the Chesapeake Bay area, did adopt agricultural reforms (Craven [1925] 2007; Gates 1960).

CONCLUSION

Between 1740 and 1860 the American economy changed in several related ways. First, the economy expanded dramatically, although it was highly turbulent throughout this time period, with wars, embargoes, financial panics, and depressions stalling—and sometimes even reversing—the general upward trajectory. Second, manufacturing increased as a share of the economy, and production shifted from rural households to small craft shops (managed by their proprietors) or large industrial factories (managed by salaried supervisors), most of which were located in urban areas. Third, commerce touched an increasing fraction of Americans—even those in frontier areas. Fourth, agriculture became much more oriented toward commercial markets, especially those in the burgeoning urban areas. Moreover, the agricultural and manufacturing output of all regions became increasing sold through a hierarchical system of markets that spanned the country rather than consumed locally. Fifth, agriculture became "scientific" as farmers sought to improve their yields by experimenting with new techniques, using innovative labor-saving machines, and raising new breeds of livestock and new kinds of plants.

But there was great regional variation in economic development. The Northeast urbanized and industrialized more rapidly than the West, while the South remained largely rural and agricultural. Regional differences in population concentration and industrialization strengthened the cultural differences that were already apparent before the Revolution. Most notably, the southern plantation elite came to view commerce and industry as vulgar (which is ironic considering that they were heavily involved in producing cash crops for trade in national and international markets), while northerners and westerners celebrated both.

Magazines played two distinct roles in economic modernization during this period. First, business magazines were rare and of limited importance until the last decade before the Civil War. The only exception was bank note reporters and counterfeit detectors, although they had mixed effects: they both wove webs of social relations among many different types of economic actors that often covered large territories *and* undermined economic actors' trust in a basic medium of exchange. Somewhat more numerous than business magazines were technical and scientific magazines, which began to affect the economy in the last two decades before the Civil War by diffusing knowledge of mathematics, chemistry, geology, and mechanics.

Second, agricultural magazines were by far the most important type of magazine for the economy, in part because agriculture was throughout this time period the largest sector of the economy but also because, starting in the

1820s, such magazines were numerous, broadly distributed, and widely read. Indeed, several agricultural magazines reached mass audiences across the country, preaching the gospel of "scientific" agriculture. They exhorted farmers everywhere to rotate crops and fertilize them with manure; amend soil with lime, gypsum, and guano; manage fields to reduce the erosion of precious topsoil and improve drainage; invest in new mechanical equipment; plant crops such as clover and timothy grass to enrich the soil and feed livestock; experiment with new plant and animal breeds from abroad and develop better breeds of their own; learn from European and American scientists; and—most important—converse with each other. In this way agricultural magazines created strong communities of practice, some of which spanned the nation, others of which were limited to specific geographic regions and supported communities of place.

The contrast between the strong effects of agricultural magazines and the weak effects of bank-note reporters suggests two scope conditions for my arguments about magazines and community. The first involves the temporal nature of information. Magazines' impact on community depends on how long the information they communicate remains valuable. In this era, commercial exchange required frequent updates about bank-note values, while scientific agriculture needed more long-lasting information flows. Information about bank notes had a very short life—perhaps too short for any magazine, even a weekly or semiweekly one, to succeed at offering, especially given the inevitable lag between getting information about the value of bank notes, writing it up, printing it, and distributing it to subscribers through the mail or in local stores.

The second scope condition involves the nature of the relations between magazines and their audiences (i.e., contributors and readers). In agriculture, audiences were united in seeking to improve farming practice. In contrast, in commerce there were two audiences with diametrically opposing interests: speculative bankers and forgers versus merchants, farmers, tradespeople, and artisans. Publishing magazines could not solve the second group's problem because the first group could use magazines to adjust their practices. As a result the problem of multiple currencies could not be solved by those engaged in commerce—it required a central (i.e., federal) solution. Given the southern states' vigorous defense of states' rights in this era, this was not politically feasible. Despite general discontent, no magazine could promulgate a strong call for a single series of federally issued paper notes: doing so would literally devalue states' ability to print money via state-chartered banks. During the Civil War, the states remaining in the Union were galvanized to unite against a common enemy, and the southern states, which had been the strongest defenders of states' rights, were gone, so representatives in Washington could accept a federal solution to the multiple currencies problem. After the war ended the Southern states had no choice but to accept the National Currency and Bank Acts that were passed during the war (US Congress 1863, 1864, 1865)—they were *faits accomplis*.

CHAPTER 8

Conclusion

*F*rom 1741, the year they first appeared, to 1860, the year before the Civil War broke out, magazines developed from a few, fragile, questionable undertakings to over a thousand robust, highly legitimate elements of print culture, some of which attracted large audiences across the nation. Over this 120-year period magazines became more heavily concentrated in New York City, but they were also published in towns and cities across the nation. Moreover, they differentiated into over a dozen distinct genres and many targeted particular demographic subgroups. All of these developments were made possible by a series of related contextual shifts that together underpinned the expansion and entrenchment of magazines in American print culture: population growth and urbanization; the emergence of specialized occupations; advances in publishing technologies; the expansion of the postal system; the gradual development of copyright law and the emergence of the convention that authors are professionals, to be paid for their contributions; the disestablishment of state religions, waves of immigration, and outbreaks of religious revivalism that together created a pluralistic but highly competitive national religious field; the efflorescence of a wide array of voluntary social reform societies and the modernization of social reform movements, many of which were supported by religious institutions; the growth of commerce; and the rise of protoscientific agriculture. American magazines displayed these social changes in their pages and patterns of growth. Moreover, they contributed to many of these changes, making possible entirely new forms of community.

Magazines literally mediated among people, facilitating frequent interactions among them and thus weaving "invisible threads of connection" (Starr 2004: 24) among them even when they were geographically dispersed and unlikely to meet face-to-face. In this way magazines helped create the modern American cultural mosaic: a wide array of distinct local and translocal communities, collections of people with common interests, values, principles, ideas, and identities. Some sought transcendence through religion, others strove to reform social ills and improve individuals' morals and behavior, and still others pursued material interests in agriculture and specialized commercial, manufacturing, and service occupations. In other words, magazines supported essentially modern communities of practice (in agriculture, commerce, and specialized occupations), purpose (in social reform), and faith (in religion), as well as more traditional or even antimodern communities of place (the readers of localistic agricultural, religious, literary, and general-interest magazines). These highly differentiated communities variously competed or cooperated with others. Moreover, these communities often intersected—most notably when particular social reform movements were affiliated with particular religious traditions. By fostering the pluralistic integration that was central to American public culture in this era (Higham 1974), magazines helped make an America that was distinct from European societies. Basically, magazines created "cross-cutting social circles" (Blau and Schwartz 1984) that made it easier for Americans to accept people who were different in one dimension (e.g., region or religion) because they were similar in another (e.g., target of social activism or specialized occupation). The existence of the dimension of similarity made it possible to accept the dimension of difference. Thus, to put it simply, magazines both pushed Americans toward a common center and pulled them apart into many distinct subgroups.

Implications for Understanding Modernity and Community

The nature of community, of the solidaristic bonds that hold both modern and traditional societies together, has always been of central concern to sociology, a discipline that coalesced shortly after Western societies began the long process of modernization. The analysis presented here shows that the evolution of community in America from the mid-eighteenth century to the mid-nineteenth was more complex and more contingent than many early sociologists would have predicted. Most basically, contra Ferdinand Tönnies ([1887] 1957) and Charles Horton Cooley ([1909] 1923), social solidarity did not disappear as America modernized and became highly differentiated: social ties were not hollowed out, individualism did not run rampant over the essential unity of traditional communities, and American did not become an atomistic society. Instead Americans were increasingly likely to be members of *both* localistic and parochial communities (communities of local place and particular faith or agricultural practice) *and* translocal communities (nationwide communities of faith, purpose, and practice). As a result, Americans' social ties multiplied and became more varied as modernization proceeded. In addition, the individuals and organizations to whom Americans were tied became both more numerous and more varied.

Moreover, essential or natural will [*Wesenwille*], which drove collective action to achieve goals that were valued for their own sake and which Tönnies ([1887] 1957) argued animated traditional community (*Gemeinschaft*) was not everywhere displaced by arbitrary or rational will (*Kürwille*), which impelled individualistic action toward goals that were valued for the ends they could bring about and which Tönnies proposed animated modern society (*Gesellschaft*). Instead, the modern communities that developed during this period often embraced both essential and rational aims, meaning collective *and* individualistic action; and goals that were valued for their own sake *and* goals that were rationally oriented toward some outcome. These findings support Max

Weber's observation that there is a blurry line between instrumentally ratio-nal (*zweckrational*), value-rational (*wertrational*), emotional (*affektual*), and tra-ditional social action ([1968] 1978: 24–26, 41). As a result, most modern, ratio-nally oriented associative institutions (*Vergesellschaftung*), such as business concerns, social reform organizations, and nonestablished religious groups, also contained elements of communal institutions (*Vergemeinschaftung*)—spe-cifically, the latter's shared feeling of belongingness based on communal val-ues, emotions, or traditions.

Although the religious, social reform, and agricultural communities that were supported by magazines were often calculatingly, instrumentally ratio-nal—they sought to achieve long-term goals that were chosen in relation to larger systems of meaning and they considered both the means to their de-sired ends and the ends themselves—many of these communities also es-poused goals that they believed would benefit others and, at their most gran-diose, society at large. Religious groups sought to build not just a "city on a hill" but a "nation on a hill," one that would stand as a beacon of godliness, a model for the rest of the world (Tuveson 1968: 90–136). Many social reform efforts sought to help others who were outside activists' own social circles: slaves and free blacks, Indians, prostitutes, seamen, the blind, the deaf and dumb, the insane, debtors, paupers, orphans, and widows. Some of these other-focused reform organizations were among the largest of this era; for example, the American Anti-Slavery Society peaked at 90,000 members (American Anti-Slavery Society 1834–40), while the American Temperance Society had a whopping 1.5 million members in 1835 (American Temperance Society 1835). Mobilizing in support of their favored reforms, many activists argued that they would cure the nation of its moral failings. Finally, farming reform-ers advocated new agricultural practices in order to enlighten other farmers—to preach to them the gospel of scientific agriculture and in doing so elevate their role in society and improve husbandry of natural resources in an early forerunner of today's "sustainability" movement.

As Émile Durkheim ([1893] 1984) argued, when and where a more mod-ern, more highly differentiated society emerged, new forms of solidarity and new types of connections between individuals developed. But this book has shown that these new forms of solidarity did not arise precisely the way Durk-heim proposed. He argued that increasing differentiation and the concomi-tant increase in interdependence *spontaneously* creates consensus about peo-ple's mutual interests and so binds people who are in diverse social positions into cohesive societies.[1] But solidarity in America did not arise naturally or inevitably out of the complementarities caused by specialization and interde-pendence; it was frequently intentional, as Robert Morrison MacIver (1917)

---

[1] Durkheim's analysis also allowed that there were antisolidaristic pathologies of the divi-sion of labor—specifically, anomic and forced responses to that process. But he argued that these were often passing phases (seen in modernization that was incomplete or came too quickly), that their effects could be ameliorated by state action, and that a new form of solidarity arising from complementarities was the norm.

contended, stemming from the "commonality of interests" of its members. Moreover, solidarity was often made possible by magazines, consonant with Charles Horton Cooley's ([1909] 1923), Karl Deutsch's (1953), and Gabriel Tarde's (1969) arguments about the expansive and connective powers of the media. Chapter 4 showed that the creation of community was the espoused purpose of many early magazines, and that the basis of the community they sought to foster shifted from the whole of American society to specific subgroups—primarily regional, religious, demographic, and occupational. Chapter 5 showed that religious leaders recognized the power of magazines to compete with and distinguish themselves from other faiths and to shepherd their far-flung flocks. Chapter 6 showed that activists self-consciously used magazines to inspire others to join their cause and effect wide-scale social change. Finally, chapter 7 showed that agricultural reforms deployed magazines to create modern (translocal and protoscientific) communities of practice, bringing together the ideas and experience of thousands of reader-contributors across the nation.

Yet magazines also supported more traditional, sometimes even antimodern, communities of place, faith, and practice. As chapter 3 revealed, the development of magazines claiming to serve communities of readers across the nation (those that adopted titles with national toponyms) spurred the rise of magazines making purely localistic claims to serve geographically bounded communities of readers (those that adopted titles with local toponyms). Thus this modern communication tool was used to reinforce traditionally local forms of community. More complexly, the communities supported by magazines could be *simultaneously* modern and antimodern.[2] The Sabbatarian movement discussed in chapter 6 had *both* rational aims *and* sought to return American society to a more traditional set of practices, with the timing of both commerce and communication constrained by strict (biblically literalist) religious tenets. By the same token, some of the farming communities discussed in chapter 7 were *both* modern in their goal of developing and diffusing what they viewed as scientific agricultural practices that suited specific climates, soils, and landscapes *and* traditional in that they were highly localistic in their focus and celebrated agriculture as the highest calling, the most noble occupation. Again, contra Durkheim, these traditional or antimodern communities of place, faith, and practice were not natural responses, anomic or forced, to the rapid division of labor that could be eliminated through state action but instead reasoned efforts to create and support particularistic subcommunities. In particular, the geographic communities studied in chapters 3 and 7 meshed with MacIver's (1917) argument that community stems from the "commonality of interests" it offers its members, as well as his view that locally circumscribed communities are often nested within communities that span larger geographic areas.

---

[2] In sustaining both modern and antimodern communities, magazines were similar to the telephone (Fischer 1992).

There are two more general lessons to take away from this book. First, understanding how culture—shared understandings of what is and ought to be—shape the evolution of media has broad implications for society. As scholars have long pointed out, how people use media, like other technologies, is shaped by culture (Bijker, Hughes, and Pinch 1987; Starr 2004; Boczkowski 2004). New media, like the magazines studied here, make it possible for different groups in society to renegotiate power and authority relations—although those negotiations are usually based on the vestiges of old cultural technologies and power relations (Marvin 1987: 4–5). Second, understanding novel media and those who produce them is vital because media in turn shape culture. Media literally mediate among people, connecting geographically dispersed individuals into cohesive communities to share knowledge, ideas, values, and principles. New media make possible novel combinations of people who can conceive of and may actually achieve innovative goals, and diffuse brand new values, worldviews, and practices.

Consider, for example religion, which has long been a central expression of American culture. Chapter 5 showed that many upstart faiths, which were often the products of revivals' extraordinary collective effervescence, developed new ideologies to shepherd their converts into religious communities that would emulate the purity of early Christianity. But these new communities were fragile—contested by longer-established faiths and threatened by the dissipation of revivalistic fervor after revival participants returned home to their everyday routines. To sustain their flocks leaders of these new upstart religious communities had to reinforce the messages that had been so forcefully and fruitfully expressed during revivals. In other words, the gains schismatic revivalist leaders made during "unsettled times" (outbreaks of revivalism) had to be solidified during "settled times" (everyday life; Swidler 1986). That was no easy task because upstart religious leaders' flocks were far-flung and travel was difficult, so new religious communities could not depend solely on local pastors to fight their theological battles or inculcate the tenets of their faith in their followers. Upstart religious leaders turned to magazines to routinize the new ideologies and practices that constituted the basis of their religious authority. The lesson to be learned is that religious revivals and the consequent increase in religious diversity and competition—cultural and structural changes that were central to American public culture during this era—created ideal conditions for the flourishing of magazines devoted to religion. Then, as magazines began to prove their value as social "glue" within religious communities, they became "naturalized" as tools for established religious groups in the battle for souls and religious authority they waged against upstart faiths. As legitimate cultural and political tools, magazines were also adopted by social reform communities, many of which were affiliated with or informally supported by particular religious communities, and then by many other specialized communities of practice and purpose. The upshot is that magazines were both causes and consequences of fundamental shifts in American culture.

These findings, from a period that ended over 150 years ago, accord with research on social and news media in the twenty-first century. Studies of the public understanding of Islam after the September 11, 2001, attacks showed that the existing array of political, civic, and religious organizations that made claims about the nature of Islam, in conjunction with the set of values and beliefs those organizations professed, determined whether, how, and which members of this organizational ecology (fringe or mainstream) were able to garner attention for their particular political stands and ideologies (Bail 2012, 2015). This is especially true in times of crisis, such as in the wake of the September 11 attacks, when culture is highly visible and explicit (Swidler 1986) and extremely powerful in justifying the worldviews and practices that people use to construct new strategies of action to suit the new situations they encounter. At such times people are not only more aware of the cultural "tools" at their disposal but are also better able to articulate their use of these tools to both motivate and justify their behavior (Vaisey 2009). In the eighteenth and nineteenth centuries there were many "unsettled" times and thus many opportunities for magazines to significantly affect American society.

Implications for Other Aspects of American Society

This book covers a wide terrain, but even so, it barely touches on several aspects of American society that were affected by and reflected in magazines: the rise of various medical schools (several types of doctors, plus pharmacists, dentists, and veterinarians) and the teaching profession, the simultaneous development of a national literature and competing regional literatures, formal politics (as distinct from the informal politics practiced by social reform movements), and the consolidation and social incorporation of ethnic immigrant communities, especially (but not only) those whose members spoke languages other than English.

Scholars of the nineteenth-century American medical profession (e.g., Weiss and Kremble 1967; Haller 1997, 2000, 2005; Whorton 2002; Whooley 2013) have rarely attended to how magazines helped create diverse communities of practice among members of this emerging profession and how they served as platforms for debates that were often as heated as those in the pages of the religious magazines surveyed in chapter 5. Literary scholars and intellectual historians who have scrutinized relationships between magazines and literature (e.g., Sedgwick 2000; Kamrath 2002; McGill 2003; Okker 2003; Jackson 2008; Gardner 2012; Tomc 2012; Spoo 2013) have focused narrowly on particular literary movements or small authorial communities and have not investigated literary life in toto. The interplay between magazines (as distinct from newspapers) and formal politics has seldom been studied, even though the earliest magazines were heavily focused on politics and later ones often took up political themes. For example, the phrase *manifest destiny*—the determination to expand the nation westward to the Pacific—was coined in the *United States Magazine and Democratic Review*, the organ of the antiaristocratic, procapitalist, territorially expansionist Young America movement (O'Sullivan 1845; see also O'Sullivan 1839).[3]

Finally, from the mid-eighteenth century to the mid-nineteenth, almost four hundred magazines were launched to appeal to speakers of Czech, Danish, French, German, Hebrew, Italian, Norwegian, Spanish, Swedish, and Welsh. Little study of how these magazines influenced the persistence or evolution of these immigrant communities ensued, although there have been several bibliographic studies (e.g., Marino 1933; Arndt and Olson 1961; Erickson 1977), from which I drew data on magazines published in these languages. Few extant histories of immigrant groups attend to the issues that are central to this book. Only one study, of German immigrants and German-language periodicals (Wittke 1957), examined their social context in detail; it showed that German-language magazines served a dual purpose, both creating community by anchoring German-speaking immigrants in their cultural heritage and introducing those immigrants to their new country and its peculiar social mores.[4] In the same vein, studies of a more recent communication medium in the late twentieth century have shown that nationwide Spanish-language television networks began to broadcast content that appealed to Cuban Americans, Mexican Americans, and Puerto Ricans alike; such broadcasting supported the development of a panethnic Hispanic ethnicity, changing how new immigrants from these countries and others farther south encountered American society (Mora 2014a, 2014b). Together these studies suggest that in the eighteenth and nineteenth centuries magazines may have helped immigrant communities forge novel identities in their new homeland, but the question remains as to whether they impelled or impeded immigrants' assimilation.

As this brief discussion reveals, much more of the story of magazines, modernization, and community in America in the eighteenth and nineteenth centuries remains to be told.

Implications for Newer Media

Although they focus on a slice of American history that ended over 150 years ago, the findings in this book have clear relevance for those who study media in the contemporary era. Most directly, studying magazines before the Civil War can offer insight into the current magazine and newspaper industries,

[3] There is a deep connection between the notion of manifest destiny and religion—expanding the United States would "redeem" a large part of the continent and create a "nation on a hill" that would stand as a beacon of godliness, a model for the rest of the world (Tuveson 1968: 90–136). This suggests that a triple focus on religion, formal politics, and magazines would prove fruitful.

[4] Among the cited examples, a history of Hispanic periodicals (Kanellos and Martell 2000) focused mostly on newspapers and covered magazines very briefly, while an unpublished study of French émigrés and French-language periodicals (Marino 1962) was more descriptive than analytical and surveyed only a fraction of the French-language magazines published in this era.

which face significant technological and economic challenges. These industries are experimenting with Internet publishing and interactive content, but many of their experiments are not (yet) yielding the same profits and audience shares that traditional print publishing once did. As chapter 7 showed, agricultural magazines thrived in the nineteenth century by opening their pages to readers, welcoming their contributions: questions about agricultural practices, answers to such questions, reports of experiments and unusual events, and responses to those reports. In turn, this give-and-take among readers, with magazines acting as go-betweens, strengthened self-identified communities of agricultural reformers by increasing members' knowledge base and introducing them to others they might never have met. So far, contemporary magazines' and newspapers' online interactions with their readers has been generally limited to readers' responses to material emanating from those media; little is being done to solicit readers' contributions in ways that would allow them to lead, rather than follow, in the conversational dance, even though newspapers recognize that letters to the editor can offer a space for public debate (Perrin and Vaisey 2008). Contemporary media might do well to emulate early agricultural magazines and experiment with reader-led conversational threads to see if they could engage existing readers more intensely and attract new ones. Such a tactical turn might help magazines and newspapers bridge the well-documented "news gap" between journalists' and readers' preferences (Boczkowski and Mitchelstein 2013).

Analysis of the origins of the magazine industry is also relevant today as we assess novel organizational and technological forms among twenty-first-century media. The recent rise social media (the so-called Web 2.0: social networking sites, video- and text-sharing platforms, blogs, and rating and discussion forums) threatens traditional media's monopoly on the production of public culture. It has already created novel forms of community, many of which are as interactive as nineteenth-century magazines. As one of the "old" new media, magazines and the story of how they developed through the eighteenth and nineteenth centuries can shed light on the possible trajectories of "new" new media. Over the first 120 years of their history, American magazines evolved in a way that would have shocked their earliest proponents: from elite-produced and elite-consumed compilations of political, cultural, and economic material that was viewed as serious literature by those elites to platforms produced and consumed by both elites (professionals, academics, the wealthy, and political insiders) and the hoi polloi (rabble-rousing revivalists, social radicals, advocates of wacky reforms, medical quacks, children, backwoods literati, and free blacks) that covered a wide array of topics, both serious and lighthearted. Recent research has shown that those who contribute to a wide array of online media are overwhelmingly highly educated elites (Schradie 2011), but as the history of the magazine industry shows, that can change in unexpected ways. Indeed, there is recent evidence that elite dominance of "new" new media is giving way: many poorer, less-educated people in less-developed countries have created vibrant communities using social media—notably, the activists in the Arab Spring uprisings of 2010–12 and the Islamic State in Iraq and Syria today (Shane and Hubbard 2014). Moreover, the present analysis has shown that launching a magazine went from being a sure way to lose money to a means of self-aggrandizement and enrichment. Such tremendous change in form and function is common for new technologies, as can be noted in the 1943 prediction attributed to IBM founder Thomas Watson Sr. that there was a world market for only five computers, or the pronouncement by British observers in the 1880s that the telephone was a device most useful for businessmen (De Sola Pool 1983: 24); these forecasters would have been shocked at the proliferation of these devices and the uses to which teenagers put them today. So this not-so-novel point about novel technologies is worth repeating and is worthy of investigation by those who study "new" new media. At present, there are some similarities between the trajectories of print magazines and these "new" new media, but such trajectories bear watching.

Final Thoughts

Magazines, like all media, bring together like-minded people, regardless of their location or what they may have in common. In America from the mid-eighteenth to the mid-nineteenth centuries, magazines engaged and empowered people who chose to be members of a host of different groups. These associative institutions were essentially modern communities: they contained individuals who may have had no connection by birth or custom but who sought to achieve common goals and forge common identities. As America became more modern and increasingly socially differentiated, magazines made it possible for people in specialized occupations, diverse faith groups, and many different social reform movements to forge strong bonds with similar and sympathetic others. People in specialized occupations could meet and learn from each other to improve their practices. Modern (nonmonopolistic) religious groups could compete against and distinguish themselves from other groups and demarcate their own niches in what became a pluralistic, nationwide religious field. And social reform movements could energize activists across the country to push for changes in personal and social life. In all these ways, magazines created modern communities—a function that their contemporary successors, both print and online, fill today.

The concept of modernization does not explain how it occurs—by what concrete actions of individuals and organizations and under what circumstances. To understand how this process unfolds on the ground we need to pay attention to media and to the other tools that tie modern community members together—especially those who are geographically dispersed. A focus on media and other social glues also allows us to understand not only how America became modern but also the functioning of the traditional and antimodern communities of faith and place that arose in response to modernization. Eighteenth- and nineteenth-century magazines were founded with the explicit intent of creating community—sometimes including all people in the colonies or the new nation, other items limited to members of specific regions, occupations, faiths, movements, or demographic subgroups. Without magazines' ability to transcend space and time, the modernization of America would have followed a very different path. And without magazines to bridge axes of modernization, the pluralistic integration that distinguished American society from European ones in this period would have been impeded.

APPENDIX 1

Data and Data Sources

*T*his appendix describes the sources of the data used in this book and the measures for the variables constructed from these data sources. I begin by explaining the sources of the core data on magazines. I then describe how I measured various attributes of magazines: founding and failure dates (discussed in several chapters); contents and genre (chapters 2 and 3); format, location, and geographic identity (chapters 2 and 3); details about financial operations (chapter 4); language (chapter 2), and founders' motivations and goals (chapter 4). Next I explain how I gathered and coded data on magazine founders' backgrounds (chapter 4). Subsequent sections of this appendix describe data sources and measures for contextual factors. In order, these are religious institutions (chapter 5), social reform organizations (chapter 6), publishing technologies and the postal system (chapter 3), population and the economy (chapters 3 and 7), and literacy and educational institutions (chapter 3).

CORE DATA ON MAGAZINES: SOURCES

The American Periodical Series Online is my main source for primary data on magazines. It contains digital images of over 1,200 magazines (for documentation, see Hoornstra and Heath 1979 or view the series at Proquest's website, which is available through many university libraries). To augment these data I searched the American Antiquarian Society's online catalog, which provides bibliographical information on thousands of magazines, and I viewed microfilm archives covering hundreds of magazines in the Columbia University, Cornell University, and New York Public Libraries. I also conducted Internet searches to tap into archival sources in other universities and scholarly institutions, including two collaborations that have created searchable pdf files of many old, out-of-copyright texts in the libraries of a number of research universities: the Hathitrust and the Google Books Library Project. Two other sets of online archives were especially helpful: Readex Corporation's Archives of Americana (Early American Imprints, Series I: Evans, 1639–1800; Early American Imprints, Series II: Shaw-Shoemaker, 1801–1819; Early American Imprints, Series I and II: Supplements from the Library company of Philadelphia, 1670–1819, and America's Historical Newspapers) and a joint venture by the Library of Congress, the University of Michigan, and Cornell University,

The Nineteenth Century in Print: The Making of America in Books and Periodicals.

Alas, many magazines left no physical trace of their existence. For many others, only a partial record remains in archives. Hence I relied heavily on secondary sources. Guided by two standard histories of the industry—an early three-volume analysis that remains a standard reference work on the industry (Mott 1930, 1938a, 1938b) and a more recent narrative (Tebbel and Zuckerman 1991)—I searched the Columbia University Library, the New York Public Library, and the University of California library system for secondary sources. I was particularly conscientious in searching for the kinds of magazines that were least likely to be tracked by historians: (a) short-lived and small-circulation magazines; (b) publications from the hinterlands (the West and the South); (c) magazines in languages other than English; (d) publications that covered something other than "serious" literary, religious, medical, scientific, or political topics; and (e) magazines for subordinated groups: women, children, students, blacks, and Native Americans. Applying such an "affirmative action" approach to gathering data revealed many magazines that were not discussed in standard accounts. In total, I used sixteen book-length histories of the industry; twenty-nine checklists, bibliographies, and catalogs prepared by historians, bibliographers, and librarians; forty-two book-length descriptions of specific types of magazines or magazines in specific locations; and thirteen articles focusing on particular types of magazines:

> *Sixteen book-length histories of the industry:* Tassin 1916; Mott 1930, 1938a, 1938b; Richardson 1931; Garwood 1931; Wood 1949; Lewis 1955; Lyon 1942; Wittke 1957; Marino 1962; Wunderlich 1962; Strohecker 1969; Edgar 1975; Bullock 1981; Tebbel and Zuckerman 1991.
>
> *Twenty-nine checklists, bibliographies, and catalogs:* Roorbach [1852] 1939; North 1884; Ford [1889] 1972; Chandler 1905; Faxon 1908; Clark 1917; Beer 1922; Gilmer [1934] 1972; Hewett 1935; Allen, Cheney, and Oursler 1941; Stuntz 1941; Millen 1949; Arndt and Olson 1961; Kenny 1961; Willging and Hatzfeld 1968; Weichlein 1970; Kribbs 1977; Erickson 1977; Hoornstra and Heath 1979; Riley 1986a; Braude 1990; Albaugh 1994; Schmidt 1999; Baker-Batsel 2001; Smith 2006; Armstrong Atlantic State University 2006; Pflieger 2013; art magazines (online index); American Antiquarian Society Online Catalog.
>
> *Forty-two book-length descriptions of particular kinds of magazines or magazines in particular locations:* Bradford 1892; Smyth 1892; Bolton 1897; Cairns [1898] 1971; Wilder 1904; Connelley 1916; Davis 1919; McLean 1928; Tinker 1933; Demaree 1941; Flanders 1944; Snodgrass 1947; Garrison and DeGroot 1948; Dillistin 1949; MacCurdy 1951; Flandorf 1952; David 1955; Roberts 1961; Howell 1970; Stratman 1970; Campbell 1970; Davison 1973; Hutton and Reed 1975; Kowalik 1978; Blassingame, Henderson, and Dunn 1980–84; Daniel 1982; Kelly 1984; Littlefield and Parins 1984; Lippy 1986; Riley 1986b; Sloane 1987; Hoerder

and Harzig 1987; Nourie and Nourie 1990; Unsworth 1990; Fisher 1991; Endres 1994; Endres and Lueck 1995, 1996; Fackler and Lippy 1995; Lora and Longton 1999; Kanellos and Martell 2000; Haller 2000. *Thirteen articles focusing on particular types of magazines: Transactions of the American Medical Association 1848; Billings 1879; Matthews 1899; Fleming 1905; Matthews 1910; Stearns 1931, 1932; Smith 1933; Shafer 1935; Garrison and DeGroot 1948; Ebert 1953; Garnsey 1954; Garcia 1976.*

My secondary data sources sometimes disagreed with each other. Most of the time I was able to resolve discrepancies by referring to primary data (when available), by taking as correct the majority opinion (when the magazines themselves were not in the archives and there were multiple secondary data sources), or by taking as correct the opinion of the secondary source that offered the richest detail. In most cases the discrepancies were small (for example, less than a year's difference in failure date or date of move from one city to another), so even an arbitrary decision would not generate much measurement error.

REFINING THE SAMPLE: DISTINGUISHING MAGAZINES FROM OTHER TYPES OF PUBLICATIONS

In the antebellum era there was a fine line between magazines and newspapers, as many magazines published articles on current events and some emphasized politics (Mott 1930; Wood 1949; Tebbel and Zuckerman 1991). Contemporaries recognized the fuzziness of the boundary between the two kinds of periodicals. For instance, Joseph Dennie, editor of the *Farmer's Weekly Museum* (1793–1810) explicitly recognized the bifurcated audience for his "literary and political paper" as "one class, who would view it merely as a newspaper, and another, who would patronize it as a repository for the belles lettres" (Dennie 1797). Similarly, John Woods, founder of the Newark, New Jersey–based weekly *Rural Magazine* (1798–99), stated,

> The object of this publication, is intended to combine the utility of a monthly magazine, with the advantages of a weekly gazette.... Newspapers, are in general, so engrossed with political intelligence and advertisements, as to afford very little room for the insertion of important literary subjects: monthly magazines, on the other hand, appear too seldom, and are too lengthy, to secure the uninterrupted attention of the generality of readers. A periodical publication, therefore, which shall unite the miscellaneous form of a monthly magazine, with the stated recurrence of a weekly paper, promises to ensure the most probably means of information and gratification. (Woods 1797)

The fuzzy boundary between magazine and newspaper persisted throughout the period under study. John Inman, editor of the *Columbian Lady's and Gen-*

tleman's Magazine (1844–49), observed in his venture's first issue that magazines had become so popular that newspapers sought to imitate them: "All literature approximates to the magazine, either in form or character … newspapers, unable to emulate [magazines] in appearance, strive to do so in the variety and nature of their contents. In fact, the word *news*paper has come to be almost a misnomer, for the purveying of news has ceased to be their characteristic vocation and object. What is the 'leading article' but an essay? What are nine-tenths of the narrative paragraphs but short tales, either of fact or fiction?" (Inman 1844: 1; emphasis in the original).

Postmasters usually distinguished between magazines and newspapers based on contents and publication frequency: they generally classified periodicals as newspapers if they contained accounts of political and other current events, were published weekly or more frequently, and were published in large format (broadsheet); they classified all other periodicals as magazines (Kielbowicz 1989: 122–32). Because antebellum postage rates favored newspapers, wily magazine publishers played with their formats (using large broadsheet pages [approximately $22\frac{3}{4}'' \times 22''$] rather than smaller folio [$12'' \times 15''$], quarto [$9\frac{1}{2}'' \times 12''$], octavo [$6'' \times 9''$], or duodecimo [$4'' \times 6\frac{3}{4}''$] pages) and their contents (for instance, adding a single column of political news) so as to qualify for cheaper newspaper postage.

The fuzzy boundary between magazines and newspapers notwithstanding, those who ran antebellum magazines sought to publish material that would have a longer shelf life than the contents of newspapers. As pioneering magazine founder Andrew Bradford explained, "We shall also subjoin Accounts, ranged under proper Titles, of the General Affairs of *Europe*, *Asia*, and *Africa*, with References from one Number to another, in order to preserve a Connection and Chain of Events. This part of the Work, digested into such Method, we presume, will yield greater Pleasure and Profit, than the scattered, unconnected Articles of News in the common Prints" (Bradford 1740: 3). In the same way, the editor of the *Boston Weekly Magazine* (1743) distinguished his publication from newspapers in his introductory essay by arguing that his magazine would not be "flung aside, as of small Use in a few Days after their first Publication"; he printed his periodical in a form that would be "convenient to be bound up in a Volume when the Year is completed" so that it could "make the whole a Piece of valuable Furniture in the Library of a Gentleman" (*Boston Weekly Magazine* 1743: 1). In the same vein, the founder-editor of the *American Magazine* (1757–58) argued in the preface to his venture that newspapers "can pretend to nothing more than account of facts as they happen"; to "trace [facts] from their causes and connect them with their consequences" one needed a more reflective form of publication—a magazine, something "that is durable in its nature, and convenient for being transmitted and preserved entire, for future as well as present reading" (Smith 1757: 4). A contributor to the *Pioneer* (1843), a literary magazine, stated flatly that "newspapers wont [sic] keep" (Neal 1843: 64). The editor of the *United States Magazine* (1854–58) complained, "The newspaper is becoming the great reservoir to receive the world's thoughts and ideas, but it is like a sieve, and cannot retain them. People read, and the paper is consigned to Biddy, who lights therewith the fire which is to broil your beefsteak" (Smith 1856: 86).

Reasoning that magazines' contents were more varied and of longer-lasting interest than those of newspapers, I used two criteria to distinguish between magazines and newspapers: the variety of contents and the degree to which those contents had a long expected life. I initially gathered data on anything that was considered a magazine by any of my sources; this included many publications that straddled the often fuzzy boundary between magazine and newspaper. I pared down the list of publications in two steps: I first excluded almanacs, as well as proceedings of annual meetings, annual reports, and annual transactions of fraternal, professional, or scholarly societies; I then excluded publications containing articles that primarily informed readers about recent events rather than entertaining them or reporting on items of more lasting interest. Because many antebellum magazines no longer exist in archives, I could not peruse them to draw this distinction; therefore, my judgments relied heavily on the work of bibliographers and historians, such as Albaugh's (1994) two-volume annotated bibliography of religious periodicals and Kribbs's (1977) annotated bibliography of literary periodicals.

After I had made these exclusions my data set still included some publications that could be classified as either newspapers or magazines. To sharpen the distinction between newspapers and magazines, I studied bibliographies of the newspaper industry (Kenny 1861; Evans 1863; Dill 1928; Brigham 1962; Rowell and Co. 1869). I excluded publications that were described by these sources as having neither of the two key characteristics of magazines: variety or long-lasting interest. I then created two indicators: one for ninety-five publications that I was very sure straddled the line between "pure" magazines and "pure" newspapers, the second for two hundred publications that may have been newspapers rather than magazines but were not in archives and so could not be classified with certainty. By their titles and descriptions in secondary sources, another seventy-six publications seemed to fall in between magazines and other kinds of print media; they may have been publishers' catalogs, commodity price lists, or pamphlets published serially, but no archived copies exist to attest to their precise nature; to account for this remaining ambiguity I created a third indicator to flag these publications. Together these three indicator variables make it possible for me to exclude from analysis publications that may not have been, strictly speaking, magazines. Such robustness checks increase my confidence that any conclusions drawn from analysis of the magazines in my data set do, indeed, represent that print medium.

After searching the primary and secondary sources, and after excluding publications that were clearly not magazines from consideration, I was able to construct detailed life histories for 5,362 magazines published between 1741 and 1860. This data set appears to be very complete, for it includes as many magazines, and often more, than estimates made by Frank Luther Mott in his three-volume history of the industry. Mott (1930: 21) counted 45 magazines founded between 1741 and 1794; my data set includes 66. He estimated that 500–600 periodicals other than newspapers were published between 1800 and 1825 (Mott 1930: 120–21); during this quarter century, my data set includes 782. Based on data from the US Post Office and the US Census Bureau, Mott calculated that about 600 magazines were published in 1839 (1930: 342, n.6), about 700 in 1850 (1930: 370), and about 575 in 1860 (1938a: 4, n.2); for those years my searches uncovered 485, 776, and 1,059, respectively.[1] Finally, between 1850 and 1865, Mott (1938a: 4) estimated that 2,500 magazines were published; my data set, which covers only the years up to 1860, includes 2,361 magazines. Given these comparisons it seems reasonable to conclude that my data set includes virtually all antebellum magazines that left any trace of their existence.

After aggregating temporal data to the calendar year, the data set includes 24,787 annual records on 5,362 magazines published between 1741 and 1860. When I drop from the data set observations on periodicals that might not have been magazines or that fell somewhere in between magazines and newspapers, 5,067 magazines remain.

Measuring Magazine Attributes

To summarize the attributes of magazines that I measured, table A1.1 lists them. It specifies not only the operational (empirically observed) variables but also the theoretical construct onto which each operational variable maps.

Vital dates in the lives of magazines. Data on major events in the lives of magazines are quite accurate. I usually have exact *founding dates*—exact to the day for magazines that published more often than once per month, exact to the month for magazines that published less often. I often have exact failure dates—dates of the last issue of a magazine. I also have dates of mergers of two magazines or absorptions of one magazine by another; I coded all subordinate partners in such mergers or acquisitions as failing on that date. But for 5 percent of magazines (269 of 5,362), data on either founding or failure dates are imprecise or missing. When imprecise dates indicated an approximate focal year (e.g., maybe 1813) for founding or failure, I took those dates as accurate. When imprecise dates involved lower- and/or upper-bound estimates (e.g., before 1839 or sometime in the 1850s), I randomly assigned magazines founding or failure dates above lower bounds and/or below upper bounds. For bounded estimates on imprecise dates and for estimates on missing date, I made judgment calls based on observed distributions of survival times for

[1] Mott (1938a) and other historians (e.g., Tebbel and Zuckerman 1991: 25–26) attributed the apparent downturn in the number of magazines between 1850 and 1860 to the Panic of 1857. But my data-gathering effort indicates that this decline was due to Mott's less than exhaustive searches and to his reliance on the US Census Bureau, which disclosed that periodicals were undercounted.

TABLE A1.1.
Description of Magazine-Specific Variables

Theoretical construct	*Operational variable(s)*
ID number	Magazine-specific variable ranging from 1 to over 5,000
Year	Calendar year
Title	Title as given, including all subtitles; when possible, updated whenever it changed
Founding date	Year (and usually month and often day) when the first issue appeared
Organizational age	Years since first issue of the magazine
Disbanding date	Year (and usually month and day) when the last issue was published and the magazine disbanded
Contents	28 categories covering subject areas and formats coded from magazine titles, bibliographers' descriptions, and perusing magazines themselves, coded as a series of binary variables: politics/government/war, law/crime, social reform, religion/morality, philosophy/ethics, news, manners/society, education, medicine/health, agriculture, science/engineering, history, biography, geography, travel, humor, commerce/industry, sports, fashion, miscellaneous (not included in any other category), long essays, literary criticism, fiction, poetry, music, theater, fine art, translations from foreign languages
Genre	21 categories: general interest, literary miscellany, literary newspaper, literature and the arts, literary review, politics journal, political miscellany, law/crime, social reform, religion, news, social commentary, education, medicine, agriculture, science/engineering, history, geography and travel, humor, business, sports and leisure; each genre coded as a categorical string variable and as a series of binary variables
Genre unknown	Binary variable = 1 when I could not determine type
Miscellaneous dummy	Binary variable = 1 if title or subtitle included any term for indicating eclectic contents, "etc.," or an ellipsis
Publication frequency	Frequency of publication (e.g., quarterly, monthly, weekly, biweekly) translated into a continuous variable—number of issues per year
Location	City and state of publication; also trichotomous indicator variable for location in one of the three biggest cities, in another urban area, or in a rural area
Geographic scope	Series of binary variables = 1 when magazine title included a term that indicated a specific geographic level: national, regional, state, or local

TABLE A1.1. (*Continued*)

Theoretical construct	Operational variable(s)
Localistic identity	Binary variable = 1 when geographic scope was national
Universalistic identity	Binary variable = 1 when geographic scope was local, state, or regional
Non-geographic identity	Binary variable = 1 when magazine's title did not include any geographic terms
Advertising	Binary variable = 1 to indicate when a magazine had paid advertising (coded for first year only)
Subscription rate	Price in local currency for an annual subscription; price converted into dollars and deflated to constant (1860 or 2014) dollars
Language	Language(s) when not published in English
Between magazine and newspaper	Binary variable = 1 when I knew that the periodical was between magazine and newspaper in terms of both format and contents
Maybe newspaper	Binary variable = 1 when the periodical may have been a newspaper, rather than a magazine, but I could not be certain because there were no copies available to read and bibliographers' descriptions were ambiguous
Other, not a magazine	Binary variable = 1 when the periodical may have been neither a magazine nor a newspaper (e.g., a series of pamphlets), but I could not be certain because there were no copies available to read and bibliographers' descriptions were ambiguous
Denom ination	Name of the religious denomination with which the magazine was affiliated; used to sort magazines by denominational group
Audience	Name of target audience: women; children; families; members of particular specialized occupations; members of literary, scholarly, or fraternal associations; Native Americans; blacks

magazines founded during each of three periods in this industry's history. I assumed that those missing founding or failure dates were frailer than better-documented ones and so had shorter than average lives. More precisely, I assumed life spans of less than one year after the last known date of publication (when the failure date was imprecise or unknown) or before the first known date of publication (when the founding date was imprecise or unknown) for magazines born before 1795, less than two years for those born between 1795 and 1825 (inclusive), and less than three years for those born after 1825. For each founding or failure date estimated, I used a random draw from a uniform distribution. I eliminated three magazines that were missing any information on both founding and failure dates.

TABLE A1.2.
Magazine Contents Categories

Politics/war/government	Travel
Law/crime	Humor
Religion/morality	Commerce and industry
Social reform	Sports
Philosophy/ethics	Fashion
News	Miscellany (not included elsewhere)
Manners and society	Long essays
Education	Literary criticism
Medicine and health	Fiction
Agriculture	Poetry
Science and engineering	Music
History	Theater
Biography	Fine art
Geography	Translations from foreign languages

Contents and genre. I coded magazine *contents* with a series of twenty-eight binary indicator variables, which covered both substantive topics (e.g., religion, politics, theater, fashion, miscellany) and modes of expression (e.g., long essays, poetry, fiction). Table A1.2 lists these categories. Each contents category variable was coded 1 if the focal magazine covered the focal topic area or included the focal type of article. I coded magazine *genre* as a categorical variable; all twenty-one genres are listed in table 2.2 and discussed in chapter 2. My judgments about contents and genre were based on magazine titles and subtitles (which, as described in chapter 2, were often quite loquacious) and, when magazines were available in the archives, on perusal of microfiche or online copies. For the many magazines that are not available in archives, I relied on descriptions by historians and bibliographers. A total of 281 annual observations on magazines (1.1 percent) were missing so much data on contents that I could not assess their genre with any precision.

I created a dummy variable for magazines whose titles explicitly noted that their contents were highly eclectic. This variable was set equal to 1 whenever a magazine's title included the terms *miscellany, miscellaneous, cabinet, eclectic, variety, various, sundry, compendium, olio, (port)folio,* or *omnibus;* it was also set equal to 1 whenever a magazine's title or subtitled ended with *et cetera, etc., &c,* or an ellipsis. This variable was specific to the magazine and year, so it varied over time when the focal magazine's title changed.

Publication frequency. I could generally pinpoint publication frequency precisely. For many magazines I was also able to record the exact timing of publication-frequency changes. This variable was specific to the magazine and date—that is, it could vary over time if magazines changed their publication frequency. If magazines suspended publication for a finite period of time, I coded frequency as "suspended" and used this to analyze the frailty of magazines in chapter 2.

Location. I was also able to gather good data on publication location, generally being able to pinpoint publication location precisely by city and state. For many magazines I was also able to record the exact timing of location changes. As with format, the variable was specific to the magazine and date.

Geographic scope. To study the impact of postal expansion on the geographic identities claimed by newly founded magazines in chapter 3, I focused on magazines' titles because they are easily observable and therefore powerful symbols of organizations' identities. As one scholar remarked, "to many people, corporations are 'nothing but a name'" (Boddewyn 1967: 39). Organizations' names convey an organization's commitment to meeting particular customers' needs and quality expectations (Ingram 1996; Glynn and Abzug 2002; Phillips and Kim 2009); they also project images for which legitimacy is granted or withheld, and upon which decisions are made to supply resources (Glynn and Abzug 1998; Phillips and Kim 2009). I thus expected new organizations' identity claims to be expressed in their names.

Many organizations signal their connection to place through their names (Fombrun 1996; Ingram 1996; Barnett, Feng, and Luo 2013). For example, *USA Today* signals nationwide delivery and readership, while the *San Francisco Chronicle* indicates a focus on that city; such toponyms are important because they anchor people's feelings and thoughts on geographic locations. The more organizations identify themselves with local toponyms, the more they signal their local place connection, and they more they can appeal to audiences that value local place attachments (Ingram 1996). Conversely, the more organizations identify themselves with nonlocal (universal) toponyms, the more they signal their disconnection from any single place and the more they make universal appeals to audiences in many different places.

I measured magazines' explicitly claimed *geographic scope* by coding four nested dummy variables based on their titles and subtitles: national, regional, state, and local. Each of these variables was coded 1 if the magazine's title or subtitle contained a reference to the focal geographic territory and 0 otherwise. This measurement strategy allows for more complete coverage of magazines than searches of magazine pages for published lists of agents or subscribers, or searches for published articles about circulation, as many magazines were not available in the archives. The national variable was coded 1 if the magazine's title used the terms *United States, America, National, North America,* or *Federal.* The regional variable was coded 1 if the magazine's title referred to North, South, East, West, or some other widely recognized region encompassing multiple states or colonies (e.g., New England, the Ohio Valley, the Mississippi Valley, the Pacific, the South). The state variable was coded 1 if the magazine's title referred to a state, a large subregion of a state (e.g., western New York), or a pair of states (e.g., New Hampshire and Vermont). This variable was also coded 1 if the magazine's title referred to the nickname of a state (e.g., Granite for New Hampshire, Old Dominion for Virginia, Palmetto for South Carolina). Finally, the local variable was coded 1 if the magazine's title referred to a city or county. All four geographic scope variables were coded 0 if the focal magazine's title did not signal its geographic reach (e.g., *Evangelical Magazine*, *Monthly Anthology*; *Agricultural Museum*). These variables were specific to the magazine and year; they varied over time when the focal magazine's title changed.

I dealt with three sources of ambiguities in toponyms. First, *New York* in the title indicated the city unless the focal magazine was published outside New York City or the title clearly referred to the state level—for instance, if the magazine was affiliated with a statewide organization. Second, I did not code magazines that referred to specific colleges (e.g., University of North Carolina, Amherst College) as making a geographic reference. Third, if a magazine's title referred to two geographic levels (e.g., *American Gleaner and Virginia Magazine*), I coded it as referring to the larger geographic entity (in this case, the nation).

I then coded magazines that included the name or nickname of a municipality, county, substate region, state, or multistate region in their titles as claiming *localistic identities*. I coded magazines that used continent- or nationwide terms in their titles as claiming *universalistic identities*. As will be explained in appendix 2, I also experimented with a more restrictive definition of localistic identity (only municipality, county, substate region, or state) and a more inclusive definition of universalistic identity (not just nation and continent but also multistate region). Finally, I coded magazines whose titles contained no geographic terms (e.g., *Lady's Magazine*, *Free-Will Baptist Magazine*, *Port-Folio*) as having *nongeographic identities*.

Magazine finances. I was able to gather data on two aspects of magazines' finances: their subscription prices and whether or not they relied on advertising for revenue. I coded subscription prices in three stages. First, I searched archives and secondary sources for information about prices. Second, I converted prices quoted per issue to annual prices.[2] Third, I converted annual prices from the diverse currencies used by magazine publishers to a single, comparable currency. Several different currencies were used in this era: the systems of pounds, shillings, and pence issued by different colonies and, later, states; the system of pounds, shillings, and pence sterling issued by the government of Great Britain, and the system of dollars, dismes (dimes), and cents issued by the new US federal government. Using a method developed by McCusker (2001), I converted prices given in colonial British currencies into the Spanish dollar (the *peso de ocho reales*, or "pieces of eight"). This silver coin had a venerable history; it was both the de facto and the de jure world currency standard from the sixteenth century to the nineteenth (McCusker 1992). Largely because of the long-term stability of its value, the Spanish dollar was the usual coin of commerce in the Atlantic world in this era. As McCusker explained about American shopkeepers, "their [colonial or state] pounds were

---

[2] For some magazines that were published at irregular interval and listed their price per issue I was able to estimate an "average" publication frequency—if I knew the price per issue, the number of issues published, and the time span of publication—and thus estimate the annual subscription price.

money of account. Dollars were their real money" (2001: 62). Indeed, when the national currency of the fledgling republic, the Continental dollar, was first issued, it was set equal to the Spanish dollar. Therefore, I left all prices denominated in US dollars alone. Fourth, using a commodity price index developed by McCusker (2001) and the gross domestic product (GDP) deflator index from the US Bureau of Economic Analysis (2014), I took inflation into account and converted contemporary prices to modern (31 March 2014) price equivalents.

I assessed whether or not magazines relied on advertisements for income by searching for advertisements in the early issues of each magazine available in the archives. If I could view the magazine itself and saw that it did not publish advertisements, I coded advertisement as *no*; if I saw that it did publish advertisements, I coded advertisement as *yes*. If I could not view the magazine, I coded this variable as *missing*. Note that this variable was coded only for first few issues of each magazine.

Other attributes of magazines. I was able to gather data on *circulation* for only a few magazines at scattered moments in their histories (1,215 magazine-year observations, or 4.9 percent of the total). Some of these numbers came from magazines themselves but most came from secondary sources—histories of magazines or descriptions of them by contemporary observers.[3] The quality of these data is at times questionable because magazine publishers and editors sometimes boasted about their circulations, so I do not make much of them in the book. Finally, for all magazines I coded *language* of publication when it was not English.

Founders' motivations and goals. I read all available magazine prospectuses and editorial statements from early issues. Most of these came from the American Periodical Series Online, others from Readex Corporation's Archives of Americana or from documents downloaded during Internet searches. I sometimes augmented the rather scant information contained in prospectuses and early editorial statements with information from other articles in the first few issues. I sorted these documents into time periods and analyzed them in chronological order of magazine founding. My analysis encompassed the period 1741 to 1825 because after 1825, prospectuses and editorial statements were available for an increasingly small fraction of magazines. Documentary evidence was available for 59 percent (88 of 148) of magazines founded in the eighteenth century and 51 percent (389 of 757) of those founded in the first quarter of the nineteenth century. After that point, the fraction of magazines with this kind of evidence plummeted as the industry expanded rapidly: 12 percent (353 of 2,862) for magazines founded 1826–50 and only 2.1 percent (33 of 1,578) for magazines founded 1851–60. Still, the data on prospectuses I analyzed are likely biased away from magazines published in the hinterlands and toward those founded by high-status people and focused on "serious"

---

[3] The Audit Bureau of Circulations (now the Alliance for Audited Media) did not start work until 1914.

subjects—that is, general-interest, literary, religious, and scientific magazines. So the results of this analysis must be interpreted with caution. Although this analysis does not span the entire history of the American magazine industry in this era, it does continue up to the start of the first golden age of magazines, 1825–50 (Mott 1930; Tebbel and Zuckerman 1991). This means that I can analyze variation in the motivations and goals expressed by founders of different types of magazines *and* assess temporal variation from the magazine industry's birth up to the time the industry began to thrive.

BACKGROUND DATA ON MAGAZINE FOUNDERS

As was explained in chapter 4, I gathered, in collaboration with Jacob Habinek, detailed data on magazine founders in two time periods: 1741–1800, during which time magazines served mostly local audiences, and 1840–60, when many magazines reached mass audiences and some had subscribers across the country. We limited our analysis to these periods to maximize the temporal contrast between the early years of this industry's history and the period in which it was well established. This temporal sampling frame also made manageable the task of gathering data on the social positions of magazine founders, which required us to pore over a large number of archival sources and categorize a mass of qualitative data. The first period is long because so few magazines were founded before 1783, and we needed a reasonable number of observations on magazines and their founders to conduct statistical analyses. For both periods the archives revealed the names of the founders, publishers, and editors of many magazines. We sought background information on the founders of all 148 magazines launched in the eighteenth century and the founders of a random sample of 150 magazines taken from the 2,678 that appeared between 1841 and 1860. Because we cannot observe the full set of people who tried to start magazines, but only those who succeeded, our analysis will be biased toward success (Aldrich and Wiedenmayer 1993). We mitigated this bias by sampling from all magazines, both those that failed after publishing a single issue and those that achieved lasting success.

To find data on founders, we searched *American National Biography* (2000), the *Oxford Dictionary of National Biography* (2006), *Who Was Who in America, 1607–1896* (1967), and *Appleton's Cyclopedia of American Biography* (Wilson, Fiske, and Klos [1887–89] 1999).[4] We also pored over histories of publishing in America (Thomas [1874] 1970; Oswald 1937; Wroth 1931; Silver 1967; McMurtrie 1936; Lehmann-Haupt 1941, 1951) and histories of intellectual and literary life (Bender 1987; Bercovitch 1994a, 1994b). We completed the search for founder background data online. Of the 148 magazines published in the

---

[4] Although *Appleton's* has many biased entries, basic data about founders' education, kith and kin, and occupations are usually reliable (Dobson 1993).

TABLE A1.3.

Descriptive Statistics on Temporal Samples of Magazine Founders

	18th century	19th century
Number of magazines in the sample	148	150
Number of magazines with unknown founders	5 (3.4%)	25 (16.7%)
Number of magazines with known founders	143 (96.6%)	125 (83.3%)
Number founded by individuals	139 (97.2%)	17 (13.6%)
Number founded by organizations	4 (2.8%)	108 (86.4%)
Number with known individual founders—information available	162 (98.2%)	104 (83.2%)
Number with known individual founders—no information available	3 (1.8%)	21 (16.8%)

Note: This table includes statistics on all founders of all 148 magazines launched between 1741 and 1800 (18th century), and a sample of 150 magazines randomly drawn from the 2,678 magazines launched between 1841 and 1860 (19th century). The first five rows compare the number of *magazines* over time; the last two rows compare the number of *founders* over time.

eighteenth century, we were able to identify the founders of 143, which were launched by four organizations and 165 men. We were able to uncover data on all but 3 of those men. For the sample of 150 magazines founded in the mid-nineteenth century, we were able to identify founders of only 125 magazines, which were launched by 17 organizations and 125 individuals (120 men and five women). We were able to gather data on 105 of these individuals. The details of these samples are summarized in table A1.3.

We created two broad measures to capture three aspects of magazine founders' social positions and thus their ability to acquire the resources needed to launch and run magazines: occupation, education, and location. Many magazine founders had multiple occupations (e.g., lawyer and writer, physician and college professor, or printer, publisher, and postmaster). We first coded all occupations held by each individual—*printer, other publishing trade, writer, minister, lawyer, doctor, other*—as a series of dummy variables. We then coded each individual's *primary occupation* as a five-category variable (*printer, other publishing trades, writer, professional, other*), based on our reading of biographies and histories. For the vast majority of cases this task was straightforward; for instance, we coded any professional who was also a college professor as a professional because the former occupation was a prerequisite for the latter. For the few ambiguous cases, we coded as primary the earliest occupation. There were seven such cases: five professionals who later embarked upon careers as writers, one lawyer who became a prominent landowner, and one author who became a social reformer and lecturer.

The American occupational structure changed greatly between the eighteenth and mid-nineteenth centuries. To take this into consideration, we gathered data on the number of professionals in 1770 and 1850, the midpoints of the two time periods. For 1850 we obtained data from the census (Sobek 2006); for 1770 we combined data from several sources. For clergy, the count for 1770 is based on analysis of prosopographies of colonial clergy (Weis 1950, 1976, 1977, 1978). For lawyers, the estimate for 1770 is based on Massachusetts counts in 1740, 1775, and an 1840 history of the legal profession in that state (Gawalt 1979: 14, table 1), combined with national and Massachusetts counts in 1850 from the census (Sobek 2006). For doctors the estimate for 1770 comes from a history of the medical profession (Starr 1982: 40). We then calculated the fraction of professionals among magazine founders in each time period relative to the fraction of professionals in the general population at the midpoint of each time period.

Because education was not fully formalized during our study period, the only data we could obtain were about college. Accordingly, we coded *education* as a dummy variable indicating whether the founder had attended college. To account the fact that there were more college-educated people in the mid-nineteenth century than in the eighteenth century, we gathered data on the number of college students per capita in 1800 (the first year for which such data are available) and 1850 (the midpoint of the second period) from Burke (1973: 22, table 2.3). We used these counts to calculate the percentage of college-educated people among magazine founders in each time period relative to the percentage of college students in the general population for that period.[5]

We also created a dummy variable for *location*—in Boston, New York, or Philadelphia, versus some other location. To take into account the increasing urbanization of America we measured the populations of the three biggest cities and the percentage of the population in urban areas in 1770 and 1850, the midpoints of the two time periods in the samples analyzed. (The sources of these data are described below.) To compare the locations where magazine founders launched their new ventures to the locations where the typical American lived, we first scaled the percentage of magazines founded in the three biggest cities in each time period by the percentage of the population in those cities at the midpoint of each time period. We then scaled the percentage of magazines founded in all urban areas (including the three biggest cities) in each time period by the percentage of the population in urban areas at the midpoint of each time period.

[5] As was explained in chapter 4, it would have been more appropriate to compare the fraction of magazine founders who were college graduates to the fraction of American who were college graduates, but that second fraction is simply not available, so we used the next best thing: the number of Americans who were in college.

DATA ON RELIGION

Religious Revivals by State

To ascertain when and where revivals occurred, I pored over a comprehensive history of American religion (Ahlstrom 1972) and several histories of revivals (Beardsley 1912; Smith 1957; Rossel 1970; Carwardine 1978; Hatch 1989; Crawford 1991; Lambert 1999; Hankins 2004). After careful reading and cross-checking I created an annual indicator variable for each state, set equal to 1 when that state witnessed one or more religious revivals in that year and 0 otherwise.

Number of Congregations in Each State

Next I sought to compile state-level time-series data on the number of members or adherents of all religious groups in America from 1740 to 1860. Unfortunately such data proved to be unavailable. Instead I was able, in collaboration with Marissa King, to gather data on *the number of congregations* affiliated with all religious groups.[6] State-level data on most religious groups were available in the 1850 and 1860 censuses (Burke 2006). The 1850 census included a number of churches as "minor sects." We followed the advice given in the census itself: "the minor sects must be divided between the denominations mentioned by name and [those very few in number] not specifically referred to in the tables" (US Census Bureau 1854: footnote, p. 133).

Two secondary sources provided information for the earliest years: Gaustad's atlas (1962: 167) had very complete data for 1750; Finke and Stark (1992: 277–88) recorded the number and type of congregations in 1776. From these two sources we obtained data for the eight largest denominations in 1750 (Baptist, Catholic, Congregational, Dutch and German Reformed, Episcopal, Lutheran, and Presbyterian) and twelve denominations in 1776 (the aforementioned eight plus Dunker, Methodist, Moravian, and Quaker). We also found data on the five largest denominations (Baptist, Congregational, Episcopal, Methodist, and Presbyterian) in official yearbooks and annual reports. We made every effort to obtain data on smaller religious groups but had only limited success. Our quest for these data was, however, aided by the fact that "smaller congregations tended to congregate, rather than scatter" (Gaustad 1962: 163). Thus, the smaller groups for which we have data at the beginning of the study period did not tend to disperse geographically before the Civil

---

[6] Finke and Stark (1992: 24–30) estimated the number of adherents from the number of congregations in 1776. I did not follow their lead because during my study period the number of people in a typical congregation changed greatly and became more varied, both across denominations and locations. Thus, trying to translate number of congregations into number of people would introduce considerable noise into the data.

War. This fact proved helpful in estimating their trajectories of growth or decline.

In the paragraphs below, I sketch the history of thirty faiths and describe the data sources that we used to piece together counts of congregations in each state for twenty-five of them. To create annual records, we filled gaps between observed data points by means of linear interpolation. Similarly, we filled gaps between the first observed data points and the start of the statistical analysis period by extrapolating backward to known origin points for each faith.

(Seventh-Day) Adventists, Millennialists, and Millerites. All of these sects shared a belief that the Second Coming of Christ (the Advent) would occur soon and the world would then end. Millerites began to congregate around 1839. When the date for this second coming prophesied by William Miller passed uneventfully in the fall of 1844, many community members drifted away; others joined a group that offered a less precise date for the Advent. In 1864 this group formally organized as the Seventh-Day Adventist Church. A separate group of Millennialists were active from about 1848 onward. Alas, we found no data on Adventists before the 1860 census.

Baptists. Although there were Baptist congregations in America from 1637 onward, almost all of this denomination's growth came from evangelism during and after the Great Awakenings. The *American Baptist Yearbook* (1874: 79) contained most of the data used in this analysis. It reported the number of Baptist congregations in 1812, 1832, and 1840 for all states in the Union. We found complete data for 1790 in Asplund (1792: 5–42). The *Abolition Intelligencer and Missionary Magazine* (1822: 5) listed the number of Baptist churches across the United States in 1822. We found two additional sources for the early nineteenth century: Sweet (1931: 24, 26, 27, 34) contained data on the number of Baptist congregations in Kentucky in 1800 and 1820, in Missouri in 1800 and 1840, and in Tennessee in 1802. Armstrong and Armstrong (1979: 111) provided the number of Baptist churches in Virginia in 1800. Since Baptists were heavily concentrated in the South, these sources greatly improved the quality of the data on this denomination.

Catholics. Although this faith was planted in America in 1634, when Maryland was granted to Lord Baltimore, its adherents were barely tolerated during the late eighteenth and early nineteenth centuries. It is not surprising, then, that there were few official sources of data on Catholic churches. To augment data from the censuses, Gaustad (1962), Finke and Stark (1992), and Dorchester (1888: 334) provided data on several states (Florida, Illinois, Kentucky, Louisiana, and Wisconsin) in 1810.

Church of God. Under the leadership of extreme revivalist John Winebrenner, this group split from the German Reformed Church in 1830. It was mostly in Pennsylvania, with a few congregations in neighboring states. Probably because it was always very small, we could find no data on this denomination apart from the 1860 census.

Congregationalists. Because this was the official state-sanctioned church in the New England colonies, excellent data were available for the years before 1850 from Quint and Cushing (1873: 103–73). While this publication first appeared before 1873, earlier editions do not list the date of establishment for each congregation but instead list only extant congregations. We used founding dates given in the 1873 edition to calculate the number of churches per state at ten-year intervals. While this method undoubtedly suffers from survivor bias, because churches that disbanded before 1873 were missing from the records, the Congregational Church experienced continuous growth after the Revolution. Thus, undercounting due to lost data on dissolved churches should be minimal. To assess the extent of undercounting we gathered data from other sources when they were available. Dorchester (1888: 278) records the number of Congregational churches in 1800 in Connecticut, Massachusetts, Maine, New Hampshire, New York, Rhode Island, and Vermont. Sweet (1936a: 22–26) contains data on the number of Congregational churches in Tennessee and Kentucky between 1750 and 1850, as well as the number in Indiana in 1834 and Illinois in 1830 and 1836. The statistics reported in these supplemental sources were consistent with the data we constructed using Quint and Cushing, which reinforces our belief that undercounting due to survivor bias is minimal.

Christadelphians. This sect was established 1848 in New York in a split from the Disciples of Christ. Originally the community had no name; members were called Thomasites after their founder, John Thomas. They took the name Christadelphian ("Brethren of Christ") in 1864. Alas, we could find no data on the number of churches established by this small sect, even in the census.

Christians/Disciples of Christ/Christian Connection. This network of religious reformers sprang up after 1792 and coalesced into a distinct denomination in the early 1830s. Despite our best efforts, which included corresponding with this denomination's official historian, we were unable to find data on any of their churches before the 1850 census. Because they were concentrated in New England, Kentucky, Ohio, Pennsylvania, and Virginia, their impact on antebellum religion is limited to a few parts of the country.

Dunkers/Tunkers/Church of the Brethren. This German Anabaptist sect first gained a foothold in Pennsylvania in 1719; by 1722, Dunker congregations had been founded in Maryland and New Jersey. Throughout the study period, Dunkers remained concentrated in Maryland, New Jersey, New York, and Pennsylvania, though they made small inroads into Kentucky, North Carolina, Tennessee, and Virginia (Mallott 1954; Drury 1924). Dunkers were always few in number. We found data for 1770 in Mallott (1954), which relies on numbers originally reported in John Lewis Gillin's *The Dunkers*. We found no other data, perhaps because, as Mallott notes, this sect did not begin keeping records until 1880.

Dutch Reformed. This church took root in America in the early seventeenth century. It was heavily concentrated in New York, New Jersey, and Pennsylvania throughout the study period: as late as 1850, nine-tenths of Dutch Reformed congregations were located in New York and New Jersey (Gaustad 1962: 97). The church did not begin to spread westward until the 1840s. Thus, data from Gaustad (1962), Finke and Stark (1992) and the censuses offer excellent coverage of this faith's evolution.

Episcopalians. This was the official state-sanctioned faith in six of the thirteen original colonies, and it had substantial footholds in most of the others. Data sources are plentiful. The number of Episcopal congregations in 1820 and 1830 are recorded in the *Journals of General Conventions of the Protestant Episcopal Church in the United States, 1785–1835* (Perry 1874). Data for most states (Delaware, Maine, Massachusetts, New Hampshire, New York, New Jersey, Ohio, Rhode Island, and Virginia) came from reports presented at the convention of 1820 (Perry 1874: 1:528–46). We also used data from reports presented at the conventions of 1817 (1:462–78) for North Carolina and 1822 (2:21–51) for Georgia. Data for most states (Connecticut, Massachusetts, Mississippi, New Hampshire, New Jersey, New York, North Carolina, Rhode Island, and South Carolina,) came from the convention of 1829 (2:247–76). We also used data from the convention of 1832 (2:382–408) for Alabama, Delaware, Georgia, Kentucky, Maine, Pennsylvania, Tennessee, and Vermont. Finally, data on all states were reported at the convention of 1835 (2:576–606).

German Evangelical Synod/Association. This faith sat theologically between the Calvinist and the Lutheran traditions. Following on the heels of mergers in Prussia and other German states, which began in 1817, this denomination was officially created in the United States in 1840, although individual congregations had been founded before that. Alas, we could find no data on this small denomination, which had most of its adherents in the upper Midwest.

German Reformed. This church also sits theologically between the Calvinist and the Lutheran traditions, and arrived in America in the early eighteenth century. Between 1740 and 1860 it was concentrated in Pennsylvania and the surrounding states. To augment data from Gaustad (1962), Finke and Stark (1992), and the censuses we found data on German Reformed congregations in the Eastern Synod (Maryland, North Carolina, Ohio, Pennsylvania, South Carolina, and Virginia) for 1820 in Klein (1943).

Jews. At the end of the colonial period the only synagogues were in Charleston, South Carolina; New York City; Philadelphia; and Savannah, Georgia (Gaustad 1962: 144). Judaism grew little until the 1840s. Between 1840 and 1850 the number of Jews swelled from four thousand to over fifty thousand (Gaustad 1962: 145). Thus, data from the 1850 and 1860 censuses largely capture the growth of Judaism in America.

Lutherans. This denomination was carried to America by immigrants from four different countries to several locations: from Sweden to Delaware and New Jersey in 1638, from Holland to New York in 1649, from Germany to New York in 1708 and Pennsylvania in 1712, and from England to several states in the early eighteenth century. Lutherans remained concentrated in a handful of states. The *American Quarterly Register* reported that "this church is confined almost exclusively to the German population of the country. The congregations, though found in more than half the States, are principally in Pennsylvania, New York, Ohio, Maryland, and North Carolina" (1832: 224). Thus, data from Gaustad (1962), Finke and Stark (1992), and the censuses capture most of the growth of this denomination.

Amish, Mennonites, and Swiss Brethren. Almost all members of these three closely related Anabaptist faiths, in this era all German speakers, lived in Pennsylvania from the late seventeenth century to the first decade of the nineteenth. These denominations spread to Indiana, Ohio, Virginia, over the eighteenth century, and experienced increases throughout the antebellum era, driven in part by waves of immigration (Gaustad 1962). We were unable to find any data on Amish congregations, probably because the Amish, who were far more socially conservative than the Mennonites or Swiss Brethren, refused to create any general church organization. (This conservative tendency and consequent lack of formal organization may also explain why the Amish published no magazines before the Civil War.) We were also unable to find any data on the number and location of Mennonite and Swiss Brethren congregations outside the 1850 and 1860 censuses. (Censuses put Mennonites and Swiss Brethren in a single category.)

Mennonite Brethren. This group was born in 1860 in Pennsylvania, in a split from the main body of Mennonites (Ahlstrom 1972). It had only a single congregation during the antebellum era.

Methodists. This faith began in America in the early 1760s as a revival movement within the Episcopal Church; it became an independent denomination in 1784. The only consistent data we could obtain counted Methodist members, not churches. This is largely a reflection of the Methodist style of organizing, which emphasized the use of circuit riders who traveled from place to place rather than the establishment of permanent churches. Membership data for 1790, 1800, and 1810 came from the *Minutes of the Methodist Conferences, Annually Held in America from 1773 to 1813, Inclusive* (Methodist Connection in the United States 1813). Membership data for 1832 are reported in the *American Quarterly Register* (1832: 224) and estimated membership data for 1773 (from the first American Methodist Conference) are reported in Gaustad (1962: 75). We have data on both number of members and number of churches for four states (Indiana, Kentucky, Mississippi, and South Carolina) in 1810. We used these data to translate from number of members to number of churches: on average, there were 343 members per church.

Moravians/Unitas Fratum. This evangelical branch of Hussites migrated from Germany to Georgia in 1735, then moved to Pennsylvania soon after. The Moravians expanded up and down the East Coast over the course of the eighteenth century, but always remained a small denomination. We found only scattered data on Moravian churches between 1776 and 1850, in the *Quarterly Register and Journal of the American Educational Society* (1829: 182).

Mormons/Church of Jesus Christ of Latter-Day Saints. This sect was born in 1830 in New York State. Its adherents moved west to Missouri and Ohio in 1831, Kentucky in 1834, Illinois in 1838, and finally Utah in 1847. We were unable to find any data on Mormon congregations outside the 1860 census, perhaps because this sect was so marginalized and vilified. To determine the exact dates of the founding and dissolution of Mormon congregations as this sect moved westward, we used narratives by Ahlstrom (1972) and Hatch (1989), as well as official church websites.

Plymouth Brethren/River Brethren. This millennialist sect came to America sometime after 1832. It split into "open" and "closed" branches in 1849 and continues to the present as a small church. Unfortunately we could find no data on this sect.

Presbyterians. By the 1740s, the Presbyterians had built churches in ten of the thirteen original colonies. Most data on Presbyterian congregations came from the *Minutes of the General Assembly of the Presbyterian Church in the United States of America* (1809, 1819). These data are presented by jurisdictional area (synod and presbytery) rather than by state. We used maps of presbyteries presented in Gaustad (1962: 88) and Sweet (1936b: 50), as well as more general maps and histories of presbyteries, to transform the number of churches per jurisdictional area into the number of churches per state. Note that jurisdictional areas are sometimes split between states. For such cases we divided the number of congregations so as to approximate the land in each state covered by the focal presbytery. To supplement these official church records, Sweet (1936b: 48–51) provides data on the number of congregations in Indiana in 1806 and 1837, Michigan in 1816, and Illinois in 1837. Dorchester (1888: 282, 385–88) is the source of data for Alabama in 1830, Florida in 1824, Illinois in 1816, Indiana in 1830, Michigan in 1816 and 1830, Missouri in 1816 and 1830, and North Carolina and Virginia in 1800.

Quakers. This denomination first came to Rhode Island in 1637. After William Penn secured his grant for Pennsylvania in 1682, most Quakers moved there. Around 1740 there were also sizable Quaker communities in the Carolinas, New Jersey, and Rhode Island. Unfortunately we could find no data on the number of Quaker congregations between 1776 and 1850, probably because this denomination's authority structure was highly decentralized.

River Brethren/Brethren in Christ. This sect was born around 1780 in a split from the main Mennonite body in Pennsylvania. Around 1861 it came to be called the Brethren in Christ. Unfortunately we could find no solid data on the location or number of River Brethren congregations, probably because this group was so small.

Shakers/Society of Believers in Christ's Second Coming. This sect was established in 1774 in New Hampshire. It remained small and concentrated in New England, but spread west to New York and Ohio by 1860. Alas, we could find no data on the number of Shaker communities before the 1860 census.

Society of the Publick Universal Friend. This sect, which closely resembled the Shakers, started in 1776 in Rhode Island, where its members founded a single utopian community. The community moved to New York in 1794 and died out in 1863 when the last member died; at its peak it had only two hundred members. Data on the single congregation came from Ahlstrom (1972).

Spiritualists. Spiritualist groups started forming in the second decade of the nineteenth century. The most active were the followers of sisters Kate, Leah, and Margaret Fox, who first came together in New York in 1848. Although Spiritualists were active in several states up to the Civil War, we could find no count of their establishments of worship, perhaps because they seldom congregated in fixed locations on a regular basis.

Swedenborgians/New Jerusalem Church/New Church. This spiritualist faith came to America in 1798, taking root first in Maryland and later in Massachusetts, New York, Pennsylvania, and other neighboring states. We could find no data on this denomination before the 1850 census, perhaps because it never numbered more than 10,000 adherents (Ahlstrom 1972).

Unitarians. This faith, which began as a liberal wing of the Congregational Church in 1787, became a separate denomination in 1825. Until the 1830s Unitarianism was almost totally confined to a single state, Massachusetts (Dorchester 1888), and John Henry Allen declared, "A radius of 35 miles from Boston as a center would sweep almost the whole field of its history and influence" (quoted in Gaustad 1962: 126). During the 1830s Unitarianism started to spread to Illinois, Kentucky, Missouri, New York, Louisiana, Ohio, and Washington, DC (Gaustad 1962: 126). We found data on Unitarian congregations for 1835 and 1840 in New England in Dorchester (1888: 635).

United Brethren in Christ. The United Brethren in Christ was a German-speaking semi-Methodist movement. This sect split from the German Reformed Church in Pennsylvania around 1767 and was formally organized in 1800. It was always small; for example, the *American Quarterly Register* (1832: 225) reported that there were only thirty United Brethren congregations in America in 1832. Perhaps that is why we could find no data on this sect.

Universalists. This denomination appeared in America in 1779. During its early years, it was highly concentrated in New England and Pennsylvania, especially Boston. Data for 1835 and 1840 presented in Dorchester (1888: 628), which were taken from Universalist yearbooks, bear out this fact. Universalism expanded geographically as conventions were organized in Ohio (in 1814), North Carolina (1824), South Carolina (1830), Virginia (1835), Illinois and Indiana (1837), and Georgia (1838). Universalist conventions followed shortly after in Michigan, Iowa, Kentucky, and Wisconsin. We used data from Gaustad (1962: 130) and the 1860 census to correct 1850 census data on Universalist congregations in Indiana.

Union churches. These were independent nondenominational congregations formed from the merger of two or more existing congregations (Meagher, O'Brien, and Aherne 1979). This category, which is a congeries rather than a religious community, is listed in the 1850 and 1860 censuses. We could find no other data on these churches, which is undoubtedly due to the fact that they were independent of each other and not part of any larger organized body. We included union churches in counts of all churches, but not in counts of churches by denominational group.

Religious Organizational Structures

I pieced together information on the organizational structures created by different religious groups from histories of religion in America (Carroll 1893; Smith 1962; Clark 1965; Mathews 1969; Ahlstrom 1972; Hood 1977; Wright 1984; Goen 1985; Mead 1985; Hatch 1989; Newman and Halvorson 2000). Specific information for some denominations came from the following denominational histories: Adventist (Olsen 1925; Tyler 1944; Loughborough [1909] 1972); Apostolic Christian (Ruegger 1949); Baptist (Newman 1894); Catholic (Dolan 1978); Church of God (Forney 1914); Disciples of Christ (Garrison and DeGroot 1948; Wrather 1968); Jewish (Faber 2008; Ashton 2008); Mennonite and River Brethren in Christ (Huffman 1920; Smith [1920] 1957); Moravian (Corwin, Dubbs, and Hamilton 1894; Hamilton 1900; Hutton 1909, 1923; Langton 1956); Shaker (Tyler 1944); Swedenborgian (Meyers 1983); and Unitarian and Universalist (Allen and Eddy 1894). Details on itinerant preachers came from Wright (1976). For each denomination I ascertained the existence of following formal mechanisms to link congregations between the end of the Revolution and the start of the Civil War: whether it established collective bodies (in America, not Europe) to ordain and discipline ministers; whether it held any conferences for clergy or, more rarely, for laity; whether it used itinerant ministers or colporteurs; and whether central or regional church authorities set up missionary societies, or external groups affiliated with the denomination set up such societies. Finally, I checked the database of magazines to determine whether each denomination ever published a magazine between 1780 and 1860.

DATA ON ANTISLAVERY ASSOCIATIONS

These data, like the data on religious institutions, were gathered in collaboration with Marissa King. We defined an antislavery association to be any organization that advocated or worked for manumissions, emancipation, or abolition, or any organization that worked to limit the spread of slavery to new states and territories. Thus, colonization organizations were excluded from the analysis because they had very different ideological dispositions, objectives, and constituencies from antislavery organizations. We examined nineteen monographs, six dissertations, three bibliographic guides, and a host of primary documents, including annual reports, almanacs, petitions, newspapers, and magazines. We found data on 1,534 antislavery associations.

Our data-gathering task began with the records of the American Anti-Slavery Society (AASS); this umbrella organization kept a detailed list of all auxiliary societies, including their founding dates, and these records were printed in the AASS's *Annual Reports* between 1834 and 1839 and in the mag-

302 | Appendix 1

azine *The Liberator*. Several other primary sources proved particularly useful, including the minutes of the American Convention for Promoting the Abolition of Slavery and Improving the Condition of the African Race (1809, 1812, 1816, 1817, 1819), the *Genius of Universal Emancipation* (1821–39), the *Herald of Freedom* (1835–41), *Niles' Weekly Register* (1814–37), the *Manumissions Intelligencer* (1819–20), the *Emancipator* (1833–42), and the *American Anti-Slavery Almanac* (1836–43). Finally, we pored over Cornell University's Samuel J. May Anti-Slavery Collection (http://dlxs.library.cornell.edu/m/mayantislavery/index .html), which contains over 300,000 pages of original antislavery documents. Two secondary sources proved especially helpful: Jason Mazzone's dissertation "Organizing the Republic: Civic Associations and American Constitutionalism 1780–1830" (2004) and Alice Dana Adams's *The Neglected Period of Anti-Slavery in America* (1908). These sources contained comprehensive lists of civic associations, including abolition organizations, founded between 1790 and 1820 (Mazzone) and abolition organizations founded between 1741 and 1830 (Adams).

Although the list of antislavery organizations is not complete, the data we gathered are highly consistent with the reports of contemporary observers. In 1827, Benjamin Lundy estimated there were a total of 130 antislavery societies with approximately 6,625 members, including colonization organizations (Finnie 1969). The *Annual Report* of the American Colonization Society listed 46 auxiliary societies in 1826. Removing these 46 societies from Lundy's count indicates that there were 84 abolitionist organizations in 1827. (The actual number is probably smaller, due to the rapid growth of the African Colonization Society between 1826 and 1827; Fox 1919: 61). Our search of the archives uncovered 64 societies operating in 1827; hence, our data set contains almost 80 percent of known abolition organizations in 1827. Our data-gathering efforts also yielded counts of antislavery organizations that either exceed or approximate estimates made by historians. For instance, our data set approximates the estimates of Locke (1901: 99), who drew on memorials to Congress, minutes of the American Convention, and a variety of newspapers and contemporary accounts to enumerate the number of societies in 1791 at 12. For 1791, our data set covers 11 organizations. And our count of antislavery organizations far exceeds that of Simms (1960: 7), who estimated that there were very few societies in 1830; 198 by 1835; 526 societies in June 1836; 1,006 in 1837; and approximately 2,000 in 1840. In contrast, we counted 429 societies in 1835; 837 in 1836; 1,310 in 1837; and 1,454 in 1840.

For each antislavery organization we recorded its name, location, and founding and dissolution dates. If an organization's founding or dissolution date was not available, we used the date of first or last mention in a data source. When we could not ascertain the dissolution date (for 65 out of 1,534 organizations) we estimated it, assuming that the focal organization had a life span equal to the average life span of organizations founded in the same period.

DATA ON SOCIAL REFORM ASSOCIATIONS

Theda Skocpol kindly shared her data on federated social movement and civic-association organizations; these data are described in her published work (Skocpol 1997, 1999, 2003; Skocpol, Ganz, and Munson 2000). I used these data to assess the scale of several of the social reform organizations described in detail in chapter 5: the General Union for Promoting the Observance of the Christian Sabbath, the American Temperance Society, the Washington Temperance Society, the Independent Order of Good Templars, and the American Anti-Slavery Society.

OTHER CONTEXTUAL DATA

Printing and papermaking. To capture advances in printing technology I compiled information on the maximum possible printing speed (number of sheets per hour) produced by the most advanced printing presses, using data from histories of printing (Thomas [1874] 1970; Berry and Poole 1966; Moran 1973). I gathered data on the spread of printing presses across America from Lehmann-Haupt (1951: 69–70), and recorded the year the first printing press existed in each colony or state.

Postal service. To measure expansion, I used annual counts of US post offices. I obtained data on the number of post offices across the nation from Miles (1855) and Daniel (1941). To create state-level measures of postal expansion I obtained data on post offices from *Annual Reports of the Post Master General to the House of Representatives.* These reports usually listed post offices alphabetically by town. Marissa King, two undergraduate students supervised by Chris Rider, and I pored over these lists and counted post offices in each state. Reports were not available for all years; we used reports for 1790–91, 1796–98, 1803–4, 1807–8, 1811, 1814–15, 1817, 1819, 1822, 1825–29, 1831–35, 1841–42, 1846–47, 1851, 1855–56, and 1859. For years before 1790 I used lists for 1763 (Franklin and Foxcroft 1763), 1775 (Franklin 1775), and 1789 (Towne 1789), plus the postmaster finder website of the US Postal Service (http://webpmt.usps.gov/pmt012.cfm, retrieved 2 April 2010). I interpolated linearly between observed data points to generate one data point for each state for each year. The number of post offices in each state increased continually, so this interpolation quite accurately approximated the missing data points. I then divided the number of post offices by the area of the state, in square miles, to allow me to assess the spatial density of the postal network. To check state counts, I used data on the number of post offices across the nation.

I proxied economic conditions that directly affected the magazine industry with the postage rate for magazines, using information on histories of the postal system (Rich 1924; Kielbowicz 1989; John 1995). The postage rate for magazines declined sharply over time, from three hundred pence in 1790 to eight cents starting in 1794; it fell occasionally after that, reaching two cents in 1832. I corrected for inflation and calculated the postage rate in constant dollars.

Population. For the years 1790 to 1860, I obtained decennial data on national and state-level population (in millions) from the census (US Census Bureau 2001) and interpolated linearly to create annual data points. For earlier years I obtained decennial national and state-level population data (also in millions) from Bogue (1985). Data on the number of slaves per state came from Cramer (1997).

Data on urban populations came from multiple sources: Purvis (1995) provided data on urban areas from 1760 to 1800, while the census (US Census Bureau 1998) provided data from 1790 to 1860. However, from 1840 to 1860, the census data listed only the hundred largest cities. To find data on smaller cities, I used data in Moffat (1992, 1996), who compiled his lists from several primary and secondary sources (Scott 1795; Morse 1797, 1810; Worcester 1818; Morse and Morse 1826; US Census Bureau 1909; Greene and Harrington 1966; Schultze 1983). I sought data on the populations of all municipalities with two thousand or more inhabitants. To make sure I had complete data on smaller urban places, which were less likely to be recorded in these published sources, I also conducted a series of Internet searches. For each location mentioned by the Census Bureau, Purvis, or Moffat that had a population over two thousand any time before 1860, I searched for its population and founding date (or date of first European settlement). I used data on founding dates to extrapolate population figures for each municipality backward in time, presuming a population of 0 in the year before founding. For each municipality I interpolated between observed data points (which were sometimes, but not always, decennial) to create annual time series for each location. Then, following Census Bureau standards for this era, I used a threshold of 2,500 inhabitants to distinguish urban areas from rural ones.

I retained records for all urban areas from the first year they had estimated or recorded populations of 2,500 or more. I calculated the number of urban areas in the nation and in each state for each year. I also calculated the total urban population in each state and in the nation as a whole, as well as the total population in the three biggest cities each year. The quality of the data is worse for earlier periods than for later periods. Data for the years before 1760 are especially poor, so I limited my analysis of urban areas to the period 1760–1860.

Economic conditions. I used the best measure of economic conditions available for this time period, gross domestic product (GDP), the total value of goods and services produced within a territory. I gathered GDP data from Sutch (2006) and used a historical commodity price index developed by McCusker (2001) and a GDP deflator index from the US Bureau of Economic Analysis (2014) to adjust for inflation. GDP data began in 1790; I was able to construct a time series for the original thirteen colonies that extended back to 1740 by using estimates from McCusker (2000) for 1720, 1774, 1781, 1793, and 1800. I based my interpolations on historians' accounts of economic trends during the colonial, revolutionary, and early republican eras (McCusker and Menard 1991; McCusker 2000).[7] The only indicator of economic conditions at the state level that is available for the entire study period is the value of foreign exports, which I obtained from Evans ([1884] 1976). This variable is particularly useful because it allows me to control for "the market revolution," meaning the expansion of commercial production rather than production for consumption, which occurred between 1815 and 1842 (Sellers 1991). Data were occasionally missing, so I interpolated linearly between observed data points. Data were not available on foreign exports for several landlocked states (Arkansas, Kentucky, Missouri, and Tennessee). For these states I set foreign exports to 0. I adjusted export data for inflation, calculating exports in constant dollars.

Educational institutions and literacy. The most comprehensive nationwide data on *Sunday schools* come from the Philadelphia Sunday and Adult School Union (PSASU), which was founded in 1817 and had activities that ranged across several northeastern states, and the American Sunday School Union (ASSU), which was formed from the PSASU in 1825. I acquired state-level counts of Sunday schools from statistics that Boylan (1988) extracted from the ASSU censuses of 1832 and 1875, which included Sunday schools from all major American Christian denominations except Roman Catholic. (Note that these censuses underrepresent Methodist Sunday schools, many of which eschewed the interdenominational ASSU for the Methodist Union and were thus not counted by the ASSU.) Aided by Adam Goldstein, I estimated annual counts of Sunday schools in three stages. First, I extrapolated backward from 1832. If the historical record (Boylan 1988; Zboray 1993) indicated the precise year the first Sunday school was founded in a state, I used that year as a starting point for my backward extrapolation. For many states, however, no precise starting year was recorded, so I estimated the starting year on the basis of white settlement patterns. This is reasonable because according to Boylan (1988: 34), Sunday schools preceded churches in up to two-thirds of northern frontier settlements. Second, I extrapolated backward from the data for 1832 to the first founding date using an exponential growth function because historical accounts suggest accelerated growth and diffusion of Sunday schools during the 1820s and early 1830s, with the national count of ASSU schools almost doubling from 2,321 in 1826 to 4,258 in 1832. Third, I interpolated from 1832 to 1875. By the mid-1830s, Sunday schools had become an institu-

---

[7] I extrapolated GDP per capita backward from McCusker's (2000) estimate for 1774 assuming 0.6 percent annual growth. I assumed no growth from 1774 to 1778, due to the nonimportation agreement (McCusker and Menard 1985: 361), and negative growth (shrinkage) from 1778 to the nadir of the depression in 1782. I assumed very low growth (less than 0.3 percent per year) from 1782 to 1789 and then faster growth (1.5 percent per year) from 1789 to 1793. Finally, I assumed 1.9 percent growth from 1793 to 1800.

tionalized part of American religious life (Boylan 1988; Zboray 1993). Previous research suggests that literacy rates increased in pace with population density (Soltow and Stevens 1981), so I based my interpolation on the rate of state population growth.

I gathered raw data on all *colleges and universities* that were founded in the antebellum era from Marshall (1995). I computed cumulative state-level counts of college foundings and colleges in operation.

Because reliable data on *literacy* are not available before 1840 (Soltow and Stevens 1981), I used data on Sunday schools and colleges and universities to construct an index of literacy for each state for each year. These variables were highly correlated, so to reduce multicollinearity I combined them by conducting a principle-components factor analysis. I used an orthogonal varimax rotation and obtained a two-factor solution; I used the predicted values of first (largest) factor, which I labeled *state literacy*.

Methods for Quantitative Data Analysis

*T*o make the arguments and evidence presented in the book flow more easily and avoid alienating qualitative researchers, I provided only brief outlines of quantitative methods. Here I explain those methods in glorious detail for those readers who are interested in such things. I begin by explaining my choice of units of analysis, then describe how I conducted each of the quantitative analyses summarized in chapters 3 through 6, arranged by chapter. I also present the tables underlying those summaries and discuss them in detail.

UNITS OF ANALYSIS

There are three basic units of analysis: the magazines themselves and the states and municipalities in which they were published. I discuss each in turn.

Magazines

Most descriptive statistics about magazines are based on all magazines published during a calendar year, not just those that were alive at year-end. Many magazines survived less than six months; indeed, 160 (3.1 percent of the total) published only a single issue. Given their often ephemeral nature, counting all magazine published during a calendar year—even those that came and went within that year—is more appropriate than taking a "snapshot" at year's end. Many descriptive statistics are based on annual observations on magazines rather than a single observation per magazine, for two reasons: because some magazines moved, annual observations provide the most reasonable basis for summarizing magazines' locations, and because some magazines survived a very long time, using annual observations weights long-lived magazines more than ephemeral ones and so provides the most accurate view of the industry at any point in time.

States

To analyze magazine founding rates and the number of magazines published in a given year I used the state as my unit of analysis, for three reasons. First and most important, in the antebellum era, the states were distinct communities (Brown 1976; Hatch 1989; Anderson [1983] 1991; Nord 2001). In the federalist system, states—not the central government—had ultimate authority over most matters of importance to ordinary people (Brown 1976). Second, states varied greatly in economic and demographic terms. Conducting analysis of states lets me take those differences into consideration explicitly by including state-specific factors in statistical analyses. Third, it was extremely difficult to locate complete, serially and cross-sectionally reliable state-level data on this time period; it would be virtually impossible to assemble complete and reliable data on smaller geographic units.

To allow for comparisons over time, it is necessary to analyze invariant units—those that do not change over time. For the antebellum era this is difficult because states were developing political and geographic entities. New states were carved out of existing ones (Vermont from New Hampshire in 1791 and Maine from Massachusetts in 1820). Moreover, new states were created from territories as they were populated by whites (e.g., Tennessee in 1796 and Ohio in 1803), entered the Union when the American government purchased land from colonial powers (e.g., Louisiana from the territory purchased from France in 1803, Florida from the territory purchased from Spain in 1819), or created when new territories were ceded by treaty (e.g., Texas in 1845, California in 1848). To allow consistent comparisons over time I imposed state boundaries as of 1860. This means that, for example, magazines founded in Maine before it was carved out of Massachusetts in 1820 were coded as being in Maine, not Massachusetts, while magazines published in what became West Virginia in 1863, when it was carved out of Virginia, were coded as being published in Virginia.

Each state entered the set of data analyzed in the year in which the first magazine was published or in the year it achieved statehood, whichever came first. In analyses that require data that are available only for states, not territories, each state entered the analysis in the year it achieved statehood. Thus, if a state was not in existence in the first year of the statistical analysis, it is included for the year it was granted statehood.

Municipalities

Location at this level was taken directly from the data on magazines. As with states, municipal boundaries changed over time as cities annexed and incorporated what had been independent settlements nearby. As with states, I used municipal boundaries as of 1860. This means, for example, that Philadelphia included Germantown, Northern Liberties township, the Southwark and

Kensington districts, Spring Gardens, and many other settlements. It also means that New York City did not include Brooklyn, which was a separate municipality until 1890.

CHAPTER 2: THE HISTORY OF AMERICAN MAGAZINES, 1741–1860

Analyzing magazine life spans. I calculated the life spans of all magazines founded before the Civil War by subtracting founding dates from failure (i.e., merger or disbanding) dates. When I did not know founding or failure dates precisely (at least to the month), I rounded up by one-half year. (For more information on these data and my coding procedures for uncertain founding and failure dates, see appendix 1.) Thirty-six magazines in my data set were still published as of July 2012.[1] For those thirty-six magazines, I calculated life spans using 2012 as the end date.

Analyzing magazines' geographic dispersion. To analyze how evenly (or unevenly) magazines were spread over geographic regions at various points in time, I used the index of qualitative variation (Mueller and Schuessler 1961: 177–79; Lieberson 1969). It is calculated thus—

$$Index\ of\ Qualitative\ Variation_t = 1 - \sum_{i=1}^{n}\left(\frac{N_{it}}{\sum_{i=1}^{n}N_{it}}\right)^2 /(1 - \frac{1}{n})$$

—where N_{it} is the number of observations on magazines in category (state) i at time t, and n is the number of categories (states). This index equals 0 when all observations are in a single state. It rises as the distribution becomes in-

[1] The *North American Review*, the *Christian Register* (now *UU World*, the magazine of the Unitarian Universalist Association), *Philadelphia Recorder* (now *Episcopalian Life*), *Zion's Herald*, the *Boston Medical and Surgical Journal* (now the *New England Journal of Medicine*), the *Yale Literary Magazine*, *Bibliotheca Sacra*, the *New Orleans Medical Journal* (now the *Journal of the Louisiana State Medical Society*), *Scientific American*, *Home Journal* (now *Town and Country*), *Harper's New Monthly Magazine* (now *Harper's*), *Pacific Magazine*, the *American Law Register and Review* (now the *University of Pennsylvania Law Review*), the *AME Christian Recorder* (now the *Christian Recorder*), *American Israelite*, the *Hardware Man's Newspaper and American Manufacturer's Circular* (now *Doors and Hardware Magazine*), the *Atlantic Monthly* (now the *Atlantic*), the *Western Recorder*, the *Southwestern Christian Advocate* (now the *Christian Advocate*), the *Texas Christian Advocate* (now the *United Methodist Reporter*), the *Gospel Messenger* (now the *Messenger*), the *Gospel Publisher and Journal of Useful Knowledge* (now the *Church Advocate*), the *Second Advent Review and Sabbath Herald* (now the *Adventist Review*), the *Boston Pilot* (now the *Pilot*, a newspaper), the *Pittsburgh Catholic* (now a newspaper), *Thompson's Bank Note Reporter* (now *American Banker*, a newspaper), the *Gospel Advocate*, the *Proceedings of the American Academy of Arts and Sciences* (now *Daedalus*), the *Journal of the American Oriental Society*, *True Wesleyan* (now the *Wesleyan Advocate*), *American Bible Society Quarterly Extracts* (now the *American Bible Society Record*), the *Quarterly Papers of the Domestic and Foreign Missionary Society* (now the *Episcopalian*), the *Kenyon Collegian*, the *Denisonian*, the *American Agriculturist*, and the *Pittsburgh Legal Journal*.

creasingly evenly spread out across states. Its maximum, which occurs when observations are evenly distributed across states, equals 1.

The other well-known index of dispersion is the Simpson index of diversity (Simpson 1949), which sociologists also refer to as the Gibbs-Martin index of dispersion (Gibbs and Martin 1962) or the Blau index of heterogeneity (Blau 1977). No matter the name, these are all the complement of the Hirschman-Herfindahl index of concentration that is used in economics (Hirschman 1964). The index of qualitative variations scales the Simpson index to make possible comparisons over time by taking into account that the number of categories (states) used in calculating magazines' geographic dispersion grew over time. The maximum of the Simpson index of dispersion is $1 - 1/n$, where n is the number of categories. The index of qualitative variation divides the Simpson index by this maximum, making the maximum equal to 1 regardless of the number of categories.

Calculating this index at the municipality level was more complex. There were many states in which magazines were published in only a single town or city, which would make it impossible to calculate the index. To avoid this situation I squared the percentage of magazines published in each town or city in the focal state, summed across all towns or cities, took the square root of this sum, and subtracted the result from 1. I then took the mean across all states and scaled it by $(1 - 1/n)$, where n is the number of states where magazines were published, to standardize the index over time and force the maximum to be 1.

Analyzing magazines' heterogeneity in terms of genre. I used the same index of heterogeneity; this time, the categories were genres rather than locations.

Spatial and Temporal Variation in Access to Printing Presses

I used data from a history of the book industry in America (Lehmann-Haupt 1951: 69–70), which listed the year printing presses were first available in each state.

CHAPTER 3: THE MATERIAL AND CULTURAL FOUNDATIONS OF AMERICAN MAGAZINES

I worked with Chris Rider to conduct the quantitative analyses reported here.

Expansion of the Post Office Affecting Magazine Founding Rates

Independent variables: local and nonlocal magazines. To account for the influences of local magazines, we counted the *number of magazines published in each state* for each year. Because this variable was highly skewed, we added 1 and log-transformed it. We also experimented with linear and quadratic terms for number of magazines. We found the expected inverted-U-shaped effect, but the peak of this effect was above the 98th percentile of state-year observations, indicating that for the vast majority of states and years the effect increased at a decreasing rate—only in the industry core near the end of our study period did we see evidence of competitive crowding. This pattern of results confirms that using the logged count is appropriate.

To capture the effects of nonlocal magazines, we constructed a *distance-scaled count of magazines outside the focal state* for each year. Scaling by physical distance takes into account persistent costs of interacting across space, which means that interactions between in-state (local) and out-of-state (nonlocal) magazines diminish with out-of-state magazines' distance from the focal state. Scaling by distance from the focal state also deals with spillovers from nearby states to the focal state. To compute this variable we first identified the latitude and longitude of the municipality in each state where the largest number of magazines were published during our study period (e.g., Charleston for South Carolina, Cincinnati for Ohio, Philadelphia for Pennsylvania). Using spherical geometry (for details, see Sorenson and Audia 2000) we then computed the distance in miles from one state's magazine center to another's. Then, for each state i in each year t, we computed the distance-scaled count of out-of-state magazines thus—

$$\textit{Distance Scaled Number of Magazines Outside State}_{it} = \sum_{j \neq i} \frac{M_{jt}}{D_{ij}}$$

—where M_{jt} is the number of magazines in any state j (other than the focal state i) in year t and D_{ij} is the distance in miles between the magazine centers of the focal state i and the other state j. We summed this distance-scaled count over all states other than the focal state. States located near the industry centers, which held the largest agglomerations of magazines, scored highest on this variable. For example, in every year, Connecticut and Delaware scored higher on this variable than Georgia and Indiana because the former were closer to the industry centers than the latter.

For a robustness check we created a *national, distance-scaled count of magazines*: the number of in-state (local) magazines plus the number of out-of-state (nonlocal) magazines. Each magazine in the focal state was given a weight of 1 and each magazine in other states was given a weight inversely proportional to its distance from the focal state. This measure varies across states in any given year.

Interactions. We tested predictions about how the impact of local organizations on founding rates changes as communication systems develop by interacting the number of magazines in the focal state with the number of US (or state) post offices. We tested predictions about how the impact of nonlocal organizations on founding rates changes as communication systems develop by interacting the distance-scaled counts of magazines outside the focal state with the number of US (or out-of-state) post offices.

Control variables. We controlled for other factors that reflected variation in states' natural attractiveness to magazine entrepreneurs, starting with the lagged dependent variable, the number of foundings in the focal state in the previous year. We controlled for state population, measured in millions. We counted miles of post roads in the focal state, scaled miles by state landmass in square miles. We controlled for the postage rate in cents charged for magazines, and used a commodity price index (McCusker 2001) to correct for inflation and express the rate in constant (1860) dollars. Finally, we controlled for each state's literacy rate to account for demand net of state population.

Modeling strategy. For this analysis we used panel data on states. The start of each state's time series depended on two events: it must have achieved statehood and it must have experienced at least one magazine founding. We excluded all state-year observations from the year 1815 because the US postmaster general barred magazines from the mail for much of that year. We lagged all explanatory variables by one year to assure temporal priority and increase confidence that we had captured the correct direction of causal processes. The data set contains 1,580 state-year observations, but our use of lagged explanatory variables and exclusion of observations from 1815 reduced the sample to 1,529 observations.

The dependent variable was a discrete event tracked over time, so we used event-count methods to analyze it (Cameron and Trivedi 1986). Because this dependent variable exhibits significant over dispersion, we estimated negative-binomial models instead of Poisson models (Cameron and Trivedi 1990). To control for the impact of unobserved and/or unmeasurable state-specific, time-invariant factors (e.g., topology), we estimated conditional fixed-effects models that group observations by state. And to avoid confounding the main effects of our key independent variable (the number of post offices) with other factors that increased similarly over time, we included decade fixed effects. Basically, this approach enabled us to identify how the magazine founding rate varied within each decade as the postal system expanded and how the effects of expansion varied with (a) the number of magazines published in each state and (b) the distance-scaled number of magazines published in other states.

Results. Table A2.1 reports descriptive statistics for all variables in the founding-rate analysis; table A2.2 presents results. Model 1 of table A2.2 includes only control variables plus state fixed effects; subsequent models add explanatory variables. Within each state founding rates increased as more roads were developed, as the state's population increased, and as the US postal system expanded. These effects are generally consistent across models.

Model 2 shows that, as expected, state-level magazine founding rates increased with the number of magazines published in the focal state and decreased with the number of magazines published in nearby states. These results reveal the benefits of local (in-state) magazines but also competitive pressures from dense clusters of nearby nonlocal (out-of-state) magazines. Model 3 includes the interactions of both magazine counts with the count of

Descriptive Statistics for Variables in Magazine Founding Rate Analyses

	Mean	St. Dev.	1	2	3	4	5	6	7	8	9	10
1 All foundings	3.31	6.12	1.00									
2 State population (millions)	0.58	0.54	0.78	1.00								
3 Roads per square mile	0.16	0.11	0.38	0.28	1.00							
4 State literacy factor	−0.13	0.83	0.66	0.88	0.39	1.00						
5 Magazine postage rate	13.2	41.5	−0.07	−0.10	−0.17	−0.13	1.00					
6 Number of US post offices (1000s)	10.2	8.11	0.21	0.36	0.40	0.58	−0.23	1.00				
7 Number of in-state post offices (100s)	3.71	4.37	0.71	0.92	0.35	0.91	−0.15	0.57	1.00			
8 Number of out-of-state post offices (100s)	97.9	78.6	0.17	0.32	0.40	0.54	−0.23	1.00	0.53	1.00		
9 Number of magazines in state	1.75	1.31	0.72	0.75	0.54	0.73	−0.17	0.45	0.74	0.42	1.00	
10 Magazines outside state, distance-weighted	1.58	1.69	0.15	0.16	0.67	0.31	−0.15	0.60	0.29	0.60	0.29	1.00

Note: This table is based on 1,529 state-year observations from 1790 to 1860.

TABLE A2.2.
Conditional Fixed-Effects Negative-Binomial Regressions
of Magazine Founding Counts by State-Year

	(1)	(2)	(3)	(4)	(5)	(6)	(7)
State foundings in prior year	0.013** (0.004)	0.002 (0.004)	0.005 (0.003)	0.004 (0.003)	0.002 (0.004)	0.000 (0.004)	0.014** (0.004)
State population (millions)	0.292** (0.112)	0.146 (0.102)	0.791** (0.120)	0.771** (0.125)	0.748** (0.128)	0.334* (0.140)	1.40** (0.186)
State roads per square mile	4.52** (0.328)	2.80** (0.385)	1.50** (0.413)	1.58** (0.459)	1.32** (0.468)	2.00** (0.462)	1.92** (0.465)
State literacy factor	−0.106† (0.062)	−0.132* (0.057)	−0.139* (0.057)	−0.129* (0.060)	−0.102 (0.062)	0.076 (0.067)	−0.024 (0.070)
Magazine postage rate	−0.002* (0.001)	−0.001 (0.001)	−0.001 (0.001)	−0.002 (0.001)			
1000s of US post offices	0.013** (0.005)	0.006 (0.007)	0.117** (0.012)	0.112** (0.015)			
Number of magazines in state		0.579** (0.051)	0.488** (0.060)	0.448** (0.064)	0.433** (0.068)	0.299** (0.066)	0.219** (0.063)
Magazines outside state, distance-weighted		−0.137** (0.033)	−0.035 (0.057)	−0.113 (0.078)	−0.189† (0.097)	−0.319** (0.047)	−0.219* (0.098)
In-state magazines × US post offices			−0.024** (0.003)	−0.023** (0.003)	−0.023** (0.003)		
Out-of-state magazines × US post offices			−0.011** (0.003)	−0.009** (0.003)	−0.006† (0.004)		
In-state post offices (100s)						−0.041† (0.022)	0.116** (0.028)
Out-of-state post offices (100s)						0.000 (0.011)	−0.001 (0.011)
In-state magazines × in-state post offices							−0.046* (0.005)
Out-of-state magazines × out-of-state post offices							0.000 (0.000)
Constant	0.693** (0.181)	0.425* (0.214)	0.367 (0.285)	0.877† (0.450)	4.66** (0.675)	3.13 (3.16)	2.75 (3.12)
N (state-years)	1,529	1,529	1,529	1,529	1,529	1,529	1,529
N (states)	31	31	31	31	31	31	31
State fixed effects	Yes	Yes	Yes	Yes	Yes	Yes	Yes
Decade fixed effects	No	No	No	Yes	No	No	No
Year fixed effects	No	No	No	No	Yes	Yes	Yes
Log likelihood	−2,425.1	−2,338.1	−2,282.7	−2,275.6	−2,245.3	−2,277.8	−2,238.
Wald χ2 (df)	942.6 (6)	1,157.8 (8)	1,240.0 (10)	1,267.0 (16)	1,383.7 (75)	1,313.7 (74)	1,362.3 (76)

Note: All covariates are lagged one year; ** $p < 0.01$; * $p < 0.05$; † $p < 0.10$; two-tailed tests.

US post offices. The positive effect of in-state magazines on the magazine founding rate decreased as the postal system expanded: there is a significant positive main effect of the number of in-state magazines and a significant negative interaction between that variable and the number of US post offices. This indicates that the benefits of dense clusters of magazines within the focal state diminished with postal system expansion. In addition, the negative effect of magazines in nearby states on the founding rate increased as the postal system expanded: there is a negative (but no longer significant) main effect of the distance-scaled number of out-of-state magazines and a significant negative interaction between that variable and the number of US post offices. This indicates that the competitive effect of nearby magazines outside the focal state increased with postal system expansion.

Model 4 tests the robustness of these results to the inclusion of unreported decade fixed effects to account for the fact that both the number of magazines and post offices increased over time. This modeling strategy restricts the empirical tests to accounting for within-decade variance in postal expansion. The parameters of interest are robust to including decade fixed effects: the main effects of in-state and out-of-state magazine counts and their interactions with the count of US post offices are in the same direction as in model 3, of the same magnitudes, and at the same levels of statistical significance. This increases confidence in the findings from model 3.

Decade fixed effects do not account for temporal changes common to all states in a given year. Therefore, model 5 replaces decade fixed effects with unreported year fixed effects. We dropped the magazine postage rate and the main effect of the number of US post offices because they vary only over time, so the year fixed effects absorb their influences. We could, however, retain the interaction terms because both in-state and out-of-state magazine counts vary across states each year. In model 5 the coefficients of interest remain robust to the inclusion of year fixed effects, although the coefficient on interaction between the count of out-of-state magazines and US post offices becomes only marginally significant ($p < .09$). This set of results further increases confidence in the findings of model 3.

Our next robustness check involves assessing whether in-state and out-of-state postal expansion have different effects on magazine founding rates. We did this by disaggregating the number of US post offices into the number of in-state and out-of-state post offices. This allowed us to include both year fixed effects and the main effects of postal expansion because both in-state and out-of-state post office counts vary across states each year. Model 6 includes the main effects of in-state and out-of-state post offices, while model 7 includes interactions between each post office count with the corresponding magazine count (in-state or out-of-state). As these models show, the competitive effects of postal expansion on magazine founding rates are primarily attributable to in-state postal expansion.

Further robustness checks. The results of this analysis rest on two modeling assumptions. First, we combined observations on the magazine industry's

316 | Appendix 2

core with observations on peripheral regions. We tested the sensitivity of our results to this aggregation by estimating separate founding-count models for the core and the periphery. These results indicated that in both subsamples of states, postal expansion reduced the influence of in-state magazines and increased the influence of magazines in nearby states on the magazine founding rate. We therefore conclude that support for our predictions was drawn from both the magazine industry's core *and* its periphery. Second, the results might be driven by the increasing physical scale of our units of analysis: the thirteen original states were much smaller than states formed later. Such increases in physical scale complicate any analysis of geography. We therefore reran the analyses, using only data for the thirteen original states. The results for these states are very similar to the results for the entire nation, suggesting that our findings are robust to increases in the physical scale of the units studied.

Expansion of the Post Office Affecting Magazines' Geographic Identities

Our predictions about identity choices for newly founded magazines were differentiated by region (core versus periphery). We therefore analyzed the identities of newly founded magazines at the core separately from those on the periphery.

Modeling strategy. For this analysis we used magazine-level data. New magazines face mutually exclusive identity choices: each must choose a localistic *or* universalistic *or* nongeographic identity. Estimating conditional logit models of the identities chosen by newly founded magazines enables accounts for this choice (McFadden 1973; Hoffman and Duncan 1988). For each magazine founded between 1790 and 1860 we created three observations, one for each of the three identity choices: localistic, universalistic, or nongeographic. We grouped observations by magazine and focused on interactions between indicators for localistic and universalistic identities (the reference category is the nongeographic identity) and the number of US (or focal state) post offices to assess how the expansion of the postal system influenced the likelihood that a newly founded magazine adopted a particular identity.

Results. Table A2.3 presents conditional logit models that test our arguments about new magazines' identity claims. Here we examine how the likelihood of a magazine being founded with a localistic or universalistic identity changed as the postal system expanded, conditional on the magazine being founded in the first place. Our prediction about the rise of localistic identities pertains to peripheral states, while our prediction about the rise of universalistic identities pertains to core states. Accordingly, we tested the first prediction by estimating models 8–10 on peripheral states and tested the second prediction by estimating models 11–15 on core states.

Model 8 shows that in peripheral states magazines were least likely to be founded with a universalistic identity and most likely to be founded with a

TABLE A2.3.
Conditional Logit Models of Magazine Identity Choice at Founding

	(8)	(9)	(10)	(11)	(12)	(13)	(14)	(15)
Localistic identity	-0.542**	-0.862**	-0.672**	-1.63**	-1.51**	-1.55**	-1.74**	-1.15**
	(0.045)	(0.096)	(0.068)	(0.055)	(0.105)	(0.099)	(0.126)	(0.168)
Universalistic identity	-2.55**	-2.24**	-2.17**	-1.93**	-2.18**	-2.41**	-2.19**	-3.38**
	(0.100)	(0.216)	(0.176)	(0.063)	(0.130)	(0.133)	(0.140)	(0.391)
Localistic × US post offices (1,000s)		0.022**			-0.009			
		(0.006)			(0.007)			
Universalistic × US post offices (1,000s)		-0.023			0.019*			
		(0.015)			(0.009)			
Localistic × in-state post offices (100s)			0.022*			-0.006	-0.005	-0.010
			(0.008)			(0.007)	(0.009)	(0.012)
Universalistic × in-state post offices (100s)			-0.078*			0.036**	0.032**	0.057*
			(0.034)			(0.008)	(0.009)	(0.023)
Scope of analysis	Periphery	Periphery	Periphery	Core	Core	Core	Boston/New York/ Philadelphia	Other core
N (observations)	6,813	6,813	6,813	8,064	8,064	8,064	5,787	2,277
N (magazines)	2,271	2,271	2,271	2,688	2,688	2,688	1,929	759
N (states)	30	30	30	3	3	3	3	3
Log pseudolikelihood	-1,854.8	-1,845.0	-1,844.8	-1,992.7	-1,988.9	-1,981.3	-1,417.8	-536.2
Wald χ2 (df)	709.9 (2)	714.8 (4)	689.9 (4)	1,586.7 (2)	1,583.5 (4)	1,573.7 (4)	1,147.3 (4)	400.9 (4)

Note: Robust standard errors in parentheses; observations grouped by magazine; ** $p < 0.01$; * $p < 0.05$; † $p < 0.10$; two-tailed tests.

nongeographic identity (the reference category), as indicated by their titles' references to place names. Model 9 supports our prediction: the interaction between the number of US post offices and the indicator for localistic identity is positive and statistically significant. As the postal system expanded, magazines in peripheral states became significantly more likely to adopt localistic identities than nongeographic identities.

Model 11 shows that magazines in core states were also least likely to be founded with a universalistic identity and most likely to be founded with a nongeographic identity (the reference category). But the difference between the probability of a universalistic and a localistic identity choice is much smaller in core states than in peripheral states, as evidenced by the difference between the magnitudes of the effect estimates on the localistic and universalistic indicators. Model 12 supports our prediction: the interaction between number of US post offices and the indicator for universalistic identity is positive and statistically significant. As the postal system expanded, magazines in core states became more likely to adopt universalistic identities than nongeographic identities.

To check the robustness of these effects, models 10 and 13 replace US-level postal counts with state-level counts. Model 10 shows that on the periphery, as the focal state's postal system expanded, more magazines were founded with localistic identities and fewer were founded with universalistic identities. Model 13 reveals that at the core, as the focal state's postal system expanded, more magazines were founded with universalistic identities. These results bolster confidence in the results shown in models 9 and 12.

To check the robustness of our results in defining the state, rather than the city, as the unit of analysis, models 14 and 15 replicate model 13 on two subsamples of the core: Boston, New York, and Philadelphia (model 14) and all other core locations (model 15). Both models show the same pattern of results as model 13: significant negative and positive main effects of localistic and universalistic identities respectively, nonsignificant negative interaction with in-state post offices, and significant positive interaction with out-of-state post offices. These results strengthen confidence in the results shown in model 13.

Final robustness check. These results were based on a key modeling assumption—that localistic identities could focus on a municipality, county, state, or multistate region while universalistic identities encompassed the entire nation or even the entire continent. But that may be an overly broad definition of localistic and an overly narrow definition of universalistic. Of particular concern is the classification of magazines with titles indicating a multistate regional identity (e.g., New England, the Mississippi Valley, the South). Such magazines might be better classified as having universalistic rather than localistic identities. We checked the robustness of our results to this more restrictive definition of localistic identity (encompassing only a municipality, county, or state) and this more inclusive definition of universalistic identity (encompassing the continent, the nation, or a multistate region). We obtained results consistent with those shown in table A2.3: the expansion of the postal system increased the rate at which magazines were founded with universalistic foundings in the industry's core and increased the rate at which magazines were founded with localistic identities in the industry's periphery.

CHAPTER 4: LAUNCHING MAGAZINES

Analyzing Magazine Founders' Backgrounds

I undertook this work jointly with Jacob Habinek and Leo Goodman.

Bivariate analysis methods. To assess whether there were statistically significant changes over time in the frequencies of founders' occupation and education, we analyzed 2 × 2 contingency tables and conducted χ^2 tests. (When cell counts are lower than five, the χ^2 test is not accurate; for tables with low cell counts, Fisher's exact test [Fisher 1922] instead, as is standard in contingency-table analysis.) The unit of analysis here was the individual founder. For each occupation we conducted a separate analysis, comparing frequencies of magazine founders in the focal occupation to frequencies of founders in *any other* occupation. This allowed us to assess the statistical significance of time trends for each occupation separately, which is necessary because historical trends in access to resources varied greatly across occupations. For location we assessed the statistical significance of time trends in the trichotomous location variable by analyzing a 3 × 2 contingency table, again using the χ^2 test. The unit of analysis here was the magazine.

The distributions of occupations, educational statuses, and locations from which founders were drawn changed greatly over our observation period. We took these changes into consideration as much as possible, given limitations on the data available. We scaled the percentage of professional and college-educated magazine founders by the percentage of professionals and college students, respectively. This allowed us to compare the likelihood of a magazine founder being a professional or having a college education, relative to the general population, in each time period. We also scaled the percentage of magazines launched in the three biggest cities and in all urban areas by the percentage of the population living in those locations. This allowed us to compare the likelihood of a magazine's founders being in those three cities or in other urban areas, relative to the typical American, in each time period.

Bivariate results. Tables A2.4a–c present the analysis of trends in occupation, education, and location: table A2.4a analyzes occupation, table A2.4b education, and table A2.4c location. For occupation and education the unit of analysis is the individual founder; for location it is the magazine. Each contingency table reports the χ^2 statistic and the statistical significance level for the difference between the two time periods.

Table A2.4a.

Changes over Time in Magazine Founders' Occupations

Occupation	18th Century	19th Century	χ^2
Publishing trades	109 (67.3%)	21 (20.3%)	55.4***
Not publishing trades	53 (32.7%)	82 (79.6%)	
Printer	81 (50.0%)	4 (3.9%)	61.5***
Not printer (includes other publishing trades)	81 (50.0%)	99 (96.1%)	
Other publishing trades	28 (17.3%)	17 (16.5%)	0.03
Other occupation (includes printer)	134 (82.7%)	86 (83.5%)	
Writer	6 (3.7%)	15 (14.6%)	10.2**
Not writer	156 (96.3%)	88 (85.4%)	
Professional	30 (18.5%)	46 (44.7%)	21.0***
Not professional	132 (81.5%)	57 (55.3%)	
Minister	14 (8.6%)	24 (23.3%)	11.0**
Not minister (includes lawyer and doctor)	148 (91.4%)	79 (76.7%)	
Lawyer	12 (7.4%)	4 (3.9%)	1.4
Not lawyer (includes minister and doctor)	150 (92.6%)	99 (96.1%)	
Doctor	4 (2.5%)	18 (17.5%)	18.6***
Not doctor (includes minister and lawyer)	158 (97.5%)	85 (82.5%)	
Other	17 (10.5%)	21 (20.3%)	5.0*
Not other (printing trade, writer, or professional)	155 (89.5%)	82 (79.7%)	

Note: This table analyzes 162 magazine founders in the eighteenth century and 103 in the nineteenth century. The nineteenth-century sample omits one magazine founder, William August Munsell, who was eight years old when he started his magazine. Each founder's occupation is assessed before he or she founded his or her first magazine. We analyzed each occupation independently by comparing the number of founders in the focal occupation to the number of founders in all other occupations; * $p < 0.05$, ** $p < 0.01$, and *** $p < 0.001$, $df = 1$. For tables that contain cells with fewer than five observations, p values are based on Fisher's exact test instead of the χ^2 test.

Table A2.4a shows a separate analysis of each occupation, using 2 × 2 contingency tables. For each subtable, the first row records frequencies of magazine founders in the focal occupation; the second, frequencies of magazine founders in *any other* occupation. Thus, the row labeled "Publishing trades" records frequencies of magazine founders in the publishing trades, while the next row records frequencies of magazine founders in all other occupations

TABLE A2.4B.
Changes over Time in Magazine Founders' Education Levels

Education	18th Century	19th Century	χ^2
College education	22 (13.6%)	17 (16.3%)	0.39
No college education	103 (86.4%)	87 (83.7%)	

Note: This table analyzes 162 founders in the eighteenth century and 104 in the nineteenth century. For the χ^2 test, $df = 1$.

TABLE A2.4C.
Changes over Time in Magazine Founders' Locations

Location	18th Century	19th Century	χ^2
Boston/New York/Philadelphia	82 (55.8%)	53 (36.1%)	
Other urban area	27 (18.4%)	65 (44.2%)	23.1***
Rural area	38 (25.9%)	29 (19.7%)	

Note: This table analyzes all magazines for which location is known: 147 magazines in both the eighteenth century and the mid-nineteenth; *** indicates $p < 0.001$, $df = 2$.

combined. The first column records frequencies in the eighteenth century; the second, in the mid-nineteenth century. It shows that magazine entrepreneurs' occupations became significantly more heterogeneous from the eighteenth century to the mid-nineteenth century. Likewise, table A2.4b shows that the likelihood of magazine founders attending college was fairly constant. Even in the second time period they were still 161 times more likely than the typical American to have attended college. Finally, table A2.4c shows that the fraction of magazines founded in the three largest cities declined substantially.

Multivariate analysis methods. To analyze interactions among occupation, education, and location we conducted a multivariate analysis of variation over time in the frequency of magazines with different combinations of these status markers. This allowed us to consider not only the change in the *prevalence* of founders from each social position but also changes in *relationships among* those social positions. Because all the variables in the analysis are categorical, we used log-linear techniques (Goodman 1970; Bishop, Fienberg, and Holland 1975),[2] which extend the analysis of two-variable contingency tables to multivariable tables, and thus allow us to analyze conditional relationships among multiple categorical variables. As with two-variable contingency tables, we assessed statistical significance using χ^2 tests.

Because many organizational scholars are not familiar with them, let me explain the basics of log-linear techniques and compare them to the more fa-

---

[2] For a straightforward comparison of this technique to linear and logistic regression, and an explanation of why log-linear techniques are preferred over regression techniques when all variables are categorical, see Knoke and Burke (1980).

miliar regression techniques. Log-linear analysis is similar to multiple regression analysis in that it assesses relationships—main effects and interactions—among a set of variables. But log-linear analysis differs from multiple regression analysis in that it starts with a fully specified ("saturated") model, one that contains all possible combinations of main effects and interactions, and subtracts parameters (interactions between two or more variables) step by step, rather than starting with a model containing main effects only and adding interaction parameters. The goal in log-linear analysis is to determine the simplest model—the one containing the simplest set of interaction parameters—that does not differ from the saturated model. Most log-linear analysis involves comparing how well a hierarchically nested set of models fits the data. The models are hierarchically nested because those containing complex interactions among a set of variables must necessarily also contain all simpler interactions among those variables; for instance, a model containing a three-way interaction must contain all of the two-way interactions among the three variables, plus the main effects of each variable and the grand mean (equivalent to the constant in multiple regression).

The unit of analysis here was the magazine. We cross-classified magazines according to five dichotomous variables: the presence or absence of a founder in the professions, the presence or absence of a founder in the publishing trades (including printing), the presence or absence of a founder with a college education, whether or not the magazine was published in one of the three biggest cities, and whether the magazine was published in the eighteenth century or the mid-nineteenth. We simplified the occupational categories to generate a cross-classification table with reasonably large cell counts; including more fine-grained occupational categories would have resulted in a prohibitively large numbers of cells with very low observed counts. As is customary in log-linear analysis, we recoded all variables to –1 when the focal attribute was absent and +1 when the focal attribute was present. Doing so yields effect estimates that are relative to category means, which simplifies interpretation.

The notation used in log-linear analysis differs from that used in multiple-regression analysis. Letters denote the variables in the cross-tabulation and a set of letters enclosed in parentheses denotes each multivariate model. For instance, C might stand for college education, L for location in a large city, and T for time period. Then {CLT} would denote a model containing the grand mean for the table, three main effects (C, L, T), three two-way interactions (C × L, C × T, and L × T), and one three-way interaction (C × L × T). A simpler model, nested within the first and denoted as {CT}{LT}, would contain the grand mean, three main effects (C, L, and T), and two two-way interactions (C × T and L × T).

Most log-linear analyses make no distinction between independent and dependent variables. But we wanted to explain variation over time in the frequency of magazines with different combinations of founder occupations, education, and location. Therefore we used Goodman's (1972) modification of multiple regression for the analysis of categorical data, which treats one categorical variable as the outcome to be predicted. Specifically, we modeled the difference between the second period and the first in the odds of newly founded magazines having founders in a given combination of social positions. Thus, we treated time period (T) as the variable to be predicted, and the four social positions—professional occupation (P), publishing trades occupation (B), college education (C), and location in one of the three biggest cities (L)—as the predictor variables. This approach is similar to logistic regression models that predict a categorical outcome (like voting or innovation adoption) using continuous variables.

We used a stepwise procedure (Goodman 1970) to select the model with the fewest parameters that that did not differ significantly from the data. We compared the observed frequencies in the five-way data table, which we created by cross-classifying the four dichotomous predictor variables and the dichotomous outcome variable, to the estimated expected frequencies under the selected model. We used two test statistics: the likelihood-ratio and goodness-of-fit χ^2 statistics. Because our sample is small (226 magazines with known founders) we also used the estimated parameters obtained from the saturated model to as a guide to selecting which parameters should be included in the final model (Goodman 1970). We then used the estimated expected frequencies from the selected model to estimate the odds of being in the second period rather than the first for each combination of predictor variables.

Multivariate results. The unsaturated model that fits the data best includes the following sets of effects: {PBCL}{PBT}{PCT}{PLT}{BCT}. Thus, this model includes four three-way interactions between the predictor variables and time (P × B × T, P × C × T, P × L × T, and B × C × T) plus the two-way interactions between the four predictor variables and time. Table A2.5 demonstrates why we selected this model, presenting a series of log-linear models of increasing complexity. For each model the table lists the parameters fitted, notes the degrees of freedom, and assesses model fit. Model 7 (boldfaced) is the selected model. It fits the data very well: likelihood-ratio $\chi^2 = 2.63$ ($df = 7$, $p = 0.917$ compared to the saturated model), Pearson's $\chi^2 = 2.78$ ($df = 7, p = 0.905$ compared to the saturated model). This means that the saturated model does not fit the data any better than the selected model, even though the selected model is more parsimonious (it contains fewer parameters). We checked to see whether any more parsimonious model would fit the data as well as model 7, but none did. For example, models 1 and 2 both exclude one of the interactions estimated in model 7 (B × C × T and P × L × T, respectively), but they do not fit the data as well as model 7. The χ^2 tests comparing models 1 and 2 to model 7 confirm that the parameters omitted in models 1 and 2 make statistically significant contributions to model fit. We then checked to see whether any equally parsimonious model (any model containing the same number of parameters) would fit the data better than model 7. Models 3–6 are equal in complexity to model 7, but none fit the data as well as model 7. Finally, we

TABLE A2.5.
Log-Linear Models of the Effects of Professional and Publishing Trades Occupations, College Education, and Location on Time Period

Model	Marginals fitted	Equivalent logistic regression interactions	Degrees of freedom	Likelihood ratio χ^2	Pearson's χ^2	AIC
1	{PBT}{PCT}{PLT}	P × B, P × C, and P × L only	8	8.55	9.6	148.21
2	{PBT}{PCT}{BCT}	P × B, P × C, and B × C only	8	10.05	7.81	149.71
3	{PCT}{PLT}{BCT}{BLT}	All except P × B and C × L	7	12.81†	12.74†	154.47
4	{PBT}{PLT}{BCT}{BLT}	All except P × C and C × L	7	14.13*	15.24*	155.79
5	{PBT}{PCT}{BCT}{BLT}	All except P × L and C × L	7	3.5	3.51	145.16
6	{PBT}{PCT}{PLT}{BLT}	All except B × C and C × L	7	6.94	6.25	148.6
7	**{PBT}{PCT}{PLT}{BCT}**	**All except B × L and C × L**	7	**2.63**	**2.78**	**144.3**
8	{PCT}{PLT}{BCT}{BLT}{CLT}	All except P × B	6	12.53†	12.3†	156.19
9	{PBT}{PLT}{BCT}{BLT}{CLT}	All except P × C	6	12.95*	13.13*	156.61
10	{PBT}{PCT}{BCT}{BLT}{CLT}	All except P × L	6	2.1	2.14	145.76
11	{PBT }{PCT}{PLT}{BLT}{CLT}	All except B × C	6	6.84	6.17	150.5
12	{PBT}{PCT}{PLT}{BCT}{CLT}	All except B × L	6	2.45	2.77	146.11
13	{PBT}{PCT}{PLT}{BCT}{BLT}	All except C × L	6	1.32	1.27	144.98
14	{PBT}{PCT}{PLT}{BCT}{BLT}{CLT}	All	5	1.06	1.07	146.72

Note: **P** indicates the presence or absence of a professional on a founding team, **B** the presence or absence of a member of the publishing trades on a founding team, **C** the presence or absence of someone with a college education on a founding team, **L** whether or not a magazine was founded in one of the three biggest cities, and **T** whether a magazine was founded between 1741 and 1800 or between 1841 and 1860. Each log-linear model also fits {PBCL}; Model 7, **boldfaced**, is the best-fitting unsaturated model.
† indicates $p < 0.10$, * $p < 0.05$.

checked to see whether more complex models (models that contain more parameters) would fit the data better than model 7. Models 8–14 are all more complex than model 7, but none offer a significant improvement in fit over model 7.

Because the sample is small we checked model selection in two ways. First, table A2.5 reports the Akaike Information Criterion for each model, which does not depend on the same large-sample assumptions as χ^2 statistics and which measures how much information is lost when a given model is used to describe the distribution of the data, compared to the saturated model containing all parameters (Akaike 1974). Among models with $df = 7$, model 7 has the lowest Akaike Information Criterion, which further supports its selection. Second, we used the estimated parameters obtained from the saturated model as a guide to which parameters should be included in the selected unsaturated model (Goodman 1970). Column 1 in table A2.6 presents effect estimates from the saturated model. It confirms the analysis of table A2.5. In the saturated model {BLT} and {CLT} are the three-way interactions that are closest to 0, so a model that drops them, as does model 7 in table A2.5, is likely to fit the data well.

Column 2 in table A2.6 presents the estimated effects of all parameters pertaining to the odds of appearing in the second time period rather than the first in the selected model. Recall that coefficients were estimated using means constraints: each effect was calculated at the sample means for all other variables. Thus, for example, the coefficient {PT} is the effect the odds of a magazine's being published in the second period rather than the first due to having a printer founder versus not having one. Both the professional and publishing-trades occupations {PT} and {BT} have negative effects on the odds of a magazine appearing in the mid-nineteenth century rather than the eighteenth century, but the effect for publishing trades is only half the size of the effect for professional occupations. Location in one of the three biggest cities {LT} has a small negative effect on these odds. The effect of founders' education {CT} is close to 0, indicating that magazines in the second period were no more likely to have college-educated founders than those in the first. This pattern of results differs from the bivariate analysis in two respects: that analysis showed that the likelihood of having a professional founder increased and the likelihood of having a college-educated founder decreased.

Differences between the bivariate and multivariate results are due to interactions between the professional and publishing trades occupations, between both occupations and college education, and between the professional occupation and location. We discuss each interaction in turn. Having professional founders *and* founders in the publishing trades {PBT} increased the odds of a magazine appearing in the mid-nineteenth century rather than the eighteenth century. While the members of each occupation on its own became less likely to found magazines (the effects for {PT} and {BT} are negative), members of the two occupations became more likely to found magazines together ({PBT} is positive). This suggests that the resources attached to these two occupations

TABLE A2.6.

Estimates of Main Effects and Interactions: The Saturated
Model and the Best-Fitting Unsaturated Model

Parameter	Equivalent logistic regression parameter	*(1)* Saturated model	*(2)* Best-fitting unsaturated model	*(3)* Equivalent logistic regression model
T	Constant	0.54	0.35	0.99
PT	Professional	−0.43	−0.27	0.44
BT	Publishing	−0.73	−0.56	−2.46
CT	College education	0.3	0.09	4.32
LT	Location (in Boston/New York/ Philadelphia)	0.36	−0.16	0.29
PBT	Professional × publishing	0.57	0.43	3.41
PCT	Professional × college	−0.73	−0.58	−4.65
BCT	Publishing × college	−0.53	−0.38	−3.13
PLT	Professional × location	−0.66	−0.23	−1.81
BLT	Publishing × location	−0.36		
CLT	College × location	0.46		
PBCT	Professional × publishing × college	0.16		
PBLT	Professional × publishing × location	0.62		
PCLT	Profl × College × Location	−0.52		
BCLT	Publng × College × Location	−0.48		
PBCLT	Profl × Publng × College × Location	0.55		

Note: **P** indicates the presence or absence of a professional on a founding team, **B** the presence or absence of a member of the publishing trades on a founding team, **C** the presence or absence of someone with a college education on a founding team, **L** whether or not a magazine was founded in one of the three biggest cities, and **T** whether a magazine was founded between 1741 and 1800 or between 1841 and 1860.

became increasingly complementary. Next, having college-educated founders *and* professionals, {PCT}, decreased the odds of a magazine appearing in the mid-nineteenth century rather than the eighteenth century, as did having college-educated founders *and* founders in publishing, {BCT}. This indicates that although the prevalence of magazine founders with a college education did not change overall (based on the near-0 effect for {CT}), magazine founders within these two occupations became significantly *less* likely to have attended college over time.

Finally, location interacted with occupation: having a professional founder *and* being located in one of the three biggest cities, {PLT}, decreased the odds of a magazine being published in the mid-nineteenth century rather than the eighteenth century. In other words, having a professional founder and being located *outside* a major urban center *increased* the odds. Note that neither the publishing-trades occupation nor college education interacted with location, as {BLT} and {CLT} were not required for the selected model to fit the data well. Taken together these results suggest that *only* those magazines with professionals among their founders became more geographically dispersed while magazines with members of the publishing trades and college-educated men remained just as concentrated in the major urban centers in the mid-nineteenth century as they were in the eighteenth century.

Analyzing Magazine Founders' Espoused Motivations

As I read magazine prospectuses and editorial statements, I took notes on what magazine founders discussed and recorded illustrative quotations. After reading documents for the first seventy magazines (with publication dates to 1798), I created a preliminary list of analytical categories and coded these magazines. Then I read documents for seventy magazines published from 1821 to 1825, took notes, revised the list of analytical categories, and coded these magazines. Using this list of analytical categories, I read all 477 magazines for which documentary evidence was available and coded them. The results of this analysis were twofold: first, qualitative data, consisting of a series of quotations and detailed notes; second, quantitative data, consisting of a series of dummy variables recording for each magazine coding (1) type of motivation espoused and (2) type of community served.

CHAPTER 5: RELIGION

Sample, Unit of Analysis, and Level of Analysis

I analyzed competitive mobilization by religious organizations with Adam Goldstein; our analysis covered all magazines affiliated with American religious organizations from 1790 to 1860. This analysis starts in 1790 because that is the first year for which good data are available on many explanatory variables. Only five religious magazines were published before this date.

This analysis focuses on denominations because they are "the fundamental church structure of this country" (Smith 1962: 97; see also Niebuhr 1929; Ahlstrom 1972; Hall 1998). We analyzed magazine publishing activity for all twenty-two denominations founded before 1860 for which good data were available on the number and location of their congregations: Adventist, Baptist, Catholic, Church of God, Congregational, Disciples of Christ, Dunker, Dutch Reformed, Episcopalian, German Reformed, Jewish, Lutheran, Mennonite, Methodist, Moravian, Mormon, Presbyterian, Quaker, Shaker, Swedenborgian, Unitarian, and Universalist.[3] Together these denominations accounted for 94.3 percent of all congregations in the United States in 1776, 98.8 percent in 1850, and 99.6 percent in 1860 (the only years for which reli-

---

[3] We followed Koçak and Carroll (2008) and distinguished among denominations rather than among groups within denominations, such as branches of the Baptists.

able national counts are available), so our data quite accurately represent the field of American religion.

We conducted analyses at two levels, local and national, because the processes we probed are theorized as occurring at these two levels. Previous research has defined the locations where competition occurs as municipalities, counties, or states (Chaves and Gorski 2001). We defined locations as states for three reasons. First, as explained above, many religious magazines circulated far beyond their sites of production. Second, prior empirical tests have shown that using a more granular definition of locations makes little difference (Chaves and Gorski 2001). Third, it was extremely difficult to find serially and cross-sectionally reliable state-level data for this time period; it would be impossible to piece together data on smaller geographic units.

For the state-level analysis our data comprised one observation per denomination per year for every state in which the denomination had congregations; for the national-level analysis they comprised one observation per denomination per year. We studied each denomination starting in 1790 (for denominations founded before that date) or the year each was founded. For the state-level analysis the start of each denomination-state time series depended on two events: the state must have entered the Union and the denomination must have at least one congregation in the state.

Measures

Dependent variable. The outcome studied here is the number of magazines affiliated with a given denomination (nationally or in a given state) in a given year. We focused on denominational magazines, those that proclaimed a doctrinal and/or organizational affiliation with a particular denomination. For magazines that were available in archives, we coded denominational affiliation on the basis of contents and editorial statements; for magazines that were not available in archives, we relied on magazine titles, industry histories (e.g., Mott 1930), and bibliographies (e.g., Albaugh 1994). Our analysis excluded nondenominational and interdenominational publications, leaving 832 denominational magazines.

Independent variables. We constructed measures of local religious market structure and denominations' shares of those markets from state-level counts of congregations as described in appendix 1. To capture local competition we measured *local pluralism* in each state for each year using the Simpson index (described above), which is complement of the Herfindahl index of market concentration. To capture each denomination's local market position we measured its *local market share* in each state for each year based on the number of congregations. To capture a denomination's position in the national market we calculated its *national market share* across all states. We measured each denomination's *spatial scale* as the number of states in which it had congregations.

We measured the degree of *contact in multiple local markets* by counting the number of markets outside the focal market in which the focal denomination meets a local rival, summed across all local rivals. We scaled this count by the number of markets in which the focal denomination operates to yield a proportion. This proportion ranges from 0, when a denomination has no contact with local rivals in any of its other markets, to 1, when a denomination meets all local rivals in all of its other markets. This measure is identical to a measure used in previous research on for-profit organizations competing in multiple geographic markets (Haveman and Nonnemaker 2000). Finally, we counted the cumulative number of *schisms* in each denomination based on standard historical reference works (Mead 1985; Williams 1998; Melton 2003). We lagged this measure by two years to capture the effects of subgroup mobilization before the schismatic event.

Control variables. In the state-level analysis we controlled for *denomination size* (number of congregations in the focal state in the focal year), *denominational growth rate* in the focal state (a five-year moving average), *state population* (in millions), the *percent state urban population* (places with over 2,500 inhabitants), a national-level control for *immigration*, and an index of *industrial production*. Finally, we included several time-varying controls related to the overall growth of literacy and infrastructure: *miles of postal roads* (in the focal state) and the *magazine postage rate* (in cents); *maximum printing speed* (in sheets per hour); and the number of *colleges* in the United States. In the national-level analyses we included the same time-varying controls, with all variables calculated for the country as a whole.

Model Specification and Estimation

State-level analyses. Our dependent variable was the number of religious magazines affiliated with each denomination in each state for each year. Because this variable is overdispersed, we estimated negative-binomial models. Because our dependent variable is the number of magazines *published*, not the number *founded*, we modeled a growth process: change over time in the number of denominational magazines in each state. Since past size affects future size we included the lagged dependent variable in our models (Heckman and Borjas 1980).

Because each denomination could have congregations in multiple states, and each state could be home to multiple denominations, we were dealing with cross-classified data rather than hierarchically clustered data (Goldstein 1987; Rabe-Hesketh and Skrondal 2008: 472–508). To accommodate this data structure we estimated mixed-effects models with crossed random effects for denomination and state. The first effect captured unobserved factors that might affect each denomination's propensity to publish magazines; the second captured unobserved factors that might affect magazine publishing in each location. The models we estimated took the form—

330 | Appendix 2

$$\lambda_{ist} = \exp[\alpha y_{ist-1} + \boldsymbol{\beta}' \boldsymbol{x}_{ist-1} + \zeta_i + \zeta_s], \sigma^2[y_{ist}] = \lambda_{ist}\tau$$

—where λ_{ist} is the fundamental parameter of the negative binomial distribution, y_{ist-1} is the lagged dependent variable, x_{ist-1} is a vector of lagged explanatory and control variables, ζ_i is the random effect for denomination i, ζ_s is the random effect for state s, and τ is the scale parameter. We estimated these models using the *glmmADMB* package in R (Bolker et al. 2012). Because these models included the lagged dependent variable, the estimated coefficients on other variables can be interpreted as dynamic effects—that is, the estimated effect of a change in one variable (e.g., local market share) on an increase or decrease in the number of denominational magazines published between that year and the prior year.

National-level analyses. Again we modeled a growth process, but because we aggregated data across many states, the average number of magazines published was 5.4 and the range was 0 to 44. Accordingly, we estimated fixed-effects linear models of the form—

$$y_{it} = \alpha y_{it-1} + \boldsymbol{\beta}' \boldsymbol{x}_{it-1} + \gamma_i + \varepsilon_{it}$$

where y_{it} is the dependent variable (the number of magazines published by denomination i across all states at time t), y_{it-1} is the lagged dependent variable, x_{it-1} is a vector of lagged explanatory and control variables, γ_i is the denomination-specific fixed effect, and ε_{it} is the error term. Again, because these models included the lagged dependent variable, the estimated coefficients on other variables can be interpreted as dynamic effects.

Because the lagged dependent variable is correlated with denomination-specific fixed effects, ordinary least squares estimates can be biased (Nickell 1981). To circumvent this problem we estimated fixed-effects instrumental-variable models via two-stage least squares, using the *xtivreg2* routine in Stata (Schaffer 2007). This estimation strategy is well suited to the structure of our data (max $t = 70, n = 22$). We followed the standard practice of instrumenting y_{it-1} with y_{it-2} since the latter was highly correlated with the former but not with the time-demeaned idiosyncratic error. We corrected for heteroskedasticity and for serial autocorrelation and estimated robust standard errors.

Results

State-level analyses. Table A2.7 presents descriptive statistics on all variables in the state-level analyses, while table A2.8 shows the results of the negative-binomial regressions. Model 1 in table A2.8 contains only control variables, while model 2 adds the main effects of all explanatory variables. Local pluralism had a significant positive effect on the number of denominational magazines published, which is consistent with religious-economies theory. There is a significant positive effect of local market share, as expected.

TABLE A2.7.
Descriptive Statistics for Variables Used in the State-Level Analyses of Religious Magazines

Variable number	1	2	3	4	5	6	7	8	9	10	11	12	13
Mean	0.43	88.1	0.173	0.756	0.121	62.7	136	103	4.84	10.1	0.742	0.099	0.739
Standard Deviation	1.15	172	0.477	0.666	0.124	54.1	103	66	3.99	31	0.098	0.14	0.131
Minimum	0	1	-0.667	0.047	0	4.82	4.28	22	0	2	0.237	0	0
Maximum	13	2341	24	3.88	0.633	159	281	258	20.4	300	0.871	0.868	1
1 Number of denominational magazines in the state													
2 Denomination size (number of congregations in state)	0.55												
3 Denomination growth rate in state	-0.039	-0.053											
4 State population/1,000,000	0.448	0.301	-0.046										
5 Percent state urban population	0.261	0.017	-0.082	0.243									
6 Index of industrial production (national)	0.148	0.156	0.04	0.316	0.332								
7 Immigration/1,000 (national)	0.157	0.147	0.045	0.284	0.266	0.721							
8 Number of colleges (national)	0.149	.160	0.038	0.316	0.33	0.972	0.703						
9 Miles of postal roads in the state/1,000	0.31	0.294	0.037	0.828	-0.031	0.426	0.405	0.433					
10 Magazine postage rate (cents)	-0.04	-0.033	-0.01	-0.063	-0.064	-0.195	-0.182	-0.188	-0.097				
11 Local pluralism (1 minus Herfindahl index)	0.169	0.004	-0.091	0.301	0.378	0.098	0.065	0.095	0.145	0			
12 Local market share	0.169	0.594	0.006	-0.159	-0.116	-0.095	-0.087	-0.09	-0.124	0.017	-0.254		
13 Contact with rivals in multiple locations	-0.24	-0.264	0.045	-0.273	-0.116	0.241	0.178	0.223	-0.146	-0.043	-0.373	-0.135	

Note: This table is based on 14,389 state-year observations on 22 American denominations in 33 states between 1790 and 1860.

TABLE A2.8.

Mixed-Effects Negative-Binomial Models (with Crossed Unit Effects) of the Number of Magazines Published by Each Denomination in Each State in Each Year

	(1)	(2)	(3)
Lagged number of denominational magazines in the state	0.578*** (0.018)	0.508*** (0.017)	0.494*** (0.017)
Denomination size (number of congregations in the state/1,000)	0.288* (0.102)	-1.33*** (0.113)	-1.48*** (0.117)
Denominational growth rate in the state	-0.098 (0.055)	-0.065 (0.053)	-0.056 (0.052)
State population/1,000,000	-0.387*** (0.078)	-0.191* (0.076)	-0.175* (0.076)
Percent state urban population	-0.485 (0.538)	-1.74** (0.539)	-0.136* (0.541)
Index of industrial production (constant $1860/100)	-0.406* (0.186)	-0.297 (0.178)	-0.309 (0.177)
Immigration (national)	1.43*** (0.272)	1.84*** (0.264)	1.79*** (0.263)
Magazine postage rate (cents/100)	-0.065 (0.082)	-0.075 (0.082)	-0.074 (0.082)
Number of colleges (national)	0.005*** (0.001)	0.006*** (0.001)	0.006*** (0.001)
Maximum printing speed/100,000 (national)	0.077 (0.731)	0.167 (0.692)	0.126 (0.69)
Miles of postal roads in state/1,000	0.111*** (0.013)	0.112*** (0.013)	0.117*** (0.013)
Local pluralism (complement of the Herfindahl index)		2.84*** (0.445)	1.39** (0.533)
Local market share		3.92*** (0.208)	0.598 (0.756)
Contact among denominations in multiple local markets		-1.02** (0.327)	-0.924** (0.327)
Local pluralism × local market share			5.35*** (1.16)
Constant	-3.47*** (0.251)	-5.34*** (0.516)	-4.42*** (0.545)
Standard deviation of the latent denomination-specific parameter	0.571	0.464	0.465
Standard deviation of the latent state-specific parameter	1.11	1.19	1.19
Log likelihood	-7,510.	-7,336.	-7,325.
Number of observations	13,990	13,975	13,975

Note: This table presents the results of multilevel mixed-effects negative-binomial regressions of the number of magazines published by a denomination in each state and year for 22 American denominations from 1790 to 1860. These models include crossed latent effects for state and denomination. Standard errors are in parentheses below parameter estimates; $* p < .05$, $** p < .01$ and $*** p < .001$; two-tailed tests.

Denominations were more likely to publish where their share of the local market was increasing; thus, mobilization occurred when and where denominations possessed growing concentrations of resources. As denominations met local rivals in more local markets, they published fewer denominational magazines locally, as predicted. This suggests that as competitive interactions became more geographically dispersed, denominations consolidated their publishing efforts.

Model 3 adds an interaction between local pluralism and local market share. The interaction term was positive, as expected, which indicates that the effect of increasing local pluralism was stronger when and where denominations had growing concentrations of resources to support mobilization. The contingent effect of local pluralism can be seen by comparing predicted counts. When local market share is low (2 percent), increasing local pluralism from one standard deviation below the mean to one standard deviation above the mean yields a 35 percent increase in the expected number of magazines published, holding all other variables and the random effects at their means. When local market share is high (30 percent), the same-magnitude increase in local pluralism yields a 91 percent increase in the expected number of magazines published. Thus, a denomination's capacity to mobilize in more pluralistic environments depended on it possessing a large local market share. In contrast, increasing a denomination's local market share had a big impact on local magazine publishing, even at low levels of pluralism. When pluralism was one standard deviation below the mean (0.644), increasing a denomination's local market share from 2 percent to 30 percent (approximately two standard deviations) yields a 230 percent increase in the expected number of magazines published, holding all other variables and the random effects at their means.

National-level analyses. Table A2.9 presents descriptive statistics on all variables in the national-level analyses, while table A2.10 shows the results of this analysis. Model 1 in table A2.10 includes only the control variables; model 2 adds all explanatory variables. National market share had a significant negative effect, as expected. This finding suggests that weakening national competitive positions mobilized denominations to publish more magazines. The effect of spatial scale (number of states where the denomination had congregations) was positive and significant. This supports the claim that denominational magazines grew in response to the challenges of organizing the faithful across space. The effect of spatial scale is independent of the effect of denominational size (number of congregations), which suggests that that the former variable taps into geographic expansion in particular, not overall denominational growth. Finally, increasing internal denominational differentiation, as measured by the cumulative number of schisms, had a significant positive effect on the number of denominational magazines. This suggests that denominations experiencing more internal discord published more magazines, as both established and splinter groups sought to distinguish themselves and mobilize supporters.

TABLE A2.9.

Descriptive Statistics for Variables Used in The National-Level Analyses of Religious Magazines

Variable number	1	2	3	4	5	6	7	8	9	10	11	12
Mean	4.97	10.1	0.045	45.9	0.066	1.08	0.229	1.14	82.4	0.052	13.3	0.381
Standard deviation	7.95	23	0.104	50.2	0.076	0.728	0.551	1.01	63.2	0.081	9.09	0.786
Minimum	0	0.015	−0.286	4.17	0.002	0.038	0.02	0.096	16	0	2	0
Maximum	44	192	2	158	0.2	0.251	3	2.82	258	0.375	35	4
1 Number of denominational magazines												
2 Denomination size (number of congregations)	0.83											
3 Denominational growth rate	−0.024	−0.028										
4 Index of industrial production	0.466	0.268	−0.003									
5 Maximum printing speed (pages/hour)	0.46	0.267	−0.016	0.98								
6 Postage rate for magazines ($)	0.496	0.273	−0.006	0.934	0.919							
7 Postal roads (millions of miles)	−0.163	−0.079	0.004	−0.252	−0.236	−0.329						
8 Immigration	0.453	0.246	0.008	0.802	0.824	0.853	−0.29					
9 Number of colleges	0.47	0.27	−0.01	0.973	0.94	0.961	−0.269	0.788				
10 National market share	0.567	0.796	−0.038	−0.052	−0.05	−0.06	0.026	−0.056	−0.055			
11 Spatial scale (number of states)	0.77	0.648	−0.023	0.371	0.374	0.371	−0.104	0.361	0.361	0.627		
12 Internal fragmentation (cumulative schisms)	0.654	0.604	−0.059	0.315	0.316	−0.12	0.356	0.35	0.327	0.408	0.452	

Note: This table is based on 1,314 annual observations of 22 American religious denominations between 1790 and 1860.

TABLE A2.10.
Two-Stage Least Squares Fixed-Effects Instrumental-Variable Models of the
Number of Magazines Published by Each Denomination Each Year

	(1)	(2)
Lagged number of denominational magazines (instrumented)	.925*** (0.012)	.866*** (0.018)
Denomination size (number of congregations/100)	.024*** (0.004)	.038*** (0.006)
Denominational growth rate	0.216 (0.225)	0.21 (0.231)
Index of industrial production (constant $1860/1,000)	−0.345 (0.487)	−1.10* (0.491)
Maximum printing speed (number of pages per hour/100,000)	1.52 (2.14)	3.98 (2.18)
Post roads/100,000	.594** (0.189)	.504* (0.227)
Magazine postage rate ($/100)	−2.06 (5.93)	−4.28 (6.01)
Immigration/1,000,000	0.41 (0.597)	−0.417 (0.683)
Number of colleges/100	−0.275 (0.303)	−0.159 (0.367)
National market share		−4.90** (1.63)
Spatial scale (number of states)		.068*** (0.014)
Internal fragmentation (cumulative schisms)		.254** (0.091)
Number of Observations	1,346	1,314

Note: This table presents regressions of the number of magazines published by a denomination across the nation in each year for 22 American denominations from 1790 to 1860. Both models are corrected for serial autocorrelation and heteroskedasticity. Standard errors are in parentheses below parameter estimates; * $p < .05$, ** $p < .01$ and *** $p < .001$; two-tailed tests.

CHAPTER 6: SOCIAL REFORM

Social Reform Topics in the American Periodical Series Online

To find out the prevalence of social reform topics in all magazine genres—general-interest magazines, specialized reform magazines, and other specialized genres, I used the American Periodical Series Online, restricting searches to issues published between 1741 and 1860. Table A2.11 shows the keywords used for these searches.

336 | Appendix 2

Table A2.11.
Keyword Searches for Social Reform Topics in the American Periodical Series Online

	Key Words	Total
Major Movements		
Antislavery	abolition OR slavery OR manumi* OR emancip*	103,467
African colonization	colonization	15,185
Temperance	temperance OR abstinence OR drunken	57,111
Missions	"domestic mission" OR "foreign mission"	37,356
Peace	"peace movement"	22,978
Sabbatarianism	"Sunday mail"	7,337
Humanitarian Movements		
Fallen women	"fallen women" OR prostitut*	37,168
The blind	blind AND assist*	13,377
Widows	widow AND assist*	13,356
Orphans	orphan AND assist*	7,701
The deaf and dumb	(deaf OR dumb) AND assist*	7,566
Debtors	(debtor OR pauper) AND assist*	4,805
The insane	insane AND assist*	3,301
Seamen	reform AND (sailor OR seamen)	2,345
Other, smaller movements		
Anti–capital punishment	"capital punishment"	10,942
Antigambling	gambling	8,630
Indian removal	"Indian removal"	7,148
Prison reform	"prison reform"	5,743
Antidueling	duelling OR dueling	3,911
Women's rights (education)	"female education"	2,480
Women's rights (dress reform)	"dress reform" OR bloomer	1,042
Women's rights (suffrage)	"women's rights" OR "female suffrage"	266
Anti-Masonry	anti-mason*	1,063
Anti–novel reading	"novel reading"	850
Workingmen's rights	(rights OR class) AND workingm* OR "labor reform"	608
Free love	"free love"	330
Vegetarianism	vegetarian*	321
Spelling reform	reform AND (phonetic OR fonetic)	294
Anti-cockfighting	cockfighting	62
Anti-bearbaiting/bullbaiting	bearbaiting OR bullbaiting	13

The Reciprocal Influence of Magazines and Reform Movements

I investigated relationships among churches, magazines, and antislavery organizations in conjunction with Marissa King.

Sample and unit of analysis. We analyzed the number of antislavery societies founded in each state in each calendar year. The time frame for this analysis spans the rise of the modern antislavery movement; it ends just as the movement began to splinter in 1840. The choice of time frame is driven by historical considerations and by limitations on data availability and reliability: almost no antislavery societies were founded before 1790 and data on some explanatory factors are impossible to obtain before that date, while accurate data on antislavery societies becomes increasingly difficult to find after 1840 because the movement fractured into competing camps.

As with the study of religious magazines, the state is the unit of analysis because it allows us to control for state-specific factors that may influence antislavery society foundings, such as the size of the slave population and the extent of slave-intensive cotton culture. Our analysis includes all twenty-six states that achieved statehood before 1840: Alabama, Arkansas, Connecticut, Delaware, Georgia, Illinois, Indiana, Kentucky, Louisiana, Maine, Maryland, Massachusetts, Michigan, Mississippi, Missouri, New Hampshire, New Jersey, New York, North Carolina, Ohio, Pennsylvania, Rhode Island, South Carolina, Tennessee, Virginia, and Vermont. The original thirteen colonies were included in the data set from 1790 to 1840. Newer states were included from the year they achieved statehood to 1840. The analysis includes virtually all foundings of antislavery societies except eight associations founded before 1790.

Modeling strategy: event-count methods. The dependent variable is a count, which we modeled using event-count methods (Cameron and Trivedi 1986). Because our data show substantial overdispersion, we estimated negative-binomial models (Cameron and Trivedi 1990) using the *xtnbreg* procedure in Stata, which corrects overdispersion by rescaling standard errors and recalculating goodness-of-fit statistics. To account for nonindependence among observations on each state we estimated models with standard errors clustered on states. To mitigate problems arising from unobserved heterogeneity not captured by our explanatory or control variables we estimated random effects.

Clarifying causality: the instrumental-variable technique. To establish that the press was a cause and not a correlate or consequence of the organized antislavery movement, we used the instrumental-variable (IV) technique, which separates the endogenous and exogenous components of the press (Angrist and Krueger 2001; Bound, Jaeger, and Baker 1995; Greene 2003: 378–401). We began by estimating a first-stage regression to predict the endogenous variable—

$$W_{st} = \alpha + \beta'X_{st} + \gamma Z_{st} + \varepsilon$$

—where W_{st} is the endogenous variable (here, magazines) in state s at time t, X_{st} is a vector comprising measures of this-worldly and otherworldly churches and all control variables in state s at time t, and Z_{st} is the value of the instrument for state s at time t. This first-stage regression purges the endogenous components, producing an exogenous variable—the predicted value of the endogenous variable ($\hat{W}$). We used this new exogenous variable in a second-stage analysis to predict the outcome of interest—

$$Y_{st} = \alpha + \beta'X_{s,t-1} + \delta \, \hat{W}_{s,t-1} + \varepsilon$$

—where Y_{st} is the number of antislavery societies founded in state s at time t and all other variables are defined above. The instrument is the number of post offices in each state. This is a good choice because the number of post offices is partially correlated with the endogenous variable, it acts only through the endogenous variable (not directly), and it is truly exogenous and uncorrelated with the error term. (For more details, see King and Haveman 2008.)

One remaining problem: event-count models are incompatible with the IV technique. Recall that our dependent variable is a count, so event-count methods are most appropriate (Cameron and Trivedi 1986). But event-count models are multiplicative, so they violate a core assumption of IV estimation—namely, that unobservables be additively separable from the parametric model (Mullahy 1997). The trick, then, is to turn a multiplicative model into an additive one. One way to do this is to log the count variable (after adding 1 to make it possible to generate a real value for 0 counts) and estimate the logged variable using an additive model (Mullahy 1997; Santos Silva and Tenreyro 2006). Accordingly, we estimated two-stage feasible generalized least squares models of the logged number of antislavery societies founded (and a first-stage model of the number of magazines published) using the *xtivreg* procedure in Stata. We dropped one control variable, the number of antislavery societies, because it is a close derivative of the dependent variable and including lagged values of the dependent variable and its close derivatives complicates the estimation using the IV technique (Angrist and Krueger 2001).

Control variables. Our analyses control for several factors that might influence both the antislavery movement and the magazine industry—specifically, the free and slave populations, urbanization, economic development in each state, and the formation of the American Anti-Slavery Society (AASS). The only state-level indicator of economic growth available for the antebellum era is the value of foreign exports. To control for the catalyzing power of the AASS we created a binary indicator variable equaling 0 from 1790 to 1831 (before the AASS was founded) and 1 from 1832 onward. Note that this indicator varies only over time; it is constant across states. Finally, we controlled for demographic processes among antislavery societies (Hannan and Freeman 1989) by including both a linear and a squared term for the number of antislavery societies operating to capture both legitimating and competitive effects.

Negative-Binomial Regression Analysis of Antislavery Society Foundings, 1790–1840

	1	2	3	4
Constant	-3.80***	-1.29***	-3.86***	-3.79***
	(0.219)	(0.298)	(0.221)	(0.230)
Free population/1,000	0.237**	0.137	0.239***	0.134***
	(0.055)	(0.107)	(0.058)	(0.041)
Number of slaves/1,000	0.461**	0.069	0.398**	0.026
	(0.154)	(0.177)	(0.154)	(0.145)
Percent urban population	0.038**	-0.003	0.016	0.001
	(0.012)	(0.020)	(0.014)	(0.011)
Exports ($1,000,000, 1840)	-0.146***	-0.084***	-0.136***	-0.156***
	(0.043)	(0.010)	(0.004)	(0.003)
AASS dummy (= 1, 1832+)	1.21***	1.73***	0.768***	1.68***
	(0.214)	(0.239)	(0.224)	(0.194)
Number of antislavery societies	0.028***	0.021***	0.020***	0.019***
	(0.005)	(0.004)	(0.004)	(0.004)
Number of antislavery societies^2/1,000	-0.009***	-0.007***	-0.007***	-0.007***
	(0.017)	(0.002)	(0.001)	(0.001)
Number of this-worldly churches/1,000	0.614	1.06	0.521	1.40
	(1.12)	(2.21)	(1.16)	(1.09)
Number of otherworldly churches/1,000	-2.71***	-2.31**	-2.18***	-2.00***
	(0.567)	(0.731)	(0.628)	(0.481)
Number of magazines		0.028**		0.014
		(0.010)		(0.009)
Number of social reform magazines			0.314***	0.200***
			(0.046)	(0.052)
χ^2	209.2	476.71	322.1	586.1

Note: These random-effects models were estimated on 989 annual observations of 1,534 foundings of antislavery societies in 26 states between 1790 and 1840, inclusive. The dependent variable is the number of antislavery societies founded. Standard errors, which are shown in parentheses below parameter estimates, are clustered within states. $^\dagger p < .10$, $^* p < .05$, $^{**} p < .01$, and $^{***} p < .001$; two-tailed tests. All explanatory variables were lagged by one year to ensure temporal priority.

Results: event-count models. Table A2.12 presents the baseline analysis of antislavery society foundings. As predicted, model 1 shows a positive effect of the number of this-worldly churches and a negative effect of the number of otherworldly churches. But only the coefficient on otherworldly churches reached statistical significance. Model 2 adds the number of magazines published in the focal state. The effect of magazines is positive and statistically significant. Both coefficients on churches remain roughly the same in size and significance level, which indicates that they had a direct influence on antislavery society foundings. In other words, their effects were not mediated by magazines. Model 3 shows that social reform magazines have a similar positive effect. Model 4 suggests that the effect of magazines in general is due primarily to social reform magazines: when both magazine counts are included in the model, only the number of social reform magazines has a statistically significant effect. In other words, social reform magazines mediated the effect of other kinds of magazines.

In preparation for the IV analysis we reestimated the models shown in table A2.12 without the counts of antislavery societies in order to avoid complications that develop when using the IV technique to estimate models containing derivatives of the dependent variable (Angrist and Krueger 2001). The coefficients on the remaining variables did not change materially.

Applying the IV technique. Table A2.13 shows more elaborate investigations of the complex causal relationships among the development of the magazine industry, the expansion of organized religion, and the founding of antislavery societies. This table is divided into two parts. Models 1 and 2 analyze the effect of all kinds of magazines; models 3 and 4 analyze the effect of magazines devoted to social reform causes. Models 1 and 3 use simple generalized least squares (GLS) techniques; models 2 and 4 use GLS and the instrumental variable (GLS-IV) to deal with the endogeneity of magazines. For all models, the dependent variable is the logged number of antislavery societies founded; this transformation turns the count into a continuous variable. We added 1 to all values before taking the log. Thus, when no antislavery society was founded in the focal state in the focal year, we could still calculate a value for the log transformation.

Comparing the results in tables A2.12 and A2.13 shows consistency across estimation methods: the parameter estimates on the four variables of central interest are always in the expected direction and, with the exception of this-worldly churches, at least marginally significant. This increases confidence in the simple GLS models. Jerry Hausman's (1978) specification tests reveal significant differences between the coefficients in the GLS and GLS-IV models (models 1 versus 2, $\chi^2 = 244.5$, $df = 8$, $p < .001$; models 3 versus 4, $\chi^2 = 151.7$, $df = 8$, $p < .001$), which indicates that the GLS estimators were inconsistent. The effects of the press are about the same magnitude in the GLS-IV models as in the GLS models, but the effects of the pulpit are consistently larger. In the GLS-IV models, the effects of this-worldly churches are also at least marginally significant. Taken together the Hausman specification tests and the increased magnitudes and significance levels demonstrate that much of the effects of churches are obscured when the endogeneity of the press is not taken into account.

Let's now compare the effects of the variables of central interest after partialing out with the endogenous component of magazines. This-worldly churches had the expected positive effects in both GLS-IV models. In contrast, otherworldly churches had the expected negative effects in both GLS-IV models. In the GLS-IV models the effects of magazines, whether we consider all magazines or only specialized reform magazines, remained positive and statistically significant.

TABLE A2.13.
Further Analysis of Antislavery Society Foundings,
1790–1840: Eliminating Endogeneity

Number	1	2	3	4
Estimation method	GLS	GLS—IV	GLS	GLS—IV
Version of magazines used	Magazines	Magazines predicted using IV	Reform magazines	Reform magazines predicted using IV
Constant	0.037	−0.006	0.002	−0.003
	(0.026)	(0.147)	(0.023)	(0.225)
Free population/1,000	0.015	−0.017	0.010	0.003
	(0.011)	(0.024)	(0.011)	(0.029)
Number of slaves/1,000	0.002	0.022	−0.012	0.004
	(0.019)	(0.075)	(0.017)	(0.084)
Percent urban population	0.002	−0.007	0.004**	−0.004
	(0.002)	(0.008)	(0.002)	(0.009)
Exports ($1,000,000, 1840)	−0.026***	−0.034***	−0.023***	−0.043***
	(0.005)	(0.009)	(0.004)	(0.011)
AASS dummy (=1, 1832+)	0.340***	0.760***	0.290***	0.714***
	(0.039)	(0.064)	(0.037)	(0.064)
Number of magazines	0.021***	0.021**	0.249***	0.309*
	(0.003)	(0.007)	(0.026)	(0.121)
Number of this-worldly churches/1,000	0.207	2.09**	0.723***	1.79†
	(0.216)	(0.765)	(0.189)	(1.08)
Number of otherworldly churches/1,000	−0.300**	−0.978***	−0.173†	−0.801***
	(0.106)	(0.225)	(0.101)	(0.224)
χ^2	404.6	607.1	429.7	613

Note: These models were estimated on 989 annual observations of 1,534 foundings of antislavery societies in 26 states between 1790 and 1840, inclusive. The dependent variable is the natural logarithm of the number of antislavery societies founded (plus 1). All models include random effects and correct for heteroskedasticity. Standard errors, which are shown in parentheses below parameter estimates, are clustered within states; † $p < .10$, * $p < .05$, ** $p < .01$, and *** $p < .001$; two-tailed tests. All explanatory variables were lagged by one year to ensure temporal priority.

Robustness checks. We assessed the robustness of these results in two ways. First, we dropped from our analysis the four landlocked states for which we could find no data on foreign exports: Arkansas, Kentucky, Missouri, and Tennessee. The results are identical to the ones reported here, with one exception: in the GLS-IV model corresponding to model 4 of table A2.13, the coefficient on social reform magazines was nonsignificant. Second, we conducted more detailed analyses of the impact of particular religious institutions. We could obtain only rough estimates of the number of congregations for many denominations. To improve the quality of the data we reestimated all models substituting counts of congregations in the largest this-worldly and otherworldly denominations for which we could gather good data: this-worldly Congregationalist churches, and otherworldly Baptist and Methodist churches. The results of this alternative analysis are very similar to the results shown here: Congregational churches had positive and generally statistically significant effects, while Baptist and Methodist churches had negative effects. In the GLS models the effects of Baptist churches were statistically significant but the effects of Methodist churches were nonsignificant. In the GLS-IV models, however, the effects of both Baptist and Methodist churches were negative and statistically significant. These results reinforce confidence in the results shown in table A2.13.

References

Abbott, Ephraim. 1849. Introductory. *Valley Farmer* 1(1): 1. http://search.proquest.com /americanperiodicals/docview/125742543/B3A72C4B2C34EF4PQ/3?accountid =14496, retrieved 13 June 2007.

Abbott, Ephraim. 1852. To the reader. *Valley Farmer* 4(1): 1–2. http://search.proquest .com/americanperiodicals/docview/125738395/3F94D8B0C13944DDPQ/2 ?accountid=14496, retrieved 13 June 2013.

Abbott, Richard H. 1968. The agricultural press views the yeoman: 1819–1859. *Agricultural History* 42(1): 35–48.

Abolition Intelligencer and Missionary Magazine. 1822. The apologist. *Abolition Intelligencer and Missionary Magazine* 1(1): 4–8. http://search.proquest.com/american periodicals/docview/88914624/2FA7161260C4D30PQ/3?accountid=14496, retrieved 30 March 2010.

Abrams, Howard B. 1983. The historic foundation of American copyright law: Exploding the myth of common law copyright. *Wayne Law Review* 29(3): 1119–91.

Abrams, Meyer Howard. 1953. *The Mirror and the Lamp*. New York: Oxford University Press.

Abzug, Robert H. 1994. *Cosmos Crumbling: American Reform and the Religious Imagination*. New York: Oxford University Press.

Adams, Alice Dana. 1908. *The Neglected Period of Antislavery in America, 1808–1831*. Boston: Ginn.

Adams, Donald R. 1968. Wage rates in the early national period: Philadelphia, 1785–1830. *Journal of Economic History* 28: 404–26.

Adams, Henry. 1921. *History of the United States*, vol. 9. New York: Charles Scribner's Sons.

Adams, Robert, Jr. 1894. Speech given June 5. *Congressional Record: The Proceedings and Debates*: 5790–5792. 53rd Congress, 3rd session. Washington DC: Government Printing Office.

Addison, Joseph. 1709. [No title.] *Tatler* 101, 1 December. http://quod.lib.umich.edu /cgi/t/text/text-idx?c=ecco;idno=004786805.0001.000, retrieved 25 July 2013.

Addison, Joseph. 1711. Genius. *Spectator* 160, 3 September 1711. http://www.gutenberg .org/files/12030/12030-h/SV1/Spectator1.html#section160, retrieved 24 July 2013.

Advocate of Peace. 1838. Tenth Annual Report of the American Peace Society. *Advocate of Peace* 2(5): 3–16. http://search.proquest.com/americanperiodicals/docview/12691 8168/D4978A05DD484D7CPQ/5?accountid=14496, retrieved 7 October 2010.

A.E. 1845. Friend Evans. *Young America* 2(22): 1. http://search.proquest.com/american periodicals/docview/126929052/114CD1E7EABB4E41PQ/9?accountid=14496, retrieved 12 August 2014.

A Female. 1845. To the editor. *Young America* 2(40): 4. http://search.proquest.com/amer

icanperiodicals/docview/126925866/114CD1E7EABB4E41PQ/31?accountid =14496, retrieved 12 August 2014.

Agricola [pseud., George W. Jeffreys]. 1819. *A Series of Essays on Agriculture and Rural Affairs*. Raleigh, NC: Gales.

Ahlstrom, Sydney E. 1972. *A Religious History of the American People*. New Haven, CT: Yale University Press.

Akaike, Hirotugu. 1974. A new look at the statistical model identification. *IEEE Transactions on Automatic Control* 19(6): 716–723.

A.K.K. 1845. To the editor. *Young America* 2(40): 4. http://search.proquest.com/american periodicals/docview/126926218/114CD1E7EABB4E41PQ/30?accountid=14496, retrieved 12 August 2014.

Albaugh, Gaylord P. 1994. *History and Annotated Bibliography of American Religious Periodicals and Newspapers Established from 1730 through 1830*. Worcester, MA: American Antiquarian Society.

Aldrich, Howard E., and Marlene Fiol. 1994. Fools rush in? The institutional context of industry creation. *Academy of Management Review* 19: 645–70.

Aldrich, Howard E., and Gabriele Wiedenmayer. 1993. From traits to rates: An ecological perspective on organizational foundings. In Jerome A. Katz and Robert H. Brockhaus Sr., eds., *Advances in Entrepreneurship: Firm Emergence and Growth*, 145–95. Greenwich, CT: JAI.

Allen, A. B., and Richard L. Allen. 1842. To our readers. *American Agriculturist* 1(1): 1–3. http://search.proquest.com/americanperiodicals/docview/89624403/pageviewPDF /25EE3273FB614F9APQ/4?accountid=14496, retrieved 29 August 2006.

Allen, Frederick Lewis, William L. Cheney, and Fulton Oursler. 1941. American magazines, 1741–1941. *Bulletin of the New York Public Library* 45: 439–56.

Allen, Joseph Henry, and Richard Eddy. 1894. *A History of the Unitarians and Universalists in the United States*. New York: Christian Literature.

American Antiquarian Society Online Catalog. http://catalog.mwa.org/webvoy.htm, retrieved January to June 2003.

American Anti-Slavery Society. 1834–40. *Annual Report of the American Anti-Slavery Society*. New York: American Anti-Slavery Society.

American Baptist Yearbook. 1874. Philadelphia: Bible and Publication Society.

American Convention for Promoting the Abolition of Slavery and Improving the Condition of the African Race. 1809. *Minutes of the Proceedings of the Twelfth American Convention for Promoting the Abolition of Slavery and Improving the Condition of the African Race*. Philadelphia: J. Bouvier.

American Convention for Promoting the Abolition of Slavery and Improving the Condition of the African Race. 1812. *Minutes of the Proceedings of the Thirteenth American Convention for Promoting the Abolition of Slavery and Improving the Condition of the African Race*. Philadelphia: Hamilton-Ville.

American Convention for Promoting the Abolition of Slavery and Improving the Condition of the African Race. 1816. *Minutes of the Proceedings of the Fourteenth American Convention for Promoting the Abolition of Slavery and Improving the Condition of the African Race*. Philadelphia: W. Brown.

American Convention for Promoting the Abolition of Slavery and Improving the Condition of the African Race. 1817. *Minutes of the Proceedings of the Fifteenth American Convention for Promoting the Abolition of Slavery and Improving the Condition of the African Race*. Philadelphia: Merritt.

American Convention for Promoting the Abolition of Slavery and Improving the

Condition of the African Race. 1819. *Minutes of the Proceedings of the Sixteenth American Convention for Promoting the Abolition of Slavery and Improving the Condition of the African Race.* Philadelphia: William Fry.

American Cotton Planter. 1853. American agriculture—What it is, and what it ought to be. *American Cotton Planter* 1(1): 175–76. http://books.google.com/books?id=YKIE AAAAYAAJandpg=PA319anddq=%22american+cotton+planter%22+1853andhl=e nandsa=Xandei=j4m1U-O_E4nDigK-iYCYAwandved=0CCoQ6AEwAA#v =onepageandq=%22american%20cotton%20planter%22%201853andf=false, retrieved 3 July 2014.

American Farmer. 1825. [No title.] *American Farmer* 7(21): 165. http://search.proquest .com/americanperiodicals/docview/90142438/78723CC5A0B04258PQ/79?accountid =14496, retrieved 1 August 2014.

American Farmer. 1839. Labour. *American Farmer* 1(5): 33. http://search.proquest.com /americanperiodicals/docview/90024852/pageviewPDF/EB5ED1AB54404B19PQ/6 ?accountid=14496, retrieved 24 April 2013.

American Farmer. 1860. A lady's letter. *American Farmer*, new series 1(7): 210. http:// search.proquest.com/americanperiodicals/docview/90068341/D34AA7C35BDB42 E9PQ/59?accountid=14496, retrieved 1 August 2014.

American National Biography Online. 2000. New York: Oxford University Press and American Council of Learned Societies. http://www.anb.org.arugula.cc.columbia. edu:2048/articles/index.html), retrieved June-October 2006.

American Quarterly Register. 1832. Ecclesiastical register. *American Quarterly Register* 4(3): 222–26. http://search.proquest.com/americanperiodicals/docview/124451742 /838C25E9B5E418BPQ/9?accountid=14496, retrieved 21 November 2007.

American Temperance Society. 1835. *Permanent Documents of the American Temperance Society.* New York: J. P. Haven.

Anderson, Benedict. (1983) 1991. *Imagined Communities: Reflections on the Origin and Spread of Nationalism.* Rev. ed. London: Verso.

Andrews, Kenneth T., and Michael Biggs. 2006. The dynamics of protest diffusion: Movement organizations, social networks, and news media in the 1960 sit-ins. *American Sociological Review* 71: 752–77.

Angrist, Joshua D., and Alan B. Krueger. 2001. Instrumental variables and the search for identification: From supply and demand to natural experiments. *Journal of Economic Perspectives* 15: 69–85.

Appleby, Joyce. 2010. *The Relentless Revolution: A History of Capitalism.* New York: W. W. Norton.

Appold, Stephen. 2005. Location patterns of US industrial research: Mimetic isomorphism and the emergence of geographic clusters. *Regional Studies* 39: 17–39.

Ariel. 1828. Miseries of authorship. *Ariel* 2(16): 124. http://search.proquest.com/amer icanperiodicals/docview/124472745/27AEE40EF0CE445BPQ/3?accountid=14496, retrieved 4 October 2008.

Armstrong Atlantic State University. 2006. *Subject Guide to Early American Periodicals.* http://www.library.armstrong.edu/subguideearlyperiodicals-APS.html, retrieved March 2006.)

Armstrong, U. K., and Marjorie Armstrong. 1979. *The Baptists in America.* Garden City, NY: Doubleday.

Ardrey, Robert L. 1894. *American Agricultural Improvements: A Review of Invention and Development in the Agricultural Implement Industry of the United States.* Chicago: Published by the author.

Arndt, Karl J. R., and Mary Olson. 1961. *German-American Newspapers and Periodicals, 1732–1955*. Deutsche Presseforschung, Bd 3. Heidelberg: Quelle und Meyer.

Art magazines. Online list. http://www.rlg.org/citadel/aaititle.html, retrieved April 2003.

Asbury, Francis. 1790. Preface. *Arminian Magazine* 2(1): iii–iv. http://search.proquest.com/americanperiodicals/docview/88497335/F553938485CC43C7PQ/11?accountid=14496, retrieved 13 May 2003.

Ashforth, Blake E., and Barrie W. Gibbs. 1990. The double-edge of organizational legitimation. *Organizational Science* 1: 177–94.

Ashton, Dianne. 2008. Expanding Jewish life in America, 1826–1901. In Marc Lee Raphael, ed., *Columbia History of Jews and Judaism in America*, 47–69. New York: Columbia University Press.

Asplund, John. 1792. *Annual Register of the Baptist Denomination in North America*. Richmond, VA: Dixon, Nicholson, and Davis.

Backes-Gellner, Uschi, and Arndt Werner. 2007. Entrepreneurial signaling via education: A success factor in innovative start-ups. *Small Business Economics* 29(1): 173–90.

Bagdikian, Ben H. (1983) 2004. *The Media Monopoly*. Rev. and updated ed. Boston: Beacon.

Bail, Christopher A. 2012. The fringe effect: Civil society organizations and the evolution of media discourse about Islam since the September 11th attacks. *American Sociological Review* 77(7): 855–79.

Bail, Christopher A. 2015. *Terrified: How Civil Society Organizations Shape Public Understandings of Islam*. Princeton, NJ: Princeton University Press.

Bailyn, Bernard. 1960. *Education in the Forming of American Society*. Chapel Hill: University of North Carolina Press.

Bainbridge, William Sims. 1997. *The Sociology of Religious Movements*. New York: Routledge.

Baker, C. Edwin. 2006. *Media Concentration and Democracy: Why Ownership Matters*. Cambridge: Cambridge University Press.

Baker-Batsel, John. 2001. *List of Serials Published by the Churches Related to the United Methodist Church*. http://s3.amazonaws.com/gcah.org/UMC_History/Bibliographies/MethList.pdf, retrieved 28 December 2014.

Baldwin, Simeon E. 1901. Private corporations, 1701–1901. In *Two Centuries Growth of American Law, 1701–1901*, 261–312. New York: Charles Scribner's Sons.

Baldwin, Thomas. 1817. To the friends and patrons. *American Baptist Magazine and Missionary Intelligencer*, new series, 1(1): 3. http://search.proquest.com/americanperiodicals/docview/880203221/96AD1D9C0AD34900PQ/3?accountid=14496, retrieved 30 March 2006.

Bardolph, Richard. 1948. A North Carolina farm journal of the middle 'fifties. *North Carolina Historical Review* 25(1): 57–89.

Barlow, Joel. 1783. Letter to Elias Boudenot, Esquire. Primary Sources on Copyright Law. http://copy.law.cam.ac.uk/cam/tools/request/showRepresentation?id=representation_us_1783bandpagenumber=1_1andshow=transcription, retrieved 15 August 2013.

Barlow, Joel, and Elisa Babcock. 1784. Prospectus of the *American Mercury*. http://www.readex.com/, retrieved 6 October 2006.

Barnes, Gilbert H. 1964. *The Antislavery Impulse, 1830–1844*. New York: Harcourt, Brace and World.

Barnes, James J. 1974. *Authors, Publishers and Politicians: The Quest for an Anglo-American Copyright Agreement, 1815–1854*. London: Routledge and Kegan Paul.

Barnett, William P., Mi Feng, and Xiaoqu Luo. 2013. Social identity, market memory, and first-mover advantage. *Industrial and Corporate Change* 22(3): 585–615.

Barnett, William P. and Michael Woywode. 2004. From Red Vienna to the Anschluss: Ideological competition among Viennese newspapers during the rise of national socialism. *American Journal of Sociology* 109: 1452–1500.

Barrett, George C. 1835. Prospectus. *Fessenden's Practical Farmer and Silk Manual* 1(1): 1. http://search.proquest.com/americanperiodicals/docview/125184933/39D733E4 92124FEFPQ/5?accountid=14496, retrieved 30 October 2006.

Basch, Norma. 1982. *In the Eyes of the Law: Women, Marriage, and Property in Nineteenth-Century New York*. Ithaca, NY: Cornell University Press.

Beach, L. 1798. To the Patrons. *The Hummingbird, or Herald of Taste* 1(1): 2–3. http://search.proquest.com/americanperiodicals/docview/88516941/90DD52FD1CEC40 30PQ/6?accountid=14496, retrieved 14 May 2003.

Beardsley, Frank Grenville. 1912. *A History of American Revivals*. 2nd ed. New York: American Tract Society.

Beecher, Lyman. 1803. *The Practicability of Suppressing Vice, by Means of Societies Instituted for That Purpose: A Sermon, Delivered before the Moral Society at East-Hampton (Long-Island)*. New London, CT: Samuel Green.

Beecher, Lyman. 1809. *The Remedy for Duelling: A Sermon, Delivered before the Presbytery of Long-Island, at the Opening of their Session at Aquebogue, April 16 1806, to Which is Annexed, the Resolutions and Address of the Anti-Duelling Association of New York*. New York: Williams and Whiting.

Beecher, Lyman. 1814. *An Address to the Charitable Society for the Education of Indigent Pious Young Men for the Ministry of the Gospel*. New Haven, CT: n.p.

Beecher, Lyman. 1827. *Six Sermons on the Nature, Occasions, Signs, Evils, and Remedy of Intemperance*. Boston: T. R. Marvin.

Beecher, Lyman. 1828. [No title.] *Spirit of the Pilgrims* 1(1): 1–20. http://search.proquest .com/americanperiodicals/docview/126197158/B4899FCDEB714E94PQ/1 ?accountid=14496, retrieved 5 September 2006.

Beer, William. 1922. Checklist of American periodicals, 1741–1899. *Proceedings of the American Antiquarian Society*. 32: 330–45.

Beers, Henry Augustus. 1885. *Nathaniel Parker Willis*. Boston: Houghton, Mifflin.

Beckwith, George C. 1837. Report of the Rev. George C. Beckwith's Agency in Behalf of the American Peace Society. *Advocate of Peace* 1(1): 31–36. http://search.proquest .com/americanperiodicals/docview/126918816/D4596CA841944856PQ/11 ?accountid=14496, retrieved 7 October 2010.

Bell, Daniel. 1976. *The Cultural Contradictions of Capitalism*. New York: Basic Books.

Bellah, Robert. 1968. Meaning and modernisation. *Religious Studies* 4(1): 37–45.

Bender, Thomas. 1978. *Community and Social Change in America*. New Brunswick, NJ: Rutgers University Press.

Bender, Thomas. 1986. Wholes and parts: The need for synthesis in American history. *Journal of American History* 73: 120–36.

Bender, Thomas. 1987. *New York Intellect: A History of Intellectual Life in New York City from 1750 to the Beginnings of Our Time*. Baltimore: Johns Hopkins University Press.

Bendix, Reinhard. 1956. *Work and Authority in Industry: Ideologies of Management in the Course of Industrialization*. Berkeley: University of California Press.

Benton, Thomas Hart. 1834. State of the currency. *Aurora* 1(32): 254–55. http://search

.proquest.com/americanperiodicals/docview/124538328/236B3C96FD804A17PQ /1?accountid=14496, retrieved 21 July 2014.

Bercovitch, Sacvan, ed. 1994a. *The Cambridge History of American Literature*, vol. 1: *1590–1820*. Cambridge: Cambridge University Press.

Bercovitch, Sacvan, ed. 1994b. *The Cambridge History of American Literature*, vol. 2: *1820–1865*. Cambridge: Cambridge University Press.

Berg, Barbara J. 1980. *The Remembered Gate: Origins of American Feminism, the Woman and the City, 1800–1860*. Oxford: Oxford University Press.

Berger, Peter L. 1986. *The Capitalist Revolution: Fifty Propositions about Prosperity, Equality, and Liberty*. New York: Basic Books.

Berger, Peter L., and Thomas Luckmann. 1967. *The Social Construction of Reality: A Treatise in the Sociology of Knowledge*. Garden City, NY: Doubleday.

Berk, Gerald, and Marc Schneiberg. 2005. Varieties *in* capitalism, varieties *of* association: Collaborative learning in American industry, 1900–1925. *Politics and Society* 33: 46–87.

Berle, Adolf A., and Gardner C. Means. 1932. *The Modern Corporation and Private Property*. New York: Macmillan.

Berry, William Turner, and Herbert Edmund Poole. 1966. *Annals of Printing: A Chronological Encyclopedia from the Earliest Times to 1950*. London: Blandford.

Beyerlein, Kraig, and John Hipp. 2006. From pews to participation: The effect of congregation activity and context on bridging civic engagement. *Social Problems* 53: 97–117.

Bijker, Wiebe E., Thomas P. Hughes, and Trevor Pinch, eds. 1987. *The Social Construction of Technological Systems: New Directions in the Sociology and History of Technology*. Cambridge, MA: MIT Press.

Billings, John S. 1879. The medical journals of the United States. *Boston Medical and Surgical Journal* 100: 1–14.

Billington, Ray Allen. (1938) 1963. *The Protestant Crusade, 1800–1860: A Study of the Origins of American Nativism*. Gloucester, MA: Peter Smith.

Bishop, Yvonne M. M., Stephen E. Fienberg, and Paul W. Holland. 1975. *Discrete Multivariate Analysis*. Cambridge, MA: MIT Press.

Blassingame, John W., Mae G. Henderson, and Jessica M. Dunn, eds. 1980–84. *Antislavery Newspapers and Periodicals*. 5 vols. Boston: G. K. Hall.

Blau, Peter M. 1977. *Inequality and Heterogeneity: A Primitive Theory of Social Structure*. New York: Free Press.

Blau, Peter M., and Joseph E. Schwartz. 1984. *Cross-Cutting Social Circles*. Orlando, FL: Academic Press.

Bledstein, Burton J. 1976. *The Culture of Professionalism: The Middle Class and the Development of Higher Education in America*. New York: W. W. Norton.

Blodget, Samuel, Jr. (1806) 1964. *Economica: A Statistical Manual for the US of A*. New York: A. M. Kelley.

Blum, Alan F., and Peter McHugh. 1936. The social ascription of motives. *American Sociological Review* 36(1): 98–109.

Blumin, Stuart M. 1973. Residential mobility within the nineteenth-century city. In Allen F. Davis and Mark H. Haller, eds., *The Peoples of Philadelphia: A History of Ethnic Groups and Lower-Class Life, 1790–1940*, 37–52. Philadelphia: Temple University Press.

Blumin, Stuart M. 1989. *The Emergence of the Middle Class: Social Experience in the American City, 1760–1900*. New York: Cambridge University Press.

Boczkowski, Pablo J. 2004. *Digitizing the News: Innovation in Online Newspapers*. Cambridge, MA: MIT Press.

Boczkowski, Pablo J., and Eugenia Mitchelstein. 2013. *The News Gap: When Information Preferences of the Media and the Public Diverge*. Cambridge, MA: MIT Press.

Boddewyn, J. 1967. The names of US industrial corporations: A study in change. *Names* 15: 39–52.

Bodenhorn, Howard. 2000. *A History of Banking in Antebellum America: Financial Markets and Economic Development in an Era of Nation-Building*. Cambridge: Cambridge University Press.

Bodenhorn, Howard. 2006. State banks—number, assets, and liabilities: 1834–1896. In Susan B. Carter, Scott Sigmund Gartner, Michael R. Haines, Alan L. Olmstead, Richard Sutch, and Gavin Wright, eds., *Historical Statistics of the United States, Millennial Edition On Line*, tables Cj149–57. New York: Cambridge University Press. http://dx.doi.org/10.1017/ISBN-9780511132971.Cj142–36110.1017/ISBN-9780511132971.Cj142–361, retrieved 8 July 2014.

Bodenhorn, Howard, and Eugene N. White. 2006. State banks—number, assets, and liabilities: 1782–1837. In Susan B. Carter, Scott Sigmund Gartner, Michael R. Haines, Alan L. Olmstead, Richard Sutch, and Gavin Wright, eds., *Historical Statistics of the United States, Millennial Edition On Line*, tables Cj142–48. http://dx.doi.org/10.1017/ISBN-9780511132971.Cj142–36110.1017/ISBN-9780511132971.Cj142–361, retrieved 8 July 2014.

Bogue, Allan G. 1963. *From Prairie to Corn Belt: Farming on the Illinois and Iowa Prairies in the Nineteenth Century*. Chicago: University of Chicago Press.

Bogue, Donald J. 1985. *Population of the United States: Historical Trends and Future Projections*. New York: Free Press.

Bolker, Ben, Hans Skaug, Arni Magnusson, and Anders Nielsen. 2012. Getting started with the glmmADMB package. http://glmmadmb.r-forge.r-project.org/glmmADMB.pdf, retrieved 12 March 2013.

Bolt, Christine, and Seymour Drescher. 1980. *Anti-Slavery: Religion and Reform*. Kent, England: Wm. Dawson and Sons.

Bolton, Henry Carrington. 1897. *Catalogue of Scientific and Technical Periodicals, 1665–1895*. 2nd ed. Washington, DC: Smithsonian Institution.

Boston Weekly Magazine. 1743. [No title.] *Boston Weekly Magazine* 1(1): 1. http://search.proquest.com/americanperiodicals/docview/88497337/pageviewPDF/696BFB946F7F4EF2PQ/1?accountid=14496, retrieved 13 May 2003.

Botein, Stephen. 1981. Printers and the American Revolution. In Bernard Bailyn and John B. Hench, eds., *The Press and the American Revolution*, 11–57. Boston: Northeastern University Press.

Botts, C. T. 1841. Machinery. *Southern Planter* 1(5): 91. http://search.proquest.com/americanperiodicals/docview/126310261/4B00D8DACDBD4527PQ/17?accountid=14496, retrieved 18 June 2013.

Botts, Charles T. 1846. Postage. *Southern Planter* 6 (6): 142–43. http://search.proquest.com/americanperiodicals/docview/126296705/fulltextPDF/A16486A1861F4601PQ/17?accountid=14496, retrieved 4 August 2010.

Bound, John, David Jaeger, and Regina Baker. 1995. Problems with instrumental variables when the correlation between the instruments and the endogenous explanatory variable is weak. *Journal of the American Statistical Association* 90: 443–50.

Bourdieu, Pierre. (1979) 1984. *Distinction: A Social Critique of the Judgement of Taste*. Translated by Richard Nice. Cambridge, MA: Harvard University Press.

Bowen, Frances. 1843. Oeuvres of d'Alexandre Dumas. *North American Review* 56: 109–11. http://search.proquest.com/americanperiodicals/docview/137094167/pageview ?accountid=14496, retrieved 4 January 2006.

Boyer, Paul. 1978. *Urban Masses and Moral Order in America, 1820–1920.* Cambridge, MA: Harvard University Press.

Boylan, Anne M. 1988. *Sunday School: The Formation of an American Institution, 1790–1880.* New Haven, CT: Yale University Press.

Bracha, Oren. 2008a. The ideology of authorship revisited: Authors, markets, and liberal values in early American copyright. *Yale Law Journal* 118(2): 186–271.

Bracha, Oren. 2008b. Commentary on John Usher's printing privilege 1672. In L. Bently and M. Kretschmer, eds., *Primary Sources on Copyright, 1450–1900.* Cambridge: University of Cambridge and Bournemouth University. http://www.copyrighthistory .org, retrieved 25 March 2013.

Bracha, Oren. 2010. The adventures of the Statute of Anne in the land of unlimited possibilities: The life of a legal transplant. *Berkeley Technology Law Journal* 25: 1426–73.

Brackenridge, Hugh Henry. 1779a. Preface. *United States Magazine* 1(1): 3–4. http:// search.proquest.com/americanperiodicals/docview/88894985/E6907744F61E423 DPQ/2?accountid=14496, retrieved 15 May 2003.

Brackenridge, Hugh Henry. 1779b. Introduction. *United States Magazine* 1(1): 9–11. http://search.proquest.com/americanperiodicals/docview/88892729/E6907744F61 E423DPQ/8?accountid=14496, retrieved 20 March 2006.

Bradburn, Norman. N., Lance J. Rips, and Steven K. Shevell. 1987. Answering autobiographical questions: The impact of memory and inference on surveys. *Science*, new series, 236(4798): 157–61.

Bradford, Andrew. 1740. The plan of an intended magazine. *American Weekly Mercury* 1088: 1–3. http://infoweb.newsbank.com/iw-search/we/HistArchive/?p_product=EANX andp_theme=ahnpandp_nbid=S5DH4BPEMTQwMzYzNDg4MS44NjMwMjQ6M ToxNToxNjkuMjI5LjE1MS4yMDUandp_action=docands_lastnonissuequeryname =3andd_viewref=searchandp_queryname=3andp_docnum=24163andp_docref =v2:10380B67EBBF3BE8@EANX-105E3E9780E666A1@2356892–105E3E978591 E756@0, retrieved 1 June 2010.

Bradford, Thomas Lindsay. 1892. *Homoeopathic Bibliography of the United States, from the Year 1825 to the Year 1891, Inclusive.* Philadelphia: Boericke and Tafel.

Bradsher, Earl L. 1929. The financial rewards of American authors. *Studies in Bibliography* 28(2): 186–202.

Brady, Dorothy S. 1964. Relative prices in the nineteenth century. *Journal of Economic History* 26: 145–203.

Braithwaite, Richard B. 1950. *Scientific Explanation: A Study of the Function of Theory, Probability and Law in Science.* Cambridge: Cambridge University Press.

Braude, Ann. 1990. *News from the Spirit World: A Checklist of American Spiritualist Periodicals, 1847–1900.* Worcester, MA: American Antiquarian Society.

Braudel, Fernand. 1980. *On History.* Translated by Sarah Matthews. Chicago: University of Chicago Press.

Braudel, Fernand. 1981. *Civilization and Capitalism, 15th–18th Century*, vol. 1: *The Structures of Everyday Life: The Limits of the Possible.* Translated by Miriam Kochan; revised by Sián Reynolds. Berkeley: University of California Press.

Braudel, Fernand. 1982. *Civilization and Capitalism, 15th–18th Century*, vol. 2: *The*

Wheels of Commerce. Translated by Sián Reynolds. Berkeley: University of California Press.

Braudel, Fernand. 1984. *Civilization and Capitalism, 15th–18th Century*, vol. 3: *The Perspective of the World*. Translated by Sián Reynolds. Berkeley: University of California Press.

Brauneis, Robert. 2008. The transformation of originality in the Progressive-Era debate over copyright in news. Working paper, Tulane University Law School.

Breckenridge, Robert J., and Andrew Boyd Cross. 1836. Advertisement. *Baltimore Literary and Religious Magazine* 2(1): 1–3. http://search.proquest.com/americanperiodicals /docview/124049954/46C5CA06BE634C08PQ/2?accountid=14496, retrieved 30 October 2006.

Brigham, Clarence S. 1962. *History and Bibliography of American Newspapers, 1690–1820, Including Additions and Corrections, 1961*. 2 vols. Hamden, CT: Archon.

Brother Jonathan. 1842. Newspaper quackery. *Brother Jonathan* 1(13): 353–54. http:// search.proquest.com/americanperiodicals/docview/125759709/2980FED34D11456 7PQ/21?accountid=14496, retrieved 18 June 2011.

Brown, Charles Brockden. 1803. Editor's address to the public. *Literary Magazine and American Register* 1(1): 3–6. http://search.proquest.com/americanperiodicals/docview /89446935/140EA8BA64113741686/2?accountid=14496, retrieved 14 May 2003.

Brown, Richard D. 1974. The emergence of urban society in rural Massachusetts, 1760–1820. *Journal of American History* 61: 29–51.

Brown, Richard D. 1976. *Modernization: The Transformation of American Life 1600–1865*. Prospect Heights, IL: Waveland.

Brown, Hugh Hale. 1826. Preface. *Hopkinsian Magazine* 2(2): iii–iv. http://search .proquest.com/americanperiodicals/docview/91313782/13C0E22BEA014AAAPQ /7?accountid=14496, retrieved 18 July 2006.

Brown, Solyman. 1844. The Leraysville Phalanx. *Phalanx: Organ of the Doctrine of Association* 1(7): 100. http://search.proquest.com/americanperiodicals/docview/13770 8442/D3434DB1BEE8472APQ/5?accountid=14496, retrieved 12 August 2014.

Brubaker, B. R. 1975. Spoils appointments of American writers. *New England Quarterly* 48(4): 556–64.

Buckingham, Joseph Tinker. 1811. Something more, from the publisher to the reader. *Comet* 1(1): 1–2. http://search.proquest.com/americanperiodicals/docview/1242461 83/5A4132C95C6949BAPQ/2?accountid=14496, retrieved 14 May 2003.

Bugbee, B. W. 1967. *The Genesis of American Patent and Copyright Law*. Washington, DC: Public Affairs Press.

Burdick, A. H. 1838. Newspaper borrowing. *Genesee Farmer and Gardener's Journal* 8(22): 173. http://search.proquest.com/americanperiodicals/docview/126097037 /ADB232F90D8C4816PQ/1?accountid=14496, retrieved 18 January 2009.

Burke, Colin B. 1973. The quiet influence: The American colleges and their students, 1800–1860. PhD diss., Washington University.

Burke, Colin B. 1982. *American Collegiate Populations: A Test of the Traditional View*. New York: New York University Press.

Burke, Colin B. 2006. Churches by state: 1850 to 1990. In Susan B. Carter, Scott Sigmund Gartner, Michael R. Haines, Alan L. Olmstead, Richard Sutch, and Gavin Wright, eds., *Historical Statistics of the United States, Millennial Edition On Line*, tables Bg349–99. New York: Cambridge University Press. http://hsus.cambridge.org /HSUSWeb/table/downloadtable.do?id=Bg349–399#, retrieved 1 April 2007.

Bullock, Penelope L. 1981. *The Afro-American Periodical Press, 1838–1909*. Baton Rouge: LSU Press.

Burnard, Trevor G. 2001. "Prodigious riches": The wealth of Jamaica before the American Revolution. *Economic History Review*, 2nd series, 54: 506–24.

Burton, M. Diane, Jesper B. Sørensen, and Christine M. Beckman. 2002. Coming from good stock: Career histories and new venture formation. *Research in the Sociology of Organizations* 19: 229–62.

Bushman, Richard Lyman. 1998. Markets and composite farms in early America. *William and Mary Quarterly* 55(3): 351–74.

Butler, Jon. 1982. Enthusiasm described and decried: The Great Awakening as interpretative fiction. *Journal of American History* 69: 305–25.

Butler, Jon. 1990. *Awash in a Sea of Faith: Christianizing the American People*. Cambridge, MA: Harvard University Press.

Bynum, William F. 1994. *Science and the Practice of Medicine in the Nineteenth Century*. Cambridge: Cambridge University Press.

Cairns, William B. (1898) 1971. *On the Development of American Literature from 1815 to 1833, with Especial Reference to Periodicals*. Madison: University of Wisconsin Press.

Calhoun, Craig. 1991. Indirect relations and imagined communities. In Pierre Bourdieu and James Coleman, eds., *Social Theory for a Changing Society*, 95–120. New York: Russell Sage Foundation.

Calhoun, Craig. 1993. "New social movements" of the early nineteenth century. *Social Science History* 17(3): 385–427.

Calhoun, Craig. 1998. Community without propinquity revisited: Communication technology and the transformation of the urban public sphere. *Sociological Inquiry* 68: 373–97.

Callow, Alexander B., Jr., ed. 1982. *American Urban History—An Interpretive Reader with Commentaries*. New York: Oxford University Press.

Cameron, A. Colin, and Pravin K. Trivedi. 1986. Econometric models based on count data: Comparisons and applications of some estimators and tests. *Journal of Applied Econometrics* 1: 29–53.

Cameron, A. Colin, and Pravin K. Trivedi. 1990. Regression-based tests for overdispersion in the Poisson model. *Journal of Econometrics* 46: 347–64.

Campbell, Alexander. 1826. The creed question. *Christian Baptist* 4(1): 323–24. http://search.proquest.com/americanperiodicals/docview/124003618/fulltextPDF/3BFE7C41842B4530PQ/44?accountid=14496, retrieved 7 December 2009.

Campbell, Laurence R. 1970. *Student Press Copes with Unrest, 1970, and Seven Other Studies*. Iowa City, IA: Quill and Scroll Society.

Carroll, Glenn R. 1985. Concentration and specialization: Dynamics of niche width in populations of organizations. *American Journal of Sociology* 90: 1262–83.

Carroll, Glenn R., and Michael T. Hannan. 2000. *The Demography of Corporations and Industries*. Princeton, NJ: Princeton University Press.

Carroll, Glenn R., and Yangchung Paul Huo. 1986. Organizational task and institutional environments in evolutionary perspective: Findings from the local newspaper industry. *American Journal of Sociology* 91: 838–73.

Carroll, H. K. 1893. *The Religious Forces of the United States: Enumerated, Classified, and Described on the Basis of the Government Census of 1890*. New York: Christian Literature.

Carter, Susan B., and Richard Sutch. 2006. Travel times between New York City and other selected cities, 1800–1857. In Susan B. Carter, Scott Sigmund Gartner, Michael

R. Haines, Alan L. Olmstead, Richard Sutch, and Gavin Wright, eds., *Historical Statistics of the United States, Millennial Edition On Line*, tables Df8–12. New York: Cambridge University Press. http://hsus.cambridge.org/HSUSWeb/toc/tableToc.do?id =Df8–12, retrieved 28 May 2007.

Carwardine, Richard J. 1978. *Transatlantic Revivalism: Popular Evangelicalism in Britain and America, 1790–1865*. Westport, CT: Greenwood.

Carwardine, Richard J. 1993. *Evangelicals and Politics in Antebellum America*. New Haven, CT: Yale University Press.

Cassedy, James H. 1969. *Demography in Early America: Beginnings of the Statistical Mind.* Cambridge, MA: Harvard University Press.

Cassedy, James H. 1984. *American Medicine and Statistical Thinking, 1800–1860.* Cambridge, MA: Harvard University Press.

Cavallo, Guglielmo, and Roger Chartier, eds. 1999. *A History of Reading in the West.* Translated by Lydia G. Cochrane. Amherst: University of Massachusetts Press.

Cave, Edward. 1731. Introduction. *Gentleman's Magazine* 1(1): n.p. http://www.otago .ac.nz/library/exhibitions/gentlemansmagazine/, retrieved 3 March 2002.

Chandler, Alfred D., Jr. 1977. *The Visible Hand: The Managerial Revolution in American Business.* Cambridge, MA: Belknap Press.

Chandler, Katherine. 1905. *List of California Periodicals Issued Previous to the Completion of the Transcontinental Telegraph: August 15, 1846–October 24, 1861.* San Francisco: Library Association of California.

Channing, William Ellery. 1872. Remarks on associations. In *The Works of William E. Channing, D.D., Twenty-Second Complete Edition*, 281–332. Boston: American Unitarian Association.

Chaplin, Joyce E. 1993. *An Anxious Pursuit: Agricultural Innovation and Modernity in the Lower South, 1730–1815.* Chapel Hill: University of North Carolina Press.

Charvat, William. 1968. *The Profession of Authorship in America, 1800–1870: The Papers of William Charvat.* Edited by Matthew J. Bruccoli. Columbus: Ohio State University Press.

Chase, Ebenezer. 1819. To the patrons. *Religious Informer* 1(1): 6–7. http://search .proquest.com/americanperiodicals/docview/137590522/A1BAD110776B4DF5PQ /11?accountid=14496, retrieved 15 May 2003.

Chaves, Mark. 1993. Denominations as dual structures: An organizational analysis. *Sociology of Religion* 54: 147–69.

Chaves, Mark, and Philip S. Gorski. 2001. Religious pluralism and religious participation. *Annual Review of Sociology* 27: 261–81.

Christian Monitor. 1814. Preface. *Christian Monitor* 1(1): 1–4. http://search.proquest .com/americanperiodicals/docview/124032215/C31441B04C94C9CPQ/2?account id=14496, retrieved 13 May 2003.

Christian Secretary. 1848. The ministry and the press. *Christian Secretary* 27(35): 1. http://search.proquest.com/americanperiodicals/docview/124273979/fulltextPDF /3FAE3E29D104418APQ/9?accountid=14496, retrieved 20 May 2013.

Christian Watchman. 1819. To patrons. *Christian Watchman* 1(1): 3. http://search.pro quest.com/americanperiodicals/docview/127212600/E0E7E25FE87F440EPQ/16 ?accountid=14496, retrieved 10 October 2006.

Chu, Pao Hsun. 1932. *The Post Office of the United States.* 2nd ed. New York: Columbia University Press.

Clark, Alvan Whitcombe. 1917. *Checklist of Indexed Periodicals.* White Plains, NY: H. W. Wilson.

Clark, Christopher. 1990. *The Roots of Rural Capitalism: Western Massachusetts, 1780–1860.* Ithaca, NY: Cornell University Press.

Clark, Elmer T. 1965. *The Small Sects in America.* Rev. ed. Nashville, TN: Abingdon.

Cloud, Noah B. 1853. Our cabinet of exchanges. *American Cotton Planter* 1(12): 370–71. http://books.google.com/books?id=YKIEAAAAYAAJandpg=PA319anddq=%22american+cotton+planter%22+1853andhl=enandsa=Xandei=j4m1U-O_E4nDigK-iYCYAwandved=0CCoQ6AEwAA#v=onepageandq=%22american%20cotton%20planter%22%201853andf=false, retrieved 3 May 2013.

Cloud, Noah B. 1857. Plantation management and practice. *American Cotton Planter and Soil of the South* 5(12): 372. http://books.google.com/books?id=X5M_AQAAMAAJandpg=PR4anddq=%22american+cotton+planter%22+%22plantation+management%22+alabamaandhl=enandsa=Xandei=BZK1U6CYOoipigLmooDACgandved=0CB4Q6AEwAA#v=onepageandq=%22american%20cotton%20planter%22%20%22plantation%20management%22%20alabamaandf=false, retrieved 3 May 2013.

Cochran, Thomas C. 1981. *Frontiers of Change: Early Industrialism in America.* New York: Oxford University Press.

Coke, Thomas, and Francis Asbury. 1789. To the subscribers. *Arminian Magazine* 1(1): iii–iv. http://search.proquest.com/americanperiodicals/docview/88496510/F9D0BE1FC5594958PQ/9?accountid=14496, retrieved 13 May 2003.

Coleman, James S. 1974. *Power and the Structure of Society.* New York: W. W. Norton.

Coleman, James S. 1982. *The Asymmetric Society.* Syracuse, NY: Syracuse University Press.

Columbian Star. 1822. To our patrons. *Columbian Star* 1(1): 3. http://search.proquest.com/americanperiodicals/docview/124260592/A7177B1483C4A80PQ/27?accountid=14496, retrieved 1 October 2012.

Commager, Henry Steele. 1973. *Documents of American History,* vol. 1: *To 1898.* Englewood Cliffs, NJ: Prentice Hall.

Commons, John R., David J. Saposs, Helen L. Sumner, E. B. Mittelman, H. E. Hoagland, John B. Andrews, Selig Perlman, Don D. Lescohier, Elizabeth Brandeis Rauschenbush, and Philip Taft. 1918. *History of Labour in the United States,* vol. 1. New York: Macmillan.

Condie, Thomas. 1798. View of the work. *Philadelphia Monthly Magazine* 1(1): 3–6. http://search.proquest.com/americanperiodicals/docview/88877072/4EC9FED91D7C4B2APQ/4?accountid=14496, retrieved 14 May 2003.

Connelley, William Elsey, Kansas Historical Society. 1916. *History of Kansas Newspapers: A History of the Newspapers and Magazines Published in Kansas from the Organization of Kansas Territory, 1854, to January 1, 1916.* Topeka: Kansas State Printing Plant.

Cooley, Charles Horton. (1909) 1923. *Social Organization: A Study of the Larger Mind.* New York: Charles Scribner's Sons.

Corwin, E. T., J. H. Dubbs, and J. T. Hamilton. 1894. *A History of the Reformed Church, Dutch, the Reformed Church, German, and the Moravian Church in the United States.* New York: Christian Literature.

Corzine, Jay. 1981. Media diffusion of subcultural elements: Comment on Fine and Kleinman. *American Journal of Sociology* 87: 170–73.

Coser, Lewis A. 1974. *Greedy Institutions.* New York: Free Press.

Cott, Nancy F. (1977) 1997. *Bonds of Womanhood: Women's Sphere in New England, 1780–1835.* 2nd ed. New Haven, CT: Yale University Press.

Coulter, E. Merton. 1930. Southern agriculture and southern nationalism before the Civil War. *Agricultural History* 4(3): 77–91.

Cramer, Clayton E. 1997. *Black Demographic Data, 1790–1860: A Sourcebook*. Westport, CT: Greenwood.

Crane, Diana. 1965. Scientists at major and minor universities: A study of productivity and recognition. *American Sociological Review* 30: 699–714.

Cranmer, H. Jerome. 1960. Canal investment, 1815–1860. In *Trends in the American Economy in the Nineteenth Century: A Report of the National Bureau of Economic Research*, 547–70. Princeton, NJ: Princeton University Press.

Craven, Avery. (1925) 2007. *Soil Exhaustion as a Factor in the Agricultural History of Virginia and Maryland, 1606–1860*. Columbia: University of South Carolina Press.

Crawford, Michael J. 1991 *Seasons of Grace: Colonial New England's Revival Tradition in the British Context*. New York: Oxford University Press.

Creighton, Andrew L. 1990. The emergence of incorporation as a legal form for organizations. PhD diss., Stanford University.

Creighton, Andrew L. 1996. Inventing the common corporation: The development of legal governance structures for US corporations in the early nineteenth century. Working paper, University of California–Berkeley.

Cremin, Lawrence A. 1970. *American Education: The National Experience, 1783–1876*. New York: Harper and Row.

Cultivator. 1853. Book farming. *Cultivator*, new series, 1(11): 353. http://search.pro quest.com/americanperiodicals/docview/124876961/fulltextPDF/BF54640EBA494 254PQ/50?accountid=14496, retrieved 20 May 2013.

Dana, Richard Henry. 1821. Preface. *Idle Man* 1(1): 3–13. http://search.proquest.com /americanperiodicals/docview/90548017/8082D70395F84B19PQ/5?accountid =14496, retrieved 14 May 2003.

Danhof, Clarence H. 1969. *Change in Agriculture: The Northern United States, 1820–1870*. Cambridge, MA: Harvard University Press.

Daniel, Edward G. 1941. United States Postal Service and postal policy, 1789–1860. PhD diss., Harvard University.

Daniel, Walter C. 1982. *Black Journals of the United States*. Westport, CT: Greenwood.

Dauber, Kenneth. 1990. *The Idea of Authorship in America: Democratic Poetics from Franklin to Melville*. Madison: University of Wisconsin Press.

David, Brother C. S. C. 1955. A history of Catholic periodical production in the US, 1830–1951. MA thesis, University of Chicago.

David, Robert J., Wesley D. Sine, and Heather A. Haveman. 2013. Seizing opportunity in emerging fields: How entrepreneurs legitimated the professional form of management consulting. *Organization Science* 24(2): 356–77.

Davidson, Cathy N. 1986. *Revolution and the Word: The Rise of the Novel in America*. New York: Oxford University Press.

Davies, Benjamin. 1799. Prospectus. *Philadelphia Magazine and Review* 1(1): ii–iv. http:// search.proquest.com/americanperiodicals/docview/88877394/918444BE1A0747FE PQ/37?accountid=14496, retrieved 15 May 2003.

Davies, John D. 1955. *Phrenology: Fad and Science, a Nineteenth-Century American Crusade*. New Haven, CT: Yale University Press.

Davis, Addison. 1845. Letter from Addison Davis. *Hangman* 1(8): 31. http://search.pro quest.com/americanperiodicals/docview/127998658/A248583FCAEC42B8PQ/18 ?accountid=14496, retrieved 2 July 2014.

Davis, Cornelius. 1796. Preface. *Theological Magazine* 1(1): n.p. http://search.proquest .com/americanperiodicals/docview/88882651/F413D46B222D44D7PQ/2?accountid =14496, retrieved 15 May 2003.

Davis, James H. 2004. An annual index of US industrial production, 1790–1915. *Quarterly Journal of Economics* 109: 1177–1215.

Davis, Joseph Stancliffe. 1917. *Essays in the Earlier History of American Corporations*, vol. 2. Cambridge, MA: Harvard University Press.

Davis, Sheldon Emmor. 1919. *Educational Periodicals during the Nineteenth Century.* US Department of the Interior, Bureau of Education, bulletin no. 28. Washington, DC:Government Printing Office.

Davison, Mary Veronica. 1973. American music periodicals in the later nineteenth century: 1853–1899. PhD dissertation, University of Minnesota Department of Musicology.

Deazley, Ronan. 2004. *On the Origin of the Right to Copy: Charting the Movement of Copyright Law in Eighteenth Century Britain, 1695–1775.* Oxford: Hart.

De Bendetti, Charles. 1980. *The Peace Reform in American History.* Bloomington: Indiana University Press.

Defoe, Daniel. 1704. *An Essay on the Regulation of the Press.* London: n.p. http://www.luminarium.org/renascence-editions/defoe2.html, retrieved 25 July 2013.

Demaree, Albert Lowther. 1941. *The American Agricultural Press, 1819–1860.* New York: Columbia University Press.

Dennie, Joseph. 1797. *An established literary and political paper: The editor of the* Farmer's Weekly Museum, *printed at Walpole, Newhampshire, offers his paper to the publick....* Walpole, NH: David Carlisle. http://www.americanantiquarian.org/, retrieved 24 March 2006.

Dennie, Joseph. 1801. Prospectus of a new weekly paper. *Port-Folio* 1(1): n.p. http://search.proquest.com/americanperiodicals/docview/89481351/135443D93F3245C9PQ/2?accountid=14496, retrieved 14 May 2003.

De Sola Pool, Ithiel. 1983. *Forecasting the Telephone.* Norwood, NJ: Ablex.

Deutsch, Karl W. 1953. *Nationalism and Social Communication: An Inquiry into the Foundations of Nationality.* Cambridge, MA: MIT Press.

DiMaggio, Paul. 1982. Cultural entrepreneurship in nineteenth-century Boston: The creation of an organizational base for high culture in America. *Media, Culture, and Society*: 4: 33–50.

DiMaggio, Paul J., and Walter W. Powell. 1983. The iron cage revisited: Institutional isomorphism and collective rationality in organizational fields. *American Sociological Review* 48: 147–60.

Dill, William Adelbert. 1928. *Growth of Newspapers in the United States: A Study of the Number of Newspapers, of the Number of Subscribers, and of the total Annual Output of the Periodical Press, from 1704 to 1925, with Comment on Coincident Social and Economic Conditions.* Lawrence: Department of Journalism, University of Kansas.

Dillistin, William H. 1949. *Bank Note Reporters and Counterfeit Detectors, 1826–1866, with a Discourse on Wildcat Banks and Wildcat Bank Notes.* New York: American Numismatic Society.

Dobson, John Blythe. 1993. The spurious articles in Appleton's Cyclopaedia of American Biography. *Biography* 16: 388–408.

Doerflinger, Thomas M. 2002. Rural capitalism in iron country: Staffing a forest factory, 1808–1815. *William and Mary Quarterly* 59(1): 3–38.

Dolan, Jay P. 1978. *Catholic Revivalism: The American Experience 1830–1900.* Notre Dame, IN: University of Notre Dame Press.

Dorchester, Daniel. 1888. *Christianity in the United States: From the First Settlement Down to the Present Time.* New York: Phillips and Hunt.

Douglas, Ann. 1977. *The Feminization of American Culture.* New York: Alfred A. Knopf.

Douglas, Mary. 1986. *How Institutions Think.* Syracuse, NY: Syracuse University Press.

Dowling, David O. 2011. *The Business of Literary Circles in Nineteenth-Century America.* New York: Palgrave-Macmillan.

Drury, A. W. 1924. *History of the Church of the United Brethren in Christ.* Dayton, Ohio: United Brethren Publishing House.

Duncan, Otis Dudley, W. R. Scott, Stanley Lieberson, Beverly Davis Duncan, and Hal H. Winsborough. 1960. *Metropolis and Region.* Baltimore: Johns Hopkins University Press.

Durkheim, Émile. (1893) 1984. *The Division of Labor in Society.* Translated by W. D. Halls. New York: Free Press.

Durkheim, Émile. (1912) 1996. *Elementary Forms of Religious Life.* Translated by Karen Fields. New York: Free Press.

Dwight, Timothy. (1822) 1969. *Travels in New England and New York.* Edited by Barbara Miller Solomon. Cambridge, MA: Belknap Press.

Ebert, Myrl L. 1953. Rise and development of the American medical periodical, 1797–1850. *Bulletin of the Medical Library Association* 40: 243–76.

Edelman, Lauren B., and Mark C. Suchman. 1997. The legal environments of organizations. *Annual Review of Sociology* 23: 479–515.

Edgar, Neal L. 1975. *A History and Bibliography of American Magazines, 1810–1820.* Metuchen, NJ: Scarecrow.

Edwards, Bob, and John McCarthy. 2004. Resources and social movement mobilization. In David Snow, Sarah Soule, and Hanspeter Kriesi, eds., *Blackwell Companion to Social Movements,* 116–52. Oxford: Blackwell.

Egerton, Douglas R. 1996. Markets without a market revolution: Southern planters and capitalism. *Journal of the Early Republic* 16(2): 207–21.

Eisenstein, Elizabeth. 1979. *The Printing Press as an Agent of Change.* Cambridge: Cambridge University Press.

Eliot, Samuel, and Joshua Blanchard. 1743. Introduction. *American Magazine and Historical Chronicle* 1(1): i–iv.

Elstein, David. 2001. The market adds choice—and quality. https://www.opendemoc racy.net/media-globalmediaownership/article_599.jsp, retrieved 22 November 2006.

Emerson, Ralph Waldo. 1837. The American Scholar. An oration delivered before the Phi Beta Kappa Society, at Cambridge, August 31. http://www.emersoncentral.com/ amscholar.htm, retrieved 16 August 2013.

Endres, Kathleen L., ed. 1994. *Trade, Industrial, and Professional Periodicals of the United States.* Westport, CT: Greenwood.

Endres, Kathleen L., and Therese L. Lueck, eds. 1995. *Women's Periodicals in the United States: Consumer Magazines.* Westport, CT: Greenwood.

Endres, Kathleen L., and Therese L. Lueck, eds. 1996. *Women's Periodicals in the United States: Social and Political Issues.* Westport, CT: Greenwood.

Enquirer. 1821. To the editor. *Genius of Universal Emancipation* 1(2): 21. http://search .proquest.com/americanperiodicals/docview/124019998/F188C99A7E54ABBPQ /2?accountid=14496, retrieved 14 August 2014.

Erickson, E. Walfred. 1977. *Swedish-American Periodicals: A Selective and Descriptive Bibliography.* New York: Arno.

Evangelical Magazine and Gospel Advocate. 1843. Thompson's Bank Note Reporter. *. Evangelical Magazine and Gospel Advocate* 14(36): 287. http://search.proquest.com

/americanperiodicals/docview/89837027/75DA25B13FAE442FPQ/43?accountid
=14496, retrieved 21 July 2014.

Evans, Charles H. 1863. *American Bibliography: A Chronological Dictionary of All Books, Pamphlets, and Periodical Publications Printed in the United States from the Genesis of Printing in 1639 to 1820.* 12 vols. Chicago: Blakely.

Evans, Charles H. (1884) 1976. *Exports, Domestic and Foreign, from the American Colonies to Great Britain from 1697 to 1789, Inclusive; Exports, Domestic and Foreign, from the United States to All Countries, from 1789 to 1883, Inclusive.* New York: Arno Press.

Everton, Michael. 2005. The would-be author and the real book-seller: Thomas Paine and eighteenth-century printing ethics. *Early American Literature* 40: 79–110.

Faber, Eli. 2008. America's earliest Jewish settlers, 1654–1820. In Marc Lee Raphael, ed., *Columbia History of Jews and Judaism in America*, 21–46. New York: Columbia University Press.

Fackler, P. Mark, and Charles H. Lippy. 1995. *Popular Religious Magazines of the United States.* Westport, CT: Greenwood.

Fanuzzi, Robert. 2003. *Abolition's Public Sphere.* Minneapolis: University of Minnesota Press.

Farmer's Register. 1843. Agricultural improvement in Norfolk county. *Farmer's Register* 1(3): 157–58. http://search.proquest.com/americanperiodicals/docview/125187342 /999EB8253D284EFEPQ/4?accountid=14496, retrieved 1 August 2014.

Fauchart, Emmannuelle, and Marc Gruber. 2011. Darwinians, communitarians, and missionaries: The role of founder identity in entrepreneurship. *Academy of Management Journal* 54: 935–57.

Faxon, Frederick Winthrop. 1908. *A Checklist of American and English Popular Periodicals to Dec. 31, 1907.* Boston: Boston Book Company.

Feather, John P. 1980. The book trade in politics: The making of the Copyright Act of 1710. *Publishing History* 8: 19–45.

Feather, John. 1988. *A History of British Publishing.* London: Routledge.

Febvre, Lucien, and Henri-Jean Martin. (1976) 1990. *The Coming of the Book: The Impact of Printing, 1450–1800.* London: Verso.

Ferguson, Adam. 1767. *An Essay on the History of Civil Society.* Edinburgh: A. Millar and T. Caddel.

Ferguson, Robert A. 1984. *Law and Letters in American Culture.* Cambridge, MA: Harvard University Press.

Fessenden, Thomas Green. 1839. *Complete Farmer and Rural Economist.* Boston: Otis, Broaders.

Field, Henry M. 1856. The pulpit and the press. *New York Evangelist* 27(28): n.p. http:// search.proquest.com/americanperiodicals/docview/125442865/fulltextPDF/C9F3D E6A64434713PQ/4?accountid=14496, retrieved 10 May 2009.

Fine, Gary Alan, and Sherryl Kleinman. 1981. Mass and specialized media. *American Journal of Sociology* 87: 173–77.

Finke, Roger, Avery Guest, and Rodney Stark. 1996. Mobilizing local religious markets: Religious pluralism in the Empire State, 1855 to 1865. *American Sociological Review* 61: 203–18.

Finke, Roger, and Rodney Stark. 1988. Religious economies and sacred canopies: Religious mobilization in American cities, 1906. *American Sociological Review* 53: 41–49.

Finke, Roger, and Rodney Stark. 1992. *The Churching of America 1776–1990: Winners and Losers in our Religious Economy.* New Brunswick, NJ: Rutgers University Press.

Finnie, Gordon. 1969. The antislavery movement in the upper South before 1840. *Journal of Southern History* 35: 319–42.

Fischer, Claude S. 1982. *To Dwell among Friends: Personal Networks in Town and City.* Chicago: University of Chicago Press.

Fischer, Claude S. 1992. *America Calling: A Social History of the Telephone to 1940.* Berkeley: University of California Press.

Fischer, David Hackett. 1989. *Albion's Seed: Four British Folkways in America.* New York: Oxford University Press.

Fisher, R. A. 1922. On the interpretation of χ^2 from contingency tables, and the calculation of P. *Journal of the Royal Statistical Society* 85(1): 87–94.

Fisher, William, ed. 1991. *Business Journals of the United States.* New York: Greenwood.

Fishlow, Albert. 1965. *Railroads and the Transformation of the Antebellum Economy.* Cambridge, MA: Harvard University Press.

Flanders, Bertram Holland. 1944. *Early Georgia Magazines: Literary Periodicals to 1865.* Athens: University of Georgia Press.

Flandorf, Vera. 1952. Music periodicals in the United States: A survey of their history and contents. MA thesis, University of Chicago.

Fleming, Herbert E. 1905. The literary interest of Chicago, I and II. *American Journal of Sociology* 11(3): 377–408.

Flexner, Eleanor, and Ellen Fitzpatrick. 1996. *Century of Struggle: The Woman's Rights Movement in the United States.* Enlarged ed. Cambridge, MA: Belknap Press.

Fligstein, Neil. 2001. Social skill and the theory of fields. *Sociological Theory* 19(2): 105–25.

Fligstein, Neil. 2008. *Euroclash: The EU, European Identity, and the Future of Europe.* New York: Oxford University Press.

Fligstein, Neil, and Doug McAdam. 2012. *A Theory of Fields.* New York: Oxford University Press.

Fogel, Robert. 1989. *Without Consent or Contract: The Rise and Fall of American Slavery.* New York: W. W. Norton.

Fogel, Robert, and Stanley Engerman. 1995. *Time on the Cross: The Economics of American Negro Slavery.* New York: W. W. Norton.

Fombrun, Charles J. 1996. *Reputation: Realizing Value from Corporate Image.* Boston: Harvard Business School Press.

Foner, Eric. 1980. *Politics and Ideology in the Age of the Civil War.* New York: Oxford University Press.

Foner, Philip S. 1947. *History of the Labor Movement in the United States from Colonial Times to the Founding of the American Federation of Labor.* New York: Industrial Publishers.

Foote, John P. 1824. [No title.] *Cincinnati Literary Gazette* 1(2): 13. http://search.proquest.com/americanperiodicals/docview/124260866/fulltextPDF/A9CF4727115844CBPQ/6?accountid=14496; retrieved 21 July 2012.

Ford, Paul Leicester. (1889) 1972. *Checklist of American Magazines Printed in the 18th Century.* New York: Macmillan.

Forney, C. H. 1914. *History of the Churches of God in the United States of America.* Harrisburg, PA: Publishing House of the Churches of God.

Foster, Charles I. 1960. *An Errand of Mercy: The Evangelical United Front, 1790–1837.* Chapel Hill: University of North Carolina Press.

Fourcade, Marion. 2009. *Economists and Societies: Discipline and Profession in the United States, Great Britain, and France.* Princeton, NJ: Princeton University Press.

Fox, Early Lee. 1919. *The American Colonization Society, 1817–1840.* Baltimore: Johns Hopkins University Press.

Fox-Genovese, Elizabeth, and Eugene D. Genovese. 1983. *Fruits of Merchant Capital: Slavery and Bourgeois Property in the Rise and Expansion of Capitalism.* New York: Oxford University Press.

Francis, Simeon. 1857. American farmers. *Illinois Farmer* 2(4): 73–77. http://idnc.library.illinois.edu/cgi-bin/illinois?a=dandd=IFR18570401.2.35#, retrieved 20 May 2013.

Freeman, Jo. 1973. The origins of the women's liberation movement. *American Journal of Sociology* 78: 792–811.

Freeman, John. 1986. Entrepreneurs as organizational products. In Gary Libecap, ed., *Advances in the Study of Entrepreneurship, Innovation, and Economic Growth,* 1:33–52. Greenwich, CT: JAI.

Freeman, John H., and Pino G. Audia. 2006. Community ecology and the sociology of organizations. *Annual Review of Sociology* 32: 145–69.

Freneau, Philip. 1797. To the public. *Time-Piece and Literary Companion* 1(1): 1. http://search.proquest.com/americanperiodicals/docview/88886625/7496F34B26BB47C8PQ/3?accountid=14496, retrieved 15 May 2003.

Friedland, Roger, and Deirdre Boden, eds. 1994. *NowHere: Space, Time, and Modernity.* Berkeley: University of California Press.

Friedland, Roger, and Donald Palmer. 1984. Park Place and Main Street: Business and the urban power structure. *Annual Review of Sociology* 10: 393–416.

Friedman, Lawrence M. 2005. *A History of American Law.* 3rd ed. New York: Simon and Schuster.

Fuller, Louis. 1986. *Crusade against Slavery: Friends, Foes, and Reforms 1820–1860.* Algonac, MI: Reference Publications.

Fuller, Margaret. 1845. *Woman in the Nineteenth Century.* New York: Greeley and McElrath.

Galambos, Louis. 1970. The emerging organizational synthesis in modern American history. *Business History Review* 44(3): 279–90.

Galbraith, John Kenneth. 1975. *Money: Whence It Came, Where It Went.* Boston: Houghton Mifflin.

Gamson, William A., David Croteau, William Hoynes, and Theodore Sasson. 1992. Media images and the social construction of reality. *Annual Review of Sociology* 18: 373–93.

Gamson, William A., and Gadi Wolfsfeld. 1993. Movements and media as interacting systems. *Annals of the American Academy of Political and Social Science* 528: 114–25.

Garcia, Hazel. 1976. Of punctilios among the fair sex: Colonial American magazines, 1741–1776. *Journalism History* 3: 48–52.

Gardner, Jared. 2012. *The Rise and Fall of Early American Magazine Culture.* Urbana: University of Illinois Press.

Garnsey, Caroline J. 1954. Ladies' magazines to 1850: The beginning of the industry. *New York Public Library Bulletin* 58(2): 74–88.

Garrison, Winfred Ernest, and Alfred T. DeGroot. 1948. *The Disciples of Christ: A History.* St. Louis, MO: Christian Board of Publication.

Garwood, Irving. 1931. *American Periodicals from 1850 to 1860.* Macomb, IL: Commercial Art Press.

Gates, Paul W. 1960. *The Farmer's Age: Agriculture, 1815–1860.* New York: Holt, Rinehart and Winston.

Gaustad, Edwin S. 1962. *Historical Atlas of Religion in America*. New York: Harper Collins.

Gawalt, Gerard W. 1979. *The Promise of Power: The Emergence of the Legal Profession in Massachusetts, 1760–1840*. Westport, CT: Greenwood.

Genius of Universal Emancipation. 1821. Letters to the editor: From Kentucky. *Genius of Universal Emancipation* 1(4): 50. http://search.proquest.com/americanperiodicals /docview/124015575/F188C99A7E54ABBPQ/4?accountid=14496, retrieved 14 August 2014.

Genius of Universal Emancipation. 1827. Letters to the editor: From South Carolina. *Genius of Universal Emancipation* 2(25): 2. http://search.proquest.com/americanperi odicals/docview/124010369/D6D375B51EEE4236PQ/40?accountid=14496, retrieved 11 August 2014.

Genovese, Eugene D. (1961) 1989. *The Political Economy of Slavery: Studies in the Economy and Society of the Slave South*. 2nd ed. Middletown, CT: Wesleyan University Press.

"The Ghost of Jacob Patchen" [pseud.]. 1845. Letter to the editor. *Subterranean* 3(3): 2. http://search.proquest.com/americanperiodicals/docview/126247654/CC6ACE9A0 0474755PQ/5?accountid=14496, retrieved 13 August 2014.

Gibbs, Jack P., and Walter T. Martin. 1962. Urbanization, technology, and the division of labor. *American Sociological Review* 27: 667–77.

Giddens, Anthony. 1990. *The Consequences of Modernity*. Palo Alto, CA: Stanford University Press.

Gilman, Samuel, and Martin Luther Hurlbut. 1822. [No title.] *Unitarian Defendant* 1(1): 1–3. http://search.proquest.com/americanperiodicals/docview/126285012/E8F 86AA8F6E648CBPQ/3?accountid=14496, retrieved 12 March 2009.

Gilmer, Gertrude C. (1934) 1972. *Checklist of Southern Periodicals to 1861*. Boston: F. W. Faxon.

Ginsburg, Jane C. 1990. A tale of two copyrights: Literary property in revolutionary France and America. *Tulane Law Review* 65(5): 991–1031.

Gitlin, Todd. 1980. *The Whole World Is Watching: Mass Media in the Making and Unmaking of the New Left*. Berkeley: University of California Press.

Glynn, Mary Ann, and Rikki Abzug. 1998. Isomorphism and competitive differentiation in the corporate name game. In Joel A. C. Baum, ed., *Advances in Strategic Management*, 15:105–28. Greenwich: JAI.

Glynn, Mary Ann, and Rikki Abzug. 2002. Institutionalizing identity: Symbolic isomorphism and organizational names. *Academy of Management Journal* 45: 267–80.

Goen, C. C. 1985. *Broken Churches, Broken Nation: Denominational Schisms and the Coming of the American Civil War*. Macon, GA: Mercer University Press.

Goldstein, Adam, and Heather A. Haveman. 2013. Pulpit and press: Denominational dynamics and the growth of religious magazines in antebellum America. *American Sociological Review* 78(5): 797–827.

Goldstein, H. 1987. Multilevel covariance components analysis. *Biometrika* 74: 430–31.

Goodman, Leo A. 1970. The multivariate analysis of qualitative data: Interactions among multiple classifications. *Journal of the American Statistical Association* 65: 225–56.

Goodman, Leo A. 1972. A modified multiple regression approach to the analysis of dichotomous variables. *American Sociological Review* 37: 28–46.

Gordon, David M., Richard Edwards, and Michael Reich. 1982. *Segmented Work, Divided Workers: The Historical Transformation of Labor in the United States.* Cambridge: Cambridge University Press.

Gordon, Robert B. 1989. Simeon North, John Hall, and mechanized manufacturing. *Technology and Culture* 30(1): 179–88.

Gordon, Robert W. 1984. Critical legal histories. *Stanford Law Review* 36: 57–125.

Gorman, Robert. 1939. *Catholic Apologetical Literature in the United States, 1784–1858.* Washington, DC: Catholic University of America Press.

Gouge, William M. 1842. The science of currency. *New York Herald* 1(20): 306–7. http://books.google.com/books?id=GB8jAQAAMAAJandpg=PA307andlpg=PA307anddq =journal+of+banking+%22the+science+of+currency%22andsource=blandots=7CC Dl2m2lhandsig=SdWbSXn3Lom21blu1u978IDvRs0andhl=enandsa=Xandei=TSY TVJ-EK-uajAL7lYDYCgandved=0CCAQ6AEwAA#v=onepageandq=journal%20of %20banking%20%22the%20science%20of%20currency%22andf=false, retrieved 12 July 2014.

Granovetter, Mark S., and Patrick McGuire. 1998. The making of an industry: Electricity in the United States. In Michel Callon, ed., *The Law of Markets*, 147–73. Oxford: Blackwell.

Gray, Alonzo. 1842. *Elements of Scientific and Practical Agriculture, or the Application of Biology, Geology, and Chemistry to Agriculture and Horticulture. Intended as a Textbook for Farmers and Students in Agriculture.* Andover, MA: Allen, Morrill, and Wardwell.

Gray, Lewis C. 1933. *History of Agriculture in the Southern United States.* Washington, DC: Carnegie Institution.

Greene, Evarts B. and Virginia D. Harrington. 1966. *American Population before the First Federal Census of 1790.* Gloucester, MA: Peter Smith.

Greene, William H. 2003. *Econometric Analysis.* New York: Prentice Hall.

Greenhood, David, and Helen Gentry. 1936. *Chronology of Books and Printing.* New York: Macmillan.

Greiggs, Samuel. 1833. [No title.] *Genesee Farmer* 3(6): 46. http://search.proquest.com /americanperiodicals/docview/126155201/D9FE07C8765146D9PQ/18?accountid =14496, retrieved 1 August 2014.

Grenell, Mary. 1845. Correspondence: From Ohio. *Circular* 1(9): 36. http://search.pro quest.com/americanperiodicals/docview/137598443/B04FE2BF91A34C46PQ/1 ?accountid=14496, retrieved 13 August 2014.

Griffin, Clifford S. 1957. Religious benevolence as social control: 1815–1860. *Mississippi Valley Historical Review* 44: 423–44.

Griffin, Clifford S. 1960. *Their Brothers' Keepers: Moral Stewardship in the United States, 1800–1865.* New Brunswick, NJ: Rutgers University Press.

Griswold, Wendy. 1981. American character and the American novel: An expansion of reflection theory in the sociology of literature. *American Journal of Sociology* 86: 740–65.

Griswold, Wendy. 2008. *Regionalism and the Reading Class.* Chicago: University of Chicago Press.

Griswold, Wendy, and Nathan Wright. 2004. Cowbirds, locals, and the dynamic endurance of regionalism. *American Journal of Sociology* 109(6): 1411–51.

Goodrich, A. T. 1819. Prospectus. *Belles-Lettres Repository* 1(1): 1. http://search.proquest .com/americanperiodicals/docview/136130354/1410ED25075961D274/27?accountid =14496, retrieved 13 May 2003.

Guatimozin. 1821. To the farmers and planters of the United States. *Farmer's and Plant-*

er's Friend 1(1): 5. http://search.proquest.com/americanperiodicals/docview/896130 80/140EA893F581E9F98F2/1?accountid=14496, retrieved 4 October 2013.

Gurevich, Michael, and Mark R. Levy, eds. 1985. *Mass Communication Review Yearbook,* vol. 5. Beverly Hills, CA: Sage.

Haber, Samuel. 1991. *The Quest for Authority and Honor in the American Professions, 1750–1900.* Chicago: University of Chicago Press.

Habermas, Jürgen. (1962) 1991. *The Structural Transformation of the Public Sphere: An Introduction into a Category of Bourgeois Society.* Translated by Thomas Burger with the assistance of Frederick Lawrence. Cambridge, MA: MIT Press.

Haines, Michael R. 2008. *Historical, Demographic, Economic, and Social Data: The United States, 1790–2002.* Ann Arbor, MI: Inter-university Consortium for Political and Social Research. Retrieved 24 September 2008.

Haites, Erik F., and James Mak. 1978. Social savings due to western river steamboats. *Research in Economic History* 3: 294.

Haites, Erik F., James Mak, and Gary M. Walton. 1975. *Western River Transportation: The Era of Early Internal Development, 1810–1860.* Baltimore: Johns Hopkins University Press.

Halbert, Sanford. 1850. Importance of circulating the repository. *African Repository* 26(5): 144. http://search.proquest.com/americanperiodicals/docview/89575747/55 AF667C9E4B4C3CPQ/13?accountid=14496, retrieved 13 August 2014.

Hale, F. Dennis. 2003. Political discourse remains vigorous despite media ownership. In Joseph Harper and Thom Yantek, eds., *Media, Profit, and Politics: Competing Priorities in a Democratic Society,* 140–57. Kent, OH: Kent State University Press.

Hall, Arthur. 1940. *The Story of Soil Conservation in the South Carolina Piedmont, 1800–1860.* Miscellaneous Publication no. 40. Washington, DC: US Department of Agriculture.

Hall, Peter Dobkin. 1984. *The Organization of American Culture, 1700–1900: Private Institutions, Elites, and the Origins of American Nationality.* New York: New York University Press.

Hall, Peter Dobkin. 1992. *Inventing the Nonprofit Sector and Other Essays on Philanthropy, Voluntarism, and Nonprofit Organizations.* Baltimore: Johns Hopkins University Press.

Hall, Peter Dobkin. 1998. Religion and the organizational revolution in the United States. In N. J. Demerath III, Peter Dobkin Hall, Terry Schmitt, and Rhys H. Williams, eds. 1998. *Sacred Companies: Organized Aspects of Religion and Religious Aspects of Organizations,* 99–115. New York: Oxford University Press.

Haller, John S. 1997. *Kindly Medicine: Physio-Medicalism in America, 1836–1911.* Kent, OH: Kent State University Press.

Haller, John S. 2000. *The People's Doctors: Samuel Thomson and the American Botanical Movement, 1790–1860.* Carbondale: Southern Illinois University Press.

Haller, John S. 2005. *The History of Homeopathy: The Academic Years, 1820–1935.* Binghamton, NY: Haworth.

Halloren, James D., Philip Elliott, and Graham Murdock. 1969. *Demonstrations and Communication: A Case Study.* Harmondsworth, England: Penguin.

Hamilton, James T. 2003. *All the News That's Fit to Sell: How the Market Transforms Information into News.* Princeton, NJ: Princeton University Press.

Hamilton, John Taylor. 1900. *A History of the Church Known as the Moravian Church, or the Unitas Fratum, or the Unity of the Brethren, during the Eighteenth and Nineteenth Centuries.* Bethlehem, PA: Times Publishing Company Printers.

Handlin, Oscar. 1959. *Boston's Immigrants, 1790–1865: A Study in Acculturation*. Cambridge, MA: Belknap Press.

Hankins, Barry. 2004. *The Second Great Awakening and the Transcendentalists*. Westport, CT: Greenwood.

Hannan, Michael T., and John Freeman. 1977. The population ecology of organizations. *American Journal of Sociology* 82: 929–64.

Hannan, Michael T., and John Freeman. 1989. *Organizational Ecology*. Cambridge, MA: Harvard University Press.

Harbinger. 1845. Letter from Broadway—No. III. *Harbinger* 1(9): 134. http://search.proquest.com/americanperiodicals/docview/125703657/98C7A97A3DED4743PQ/2?accountid=14496, retrieved 12 August 2014.

Harbinger. 1846. Letter to the editor. *Harbinger* 3(2): 18. http://search.proquest.com/americanperiodicals/docview/125701931/98C7A97A3DED4743PQ/10?accountid=14496, retrieved 12 August 2014.

Haroutunian, Joseph. 1970. *Piety versus Moralism: The Passing of the New England Theology*. New York: Harper Torchbooks.

Hart, James. (1950) 1963. *The Popular Book: A History of America's Literary Taste*. Berkeley: University of California Press.

Harvey, David. (1975) 2001. *Spaces of Capital: Towards a Critical Geography*. Edinburgh: Edinburgh University Press.

Hatch, Nathan O. 1989. *The Democratization of American Christianity*. New Haven, CT: Yale University Press.

Hausman, Jerry. 1978. Specification tests in econometrics. *Econometrica* 46: 1251–71.

Haveman, Heather A. 2004. Antebellum literary culture and the evolution of American magazines. *Poetics* 32: 5–28.

Haveman, Heather A., Jacob Habinek, and Leo A. Goodman. 2012. How entrepreneurship evolves: The founders of new magazines in America, 1741–1860. *Administrative Science Quarterly* 57: 585–624.

Haveman, Heather A., and Daniel N. Kluttz. 2014. Property in print: Copyright law and the American magazine industry. Working paper, University of California—Berkeley.

Haveman, Heather A., and Lynn Nonnemaker. 2000. Competition in multiple geographic markets: The impact on market entry and growth. *Administrative Science Quarterly* 44: 232–67.

Haveman, Heather A., Hayagreeva Rao, and Srikanth Paruchuri. 2007. The winds of change: The progressive movement and the bureaucratization of thrift. *American Sociological Review* 72: 117–42.

Haveman, Heather A., and Christopher I. Rider. 2014a. The spatial scope of competition and the geographic distribution of entrepreneurship: Magazine foundings and the US post office. *Sociological Science* 1(3): 111–27.

Haveman, Heather A., and Christopher I. Rider. 2014b. Place *and* space: The development of communication systems and competitive differentiation among startups. Working paper, University of California–Berkeley Department of Sociology.

Hawley, Amos H. 1968. *Human Ecology: A Theoretical Essay*. Chicago: University of Chicago Press.

Hay, William D. 1855. *A History of Temperance in Saratoga County, N.Y.* Saratoga Springs, NY: G. M. Davison.

Hayter, Earl W. 1968. *The Troubled Farmer, 1850–1900: Rural Adjustment to Industrialization*. DeKalb: Northern Illinois University Press.

Headd, Brian. 2001. Business success: Factors leading to surviving and closing successfully. Working Paper #CES-WP-01-01. Washington, DC: Center for Economic Studies, US Census Bureau.

Heckman, James, and George Borjas. 1980. Does unemployment cause future unemployment? *Economica* 47: 247–83.

Helgerson, Richard. 1983. *Self-Crowned Laureates: Spenser, Jonson, Milton, and the Literary System*. Berkeley: University of California Press.

Helleiner, Eric. 1999. National currencies and national identities. *American Behavioral Scientist* 41: 1409–36.

Henkin, David. 1998. *City Reading: Written Words and Public Spaces in Antebellum New York*. New York: Columbia University Press.

Henkin, David. 2006. *The Postal Age: The Emergence of Modern Communications in Nineteenth-Century America*. Chicago: University of Chicago Press.

Henkle, Saul. 1823. Introductory observations. *Gospel Trumpet* 2(1): 1–2. http://search.proquest.com/americanperiodicals/docview/126084195/BB547C354B634188PQ/4?accountid=14496, retrieved 14 May 2003.

Hepburn, Alonzo Barton. 1903. *History of Coinage and Currency in the United States and the Perennial Contest for Sound Money*. New York: Macmillan.

Herbert, Henry William, and Andrew D. Patterson. 1833. Introduction: Writers and critics. *American Monthly Magazine* 2(1): 1–7. http://search.proquest.com/americanperiodicals/docview/89572706/fulltextPDF/141054DBD236002C92C/2?accountid=14496, retrieved 1 June 2009.

Hewett, Daniel. 1935. Daniel Hewett's list of newspapers and periodicals in the US in 1828. *American Antiquarian Society Proceedings*, new series, 44: 365–98.

Higham, John. 1974. Hanging together: Divergent unities in American history. *Journal of American History* 61: 5–28.

Hindle, Brooke, and Steven Lubar. 1986. *Engines of Change: The American Industrial Revolution, 1790–1860*. Washington, DC: Smithsonian Institution Press.

Hirrel, Leo P. 1998. *Children of Wrath: New School Calvinism and Antebellum Reform*. Lexington: University Press of Kentucky.

Hirschman, Albert O. 1964. The paternity of an index. *American Economic Review* 54: 761–62.

H.J. 1833. Change of sentiment. *Abolitionist* 1(4): 60–61. http://search.proquest.com/americanperiodicals/docview/124720515/A18A3E80F6F348A8PQ/2?accountid=14496, retrieved 12 August 2014.

Hobbes, Thomas. (1651) 1962. *Leviathan*. New York: Collier.

Hobsbawm, Eric J. 1959. *Primitive Rebel: Studies in Archaic Forms of Social Movements in the 19th and 20th Centuries*. Manchester, England: Manchester University Press.

Hoerder, Dirk, and Christiane Harzig. 1987. *The Immigrant Labor Press in North America, 1840s–1970s: An Annotated Bibliography*. 3 vols. New York: Greenwood.

Hoffman, Saul D., and Greg J. Duncan. 1988. Multinomial and conditional logit discrete-choice models in demography. *Demography* 25: 415–27.

Hofstadter, Richard. 1955. *The Age of Reform*. New York: Vintage.

Hodges, Samuel W. 1877. Sons of Temperance—Historical Record of the Order. In *Centennial Temperance Volume: A Memorial of the International Temperance Conference Held in Philadelphia, June, 1876*. New York: National Temperance Society and Publications House.

Home Magazine. 1853. Magazine literature. *Home Magazine* 2(3): 235–36. http://search

.proquest.com/americanperiodicals/docview/124501023/EC82EC7D04A34753PQ /3?accountid=14496, retrieved 28 July 2014.

Hood, Fred J. 1977. Evolution of the denomination among the Reformed of the middle and southern states, 1780–1840. In Russell E. Richey, ed., *Denominationalism*, 139–60. Nashville, TN: Abingdon.

Hoornstra, Jean, and Trudy Heath, editors. 1979. *American Periodicals, 1741–1900: An Index to the Microfilm Collections.* Ann Arbor, MI: University Microfilm International.

Hounshell, David A. 1984. *From the American System to Mass Production.* Baltimore: Johns Hopkins University Press.

Howell, Warren R. 1970. *Early Newspapers and Periodicals of California and the West.* San Francisco: John Howell.

Huffman, Jasper Abraham. 1920. *History of the Mennonite Brethren in Christ Church.* New Carlisle, OH: Bethel.

Humanitas. 1831. Messrs. Editors. *Genius of Universal Emancipation* 2(7): 112. http:// search.proquest.com/americanperiodicals/docview/124022635/F188C99A7E54AB BPQ/331?accountid=14496, retrieved 14 August 2014.

Hunter, David. 1952. *Papermaking in Pioneer America.* Philadelphia: University of Pennsylvania Press.

Hurst, James Willard. 1973. *A Legal History of Money in the United States, 1774–1970.* Lincoln: University of Nebraska Press.

Hutton, Frankie, and Barbara Strauss Reed, eds. 1975. *Outsiders in 19th-Century Press History: Multicultural Perspectives.* Bowling Green, OH: Bowling Green State University Popular Press.

Hutton, Joseph Edmond. 1909. *A History of the Moravian Church.* 2nd ed., rev. and enlarged. London: Moravian Publication House.

Hutton, Joseph Edmond. 1923. *A History of Moravian Missions.* London: Moravian Publication House.

Iannaccone, Laurence. 1994. Why strict churches are strong. *American Journal of Sociology* 99: 1180–1211.

Illinois Monthly Magazine. 1831. Periodicals. *Illinois Monthly Magazine* 1(7): 302–4. http://search.proquest.com/americanperiodicals/docview/90536646/F5145CD4F3 CC4BD9PQ/3?accountid=14496, retrieved 27 May 2014.

Ingram, Paul. 1996. Organizational form as a solution to the problem of credible commitment: The evolution of naming strategies among US hotel chains, 1896–1980. *Strategic Management Journal* 17: 85–98.

Inkeles, Alex, and David H. Smith. 1974. *Becoming Modern: Individual Change in Six Developing Countries.* Cambridge, MA: Harvard University Press.

Inman, John. 1844. Magazine literature. *Columbian Lady's and Gentleman's Magazine* 1(1): 1–6. http://search.proquest.com/americanperiodicals/docview/124775479/8A 97F3221EC4A4BPQ/4?accountid=14496, retrieved 14 May 2003.

International Weekly Miscellany. 1850. Introduction. *International Weekly Miscellany* 1(1): 1.

Jackson, Leon. 2008. *The Business of Letters: Authorial Economics in Antebellum America.* Stanford, CA: Stanford University Press.

Janelle, Donald G. 1968. Central-place development in a time-space framework. *Professional Geographer* 20: 5–10.

Janelle, Donald G. 1969. Spatial reorganization: A model and concept. *Annals of American Geographers* 59: 348–64.

Jasper, James. 2011. Emotions and social movements: Twenty years of theory and research. *Annual Review of Sociology* 37: 285–303.

Jaszi, Peter. 1991. Towards a theory of copyright: The metamorphoses of "authorship." *Duke Law Journal* 1991(2): 455–502.

John, Richard R. 1990. Taking Sabbatarianism seriously: The postal system, the Sabbath, and the transformation of American political culture. *Journal of the Early Republic* 10: 517–67.

John, Richard R. 1995. *Spreading the News: The American Postal System from Franklin to Morse.* Cambridge, MA: Harvard University Press.

Johnson, Paul E. 1978. *A Shopkeeper's Millennium: Society and Revivals in Rochester, New York, 1815–1837.* New York: Hill and Wang.

Jones, Alice Hanson. 1980. *Wealth of a Nation to Be: The American Colonies on the Eve of the Revolution.* New York: Columbia University Press.

Jones, E. L. 1974. Creative disruptions in American agriculture, 1620–1820. *Agricultural History,* 48: 510–528.

Jones, Eric. 1968. Agricultural origins of industry. *Past and Present* 40: 58–71.

Jones, James W., and William S. Jones. 1843. To southern planters. *Southern Cultivator* 1(1): 6. http://search.proquest.com/americanperiodicals/docview/137966049/783E5 D80B2644C86PQ/14?accountid=14496, retrieved 9 June 2007.

Jordan, Weymouth T. 1957. Noah B. Cloud and the *American Cotton Planter. Agricultural History* 31(4): 44–49.

Journal of Health. 1829. Prospectus. *Journal of Health* 1(1): 1–2. http://search.proquest .com/americanperiodicals/docview/136123106/88E941B7C948C0PQ/3?accountid =14496, retrieved 14 May 2003.

Kaestle, Carl F. 1983. *Pillars of the Republic: Common Schools and American Society, 1780–1860.* New York: Hill and Wang.

Kaestle, Carl F. 1991a. Studying the history of literacy. In Carl F. Kaestle, Helen Damon-Moore, Lawrence C. Stedman, Katherine Tinsley, and William Vance Trollinger, Jr., *Literacy in the United States: Readers and Reading since 1880,* 3–32. New Haven, CT: Yale University Press.

Kaestle, Carl F. 1991b. The history of readers. In Carl F. Kaestle, Helen Damon-Moore, Lawrence C. Stedman, Katherine Tinsley, and William Vance Trollinger Jr., *Literacy in the United States: Readers and Reading since 1880,* 33–72. New Haven, CT: Yale University Press.

Kamrath, Mark. 2002. *Eyes Wide Shut* and the cultural poetics of eighteenth-century American periodical literature. *Early American Literature* 37: 497–536.

Kanellos, Nicolas, and Helvetia Martell. 2000. *Hispanic Periodicals in the United States, Origins to 1960: A Brief History and Comprehensive Bibliography.* Houston, TX: Arte Publico.

Kanter, Rosabeth Moss. 1972. *Commitment and Community: Communes and Utopias in Sociological Perspective.* Cambridge, MA: Harvard University Press.

Katan, George, and James N. Morgan. 1952. A quantitative study of factors determining business decisions. *Quarterly Journal of Economics* 66: 67–90.

Katz, Michael B. 1986. *In the Shadow of the Poorhouse: A Social History of Welfare in America.* New York: Basic Books.

Kaufman, Jason. 2008. Corporate law and the sovereignty of states. *American Sociological Review* 73: 402–25.

Kaufman, Jason, and Matthew E. Kaliner. 2011. The re-accomplishment of place in twentieth century Vermont and New Hampshire: History repeats itself, until it doesn't. *Theory and Society* 40: 119–54.

Kelly, R. Gordon, ed. 1984. *Children's Periodicals of the United States.* Westport, CT: Greenwood.

Kennard, Timothy. 1809. [No title.] *Omnium Gatherum* 1(1): 1–2. http://search.proquest .com/americanperiodicals/publication/24544/citation/9FEA3C09E1D4899PQ /1?accountid=14496, retrieved 14 May 2003.

Kenny, Daniel J. 1861. *The American Newspaper Directory and Record of the Press. Containing an Accurate List of all the Newspapers, Magazines, Reviews, Periodicals, etc., in the United States and British Provinces of North America.* New York: Watson.

Kern, Stephen. 1983. *The Culture of Time and Space, 1880–1918.* Cambridge, MA: Harvard University Press.

Kernan, Alvin. 1987. *Printing Technology, Letters, and Samuel Johnson.* Princeton, NJ: Princeton University Press.

Khan, B. Zorina. 2005. *The Democratization of Invention: Patents and Copyright in American Invention, 1790–1920.* New York: Cambridge University Press.

Khan, B. Zorina, and Kenneth L. Sokoloff. 2001. Intellectual property institutions in the United States: Early development. *Journal of Economic Perspectives* 15: 233–46.

Kielbowicz, Richard B. 1989. *News in the Mail: The Press, Post Office, and Public Information, 1700–1800s.* New York: Greenwood.

Kim, Hyojoung, and Steven Pfaff. 2012. Structure and dynamics of religious insurgency: Students and the spread of the Reformation. *American Sociological Review* 77: 188–215.

Kimball, L. 1845. Practical papers. *Prairie Farmer* 5(9): 213. http://search.proquest.com /americanperiodicals/docview/127488317/28D43115A7074759PQ/5?accountid =14496, retrieved 1 August 2014.

King, Marissa D., and Heather A. Haveman. 2008. Antislavery in America: The press, the pulpit, and the rise of antislavery societies. *Administrative Science Quarterly* 53: 492–528.

Klein, H. M. 1943. *History of the Eastern Synod of the Reformed Church in the United States.* Lancaster, PA: Rudsill and Smith.

Kline, Ronald R. 2000. *Consumers in the Country: Technology and Social Change in Rural America.* Baltimore: Johns Hopkins University Press.

Knoke, David, and Peter J. Burke. 1980. *Log-Linear Models.* Newbury Park, CA: Sage.

Knowles, James D. 1836. Introduction. *Christian Review* 1(1): 5–14. http://search .proquest.com/americanperiodicals/docview/89785949/7DD6B558EEA94E7FPQ/2 ?accountid=14496, retrieved 14 May 2003.

Koçak, Özgecan, and Glenn Carroll. 2008. Growing church organizations in diverse US communities, 1890–1926. *American Journal of Sociology* 113: 1272–1315.

Koch, Adrienne. 1965. *The American Enlightenment: The Shaping of the American Experiment as a Free Society.* New York: George Braziller.

Koek, Joost. 1999. Reconsidering the reading revolution: The thesis of the "reading revolution" and a Dutch bookseller's clientele around 1800. *Poetics* 26: 289–307.

Kollock, Shepard, and David Austin. 1789a. [No title.] *Christian's, Scholar's, and Farmer's Magazine* 1(1): n.p. http://search.proquest.com/americanperiodicals/docview/88 493815/5AFE7561DD7941C8PQ/3?accountid=14496, retrieved 21 March 2006.

Kollock, Shepard, and David Austin. 1789b. To subscribers. *Christian's, Scholar's, and Farmer's Magazine* 1(1): n.p. http://search.proquest.com/americanperiodicals/docview /88882651/F413D46B222D44D7PQ/2?accountid=14496, retrieved 21 March 2006.

Kono, Cliff, Donald Palmer, Roger Friedland, and Matthew Zafonte. 1998. Lost in space: Understanding the geography of corporate interlocking directorates. *American Journal of Sociology* 103: 863–911.

Kowalik, Jan. 1978. *The Polish Press in America.* San Francisco: R and E Research Associates.

Kribbs, Jayne K., ed. 1977. *An Annotated Bibliography of American Literary Periodicals, 1741–1850.* Boston: G. K. Hall.

Kronick, David A. 1962. *A History of Scientific and Technical Periodicals: The Origins and Developments of the Scientific and Technological Press, 1665–1790.* New York: Scarecrow.

Krugman, Paul. 1991. Increasing returns and economic geography. *Journal of Political Economy* 99: 483–99.

Kulikoff, Allan. 1992. *The Agrarian Origins of American Capitalism.* Charlottesville: University of Virginia Press.

Lambert, Frank. 1999. *Inventing the Great Awakening.* Princeton, NJ:Princeton University Press.

Lamoreaux, Naomi R. 1994. *Insider Lending: Banks, Personal Connections, and Economic Development in Industrial New England.* Cambridge: Cambridge University Press.

Langton, Edward. 1956. *History of the Moravian Church: The Story of the First International Protestant Church.* London: Allen and Unwin.

Larson, John Lauritz. 1987. "Bind the republic together": The national union and the struggle for a system of internal improvements. *Journal of American History* 74: 363–87.

Larson, John Lauritz. 2010. *The Market Revolution in America: Liberty, Ambition, and the Eclipse of the Common Good.* New York: Cambridge University Press.

Larson, Magali S. 1977. *The Rise of Professionalism.* Berkeley: University of California Press.

Latter Day Luminary. 1818. Introduction. *Latter Day Luminary* 1(1): iii–viii. http://search.proquest.com/americanperiodicals/docview/90542638/pageviewPDF/4218E BBC30A2474CPQ/1?accountid=14496, retrieved 14 May 2003.

Lazear, Edward P. 1977. Academic achievement and job performance: Note. *American Economic Review* 67: 252–54.

Lebergott, Stanley. 1964. *Manpower in Economic Growth: The American Record since 1800.* New York: McGraw-Hill.

Lebergott, Stanley. 1966. Labor force and employment. In National Bureau of Economic Research, *Studies in Income and Wealth* 30: 117–204. New York: Columbia University Press.

Lehmann-Haupt, Helmut. 1941. *Bookbinding in America.* New York: R. R. Bowker.

Lehmann-Haupt, Helmut, ed. 1951. *The Book in America: A History of the Making and Selling of Books in the United States.* New York: R. R. Bowker.

Lehrman, William G. 1994. Diversity in decline: Institutional environment and organizational failure in the American life insurance industry. *Social Forces* 73: 605–35.

Lemmer, George F. 1957. Early agricultural editors and their farm philosophies. *Agricultural History* 31: 3–22.

Lemon, James T. 1967. Household consumption in eighteenth-century America and its relationship to production and trade: The situation among farmers in southeastern Pennsylvania. *Agricultural History* 16: 59–70.

Lewis, Benjamin Morgan. 1955. A history and bibliography of American magazines, 1800–1810. PhD diss., University of Michigan.

Lieberson, Stanley. 1969. Measuring population diversity. *American Sociological Review* 34: 850–62.

Liebman, Robert C., John R. Sutton, and Robert Wuthnow. 1988. Exploring the social sources of denominationalism: Schisms in American protestant denominations, 1890–1980. *American Sociological Review* 53: 343–52.

Lincoln, Levi, Jr. 1823. Address delivered before the Worcester County Agricultural Society. *New England Farmer* 1(23): 180. http://www.biodiversitylibrary.org/item/77782#page/7/mode/1up, retrieved 13 June 2013.

Linklater, Andro. 2002. *Measuring America: How an Untamed Wilderness Shaped the United States and Fulfilled the Promise of Democracy.* New York: Walker.

Lippy, Charles H. 1986. *Religious Periodicals of the United States: Academic and Scholarly Journals.* Westport, CT: Greenwood.

Lipsky, Michael. 1968. Protest as a political resource. *American Political Science Review* 62: 1144–58.

Literary Tablet. 1833. Anonymous writings. *Literary Tablet* 1(24): 188. http://search.proquest.com/americanperiodicals/docview/90040624/141057A667B3AA265B5/6?accountid=14496, retrieved 1 June 2009.

Littlefield, Daniel, and James W. Parins. 1984. *American Indian and Alaska Native Newspapers and Periodicals, 1826–1924.* Westport, CT: Greenwood.

Locke, John. 1690a. *Second Treatise of Civil Government.* Chap. 5, Of property, sec. 27. http://www.constitution.org/jl/2ndtr05.htm, retrieved 23 July 2013.

Locke, John. 1690b. *An Essay concerning Human Understanding.* Hazleton, PA: Pennsylvania State University Press.

Locke, Mary Stoughton. 1901. *Anti-Slavery in America: From the Introduction of African Slaves to the Prohibition of the Slave Trade (1619–1808).* Boston: Ginn.

Loehr, Rodney C. 1952. Self-sufficiency on the farm. *Agricultural History* 26(2): 37–41.

Lomi, Alessandro, and Erik R. Larsen. 1996. Interacting locally and evolving globally: A computational approach to the dynamics of organizational populations. *Academy of Management Journal* 36: 1287–1321.

Long, Kathryn Teresa. 1998. *The Revival of 1857–58: Interpreting an American Religious Awakening.* New York: Oxford University Press.

Longworth's American Almanack, New-York Register, and City Directory. 1799. New York: J. C. Totten.

Lora, Ronald, and William Henry Longton, eds. 1999. *The Conservative Press in 18th and 19th Century America.* Westport, CT: Greenwood.

Loughborough, J. N. (1909) 1972. *The Great Second Advent Movement: Its Rise and Progress.* New York: Arno.

Loveland, Anne C. 1966. Evangelicalism and "immediate emancipation" in American antislavery thought. *Journal of Southern History* 32: 172–88.

Lucas, Peter J. 1982. The growth and development of English literary patronage in the later Middle Ages and early Renaissance. *The Library: The Transactions of the Bibliographical Society,* 6th series, 4: 218–48.

Lundy, Benjamin. 1821. Address to the public. *Genius of Universal Emancipation* 1(1): 1–3. http://search.proquest.com/americanperiodicals/docview/124015901/BE115E7BEABF42B2PQ/4?accountid=14496, retrieved 14 May 2003.

Luraghi, Raimondo. 1962. The Civil War and the modernization of American society: Social structure and industrial revolution in the Old South before and during the war. *Civil War History* 18: 230–50.

Lyon, Betty Longenecker. 1942. A history of children's secular magazines published in the United States from 1789–1899. PhD diss., Johns Hopkins University.

MacCurdy, Raymond R. 1951. *A History and Bibliography of Spanish-Language Newspapers and Magazines in Louisiana, 1808–1949.* Albuquerque: University of New Mexico Press.

MacIver, R. M. 1917. *Community: A Sociological Study.* London: Macmillan. http://www.unz.org/Pub/MacIverRobert-1917?View=ReadIt, retrieved May 2014.

Macpherson, C. B. 1962. *The Political Theory of Possessive Individualism: Hobbes to Locke.* Oxford: Clarendon Press.

Mallott, Floyd. 1954. *Studies in Brethren History.* Elgin, IL: Brethren Publishing House.

Margo, Robert A. 2000. *Wages and Labor Markets in the United States, 1820–1860.* Chicago: University of Chicago Press.

Margo, Robert A., and Georgia C. Villaflor. 1987. The growth of wages in antebellum America: New evidence. *Journal of Economic History* 47: 873–95.

Marilley, Suzanne. 1997. *Woman Suffrage and the Origins of Liberal Feminism in the United States, 1820–1920.* Cambridge, MA: Harvard University Press.

Marin, Margaret E. 1938–39. *Merchants and Trade of the Connecticut River Valley, 1750–1820.* Northampton, MA: Smith College.

Marino, Samuel Joseph. 1962. The French refugee newspapers and periodicals in the United States, 1789–1825. PhD diss., University of Michigan.

Marquis, Christopher. 2003. The pressure of the past: Network imprinting in intercorporate communities. *Administrative Science Quarterly* 48: 655–89.

Marquis, Christopher, and Julie Battilana. 2009. Acting globally but thinking locally? The enduring influence of local communities on organizations. *Research in Organizational Behavior* 29: 283–302.

Marquis, Christopher, and Michael Lounsbury. 2007. Vive la résistance: Competing logics and the consolidation of US community banking. *Academy of Management Journal* 50: 799–820.

Marshall, Alfred. 1920. *Principles of Economics: An Introductory Volume.* London: Macmillan.

Marshall, Gloria J. 1995. The survival of colleges in America: A census of four-year colleges in the United States 1636–1973. PhD diss., Stanford School of Education.

Marti, Donald B. 1979. *To Improve the Soil and the Mind: Agricultural Societies, Journalism, and Schools in the Northeastern States, 1791–1865.* Ann Arbor, MI: University Microfilms International.

Marti, Donald B. 1980. Agricultural journalism and the diffusion of knowledge: The first half-century in America. *Agricultural History* 54(1): 28–37.

Martin, Margaret E. 1939. *Merchants and Trade of the Connecticut River Valley, 1750–1820.* Northampton, MA: Smith College Studies in History.

Marty, Martin E. 1963. The Protestant press: Limitations and possibilities. In Martin E. Marty, John G. Deedy Jr., and David Wolf Silverman, *The Religious Press in America*, 3–63. New York: Holt, Rinehart and Winston.

Marty, Martin E. 1976. Living with establishment and disestablishment in nineteenth-century America. *Journal of Church and State* 18(1): 61–77.

Marty, Martin E. 1987. *Religion and Republic: The American Circumstance.* Boston: Beacon.

Marty, Martin E., John G. Deedy Jr., David Wolf Silverman, and Robert Lekachman. 1963. *The Religious Press in America.* New York: Holt, Rinehart and Winston.

Marvin, Carolyn. 1987. *When Old Technologies Were New: Thinking about Electric Communication in the Late Nineteenth Century.* New York: Oxford University Press.

Marx, Karl. (1857–61) 2002. *Grundrisse der Kritik der Politischen Ökonomie* [Outlines of the Critique of Political Economy]. Marxists' Internet Archive. https://www.marxists.org/archive/marx/works/1857/grundrisse/ch10.htm, retrieved 9 January 2010.

Marx, Karl. (1867) 1977. *Capital: A Critique of Political Economy*, vol. 1. Translated by Ben Fowkes. New York: Vintage.

Marx, Karl, with Friedrich Engels. (1846) 1947. *The German Ideology: Critique of Modern German Philosophy According to Its Representatives Feuerbach, B. Bauer and Stirner, and of German Socialism According to Its Various Prophets.* Edited by Roy Pascal. New York: International Publishers.

Marx Ferree, Myra. 2012. *Varieties of Feminism: German Gender Politics in Global Context.* Stanford, CA: Stanford University Press.

Mason, John Mitchell. 1806. Introduction. *The Christian's Magazine* 1(1): iii–xvi. http://search.proquest.com/americanperiodicals/docview/89410264/653873B64F304700PQ/15?accountid=14496, retrieved 14 May 2003.

Masonic Mirror and Mechanics' Intelligencer. 1825. Counterfeiting. *Masonic Mirror and Mechanics' Intelligencer* 1(4): 2. http://search.proquest.com/americanperiodicals/docview/124924100/4059338C87C04BF6PQ/7?accountid=14496, retrieved 18 July 2014.

Mathews, Donald G. 1969. The Second Great Awakening as an organizing process, 1780–1830: An hypothesis. *American Quarterly* 21(1): 23–43.

Matthews, Albert. 1910. *Lists of New England Magazines, 1743–1800.* Cambridge, MA: John Wilson and Son.

Matthews, Harriet L. 1899. Magazines for children. *Bulletin of Bibliography* 1: 133–36.

Mazzone, Jason. 2004. Organizing the republic: Civic associations and American constitutionalism 1780–1830. PhD diss., Yale University Law School.

McAdam, Doug. 2003. Beyond structural analysis. In Mario Diani and Doug McAdam, eds., *Social Movements and Social Networks: Relational Approaches to Collective Action*, 281–98. Oxford: Oxford University Press.

McCarthy, John D., and Mayer Zald. 1977. Resource mobilization and social movements: A partial theory. *American Journal of Sociology* 82: 1212–41.

McCarthy, Kathleen D. 2003. *American Creed: Philanthropy and the Rise of Civil Society, 1700–1865.* Chicago: University of Chicago Press.

McChesney, Robert. 2001. Policing the unthinkable. https://www.opendemocracy.net/media-globalmediaownership/article_56.jsp, retrieved 25 October 2007.

McChesney, Robert W. 2004. *The Problem of the Media: US Communication in the 21st Century.* New York: Monthly Review Press.

McClelland, Peter D. 1997. *Sowing Modernity: America's First Agricultural Revolution.* Ithaca, NY: Cornell University Press.

McCusker, John J. 1992. *Money and Exchange in Europe and America, 1600–1775: A Handbook.* 2nd ed. Chapel Hill: University of North Carolina Press.

McCusker, John J. 2000. Estimating early American gross domestic product. *Historical Methods* 33: 155–62.

McCusker, John J. 2001. *How Much Is That in Real Money? A Historical Commodity Price Index for Use as a Deflator of Money Values in the Economy of the United States.* 2nd ed., rev. and enlarged. Worcester, MA: American Antiquarian Society.

McCusker, John J. 2005. The demise of distance: The business press and the origins of the information revolution in the early modern Atlantic world. *American Historical Review* 110(2): 295–321.

McCusker, John J., and Russell R. Menard. 1991. *The Economy of British America, 1607–1789.* 2nd ed. Chapel Hill: University of North Carolina Press.

McFadden, Daniel. 1973. Conditional logit analysis of qualitative choice behavior. In Paul Zarembka, ed., *Frontiers in Econometrics*, 105—35. New York: John Wiley.

McGill, Meredith L. 2003. *American Literature and the Culture of Reprinting, 1834–1853.* Philadelphia: University of Pennsylvania Press.

McKivigan, John R. 1984. *The War against Proslavery Religion: Abolitionism and the Northern Churches, 1830–1865.* Ithaca, NY: Cornell University Press.

McLean, Elliott Hall. 1928. Periodicals published in the South before 1880. Manuscript, University of Virginia.

McLoughlin, William G. 1978. *Revivals, Awakenings, and Reform: An Essay on Religion and Social Change in America, 1607–1977.* Chicago: University of Chicago Press.

McLuhan, Marshall. 1962. *The Gutenberg Galaxy: The Making of Typographic Man.* Toronto: University of Toronto Press.

McMurry, Sally. 1989. Who read the agricultural journals? Evidence from Chenango County, New York, 1839–1865. *Agricultural History* 63(4): 1–18.

McMurtrie, Douglas C. 1936. *A History of Printing in the United States.* New York: R. R. Bowker.

M'Donald, Alexander. 1836. On keeping agricultural books. *Southern Agriculturist and Register of Rural Affairs* 9(8): 411–12. http://search.proquest.com/americanperiodicals/docview/137649211/DEE9E7A1511847A5PQ/50?accountid=14496, retrieved 1 August 2014.

Mead, Frank S. 1985. *Handbook of Denominations in the United States.* New 9th ed., rev. Samuel S. Hill. Nashville, TN: Abingdon.

Meagher, Paul Kevin, Thomas O'Brien, and Consuelo Maria Aherne, eds. 1979. *Encyclopedic Dictionary of Religion.* Washington, DC: Corpus.

Meigs, Josiah, and Eleutheros Dana. 1786. To the public. *New Haven Gazette, and Connecticut Magazine* 1(1): iii–iv. http://search.proquest.com/americanperiodicals/docview/88859800/992D392EDB2E4B91PQ/2?accountid=14496, retrieved 13 July 2012.

Melder, Keith E. 1977. *Beginnings of Sisterhood: The American Woman's Rights Movement, 1800–1850.* New York: Schocken.

Melton, Gordon. 2003. *Encyclopedia of American Religions.* 7th ed. Detroit: Gale Research.

Merchants' Magazine. 1852. A national currency: Confidence its basis. *Merchants' Magazine* 26(5): 616–17. http://search.proquest.com/americanperiodicals/docview/127933789/2349D709610949C7PQ/117?accountid=14496, retrieved 11 August 2014.

Merton, Robert K. 1968. *Social Theory and Social Structure.* Enlarged ed. New York: Free Press.

Methodist Connection in the United States. 1813. *Minutes of the Methodist Conferences, Annually Held in America from 1773 to 1813, Inclusive.* New York: Hitt and Ware.

Meyer, David, and Suzanne Staggenborg. 1996. Movements, countermovements, and the structure of political opportunity. *American Journal of Sociology* 101: 1628–60.

Meyer, John W., and Patricia Bromley. 2013. The worldwide expansion of "organization." *Sociological Theory* 31(4): 366–89.

Meyer, John W., and Brian Rowan. 1977. Institutionalized organizations: Formal structure as myth and ceremony. *American Journal of Sociology* 83: 340–63.

Meyers, Mary Ann. 1983. *A New World Jerusalem: The Swedenborgian Experience in Community Construction.* Westport, CT: Greenwood.

Meyrowitz, Joshua. 1985. *No Sense of Place: The Impact of Electronic Media on Behaviour.* Oxford: Oxford University Press.

Mihm, Stephen. 2007. *A Nation of Counterfeiters: Capitalists, Con Men, and the Making of the United States.* Cambridge, MA: Harvard University Press.

Miles, Pliny. 1855. *Postal Reform: Its Urgent Necessity and Practicability.* New York: Stringer and Townsend.

Millen, Irene. 1949. American musical magazines, 1786–1865. MLS thesis, Carnegie Institute of Technology.

Miller, Perry. 1965. *The Life of the Mind in America, from the Revolution to the Civil War.* New York: Harcourt, Brace and World.

Miller, Floyd J. 1975. *The Search for a Black Nationality: Black Emigration and Colonization, 1787–1863.* Urbana: University of Illinois Press.

Milligan, Joseph. 1822. Preface. *American Museum and Repository of Arts and Sciences* 1(1): 1. http://search.proquest.com/americanperiodicals/docview/89583215/915A4E2B95FB4C67PQ/5?accountid=14496, retrieved 5 March 2009.

Mills, C. Wright. 1939. Language, logic, and culture. *American Sociological Review* 4: 670–80.

Mills, C. Wright. 1940. Situated actions and vocabularies of motive. *American Sociological Review* 5: 904–13.

Mimin. 1845. Amateur authors and small critics. *United States Magazine, and Democratic Review* 17(85): 62–66. http://search.proquest.com/americanperiodicals/docview/126370080/fulltextPDF/141050D29F232204AB9/14?accountid=14496, retrieved 2 August 2013.

Ming, Alexander. 1817. [No title.] *Weekly Visitor, and Ladies' Museum* 1(1): 16. http://search.proquest.com/americanperiodicals/docview/126337652/11DD8091E6724A9APQ/16?accountid=14496, retrieved 26 February 2009.

Mintz, Steven. 1995. *Moralists and Modernizers: America's Pre–Civil War Reformers.* Baltimore: Johns Hopkins University Press.

Minutes of the General Assembly of the Presbyterian Church in the United States of America. 1809. Philadelphia: Presbyterian Church in the United States of America.

Minutes of the General Assembly of the Presbyterian Church in the United States of America. 1819. Philadelphia: Presbyterian Church in the United States of America.

Mirror of Taste and Dramatic Censor. 1810. Preface. *Mirror of Taste and Dramatic Censor* 4(1): i–vii. http://search.proquest.com/americanperiodicals/docview/136965794/pageviewPDF/30E6B992CAB4A76PQ/1?accountid=14496, retrieved 14 May 2003.

M'Nemar, Richard. 1807. *The Kentucky Revival, or, a Short History of the Late Extraordinary Out-Pouring of the Spirit of God, in the Western States of America, Agreeably to Scripture Promises, and Prophesies Concerning the Latter Day.* Cincinnati, OH: John W. Browne.

Moffat, Riley. 1992. *Population History of Eastern US Cities and Towns, 1790–1870.* Metuchen, NJ: Scarecrow.

Moffat, Riley. 1996. *Population History of Western US Cities and Towns, 1850–1990.* Lanham, MD: Scarecrow.

Mohl, Raymond A. 1972. Poverty, pauperism, and social order in the preindustrial American city, 1780–1840. *Social Science Quarterly* 52(4): 934–48.

Mohr, John W. 1998. Measuring meaning structures. *Annual Review of Sociology* 24: 345–70.

Molotch, Harvey. 1973. Media and movements. In John D. McCarthy and Mayer N. Zald, eds., *The Dynamics of Social Movements*, 71–93. Cambridge, MA: Winthrop.

Molotch, Harvey. 1976. The city as a growth machine: Toward a political economy of place. *American Journal of Sociology* 82: 309–31.

Molotch, Harvey, William Freudenberg, and Krista E. Paulsen. 2000. History repeats itself, but how? City character, urban tradition, and the accomplishment of place. *American Sociological Review* 65: 791–823.

Moore, R. Laurence. 1989. Religion, secularization, and the shaping of the culture industry in antebellum America. *American Quarterly* 41: 216–42.

Mora, G. Cristina. 2014a. Cross-field effects and pan-ethnic classification: The institutionalization of Hispanic panethnicity, 1965 to 1990. *American Sociological Review* 79(2): 183–210.

Mora, G. Cristina. 2014b. *Making Hispanics: How Activists, Bureaucrats, and Media Constructed a New American.* Chicago: University of Chicago Press.

Moran, James. 1973. *Printing Presses: History and Development from the Fifteenth Century to Modern Times.* Berkeley: University of California Press.

Morris, Aldon D. 1984. *The Origins of the Civil Rights Movement: Black Communities Organizing for Change.* New York: Free Press.

Morse, Jedidiah. 1797. *The American Gazetteer.* Boston: Thomas and Andrews.

Morse, Jedidiah. 1810. *The American Gazetteer.* 3rd ed. Boston: Thomas and Andrews.

Morse, Jedidiah, and Richard C. Morse. 1826. *The Traveller's Guide; or, Pocket Gazetteer of the United States.* New Haven, CT: S. Wadsworth.

Morss, James, Asa Eaton, Charles Burroughs, and Thomas Carlisle. 1820. Introduction. *Churchman's Repository for the Eastern Diocese* 1(1): 3–6. http://search.proquest.com /americanperiodicals/docview/90542638/pageviewPDF/4218EBBC30A2474CPQ/1 ?accountid=14496, retrieved 14 May 2003.

Moss, Roger W. 1972. Master builders: A history of the colonial Philadelphia building trades. PhD diss., University of Delaware.

Mott, Frank Luther. 1930. *A History of American Magazines, 1741–1850.* Cambridge, MA: Harvard University Press.

Mott, Frank Luther. 1938a. *A History of American Magazines, 1850–1865.* Cambridge, MA: Harvard University Press.

Mott, Frank Luther. 1938b. *A History of American Magazines, 1865–1885.* Cambridge, MA: Harvard University Press.

Mott, Frank Luther. 1941. *American Journalism: A History of Newspapers in the United States through 250 years, 1690–1940.* New York: Macmillan.

Mueller, Eva, and James N. Morgan. 1962. Location decisions of manufacturers. *American Economic Review* 52: 204–17.

Mueller, J. E., and Karl F. Schuessler. 1961. *Statistical Reasoning in Sociology.* Boston: Houghton Mifflin.

Muir, Diana. 2000. *Reflections in Bullough's Pond: Economy and Ecosystem in New England.* Hanover, NH: University Press of New England.

Mullahy, John. 1997. Instrumental variable estimation of count data models: Applications of models to cigarette smoking behavior. *Review of Economics and Statistics* 79: 586–93.

Murphy, Stephen Wills. 2008. "It is a sacred duty to abstain": The organizational, biblical, theological, and practical roots of the American Temperance Society, 1814–1830. PhD diss., University of Virginia.

Museum of Foreign Literature, Science, and Art. 1824. American literature. *Museum of*

Foreign Literature, Science, and Art 5(25): 87–106. http://search.proquest.com/ameri canperiodicals/docview/135931457/14109D353141D39FFD4/17?accountid=14496, retrieved 12 May 2009.

Nagel, Ernest. (1961) 1979. *The Structure of Science: Problems in the Logic of Scientific Explanation.* Indianapolis: Hackett.

Nagle, Paul C. 1964. *One Nation Indivisible.* New York: Oxford University Press.

Neal, John. 1843. Newspapers. *Pioneer* 1(2): 61–65. http://search.proquest.com/ameri canperiodicals/docview/137771372/4DAE4E00D2E04560PQ/1?accountid=14496, retrieved 29 September 2008.

Neill, William. 1822. Hints to patrons. *Presbyterian Magazine* 2(1): 44–45. https:// archive.org/details/presbyterianmag00neilgoog, retrieved 17 April 2006.

Nettles, Curtis P. 1938. *The Roots of American Civilization.* New York: Appleton-Century-Crofts.

Nevins, William. 1839. Do you pay for a religious newspaper? *Episcopal Recorder* 17(38): 152.   http://search.proquest.com/americanperiodicals/docview/89893015/fulltext PDF/4651D4328D124523PQ/9?accountid=14496, retrieved 27 February 2010.

New England Farmer. 1852. A new volume. *New England Farmer* 4(1): 1. http://search .proquest.com/americanperiodicals/docview/127820215/pageviewPDF/18085961A 8444F7BPQ/1?accountid=14496, retrieved 17 April 2014.

New York Herald. 1842. Bank note reporter. *New York Herald* 7(330): 2. http://infotrac. galegroup.com/itw/infomark/335/305/27983389w16/purl=anddyn=9!pdy _2_5AJW-1842-FEB19–002-F?sw_aep=berk89308, retrieved 17 July 2014.

Newman, Abel Henry. 1894. *A History of the Baptist Churches.* New York: Christian Literature.

Newman, Richard, Patrick Rael, and Phillip Lapsansky. 2000. *Pamphlets of Protest: An Anthology of Early African American Protest Literature, 1790–1860.* New York: Routledge.

Newman, Richard S. 2002. *The Transformation of American Abolitionism: Fighting Slavery in the Early Republic.* Chapel Hill: University of North Carolina Press.

Newman, Richard S., and Peter L. Halvorson. 2000. *Atlas of American Religion: The Denominational Era, 1776–1990.* Lanham, MD: Rowman and Littlefield.

Nickell, Stephen. 1981. Biases in dynamic models with fixed effects. *Econometrica* 49: 1417–26.

Niebuhr, H. Richard. 1929. *The Social Sources of Denominationalism.* New York: Henry Holt.

Nisbet, Robert A. 1966. *The Sociological Tradition.* New York: Basic Books.

Noll, Mark A. 2002. *America's God: From Jonathan Edwards to Abraham Lincoln.* New York: Oxford University Press.

Nord, David Paul. 2001. *Communities of Journalism: A History of American Newspapers and their Readers.* Urbana: University of Illinois Press.

Nord, David Paul. 2004. *Faith in Reading: Religious Publishing and the Birth of Mass Media in America.* New York: Oxford University Press.

North, Douglass C. 1961. *The Economic Growth of the United States, 1790–1860.* Englewood Cliffs, NJ: Prentice Hall.

North, Simon Newton Dexter. 1884. *History and Condition of the Newspaper and Periodical Press of the United States, with a Catalogue of the Publications of the Census Year.* Washington DC: Government Printing Office.

Norton, John Pitkin. 1855. *Elements of Scientific Agriculture, or the Connection between*

Science and the Art of Practical Farming, Prize Essay of the New York State Agricultural Society. New York: C. M. Saxton.

Nourie, Alan, and Barbara Nourie, eds. 1990. *American Mass-Market Magazines.* New York: Greenwood.

Nussbaum, Arthur. 1957. *A History of the Dollar.* New York: Columbia University Press.

Okker, Patricia. 2003. *Social Stories: The Magazine Novel in Nineteenth-Century America.* Charlottesville: University of Virginia Press.

Oleson, Alexandra, and Sanborn C. Brown, eds. 1976. *The Pursuit of Knowledge in the Early American Republic: American Scientific and Learned Societies from Colonial Times to the Civil War.* Baltimore: Johns Hopkins University Press.

Olmsted, Frederick Law. (1862) 1953. *The Cotton Kingdom: A Traveller's Observations on Cotton and Slavery in the American Slave States.* Edited and with an introduction by Arthur M. Schlesinger. New York: Alfred A. Knopf.

Olsen, M. Ellsworth. 1925. *A History of the Origin and Progress of Seventh-Day Adventists.* Takoma Park, MD: Review and Herald Publishing Association.

Olson, Daniel. 1998. The influence of religious pluralism on close social ties and religious involvement. Paper presented at the annual meeting of the Society for the Scientific Study of Religion, Montreal, 6–8 November 1998.

Ornstein, Martha. (1938) 1963. *Rôle of Scientific Societies in the Seventeenth Century.* Hamden, CT: Archon.

Oswald, John Clyde. 1937. *Printing in the Americas.* New York: Gregg.

O'Sullivan, John L. 1839. The great nation of futurity. *United States Magazine and Democratic Review* 6(23): 426–30. http://digital.library.cornell.edu/cgi/t/text/text-idx?c =usde;cc=;view=toc;subview=short;idno=usde0006-4, retrieved 12 May 2014.

O'Sullivan, John L. 1845. Annexation. *United States Magazine and Democratic Review* 17(1): 5–10. http://web.grinnell.edu/courses/HIS/f01/HIS202-01/Documents /OSullivan.html, retrieved 12 May 2014.

Oxford Dictionary of National Biography. 2006. New York: Oxford University Press. http://www.oxforddnb.com/subscribed/?_fromAuth=1, retrieved May–August 2006.

Pabst, Margaret Richards. 1940–41. *Agricultural Trends in the Connecticut Valley Region of Massachusetts, 1800–1900.* Northampton, MA: Smith College.

Panoplist, and Missionary Magazine. 1816. To patrons and correspondents. *Panoplist, and Missionary Magazine* 12(1): 48. http://search.proquest.com/americanperiodicals/doc view/136972145/140EAA6470345155611/11?accountid=14496, retrieved 4 October 2013.

Park, Robert E. 1940. News as a form of knowledge. *American Journal of Sociology* 45: 675–77.

Parson, Theophilous. 1824. Prospectus. *United States Literary Gazette* 1(1): 1. http:// search.proquest.com/americanperiodicals/docview/126331385/AE472DB8293943E 7PQ/3?accountid=14496, retrieved 15 May 2003.

Parsons, Talcott. (1922) 1993. "Introduction." In *The Sociology of Religion,* xxix–lxxvii. Boston: Beacon.

Patterson, Lyman Ray. 1968. *Copyright in Historical Perspective.* Nashville, TN: Vanderbilt University Press.

Paul, T. V., G. John Ikenberry, and John Hall, eds. 2003. *The Nation-State in Question.* Princeton, NJ: Princeton University Press.

Pearson, Eliphalet. 1816. *Constitution and Address of the American Society for Educating Pious Youth for the Gospel Ministry.* Boston: American Society.

Pedder, Laura Green. 1936. *The Letters of Joseph Dennie*. Orono: University of Maine Press.

Pelanda, Brian Lee. 2011. Declarations of cultural independence: The nationalistic imperative behind the passage of early American copyright laws, 1783–1787. *Journal of the Copyright Society of the USA* 58: 431–54.

Perl, Paul, and Daniel Olson. 2000. Religious market share and intensity of church involvement in five denominations. *Journal for the Scientific Study of Religion* 39: 12–31.

Perrin, Andrew J., and Stephen Vaisey. 2008. Parallel public sphere: Distance and discourse in letters to the editor. *American Journal of Sociology* 114: 781–810.

Perrow, Charles. 1991. A society of organizations. *Theory and Society* 20: 725–62.

Perrow, Charles. 2002. *Organizing America: Wealth, Power, and the Origins of Corporate Capitalism*. Princeton, NJ: Princeton University Press.

Perry, William Stevens, ed. 1874. *Journals of General Conventions of the Protestant Episcopal Church in the United States, 1785–1835*. 3 vols. Claremont, NH: Claremont Manufacturing.

Pew Research Center. 2010. *Public Sees a Future Full of Promise and Peril*. Washington DC: Pew Research Center. http://www.people-press.org/2010/06/22/public-sees-a-future-full-of-promise-and-peril/, retrieved 28 August 2014.

Pflieger, Pat. 2013. American Children's Periodicals, 1789–1872. http://www.merrycoz.org/bib/intro.htm, retrieved 27 September 2013.

Philadelphia Magazine and Review. 1799. Prospectus. *Philadelphia Magazine and Review* 1(1): ii–iv. http://search.proquest.com/americanperiodicals/docview/88877394/141 2CE255B7400F9502/2?accountid=14496, retrieved 14 May 2003.

Phillips, Brenda Diane. 1985. The decade of origin: Resource mobilization and women's rights in the 1850s. PhD diss., Ohio State University.

Phillips, Damon J., and Young-Kyu Kim. 2009. Why pseudonyms? Deception as identity preservation among jazz record companies, 1920–1929. *Organization Science* 20: 481–99.

Pinkett, Harold T. 1950. The "American Farmer," a pioneer agricultural journal, 1819–1834. *Agricultural History* 23(3): 146–51.

Pitcher, Edward William R. 2000. *An Anatomy of Reprintings and Plagiarisms: Finding Keys to Editorial Practices and Magazine History, 1730–1820*. Lewiston, NY: Edwin Mellen.

Podolny, Joel M. 1993. A status-based model of market competition. *American Journal of Sociology* 98: 829–72.

Poe, Edgar Allan. 1835. Letter to Thomas Willis White, April 30. http://www.eapoe.org/works/letters/p3504300.htm, retrieved 14 October 2013.

Popper, Karl R. (1934) 1968. *The Logic of Scientific Discovery*. New York: Harper and Row.

Porter, Theodore M. 1986. *The Rise of Statistical Thinking, 1820–1900*. Princeton, NJ: Princeton University Press.

Port-Folio. 1815. Anecdote. *Port-Folio* 6(2): 201. http://search.proquest.com/american periodicals/docview/89477793/1B86A57E2BEF4EB4PQ/17?accountid=14496, retrieved 7 September 2011.

Poulson, Barry W. 1969. Estimates of the value of manufacturing output in the early nineteenth century. *Journal of Economic History* 29(3): 521–25.

Pred, Allan R. 1973. *Urban Growth and the Circulation of Information: The United States System of Cities, 1790–1840*. Cambridge, MA: Harvard University Press.

References | 379

Pred, Allan R. 1980. *Urban Growth and City-Systems in the United States, 1840–1860.* Cambridge, MA: Harvard University Press.

Prescott, W. H., Edward Everett, F. Dexter, and John Ware. 1820. Club-Room. *Club-Room* 1(1): 3–13. http://search.proquest.com/americanperiodicals/docview/124230 617/C4AF7C0D890A4EC0PQ/3?accountid=14496, retrieved 14 May 2003.

Price, Jacob M. 1964. The economic growth of the Chesapeake and the European market, 1697–1775. *Journal of Economic History* 24(4): 496–511.

Prude, Jonathan. (1983) 1999. *The Coming of Industrial Order; Town and Factory Life in Rural Massachusetts, 1810–1860.* Amherst: University of Massachusetts Press.

Purvis, Thomas. 1995. Population of American urban centers, 1760–1800 (table). In *Revolutionary America 1763 to 1800,* 253. New York: Facts on File.

Putnam. 1841. Book farming. *Union Agriculturist and Western Prairie Farmer* 1(1): 3. http://search.proquest.com/americanperiodicals/docview/127589185/92EDDC762 7AB4806PQ/14?accountid=14496, retrieved 13 June 2013.

Quarterly Register and Journal of the American Educational Society. 1829. Statistical register of religious denominations in the United States for January 1829: United Brethren, or Moravians. *Quarterly Register and Journal of the American Educational Society* 1(7): 182.

Quimby, G. W. 1845. Letter from Rev. G. W. Quimby. *Hangman* 1(8): 31. http://search .proquest.com/americanperiodicals/docview/127987621/8AD6710B156A4B55PQ /5?accountid=14496, retrieved 13 August 2014.

Quint, Alonzo, and Christopher Cushing. 1873. *Congregational Quarterly,* vol. 15. Boston: American Congregational Union.

Rabe-Hesketh, Sophia, and Anders Skrondal. 2008. *Multilevel and Longitudinal Modeling Using Stata.* 2nd ed. College Station, TX: Stata Press.

Randall, Henry S. 1844. Letter from Col. H. S. Randall. *Ohio Cultivator* 1(1): 3. http:// search.proquest.com/americanperiodicals/docview/137065418/E414DD69504F434 3PQ/12?accountid=14496, retrieved 1 August 2014.

Rao, Hayagreeva. 1998. Caveat emptor: The construction of nonprofit consumer watchdog organizations. *American Journal of Sociology* 103: 912–61.

Religious Instructor. 1810. Advertisement. *Religious Instructor* 1(1): 3. http://search.pro quest.com/americanperiodicals/publication/35167/citation?accountid=14496, retrieved 15 May 2003.

Rendall, Jane. 1984. *The Origins of Modern Feminism: Women in Britain, France, and the United States, 1780–1860.* New York: Schocken.

Rich, Wesley Everett. 1924. *The History of the United States Post Office to the Year 1829.* Cambridge, MA: Harvard University Press.

Richards, George. 1811. Prospectus and Preface. *Freemasons Magazine and General Miscellany* 1(1): 1–3. http://search.proquest.com/americanperiodicals/docview/89614511 /75467873E5984327PQ/2?accountid=14496, retrieved 14 May 2003.

Richardson, Lyon N. 1931. *A History of Early American Magazines, 1741–1789.* New York: Thomas Nelson and Sons.

Riley, Dylan J. 2010. *The Civic Foundations of Fascism in Europe: Italy, Spain and Romania 1870–1945.* Baltimore: Johns Hopkins University Press.

Riley, Sam G. 1986a. *Index to Southern Periodicals.* New York: Greenwood.

Riley, Sam G. 1986b. *Magazines of the American South.* New York: Greenwood.

Ringwalt, J. Luther. 1888. *Development of Transportation Systems in the United States, Comprising a Comprehensive Description of the Leading Features of Advancement, from* the *Colonial Era to the Present Time, in Water Channels, Roads, Turnpikes, Canals, Railways, Vessels, Vehicles, Cars and Locomotives*. Philadelphia, PA: Railway World Office.

Roberts, Helene Emmylou. 1961. American art periodicals of the nineteenth century. MLS thesis, University of Washington.

Robertson, Stephen. 2006. Seduction, sexual violence, and marriage in New York City, 1886–1955. *Law and History Review* 24(2): 331–73.

Romo, Frank P., and Michael Schwartz. 1995. The structural embeddedness of business decisions: The migration of manufacturing plants in New York state, 1960 to 1985. *American Sociological Review* 60: 874–907.

Roorbach, Orville Augustus. (1852) 1939. *Bibliotheca Americana: Catalogue of American Publications, Including Reprints and Original Works, from 1820 to 1852, Inclusive. Together with a List of Periodicals Published in the United States*. New York: Peter Smith.

Rorabaugh, W. J. 1979. *The Alcoholic Republic: An American Tradition*. New York: Oxford University Press.

Roscigno, Vincent J., and William F. Danaher. 2001. Media and mobilization: The case of radio and southern textile worker insurgency, 1929 to 1934. *American Sociological Review* 66: 212–48.

Rose, Mark. 1993. *Authors and Owners: The Invention of Copyright*. Cambridge, MA: Harvard University Press.

Rossel, Robert D. 1970. The Great Awakening: An historical analysis. *American Journal of Sociology* 75: 907–25.

Rosenthal, Naomi, Meryl Fingrutd, Michele Ethier, Roberta Karant, and David McDonald. 1985. Social movements and network analysis: A case study of nineteenth-century women's reform in New York State. *American Journal of Sociology* 90: 1022–54.

Rossi, Alice S. 1973. Social roots of the woman's movement in America. In Alice S. Rossi, ed., *The Feminist Papers: From Adams to de Beauvoir*, 241–81. New York: Columbia University Press.

Rossiter, Margaret. 1975. *The Emergence of Agricultural Science*. New Haven: Yale University Press.

Roth, Randolph. 1987. *The Democratic Dilemma: Religion, Reform, and the Social Order in the Connecticut River Valley of Vermont, 1791–1850*. New York: Cambridge University Press.

Rothenberg, Winifred Barr. 1992. *From Market-Places to a Market Economy: The Transformation of Rural Massachusetts, 1750–1850*. Chicago: University of Chicago Press.

Rothman, David J. 1971. *Discovery of Asylum: Social Order and Disorder in the New Republic*. Boston: Little, Brown.

Rowell, George P. and Co. 1869. *Rowell's American Newspaper Directory*. New York: George P. Rowell and Co.

Roy, William G. 1997. *Socializing Capital: The Rise of the Large Industrial Corporation in America*. Princeton, NJ: Princeton University Press.

R. T____x. 1825. Communication. *African Repository and Colonial Journal* 1(1): 5–6. http://search.proquest.com/americanperiodicals/docview/89421077/EB6F1A9766C B425DPQ/3?accountid=14496, retrieved 5 May 2003.

Rudé, George F. E. 1981. *The Crowd in History: A Study of Popular Disturbances in France and England, 1730–1848*. London: Lawrence and Wishart.

Ruegger, Herman. 1949. *Apostolic Christian Church History*, vol. 1. Chicago: Apostolic Christian Publishing.

Ruffin, Edmund. 1852. *An Essay on Calcareous Manures.* Richmond, VA: J. W. Randolph.

Russell, Ezekiel. 1771. The printer and publisher of the *Censor* to the publick. *Censor* 1(2): 1–5. http://search.proquest.com/americanperiodicals/docview/88499309/4FE DDBE7AF24446DPQ/3?accountid=14496, retrieved 16 March 2006.

Rutman, Darrett B. 1980. Community study. *Historical Methods* 13(1): 29–41.

Sampson, Ezra, George Chittenden, and Henry Crosswell. 1802. To the public. *Balance and Columbian Repository* 1(2): 1. http://search.proquest.com/americanperiodicals /docview/88902023/1410EC6039045C7ED89/5?accountid=14496, retrieved 13 May 2003.

Santos Silva, J. M. C., and Silvana Tenreyro. 2006. The log of gravity. *Review of Economics and Statistics* 88: 641–58.

Sarjent, Abel. 1807a. Introductory discourse. *Halcyon Itinerary* 1(1): vii–xix. http:// search.proquest.com/americanperiodicals/docview/89328967/30DF3AD356DA421 EPQ/8?accountid=14496, retrieved 4 March 2009.

Sarjent, Abel. 1807b. An Address to America. *Halcyon Itinerary* 1(3): 100–108. http:// search.proquest.com/americanperiodicals/docview/89328967/30DF3AD356DA421 EPQ/8?accountid=14496, retrieved 11 September 2002.

Saunders, David. 1992. *Authorship and Copyright.* London: Routledge.

Saunders, J. W. 1951. The stigma of print: A note on the social bases of Tudor poetry. *Essays in Criticism* 1: 139–64.

Savage, William Sherman. 1938. *The Controversy over the Distribution of Abolition Literature.* Washington, DC: Association for the Study of Negro Life and History.

Sawyer, John York. 1831. Prospectus of the *Western Ploughboy. Illinois Advocate* 1(2): 4.

Saxenian, Annalee. 1994. *Regional Advantage: Culture and Competition in Silicon Valley and Route 128.* Cambridge, MA: Harvard University Press.

Scaff, Lawrence. 2011. *Max Weber in America.* Princeton, NJ: Princeton University Press.

Schaffer, Mark. 2007. XTIVREG2: STATA module to perform extended IV/2SLS, GMM and AC/HAC, LIML and K-class regression for panel data models. http://ideas .repec.org/c/boc/bocode/s456501.html, retrieved 1 February 2008.

Scheiber, Harry N. 1972. Government and the economy: Studies of the "commonwealth" policy in nineteenth-century America. *Journal of Interdisciplinary History* 3: 135–51.

Schlesinger, Arthur M. 1944. Biography of a nation of joiners. *American Historical Review* 50: 1–25.

Schlesinger, Arthur M., Jr. 1958. *Prelude to Independence: The Newspaper War on Britain, 1764–1776.* New York: Alfred A. Knopf.

Schlesinger, Arthur M., Jr. 2000. Foreword. *One Hundred and Fifty Years of Harper's Magazine,* viii–ix. New York: Franklin Square.

Schmidt, Mary. 1999. *Index to Nineteenth Century American Art Periodicals.* 2 vols. Madison, CT: Sound View.

Schneiberg, Marc. 2002. Organizational heterogeneity and the production of new forms: Politics, social movements and mutual companies in American fire insurance, 1900–1930. *Research in the Sociology of Organizations* 19: 39–89.

Schradie, Jen. 2011. The digital production gap: The digital divide and Web 2.0 collide. *Poetics* 39: 145–68.

Schudson, Michael. 1978. *Discovering the News: A Social History of American Newspapers.* New York: Basic Books.

Schultze, Suzanne. 1983. *Population Information in Nineteenth Century Census Volumes.* Phoenix, AZ: Oryx.

Schumacher, Max George. 1975. *The Northern Farmer and His Markets during the Late Colonial Period.* New York: Arno.

Schumpeter, Joseph A. (1934) 1983. *The Theory of Economic Development.* Translated by Redvers Opie. New Brunswick, NJ: Transaction.

Scott, Anne Firor. 1991. *Natural Allies: Women's Associations in American History.* Champagne: University of Illinois Press.

Scott, Joseph. 1795. *The United States Gazetteer.* Philadelphia: F. and R. Bailey.

Scott, Marvin B., and Stanford M. Lyman. 1968. Accounts. *American Sociological Review* 33(1): 46–62.

Scott-Morton, Fiona M., and Joel M. Podolny. 2002. Love or money? The effects of owner motivation in the California wine industry. *Journal of Industrial Economics* 50: 431–56.

Seavoy, Ronald E. 1978. The public-service origins of the American business corporation. *Business History Review* 52: 31–60.

Seavoy, Ronald E. 1982. *The Origins of the American Business Corporation, 1784–1855: Broadening the Concept of Public Service during Industrialization.* Westport, CT: Greenwood.

Sedgwick, Ellery. 2000. Magazines and the profession of authorship in the United States, 1840–1900. *Papers of the Bibliographical Society of America* 94(3): 399–425.

Sellers, Charles C. 1991. *The Market Revolution: Jacksonian America, 1815–1846.* New York: Oxford University Press.

Sewell, William H., Jr. 1996. Historical events as transformations of structures: Inventing revolution at the Bastille. *Theory and Society* 25: 841–81.

Shafer, Henry Burnell. 1935. Early medical magazines in America. *Annals of Medical History* 7: 480–91.

Shane, Scott, and Ben Hubbard. 2014. ISIS displaying a deft command of varied media. *New York Times*, 31 August. http://www.nytimes.com/2014/08/31/world/middle east/isis-displaying-a-deft-command-of-varied-media.html?_r=0, retrieved 31 August 2014.

Shane, Scott, and Rakesh Khurana. 2003. Bringing individuals back in: The effects of career experience on new firm founding. *Industrial and Corporate Change* 12: 519–43.

Shepherd, Thomas W., and Thomas Green Fessenden. 1822a. Prospectus. *New England Farmer and Horticultural Register* 1(1): 1. http://search.proquest.com/americanperi odicals/publication/24525/citation/44EACBB0209648F1PQ/2?accountid=14496#, retrieved 14 May 2003.

Shepherd, Thomas W., and Thomas Green Fessenden. 1822b. To the public. *New England Farmer and Horticultural Register* 1(1): 6. http://search.proquest.com/american periodicals/publication/24525/citation/44EACBB0209648F1PQ/2?accountid =14496#, retrieved 18 July 2006.

Shore, Laurence. 1986. *Southern Capitalists: The Ideological Leadership of an Elite, 1832–1885.* Chapel Hill: University of North Carolina Press.

Shriver, Augustus. 1860. Chester County Hogs. *American Farmer*, new series, 2(1): 24. http://search.proquest.com/americanperiodicals/docview/90086122/D34AA7C35B DB42E9PQ/24?accountid=14496, retrieved 1 August 2014.

Silliman, Benjamin. 1820. Preface. *American Journal of Science and Arts* 2(2): 176. http:// search.proquest.com/americanperiodicals/docview/89586214/E4B9BEB722324C22 PQ/2?accountid=14496, retrieved 7 September 2011.

Silver, Rollo G. 1967. *The American Printer, 1787–1825.* Charlottesville: University of Virginia Press.

Simmel, Georg. (1900) 1990. *The Philosophy of Money.* 2nd enlarged ed. London: Routledge.

Simms, Henry H. 1960. *Emotions at High Tide: Abolition as a Controversial Factor, 1830–1845.* Baltimore: Moore.

Simpson, E. H. 1949. Measurement of population diversity. *Nature* 163: 688.

Simpson, Lewis P. 1954. A literature adventure of the early republic: The Anthology Society and the *Monthly Anthology. New England Quarterly* 27: 168–90.

Sine, Wesley D., Heather A. Haveman, and Pamela S. Tolbert. 2005. Risky business? Entrepreneurship in the new independent-power sector. *Administrative Science Quarterly* 50: 200–232.

Skillman, Thomas. 1824. Prospectus. *Western Luminary* 1(1): 1–5. http://search.pro quest.com/americanperiodicals/docview/126854011/5B929A68E267496BPQ/3 ?accountid=14496, retrieved 29 August 2006.

Skinner, John S. 1819. To the public. *American Farmer* 1(1): 5. http://search.proquest .com/americanperiodicals/docview/90209461/2B06DF4566EE49D3PQ/22?account id=14496, retrieved 17 April 2006.

Skinner, John S. 1857. Our past and our future. *The Plough, the Loom, and the Anvil* 10(1): 1. http://search.proquest.com/americanperiodicals/docview/125742516/6E16 C55A50AD4026PQ/5?accountid=14496, retrieved 20 May 2013.

Skocpol, Theda. 1997. The Tocqueville problem: Civic engagement in American democracy. *Social Science History* 21: 455–79.

Skocpol, Theda. 1999. How Americans became civic. In Theda Skocpol and Morris P. Fiorina, eds., *Civic Engagement in American Democracy*, 27–80. Washington DC: Brookings Institution Press and the Russell Sage Foundation.

Skocpol, Theda. 2003. *Diminished Democracy: From Membership to Management in American Civic Life.* Norman: University of Oklahoma Press.

Skocpol, Theda, Marshall Ganz, and Ziad Munson. 2000. A nation of organizers: The institutional origins of civic voluntarism in the United States. *American Political Science Review* 94: 527–46.

Sloane, David E. E., ed. 1987. *American Humor Magazines and Comic Periodicals.* New York: Greenwood.

Smith, Adam. (1776) 1981. *An Inquiry into the Nature and Causes of the Wealth of Nations.* Edited by W. B. Todd. Indianapolis: Liberty Classics.

Smith, C. Henry. (1920) 1957. *The Story of the Mennonites.* 4th ed., rev. and enlarged by Cornelius Krahn. Newton, KS: Mennonite Publication Office.

Smith, Christian, ed. 1996. *Disruptive Religion: The Force of Faith in Social Movement Activism.* New York: Routledge.

Smith, David, Ryan Cordell, and Elizabeth Dillon. 2013. Infectious texts: Modeling text reuse in nineteenth-century newspapers. Working paper, Northeastern University.

Smith, David C. 1970. *History of Papermaking in the United States (1691–1969).* New York: Lockwood.

Smith, David Eugene. 1933. Early American mathematical periodicals. *Scripta Mathematica* 1: 277–85.

Smith, Elias. 1808. Liberty No. 1. *Herald of Gospel Liberty* 1(1): 2. http://search.proquest .com/americanperiodicals/docview/89329057/646EFE6D334040C0PQ/3?account id=14496, retrieved 14 May 2003.

Smith, Elwyn A. 1962. The forming of a modern American denomination. *Church History* 31: 74–91.

Smith, Natalia. 2006. Southern Literary Magazines 1727–1900. Online database at the University of North Carolina, Chapel Hill. http://www.lib.unc.edu/edd/people /smith/southbib/southbr, retrieved 14 March 2006.

Smith, Seba. 1856. The newspaper. *United States Magazine*, new series, 1(1): 86. http:// search.proquest.com/americanperiodicals/docview/89791317/1F20B6E25A8E4D4 0PQ/1?accountid=14496, retrieved 13 June 2007.

Smith, Timothy. 1957. *Revivalism and Social Reform in Mid-Nineteenth Century America*. Nashville, TN: Abingdon.

Smith, Timothy. 1968. Congregation, state, and denomination: The forming of the American religious structure. *William and Mary Quarterly* 25: 155–68.

Smith, Timothy. 1978. Religion and ethnicity in America. *American Historical Review*, 83: 1155–85.

Smith, Walter Buckingham, and Arthur Harrison Cole. 1935. *Fluctuations in American Business 1790–1860*. Cambridge, MA: Harvard University Press.

Smith, William. 1757. Preface. *American Magazine and Monthly Chronicle* 1(1): 3–7. http://search.proquest.com/americanperiodicals/docview/88877394/918444BE1A0 747FEPQ/37?accountid=14496, retrieved 28 May 2010.

Smith-Rosenberg, Carroll. 1971. *Religion and the Rise of the American City: The New York City Mission Movement, 1812–1870*. Ithaca, NY: Cornell University Press.

Smyth, Albert H. 1892. *Philadelphia Magazines and their Contributors, 1841–1850*. Philadelphia: Robert M. Lindsay.

Snodgrass, Isabelle S. 1947. American musical periodicals of New England and New York, 1786–1850. MLS thesis, Columbia University.

Snow, David A., and Robert D. Benford. 1992. Master frames and cycles of protest. In Aldon D. Morris and Carol McLung Mueller, eds., *Frontiers of Social Movement Theory*, 133–55. New Haven, CT: Yale University Press.

Snow, David A., E. Burke Rochford, Steven K. Worden, and Robert D. Benford. 1986. Frame alignment processes, micromobilization, and movement participation. *American Sociological Review* 51: 464–81.

Snow, Louis Franklin. 1907. *The College Curriculum in the United States*. New York: Teacher's College Press.

Sobek, Matthew. 2006. Detailed occupations—all persons: 1850–1990. In Susan B. Carter, Scott Sigmund Gartner, Michael R. Haines, Alan L. Olmstead, Richard Sutch, and Gavin Wright, eds., *Historical Statistics of the United States, Earliest Times to the Present: Millennial Edition*, tables Ba1159–1439. New York: Cambridge University Press. http://hsus.cambridge.org/HSUSWeb/table/citation.do?id=Ba1159–1395 and http:// hsus.cambridge.org/HSUSWeb/toc/tableToc.do?id=Ba1396–1439, retrieved 2 February 2009.

Soltow, Lee, and Edward W. Stevens. 1981. *The Rise of Literacy and the Common School in the United States: A Socioeconomic Analysis to 1870*. Chicago: University of Chicago Press, 1981.

Sorenson, Olav, and Pino G. Audia. 2000. The social structure of entrepreneurial activity: Geographic concentration of footwear production in the United States, 1940–1989. *American Journal of Sociology* 106: 424–62.

Southern Agriculturist and Register of Rural Affairs. 1836. Agricultural reports. *Southern Agriculturist and Register of Rural Affairs* 9(1): 19–21. http://search.proquest.com

/americanperiodicals/docview/137594772/DEE9E7A1511847A5PQ/46?account id=14496, retrieved 1 August 2014.

Southwick, Solomon. 1819. Original. *Plough Boy*, June 5 1819 1(1): 1–2. http://search .proquest.com/americanperiodicals/docview/137784800/A037CD37BD6D47C2PQ /2?accountid=14496, retrieved 14 May 2003.

Spence, Michael. 1973. Job market signaling. *Quarterly Journal of Economics* 87: 355–79.

Spoo, Robert. 2013. *Without Copyrights*. Oxford: Oxford University Press.

Sprigman, Christopher. 2004. Reform(aliz)ing copyright. *Stanford Law Review* 52(20): 485–568.

Stark, Rodney, and William Sims Bainbridge. 1980. Networks of faith: Interpersonal bonds and recruitment to cults and sects. *American Journal of Sociology* 85: 1376–95.

Stark, Rodney, and Roger Finke. 2000. *Acts of Faith: Explaining the Human Side of Religion*. Berkeley: University of California Press.

Stark, Rodney, and James C. McCann. 1993. Market forces and Catholic commitment: Exploring the new paradigm. *Journal for the Scientific Study of Religion* 32: 111–24.

Starnes, Rebekah. 2009. From the periodical archives: The entertaining companion: *Philadelphisches Magazin*, the first German-American literary journal. *American Periodicals: A Journal of Criticism, History, and Bibliography* 19(1): 85–89.

Starr, Paul. 1982. *The Social Transformation of American Medicine*. New York: Basic Books.

Starr, Paul. 2004. *The Creation of the Media: Political Origins of Modern Communications*. New York: Basic Books.

Staudenraus, Philip J. (1961) 1980. *The African Colonization Movement, 1816–1865*. New York: Octagon.

Stearns, Bertha Monica. 1931. Early western magazines for ladies. *Mississippi Valley Historical Review* 18: 319.

Stearns, Bertha Monica. 1932. Reform periodicals and female reformers, 1830–1860. *American Historical Review* 37: 678–99.

Stern, Robert N., and Stephen R. Barley. 1996. Organizations and social systems: Organizational theory's neglected mandate. *Administrative Science Quarterly* 41: 146–52.

Stewart, James Brewer. 1997. *Holy Warriors: The Abolitionists and American Slavery*. Rev. ed. New York: Hill and Wang.

Stigler, Stephen M. 1986. *The History of Statistics: The Measurement of Uncertainty before 1900*. Cambridge, MA: Belknap Press.

Stinchcombe, Arthur L. 1965. Social structure and organizations. In James G. March, ed., *Handbook of Organizations*, 142–93. Chicago: Rand McNally.

Stoll, Steven. 2002. *Larding the Lean Earth: Soil and Society in Nineteenth-Century America*. New York: Hill and Wang.

Storper, Michael. 1995. The resurgence of regional economies, ten years later: The region as the nexus of untraded interdependencies. *European Urban and Regional Studies* 2: 191–221.

Stott, Richard B. 1990. *Workers in the Metropolis: Class, Ethnicity, and Youth in Antebellum New York City*. Ithaca: Cornell University Press.

Stout, Harry S., and D. Scott Cormode. 1998. Institutions and the story of American Religion. In N. J. Demerath III, Peter Dobkin Hall, Terry Schmidt, and Rhys Williams, eds., *Sacred Canopies: Organizational Aspects of Religion and Religious Aspects of Organizations*, 62–78. New York: Oxford University Press.

Strang, David, and John W. Meyer. 1993. Institutional conditions for diffusion. *Theory and Society* 22: 487–511.

Stratman, Carl J. 1970. *American Theatrical Periodicals, 1798–1967: A Bibliographical Guide.* Durham, NC: Duke University Press.

Strickland, William. 1801. *Observations on the Agriculture of the United States of America.* London: W. Bulmer.

Strohecker, Edwin Charles. 1969. American juvenile literary periodicals, 1789–1826. PhD diss., University of Michigan.

Stuntz, Stephen Conrad. 1941. *List of Agricultural Periodicals of the United States and Canada Published during the Century July 1810 to July 1910.* US Department of Agriculture miscellaneous publication no. 398. Washington, DC: Government Printing Office.

Suchman, Mark C. 1995. Managing legitimacy: Strategic and institutional approaches. *Academy of Management Review* 20: 571–610.

Suire, Raphaël, and Jérôme Vincente. 2009. Why do some places succeed when others decline? A social interaction model of cluster viability. *Economic Geography* 9: 381–404.

Sutch, Richard. 2006. Gross domestic product: 1790–2002 (continuous annual series). In Susan B. Carter, Scott Sigmund Gartner, Michael R. Haines, Alan L. Olmstead, Richard Sutch, and Gavin Wright, eds., *Historical Statistics of the United States, Earliest Times to the Present: Millennial Edition On Line,* tables Ca9–19. New York: Cambridge University Press. http://dx.doi.org/10.1017/ISBN-9780511132971.Ca1–26, retrieved 17 May 2007.

Sutton, John R., and Mark Chaves. 2004. Explaining schisms in American Protestant denominations, 1890–1990. *Journal for the Scientific Study of Religion* 43: 171–90.

Sweet, William Warren. 1931. *Religion on the American Frontier: The Baptists, 1783–1830.* New York: Henry Holt.

Sweet, William Warren. 1936a. *Religion on the American Frontier: The Congregationalists, 1783–1850.* Chicago: University of Chicago Press.

Sweet, William Warren. 1936b. *Religion on the American Frontier: The Presbyterians, 1783–1832.* New York: Henry Holt.

Swidler, Ann. 1973. The concept of rationality in the work of Max Weber. *Sociological Inquiry* 43(1): 35–42.

Swidler, Ann. 1986. Culture in action: Symbols and strategies. *American Sociological Review* 51: 273–86.

Swidler, Ann. 2001. *Talk of Love: How Culture Matters.* Chicago: University of Chicago Press.

Swords, Thomas, and James Swords. 1800. Introduction. *New-York Missionary Magazine* 1(1): 2–5. http://search.proquest.com/americanperiodicals/docview/89580363/2508 5953A2CF4E44PQ/2?accountid=14496, retrieved 14 May 2003.

Sylla, Richard. 1976. Forgotten men of money: Private bankers in early US history. *Journal of Economic History* 36(1): 173–88.

Szatmary, David P. 1980. *Shays' Rebellion: The Making of an Agrarian Insurrection.* Amherst: University of Massachusetts Press.

Tarde, Gabriel. 1969. *Gabriel Tarde on Communication and Social Influence.* Edited and with an introduction by Terry N. Clark. Chicago: University of Chicago Press.

Tarrow, Sidney G. 1993. Modular collective action and the rise of the protest event. *Politics and Society* 61: 69–90.

Tarrow, Sidney G. 1998. *Power in Movement: Social Movements and Contentious Politics.* Cambridge: Cambridge University Press.

Tassin, Algernon de Vivier. 1916. *The Magazine in America.* New York: Dodd, Mead.

Taylor, Charles Alan. 1996. *Defining Science: A Rhetoric of Demarcation.* Madison: University of Wisconsin Press.

Taylor, George Rogers. 1951. *The Transportation Revolution 1815–1860.* New York: Rinehart.

Taylor, John. (1813) 1977. *Arator: Being a Series of Agricultural Essays, Practical and Political, in Sixty-Four Numbers.* Edited and with an introduction by M. E. Bradford. Indianapolis, IN: Liberty Fund.

Taylor, Mendell. 1964. *Exploring Evangelism.* Kansas City, MO: Beacon Hill.

Tebbel, John, and Mary Ellen Zuckerman. 1991. *The Magazine in America, 1741–1990.* New York: Oxford University Press.

Thernstrom, Stephan, and Peter Knights. 1970. Men in motion: Some data and speculations about urban population mobility in nineteenth-century America. *Journal of Interdisciplinary History* 1: 7–35.

Thomas, Isaiah. 1794. To the public. *Worcester Intelligencer* 1(1): 1. http://infoweb.newsbank.com/iw-search/we/HistArchive/HistArchive?d_viewref=docandp_docnum=-1andp_nbid=C5BT5DFUMTQwNzM3MDIyNi44ODczODY6MToxNToxNjku MjI5LjE1MS4yMDUandf_docref=v2:109E89E841FC8798@EANX-10B8421 F8F75AC10@2376585–10B8421F9E36C978@0andp_docref=v2:109E89 E841FC8798@EANX-10B8421F8F75AC10@2376585–10B8421F9E36C978@0, retrieved 6 October 2006.

Thomas, Isaiah. (1874) 1970. *The History of Printing in America, with a Bibliography of Printers and an Account of Newspapers.* 2nd ed. New York: Weathervane.

Thomas, Isaiah, Ebenezer Turrell Andrews, and John Sprague. 1788. Proposal for a new magazine. Worcester, MA: Isaiah Thomas. Early American Imprints, series 1: Evans, 1639–1800, document 21492, http://infoweb.newsbank.com/iw-search/we/Evans ?p_action=docandp_theme=eaiandp_topdoc=1andp_docnum=1andp_sort=YMD _date:Dandp_product=EVANLandp_text_direct-0=u433=%28%2021492%20 %29|u433ad=%28%2021492%20%29andp_nbid=D64D52XLMTQwMzYzMTM0Ni4 3OTkyOTk6MToxNToxNjkuMjI5LjE1MS4yMDUandp_docref=, retrieved 24 March 2006.

Thompson, E. P. 1967. Time, work-discipline, and industrial capitalism. *Past and Present* 38: 56–97.

Thompson, John B. 1995. *The Media and Modernity: A Social Theory of the Media.* Stanford, CA: Stanford University Press.

Tilly, Charles. 1984. *Big Structures, Large Processes, Huge Comparisons.* New York: Russell Sage Foundation.

Tilly, Charles. 1986. *The Contentious French.* Cambridge, MA: Belknap Press.

Tilly, Charles. 1995. *Popular Contention in Great Britain, 1758–1834.* Cambridge, MA: Harvard University Press.

Tinker, Edward Larocque. 1933. *Bibliography of the French Newspapers and Periodicals of Louisiana.* Worcester, MA: American Antiquarian Society.

Tocqueville, Alexis de. (1848) 2000. *Democracy in America.* Translated and edited by Harvey C. Mansfield and Delba Winthrop. Chicago: University of Chicago Press.

Tomc, Sandra. 2012. *Industry and the Creative Mind: The Eccentric Writer in American Literature and Entertainment, 1790–1860.* Ann Arbor: University of Michigan Press.

Tonn, Mari Boor. 1991. The *Una*, 1853–1855: The premiere of the woman's rights press.

In Martha M. Solomon, ed., *A Voice of Their Own: The Woman Suffrage Press, 1840–1910*, 48–70. Tuscaloosa: University of Alabama Press.

Tönnies, Ferdinand. (1887) 1957. *Community and Society*. Translated by Charles P. Loomis. New Brunswick, NJ: Transaction.

Towne, Marvin, and Wayne Rasmussen. 1960. Farm gross product and gross investment in the nineteenth century. In Conference on Research in Income and Wealth, Economic History Association, *Trends in the American Economy in the Nineteenth Century*, 255–315. National Bureau of Economic Research reprint. New York: Arno.

Tracy, E. C. 1845. *Memoir of the Life of Jeremiah Evarts, Esq.: Late Corresponding Secretary of the American Board of Commissioners for Foreign Missions*. Boston: Crocker and Brewster.

Transactions of the American Medical Association. 1848. Periodical medical publications of the United States. *Transactions of the American Medical Association* 1: 250–70. http://ama.nmtvault.com/jsp/viewer.jsp?doc_id=Transactions%2Fama_arch%2FAD200001%2F00000001andquery1=andrecoffset=0andcollection_filter=Allandcollection_name=Transactionsandinit_width=640andsort_col=date+, retrieved 10 July 2004.

Treat, Payson Jackson. 1910. *The National Land System, 1785–1820*. New York: E. B. Treat.

Tryon, Rolla M. 1917. *Household Manufactures in the United States, 1640–1860*. Chicago: University of Chicago Press.

Tucker, Luther, and Ambrose Stevens. 1831. To the public. *Genesee Farmer and Gardener's Journal* 1(1): 2. http://search.proquest.com/americanperiodicals/docview/126153068/13AC0DBFCBE642AFPQ/5?accountid=14496, retrieved 2 October 2006.

Tucker, Mark. 1833. Means of a revival of religion. *American National Preacher* 9(7): 129–38. http://books.google.com/books?id=oCUPAAAAIAAJandpg=PA129andlpg=PA129anddq=%22mark+tucker%22+1833+%22means+of+a+revival+of+religion%22andsource=blandots=iugh4zVeiUandsig=_lw00e0k_p9jH6v5DakdvWJBnfIandhl=enandsa=Xandei=A9KAVKnUOZCpogSV8IDQAQandved=0CCAQ6AEwAA#v=onepageandq=%22mark%20tucker%22%201833%20%22means%20of%20a%20revival%20of%20religion%22andf=false, retrieved 3 December 2014.

Turner, Ralph H. 1969. The public perception of protest. *American Sociological Review* 34: 815–31.

Tuveson, Ernest Lee. 1968. *Redeemer Nation: The Idea of America's Millennial Role*. Chicago: University of Chicago Press.

Tyack, David, Thomas James, and Aaron Benavot, eds. 1987. *Law and the Shaping of Public Education, 1785–1954*. Madison: University of Wisconsin Press.

Tyler, Alice Felt. 1944. *Freedom's Ferment: Phases of American Social History from the Colonial Period to the Outbreak of the Civil War*. New York: Harper Torchbooks.

Tyrrell, Ian. 1979a. *Sobering Up: From Temperance to Prohibition in Antebellum America, 1800–1860*. Westport, CT: Greenwood.

Tyrrell, Ian. 1979b. Temperance and economic change in the antebellum north. In Jack S. Blocker, ed., *Alcohol, Reform, and Society: The Liquor Issue in Social Context*, 45–68. Westport, CT: Greenwood.

Unsworth, Michael. 1990. *Military Periodicals: US and Selected International Periodicals*. New York: Greenwood.

Upham, Thomas C. 1846. Letter from Prof. Upham. *Hangman* 1(2): 6. http://search.proquest.com/americanperiodicals/docview/127996879/8AD6710B156A4B55PQ/35?accountid=14496, retrieved 13 August 2014.

US Bureau of Economic Analysis. 2014. GDP deflator table. http://www.multpl.com /gdp-deflator/table, retrieved 12 June 2014.

US Census Bureau. 1909. *A Century of Population Growth: From the First Census of the United States to the Twelfth, 1790–1900.* Washington, DC: Government Printing Office.

US Census Bureau. 1975. Annual Population Estimates for the United States: 1790 to 1970. In *Historical Statistics of the United States, Colonial Times to 1970,* tables A-6–8. Washington, DC: Government Printing Office.

US Census Bureau. 1998. *Population of the 100 Largest Cities and Other Urban Places in the United States: 1790 to 1990.* Working paper no. 27. http://www.census.gov/popu lation/www/documentation/twps0027.html, retrieved 22 June 2002.

US Census Bureau. 2001. *Statistical Abstract of the United States, Online Edition.* Washington, DC: Government Printing Office. http://www.census.gov/statab/www/, retrieved April 2004.

US Congress. 1790a. *An Act for the Encouragement of Learning, by Securing the Copies of Map, Charts, and Books, to the Authors and Proprietors of Such Copies, during the Times Therein Mentioned.* 1 Stat. 124 (31 May 1790).

US Congress. 1790b. *An Act to Promote the Progress of the Useful Arts.* 1 Stat. 109–12 (10 April 1790).

US Congress. 1792a. *An Act to Establish the Post-Office and Post Roads within the United States.* 1 Stat. 232 (20 February 1792).

US Congress. 1792b. *An Act Establishing a Mint, and Regulating the Coins of the United States.* 1 Stat. 246 (2 April 1792).

US Congress. 1794. *An Act to Establish the Post-Office and Post Roads within the United States.* 1 Stat. 354 (8 May 1794).

Vaisey, Stephen. 2009. Motivation and justification: A dual-process model of culture in action. *American Journal of Sociology* 114: 1675–1715.

Virginia Religious Magazine. 1804. Preface. *Virginia Religious Magazine* 1(1): i–iv. http:// search.proquest.com/americanperiodicals/docview/124032215/C31441B04C94C9 CPQ/2?accountid=14496, retrieved 15 May 2003.

Voas, David, Alasdair Crockett, and Daniel V. A. Olson. 2002. Religious pluralism and participation: Why previous research is wrong. *American Sociological Review* 67: 212–30.

Walsh, Alexander. 1840. Agriculture and its improvement. *Cultivator* 7(2): 34–35. http://search.proquest.com/americanperiodicals/docview/124879435/fulltextPDF /1D811F1506444F8PQ/27?accountid=14496, retrieved 13 June 2013.

Warburton, William (1747) 1788. A letter from an Author to a member of Parliament; concerning literary property. In Richard Hurd, ed., *The Works of the Right Reverend William Warburton,* 12:405–16. London: Cadell and Davies.

Warfel, Harry R., ed. 1953. *Letters of Noah Webster.* New York: Library Publishers.

Warner, Sam Bass, Jr. 1972. *The Urban Wilderness: A History of the American City.* New York: Harper and Row.

Watt, Ian. (1957) 2001. *The Rise of the Novel: Studies in Defoe, Richardson, and Fielding.* Berkeley: University of California Press.

Wayland. 1841. [No title.] *Union Agriculturist and Western Prairie Farmer* 1(1): 3. http:// search.proquest.com/americanperiodicals/docview/127588169/92EDDC7627AB48 06PQ/19?accountid=14496, retrieved 13 June 2013.

Weber, Max. (1922) 1993. *The Sociology of Religion.* Translated by Ephraim Fischoff. Boston: Beacon.

Weber, Max. (1968) 1978. *Economy and Society: An Outline of Interpretive Sociology*. Translated and edited by Guenther Roth and Claus Wittich. Berkeley: University of California Press.

Webster, Noah. (1783) 2011. Introduction. *A Grammatical Institute of the English Language*. Hartford, CT: Hudson and Gibson. Reprinted and made available online by Donald L. Porter. http://www.donpotter.net/PDF/webster-1783.pdf, retrieved 11 August 2014.

Webster, Noah. 1788. Acknowledgements. *American Magazine* 1(3): 130. http://search .proquest.com/americanperiodicals/docview/88511527/B398199D20F540E7PQ/2 ?accountid=14496, retrieved 2 August 2012.

Webster, Noah. 1790. Introductory essay. *New York Magazine* 1(4): 195–98. http://search .proquest.com/americanperiodicals/docview/88867285/9FDC46601DD94214PQ /3?accountid=14496, retrieved 28 July 2010.

Webster, Noah. 1843. Origin of the copy-right laws of the United States. In *A Collection of Papers on Political, Literary and Moral Subjects*, 173–78. New York: Webster and Clark.

Weeden, Kim A. 2002. Why do some occupations pay more than others? Social closure and earnings inequality in the United States. *American Journal of Sociology* 108: 55–101.

Weeks, Lyman H. 1916. *A History of Papermaking in the United States: 1690–1916*. New York: Lockwood Trade Journal.

Weichlein, William J. 1970. *A Checklist of American Musical Periodicals, 1850–1900*. Detroit: Information Coordinators.

Weis, Frederick. 1950. *The Colonial Clergy of Maryland, Delaware, and Georgia*. Baltimore: Genealogical Publishing.

Weis, Frederick. 1976. *The Colonial Clergy of Virginia, North Carolina, and South Carolina*. Baltimore: Genealogical Publishing.

Weis, Frederick. 1977. *The Colonial Clergy of New England*. Baltimore: Genealogical Publishing.

Weis, Frederick. 1978. *The Colonial Clergy of the Middle Colonies: New York, New Jersey, and Pennsylvania, 1628–1776*. Baltimore: Genealogical Publishing.

Weiss, Thomas G. 1992. US labor force estimates and economic growth, 1800–1860. In Robert Gallman and John Wallis, eds., *American Economic Growth and Standards of Living before the Civil War*, 19–78. Chicago: University of Chicago Press.

Weld, Isaac, Jr. 1807. *Travels through the States of North America . . . during the Years 1795, 1796, and 1797*. London: J. Stockdale.

Welter, Barbara. 1966. The cult of true womanhood, 1820–1860. *American Quarterly* 18: 151–74.

Wertenbaker, Thomas J. 1922. *The Planters of Colonial Virginia*. Princeton, NJ: Princeton University Press.

Wesler, T. 1852. Letter from Indiana. *Ohio Cultivator* 8(3): 43. http://search.proquest .com/americanperiodicals/docview/137198557/E414DD69504F4343PQ/6?account id=14496, retrieved 1 August 2014.

Wheeler, James O. 1988. Spatial ownership links of major corporations: The Dallas and Pittsburgh examples. *Economic Geography* 64: 1–16.

White, Harrison C. 1981. Where do markets come from? *American Journal of Sociology* 87: 517–47.

White, Harrison C., and Cynthia A. White. 1965. *Canvases and Careers: Institutional Change in the French Painting World*. Chicago: University of Chicago Press.

White, Ronald, and C. Howard Hopkins. 1976. *The Social Gospel: Religion and Reform in Changing America*. Philadelphia: Temple University Press.

Who Was Who in America, Historical Volume, 1607–1896. 1967. Rev. ed. Chicago: Marquis.

Whooley, Owen. 2013. *Knowledge in the Time of Cholera: The Struggle over American Medicine in the Nineteenth Century*. Chicago: University of Chicago Press.

Wiebe, Robert. 1984. *The Opening of American Society: From the Adoption of the Constitution to the Eve of Disunion*. New York: Alfred A. Knopf.

Wilde, Melissa. 2007. *Vatican II: A Sociological Analysis of Religious Change*. Princeton, NJ: Princeton University Press.

Wilder, Alexander. 1904. *History of Medicine: A Brief Outline of Medical History from the Earliest Historic Period, with an Extended Account of the Various Sects of Physicians and New Schools of Medicine in Later Centuries*. Augusta, ME: Maine Farmer.

Wiley, Dan. 1810. Introduction. *Agricultural Museum* 1(1): 1–3. https://play.google.com/books/reader?id=JQECAAAAYAAJandprintsec=frontcoverandoutput=readerand authuser=0andhl=enandpg=GBS.PP8, retrieved 13 May 2003.

Willging, Eugene P., and Herta Hatzfeld. 1959–68. *Catholic Serials of the 19th Century in the United States: A Descriptive Bibliography and Union List*. 12 vols. Washington, DC: Catholic University of America Press.

Williams, Peter. 1998. *America's Religions*. Urbana: University of Illinois Press.

Wilson, James Grant, John Fiske, and Stanley L. Klos, eds. (1887–1889) 1999. *Appleton's Cyclopedia of American Biography*. 6 vols. New York: D. Appleton.

Wilson, William. 1831. Remarks on the cultivation and diseases of peach trees. *New York Farmer* 4(2): 33–34. http://search.proquest.com/americanperiodicals/docview/137142259/2F37129FAD16494FPQ/2?accountid=14496, retrieved 1 August 2014.

Winship, Michael. 2001. Hawthorne and the "scribbling women": Publishing *The Scarlet Letter* in the nineteenth-century United States. *Studies in American Fiction* 29(1): 3–11.

Wittke, Carl. 1957. *The German-Language Press in America*. Lexington: University Press of Kentucky.

Wood, Gordon. 1969. *The Creation of the American Republic, 1776–1787*. Williamsburg, VA and Chapel Hill: Institute of Early American History and Culture and University of North Carolina Press.

Wood, James Playstead. 1949. *Magazines in the United States*. New York: Ronald.

Wood, Richard. 1999. Religious culture and political action. *Sociological Theory* 17: 307–22.

Woodmansee, Martha. 1984. The genius and the copyright: Economic and legal conditions for the emergence of the author. *Eighteenth-Century Studies* 17: 425–48.

Woods, John. 1797. Proposals for publishing (by the proprietors of the *Newark Gazette*) by subscription, a weekly paper, to be entitled *The Rural Magazine*. Newark, NJ: John H. Williams. Early American Imprints, Series I: Evans, 1639–1800, document 48321. http://infoweb.newsbank.com/iw-search/we/Evans/?p_product=EAIXandp _theme=eaiandp_nbid=F60I50EIMTQwNjEzNzAxNS4zNzQ4NzI6MToxNToxMz YuMTUyLjIlwOC4xMTIandp_action=docandp_docnum=1andp_queryname =2andp_docref=v2:0F2B1FCB879B099B@EAIX-0F2F82C7913A0CA8@48321-@1, retrieved 24 March 2006.

Woodward, Carl R. 1927. *The Development of Agriculture in New Jersey, 1660–1880*. New Brunswick, NJ: Rutgers University Press.

Worcester, Joseph Emerson. 1818. *A Gazetteer of the United States*. Andover, MA: Flagg and Gould.

Wrather, Eva Jean. 1968. *Creative Freedom in Action: Alexander Campbell on the Structure of the Church*. St. Louis, MO: Bethany.

Wright, Conrad. 1984. The growth of denominational bureaucracies: A neglected aspect of American church history. *Harvard Theological Review* 77(2): 177–94.

Wright, John S., and J. Ambrose Wright. 1849. The agricultural press. *Prairie Farmer* 9(1): 36. http://search.proquest.com/americanperiodicals/docview/127529966/5B85 068C568D4331PQ/47?accountid=14496, retrieved 13 June 2013.

Wright, Richardson. 1976. *Hawkers and Walkers in Early America*. New York: Arno.

Wright, Robert E. 2012. Capitalism and the rise of the corporation nation. In Michael Zakim and Gary J. Kornblith, eds., *Capitalism Takes Command: The Social Transformation of Nineteenth-Century America*, 145–68. Chicago: University of Chicago Press.

Wright, Robert E. 2014. Corporations dataset. http://faculty.augie.edu/~rwright/, retrieved 19 July 2014.

Wroth, Lawrence C. 1931. *The Colonial Printer*. Charlottesville: University of Virginia Press.

Wroth, Lawrence C., and Rollo G. Silver. 1951. Book production and distribution from the American Revolution to the war between the states. In Helmut Lehmann-Haupt, ed., *The Book in America: A History of the Making and Selling of Books in the United States*, 63–136. New York: R. R. Bowker.

Wunderlich, Charles Edward. 1962. A history and bibliography of early American musical periodicals, 1782–1852. PhD diss., University of Michigan.

Wuthnow, Robert. 1999. Mobilizing civic engagement: The changing impact of religious involvement. In Theda Skocpol and Morris P. Fiorina, eds., *Civic Engagement in American Democracy*, 331–63. Washington, DC, and New York: Brookings Institution Press and the Russell Sage Foundation.

Wyatt-Brown, Bertram. 1971. Prelude to abolitionism: Sabbatarian politics and the rise of the second party system. *Journal of American History* 63: 316–41.

Young, Michael P. 2002. Confessional protest: The religious birth of US national social movements. *American Sociological Review* 67: 660–88.

Young, Michael P. 2006. *Bearing Witness against Sin: The Evangelical Birth of the American Social Movement*. Chicago: University of Chicago Press.

Zald, Mayer N. 1990. History, sociology, and theories of organization. In John E. Jackson, ed., *Institutions in American Society: Essays in Market, Political, and Social Organizations*, 81–108. Ann Arbor: University of Michigan Press.

Zald, Mayer N. 1996. More fragmentation? Unfinished business in linking the social sciences and the humanities. *Administrative Science Quarterly* 40: 251–61.

Zald, Mayer N., and Bert Useem. 1987. Movement and countermovement interaction: Mobilization, tactics, and state involvement. In Mayer N. Zald and John D. McCarthy, eds., *Social Movements in an Organizational Society*, 247–72. New Brunswick, NJ: Transaction.

Zboray, Ronald J. 1993. *A Fictive People: Antebellum Economic Development and the American Reading Public*. New York: Oxford University Press.

Zelizer, Viviana A. 1994. *The Social Meaning of Money: Pin Money, Paychecks, Poor Relief, and Other Currencies*. New York: Basic Books.

Zerubavel, Eviatar. 1981. *Hidden Rhythms: Schedules and Calendars in Social Life*. Berkeley: University of California Press.

Zerubavel, Eviatar. 1985. *The Seven Day Circle*. Chicago: University of Chicago Press.

Zhou, Xueguang. 1993. Occupational power, state capacities, and the diffusion of licensing in the United States: 1890 to 1950. *American Sociological Review* 58: 536–52.

Zhou, Xueguang. 2005. The institutional logic of occupational prestige ranking: Reconceptualization and reanalyses. *American Journal of Sociology* 111: 90–140.

Zilversmit, Arthur. 1967. *The First Emancipation: The Abolition of Slavery in the North.* Chicago: University of Chicago Press.

Zucker, Lynne G. 1986. Production of trust: Institutional sources of economic structure, 1840–1920. In B. Staw and L. Cummings, eds., *Research in Organizational Behavior*, 8:53–111. Greenwich, CT: JAI Press.

Index

Philadelphia (*cont.*)
37–38; population statistics, 75–76; printing technologies, 50; religious communities, 169, 297; in research methodology, 305, 308–9, 316–18; Sunday school movement, 79

Philadelphia, magazine publishing: agricultural periodicals, 255–56, 259; business periodicals, 242, 243, 244; as concentrated center, 31, 35, 36, 113; content variety, 43, 44–45; distribution times from, 62; editorial statements, 135; religious periodicals, 170; reprinting practices, 95, 96, 103; in research methodology, 293; special interest periodicals, 50; stratification of, 59, 104. *See also* location element, founders' status

Philadelphia Magazine, 97
Philadelphia Magazine and Review, 96, 135
Philadelphia Monthly Magazine, 5
Philadelphia Repository, 95
Philadelphia Repository and Weekly Register, 43
Philadelphisches Magazin, 50
Philosophical Transactions, 24
physician occupation, 112, 115–17, 292–93
Pioneer, 282
Plan of Union, 165
The Plough, the Loom, and the Anvil, 264
Plough Boy, 98, 257, 264
Plymouth Brethren, 157, 299
Poe, Edgar Allan, 90, 95, 101, 102
politics category, 45–48, 274–75
Polyanthos, 98
Pomologist Magazine, 86
Popper, Karl R., 246
population statistics, 15–16, 35, 75–77, 147, 304
Port-Folio, 44–45, 99, 132, 203
Postal Act (1792), 64, 94
Postal Act (1794), 16, 62, 64, 65
Postal Act (1810), 188
postal system: acceptance of magazines, 64–66; data and methodology overview, 303–4, 310–19; growth of, 16, 61–64; impact on magazines, 66–74, 257; newspaper classification, 282; in reprinting culture, 94; Sabbatarian protests, 188–89
post-colonial era, overview of unification challenges, 2–3
Powell, Walter W., 42
Powers, John, 169
practical science, 247–48
Prairie Farmer, 257, 259, 264
Presbyterian Church: membership patterns,

144, 150, 151, 177; national structure, 156, 157; in research methodology, 294, 299, 327; in revivalist activity, 145, 148, 149, 150; in social reform movement, 159, 197, 200, 214–15; as this-worldly religion, 214–15, 218

Presbyterian Church, magazines: anti-Catholicism in, 168; endorsement tactics, 141; founders, 120; market share, 163, 170; purpose statements, 140, 164, 165–66, 169, 175

Presbyterian Magazine, 139
prices, subscription, 83–84, 140, 242, 289–90
Prince, Thomas, 117
Prince, Thomas, Sr., 160
printing technologies, 16, 56–61, 303
prison reform, 207, 208
probability theory, 246–47
professional occupations. *See* occupation element, founders' status
profit motivation, 129–32
Protestant, 167–68
Protestant Magazine, 169
Protestant Reformation Society, 168
publication schedules, 29, 51–52, 242, 287
publicity function, social reform magazines, 206–8
public sphere, overview of media roles, 1–2, 273–74, 276–77
publishing occupations. *See* occupation element, founders' status
publishing technologies, 16, 57–61, 303
Putnam's Monthly Magazine, 102

Quakers, 191, 299

railroad construction, 63–64, 236
Randolph, Edmond, 140
rates, postal, 65–66, 312
Reader's Digest, 94n16
readership: agricultural magazine growth, 258; attraction and retention strategies, 136–42; audience variety, 49–51, 84–86; measurement methodology, 290; statistics as vitality indicator, 29–30. *See also* geography-based patterns, magazine industry
reading public, changes, 74–89
Red Book, 99
Reformed Dutch Church, 157
Reformer, 176
regional patterns. *See* geography-based patterns
religion: data and methodology overview,

Princeton Studies in Cultural Sociology

Paul J. DiMaggio, Michèle Lamont, Robert J. Wuthnow, and Viviana A. Zelizer, Series Editors